MW00609850

Spies, Scouts, and Secrets in the Gettysburg Campaign

How the Critical Role of Intelligence Impacted
the Outcome of Lee's Invasion of the North, June-July, 1863

Thomas J. Ryan

SB

Savas Beatie
California

Library of Congress Cataloging-in-Publication Data

Ryan, Thomas J., 1934-
Spies, scouts and secrets in the Gettysburg campaign : how the critical role of intelligence impacted the outcome of Lee's invasion of the north, June-July, 1863 / by Thomas J. Ryan.
pages cm
Includes bibliographical references and index.
ISBN 978-1-61121-178-8 (hardcover : alk. paper)
1. Gettysburg Campaign, 1863. 2. United States—History—Civil War, 1861-1865—Military intelligence. 3. United States—History—Civil War, 1861-1865—Secret service. 4. Military intelligence—United States—History—19th century. I. Title.
E475.51.R93 2015
973.7'349—dc23
2015000010

SB

Published by
Savas Beatie LLC
989 Governor Drive, Suite 102
El Dorado Hills, CA 95762

Phone: 916-941-6896
E-mail: sales@savasbeatie.com

05 04 03 02 01 5 4 3 2 1
First edition, first printing

Savas Beatie titles are available at special discounts for bulk purchases in the United States by corporations, institutions, and other organizations. For more details, please contact Special Sales, P.O. Box 4527, El Dorado Hills, CA 95762, or you may e-mail us at sales@savasbeatie.com, or visit our website at www.savasbeatie.com for additional information.

Proudly published, printed, and warehoused in the United States of America.

To Fil for all we've done together

Also, to the late Edwin C. Fishel and William A. Tidwell,
Civil War intelligence research pioneers.

Table of Contents

Table of Contents (continued)

List of Maps

List of Maps (continued)

List of Illustrations

List of Illustrations (continued)

In 1868 a Virginian named William M. McDonald wrote to Robert E. Lee seeking comment on the general's battles in the late war for use in a school history he was writing. Lee obliged him. When he came to the battle of Gettysburg, Lee explained that "Its loss was occasioned by a combination of circumstances." He was blunt about the first of those circumstances: "It was commenced in the absence of correct intelligence." By contrast, as Thomas J. Ryan observes, had Mr. McDonald made inquiry of George Gordon Meade, Lee's Gettysburg opponent, Meade might have responded, "The battle was won because of the timeliness and accuracy of intelligence."

As Ryan makes clear in this definitive study of military intelligence in the Gettysburg campaign, the Union's clear-cut edge in intelligence-gathering in the early summer of 1863 was only a recent phenomenon. Indeed, for much of the war to that point, the intelligence game was in bad odor in the Army of the Potomac.

One of General George B. McClellan's first actions on taking command of the Potomac army in July 1861 was to hire as his personal intelligence chief the Chicago detective Allan Pinkerton. On reaching Washington, Pinkerton found that McClellan had already, entirely on his own hook, compiled a count (a huge overcount) of the Confederate army facing him. Pinkerton was a sycophant, with no thought of undercutting his boss's delusions. For the next sixteen months, Pinkerton furnished "general estimates" of the Army of Northern Virginia that were two and three times its actual size. This being just what McClellan expected to hear, his naturally cautious nature grew ultra-cautious. McClellan had "the slows," said Mr. Lincoln. In November 1862, with the war in the East stalled, the president fired McClellan. Pinkerton departed with him, leaving the Potomac army virtually bereft of an intelligence arm.

Pinkerton's close-held system had relied on spies and on interrogation of those from "the other side"—deserters, prisoners, refugees, contraband slaves. This raw data, unsound, unsorted, unevaluated, went directly to McClellan. Comparatively little came from other sources, cavalry or signalmen, for example. The McClellan-Pinkerton era furnished the worst sort of precedent for intelligence-gathering. It took Joseph Hooker, Meade's predecessor in command of the Army of the Potomac, to turn matters around with the bureau of military information. The BMI was designed to collect, collate, and evaluate intelligence from all sources—spies, cavalry, interrogation, signalmen, and so on—for the commander's use. To be sure, the system did not always work faultlessly in the Gettysburg campaign—in pursuit of the Rebels after the battle Meade complained to his wife, "I can get no reliable information of the enemy and have to grope my way in the dark. It is wonderful the difficulty I have in obtaining correct information." Still, over all, from start to finish, General Meade was better informed than was General Lee.

Lee did not have anything like the BMI; he did not even have an intelligence officer on staff. But he did have as his cavalry chief J. E. B. Stuart. Jeb Stuart was a master of using cavalry for intelligence-gathering. Lee had depended on him to paint a true picture of the enemy in every campaign before Gettysburg, and Stuart did not disappoint. Lee also learned much from security-unconscious Northern newspapers and from spies (which he euphemistically called scouts) and other loyalists when operating in Virginia. Operating in Pennsylvania, however, lost him these sources, and he became more dependent than ever on Stuart and his cavalry. How that worked out receives Ryan's careful analysis.

Spies, Scouts, and Secrets in the Gettysburg Campaign is the first book to detail how the intelligence game was played, by both sides, in this momentous campaign, and Thomas Ryan's experience as an intelligence officer for the Department of Defense brings context to this story it has not had before.

Stephen W. Sears

Introduction

This project emanated from a series of articles, published from 1998-2007, for "The Civil War Page" of the *Washington Times* newspaper about intelligence operations in general, and those during the Gettysburg campaign in particular. Additional investigation into Union and Confederate intelligence operations resulted in a number of articles for *Gettysburg Magazine.* This combined material published over more than a decade formed the basis for this study and prompted further in-depth research.

Before the Civil War, the United States did not have a viable intelligence organization in place. This was the legacy of attitudes dating from the American Revolution that it was improper or unnecessary for the federal government to engage in spying. Even though Gen. George Washington employed spies liberally during the revolution, no permanent intelligence apparatus survived the war's end. Little was done subsequently to rectify this shortcoming. Consequently, the U.S. found itself at an intelligence disadvantage during the War of 1812 and the Mexican War.

When the North-South conflict erupted in 1861, the Federal government and the Confederacy established rudimentary information gathering efforts at the national levels in Washington and Richmond, and individual commands organized military intelligence operations. There was virtually no central direction and only limited coordination among commands on either side until the latter part of the war regarding what was generally referred to as "secret service" activities.

Captain Arthur L. Wagner, an instructor in the art of war at the U.S. Infantry and Cavalry School, Fort Leavenworth, Kansas, neatly encapsulates the importance of a viable intelligence-gathering operation: "Information in regard to the enemy is the indispensable basis of all military plans, and nothing but faulty dispositions of the security of an army can be expected if such information is lacking."

Military intelligence is information significant to military policymaking or the planning and conduct of military operations and activities. Counterintelligence is information gathered and activities conducted to identify, deceive, exploit, disrupt, or protect against enemy intelligence activities. Security operations, of which counterintelligence is a part, encompasses any measures taken by a military unit to protect itself against all acts designed to impair its effectiveness.

In his groundbreaking publication The Secret War for the Union: The Untold Story of Military Intelligence in the Civil War, Edwin C. Fishel accurately observed that "intelligence . . . has not been a favorite subject of those who study the Civil War." The impact that intelligence, or the lack thereof, had on the outcome of events is seldom considered, and even when it is, it usually receives cursory notice.

Fishel provided an extensive rendering of the evolution of Union intelligence operations up through the Gettysburg campaign in 1863. Comprehensive documentation of Confederate intelligence efforts during specific battles, however, is still lacking. Our knowledge about how intelligence impacted commanders' decisions in combat and the outcome of Civil War campaigns is also limited. Counterintelligence or security operations have not received the attention they deserve. Historical accounts generally examine battles in minute detail, but they seldom focus on intelligence as a key, often the key, element in success or failure of Union and Confederate operations.

With this in mind, this study discusses the resources available to both sides for conducting intelligence operations during the Gettysburg campaign and compares how the respective army commanders Gen. Robert E. Lee and Maj. Gens. Joseph Hooker and George G. Meade planned and implemented the gathering and reporting of intelligence to achieve specific objectives during the campaign. The study identifies and discusses the individuals who played important intelligence-related roles on both sides and assesses their contributions.

It examines the Gettysburg campaign day-by-day, hour-by-hour from mid-May to mid-July 1863 focusing on the Union and Confederate leadership's intense efforts to decipher the movements and objectives of their opponents, and maneuver to gain the advantage. It includes information-gathering affecting the outcome of cavalry clashes and infantry engagements along the invasion route, and it describes the army commanders' recurrent attempts to outwit their counterparts with unorthodox tactics, surprise, and deception. Specially trained personnel, such as scouts and spies, played leading roles in these endeavors. Among the objects of these stratagems was raising the anxiety level of the authorities in Washington and Richmond provoking them to withhold or withdraw units from the armies for defense of the capitals.

At the outset of Lee's invasion, the Union cavalry failed to provide early warning of Lee's army stealing a march northward by a surreptitious route through the Shenandoah Valley. This shifted the burden to the newly organized intelligence staff, the bureau of military information (BMI), to inform Union commander Hooker about Lee's movements. The quality of intelligence reports on either side varied greatly, depending on the source. It ran the gamut of professionally-written tabulations of enemy unit locations and estimation of enemy intentions to speculative commentary with little or no supporting evidence. The most effective reports usually came from eye-witness or first-hand accounts delivered directly by the observer to headquarters. Regardless of the source or content, however, the burden fell on individual commanders to judge the reliability of every report received.

Throughout the campaign, teams from the Union signal corps—which had operated since 1861 but was not officially established until two years later—maintained communications between army headquarters and the infantry and cavalry and kept close watch on the enemy and reported on their movements. Conversely, the Confederate signal corps was neither as productive nor cohesive. Lee preferred to operate with a small staff and chose not to assign an officer to direct overall signal operations for the army. This proved to be a handicap to rapid communications between Lee and his subordinates especially later in the campaign.

Normally cavalry served as the primary information gatherer while armies were on the march. But the Union cavalry proved unequal to the task during the march toward Gettysburg. Its commander, Brig. Gen. Alfred Pleasonton, often provided unsubstantiated and inaccurate information to Hooker. Were it not for alternate sources of intelligence, Hooker would have had considerable difficulty tracking Lee's march toward Pennsylvania.

Pleasonton's incompetence was offset, however, by the separation of the Confederate cavalry under Maj. Gen. James Ewell Brown "Jeb" Stuart from the Army of Northern Virginia for several critical days during Lee's invasion. It severely crippled Lee's knowledge of the whereabouts of his enemy, and hence his ability to maneuver, a deficiency Hooker did not experience because a variety of Federal intelligence functions tracked Lee's movements northward.

The dramatic unfolding of this critical military campaign, in particular a comparison of Union and Confederate intelligence operations and their effectiveness in support of the armies, is the subject of this story. How each side employed its resources and gathered information about the enemy's strength, disposition, and intentions played a major role in the outcome of a momentous confrontation between these two powerful forces, and consequently on the future history of the United States. It's a story that needs to be told.

Acknowledgments

This book evolved from articles I wrote for the *Washington Times* dealing with intelligence operations during the Gettysburg campaign. The late Woody West, editor of the *Times'* weekly Civil War page and his successor, Greg Pierce, encouraged my work as a special contributor to the *Times*.

Publisher Bob Younger and his editor, Andy Turner, supported the idea of expanding the *Washington Times* articles into a five-part series for *Gettysburg Magazine*. This study is a comprehensive elaboration of these magazine articles, and many people had a hand in the outcome.

As a member of the Friends of the National Parks at Gettysburg for the past 20 years, I have attended dozens of seminars and musters conducted by talented specialists, such as licensed battlefield guides Phil Lechak, Dr. Charles C. Fennell, Jr., Wayne Wachsmuth, Tom Vossler, Kavin Coughenour and Stuart Dempsey, and park rangers Scott Hartwig, Troy Harman and Eric Campbell—among many others. I also attended several Gettysburg national military park seminars, all of which have been valuable learning experiences. A course at the Army War College, Carlisle, Pennsylvania, that included a "staff ride" at Gettysburg to learn about strategy and tactics during the battle, and a friends of the Gettysburg park "how to" course on conducting research presented by the inimitable licensed battlefield guide Wayne Motts (currently director of the National Civil War museum in Harrisburg, Pennsylvania) paid dividends as the project progressed. The seminar featured tours to research institutions and introductions about their collections including the National Archives, the Gettysburg National Military Park library, Adams County Historical Society, Gettysburg College library, and U.S. Army Military History Institute, Carlisle, Pennsylvania.

Membership in the Central Delaware Civil War Round Table, Dover, Delaware, has provided additional background for my research. Gettysburg has been a frequent subject of speakers at our monthly meetings, and our annual trips to Civil War battlefields included Gettysburg on three occasions. Additional knowledge and experience has been gained from longtime membership in the Fort Delaware Society. Fort Delaware was the location of a Civil War prison that housed Confederate POWs, including thousands captured at Gettysburg.

During the research phase of this project, the staff at the National Archives in Washington, DC, was extremely helpful in providing access to the bureau of military information (BMI) files. The Library of Congress staff was equally skillful in directing me to documents relating to selected individuals involved in this story, especially BMI operative John Babcock and Union cavalry commander Alfred Pleasonton. John Heiser, Director, GNMP Library, was particularly responsive in identifying documents related to my research. Ben Neely and Lisa Shower of the Adams County Historical Society graciously located information about activities and people in the town of Gettysburg. Karen Drickamer, director of special collections, hosted my visit to the Musselman Library, Gettysburg College, and her staff helped identify numerous out-of-print sources—especially dealing with Union and Confederate cavalry operations. The U.S. Army Military Institute staff guided my research, and supplied useful source material.

Deana Preston, research assistant, Senate House state historic site, Kingston, New York, graciously answered my many questions and provided material dealing with the life and military service of BMI commander George H. Sharpe. Danelle Moon, manuscripts and archives, Yale University library, researched and helpfully provided information about Sharpe and William Norris, chief, Confederate signal and secret service, both of whom graduated from Yale. Manuscripts archivist Scott Taylor, special collections, Georgetown University library, painstakingly facilitated my review of the Edwin C. Fishel collection. James Scott, Sacramento (California) public library, most helpfully researched, copied and forwarded articles written by Noah Brooks, newspaper correspondent and friend of Abraham Lincoln. Olga Otsapina, Norris Foundation curator of American historical manuscripts, The Huntington Library, San Marino, California, demonstrated interest in my project, researched the Joseph Hooker collection and provided pertinent documents.

Research librarians Sue Keefe and Barbara Litzau at the South Coastal library in Bethany Beach, Delaware, always graciously responded to my innumerable requests and located numerous sources via the interlibrary loan system. Other institutions that contributed time and effort locating sources include Coyle free library in Chambersburg, Pennsylvania, Frederick county (Maryland) public libraries, and Washington county (Maryland) historical society. The staff of the Culpeper public library provided information about the Eugene M. Scheel historical map of Culpeper county, Virginia. Cindy Arbelbide, Rappahannock county public library, shared information about the location of Rock Ford, a Rappahannock River crossing point for Confederate cavalry.

Virginia Beard Morton, author of *Marching Through Culpeper*, conducted a personal tour of the town of Culpeper, Brandy Station battlefield, and Kelly's Ford. Pete Estes shared his extensive knowledge of Rappahannock county on a personal driving tour of the roads on which the Army of Northern Virginia marched toward the Blue Ridge Mountains from Culpeper Court House, and Ashby's Gap leading to the Shenandoah Valley. Loudoun county, VA, expert and author Steve Meserve guided me on tours of Aldie, Middleburg, and Upperville in the Loudoun valley where cavalry battles occurred during the march northward; the area dubbed "Mosby's Confederacy" in Loudoun and Fauquier counties, important routes of the Confederate's march northward; and Guilford Hill just north of Leesburg, the site of a Union signal station that figured importantly in the campaign.

During a visit to The Homestead in Union Mills, Maryland, the property of Andrew and William Shriver during the Civil War, a docent alerted me to Frederic Shriver Klein's "Just South of Gettysburg: Carroll County, Maryland in the Civil War," and described Jeb Stuart's cavalry camping on the property in June 1863 on the way to Pennsylvania. Ronald Kuehne, outreach coordinator, Pipe Creek Civil War Round Table, shared information about a Union observation post and signal station at the Trinity Lutheran church in Taneytown, Maryland.

The staff of the Hanover public library, Hanover, Pennsylvania, provided documentation dealing with the battle of Hanover on June 30, 1863 involving Stuart's Confederate cavalry and Kilpatrick's Union cavalry. Licensed battlefield guide Larry Wallace conducted a bus tour of the battlefield in and around Hanover that was most helpful in identifying key locations where the fighting took place. Don Lehman, founder of the organization Historic Wrightsville, guided me on a comprehensive tour of the route Confederate troops followed from York toward Wrightsville, Pennsylvania, pointed out locations where Confederate troops and Union militia became engaged, and described how the Union army burned the mile-long covered bridge over the Susquehanna River.

Eric Wittenberg, J. D. Petruzzi, and Mike Nugent generously provided driving tour guides for the routes of the Army of Northern Virginia's retreat from Gettysburg from their yet to be published book "One Continuous Fight: The Retreat from Gettysburg." Mark Snell, director of the George Tyler Moore Civil War Center at Shepherd University, led a tour of Shepherdstown and Harper's Ferry, West Virginia, and the surrounding area—locations that had an important bearing on the Gettysburg campaign. Along with friend and fellow Civil War devotee, Larry Arena, I took a self-guided tour to the top of the steep Maryland Heights across the river from Harper's Ferry, and examined the remains of the Civil War-era fortifications. From this vantage point, a Union signal corps station observed and transmitted information about Lee's army marching down the

Shenandoah Valley and across the Potomac River. Dave Shultz led a tour of the area of the Gettysburg battlefield where Capt. Samuel Johnston, an engineer on Gen. Robert E. Lee's staff, conducted his controversial reconnaissance of the Union lines on the morning of July 2, 1863.

My friend and colleague Rick Schaus read and commented on the entire manuscript, and readily responded to many inquiries. Many thanks also to Scott Mingus who commented on the manuscript, and willingly shared information from his storehouse of knowledge about the Gettysburg campaign. Alan Brunelle, David Gaddy, Jim Cameron and Dave McGowan also took time from their busy schedules to comment on selected chapters.

The ever gracious Scott Mingus and J.D. Petruzzi answered frequent questions about the publication process based on their experience in this field. Others who contributed their expertise in a variety of ways to this book include Dean Shultz, Steve French, Don Wiles, Larry Freiheit, Chuck Teague, Andy Waskie, David G. Smith, Greg Biggs, and Bob Huddleston.

My learning curve has been augmented greatly by monitoring and participating in the online Gettysburg discussion group and military history online whose talented, helpful, and gregarious members post insightfully about the Gettysburg campaign. Logging on to the signal corps association website and posting comments and questions for this astute group has been helpful in learning more about signal corps operations during the Gettysburg campaign. My apologies to everyone else who contributed to this project; but, because of the passage of time, have inadvertently been omitted from this list.

The entire team at Savas Beatie has my heartfelt appreciation. Publisher Theodore P. Savas has been continually supportive throughout the process. Editor Tom Schott patiently guided this neophyte author and transformed my raw text into a flowing recitation of the story. Production Manager Lee Merideth expertly took charge of the design and layout of the chapters. Marketing Director Sarah Keeney and Media Specialist Michele Sams affably handled the indispensable administrative and public relations endeavors on which marketing success is so dependent. My longtime colleague Phil Laino professionally drew the maps that accompany this narrative. I am also grateful to my friend and neighbor Fulton Loppatto who voluntarily applied his considerable expertise in designing my website which features this book.

Special thanks go to Stephen W. Sears, a gifted and prolific historian with consummate writing skills, for contributing the foreword. He is the author of Gettysburg, a recognized standard in the field, and many other publications dealing with the Civil War.

This book is dedicated to my wife Felicetta ("Fil") who steadfastly supported this project, and participated in many research trips following the paths of the two armies to see firsthand the sites where the Gettysburg campaign unfolded. It is also a memorial to the late Edwin C. Fishel and William A. Tidwell, pioneers in Union and Confederate intelligence operations research respectively—both of whom I suspect are continuing their research on a more celestial level.

Thomas J. Ryan
Bethany Beach, Delaware

Abbreviations

AAG—Assistant Adjutant General
B&L—Battles and Leaders of the Civil War
BMI—Bureau of Military Information
GNMP—Gettysburg National Military Park
JCCCW—Joint Congressional Committee on the Conduct of the War
NA—National Archives
PMG—Provost Marshall General
RG—Record Group
SHSP—Southern Historical Society Papers

Chapter One

Intelligence Resources:
The Army of the Potomac

I hope our friends understand that in the great game that is now being played,
everything in the way of advantage depends upon which side gets the best information.

— *Col. George H. Sharpe[1]*

At the outset of the war, the Union Army of the Potomac commanders organized what was referred to as secret service units for information-gathering purposes, but it was not until early 1863 that commander Maj. Gen. Joseph Hooker created a viable military intelligence capability. By the outset of the Gettysburg campaign in June 1863, Hooker had operational intelligence resources in place to support his strategic and tactical objectives.[2]

After his army's defeat at Chancellorsville in May 1863, Hooker knew he had little time to prepare for another engagement with Gen. Robert E. Lee's Army of Northern Virginia. Accordingly, he needed to learn about the enemy's plans and resources, and deny Lee information about his own operations.[3]

To accomplish these objectives, Hooker had available a variety of resources, including the Provost Marshal General, Bureau of Military

---

1 Sharpe to McConaughy, June 29, 1863, Gettysburg National Military Park Library. David McConaughy was a Gettysburg lawyer who was leading a team of civilians gathering information about Confederate movements in Pennsylvania.

2 Ibid.; Edwin C. Fishel, *The Secret War for the Union: The Untold Story of Military Intelligence in the Civil War* (New York, 1986), 286-88.

3 Hooker to Lincoln, Lincoln to Hooker, Halleck to Hooker, June 5, 1863, OR 27, pt. 1, 30-32.

Information, Cavalry Corps, Signal Corps, Balloon Corps, U.S. Military Telegraph, special units, spy networks, and topographical experts.[4]

Provost Marshal General

> [T]he gathering of information about the enemy . . . became increasingly important and absorbed more and more of [the provost marshal general's] time and energy.
> David S. Sparks[5]

Although the American army employed provost marshals to control the discipline of its troops since the days of the Revolution, the practice had all but elapsed before the Civil War. A centralized system of provost marshals was impractical with U. S. army units scattered throughout the country.

After the Civil War began and Maj. Gen. George McClellan took command of the federal army, he appointed Col. Andrew Porter as provost marshal for Washington, D.C., and later as provost marshal general (PMG) for the Army of the Potomac. Besides standard military police functions, McClellan gave Porter administrative oversight of a civilian intelligence staff with a former head of a detective agency, Allan Pinkerton, in charge. Pinkerton's job was to gather information about the enemy and report directly to McClellan who served as his own intelligence officer.[6]

---

4   Although airborne balloons had been part of the Army of the Potomac's intelligence tools since soon after the war began, for administrative and logistical reasons the balloon program was dropped following the battle of Chancellorsville. Therefore, air balloons were not in service during the Gettysburg campaign. Charles M. Evans, *War of the Aeronauts: A History of Ballooning in the Civil War* (Mechanicsburg, PA, 2002), 88-287; Fishel, *The Secret War*, 5, 442-43.

5   David S. Sparks, *Inside Lincoln's Army, The Diary of General Marsena Rudolph Patrick, Provost Marshal General, Army of the Potomac* (New York, 1964) 18.

6   Wilton P. Moore, "Union Army Provost Marshals in the Eastern Theater," *Military Affairs* (Autumn, 1962), 26:120-21; Fishel, *The Secret War*, 114, 238. Not until March 1863 did Congress create the office of provost marshal general (PMG) within the war department. Colonel James B. Fry received an appointment to that position. The primary responsibilities of the PMG were "the arrest of deserters, the enrollment of the national forces for draft, and the enlistment of volunteers." In addition, the PMG was "to detect, seize, and confine" enemy spies officially defined as "a person who secretly, in disguise, or under false pretenses, seeks information, with the intention of communicating it to the enemy." Assistant provost marshal generals in the various states were to use special precautions in conducting suspected spies to the commanding general of the local department for investigation and trial. This essentially was a counterintelligence function of the PMG's office. OR series III, 2:586; 3:74, 88-89, 93, 131; 5:599; series IV, 4:656.

Brig. Gen. Marsena Patrick (center)
and staff
Library of Congress

In October 1862, Brig. Gen. Marsena Patrick replaced Porter as PMG. Patrick recorded in his diary that his assignment included responsibility for "secret service," meaning that Pinkerton's staff would remain as part of the PMG's office. But when President Lincoln replaced McClellan with Maj. Gen. Ambrose E. Burnside in November 1862, Pinkerton resigned and took most of his staff with him.[7]

Once Pinkerton's team departed, in addition to various military police responsibilities, Patrick directed a team of scouts and spies he called "operatives." He was responsible for gathering information by "examining" or interrogating Confederate prisoners, enemy deserters, and escaped slaves or "contrabands." Patrick's scouts conducted reconnaissance, and his spies, some of whom he personally recruited, operated behind enemy lines.[8]

---

7   McClellan chose Patrick for this assignment following his successful stint as military governor of Fredericksburg, Virginia, during the Union occupation. Patrick remained as PMG under the new command and expanded his role by assigning provost marshals to the army's new Grand Divisions. Sparks, *Inside Lincoln's Army*, 15-18, 156-58, 160-61, 165, 179, 184; Moore, "Union Army Provost Marshals in the Eastern Theater," 123; David S. Sparks, "General Patrick's Progress: Intelligence and Security in the Army of the Potomac," *Civil War History* (December 1964), 10:376; Allan Pinkerton, *The Spy of the Rebellion* (Lincoln, NE, 1989), 235; Patricia L. Faust, ed., *Historical Times Illustrated Encyclopedia of the Civil War* (New York, 1986), 561. When McClellan first established the provost marshal department, the list of duties he prescribed did not address secret service activities. He evidently made private arrangements for those with Patrick, or Patrick assumed those duties on his own. *OR* 5, ser. I, 30. Since there is no evidence that Patrick collaborated with Allen Pinkerton, McClellan's civilian intelligence chief, it appears that both reported directly to McClellan about intelligence matters. For more on Pinkerton's intelligence responsibilities, see Fishel, *The Secret War*, 53-55. On Patrick, see Sparks, *Inside Lincoln's Army*, 11-24.

8   Ibid., 169, 175-76, 179. 181, 186, 193, 203; Sparks, "General Patrick's Progress," 376-77. "[The] provost units [of] the separate divisions of the Army of the Potomac . . . assumed certain intelligence responsibilities, collecting and disseminating information on enemy forces." Robert K. Wright, Jr., *Military Police* (Washington D.C., 1992), 4.

Maj. Gen. Joseph Hooker
Library of Congress

The PMG maintained depots to hold and interrogate enemy prisoners. He offered incentives for prisoners to reveal desired military information. In exchange for militarily useful information, cooperative prisoners were paroled and allowed to live and work in the North.[9]

9 Sparks, *Inside Lincoln's Army*, 170. Positive inducements or incentives continue to be a legal method of interrogation to this day. See "Interrogation and the Collection of Intelligence,"

Patrick also questioned Union officers and loyal citizens about the surrounding terrain and briefed Burnside and his commanders before a military action or campaign. Patrick also conducted counterintelligence operations, such as arresting suspected spies within Union lines and local residents who were known to have served as guides for the enemy. Patrick arrested newspaper correspondents who reported sensitive military information and detained citizens of doubtful loyalty before combat operations, thereby preventing informers from alerting the enemy about Union army movements. At times, Patrick found the workload of his combined secret service and military police duties more than he could handle.[10]

When Maj. Gen. Joseph Hooker replaced Burnside as Army of the Potomac commander in early 1863, he instructed Patrick to perform his provost duties as he had in the past and also ordered him to establish a dedicated military intelligence unit within the PMG's department. However, just as McClellan had done with Pinkerton, Hooker maintained operational control over this new organization, the bureau of military information (BMI), through his chief of staff. The BMI's mission was to collect information about the enemy from all available sources, evaluate and process this data, and report the resulting intelligence directly to the army commander.[11]

The establishment of the BMI transformed the way information about the enemy was evaluated. Under McClellan, information from enemy deserters, prisoners, and spies, as well as escaped slaves, was sent directly to his headquarters for analysis. McClellan's staff or, more likely, the general himself did the analysis. Apparently McClellan had information about the enemy channeled directly to him to preclude line and staff officers from forming opinions that differed from his own. John Babcock, a BMI civilian intelligence staff member who served under both McClellan and Hooker, cited the absence of an in-depth analytical effort while McClellan was in command. Under the

---

International Encyclopedia of the Social Sciences, 2008, accessed July 31, 2014, www.encyclopedia.com/topic/Questioning.aspx.

10 Sparks, *Inside Lincoln's Army*, 169-70, 183-86, 202-203, 204-205, 207; Sparks, "General Patrick's Progress," 375-76, 378-79. Conflict between Patrick's department and Col. Lafayette C. Baker, the war department's special provost marshal in Washington, hindered efficient operations. Because Baker suspected Patrick's department of issuing permits for contraband goods being sent into the South, he ordered detectives to investigate; Patrick countered by having the detectives arrested. Fishel, *The Secret War*, 284-86.

11 Sparks, *Inside Lincoln's Army*, 208, 212; Fishel, *The Secret War*, 3-4, 318-22.

Col. George H. Sharpe
Library of Congress

new system, the BMI performed the
analysis and reported the results.
Hooker therefore stood to benefit
greatly from the informed opinion of a
professional intelligence staff.[12]

Bureau of Military Information

> I have made some arrangements about
> [the] secret service Department . . . with
> Col. Sharp[e] . . . for its Chief.
>   Brig. Gen. Marsena Patrick[13]

When Hooker established the BMI and placed it within the PMG's
department, Patrick appointed Col. George H. Sharpe, a veteran infantry
regimental commander, as deputy provost marshal general to direct the new
bureau. The BMI was intended to be a cohesive intelligence operation
responsible for collecting and analyzing data about the organization, strength,
disposition, movement, and morale of the enemy.[14]

The 35-year-old Sharpe had excellent credentials to head the BMI. From
the Hudson River town of Kingston, New York, he received a B.A. from
Rutgers in 1847, and studied law at Yale in 1847-48. He joined the 20th New
York state militia as a captain in May 1861, and served at First Bull Run. By
August, he became colonel of the 120th New York, for which he had recruited
over a thousand men. Before the war, Sharpe served as a diplomat at U.S.
legations in Vienna and Rome, traveled widely, and was versed in several

---

12 *OR* 5, 52. See Fishel, *The Secret War*, 112-13, 322.

13 Sparks, *Inside Lincoln's Army*, 211-12.

14 General Orders No. 32, March 30, 1863, *OR* 25, pt. 2, 167. Information about the BMI
mission can be found in Sparks, *Inside Lincoln's Army*, 212; Fishel, *Secret War*, 3-4, 286-87, 298;
Francis Trevelyan Miller, ed., "Soldier Life and Secret Service," *The Photographic History of the Civil
War*, 5 vols. (Secaucus, NJ, 1987), 4:264-65, 276, 278-79; Feis, "Secret Service USA," 725.

languages. He had a limited but unblemished combat record and was touted for brigade command before Patrick chose him to head the intelligence organization.[15]

According to Edwin C. Fishel, the new intelligence organization under Sharpe "was a sophisticated 'all-source' operation, decades ahead of its time." The term "all source" intelligence refers to information gathered and processed from a variety of organizations, such as the BMI, Signal Corps, cavalry, etc. Edwin B. Coddington commented about Sharpe's work prior to Lee's invasion of the North in June 1863, "Among the early estimates of enemy intentions the shrewdest and most accurate came from a man whose name reflected the cast of his abilities and the character of his work: Colonel G. H. Sharpe." Stephen W. Sears, too, testified to the excellence of the new bureau, describing it as "an espionage network to spy on General Lee's army as it had never been spied on before. The results were extraordinary." Arthur L. Wagner described the specific nature of an intelligence chief's job: "The management of the secret service of an army requires a profound insight into human nature, and an ability to estimate at once the military worth of the information brought in." Sharpe would prove equal to the task.[16]

Two capable assistants helped him manage the bureau. One was John C. Babcock, who was a Chicago architect when war came in 1861. Babcock enlisted in the Sturgis Rifles, an infantry company that served as McClellan's bodyguard. Pinkerton had recruited Babcock as a mapmaker and an interrogator of prisoners and deserters, skills that proved valuable in future assignments.[17] Given Babcock's background, Sharpe assigned him as an

---

15 Cathy Hoyt, *Pvt. William H. Ellsworth, 120th Regiment NYS Volunteers* (Woodstock, VT, n.d.), 1-2; Sparks, *Inside Lincoln's Army*, 212; Fishel, *The Secret War*, 286-88, 290, 293; Miller, "Soldier Life and Secret Service," 4, 264-65, 287-88; *OR* 21, 379-80, 388-89. Sharpe's counterpart as the head of the Confederate secret service, William Norris, also graduated from Yale, in 1840, and later studied law in Baltimore. See also David Winfred Gaddy's "Foreword" to Dr. Chas. E. Taylor, *The Signal and Secret Service of the Confederate States* (Harmans, MD, 1986), v. The choice of Sharpe and Norris as intelligence chiefs set precedent: during World War II almost the entire Pentagon top-level intelligence operation was staffed by lawyers. Fishel, *The Secret War*, 647-59.

16 Fishel, *The Secret War*, 3; Edwin B. Coddington, T*he Gettysburg Campaign: A Study in Command* (New York, 1968), 49; Stephen W. Sears, *Chancellorsville*, (Boston, 1996), 101; Wagner, *The Service of Security and Information*, 210-11.

17 Fishel, *The Secret War*, 153-54, 215, 257-62; Susan Tortorelli (trans.), *Illinois Sturgis Rifles Regiment History*, accessed July 31, 2014, www.civilwar.illinoisgenweb.org/history/misc-003.html. After Lincoln relieved McClellan of command, Babcock received orders to return to his former company, the Sturgis Rifles, which had been serving as McClellan's personal guard.

John C. Babcock
Miller's Photographic History

interrogator, analyst, and the primary report writer. The quality of his reports reflected his ability to evaluate information from a variety of sources and to translate it into useful intelligence. Babcock demonstrated these skills during the Chancellorsville campaign in April/May 1863 by estimating the size of Lee's forces within a small margin of error.[18]

Sharpe's other assistant was Capt. John McEntee, a former merchant in Rondout, New York, near Kingston, who had had business dealings with Sharpe before the war. He joined the Ulster Guard, a regiment Sharpe formed in 1861, and became a quartermaster sergeant. Battlefield experience in 1862 gained him a captaincy. Sharpe selected the 27-year- old McEntee for the BMI to lead scout and spy teams in the field and also to serve as an interrogator and report writer.[19]

Sharpe, Babcock, and McEntee assumed the responsibility for developing the BMI into an effective intelligence organization. At the time of the Gettysburg campaign, the bureau had 21 people assigned, and it was primarily engaged in deploying scouts and spies to gather information.[20]

One of its most capable scouts was Sgt. Milton W. Cline, a member of the 3rd Indiana Cavalry who came recommended to the BMI based on his

---

Before leaving his post McClellan ordered the company mustered out of the army, and Babcock returned to civilian status. When Burnside took command in late 1862, he hired the 26-year-old Babcock as his intelligence chief but neglected to give him enough authority to carry out his mission. Fishel, *The Secret War*, 153-54, 257, 273, 300, 375; Miller, *Soldier Life and Secret Service*, 4.

18 Fishel, *The Secret War*, 153-54, 257, 273, 300, 375; Miller, "Soldier Life and Secret Service," 4.

19 Fishel, *The Secret War*, 293.

20 Records of the Bureau of Military Information, Record Group (RG) 393, National Archives (NA), June 20, 1863; ibid., 459-60.

Capt. John McEntee
Library of Congress

experience with Hooker's command in Maryland in late 1861-early 1862. He often scouted disguised as a Rebel cavalryman. He operated solo or with a small team, and roamed behind enemy lines mixing in with Rebel troops for days at a time. As a trusted scout in Sharpe's unit, Cline performed valuable service during the campaign.[21]

Interrogation of prisoners, deserters, refugees, and contrabands or escaped slaves provided important intelligence for the BMI. The amount and quality of information derived through this method was enhanced by incentives offered to reveal strategic and tactical military knowledge about the enemy, a practice begun by Patrick. These enticements included better treatment, avoidance of prison time, job opportunities in the North, and release to return home under controlled conditions. Sharpe's success in motivating prisoners and deserters to assist him by making a "full discovery of their knowledge of the enemy" evidently helped spur the War Department to adopt this incentive program as official government policy.[22]

In light of inaccurate information often derived through this process in the past, these improved interrogation techniques would prove valuable. The BMI would have ample opportunity to demonstrate its proficiency during Lee's invasion. In addition to its own capabilities, the BMI relied on various other resources to collect information, particularly the cavalry. Unfortunately, the

21 Sharpe to Butterfield, June 23, 1863, *OR* 27, pt. 3, 266; Fishel, *The Secret War*, 292, 306-10, 553.

22 Quote from Sharpe to Brig. Gen. John Henry Martindale, military governor, District of Columbia, Dec. 12, 1863, RG 393, NA; Sparks, *Patrick's Diary*, 199; General Orders No. 64, February 18, 1864, *OR* 4, ser. 3, 118.

Army of the Potomac was not blessed with the most skillful of cavalry leaders for most of the campaign.[23]

Cavalry Corps

> Cavalry should extend well away from the main body on the march like antennae to mask its movements and to discover any movement of the enemy.
> Brig. Gen. William Woods Averell[24]

The cavalry performed vital intelligence and counterintelligence roles in addition to its combat mission. Its mobility enabled cavalry to gather information and screen the army's movements from the eyes of the enemy, roles that increased in importance when the army was on the march. Despite these scouting and security responsibilities, however, the cavalry forces still had to be able to concentrate rapidly for combat duty when necessary. D. H. Mahan, professor of military and civil engineering and of the art of war at the United States Military Academy during the Civil War years, taught his students: "To keep an enemy in ignorance of the state of our forces and the character of our position is one of the most indispensable duties of war." Captain Arthur L. Wagner, an instructor at the U.S. Infantry and Cavalry School at Ft. Leavenworth, Kansas, commented that it was the duty of the cavalry "to gain and keep contact with the enemy, and in their movements everything should be subordinated to the one object of gaining information."[25]

Following the standard European model of the time, Union manuals and military classes emphasized cavalry primarily as an offensive weapon. It was

---

23 Cavalry commander Maj. Gen. Alfred Pleasonton was particularly prone to passing along inaccurate and misleading information derived from interrogating enemy prisoners and deserters, escaped slaves, and civilians. For commentary on this issue during an earlier campaign, see Stephen W. Sears, *Landscape Turned Red: The Battle of Antietam* (New York, 1983), 113-17.

24 Eric J. Wittenberg, *The Union Cavalry Comes of Age* (Washington, D.C., 2003), 4. Averell commanded the Second Division of the Army of the Potomac Cavalry Corps until May 1863.

25 D. H. Mahan, *Advanced-Guard, Out-Post, and Detachment Service of Troops, with the Essential Principles of Strategy, and Grand Tactics for the use of Officers of the Militia and Volunteers* (New York, 1863), 83, 105; Edward G. Longacre, *Lincoln's Cavalrymen: A History of the Mounted Forces of The Army of the Potomac, 1861-1865* (Mechanicsburg, PA, 2000), 28; Wagner, *The Service of Security and Information*, 148, 157-58.

some time before the army understood its vital intelligence and counterintelligence roles.[26]

The Confederates recognized early on the valuable role of cavalry in gathering information and screening the army from the eyes of the enemy. Early in the war, however, the Union cavalry's ability to conduct intelligence and counterintelligence operations was limited, because Federal authorities failed to promote its development, and military commanders often inhibited its role in the field. The cavalry was insufficiently armed, and the weapons received were often inferior. There were not enough mounts, and horses supplied by the war department were generally of poor quality that broke down after limited duty.[27]

To its detriment, both McClellan and Burnside retained operational control over the cavalry, while limiting its leaders to administrative responsibilities. They dispersed cavalry in small units throughout the army, thereby preventing improving tactical competence and esprit de corps. In addition, infantry commanders to whom cavalry units were assigned often misused them as personal orderlies and messengers. As a result, Union cavalry lagged behind and could not contend with the better organized and more capable Rebel horsemen that frequently operated behind their lines with impunity. An embarrassing example of this occurred during McClellan's first major campaign on the Virginia peninsula. The ineffectual Union cavalry proved helpless as Stuart's troopers circled McClellan's forces gathering valuable information about their disposition for Lee.[28]

Lieutenant Edward P. Tobie of the 1st Maine Cavalry attempted to put this situation in perspective:

26 Longacre, *Lincoln's Cavalrymen*, 8-11; J. A. Roberts, "Blind Man's Bluff: Reconnaissance and Counter-Reconnaissance Efforts in the Gettysburg Campaign," accessed July 31, 2014, www.globalsecurity.org/military/library/report/1992/RJA.htm; William C. Davis, *Rebels & Yankees: The Fighting Men Of The Civil War* (New York, 1991), 75-76, 84.

27 Eric Wittenberg, "Learning the Hard Lessons of Logistics: Arming and Maintaining the Federal Cavalry," *North & South* (January 1999), 62-66; Roberts, *Reconnaissance and Counter-Reconnaissance*, 5-6; Stephen Z. Starr, *The Union Cavalry in the Civil War*, 3 vols. (Baton Rouge, LA, 1979), 1:234-59.

28 Starr, *The Union Cavalry*, 1:234-40, 265-74, 324-25; Longacre, *Lincoln's Cavalrymen*, 53-129; Roberts, *Reconnaissance and Counter-Reconnaissance*, 5-6. Cavalry commander Brig. Gen. George Stoneman complained to McClellan during the campaign that officers were using men that were needed for scouting parties as orderlies and other incidental duties. OR 11, pt. 2, 930; Starr, *The Union Cavalry*, 266.

Maj. Gen. George B. McClellan
Library of Congress

Up to the spring of 1863 the cavalry of the Army of the Potomac, at least, had been of little use as a separate branch of the service. In the first place, the regular army officers had no faith in volunteer cavalry, characterizing it as a 'mounted mob' . . . Thus there was the prejudice against cavalry in general, and volunteer cavalry in particular, to overcome . . . [and] the work of making volunteer regiments of cavalry into good troopers was necessarily one which required much time and . . . actual experience. . . . The cavalry had been broken up and divided,—a regiment with this division or brigade, a company at this or that general's headquarters . . . till it was rare to see a large body together. . . . The history of [the 1st Maine] shows that it had served together but little of the time. . . . A portion of it had served all over the Army of the Potomac, on all sorts of service. And the different companies had been broken up by the general desire on the part of commanding officers to have orderlies, clerks, etc. . . . which . . . interfered with the efficiency of the regiment.[29]

The situation had begun to improve before Lee's invasion of the North got underway in early June 1863. With general orders no. 6 on February 5, about the same time he established the BMI, Hooker had revamped the cavalry into a single unit. The 1st New Jersey Cavalry's chaplain, Henry R. Pyne, exulted. The cavalry "owe a debt of gratitude . . . to [Hooker] . . . [f]or the first time the cavalry found themselves made useful by their general, and treated as something better than military watchmen for the army."[30]

Under the reorganization, the cavalry had a variety of missions: picketing the perimeter of encampments to give early warning in the event of attacks and to prevent intruders from penetrating the lines; scouting in small squads searching out the enemy and gathering useful information for army commanders; keeping enemy patrols at a distance from Union army positions; observing and arresting local civilians suspected of passing information to the enemy; uncovering civilian networks smuggling medical and other war-related goods to the Confederates; and guarding and escorting prisoners of war. [31]

In his memoirs, J. H. Kidd of the 6th Michigan described a cavalry picket established around Washington, D.C., in a semi-circular line with the right and left resting on the Potomac above and below the city. Along a creek two miles in front of the pickets a line of vedettes prevented the enemy from making a surprise attack. Well out from the main camp two large reserves commanded by captains were stationed, with smaller ones under a lieutenant or sergeant even farther out toward the vedettes.[32]

29 Edward P. Tobie, *History of the First Maine Cavalry, 1861-1865* (Boston, 1887), 122-23.

30 Hdqrs. Army of the Potomac, General Orders, No. 6, February 5, 1863, *OR* 25, pt. 2, 51; Henry R. Pyne, *The History of the First New Jersey Cavalry* (New Brunswick, NJ, 1961), 117.

31 Abner Hard, M.D., *History of the Eighth Cavalry Regiment Illinois Volunteers* (Dayton, OH, 1984), 226-28; Louis N. Boudrye, *Fifth New York Cavalry* (Albany, NY, 1865), 58-60; James Penfield, *1863-64 Civil War Diary* (Ticonderoga, NY, 1999), 60-61; William O. Lee, *Seventh Regiment Michigan Volunteer Cavalry, 1862-1865* (Detroit, MI, 1990), 90-95, 129-32, 161-63, 209; Eric Wittenberg, ed., *One of Custer's Wolverines: The Civil War Letters of Brevet Brigadier General James H. Kidd, 6th Michigan Cavalry* (Kent, OH, 2000), 20. Captain James H. Kidd, 6th Michigan Cavalry, wrote the job description of a Union cavalryman: "scout by day and vigilant watch by night." Wittenberg, *One of Custer's Wolverines*, 36.

32 J. H. Kidd, *Personal Recollections of a Cavalryman with Custer's Michigan Cavalry Brigade in the Civil War* (Grand Rapids, MI, 1969), 101-102. The necessity for effective picketing in hostile territory

One of the cavalry's more difficult duties was to contend with troublesome Rebel guerrillas, particularly those of Maj. John S. Mosby, "Mosby's Rangers," who attacked military targets without warning before vanishing into the countryside. Mosby's men, as cavalry historian Edward G. Longacre has pointed out, were adept at "slipping through the lines—sometimes in disguise, sometimes boldly in Rebel gray—to gather critical intelligence." Guerrillas also hampered the work of Union scouting detachments and ambushed cavalry patrols—killing, wounding, and capturing significant numbers. Though important, the duty was onerous as one Union cavalry officer lamented:

> Guerillas were numerous and bold at this time, hovering around the rear of the army, picking up stragglers, tearing up rails and destroying culverts on the railroad, attacking small bodies of troops, now and then capturing a wagon or a whole train, and occasionally charging into a camp and carrying off whatever they could. . . . the boys soon found...that picketing against guerillas was the most despicable part of the service.[33]

Mosby's unorthodox tactics often allowed his rangers to outmaneuver the Union cavalry's more formal, cumbersome responses. Focusing on the depredations of guerrillas distracted from other critical cavalry duties, especially scouting the enemy's disposition, strength, and intentions, and screening the army from enemy observation and sudden attack. When the cavalry was in camp, "constant watchfulness was required," because of the guerrillas.[34]

The Union cavalry reorganization helped foster a much-needed sense of identity among the Union horse soldiers. By June, the cavalry consisted of a two-division corps (soon to be increased to three) with newly promoted Brig.

---

was demonstrated when the 1st Pennsylvania deployed three of its 11 companies (about 115 of its 418 men) and the 3rd Pennsylvania four of its 12 companies (about 140 of its 394 men) on picket duty when the cavalry regiments camped near Warrenton, Virginia, in mid-June to counter the threat of attack by enemy cavalry and guerrillas in the area. William Brooke Rawle, *History of the Third Pennsylvania Cavalry* (Philadelphia, 1905), 251; George D. Bayard, Owen Jones, and John P. Taylor, *History of the First Reg't Pennsylvania Reserve Cavalry* (Philadelphia, 1864), 56-57.

33 Edward G. Longacre, *Custer and His Wolverines: The Michigan Cavalry Brigade, 1861-1865* (Conshohocken, PA, 1997), 102-103. See also Wittenberg, *One of Custer's Wolverines*, 17-39; William Hyndman, *History of a Cavalry Company: A Complete Record of Company "A," 4th Penn's Cavalry* (Philadelphia, 1870), 96; William H. Beach, *The First New York (Lincoln) Cavalry* (Milwaukee, WI, 1902), 222-26. Union cavalry officer quoted in Tobie, *First Maine Cavalry*, 145.

34 Eric J. Wittenberg, *Under Custer's Command: The Civil War Journal of James Henry Avery* (Washington, DC, 2000), 26; Tobie, *First Maine Cavalry*, 145.

Gen. Alfred Pleasonton in command. Brigadier Generals John Buford and David M. Gregg headed the divisions.[35]

As senior division commander, Pleasonton assumed temporary command of the corps when Maj. Gen. George Stoneman went on medical leave following his raid behind enemy lines in Virginia. The caliber of corps leadership, however, was suspect. Pleasonton had obtained his position through an ingratiating personality with his commanders, seniority in rank, exaggerated claims of success on the battlefield, and political connections. Surgeon Abner Hard of the 8th Illinois Cavalry noted that Pleasonton "had already cultivated the favor of the powerful Radical Republicans in Congress," including Congressman John Farnsworth, a former colonel of the 8th Illinois. Hard implied that Pleasonton curried favor with Farnsworth by arranging the unprecedented promotion of the congressman's nephew, a member of Pleasonton's staff, from captain to brigadier general, while, at the same time, requesting Farnsworth to lobby for Pleasonton's promotion to major general. Questions about Pleasonton's decisiveness and judgment in combat also raised doubts about his ability to perform at a higher level. In particular, Pleasonton's inability to collect accurate information about the enemy and assess it objectively often left army commanders without reliable data to conduct successful operations. Opinions were mixed in this regard, however, since Hard thought that "despite his flaws of character," Pleasonton "knew how to fight cavalry."[36]

---

35 OR 25, pt. 2, 51; Starr, *The Union Cavalry*, 1:339; Longacre, *Lincoln's Cavalrymen*, 127, 163; Longacre, *The Cavalry at Gettysburg*, 49-50; Roberts, *Reconnaissance and Counter-Reconnaissance*, 6-7. Hooker initially assigned Brig. Gen. George Stoneman as cavalry corps commander, then replaced him with Pleasonton following the battle of Chancellorsville. Starr, *The Union Cavalry*, 1:367-68.

36 Hdqrs. Cav. Corps, Army of the Potomac, General Orders, No. 11, May 22, 1863, OR 25, pt. 2, 513; Hard, *Eighth Cavalry Regiment Illinois Volunteers*, vii, ix. See also Pleasonton to Farnsworth, June 23, 1863, Pleasonton Papers, Library of Congress; Longacre, *Lincoln's Cavalrymen*, 28, 145; Roberts, *Reconnaissance and Counter-Reconnaissance*, 6-7. For a profile of Pleasonton's life and military career, see, J. David Petruzzi, "The fleeting fame of Alfred Pleasonton," *America's Civil War* (March 2005), 22-28. After Chancellorsville, Hooker looked for scapegoats and hit on Stoneman for one. Apparently seeing the writing on the wall, Stoneman decided to take medical leave. Ben F. Fordney, *Stoneman at Chancellorsville: The Coming of Age of Union Cavalry* (Shippensburg, PA, 1998), 47; Starr, *The Union Cavalry*, 1:361-62, 367-68. Special Orders No. 153 granted Stoneman a leave of absence "for the benefit of his health." But directions for him to report to the Adjutant-General of the Army for further instructions at the end of his leave of absence evinced Hooker's intention to sack Stoneman. Hdqrs, Army of the Potomac, Special Orders, No. 153, June 5, 1863, OR 27, pt. 3, 10-11. Rumors in camp about

Maj. Gen. Alfred Pleasonton
Library of Congress

Like Jeb Stuart, his Confederate counterpart, Pleasonton was a product of West Point. Following graduation in 1844, he served in the Mexican War and on the American frontier where he gained experience in scouting hostile Indian tribes. As a captain in the 2nd U.S. Dragoons, he led the regiment from Utah to Washington, D.C., after the Civil War commenced. Pleasonton's performance during the Peninsula campaign in 1862 caught McClellan's attention and led to his promotion to brigadier general.[37]

During Lee's Maryland campaign in September 1862, while Pleasonton commanded the operational arm of McClellan's cavalry, he sent Union headquarters inflated estimates of enemy strength derived from dubious sources. In part this was the result of the Union cavalry's inability to penetrate the enemy's screen that prevented them from observing Lee's army, and capturing prisoners for interrogation.[38]

---

this were noted in a May 12, 1863, entry in the diary of Capt. Charles Francis Adams, Jr., 1st Massachusetts Cavalry, "They . . . say that Hooker wishes to depose Stoneman and hand the command over to Pleasonton." Quoted in Starr, *The Union Cavalry,* 1:368.

37 Ezra J. Warner, *Generals in Blue: Lives of Union Commanders* (Baton Rouge, LA, 1992), 373; Petruzzi, "The fleeting fame of Alfred Pleasonton," 24.

38 Pleasonton to Marcy, September 6 and 7, 1862, OR 19, pt. 2, 192-4, 200-201; McClellan to Halleck, September 9, 1862, 219; McClellan to [Lincoln], September 10, 182, 233. It also reflected McClellan's belief that the Army of Northern Virginia was two to four times larger than its actual size, which undoubtedly influenced Pleasonton's perception. Neither man displayed proper skepticism about exaggerated enemy strength figures. During the Peninsula campaign in July 1862, McClellan concluded without substantiation that the enemy had "perhaps double my numbers." Stephen W. Sears, *To the Gates of Richmond: The Peninsula Campaign* (Boston, 1992), 99.

Pleasonton also at times gratuitously offered strategic advice to his commander, rather than limiting his input to information derived from scouting and reconnaissance. His questionable judgment in evaluating information and a penchant for overreaching his authority would handicap the upcoming campaign. To his credit, however, on December 1, 1862, Pleasonton had recommended reorganization of the cavalry to Burnside. It should, he wrote, be formed into brigades and divisions within a corps organization. Pleasonton accurately pointed out that: "The rebel cavalry owe their success to their organization, which permits great freedom and responsibility to its commanders, subject to the commanding general." Even though Burnside did not implement these recommendations during his short tenure as Army of the Potomac commander, Pleasonton must have been pleased when, shortly after his appointment, Hooker announced the cavalry reorganization—although there is no evidence that he had seen or specifically acted upon Pleasonton's memorandum.[39]

Pleasonton's first opportunity to perform as a division commander under Stoneman in the new reorganization proved less than successful. During an engagement with Rebel cavalry at Hartwood Church, Virginia, in February, Pleasonton either misunderstood or did not follow his orders. Chief of staff Maj. Gen. Daniel Butterfield reprimanded him for not pursuing the enemy as instructed. This established a pattern of failing to follow orders that would be repeated during the Gettysburg campaign.[40]

Before the battle of Chancellorsville, Stoneman took his corps on a raid behind enemy lines. He left Pleasonton in support of the army, but with only one of his two brigades. Pleasonton's failure to clarify whether he or his brigade commander Col. Thomas C. Devin was in charge of this detachment led to confusion. This was especially evident when the three regiments of this brigade were doled out individually in support of infantry units, rather than fighting as a unit. It also led to heavy casualties among these cavalrymen. Pleasonton also made outlandish claims about saving the Union army from defeat at

---

39 Pleasonton to Burnside, December 1, 1862, OR 21, 815. See also, Starr, *The Union Cavalry*, 1:327; Wittenberg, *The Union Cavalry Comes of Age*, 7-8, 13-14.

40 Butterfield to Pleasonton, February 26, 1863, OR 25, pt. 2, 108; Wittenberg, *The Union Cavalry Comes of Age*, 60-62; Starr, *The Union Cavalry*, 1:343-45.

Brig. Gen. John Buford
Library of Congress

Chancellorsville; however, those who knew better challenged these exaggerations.[41]

Evaluating Pleasonton's performance after he assumed the critical post as his army's cavalry commander, and, perhaps having second thoughts about this appointment, Hooker later spelled out the scope of Pleasonton's primary mission. He relied, he wrote, on his cavalry force to provide information about the location, strength and movements of the enemy—all of which was to be communicated promptly. Hooker would soon learn that Pleasonton was neither well-equipped nor well-disposed to fulfill these requirements.[42]

John Buford and David Gregg were Pleasonton's division commanders, both with reputations as capable cavalry leaders. Buford's combat tactics, reconnaissance, and information-gathering abilities were highly respected. A member of his staff described him as:

> a thoroughly trained officer, a gentleman of truly modest and retiring deportment, cool and self-possessed at all times, his orders on the field marvels of precision, his power of perception quick, combining with an admirable grasp of mind that courage and caution which made him one of the most promising officers of the cavalry corps, and justly entitled him to the command of the First Division.[43]

41 Wittenberg, *The Union Cavalry Comes of Age*, 145-46, 158-64, 168-71; Petruzzi, *The Fleeting Fame of Alfred Pleasonton*, 26.

42 Williams to Hooker, June 17, 1863, *OR* 27, pt. 3, 172.

43 Theo. W. Bean, "General Buford at Gettysburg—The Cavalry Ride into Pennsylvania and the Choice of the Field of Battle—The First Day on the Outposts Before the Arrival of the Infantry," *Gettysburg Sources*, 3 vols. (Baltimore, MD, 1990), 3:73; Longacre, *Lincoln's Cavalrymen*, 16, 99, 101, 151.

Brig. Gen. David McM. Gregg
Library of Congress

Born in Kentucky, Buford received an appointment to West Point while living in Illinois. Upon graduation in 1848, he performed frontier service out west for several years with the 2nd Dragoons (later the 2nd Cavalry). Buford received a brigadier general's commission after serving staff duty in Washington and took command of the reserve cavalry brigade. He was badly wounded at Second Bull Run, but recovered in time to serve as chief of the Army of the Potomac's cavalry during the Maryland campaign. At Chancellorsville, Buford took part in Stoneman's raid once again in command of the reserve brigade. He took division command under Pleasonton before the Gettysburg campaign.[44]

David Gregg, a dedicated professional of battle-tested leadership qualities, was a Pennsylvanian by birth and cousin of that state's governor, Andrew Gregg Curtin. At West Point, Gregg was an underclassman to Jeb Stuart and Philip Sheridan. He graduated eighth in the class of 1855, and gained a reputation as one of the best horsemen in the corps of cadets. Gregg also served on the Indian frontier, and several months after the outset of the Civil War he became colonel of the 8th Pennsylvania Cavalry. He later received an appointment as a volunteer brigadier general, and commanded a division during Stoneman's raid in Virginia.[45]

At the outset of the campaign, the Union cavalry corps numbered just under 8,000 troops. It would soon be increased to nearly 11,500 with the addition of a third division under Brig. Gen. Hugh Judson Kilpatrick, detached

44 Longacre, *Lincoln's Cavalrymen*, 95, 151; Warner, *Generals in Blue*, 52-53.

45 Ibid., 187-88; Maj. Gen. David McMurtrie Gregg, accessed August 1, 2013, www.oocities. org/mwkop/GenGregg.html; Sears, *Chancellorsville*, 466.

from the Department of Washington.[46] The 27-year-old Kilpatrick had graduated from West Point in 1861 and rose rapidly in the volunteer army. During his brief career as a cavalry officer, he gained a reputation of ambition and vanity. He also was reckless with the lives of his subordinates, thereby earning the moniker "Kill-cavalry." Pleasonton apparently appreciated his aggressiveness, despite his lack of self-discipline.[47]

Along with the BMI, Hooker relied on his cavalry to keep him informed about the activities of the Rebel army. Once Hooker suspected that Lee planned to move northward away from the Rappahannock, he sent the cavalry up river to reconnoiter for enemy activity in that area. How well the Army of the Potomac's new cavalry corps performed its assignments would be a key factor in determining who would gain the upper hand as Lee's invasion of the North got underway.[48]

Signal Corps

> In every important campaign and on every bloody Ground [of the Civil War], the red
> flags of the Signal Corps . . . were seen on the advanced lines.
>   Maj. Gen. Adolphus W. Greely[49]

46 Field report of the Cavalry Corps, Army of the Potomac, June 28, 1863, *OR* 27, pt. 1, 154; Statement showing strength of Pleasonton's command, June 9, 1863, 906; Busey and Martin, *Regimental Strengths and Losses at Gettysburg*, 16, 244; Longacre, *The Cavalry at Gettysburg*, 166. The expanded corps would number about 1,000 fewer than the reinforced Army of Northern Virginia's cavalry force. The seven cavalry brigades assigned to the Army of Northern Virginia by June 1863 totaled just over 12,500.

47 Cavalry Corps, Special Orders, No. 98, June 28, 1863, *OR* 27, pt. 3, 376; Warner, *Generals in Blue*, 266-67; Samuel J. Martin, *Kill-Cavalry: The Life of Union General Hugh Judson Kilpatrick* (Mechanicsburg, PA, 2000).

48 It remained to be seen whether Pleasonton would dedicate his cavalrymen to the exacting work of acquiring information about the enemy and screening the army from observation. He had made the case to Burnside several months earlier that the cavalry's duties were "to cover the front and flanks of the army[,] form advanced guards, rear guards, [and] gain information of the enemy's movements" Pleasonton to Burnside, December 1, 1862, *OR* 21, 815; Sears, *Chancellorsville*, 465. For a discussion of the evolution, performance and leadership of cavalry units prior to the Gettysburg campaign, see Davis, *The Fighting Men*, 67-82.

49 A. W. Greely, "The Signal Corps," *The Photographic History of the Civil War* (Secaucus, NJ, 1987), 318. Greely enlisted in the 19th Massachusetts Volunteer Infantry and served throughout the war. He fought in several major battles, was seriously wounded three times, and rose in rank from private to brevet major of volunteers. In 1887, he became chief of the signal corps of the U.S. Army. See Arlington National Cemetery Site, accessed August 3, 2014, www.arlingtoncemetery.net/awgreely.htm.

Albert J. Myer, the founder of the U.S. Army signal corps, received a medical degree from the University of Buffalo in New York before joining the army in 1854 as an assistant surgeon. While stationed in Texas, Myer developed a military signaling system based on his medical dissertation "A New Sign Language for Deaf Mutes." While attending medical school, Myer had worked for the New York State Telephone Company as a telegraph operator. This experience, as well as his interest in sign language, aided him in developing a system for signaling "to communicate between detachments of troops…or ships at sea." After a period of field trials and overcoming military and governmental bureaucratic hurdles, the signal corps came into being on June 21, 1860.[50]

Soon after the Civil War began, Myer instituted a program for the Federal military forces. He established a training program and arranged for signal parties to be attached to all Union departments and armies. Military units communicated with each other in a variety of ways, including by flag signals during the day and torches at night to send coded messages (informally referred to as the "wigwag" system).[51]

The chief signal officer of the Army of the Potomac at the outset of the Gettysburg campaign, Capt. Benjamin Franklin Fisher, assigned a signal party to every corps as well as to army headquarters. In addition to sending and receiving messages, the signal corps also was responsible for intercepting enemy communications, observing their movements, conducting reconnaissance, and exploring terrain.[52]

Signal equipment included flags of different sizes and colors (depending on the background and distance involved), torches, fuel, and other paraphernalia. Since both sides used similar signal codes to transmit messages, they employed ciphers with prearranged keywords to secure the contents from enemy

---

50 Brown, *The Signal Corps*, 20-22; Rebecca Robbins Raines, *Getting the Message Through: A Branch History of the U.S. Army Signal Corps* (Washington, D.C., 1999), 5; Paul J. Scheips, "Union Signal Communications: Innovation and Conflict," *Civil War History* (December 1963), IX:.

51 Brown, *The Signal Corps*, 19-37, 160.

52 Myer's report to the Adjutant General, Army of the Potomac, October 21, 1862, OR 5, 69-72; Brown, The Signal Corps, U.S.A., 145, 297, 357-60; Bill Cameron, "Signal Corps," in David Stephen Heidler and Jeanne T. Heidler, eds., *Encyclopedia of the American Civil War: A Political, Social, and Military History*, 5 vols. (New York, 2002), 4:1788; Cameron, "The Signal Corps at Gettysburg," 10; Raines, Getting the Message Through, 25; Greely, "The Signal Corps," 326, 328.

Col. Albert J. Myer
Library of Congress

interception. With proper conditions and the use of telescopes, communication could regularly be sustained over distances of 10-15 miles, even farther if conditions were right.[53]

The Signal Corps supplemented flag and torch signals with a system of field telegraphy. Insulated wire on reels carried in wagons allowed units to communicate in all weather conditions over long distances. Each telegraph wagon train carried at least five miles of wire and 200 poles. The Beardslee Machine, a magneto-electric generator, facilitated use of the telegraph for tactical purposes—replacing heavier lead batteries that limited vital mobility in the field. During the march northward in June 1863, the Signal Corps provided field telegraph service connecting Hooker's headquarters with the various army corps.[54]

Since their outposts were often isolated, signal personnel were vulnerable to attack and capture. On a fog-shrouded morning in October 1862, for example, Confederate cavalry overran a Union signal station on Fairview Heights near Clear Spring, Maryland, during a raid into Pennsylvania, and captured two members of the signal party. In addition, signal positions located

53 Cameron, "Signal Corps," Heidler & Heidler, 4:1788; Greely, "The Signal Corps," 316, 318. Although each corps was authorized a captain, eight lieutenants, seven sergeants, 25 first-class privates, and 34 second-class privates–a total of 75 signal personnel–the actual size of these units during the Gettysburg campaign was significantly smaller. Cameron, "A Signal Sergeant at Gettysburg: The Diary of Luther C. Furst," *Gettysburg Magazine* (January 1994), no. 10, 43.

54 Scheips, "Union Signal Communications," 9-11; William R. Plum, *The Military Telegraph during the Civil War in the United States*, 2 vols. (Chicago, 1882), 2:9-24; OR 25, pt. 2, 457-58. Sometimes the Beardslee Machines failed to perform adequately during combat conditions, such as during the battle of Chancellorsville in early May 1863 when lightning strikes disrupted the machines' synchronization. And at times they proved inadequate over distances longer than five miles. Consequently, chief of staff Butterfield ordered United States Military Telegraph operators to provide service at critical points on the field during Chancellorsville. Sears, *Chancellorsville*, 194-96; Brown, *The Signal Corps*, 358-60.

near the enemy often were within the range of their artillery and sharpshooters.[55]

Before the Gettysburg campaign, the signal corps had gained valuable experience on all the army's previous fields, from the Peninsula to Chancellorsville. A tested veteran organization by June 1863, it was more than capable of providing reliable communications and information about the enemy. Signal messages could also be used to deceive the enemy. Before Chancellorsville, the Federals concocted a ruse to fool Lee into believing that the Union cavalry were moving into the Shenandoah Valley via an unencrypted message. The ruse worked: Lee sent Stuart's cavalry upriver to interdict this supposed Union movement, thereby leaving a gap in the line that permitted the Union infantry to make a turning movement against Lee's right flank around Fredericksburg.[56]

Chief signal officer Benjamin Fisher, one of the most talented and experienced officers in the Signal Corps with "a brilliant record," was captured by Mosby's Rangers near Aldie, Virginia, on June 17, 1863, and sent to Libby Prison in Richmond. Captain Lemuel B. Norton assumed command of the army's Signal Corps detachment, which would perform singular service under his leadership in the ensuing campaign.[57]

Balloon Corps

---

55 Lee's post-action reports, August 19, 1863, October 14, 1862, *OR* 19, pt. 1, 152, pt. 2, 51; Cameron, "Signal Corps," 1788; Greely, "The Signal Corps," 318, 322; John W. Thomason, Jr., *Jeb Stuart* (New York, 1930), 300.

56 Greely, "Signal Corps," 322, 324, 326, 328; Brown, *The Signal Corps*, 289-357. For a discussion of the ruse, see Fishel, *The Secret War*, 347-48.

57 Beginning in August 1861, Fisher served as assistant to Major Myer on detail from the 3rd Pennsylvania Regiment and soon became an instructor at the signal camp in the capital. Later he was in charge of signal detachments in Brig. Gen. Joseph Hooker's command on the lower Potomac, Maj. Gen. Erasmus D. Keyes' IV Corps on the Peninsula, and during the Maryland campaign before receiving appointment as the army's chief signal officer in September 1862. Fisher managed to escape from Libby Prison in February 1864 and returned to service with the Signal Corps. In December 1864, he succeeded Lt. Col. W. J. L. Nicodemus (who had succeeded Major Myer on November 10, 1863) as chief of the Union Signal Corps. Norton had joined Myer in August 1861 at the signal camp in Georgetown on detail from the 10th Pennsylvania Reserve Regiment and served as an instructor. He also served on the Peninsula in March 1862 and at Fredericksburg in December. Brown, *The Signal Corps*, 57, 60, 69, 71, 77, 83, 87, 164-65, 291, 293, 342, 358, 364, 370, 769-70, 842-43.

[Based on my observations from the balloon], the enemy's line of battle is formed in
the edge of the woods, at the foot of the heights, from opposite Fredericksburg to
some distance to the left of our lower crossing. Their line appears quite thin, compared
with our force. Their tents all remain as heretofore, as far as I can see.

T. S. C. Lowe, Chief of Aeronaut (aloft)[58]

Another method for enemy observation was the use of gas-filled balloons
that floated high above their positions. The brainchild of aeronaut Thaddeus S.
C. Lowe, an aeronautical corps with Lowe in charge came into being when
President Lincoln unofficially sanctioned it in August 1861 as a part of the
Union army. In addition to gathering information about enemy strength,
position, and movements, balloons sometimes served to coordinate artillery fire
against enemy targets.[59]

The army tested various methods of signaling, including the use of flags
and colored flares, to facilitate air-to-ground communications and
experimented with sending messages over telegraph wire also. Army lethargy,
civilian–military friction and prejudice, and logistical problems in transporting
and maintaining the balloons, however, doomed the program. By April 1863,
Lowe resigned his position, and the remnants of the balloon corps did not
accompany the Army of the Potomac during the Gettysburg campaign. It soon
faded out of existence.[60]

In his book *War of the Astronauts: A History of Ballooning During the Civil War,*
Charles M. Evans concluded, "If the [Balloon Corps] had been allowed to
continue their efforts with the Army of the Potomac, the timing may have
proved propitious. A new battlefront was forming to the north, as Robert E.
Lee pulled his men from the vicinity of Fredericksburg and began a long march
toward Pennsylvania."[61]

---

58 Lowe to Butterfield, April [29], 1863, *OR* 25, pt. 2, 289. Thaddeus S. C. Lowe was the
civilian head of the U.S. Army Balloon Corps. He transmitted this message from a "Balloon in
the Air" on April 29, 1863, prior to the battle of Chancellorsville. Lowe probably sent this
message to the ground via a telegraph wire that ran along one of the tethers anchoring the
balloon to the ground. See Evans, *Aeronauts,* 69.

59 Ibid., 87; 112-13; Faust, *Historical Times Encyclopedia,* 35.

60 Evans, *Aeronauts,* 68-71, 166, 288-93; Fishel, *The Secret War,* 442-43.

61 Evans, *Aeronauts,* 200.

U.S. Military Telegraph

> The successful operation of army movements often [depends] upon the reliability and promptness of the telegraph and its operators.
>
> Maj. Thomas T. Eckert[62]

The Civil War saw the first extensive military application of the telegraph. In addition to the Signal Corps, the U.S. Military Telegraph Service supplied the Army of the Potomac's communications requirements. The telegraph service, essentially a civilian bureau adapted for military purposes, had as its primary mission providing strategic and administrative communications to commanders. The Signal Corps, on the other hand, mainly supported tactical operations with its flag and field telegraph system.[63]

In February 1862, Lincoln took control of all telegraph lines in the U.S. Although attached to the quartermaster department, the telegraph service unofficially took its direction from the secretary of war, Edwin M. Stanton. From an intelligence perspective, the telegraph permitted the Army of the Potomac to exchange information with other commands and the government at Washington. In addition, the telegraph service employed ciphers to guard the secrecy of communications against wiretapping. To help maintain security, access to cipher books was limited to civilian telegraph experts assigned to the military units. No exceptions to this rule were permitted, not even for army commanders.[64]

When the campaign began in early June, while the armies faced each other across the Rappahannock River, the Army of the Potomac at Falmouth was in communication by telegraph with the commands of the Middle Depart- ment at Baltimore, the Department of Washington, and the Department of Virginia and North Carolina at Fort Monroe and Suffolk. It also was able to communicate with the Union cavalry operating northwest of army headquarters at Bealeton, Virginia. As the Union army moved northward in pursuit of the Confederates,

---

62 Quoted in Plum, *The Military Telegraph During the Civil War*, 2:24. Eckert was chief of the military telegraph office at the war department in Washington. See David Homer Bates, *Lincoln in the Telegraph Office: Recollections of the United States Military Telegraph Corps During the Civil War* (Lincoln, NE, 1995), 124, 137.

63 G. J. A. O'Toole, *The Encyclopedia of American Intelligence and Espionage: From the Revolutionary War to the Present* (New York, 1988), 496.

64 Scheips, *Union Signal Communications*, 4; ibid.; Greely, "Signal Corps," 348-49.

Col. Hiram Berdan
Library of Congress

civilian telegraph operators helped
maintain communications throughout
the campaign.[65]

Special Units

> I received orders to send forward a
> detachment of 100 sharpshooters to
> discover, if possible, what the enemy was
> doing.
>   Col. Hiram Berdan[66]

The Army of the Potomac had
other means for gathering information
and denying the enemy knowledge of its strength and movements.
Sharpshooter units could be used as well. Their main function in combat was to
serve as skirmishers forming a defense line in front of the army while
reconnoitering enemy positions. They also confronted enemy troops
attempting to reconnoiter Union lines. Most notable of these special units were
the 1st and 2nd United States Sharpshooters, otherwise known as "Berdan's
Sharpshooters" after their founder and commander Col. Hiram Berdan.[67]

Berdan's Sharpshooters established their reputation during the Peninsula
campaign in March 1862 by leading the army when it was on the move,
searching for the location of the enemy, and harassing them with accurate
gunfire. At times, Berdan's men also conducted nighttime scouting operations.
One New York soldier opined, "Berdan's Sharp Shooters prove themselves to
be one of the most useful organizations of our service." They participated in all

---

65 Plum, *The Military Telegraph*, 9-24; Scheips, *Union Signal Communications*, 9-11.

66 OR 27, pt. 1, 515; R. L. Murray, *Berdan's Sharpshooters in Combat: The Peninsula Campaign and Gettysburg* (Wolcott, NY, 2005), 62.

67 Murray, *Berdan's Sharpshooters*, preface, 1-2 (unnumbered).

subsequent Army of the Potomac engagements thereby gaining experience that would prove valuable during the Gettysburg campaign.[68]

Another unit with special qualifications available to the army was the Loudoun Rangers. In June 1862, Secretary of War Edwin Stanton recruited Samuel C. Means, a successful businessman from Waterford, Virginia, to organize the independent Loudoun Rangers and assigned him as commander with the rank of captain. The Rangers' mission was to serve as scouts and guides for regular army units and to counteract Confederate raiding parties in northern Virginia, particularly Mosby's Rangers.[69]

The members of this group were disaffected Virginians, mostly Germans and Quakers who opposed slavery and secession. They hailed from Loudoun, Clarke, and Jefferson counties, and established their base around Waterford about 10 miles north of Leesburg. The Loudoun Rangers peak strength was about 200 organized into two companies, but they generally operated with a smaller force.

A detachment of Loudoun Rangers saw action as scouts and guides for the Harpers Ferry garrison during the Antietam campaign in September 1862, and also for Maj. Gen. George B. McClellan's army following the battle. During the Gettysburg campaign, the commander at Harper's Ferry, Maj. Gen. William French, employed the Loudoun Rangers as scouts. Captain Means and his men were also available during the upcoming campaign.[70]

Couriers, guides, and escorts assigned to army units also gathered information. Several units carried out these essential duties for army headquarters including the 2nd Pen- nsylvania Cavalry, two companies of the 6th Pennsylvania Cavalry, and detachments from the 1st, 2nd, 5th, and 6th U.S. Cavalry. These units scouted the best routes for movement of the army and kept watch for enemy spies and informers operating in or near the Union encampment. Other units functioned in similar capacity at the corps level and below.[71]

---

68 Ibid., 3-19.

69 Briscoe Goodhart, *History of the Independent Loudoun Virginia Rangers, U.S. Vol. Cav. (SCOUTS), 1862-65* (Washington, 1896), 1-8, 27.

70 Ibid., 51-58, 77-78, 88-91, 98-102; Virgil Carrington Jones, *Ranger Mosby*, (Chapel Hill, NC, 1944), 89-91; Thomas J. Ryan, "A Battle of Wits: Intelligence Operations during the Gettysburg Campaign," *Gettysburg Magazine* (July 2004), no. 31, 25.

71 Coddington, *The Gettysburg Campaign*, 575, 577, 580-81, 583-84.

Allan Pinkerton
Miller's Photographic History

Spy Networks

> The rebels are shortly in advance of us—but if thro' the districts they threaten our friends will organize & send us information with the precision you have done, they may rest secure in the result.
>
> Col. George H. Sharpe[72]

A potentially lucrative source of strategic military and political intelligence was the capital of the Confederacy. But, unlike the Confederates who had established spy networks in Washington early in the war, little effort was made to exploit anti-secessionist and pro-Union sympathy in Richmond by creating networks to serve the Northern cause.[73]

McClellan's intelligence chief, Allen Pinkerton, had some success in penetrating Richmond with his agents. By March 1863, the BMI's Sharpe hired a civilian, Joseph H. Maddox, to operate in Richmond; however, this effort produced little of value. A viable Union spy network would not be created in Richmond until several months following the Gettysburg campaign.[74]

The movement away from the Rappahannock River in Virginia in June 1863 to friendlier regions in Maryland and Pennsylvania, however, meant that

---

72 Sharpe to David McConaughy, June 29, 1863, quoted in Fishel, *The Secret War*, 503. McConaughy was a resident of Gettysburg who organized a group of civilians to scout and spy on Lee's army in Pennsylvania.

73 William A. Tidwell, et al., *Come Retribution: The Confederate Secret Service and the Assassination of Lincoln* (Jackson, MS, 1988), 51-75.

74 Elizabeth R. Varon, *Southern Lady, Yankee Spy: The True Story of Elizabeth Van Lew, A Union Agent in the Heart of the Confederacy* (Oxford, UK, 2003), 74-76, 97-98, 109-12; Fishel, *The Secret War*, 555.

the army could depend more on the local populace for information. During the campaign, a number of civilians actively observed Lee's troops and informed the Union army about their movements. Major General Darius N. Couch, the Department of the Susquehanna commander in Pennsylvania, established one civilian group, and Maj. Gen. Robert C. Schenck, VIII Corps commander also sent out civilian scouts in search of Lee's army.[75]

The widely dispersed positions of the Army of Northern Virginia during the invasion made it difficult for the Union cavalry and BMI scouts to maintain contact with the enemy. So Federal authorities welcomed civilian help in tracking and reporting on their movements.[76]

Topographical Experts

> [Gen. Kilpatrick] asked . . . where Jacob Wirt lived [in Hanover] . . . One officer came out carrying a large wall map of York County.
> Robert E. Spangler[77]

Reliable maps of the regions in which they were operating were one potential, but rarely seen, source of useful information to military commanders. Most maps existing at the outset of hostilities not only lacked accuracy, but also the details needed for military purposes. Given a paucity of maps to guide them, the Union army was at a disadvantage in Southern territory because Confederates were more familiar with the landscape.

This disparity impacted military operations, particularly in the east. At the same time, information derived from blacks in the South who had an intimate familiarity with the areas they inhabited partially offset the difficulty. This information had to be handled with some discretion, however, since blacks, in their exuberance to help, had a tendency to embellish the facts.

Thanks to the writings of participants in the mid-nineteenth century conflict, we have an understanding of important topographical activities and advancements. The Federal government was better prepared than the Confederacy to produce wartime maps through its corps of topographical

---

75 Fishel, *The Secret War*, 456-57, 471-72, 503-04.

76 Hooker to Lincoln, June 15, 1863, *OR* 27, pt. 1, 43-44.

77 William Anthony, "Reminiscences Told by Robert E. Spangler," in *Battle of Hanover* (Hanover, PA, 1945), 143.

engineers, the U.S. Coast Survey, and other agencies. These organizations produced general or strategic maps, but they often based their work on existing and, therefore, unreliable maps.

Commanders in the field also required narrowly focused maps of their operational areas. Experience demonstrated timeliness more important than accuracy in preparing these maps for tactical purposes, because in combat the enemy often overran a position before a map could be completed. While reconnoitering the countryside, army engineers exploring the terrain were vulnerable to enemy fire or capture. Even friendly scouts and outposts at times frustrated their work and marched them to camp for identification.

At times, not knowing the terrain, commanders employed a reconnaissance in-force literally to capture the ground so engineers could sketch and map the area. The information obtained and graphically depicted was a key ingredient in combat decisions, especially since successful operations frequently depended on the availability and condition of roads. It helped if commanders were a "quick study" being able to examine detailed maps and readily retain the information.

One of the main duties of staff engineers was to reconnoiter the enemy and produce accurate topographical sketches of their position and strength. They especially noted the extent and nature of wooded areas where the enemy could be hiding, and where it was difficult to employ cavalry and artillery. Other natural features, such as hills and mountains, were also observed because they were keys to holding ground and winning battles.

Since marching armies often lived off of the land, maps routinely included potential sources of supply such as taverns, hotels, stables, general stores, blacksmiths, etc. Questioning enemy stragglers or local residents about surrounding terrain proved valuable, especially if done by a resourceful and perceptive interrogator. If civilians resisted, threats to their safety helped elicit the desired information. Enterprising topographical engineers were also able to fix the exact location of towns on their maps by examining data acquired from local clerks.

The result of this combined activity generally included a sketch of the terrain the army would travel, a better understanding of the enemy's intentions, and identification of the potential battlefield. Multiple sources, such as surveys, reconnaissance, interviews of knowledgeable people, existing maps, related documents, and engineering reviews, combined to produce these results.[78]

Summation

As the Gettysburg campaign got underway in early June 1863, the Army of the Potomac had extensive intelligence and communications resources in place. Specialists in these areas were called upon to support the Union commanders and their operations. How well the army leaders understood and applied these resources would have a decided effect on the outcome of the campaign.

In particular, Major General Meade, who would take command of the army on June 28, was not only new to command of the army, but unfamiliar with the inner workings of the BMI. Meade's approach to information gathering differed from Hooker's; therefore, his expectations would modify the types of reports flowing to army headquarters from the intelligence staff. Meade preferred to receive raw information rather than processed data. The type of information he received, or did not receive in certain instances, influenced his approach to combat with the enemy.

78 Earl B. McElfresh, *Maps and Mapmakers of the Civil War* (New York, 1999), 17-22, 24, 26, 29-31, 33-34, 36-37, 45-46, 49, 51-52, 54, 56, 58, 65-66.

Chapter Two

Intelligence Resources:
Army of Northern Virginia

Washington had seemed to offer a perfect place of concealment and field of
operations for Confederate spies [and] domestic conspirators.

— *Senator Charles Sumner*[1]

Robert E. Lee: Intelligence Officer

Lee excelled in putting intelligence to use. Given a piece of significant tactical
information, he knew what action to take, and he took it, and saw it through.
Edwin C. Fishel[2]

When
Lee assumed command of the Army of Northern
Virginia in July 1862, he recognized the importance
of learning about the location, strength, and intentions of the enemy. For this
Lee mainly relied on his cavalry commander, Maj. Gen. James Ewell Brown
"Jeb" Stuart.[3]

By early 1863, Lee began to use his cavalry primarily for information
gathering. This was especially true after Hooker, the new Army of the Potomac
commander, tightened security around his encampments and dried up

---

1 Massachusetts Senator Charles Sumner in a speech before the U.S. Senate during the early
months of the war. See George Fort Milton, *Abraham Lincoln and The Fifth Column* (Washington,
1943), 25. According to Sumner, Washington was "notorious [for having] . . . a very disloyal
population."

2 Fishel, *Secret War for the Union*, 571.

3 Clifford Dowdey and Louis H. Manarin, *The Wartime Papers of Robert E. Lee* (New York,
1961) 181-84, 192.

Gen. Robert E. Lee
Library of Congress

information from scouts and spies. Lee ordered the 30-year-old Stuart to disrupt Union communications north of their headquarters at Falmouth, Virginia. Stuart's job was to penetrate Union lines, observe their forces, gather information, and capture prisoners for interrogation, a task he accomplished with relative impunity because of the poor organization and ineffectiveness of Union cavalry at the time.[4]

While Lee relied on cavalry to gather intelligence about Union forces, he had other resources available: scouts and spies, special operations units, the Signal Corps, the secret service bureau, the telegraph, terrain exploration and mapmaking, and provost guards. But Lee lacked a dedicated headquarters unit, similar to the Army of the Potomac's BMI, to collate and analyze collected data and provide him with succinct reports. Instead, in keeping with his concept of maintaining a small staff, Lee personally examined and evaluated information about the enemy for planning purposes.

One advantage Lee had over his adversaries was information from Maj. William Norris' secret service unit in Richmond. In charge of the Confederate Signal Corps, Norris operated a spy and communications network extending to the enemy capital in Washington and beyond. No counterpart organization existed in the North. Southern sympathizers, some employed in the Federal war department, alerted Norris via a communications system referred to as the "Secret Line" about the strength, deployment, and intentions of Union forces. Northern newspapers arriving in Richmond along this line a day or two after publication also proved useful sources of information.[5]

Lee gained practical experience in gathering intelligence as a young army officer during the Mexican War. He spent considerable time reconnoitering the enemy and cultivated an appreciation for these operations. His commanders during that period, Brig. Gen. John C. Wool and Maj. Gen. Winfield Scott, recognized his abilities and relied on his resourcefulness in pinpointing enemy locations and attack routes. After the American victory at Cerro Gordo in 1847, Scott wrote in his report that Lee "was again indefatigable during these operations in reconnoissances [sic] as daring as laborious, and of the utmost value."[6]

By 1856, Lee was serving in Texas as commander of a cavalry detachment engaged in Indian operations along the frontier. He reconnoitered extensively to become familiar with the territory and remained alert to Comanche attempts

---

4   Sears, *Chancellorsville*, 47-49.

5   Taylor, *The Signal and Secret Service*, 1-24; William A. Tidwell, et al., *Come Retribution: The Confederate Secret Service and the Assassination of Lincoln* (Jackson, MS, 1988), 80-104.

6   A. L. Long, *Memoirs of Robert E. Lee: His Military and Personal History* (Edison, NJ, 1983), 47-71; Tidwell, *Come Retribution*, 105-06.

to bypass the cavalry outpost unseen. One observer noted that Lee "examined everything thoroughly and conscientiously until master of every detail."[7]

During this period Lee also had to plan the defense of an expansive geographic area against attack by a much larger enemy force. To help him accomplish this task, he employed local Indian scouts familiar with the territory. Survival at remote army outposts in hostile and barren regions required considerable fortitude and determination. His experience of fighting against considerable odds in Texas would prepare him for later challenges.[8]

Lee was a complex person. For more than 30 years he served with loyalty and distinction in the U.S. army before changing sides and fighting against his former countrymen with unequaled tenacity. His speech was enriched with God-fearing language, yet he embraced a cause that aimed to keep an entire race enslaved. But he was also a family man who rarely spent time at home for many years while serving at distant military posts. He spoke to his wife in endearing terms when he found time to write, which was on a haphazard basis. He was a man absorbed in his profession, figuring out ways to attack and annihilate the enemy, whether Santa Anna's army in Mexico, hostile Indians along the frontier, or Union soldiers—his former comrades in arms whom he referred to impersonally as "those people."

Lee had an excellent command of the English language. His writing was concise, purposeful, and respectful. A true paradox, he wrote with clarity on most occasions, yet at times gave his subordinate officers ambiguous discretionary orders. This usually worked well with experienced officers, but led to confusion and hesitation with those who were less self-assured.

Lee applied the knowledge gained over the years and, emulating his idol Gen. George Washington, served as his own intelligence chief during the Civil War while delegating certain intelligence duties to staff members such as Majs. Walter H. Taylor and Charles S. Venable. However, Stuart's performance in gathering information about Union forces and countering enemy efforts to gain

---

7   Carl Coke Rister, *Robert E. Lee in Texas*, (Norman, OK, 2004 reprint), 37-52; Long, *Memoirs of Robert E. Lee*, 75-79; "Robert Edward Lee," *The Handbook of Texas Online*, accessed on March 2, 2014, http://www.tshaonline.org/handbook/online/articles/fle18; Thomas T. Smith, *The Old Army in Texas: A Research Guide to the U. S. Army in Nineteenth-Century Texas* (Austin, TX, 2000), 99-100; Robert E. Lee, Jr., *Recollections and Letters of General Robert E. Lee* (Garden City, NY, 1924), 21, 23.

8   Rister, *Lee in Texas*, 13, 40-52; Long, *Memoirs of Robert E. Lee*, 78-81; *The Handbook of Texas Online*, see note above.

the advantage led to close collaboration in intelligence operations between Lee and Stuart that served the army well during the upcoming campaigns.[9]

The Cavalry Division

> [W]e were the eyes and ears of the army and . . . upon our vigilance depended the safety of the army.
>
>   J. E. B. Stuart[10]

From the outset of the war, Jeb Stuart performed vital scouting and screening activities for his commanders, initially Gen. Joseph Johnston and later Lee. He graduated from West Point in 1854 (13th of 46), where he learned the fundamentals of reconnaissance and outpost duty. Stuart developed these skills during assignments on the Texas frontier and in Kansas Territory. Much like his future commander and mentor Robert E. Lee experienced out West, Stuart encountered difficulty in tracking elusive Indian bands that roamed the countryside and ravaged vulnerable settlements. Rather than complain about these isolated assignments, Stuart made the best of the situation. He realized early on that to reach the position in life to which he aspired would require hard work, determination, and personal integrity. This philosophy translated into a high-spirited, flamboyant cavalryman who gained recognition through his accomplishments and assertive promotion of his military career. Stuart also benefited from assignment to the newly established 1st Cavalry in 1855, a unit specifically trained for scouting and outpost duty. Scouts explored surrounding roads and terrain, and reconnoitered enemy positions. Outpost detachments protected against surprise by observing enemy movements, and preventing them from pinpointing the army's location. They gave early warning and hindered attacks, allowing the main force to prepare for action. Stuart would later show he had learned his scouting and outpost lessons well.[11]

---

9 Tidwell, *Come Retribution*, 105; Sears, *Chancellorsville*, 47. Evidence of Veneble's staff role for intelligence includes a number of intelligence reports he retained after the war, now part of collection #2213 at the University of North Carolina at Chapel Hill. All but a few of these reports post-date the Gettysburg campaign.

10 Robert J. Driver, Jr., *1st Virginia Cavalry* (Lynchburg, VA, 1991), 29.

11 Emory M. Thomas, *Bold Dragoon: The Life of J. E. B. Stuart* (New York, 1988), 37-52, 59-61, 88-89, 105-16; John W. Thomason, Jr., *Jeb Stuart* (New York, 1995 reprint), 20-32; Wagner, *The Service and Security of Information*, 40, 139.

Stuart's service in Texas and on the plains also taught him valuable campaigning skills. He discovered what it took to survive in a hostile atmosphere while on patrol in unfamiliar territory. By the time the Civil War began, Stuart had gained a thorough introduction to the complexities and difficulties of military life, including command experience. Exposure to the fundamentals of information gathering was a key ingredient.[12]

In 1861, acknowledging Stuart's success with the old army out West, and in response to his inquiries for a position commensurate with his abilities, the newly established Confederate government rewarded him with an appointment as commander of the 1st Virginia Cavalry with the rank of lieutenant colonel. (Initially, Stuart was commissioned a major in the Virginia State Forces cavalry on May 6, 1861, and assigned to Winchester within Joseph E. Johnston's Army of the Shenandoah.) He proved adept in this role when he reconnoitered Maj. Gen. Robert Patterson's Union army operating near Smithfield, Virginia, in mid-1861. The information he collected, coupled with Stuart's effective screening of the movements of General Johnston's forces, permitted Johnston to reinforce Brig. Gen. Pierre G. T. Beauregard's outnumbered troops at Manassas Junction, which led to a Confederate victory at the initial battle of Bull Run.[13]

The period of relative quiet following Bull Run provided the Confederate cavalrymen an opportunity to receive instruction from Stuart and gain experience in reconnaissance and outpost duty. Of Stuart, Johnston said, "I know no one more competent than he to estimate the occurrences before him at their true value." In other words, he thought Stuart excelled at gathering reliable information about the enemy. High praise indeed! Soon thereafter Stuart received a promotion to brigadier general in command of six regiments of cavalry. Johnston, meanwhile, wrote to President Jefferson Davis recommending expansion of the cavalry to a brigade of three to four thousand men, with Stuart in command. Without more cavalry, Johnston believed he

---

12 H. B. McClellan, *The Campaigns of Stuart's Cavalry* (Edison, NJ, 1993 reprint), 10-27, 29-31.

13 Johnston's reports, OR 2, 185-86, 471-73, 476-77; Adele H. Mitchell (ed.), *The Letters of Major General James E. B. Stuart* (Centreville, VA, 1990), 199, 207-08; Charles Wells Russell, *Gray Ghost: The Memoirs of Colonel John S. Mosby* (New York, 1992), 36; Driver, *1st Virginia Cavalry*, 1-15; W. W. Blackford, *War Years with Jeb Stuart* (Baton Rouge, LA, 1993), 19; McClellan, *Stuart's Cavalry*, 32-34, Edward G. Longacre, *Lee's Cavalrymen: A History of the Mounted Force of the Army of Northern Virginia, 1861-1865* (Mechanicsburg, VA), 1-4; Thomason, *Jeb Stuart*, 46, 65.

would have to rely on the people in the countryside for information about enemy movements.[14]

During McClellan's Peninsula campaign in mid-1862, Johnston suffered a serious wound and Robert E. Lee assumed command of the Confederate army. Based on information that scout John Mosby had discovered, Lee ordered Stuart to employ secrecy and surprise in finding the rear of the enemy, gathering information about his operations, interrupting his communications, and pinpointing the location of his right flank. In a publicly acclaimed feat that Lee praised as a "brilliant exploit," and which set the pattern for future cavalry operations, Stuart led a detachment on this precarious expedition that completely circled McClellan's army, thereby accomplishing his commander's objectives in grand style.[15]

Soon after Stuart's exploit against McClellan, the cavalry reorganized into a two-brigade division, and the Confederacy awarded Stuart the rank of major general. Lee and Stuart both recognized the importance of a powerful, unified mounted arm that would actively pursue the army's needs for gathering information about the enemy's plans and objectives, and preventing them from returning the favor.[16]

A new threat loomed in August 1862 with the advance of Union Maj. Gen. John Pope's Army of Virginia. Assisted by some errors by Stuart's cavalry in carrying out their assignments, Pope's forces were able to evade a trap Lee had set for them. Stuart made amends by staging a raid into the rear of the Union army, gaining information that helped Lee rout Pope's forces at the second battle of Bull Run in which Stuart performed key tactical and intelligence roles. His troopers destroyed a supply depot and captured documents that yielded information about the size, intentions, and planned reinforcement of the Union army. After driving Pope's army into the fortifications around Washington, in September 1862 Lee decided to bring the war to the North by moving into Maryland. The complexity of Lee's maneuvers and a lost copy of his orders that

14 Johnston to [Davis], OR 5, 777; HQ Dept. of Northern Virginia, Special Orders, No. 120, May 28, 1862, OR 11, pt. 3, 558; McClellan, *Stuart's Cavalry*, 42-43; Blackford; *War Years*, 48-49.

15 Post-action reports: Stuart's, June 17, 1862, OR 11, pt. 1, 1036-40; Lee's, March 6, 1863, pt. 2, 489-90; Lee to Stuart, June 11, 1862, pt. 3, 590-91; Russell, *Gray Ghost*, 84-90; McClellan, *Stuart's Cavalry*, 52-67, 70; Driver, *1st Virginia Cavalry*, 36-39; Sears, *To the Gates of Richmond*, 167-73, Ezra J. Warner, *Generals in Gray* (Baton Rouge, LA, 1959), 181.

16 Longacre, *Lee's Cavalrymen*, 104; Thomason, *Jeb Stuart*, 214.

Maj. Gen. James E. B. Stuart
Library of Congress

fell into McClellan's hands caused Stuart to make quick decisions based on scant information. Although his actions later came under scrutiny, Stuart had acted according to his best judgment at the time. Despite these lapses, Stuart and his cavalry conducted reconnaissance and acquitted themselves reasonably well during the bloody fighting at Sharpsburg.[17]

In early October 1862, authorities in Richmond desired information on what McClellan's intentions were following the battle along Antietam Creek. Lee directed Stuart to lead a cavalry detachment on an expedition into Maryland and Pennsylvania to damage McClellan's combat capability, especially his transportation facilities, and to gather information of the position, force, and probable intentions of the enemy. Stuart enhanced his reputation by duplicating in some respects his ride around McClellan's army on the Virginia Peninsula earlier in the year. Lee had high praise for Stuart's "boldness, judgment, and prudence" in the execution of the expedition, despite his cavalry's inability to destroy a major railroad bridge that was the key link in McClellan's supply chain.[18]

By the end of 1862, the Army of Northern Virginia's cavalry division had expanded to four brigades comprising over 9,000 men. When Maj. Gen. Ambrose E. Burnside replaced McClellan as commander of the Army of the Potomac in October, Stuart informed Lee that the Union army had relocated to the area of Fredericksburg, Virginia, where a bloody battle would soon be fought. It was during the Fredericksburg campaign that Stuart first began to notice improvement in his mounted Union foes. While screening his army's movement to that area, Stuart had difficulty holding off a persistent Union cavalry—an unexpected turn of events that would become a recurring and escalating problem over time. In practical terms, this challenge to the supremacy of Confederate cavalry materialized in early 1863 when Gen. Joseph

---

17 Taylor to Stuart, August 13, 1862, *OR* 11, pt. 3, 674; Lee's post-action report, June 8, 1863, *OR* 12, pt. 2, 552-53, 558-59; Lee to Stuart, July 18 & July 30, 1862, pt. 3, 916, 920; Stuart to Lee, August 5, 1862, 924-25; Taylor to Stuart, August 13, 1862, 928; Lee to Stuart, August 18, 1862, 934; Russell, *Gray Ghost*, 103-08; Blackford, *War Years*, 97-138; McClellan, *Stuart's Cavalry*, 94-109; Longacre, *Lee's Cavalrymen*, 115-24

18 Lee to Stuart, October 8, 1862, *OR* 19, pt. 2, 55; Blackford, *War Years*, 164, 184-96, 202-03; Driver, *1st Virginia Cavalry*, 51; Longacre, *Lee's Cavalrymen*, 153-57; McClellan, *Stuart's Cavalry*, 136-37; John W. Thompson, IV, *Horses, Hostages, and Apple Cider: J. E. B. Stuart's 1862 Pennsylvania Raid* (Mercersburg, PA, 2002), 7-12.

Hooker, the new Army of the Potomac commander, consolidated the Union horsemen into a single corps-level organization.[19]

When the Confederates intercepted a ruse Union message in April, Stuart moved out of position as the Union army crossed the Rappahannock River prior to the battle of Chancellorsville. Stuart recovered in time to determine and notify Lee of the movements of this Union force. Stuart and his cavalry benefited when Hooker sent the bulk of his cavalry corps on a raid, instead of keeping them available to scout and screen for his army. [20]

In the absence of the Union cavalry, the Confederate horsemen controlled all of the roads. As a result, Stuart provided Lee with the intelligence he needed to conduct a flank attack on the Union position and win a victory against great odds. As the Chancellorsville campaign came to an end, and Lee's thoughts turned to preparation for an invasion of the North, Stuart could look back on his two years of Confederate service with pride. He had become adept at intelligence collection, counterintelligence operations, maintaining security, deception and disinformation, and field communications, the primary duties of cavalry in the field. Indeed, Stuart was responsible for the development of the cavalry into an efficient and lethal force capable of responding to the army's growing needs for information about the enemy and protection from surprise encounters.[21]

Intelligence Collection

Stuart employed a variety of methods to gather information, including reconnoitering enemy positions, sending scouts to penetrate their lines, picketing roads, deploying signal corps personnel to observe the enemy, taking reports from citizen informers, intercepting enemy messages by tapping telegraph lines, capturing couriers with dispatches, and raiding Union encampments for confidential correspondence. After an initial screening for perishable information, Stuart forwarded seized documents directly to the

19 Blackford, *War Years*, 184-96, 202-03; Driver, *1st Virginia Cavalry*, 51; Thomas, *Bold Dragoon*, 191; Longacre, *Lee's Cavalrymen*, 153-57.

20 Stuart's post-action report, May 8, 1863, *OR* 25, pt. 1, 1045-46; Fishel, *The Secret War*, 348-49; Sears, *Chancellorsville*, 163, 173-74; 190-91.

21 Post-action reports: Lee's, September 21, 1863, *OR* 25, pt. 1, 804; Stuart's, May 8, 1863, 1045-48; Sears, *Chancellorsville*, 230, 232.

commanding general for further analysis. He also forwarded Northern newspapers that came into his hands that might yield useful information.

The cavalry commander captured and interrogated prisoners, examining them individually to corroborate their stories, and tabulated order of battle data by collecting information about their unit designation and subordination, and the names of their commanders. He questioned local citizens and slaves and was not averse to using threats to force compliance. He debriefed escaped Confederate soldiers or those recovered after capture on the battlefield, for information about enemy activities. His objective was to learn the enemy's strength, composition, deployment, and intentions.[22]

At times, Stuart personally reconnoitered the enemy. He scouted areas where combat was likely to occur and thoroughly studied the features of the surrounding country. He particularly noted if enemy fortifications existed, and whether the enemy's disposition would allow them to repel an attack. When ordered to conduct a reconnaissance-in-force, Stuart used discretion to minimize casualties.

Stuart's topographical engineers drew sketches of the terrain for use by commanders for tactical purposes, and maps for later inclusion in after-action reports. Part of this process included studying the field after the battle for the relative strength of positions and the effect of fire.[23]

Counterintelligence Operations

Stuart "masked" or screened the location and activities of the Army of Northern Virginia from the enemy by placing cavalry detachments at the front, rear, and flanks of the army, making sure no hint of their movements reached the enemy. Strategically placed outposts, pickets, and vedettes provided early warning of the enemy's approach. These forward elements skirmished with enemy pickets to delay and discourage their progress, while coordinating with each other and constantly sending couriers to the rear to keep commanders

---

22 For examples of Stuart's intelligence operations before the Gettysburg campaign, see *OR* 2, 472; *OR* 5, 402-03; *OR* 11, pt. 1, 444; pt. 2, 513-20; pt. 3, 402; *OR* 12, pt. 1, 415-17; pt. 2, 118-20; pt. 3, 916; *OR* 19, pt. 1, 140; pt. 2, 52-54; *OR* 25, pt. 1, 1045-48; Blackford, *War Years*, 34-35, 101, 107; McClellan, *Stuart's Cavalry*, 40-41; 52-53.

23 Examples include: *OR* 5, 400; *OR* 11, pt. 2, 514; *OR* 12, pt. 2, 728; *OR* 19, pt. 2, 54; Blackford, *War Years*, 44, 148-49.

informed. Sharpshooters on the skirmish line added firepower and skill that helped keep the enemy at a safe distance.

With the army on the march, Stuart sent detachments ahead to seize and hold bridges and river crossings to deny them to the enemy. Cavalry vedettes positioned well forward on eminences also supplied fire-control information for artillery batteries. When the infantry withdrew from the field, the cavalry provided cover to prevent the enemy from being aware of their movement.[24]

Maintaining Security

When reconnoitering close to or within enemy lines, Stuart cautioned his scouts to avoid disclosing their presence to the enemy. His engineer, Captain Blackford, learned that small teams worked best for this activity. Stuart also ordered that sabers instead of firearms be used behind enemy lines to avoid alerting the enemy. He detained citizens who could give information to the enemy about his movements and of course arrested suspected spies and sent them to headquarters for further questioning. And naturally, upon entering a town, his forces quickly took hold of the local telegraph operator and confiscated his key and battery to thwart an alarm going forth. On occasion, Stuart safeguarded information by not informing his subordinates of the destination and purpose of the expedition.[25]

Deception and Disinformation

Stuart attempted to avoid detection or capture by anticipating enemy reaction and maneuvering accordingly. During his information-gathering expedition prior to the Seven Days' campaign in June 1862, he passed completely around the Union army because it was a route the enemy would not expect him to take. In similar fashion, during his cavalry expedition into Pennsylvania after the battle of Antietam in October 1862, he moved in such a way as to confuse local inhabitants about his actual route of travel so that they would be unable to inform Union pursuers. Stuart also used local guides to lead

24 *OR* 5, 400-02; *OR* 11, pt. 2, 521, 523; *OR* 12, pt. 1, 415-16; *OR* 19, pt. 1, 822, 828; pt. 2, 141-42; Blackford, *War Years*, 26, 170-71; McClellan, *Stuart's Cavalry*, 87, 110.

25 *OR* 11, pt. 1, 1036; pt. 3, 407; *OR* 19, pt. 2, 55-56; *OR* 21, 12, 690, 734; Blackford, *War Years*, 83.

the way in unfamiliar territory and spread false information about the Rebel army's strength and intentions to mislead the enemy. For example, in December 1862, he created the impression that a raid into the North was about to take place, causing a debilitating and fruitless chase by Union cavalry.[26]

The cavalry leader also employed maneuvers such as raising dust columns to deceive the enemy regarding the strength of opposition, and deploying units or skirmishers away from the main point of attack to divert the enemy's attention. He would also expose his mounted cavalry, especially the feared "Black Horse," in full view of the enemy to dissuade them from attacking. Or conspicuously display his unit flag with a small number of skirmishers to make the enemy think they opposed a larger force. He deceived the enemy by building campfires before leaving the area, which would often draw harmless artillery fire while Stuart made his getaway. These practices, together with crippling the enemy's communications, often allowed Lee to maneuver and gain the advantage and element of surprise.[27]

Field Communications

To keep Lee informed of enemy activity, Stuart used written or "pencil communications" by courier, or sent messages by telegraph when this was available or courier communication too hazardous. When the situation required special handling, he used his staff officers as couriers rather than his assigned team of enlisted men. Sometimes Stuart sent reports to the nearest infantry commander for action, or to the commanding general through subordinate commanders. And when convenient and necessary, he reported in person.[28]

---

26 Stuart's post-action reports, June 17, 1862, OR 11, pt. 1, 1038-39; OR 19, pt. 2, 53; Lee to Stuart, October 8, 1862, OR 19, pt. 2, 55; Blackford, *War Years*, 25, 71, 83, 140, 142, 151, 171-72, 175, 221; McClellan, *Stuart's Cavalry*, 34, 36, 62, 138, 142, 147, 149, 163-64. To maintain security, Stuart did not disclose to his men the purpose and destination of his expedition in October 1862. Stuart to Soldiers, October 9, 1862, OR 19, pt. 2, 55-56.

27 See for example, OR 2, 472-73; OR 5, 183; OR 11, pt. 1, 572; pt. 2, 513-20; OR 12, pt. 1, 416; pt. 2, 119; pt. 3, 925; OR 19, pt. 1, 142; OR 19, pt. 2, 52-55; OR 25, pt. 1, 1046-48; Blackford, *War Years*, 103-04; McClellan, *Stuart's Cavalry*, 60-61, 94; Robert J. Driver and H. E. Howard, *2nd Virginia Cavalry* (Lynchburg, VA, 1995), 68.

28 See for example, OR 5, 401; OR 11, pt. 1, 444-45; pt. 2, 513; pt. 3, 416; OR 12, pt. 2, 118-19; pt. 3, 924-25; OR 19, pt. 1, 819; OR 19, pt. 2, 52; Blackford, *War Years*, 50-51, 148; McClellan, *Stuart's Cavalry*, 66, 147. Before the battle of Sharpsburg, Stuart sent a report to Lee through Maj. Gen. D. H. Hill, a division commander. OR 19, pt. 1, 816-17.

During battle Stuart observed the enemy and kept commanders informed of their disposition. He also helped coordinate the placement of infantry and artillery by providing liaison between commanders and their units and guiding units to their respective positions. His reconnaissance teams observing the enemy had couriers assigned to keep him instantly informed of their movements.[29]

By June 1863, Jeb Stuart had at his command an expanded cavalry force for the most part well-trained and experienced. Over the previous two years, Stuart had proven to be a daring and resourceful leader. Although the enemy would be able to field a cavalry force of near equal size, the experience level of their troops and leaders did not match that of the Confederates.

Scouts and Spies

> General 'Jeb's scouts were to his superior officer the very eyes and ears of the army.
> Capt. Thomas N. Conrad[30]

Lee's personal experience conducting reconnaissance during 1840s and 1850s taught him the importance of having reliable scouts available. In Texas he employed the celebrated multi-lingual Delaware Indian Jim Shaw and his "trailers" or scouts to help reconnoiter unfamiliar frontier territory. During the Civil War, although the Confederate signal corps and secret service bureau provided strategic intelligence to Lee, for tactical purposes the general also sent out his own scouts and agents to observe the enemy and operate behind their lines, a practice that allowed him to supplement and verify data received from other sources.[31]

Stuart, Lee's primary source of tactical intelligence, also employed scouts, particularly from the 1st and 4th Virginia, to gather information. To operate behind enemy lines more effectively, they sometimes dressed in Federal

---

29 See for example, OR 11, pt. 1, 570-74; pt. 2, 519-20; Blackford, *War Years*, 191-93; McClellan, *Stuart's Cavalry*, 50.

30 Thomas N. Conrad, *A Confederate Spy: A Story of the Civil War* (New York, 1892), 4.

31 Lee to Seddon, March 29, 1863, OR 25, pt. 2, 691; Tidwell, *Come Retribution*, 109-11; O'Toole, *Honorable Treachery*, 113; Rister, *Robert E. Lee in Texas*, 37-52. On Shaw, see *Handbook of Texas Online*, "SHAW, JIM," accessed October 29, 2014, www.tshaonline.org/handbook/online/articles/fsh11.

uniforms or mufti—which only increased their peril because discovery meant execution as spies.[32]

A scout who served Stuart well was Lt. Benjamin Franklin Stringfellow. In 1861, the 21-year-old from Culpeper County joined the 4th Virginia as a private. Because he proved both brave and resourceful—his scouting led to the capture of Gen. John Pope's encampment before the second battle of Bull Run—Stuart assigned him to his staff for special operations including missions into enemy territory. Following trusted scout William D. Farley's death at Brandy Station, Stringfellow assumed a more important role for Stuart during the Northern invasion.[33]

Another of Stuart's scouts was Thomas Nelson Conrad, a former headmaster of a boy's school in Washington, D.C. He went South in 1861 to enlist and became chaplain of the 3rd Virginia Cavalry. However, he soon engaged mostly in reconnaissance and espionage, including observing the enemy, and reporting numbers and movements. According to Conrad, he received special orders prior to the Gettysburg campaign to go to Washington, D.C., acquire intelligence, and contact Southern sympathizers.[34]

Henry Thomas Harrison, who scouted for Lt. Gen. James Longstreet, would have considerable influence on the sequence of events during the Gettysburg campaign. As the Confederates prepared to move north, Longstreet gave secret orders to this "active, intelligent, enterprising scout." Longstreet instructed Harrison to work his way into the Federal capital, and he was to return to the army on the march only after he had obtained important information.[35]

---

32 Stuart's post-action reports, August 20, 1863, OR 27, pt. 2, 701, 710; June 13, 1863, 684-85; Longacre, *Lee's Cavalrymen*, 30-31, 87, 90, 95; Blackford, *War Years*, 202; OR 27, pt. 2; Robert J. Trout, *With Pen and Saber: The Letters and Diaries of J. E. B. Stuart's Staff Officers* (Mechanicsburg, PA, 1995), 63; Robert J. Trout (ed.), *In The Saddle With Stuart: The Story of Frank Smith Robertson of Jeb Stuart's Staff* (Gettysburg, 1998), 63; OR 27, pt. 2, 684-85.

33 R. Shepard Brown, *Stringfellow of the Fourth* (New York, 1960), 3-4, 12-15, 54-62, 151-166; John Bakeless, *Spies of the Confederacy* (Mineola, NY, 1970), 90-91; Stuart's post-action report, February 28, 1863, OR 12, pt. 2, p. 738.

34 Bakeless, *Spies of the Confederacy*, 64-128; Tidwell, *Come Retribution*, 109-111; Conrad, *A Confederate Spy*, 5.

35 Quoted comments about Harrison from James Longstreet, *From Manassas to Appomattox: Memoirs of the Civil War in America* (New York, 1994 reprint), 324, 333. See also G. Moxley Sorrell, *At the Right Hand of Longstreet: Recollections of a Confederate Staff Officer* (Lincoln, NE, 1999), 161, 164; Jeffry D. Wert, *General James Longstreet: The Confederacy's Most Controversial Soldier* (New

Maj. John S. Mosby
Library of Congress

Special Operations

John S. Mosby . . . is en route to scout beyond the enemy's lines toward Manassas and Fairfax. He is bold, daring, intelligent, and discreet.

J. E. B Stuart [36]

Jeb Stuart often called upon Maj. John S. Mosby and his partisan rangers for intelligence gathering. Raised in Virginia, Mosby attended the University at Charlottesville. He was practicing law in Bristol when war came in 1861. He joined a cavalry company, and his talent for scouting operations eventually led to a position on Jeb Stuart's staff.

A person of short stature, slight build, and unimpressive appearance, Mosby nonetheless was able to impose his will on others through his intense personality. He established a reputation for being daring and reliable when he reported the configuration of enemy lines and helped guide Stuart's ride around McClellan's army gathering intelligence during the Peninsula campaign in mid-1862.[37]

Later in 1862, not content with the normal cavalry routine, the restless Mosby proposed to Stuart that he take a detail of men and conduct guerrilla activity behind enemy lines. Given approval, the 29-year-old Mosby recruited

York, 1993), 254-55; James Longstreet, "Lee's Invasion of Pennsylvania," in Robert Underwood Johnson and Clarence Clough Buel, eds., *Battles and Leaders of the Civil War*, 4 vols. (New York, 1956), 3:244, 249-50; James O. Hall, "The Spy Harrison," *Civil War Times Illustrated*, No. 10, 24:23; Tony Trimble, "Harrison: Spying for Longstreet at Gettysburg," *Gettysburg Magazine* (July 1997), No. 17, 17.

36 Stuart to Jackson, July 19, 1862, *OR* 51, pt. 2, 594.

37 Charles Wells Russell, ed., *Gray Ghost*, xiii-xx; Mark M. Boatner III, *The Civil War Dictionary* (New York, 1959), 634, 816; James M. McPherson, *Battle Cry of Freedom: The Civil War Era* (New York, 1988), 462-64; Thomas, *Bold Dragoon*, 110-11, 115, 118-19, 128.

and organized the 43rd Virginia Cavalry Battalion that served primarily in Loudoun and Fauquier Counties in northern Virginia, an area that straddled major Union communications lines. Mosby's Rangers destroyed supply trains and depots, attacked small Union detachments and outposts, disrupted communications, and gathered intelligence. They proved a major thorn in the side of the Federal army during the Gettysburg campaign as indeed throughout the entire war.[38]

Sharpshooter battalions were another resource available to Lee's army for gathering information. The Confederate Congress authorized the establishment of such units in May 1862, and by January 1863 these battalions began to take shape. In the forthcoming Gettysburg campaign, sharpshooters would be employed primarily for their offensive firepower, but they were used more for reconnaissance and screening during the latter part of the campaign.[39]

Still another special operations unit, the 39th Virginia Cavalry Battalion, performed courier, escort, and guide duty for the Army of Northern Virginia. Since it had training in intelligence-related matters, the battalion also played an important scouting role during the Gettysburg campaign. This included accompanying army engineers on reconnaissance missions, and seeking out roads for the army to travel.[40]

---

38 Russell, *Gray Ghost*, xvi-xviii, 1; Virgil Carrington Jones, *Gray Ghosts and Rebel Raiders* (New York, 1956), 21, 76-77, 80.

39 Brigadier General Robert Rodes was the prime mover for the establishment of sharpshooter battalions in Lee's army. Initially these units were small in size, numbering from 100-125. Sharpshooters' duties, generally, were similar to those of the cavalry: to warn, protect, and screen the main body, while at the same time scouting and harassing the other side's movements. Fred L. Ray, *Shock Troops of the Confederacy: The Sharpshooter Battalions of the Army of Northern Virginia* (Asheville, NC, 2006), 1, 29, 49-50, 62-74.

40 Captain Samuel B. Brown's Company C, 39th Battalion, known as "Lee's Body Guard," maintained a perimeter guard around army headquarters. The battalion also guarded enemy prisoners and escorted them to depots and prisons. It also performed a counterintelligence role by arresting suspicious persons in and around military encampments. The operating strength of the battalion was about 150 men. Robert K. Driver, Jr., *1st Battalion Virginia Infantry, 39th Battalion Virginia Cavalry, 24th Battalion Virginia Partisan Rangers* (Lynchburg, VA, 1996), 51, 53-54, 56-57, 59-60; Tidwell, et al., *Come Retribution*, 110. See also Kenneth Radley, *Rebel Watchdog: The Confederate States Army Provost Guard* (Baton Rouge, LA, 1989), 37, 300. For more information on the 39th Battalion's role within the Army of Northern Virginia, see Boone Bartholomees, Jr., *Buff Facings and Gilt Buttons: Staff and headquarters Operation in the Army of Northern Virginia, 1861-1865* (Columbia, SC, 1998), 202, 206-09.

Signal Corps

> There is a flag as yet unsung, a banner bright and fair,
> It moves in waves of right and left, that banner in the air.
> To comrades true, far, far away, who watch with anxious eye,
> These secret signs an import bear, when waved against the sky.
> Confederate signal corps song[41]

Soon after the outset of the war, President Jefferson Davis assigned Capt. Edward Porter Alexander the task of establishing a signal capability for the Confederate army. Alexander was able to organize signal operations at Manassas before the first battle of Bull Run, and while instructing a signal team, he studied the topography of the land where the battle would be fought. From a signal station on nearby Wilcoxen's Hill (present-day Signal Hill), Alexander demonstrated the value of signaling by providing early warning of a pending enemy flank attack.[42]

Major Norris became chief signal officer of Confederate forces when Alexander declined the job in order to stay in the field. Norris assigned signal parties to each of the Rebel armies, including the Army of Northern Virginia. As the Gettysburg campaign got underway in early June 1863, the signalmen serving Lee's army had the benefit of two years' experience in the field. Each corps and division in the army had a signal party operating under the command of an officer or sergeant. But Lee's headquarters had no officer assigned to direct signal operations, a distinct disadvantage at Gettysburg.[43]

---

41 Brown, *The Signal Corps*, 224.

42 Edward Porter Alexander, *Military Memoirs of a Confederate: A Critical Narrative* (New York, 1993), 13-14; Gary W. Gallagher, ed., *Fighting for the Confederacy: The Personal Recollections of General Edward Porter Alexander* (Chapel Hill, NC, 1989), 37-40, 45-46, 50-51; ibid., 43-45; J. Bartholomees, *Buff Facings and Gilt Buttons*, 113-14. Based on this success and a demand within the army for more signal units, the Confederate Congress officially created the signal corps in April 1862, and the following month the war department authorized a staff signal officer at corps and division level, assisted by as many signal non-commissioned officers and privates as necessary. Cavalry brigades had signal corps teams assigned as well. The Confederate signal corps used the same "wigwag" system as the Union's employing flags and torches. General Orders No. 40, *OR* 1, ser. 4, 1131-32; Chas. E. Taylor, *The Signal and Secret Service of the Confederate States* (Harmans, MD, 1986), iv, 4-5,14-24; David Winfred Gaddy, "The Confederate Signal Corps at Gettysburg," *Gettysburg Magazine* (January 1991), No. 4, 110-11.

43 Taylor, *The Signal and Secret Service*, 4-5; Gaddy, "The Confederate Signal Corps," 110-11; Gallagher, *Fighting for the Confederacy*, 61; Brown, *The Signal Corps*, 205. On Norris, see David

Secret Service Bureau

[T]he necessity of having points on the Potomac river, at which Government agents and army scouts might . . . cross to and from the United States . . . the Secretary of War suggested . . . establishing . . . camps in King George and Westmoreland counties, Va., with an especial eye to such transportation.

Maj. William Norris[44]

An advantage Lee enjoyed over the Army of the Potomac was the secret service bureau in Richmond that regularly provided strategic intelligence. When the war began, the government of Virginia supported an espionage ring in Washington following the state's secession from the Union in April 1861. This network conveyed information to Virginia and later the Confederacy via couriers who made their way through Union lines.[45]

The Federal government eventually tightened security along these routes, forcing the Confederates to establish an improved communications capability. By September 1862, it had evolved into the "secret line," a covert activity of the Confederate signal corps, a part of the secret service bureau that controlled agents who smuggled mail, newspapers, contraband, and personnel into the South. The secret line, which had been established by Norris, operated over various routes into the U.S., at least two of which crossed the Potomac into Maryland. Couriers, agents, recruits, and foreign visitors, as well as information from spies in the North, some reportedly located at the federal war department, traveled along this route to Richmond and on to Lee and other commanders in the field.[46]

Winfred Gaddy, "William Norris and the Confederate Signal and Secret Service, *Maryland Historical Magazine* (Summer 1975), 70:167-88.

44 Taylor, *The Signal and Secret Service*, 18-19.

45 Conrad, *A Confederate Spy*, 5; Tidwell, *Come Retribution*, 62-75.

46 Taylor, *The Signal and Secret Service of the Confederate States*, 6, 17-24; Gaddy, "William Norris and the Confederate Signal and Secret Service," 173, 178; R. Shepard Brown, *The Amazing Career of the most successful Confederate Spy* (New York, 1960), 172-86; John Bakeless, *Spies of the Confederacy* (Mineola, NY, 1970), 109-14. The Confederate secret service bureau also maintained control over the ciphers, which used a key word system for securing the cipher. Special messengers periodically communicated new key words orally to the various military departments. However, Union war department cipher operators were often able to solve the unsophisticated Confederate cipher system and read the messages. Taylor, *The Signal and Secret Service*, 14-17; Bates, *Lincoln in the Telegraph Office*, 68-85.

For example, in a message dated April 27, 1863, a few days before the battle of Chancellorsville, Norris notified Lee at Fredericksburg, Longstreet at Suffolk, and apparently the president in Richmond that "a special scout" of the signal corps, who had arrived from Washington the previous night, reported that Hooker's Army of the Potomac had received a large number of reinforcements, and that additional reinforcements were on their way to Union forces in the Suffolk area.[47]

The secret line depended on agents in Northern territory. Friendly postmasters in southern Maryland allowed mail to and from the Confederacy to flow through the U.S. postal system. Country doctors sympathetic to the Southern cause transported mail and other important items. Signal corps personnel on the Virginia side of the Potomac operated out of camps along the river, shuttling personnel and material by boat across into Maryland. The system was highly efficient. According to Charles E. Taylor, who worked in the signal corps:

> Every afternoon a courier would arrive in Richmond . . . bringing files of newspapers, letters and reports in cipher from parties in Canada and various portions of the United States. So regular was this service . . . the authorities in Richmond [were] put in possession of Washington and Baltimore newspapers of the day before. The New York papers came a day later.[48]

Lee frequently gleaned valuable information from Northern newspapers that often printed details about the composition, location, and plans of Union military units. Hooker, painfully aware of the potential harm from an unrestrained press corps, issued specific guidelines in mid-June 1863 to editors on what could and could not be published. During the campaign, however, Lee continued to rely on Northern newspapers as sources of intelligence.[49]

47 Wm. Norris to. J. Longstreet, April 27, 1863, in Eli Duvall message book, Museum of the Confederacy, Richmond, VA. See also Dowdey, *The Wartime Papers*, 440-41; Lynda L. Crist, et al., eds., *The Papers of Jefferson Davis*, 9:154-55.

48 Taylor, *The Signal and Secret Service*, 17-24. Intelligence derived from Northern newspapers included "reports of battles, battlefield maps, lists of casualties, and sometimes word of military plans, troop movements, troop strengths, and other information to the Confederates." O'Toole, *Honorable Treachery*, 131.

49 Lee's exploitation of Northern newspapers in OR 25, pt. 2, 790-92, 827, 844; OR 27, pt. 3, 924, 931-32; Hooker's guidelines to editors, OR 27, pt. 3, 192.

Of course, information from Norris' secret service operations in Richmond had to be evaluated and contextualized. In the case of the April 27 report, for example, Lee immediately wrote to Davis that he believed the figures in Norris' report of 150–160,000 troops now under Hooker's command to be "much exaggerated." Nonetheless, in light of what he already knew of his enemy's strength, Lee stated his belief that "bodies of [Union] troops heretofore retained in Maryland to keep that State in subjection . . . have been forwarded to General Hooker."[50]

The "scout" who brought the information about the size of Hooker's army may have been Capt. Thomas Nelson Conrad, who travelled frequently between the two capitols. According to Conrad, toward the end of 1862, he received orders from Secretary of War James A. Seddon to set up an independent clandestine route into the North to supplement the signal corps' secret line. This was done to provide a redundancy for the critical communications channel between Richmond and its agents in the North.[51]

Early in 1863, in anticipation of an invasion of the North, General Lee decided to strengthen his strategic intelligence resources. There is evidence that he instructed Stuart to establish a direct communications line from Washington to receive information about Union military plans and movements.[52]

Telegraph

[E]ver since the affair at Beaver Dam, Lee had been afraid to trust the telegraph.
John S. Mosby[53]

---

50 Lee to Davis, April 27, 1863, OR 25, pt. 2, 752.

51 Conrad, *A Confederate Spy*, 38; Taylor, *The Signal and Secret Service*, 8, 17-23; Tidwell, *Come Retribution*, 9-11, 61-65, 89-90, 96-98; Margaret Leech, *Reveille in Washington* (New York, 1969 reprint), 94-96.

52 According to Frank Stringfellow, Stuart sent him to Washington to recruit a spy team among Southern sympathizers and create a supplementary communications route that terminated at Stuart's headquarters. Brown, *Stringfellow of the Fourth*, 172-86; Bakeless, *Spies of the Confederacy*, 109-14. Lee's desire to strengthen his strategic intelligence capability may reflect concerns about the reliability of communications routes serving Confederate spy networks. It may also reflect the fact that the terminus of the communication lines into the North was Richmond, and therefore not under Lee's direct control.

53 Russell, *Gray Ghost*, 101.

Although the Confederacy had a long-distance telegraph system in place, it did not extend farther north than Culpeper, Virginia, obviously of no strategic use to Lee during his invasion of the North. Communications between the invading army in Maryland or Pennsylvania and the Confederate capital would require a one-way courier trip of four to six days. Moreover, unlike its Northern adversaries, there is no evidence that Lee employed field telegraph during the campaign, including the battle of Gettysburg.[54]

Even had there been better facilities in the South, Lee did not trust the telegraph, believing it too insecure to pass military operations-related traffic. Lee had been wary of using the telegraph to send operational data since the Peninsula campaign in July 1862 when Union troops had commandeered and cut his telegraph lines. In March, he had instructed Brig. Gen. John Imboden, who led a brigade in western Virginia, not to send "dispatches by telegraph relative to your movements . . . [because] they will become known." Instead, Lee's preferred method of communication was a relay line of couriers on horseback.[55]

Terrain Exploration and Mapmaking

> Gen. R.E. Lee came up to our Hd. Qrs this morning and he and Gen. Jackson are having a long conversation aided [by] my maps of Maryland and Pennsylvania. No doubt another expedition is on foot.
> Jedediah Hotchkiss[56]

To conduct an invasion of the North, Lee needed reliable information about the roads and routes his army would follow. In early 1863, he assigned Jed Hotchkiss, a civilian topographical engineer on Stonewall Jackson's staff the task of preparing maps for the invasion. A self-taught amateur, Hotchkiss brought not only talent and resourcefulness to his work; he had added advantages not only by being a Northerner by birth but also by having

---

54 Plum, *The Military Telegraph*, 10; *OR* 27, pt. 3, 923-24; 1, 75-77.

55 Lee to Imboden, March 21, 1863, *OR* 25, pt. 2, 679; Russell, *Gray Ghost*, 110; A. W. Greeley, "The Military-Telegraph Service," accessed July 30, 2014, www.civilwarsignals.org/pages/tele/telegreely/telegreely.html.

56 Archie P. McDonald (ed.), *Make Me a Map of the Valley: The Civil War Journal of Stonewall Jackson's Topographer* (Dallas, TX, 1973), 87, 116, 142, 145-46.

personally explored Pennsylvania's Cumberland Valley and western Virginia as a youth.[57]

Above all, tactical maps had to be timely, but long range planning allowed Hotchkiss to produce a more elaborate and detailed product. Like the maps he had provided for Jackson for the 1862 Valley campaign, his maps for Lee's invasion of Pennsylvania were strikingly good, providing many crucial topographical details, especially practical stream and river crossings.[58] Creating maps was not the only way commanders got them. Both sides also captured them in raids of enemy camps, or took them from prisoners or casualties on the battlefield. Also, as the army moved through the countryside local citizens provided maps, either voluntarily or otherwise. Such maps were then used outright or as the template for creating other maps of a specific area. A Union newspaper correspondent who observed Lee and his army in Greencastle, Pennsylvania, reported that Lee's large staff all worked "incessantly at the country maps they have secured from citizens of the Cumberland Valley."[59]

Provost Guards

[The provost marshal] received and placed under guard 324 prisoners of war ... I took names, regiments, brigades, and corps ... in obedience with [Lee's] order.
Maj. David B. Bridgford[60]

Before launching an invasion of the North, Lee assigned the 1st Battalion Virginia Infantry, an outfit that had previously served as provost guard, to serve as the provost guard for the Army of Northern Virginia headquarters. In previous assignments, the 1st Battalion had performed a number of intelligence-related functions. Major David B. Bridgford, the battalion commander, assumed the job of army provost marshal. Bridgford's responsibilities included operating prisoner-of-war camps and interrogating prisoners to obtain information of military value. Specifically, this entailed

---

57 Ibid., xv-xvii; McElfresh, *Maps and Mapmakers*, 19, 25-26, 29, 160. The Confederacy did not have a mapmaking unit until mid-1862. While not nearly as proficient as its Northern counterpart, it did strive to acquire materials for its mapmakers.

58 See note above: McDonald, 10, 116; McElfresh, 27-29, 39-44.

59 McElfresh, *Maps and Mapmakers*, 64-65; *The Philadelphia Press*, July 12, 1863.

60 Bridgford's report, January 9, 1863, OR 21, 641.

learning names, unit designations, and chains of command up to corps level for use in discerning the enemy's order of battle.[61]

The provosts also performed counterintelligence duties such as keeping watch for escaped slaves who the Union military sometimes sent back into Confederate lines for spying or other subversive purposes, and monitoring civilians to prevent them from passing information to the enemy. Sometimes they were even known to supervise the activities of scouts and spies.[62]

Summation

By the outset of the Gettysburg campaign, Lee had gained a full year's experience as commander of the Army of Northern Virginia. He was adept at gathering information about the enemy using a variety of sources and relied on his cavalry commander, Jeb Stuart, to provide much of the information he required for operational planning.

The complexity of the upcoming expedition into the North would create impediments not experienced in earlier campaigns. Timely and accurate decisions about Confederate movements and dispositions absolutely required detailed knowledge of the enemy's whereabouts and intentions. Lee would thus have to employ all of his intelligence and counterintelligence capabilities to maximum effectiveness to ensure success during this campaign. These resources would be constantly competing with those of the Army of the Potomac, and the side that applied the greatest skill and ingenuity in this intelligence-related contest would likely be victorious in the campaign.

---

61 Ibid., 641; HQ Dept. of Northern Virginia, Special Orders, No. 151, June 4, 1863, OR 51, pt. 2, 721; Driver and Ruffner, *1st Battalion Virginia Infantry*, 32, 35-36; Bartholomees, *Buff Facings*, 144; Radley, *Rebel Watchdog*, 168.

62 OR 21, 33, 641-42; Radley, *Rebel Watchdog*, 164-65, 168, 201, 230-31, 251-52. The intelligence contributions of Bridgford's battalion were curtailed during the Gettysburg campaign, however, because Lee left it behind in Winchester as provost guard following the town's capture from Union forces on June 15, 1863. As a result, the army had to rely on provost guards assigned to units down to the brigade level to carry out intelligence duties the 1st Battalion normally provided. Driver and Ruffner, *1st Battalion Virginia Infantry*, 36; Radley, *Rebel Watchdog*, 258; Bartholomees, *Buff Facings*, 143.

Chapter Three

Intelligence Plans and Operations

What enables the wise sovereign and the good general to strike and conquer,
and achieve things beyond the reach of ordinary men, is foreknowledge.

—*Sun Tzu*[1]

Confederate Planning Overview

On April 6, 1863, Secretary of War James Seddon asked Lee's advice and approval to send two brigades from Maj. Gen. George Pickett's division to reinforce Lt. Gen. Braxton Bragg's army in the west. Lee replied that the best way to relieve the pressure on Confederate armies in that region was for the Army of Northern Virginia to go on the offensive and cross into Maryland. Following the battle of Chancellorsville in early May, when Seddon reiterated a desire to send Pickett's division to shore up the situation in the West, Lee responded that, if troops were removed, his army might have to withdraw into the defenses of Richmond.[2]

Lee also informed President Davis that he had learned Hooker's army was being reinforced, and to counter this, he proposed to advance his army "beyond the Rappahannock" in order to draw Union troops away from other threatened areas of the Confederacy.[3]

---

1   Sun Tzu, *The Art of War* (New York, 1988), 77.

2   Seddon to Lee, April 6, 1863, OR 25, pt. 2, 708-9; Lee to Seddon, April 9, 1863, 713, Lee to Seddon, May 10, 1863, 790.

3   Lee to Davis, May 11, 1863, ibid., 791-92; Stephen W. Sears, *Gettysburg* (Boston, 2003), 12-17. On Confederate invasion strategy, see James A. Kegel, *North with Lee and Jackson: The Lost Story of Gettysburg* (Mechanicsburg, PA, 1996), 11-234.

Col. Armistead L. Long
Library of Congress

Lee had several goals for moving his army out of Virginia and invading the North, and he planned to achieve these by accomplishing specific objectives. Since Hooker's position along the Rappahannock River opposite Fredericksburg was too strong to attack, Lee intended to draw Hooker away from that location. In so doing, he saw an opportunity to relieve the lower Shenandoah Valley from Union occupation by attacking the main garrison at Winchester as his army marched northward.

Lee also wanted to transfer the battleground north of the Potomac and look for an opportunity to attack the Union army. According to Col. Armistead L. Long who served on Lee's staff as military secretary and artillery advisor, about two weeks before the movement began Lee discussed his plans with him using a map of the theater of operations (probably the Jed Hotchkiss map). Long says Lee traced the proposed route of the army on the map and its destination in Pennsylvania at Chambersburg, York, or Gettysburg.[4]

Lee believed his movement would lure the enemy away from northern Virginia, devastated by the protracted presence of two large armies. At the same time, it would draw Union troops operating in other parts of the country to support of the Army of the Potomac. Unless he diverted the enemy away from their current position, Lee believed they would eventually be strengthened and

---

4 Long, *Memoirs of Lee*, 268-69. According to Long, Lee thought that a battle would likely take place in one of these vicinities, but that Gettysburg was the much better location since it was nearest the Potomac and allowed him to keep open the passes to protect his lines of communication. The accuracy of Long's memory, recorded long after the war, has to be considered.

move on Richmond thus requiring his army to fall back into the city's fortifications and undergo a siege.[5]

Another key part of Lee's agenda was the pressing need to acquire provisions for his army. Saddled with the inadequate Confederate supply system and a theater in Virginia virtually scoured clean by two years of war, Lee planned to seize sufficient livestock and foodstuffs during the invasion to feed his men not only during the campaign but beyond.[6]

Acutely aware of the growing odds against a victory for the South in this sectional conflict, Lee, in a letter to Davis, conceded Northern superiority in strength, resources, and the means for carrying on the war, and acknowledged the potential consequences of the enemy's use of these advantages. He also admitted that diminishing aggregate returns for his army showed that its ranks were growing weaker—by battlefield attrition and desertion—and recruits were not replenishing its losses.[7]

Consequently Lee's thoughts had turned to a political solution to counteract the military disadvantages besetting the South. He advocated that President Davis encourage the "friends of peace at the North" to believe that a settlement between North and South would bring about reunification—despite that being a false hope. Lee implied that holding out the prospect of a favorable peace settlement could help to undermine support for the war in the North.[8]

If he could achieve his main objective, a decisive battlefield victory on Northern soil, Lee confidently expected to reach his ultimate goal: independence for the Confederacy. But to achieve this objective and its goal, Lee's army had to reach the North safely in advance of the enemy; it was imperative that he conceal his movements and deceive Hooker about his

---

5 Lee was mistaken about the enemy's overarching plans, because Northern military strategy had downgraded the east in favor of focusing on victory in the west. Richard E. Beringer, Herman Hattaway, Archer Jones, William N. Still, Jr., *Why the South Lost the Civil War* (Athens, GA, 1986), 259; Walter H. Taylor, *General Lee: His Campaigns in Virginia, 1861-1865* (Lincoln, NE, 1994), 180.

6 Lee to Seddon, OR 25, pt. 2, , 713-14, 790; pt. 3, 868-69; Lee's post-action report, pt. 2, 27:305; Sears, *Gettysburg*, 12-13; W. H. Taylor, "The Campaign in Pennsylvania," in *The Annals of the Civil War, Written by Leading Participants North and South* (New York, 1994), 305-06.

7 Lee to Davis, June 10, 1863, OR 27, pt. 3, 880-82.

8 The fact that Lee chose to raise this political issue with the president just as he was launching an invasion indicates he was confronting the reality of increasing odds against a military victory for the South and suggests that his confidence level was not as high as is sometimes depicted as the Gettysburg campaign got underway. Ibid.

destination and intentions. Lee assigned this crucial task to Stuart and his cavalry.[9]

Union Planning Overview

The Army of the Potomac's grand strategy evolved as events unfolded. General in chief Henry Halleck instructed Hooker, or "Fighting Joe" as the press dubbed him following his gutsy performance during the Peninsula campaign, at all costs to defend Washington and Harpers Ferry from attack by enemy's forces. Otherwise, Hooker was free to maneuver his army to the greatest advantage and act as circumstances might require against Lee's forces. Lincoln advised Hooker that Lee's army was his primary objective. He was to "follow on his flank" and engage him in battle when opportunity presented itself. Because these two responsibilities of fighting battles and protecting the capital were not necessarily compatible, Hooker had to figure out a way to accomplish both.[10]

Following Lee's thumping defeat of Hooker's army at Chancellorsville in May, the atmosphere in the North was edgy and anxious. Both Lee and Hooker had good intelligence during the Chancellorsville campaign. The difference was that Lee acted while Hooker hesitated, and so the Union army lost momentum and the battle. Hooker also made the mistake of sending most of his cavalry under Maj. Gen. George Stoneman on a raid right before the battle, thus denying himself his key information gathering capability so critical to the success of a major military maneuver.[11]

His defeat at Chancellorsville led some of Hooker's subordinate generals and the authorities in Washington to lose faith in the Union army commander. In fact, the general's stock had not been particularly high before his selection as commander. Secretary Stanton had not favored Hooker's appointment because of the general's rather sordid reputation, and a number of the army's general

9   Lee's post-action report, ibid. pt. 2, 316; Stuart's post-action report, 687; Long, *Memoirs of Robert Lee*, 267-69; Richard Rollins, "Lee's Grand Strategy and Pickett's Charge," *North & South* (July 2002), 82.

10 Halleck to Hooker, June 5, 1863, *OR* 27, pt. 1, 31-32; Lincoln to Hooker, 35.

11 Jay Luvaas and Harold W. Nelson, "Intelligence in the Chancellorsville Campaign," in *The U.S. Army War College Guide to the Battles of Chancellorsville & Fredericksburg* (Carlisle, PA,1988), 299-314. On Stoneman's raid, see Sears, *Chancellorsville*, 367-70, 438-40; Walter H. Hebert, *Fighting Joe Hooker* (Lincoln, NE, 1999), 190, 193, 198, 220, 222-23, 225.

officers questioned his moral character and personal conduct as well. General Meade, for one, doubted Hooker's qualifications to command a large army. Indeed, of the seven corps commanders in the army, Hooker could count on the support of only one, III Corps commander Daniel E. Sickles. But cavalry commander Pleasonton and his chief of staff Maj. Gen. Daniel Butterfield remained loyal to Hooker.[12]

Despite Hooker's poor implementation of his strategy at Chancellorsville and the resulting defeat, he had nevertheless demonstrated an ability to deceive and outmaneuver Lee and his commanders. This experience provided a foundation for strategic planning for the upcoming campaign. One worrisome point was Hooker's misuse of his cavalry during the Chancellorsville campaign—and whether he learned from this experience remained to be seen.[13]

Union Intelligence Plans and Operations

> Reliable information of the enemy's position or movements, which is absolutely necessary to the commander of an army to successfully conduct a campaign, must be largely furnished by the cavalry. [14]
>
> Brig. Gen. William W. Averell

Hooker had experimented with different methods of intelligence gathering and counterintelligence. In early 1862, he commanded a division that included the 3rd Indiana, a cavalry regiment he assigned to scout enemy forces and track down smugglers and blockade-runners carrying mail, newspapers, and contraband through pro-secessionist southern Maryland into the South. To impede this he established a cavalry picket line along the Potomac River in southern Maryland south to Point Lookout. However, his early attempts to gain information about Confederate activities from the local population, almost entirely pro-secessionist, met without success.[15]

---

12 Hooker to Lincoln, June 16, 1863, OR 27, pt. 1, 45; Lincoln to Hooker, May 14, 1863, pt. 2, 25:479; Sandburg, *Abraham Lincoln*, 2:77; Hebert, *Fighting Joe Hooker*, 167-68, 229; Stephen W. Sears, "Meade Takes Command," *North & South* (September 2002), 12-15, 17-18; T. Harry Williams, *Lincoln and His Generals* (New York, 1952), 211.

13 Longacre, *The Cavalry at Gettysburg*, 46-47.

14 Edward K. Eckert and Nicholas J. Amato, eds., *Ten Years in the Saddle: The Memoir of William Woods Averell 1851-1862* (San Rafael, CA, 1978), 328.

15 Hooker to Williams, December 6, 1861, OR 5, 675-76.

Hooker also employed agents in an attempt to halt the smuggling, and he was one of the first to use balloons to observe enemy positions. He also cooperated and exchanged information about the enemy with Union naval forces in the area. These experiences gave him an appreciation for the value of a dedicated intelligence unit—hence the creation of the BMI.[16]

Deserters from enemy ranks, fed up with the poor living conditions they endured, proved a boon to the process of gathering information. The inability of the Army of Northern Virginia to feed, clothe, and equip its men adequately and provide sufficient forage for its horses caused considerable hardship among the troops, not to mention the death of many animals from starvation. In late March, when asked by his Union captors why he deserted, a member of the 5th Virginia Cavalry responded "no pay, no clothing and only one-fourth pound of meat a day."[17]

Intelligence reports Sharpe and Babcock generated during the BMI's initial stages were models of thoroughness and objectivity. Information about the size, location, and condition of Lee's army had been an important ingredient in Hooker's strategy from the outset of the Chancellorsville campaign. But gathering information about a stationary army was one thing. Getting it from Lee's forces while on the move northward, however, was quite another. It would test the BMI's skill and strain their resources.[18]

At the beginning of the Gettysburg campaign, Hooker focused on locating Lee's army, identifying the type, organization, size, and leadership of Confederate forces, and understanding the significance of their movements. As indicators of a possible Rebel invasion emerged, Hooker particularly wanted to find out whether Lee's forces intended to cross the Potomac. This information would dictate what Hooker would do with his forces: place them in a protective array around the capital or pursue the Rebels north of the river. If Lee planned to move across the Potomac, Hooker wanted to overtake and engage him in battle. BMI chief Sharpe, who was coordinating the effort to locate Lee's army,

---

16 Ibid., October 31, 1861, 635; November 4, 5, 1861, 642-43; November 11, 1861, 649; November 16, 1861, 653-4; November 22, 1863, 663; December 13, 1861, 686; December 20, 1861, 690; January 27, 1862, 711; February 20, 1862, 724-25; Hebert, *Fighting Joe Hooker*, 53, 59, 62.

17 Driver, *5th Virginia Cavalry*, 50.

18 Sears, *Chancellorsville*, 68-70, 84, 100-102, 130-31, 151, 201, 210, 391-92, 427; Fishel, *The Secret War*, 318-22.

wrote to his uncle on June 20, 1863, that Lee "must whip us before he goes in force into M[aryland] or Penn[sylvania]. If he doesn't, we propose to let him go, and when we get behind him, we would like to know how many men he will take back [to Virginia]."[19]

Hooker's intelligence operations at first were perforce more reactive than proactive, since Lee had taken the initiative during the early stages of the campaign. Once he suspected Lee's army on the move, Hooker directed his cavalry to pinpoint its location. Since cavalry commander Pleasonton typically submitted confusing or speculative reports, Hooker stressed the need for gathering accurate information.[20]

At army headquarters, chief of staff Butterfield coordinated Pleasonton's reports along with other information and shared it with Sharpe's bureau. Throughout the campaign, the BMI collated and processed this information and sent finished product reports to the commanding general through his chief of staff.[21]

Since March 1863, the BMI had been using all available sources to produce intelligence; this led Hooker to put a stop to trading information with the enemy, a practice that had routinely taken place under flags of truce while pickets exchanged newspapers. The Army of the Potomac no longer needed to rely on such tenuous sources that required giving up as much, if not more, information than it got from the enemy.[22]

Forwarding information obtained in the field to headquarters had been experiencing delays though, and inaccurate reporting on the size of enemy forces was also a problem. To remedy this, Hooker issued general orders no. 40 that specified everyone's duty to forward to headquarters without delay: deserters, contrabands, prisoners, and citizens captured or coming into the lines of the army. All these along with all newspapers, enemy communications, or other captured articles, were to be sent, directly to the provost marshal general

19 Hooker to Babcock, June 20, 1863, OR 27, pt. 3, 225; Sharpe to "My dear uncle," June 20, 1863, in George Sharpe Collection, Senate House State Historic Site, Kingston, NY.

20 Williams to Pleasonton, June 17, 1863, OR 27, pt. 3, 171-72.

21 Butterfield to Meade, June 10, 1863, ibid., 448-49; Pleasonton to Butterfield, June 10, 1863, 49; Fishel, *The Secret War*, 300.

22 Ibid., 322, 332.

so that the BMI could interrogate or examine them and produce timely intelligence for Hooker's use [23]

These general orders also charged officers at outposts and on the front lines with sending accurate information to headquarters. Officers should know about events in their vicinity, and they must not magnify the size of enemy forces—something Hooker himself would himself do in the near future. To scotch inaccurate information coming in from the picket lines, Hooker stipulated that all officers' "reports from the front [had to be] perfectly reliable."[24]

Hooker also took steps to prevent the press from disclosing his plans. He issued general orders no. 48 that required their signatures or bylines on correspondents' stories, hoping that loss of anonymity would prevent irresponsible reporters from betraying the army's movements to the enemy.[25]

In February 1862, Congress authorized the president to take control of the telegraph and railroad lines in the U.S. Secretary of War Stanton assumed this function and appointed E. S. Sanford of the American Telegraph Company to the rank of colonel charged with implementing censorship as military supervisor of telegrams. But when newspaper leaks persisted and Hooker complained to Stanton, the secretary replied he would support "any measure you are pleased to take on the subject." The action Hooker took was to issue general orders no. 48 to control the content of newspaper dispatches sent over telegraph lines.[26]

Hooker rather optimistically thought this order would encourage correspondents to be more circumspect about the content of their dispatches. He threatened to dismiss beyond the lines of the army anyone who ignored this requirement. The commanding general also issued publication guidelines to the editors of newspapers stating that the location of any corps, division, brigade, or regiment should not be published, and especially not the location of army

---

23 General Orders No. 40, Headquarters Army of the Potomac, April 10, 1863, OR 25, pt. 2, 197.

24 Ibid.

25 Ibid., 316.

26 Stanton to Hooker, April 30, 1863, ibid.; General Orders No. 48, 316; Brayton Harris, *Blue & Gray in Black & White: Newspapers in the Civil War* (Washington, D.C., 2000), 141-42, 254; Greely, *The Military-Telegraph Service*, 346.

headquarters. In addition, official military reports were not to be published without the sanction of the war department.[27]

Even while working to control what the press reported, Hooker did not hesitate to contrive false news stories to confuse the enemy. As he prepared to move northward, Hooker requested Stanton have the newspapers announce that he was moving south toward the James River, to divert attention from his actual intentions.[28]

Hooker's restrictions did not easily cow The New York *Tribune's* chief reporter, Josiah R. Sypher. In one instance, Sypher threatened to expose "the doings of the orderlies or of the General officers" if he were not allowed to accompany the army. Since Hooker's headquarters had a deserved reputation for rather loose behavior, Sypher's threat had the desired effect, and he was permitted privileges other reporters were denied. But Sypher and other reporters such as Lorenzo L. Crounse also circumvented Hooker's restrictions by submitting their stories and reports in code. They also avoided the army's telegraphic censorship by simply sending their reports by mail or messenger or delivering them personally.[29]

The Union army also conducted population control as a counterintelligence measure. Hooker directed cavalry leader Pleasonton to warn local residents under pain of summary punishment against aiding and abetting Rebel raids against Union positions. In addition to issuing stringent regulations regarding personal passes and trade, Hooker instructed provost marshal Patrick to examine every person moving through the lines to prevent the passing of military secrets to the enemy.[30]

Hooker also sent a request to Lee to prevent "non-combatants" from fishing on the south side of the Rappahannock. This presumably afforded an

---

27 Hooker to Gobright, June 18, 1863, *OR* 27, pt. 3, 192; Starr, *Bohemian Brigade*, 196.

28 Hooker to Stanton, June 16, 1863, *OR* 27, pt. 1, 47-48. Confederate authorities were on guard against Northern disinformation efforts. See Seddon to D. H. Hill, May 30, 1863, ibid., pt. 2, 25:834.

29 Louis M. Starr, *Bohemian Brigade: Civil War Newsmen in Action* (Madison, WI, 1987), 197, 200; Harris, *Blue & Gray in Black & White*, 151.

30 Williams to [Pleasonton], May 23, 1863, *OR* 25, pt. 2, 516-17. Hooker also reduced the large number of camp followers traveling with the army. Those without proper permits were to be arrested and sent to headquarters for further disposition. General Orders No. 56, May 23, 1863; Cohen to Gregg, Cohen to Buford, May 24, 1863, *OR* 25, 519, 521-22.

opportunity to communicate with spies or informers on the opposite bank of the river.[31]

At the outset of the Gettysburg campaign, the Union commander's strategy was to locate Lee and determine his intentions. At the same time, he wanted to prevent the enemy from learning about and disrupting his own operations. While implementing this general plan, Hooker also had to keep in mind his paramount responsibility was to ensure the safety of the capital at Washington.[32]

Hooker was determined to learn Lee's intentions by gathering information from a variety of sources that would allow him to track enemy movements. The cavalry, with support from BMI scouts, were to collect this data. He also planned to keep Lee from discovering his strategy by controlling the press, halting exchange of newspapers with the Confederates, restricting civilian movements, maintaining communications security, and keeping his plans confidential.

Confederate Intelligence Plans and Operations

> There is nothing more necessary than good Intelligence to frustrate a designing enemy, & nothing that requires greater pains to obtain.
>
> Gen. George Washington[33]

After the battle of Chancellorsville, Lee focused his attention on reorganizing and strengthening his army and planning an invasion of the North. Lee ordered Stuart to move into Culpeper County where he could better observe the enemy. He also wanted him to find out how many cavalry brigades the Army of the Potomac had, and the names of their commanders. Lee read in the Washington newspapers that Hooker was contemplating a new movement, and told Stuart to keep his scouts on the alert.[34]

---

31 Hooker to Lee, May 24, 1863, ibid., 521. These policies were reflected in Fifth Corps commander Meade's order to keep citizens under guard if there was suspicion they might communicate information to the enemy. Meade to Barnes, June 1, 1863, OR 27, pt. 3, 47; Fishel, *The Secret War*, 322; Sparks, *Inside Lincoln's Army*, 213.

32 Lincoln to Hooker, June 10, 1863, OR 27, pt. 1, 35; Halleck to Hooker, June 5, 1863, 31.

33 Washington quoted on the dust jacket of Thomas B. Allen, *George Washington, Spymaster: How the Americans Outspied the British and Won the Revolutionary War* (Washington, 2004).

34 Lee to Stuart, May 11, 1863, OR 25, pt. 2, 792.

The absence of an intelligence staff at Lee's headquarters meant that Lee, by default, had to take on a heavy responsibility for intelligence matters. His small personal staff was not in a position to assume the intelligence burden. Since the Army of Northern Virginia commander served as his own intelligence chief, a variety of operations came within his purview. These included intelligence collection, counterintelligence, information security, deception, disinformation, and covert operations—specifically the recruiting and handling of spies.[35]

Lee ordinarily left little to chance when it came to dealing with his opponents. Before engaging in battle he took the measure of Union officers he would be facing, many of whom he knew from serving with them previously. He also scoured Northern newspapers for valuable information about enemy plans and activities. Thomas Conrad of the 4th Virginia Cavalry, who frequently operated undercover in Washington, commented, "The [Northern] newspapers were a source of much information, and it was important to make an arrangement by which they could be forwarded to Richmond regularly. This was done."[36]

Like Hooker, Lee was concerned that Southern newspapers revealed information that benefited the Northern cause. His misgivings in this regard were reflected sometime later when Union cavalry commander Alfred Pleasonton informed army headquarters that the Richmond papers reported Lee's army in motion. At the same time, also like Hooker, Lee was not averse to planting stories in Southern newspapers to deceive the North about his true intentions.[37]

---

35 Taylor, *General Lee:*, vii-viii; Tidwell, *Come Retribution*, 105-13.

36 Dowdey, The Wartime Papers, 294-95, 440-41, 482-83, 503, 507-08, 527, 531; Daniel E. Sutherland, *Seasons of War: The Ordeal of a Confederate Community, 1861-1865* (Baton Rouge, LA, 1995), 236-37; Thomas Nelson Conrad, *The Rebel Scout: A Thrilling History of Scouting Life in the Southern Army* (Washington, 1904), 61.

37 Lee's report, July 28, 1862, OR 11, pt. 2, 936; Ingalls to Sawtelle, pt. 3, 27:42; Dowdey, *The Wartime Papers*, 507-08, 513, 528. According to one source, the Southern press association had worked out a compromise with military commanders early in the war. Reporters could avoid censorship if they refrained from offering opinions, refused to pass along rumors, and did not divulge information that would aid the enemy. Over time, however, editors, especially those in opposition to the Davis administration, would put this agreement to the test. R. J. Brown, "How the South Gathered News During the Civil War," *The History Buff*, accessed July 29, 2014, http://www.historybuff.com/library/refgather.html. For a discussion of Lee's approach to intelligence operations, see Tidwell, *Come Retribution*, 105-14.

From a counterintelligence perspective, Lee planned to have his cavalry screen the army's march from Culpeper, Virginia, the invasion launching point, northward into Maryland and Pennsylvania to prevent the Union army from discovering his movements and intentions. Simultaneously the horsemen would gather information about enemy activities along the march route.[38]

Lee's intelligence plan for the invasion placed heavy reliance on Stuart and his cavalry. Since Stuart had performed intelligence responsibilities capably since early in the war, Lee had faith in the timeliness and accuracy of his reports. He was concerned, however, that his army lacked sufficient cavalry to screen its movements away from the Rappahannock and, at the same time, reconnoiter the enemy.[39]

Given his reliance on cavalry for intelligence and counterintelligence activities, Lee paid particular attention to the reorganization of this arm. He retained the existing single division framework to be expanded from three to five brigades.[40]

---

38 Lee's post-action report, January 1864, *OR* 27, pt. 2, 321; Stuart's post-action report, 687.

39 Lee voiced this concern to President Davis on May 7, and sought cavalry reinforcements from North Carolina, and southern and western Virginia. Lee to Davis, May 7, 1863, *OR* 25, pt. 2, 782; Lee to D. H. Hill, May 25, 1863, in Dowdey, *The Wartime Papers*, 494; Tidwell, *Come Retribution*, 10-11, 109-10. For the role of Lee's cavalry during the Civil War, see Longacre, *Lee's Cavalrymen*; William C. Davis, "Join the Cavalry," *Rebels & Yankees: The Fighting Men of the Civil War* (London, 1999), 72-84. Lee had requested cavalry reinforcements from Davis as early as April 20, and learned from adjutant and inspector general Samuel Cooper that the president had approved the transfer of 10 regiments of cavalry to Lee's army. Lee to Davis, April 20, 1863, Cooper to Lee, April 21, 1863, Lee to Cooper, Cooper to Jones, Jones to Cooper, April 23, 1863, Jones to Lee, April 25, 1863, *OR* 25, pt. 2, 740, 742, 745, 747-48, 750-51.

40 Lee disapproved Stuart's request to restructure the cavalry into a corps, because separate divisions would have too many high-ranking officers with too few troops to command. Motivation for Stuart's corps proposal undoubtedly contained a desire to raise his status to the level of the infantry corps commanders, and increase the likelihood of promotion to lieutenant general. Also, because of the scarcity of horses, a problem that had become endemic within the army, Lee discouraged Stuart from adding two guns to his existing four-gun artillery batteries. Mitchell, *Stuart's Letters*, 320-22; Lee to Stuart, May 30, 1863, *OR* 25, pt. 2, 835-36. The news that Lee rejected his proposal to reorganize his cavalry as a corps followed Stuart's chagrin earlier in the month that he did not get, in his opinion, sufficient acclaim for his performance as temporary commander of the Second Corps after Stonewall Jackson and A. P. Hill fell wounded during the battle of Chancellorsville. It is possible that Stuart hoped to be named the new corps commander following Jackson's death, but instead the job went to Ewell. E. P. Alexander commented that if Lee had seen Stuart in action leading the Second Corps at Chancellorsville, he may have promoted him on the spot to the command. Lee to Stuart, May 11, 1863, *OR* 25, pt. 2, 792; Alexander, *Military Memoirs*, 360.

Brig. Gen. Wade Hampton
Library of Congress

Brig. Gen. William Henry Fitzhugh
"Rooney" Lee
Library of Congress

Brig. Gen. Fitzhugh Lee
Library of Congress

Brig. Gen. Beverly Robertson
Library of Congress

In addition to Fitz Lee's, W. H. F. "Rooney" Lee's, and Wade Hampton's brigades, Lee's army would gain another small, two-regiment brigade from North Carolina with Brig. Gen. Beverly Robertson in command, and another from the Shenandoah Valley with Brig. Gen. William "Grumble" Jones in charge. While Stuart was more than pleased to have two additional brigades, he had low regard for both of their commanders. In Robertson's case, Stuart lobbied Lee to assign him elsewhere, since he had proven to be a burden in the past.[41]

Lee and Stuart's wariness of Robertson's return turned out to be prescient, for during the upcoming invasion Robertson's failure to follow orders led to a breakdown in Lee's early warning system of the approaching enemy, not to mention the screening and reconnaissance services necessary for maneuvering his forces. To his chagrin, Lee would discover that the transfer of 1,000 additional cavalrymen to his army would not be worth the price of one Beverly Robertson.

Stuart also reacted negatively to Jones joining his division, but Lee overrode the objections. The two cavalry officers had an instinctive personality conflict—Stuart always upbeat and jovial, while Jones cantankerous and blunt in his mannerisms. Nonetheless, Stuart recognized that Jones was a competent leader in the field and labeled him the best outpost officer in the army. Despite their personal differences, Jones' brigade added strength to Stuart's division.[42]

Lee also had available two independent cavalry brigades, both under his—not Stuart's—direct command at this point in the campaign because he had combat and intelligence missions in mind for these irregular units.[43] Their

---

41 Lee to Jones, May 23, 1863, Lee to Davis, June 2, 1863, OR 25, pt. 2, 820, 848. Captain William W. Blackford, an engineer on Stuart's staff and an astute observer of his fellow officers, succinctly identified the problem: "General Robertson was an excellent man in camp to train troops, but in the field, in the presence of the enemy, he lost all self-possession, and was perfectly unreliable." Blackford, *War Years With Jeb Stuart*, 229.

42 OR 25, pt. 2, 788-89. Jones's dislike for Stuart was palpable, not the least because of jealousy stemming from Stuart's promotion to a higher grade despite Jones having graduated from West Point two years earlier than Stuart. See Robertson, *In the Saddle With Stuart*, 53-54; Blackford, *War Years With Jeb Stuart*, 16, 51-54, 62-63; Faust, *Historical Times Encyclopedia*, 404.

43 Stuart would not take operational control of Jenkins' brigade until July 3, the last day of the battle at Gettysburg. By then it was under the command of Col. M. J. Ferguson since Jenkins had been wounded on July 2. Imboden remained directly under Lee's command throughout the campaign, including during the retreat from Gettysburg when he was in charge of the wagon train of wounded soldiers. Brigadier General John D. Imboden, "The Confederate

Brig. Gen. William "Grumble" Jones   Brig. Gen. Albert G. Jenkins
Library of Congress   *Library of Congress*

commanders, Brig. Gens. Albert G. Jenkins and John D. Imboden, had been
lawyers and politicians in private life and were not formally trained in cavalry
tactics. Jenkins, an articulate Harvard Law School graduate and congressman
from the mountains of western Virginia, had about 1,300 men in his brigade.
Imboden, an arch-secessionist lawyer and state legislator from Staunton in the
Shenandoah Valley, commanded a force of 1,300 to 1,400.[44]

Special assignments were in store for two additional battalion-sized cavalry
units assigned to the army. Lieutenant Colonel Elijah White's 35th Virginia
Battalion often functioned as independent partisans, and this unit would
accompany Ewell's corps during its march northward. In addition, Maj. Harry

Retreat From Gettysburg," in Robert Underwood Johnson & Clarence Clough Buel, eds.,
Battles and Leaders of the Civil War, 4 vols. (New York, 1956), 3:420-29.

44 Lee to Jenkins, Lee to Imboden, June 10, 1863, in Dowdey, *The Wartime Papers*, 510;
Longacre, *The Cavalry at Gettysburg*, 94; Jones to Lee, May 15, 1863, OR 25, pt. 2, 804; Lee to
Jones, June 7, 1863, pt. 3, 27:866; Busey and Martin, *Regimental Strengths and Losses*, 244; Steve
French, *Imboden's Brigade in the Gettysburg Campaign* (Berkeley Springs, WV, 2008), 10. Jenkins'
previous commander, Maj. Gen. Samuel Jones, thought him bold and gallant but, being a
politician whose troops were also constituents, not a good disciplinarian.

Gilmor's six companies of the 1st Maryland Battalion of Fitz Lee's brigade awaited the Confederate army in the Shenandoah Valley, and would also travel with Ewell's corps. Both of these battalions would help to collect supplies and gather information.[45]

General Lee minded security. Before the invasion, he issued a general order to halt the custom of providing newspaper correspondents the number of men taken into battle along with a list of casualties. Publication of this information, he realized, afforded the enemy the opportunity to learn the strength of the army. In addition, Lee ordered discretion in the reporting of the numbers of casualties, limiting it only to those considered unfit for duty. He feared casualty reports would "mislead our friends and encourage our enemies." Lee's attention to information security was also seen in his instructions to Imboden to destroy all of his letters to prevent them from falling into the hands of the enemy.[46]

Disinformation was another of Lee's tools. At times, he instructed his corps commanders to tell citizens in the local area that their advance was to be in a certain direction, when the actual intention was to move in another. He also sent carefully coached "deserters" and "refugees" into Union lines to disseminate false information. As he informed Lt. Col. J. Critcher, 15th Virginia Cavalry, Lee was also well aware that the best sources of information for the Yankees were escaped slaves, and the best way to counter this, he believed, was to deceive the slaves about Confederate plans, so they would pass along inaccurate information to the enemy. But deceiving all the slaves was a near impossible task, given the sheer number of them traveling with the Army of Northern Virginia.[47]

Lee also recognized the value of covert operations. He ordered an additional spy network established in Washington to supply information about

---

45 The 35th was part of Jones's brigade that normally operated in the Shenandoah Valley. Frank K. Myers, *The Comanches: A History of White's Battalion, Virginia Cavalry* (Marietta, GA, 1956), 187-88; Longacre, *The Cavalry at Gettysburg*, 17-18, 31, 94; Ted Alexander, "Gettysburg Cavalry Operations, June 27-July 3, 1863," *Blue & Gray Magazine*, no. 8, 6:13; Longacre, *Lee's Cavalrymen*, 158.

46 General Orders No. 63, Hdqrs. Army of Northern Virginia, May 14, 1863, *OR* 25, pt. 2, 798; Lee to Imboden, June 20, 1863, pt. 3, 27:906; Sears, *Landscape Turned Red*, 381-86.

47 Fishel, *The Secret War*, 296-97; Lee to Critcher, May 26, 1863, *OR* 25, pt. 2, 826; Luvaas, "Intelligence in the Chancellorsville Campaign," 310. For passing on inaccurate information, see Lee to Longstreet, June 17, 1863, *OR* 27, pt. 3, 900.

the organization and disposition of Union forces. This information would travel down a communication line from the capital directly to his headquarters. With this line of communication in place, Lee no longer had to depend exclusively on information relayed to him from Richmond, the terminus of communication lines from existing spy networks in the North. Lee preferred to have experienced scouts and spies working for him, because he believed they made a calm assessment of the situation and were "not liable to excitement or exaggeration." From experience he knew that reports from citizens could not always be trusted, because they frequently distorted the facts and inflated the size of enemy forces.[48]

Lee's immediate plan was to reach Pennsylvania before Hooker learned of his intentions. Cavalry commander Jeb Stuart would be responsible for screening the army's movements, and gathering information about the enemy's response. Lee had maps of the invasion route to guide his army. He also had taken steps to impose limitations about what Southern newspapers would publish about the army. Along the way, Lee would obtain Northern newspapers to glean useful facts about the enemy. He would also broadcast misleading stories among the local citizenry about his destination and intentions, and interrogate civilians and captured Union soldiers about enemy activities in the surrounding areas. Strategic information from spy networks would reach him by courier. Lee's operational and intelligence plans were in place and ready for implementation.[49]

---

48 Tidwell, Come Retribution, 109, 111; Brown, *Stringfellow of the Fourth*, 172-86; Bakeless, *Spies of the Confederacy*, 109-114; Conrad, *The Rebel Scout*, 61, 81; Lee to Seddon, January 5, 1863, in Dowdey, *The Wartime Papers*, 387. Sometime later, probably in May, Longstreet sent "a person," to obtain information in Washington. Lee to Davis, May 30, OR 25, part 2, 832.

49 Lee would be linked to Richmond by a courier line to receive intelligence and exchange information. The line essentially followed the route the army was traveling. See Walter Lord, *The Fremantle Diary: Being the Journal of Lieutenant Colonel Arthur James Lyon Fremantle, Coldstream Guards, on his three Months in the Southern States* (Short Hills, NJ, 1954), 176-81, 186-90.

Chapter Four

Analyzing the Enemy's Intentions:
Mid-May to Early June

A power…will always find it advantageous to carry the war upon hostile soil. This course will spare its territory from devastation, carry on the war at the expense of the enemy, excite the ardor of its soldiers, and depress the spirits of the adversary.

Baron Antoine Henri De Jomini[1]

Preparation for Invasion

Stuart's men . . . are wildly enthusiastic over the prospect of an invasion of the North.
Capt. Thomas N. Conrad [2]

Lincoln

and Hooker knew that if Lee stole a march into the North through the Shenandoah Valley, he could move into Maryland and across Pennsylvania and threaten Philadelphia, Baltimore, and Washington. The loss of any of these major cities would be a serious, if not fatal, blow to the Union cause. Hooker informed Halleck that he had about 100,000 troops, all that he needed or could use to advantage in another confrontation with Lee's army. Halleck passed this

---

1 Baron De Jomini, *The Art of War* (El Paso, TX, 2005), 13. Lee was exposed to Jomini's writings on military tactics while at West Point, which are believed to have had a significant influence on his thinking during his military career. Elizabeth Brown Pryor, *Reading the Man: A Portrait of Robert E. Lee through His Private Letters* (New York, 2007), 67-68.

2 Conrad, *A Confederate Spy*, 50.

Abraham Lincoln
Library of Congress

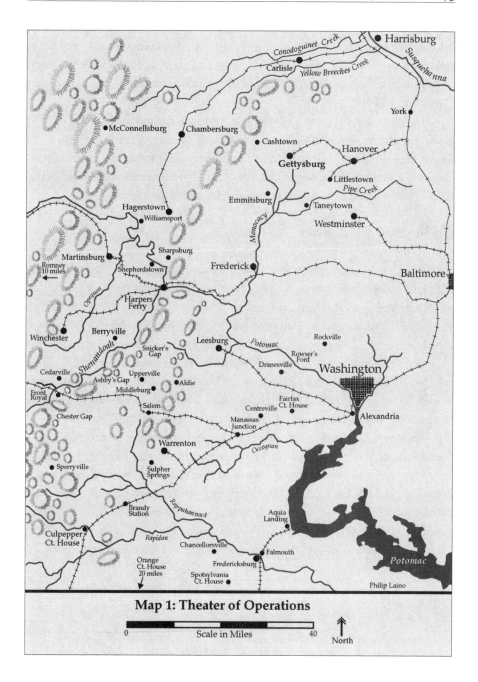

Map 1: Theater of Operations

0   Scale in Miles   40

North

information along to Stanton, commenting that Hooker had not at any point estimated the size of Lee's army at more than 70,000. Others with the "best opportunity of observation" believed that enemy strength did not exceed 60,000, he added.[3]

Hooker knew, or, at least, should have known, the numerical odds were in his favor, but he would have to depend on his cavalry to track Lee's army. A recent reorganization had unified and solidified the Union cavalry. However, cavalry commander Pleasonton had a penchant for focusing on combat activity rather than his primary information-gathering mission.[4]

Union Cavalry Initiatives

Based on his experience as a division commander operating in southern Maryland in late 1861 and early 1862, Hooker was familiar with the smuggling of contraband by Confederate agents from that secession-friendly area through the Union blockade on the Potomac River to the Northern Neck—Lancaster, Northumberland, Richmond, and Westmoreland counties. And since the majority of the citizens in southern Maryland favored the South, the smuggling continued unabated. Units of the Confederate Signal Corps established bases along the south side of the river, cooperating with private citizens to facilitate the passage of agents and contraband between Maryland and Virginia.[5]

On May 17, 1863, Hooker sent a 500-man detachment of the 8th Illinois Cavalry, with BMI scouts as guides, to sweep down the Northern Neck of Virginia, seize mail and cargo and destroy vessels that could be used for carrying contraband to the enemy. The objective was to obtain as much information as possible about enemy activities, and to interdict the enemy's system of acquiring supplies and intelligence, and, if the opportunity presented itself, inflict "summary punishment" on the "citizen marauders" of the unfriendly area.[6]

---

3   Halleck to Stanton, May 18, 1863, *OR* 25, pt. 2, 505-06.

4   Longacre, *The Cavalry at Gettysburg*, 9-11, 43-60, 273-75; George A. Rummel III, *Cavalry on the Roads to Gettysburg: Kilpatrick at Hanover and Hunterstown* (Shippensburg, PA, 2000), vii:382-83.

5   Baker, *The Secret Service*, 111, 122-27.

6   Butterfield to Pleasonton, May 16, 1863, *OR* 25, pt. 2, 494-95; D. R. Clendenin to A. J. Cohen, May 27, 1863, RG 393, NA; Hard, *History of the Eighth Cavalry Regiment Illinois Volunteers*, 238, quoted; Tidwell, *Come Retribution*, 80-104.

Gregg's cavalry division, operating out of Bealeton, was to protect the Orange and Alexandria Railroad from Rappahannock Station to Cedar Run against bushwhackers and guerillas in that the area, picket the Rappahannock River, guard the railroad bridge, and screen the army's right flank against enemy raids. The 40-mile long patrol area was a formidable assignment for his 2,000 troopers, many of them on tired mounts. Colonel Alfred N. Duffié's cavalry division received orders to clear out bushwhackers and guerrillas operating to the army's right from Morrisville to Dumfries, a distance of about 16 miles.[7]

Accumulating evidence that Stuart's cavalry was concentrated to the west and north of the Union army to conduct a raid or screen Lee's anticipated movement led Hooker to shift Brig. Gen. John Buford's cavalry to Bealeton on the army's right flank. And if he had sufficient force, Buford was to move south of the Rappahannock and drive the enemy from Culpeper across the Rapidan River. These orders were the prelude to what would soon be the largest cavalry battle of the Civil War.[8]

Decision to Invade

> There is some purpose on the part of Gen. Lee to have a raid in the enemy's country, surpassing all other raids...they may penetrate to the Hudson River; and then . . . Philadelphia, even, may be taken.
> John B. Jones, War Clerk[9]

Lee reported the latest intelligence to President Davis on May 11: citing articles in the Northern papers, including the Washington *Chronicle*, New York *Herald*, and *New York World*, that the Lincoln administration intended to reinforce Hooker with some additional 48,000 troops. He also referenced scouting reports from Fort Monroe and Suffolk indicating that Union troops had left these locations to reinforce Hooker.[10]

---

7 Alexander to Gregg, May 14, 1863, OR 25, pt. 2, 480; Gregg to Taylor, May 23, 1863, 518-19; Cohen to Gregg, May 24, 1863, 521; Gregg to Cohen, May 25, 1863, 524-25; Barstow to Pleasonton, May 21, 1863, 511.

8 Cohen to Buford, May 24, 1863, ibid., 522; Williams to Pleasonton, May 28, 1863, 537.

9 John B. Jones, *A Rebel War Clerk's Diary at the Confederate States Capital*, 2 vols. (Philadelphia, 1866), 1:326.

10 OR 25 pt. 2, 791; Taylor, *The Signal and Secret Service of the Confederate States*, 22.

Jefferson Davis
Library of Congress

After Lee recommended a movement northward, while his army still confronted Hooker near Fredericksburg on the Rappahannock, he began lobbying Davis for his army to be strengthened. "I think you will agree with me that every effort should be made to re-enforce this army in order to oppose the large force which this enemy seems to be concentrating against it," he told the president.[11]

To situate Stuart's cavalry in better position to observe the enemy, Lee requested that he move his division from its grazing grounds near Orange Court House north to Culpeper as soon as possible. Lee told Stuart that he would increase his force's size and reliability by having Jones's brigade join him, while Jenkins' brigade operated in the Valley. The larger force would increase Stuart's flexibility to "re-enforce either flank" of the army. Lee hoped that Stuart, in coordination with Hood's nearby infantry division, could "scatter" the Union cavalry.[12]

The orders for Stuart's cavalry to move northward from the vicinity of Orange Court House to Culpeper roused curiosity among the troops; rumors of a possible invasion were in the air. Captain Jesse Heath of the 4th Virginia of Fitz Lee's brigade wrote home on May 18, "Stuart is collecting a great deal of Cavalry for what purpose I do not know. The men are all very anxious for a big Pennsylvania Raid and they will give them fits if they do not go." These rumors and speculation about a cavalry raid into Pennsylvania would reach the ears of

11 Lee to Davis, May 11, 1863, *OR* 25, pt. 2, 791-92.

12 Lee to Stuart, May 11, 1863, ibid., 792; Blackford, *War Years*, 206, 210.

Union information gatherers and mislead them about Lee's actual intentions. As Stuart moved his brigades toward Culpeper, he assigned the 4th Virginia to picket the lower Rappahannock near Fredericksburg.[13]

Lee needed to communicate personally with Davis, so he went to Richmond for three days in mid-May. There, in consultation with Davis and Seddon, agreement was reached on an invasion of the North. It would be carried out by a reorganized army, for as a result of the death of Stonewall Jackson at Chancellorsville, Lee decided to reorganize his army from two to three corps to make them more manageable. On May 20, he nominated Richard Ewell and A. P. Hill as corps commanders in addition to James Longstreet.[14]

During the heat of the battle of Chancellorsville, a member of Lee's staff reportedly had asked him what he believed the enemy's next move would be. Lee, whose confidence in himself and his army bordered on condescension toward his enemy, replied that it made little difference what the enemy might do, as long as "I can but get at them with my infantry all will be well."

However, now under the pressure of preparing to invade the North and at the same time anticipating the potential for a renewed Union attack that could force him out of his present position, Lee began showing signs of stress. He needed information about the location and intentions of his adversaries to evaluate the possibility that Hooker would cross the river to attack his rear or move against Richmond. Indeed, upon learning of the Union cavalry's move to Warrenton, Lee grew even more concerned about an attack on the capital. He heard from citizens and spies north of the Rappahannock that Hooker was contemplating a change of base to the James River area.[15]

Invasion Rumors

A letter sent to Stanton on May 20 from a citizen named L. Thomas Prince, who lived in Baltimore, alerted Stanton that the Rebels intended to invade

---

13 Kenneth L. Stiles, *4th Virginia Cavalry* (Lynchburg, VA, 1985), 27-28.

14 Coddington, *The Gettysburg Campaign*, 6-7; Lee to Davis, May 7, 1863, OR 25, pt. 2, 783, 810-11; Special Orders No. 146, OR 25, pt. 2, 840; Dowdey, *The Wartime Papers*, 485.

15 Lee's quote cited in William B. Styple, ed., *Writing & Fighting the Confederate War: The Letters of Peter Wellington Alexander, Confederate War Correspondent* (Kearny, NJ, 2002), 146; Lee to Davis, May 20, 1863, OR 25, pt. 2, 811, Lee to Elzey, May 27, 1863, 826-27, Lee to Davis, May 30, 1863, 832-33.

Maj. Gen. Henry W. Halleck
Library of Congress

Maryland, and their goal was to capture Baltimore and Washington. The citizen said his information came from a relative who lived in the South, and that the invasion was to begin in about three weeks. The following day, an informant in New York alerted Halleck there was no doubt the Rebels were preparing to invade Washington and Baltimore very soon.

Also on May 20, in anticipation of Lee's march toward the Blue Ridge, Stuart moved his headquarters from Orange Court House to the Culpeper area. Upon arrival, he decided to hold a grand review of his cavalry that would not only benefit local citizens, but reflect his personal pride in his command. On May 22, Stuart's aide Frank Robertson described in a letter to his father "one of the most imposing scenes I ever witnessed." Invitations had gone out and trainloads of visitors came to witness a parade of Stuart's cavalry at Brandy Station with some 5,000 men and horses as well as artillery passing in review.[16]

The BMI's Sharpe reported to Hooker's headquarters on May 22 information his operatives had gathered the past three days. A deserter from Brig. Gen. Cadmus M. Wilcox's brigade revealed that the divisions of Longstreet's corps were near Chancellorsville, having come up from Suffolk. Sharpe gave the locations for Wilcox, Brig. Gens. William Barksdale, and Carnot Posey's brigades. He also made the point that Wilcox's brigade had some 1,500 men, which "with the reported loss [of 50 killed and 400 wounded during the battle of Chancellorsville] agrees with our estimate prior to the battle." In other words, Sharpe, whose intelligence organization was still in its

---

16 Wilbur Sturtevant Nye, *Here Come the Rebels!* (Dayton, OH, 1988), 26; Robertson, *In the Saddle with Stuart*, 60; Roger H. Harrell, *The 2nd North Carolina Cavalry* (Jefferson, NC, 2004), 109; Blackford, *War Years with Jeb Stuart*, 211.

infancy, was establishing credibility with Hooker by letting him know that the BMI's analysis of the enemy's order-of-battle could be relied upon.[17]

Another Rebel deserter from Brig. Gen. Henry Heth's brigade provided locations for elements of A. P. Hill's division, and confirmed that Longstreet's troops were marching about five miles south of Fredericksburg near Hamilton's Crossing coming from Richmond, and that Stuart's cavalry was "making great exertions" to prepare for action. Further evidence that Longstreet was in the area came from a Union chaplain of the 20th New York regiment who had just returned to the encampment north of the river after being left behind with the wounded following Chancellorsville. He had learned that Longstreet dined with Brig. Gen. William Barksdale of Lee's army following the battle. Also, a BMI scout provided information that an enemy infantry division had moved into the Culpeper area, although Sharpe had not yet been able to substantiate this. (This was probably a reference to Hood's division of Longstreet's corps that was approaching Culpeper from the south.)[18]

The Richmond press fed the rumor mill as well. An *Examiner* editorial stated that a decision about what the campaign of 1863 would comprise would likely come within the next two weeks. In the *Examiner's* tantalizing opinion, the "most important movement of the war will probably be made in that time," and added cryptically that this will lead to "greater events elsewhere."[19]

By May 23, Union Third Cavalry Division commander David Gregg alerted Pleasonton's chief of staff, Col. J. H. Taylor, that recently acquired information suggested that Lee was preparing to march away from his current base in the Fredericksburg area. An escaped slave, a former servant of an officer in the 13th North Carolina, revealed that his master had told another officer that Rebel cavalry regiments were going to join other cavalry that were already at Culpeper, and that "they were going to make a great raid through Maryland."[20]

One of the major concerns for Hooker's army was dealing with irregular warfare activity on its flanks. Small bands of attackers could tie up large segments of the army attempting to drive them off while protecting

---

17 Sharpe to Williams, May 22, 1863, RG 393, NA.

18 Ibid.

19 Ibid., May 24, 1863, quoted in Fishel, *The Secret War*, 416.

20 Gregg to Taylor, May 23, 1863, *OR* 27, pt. 2, 518-19.

infrastructure such as railroads and bridges. Gregg reported that "depredations of guerrillas and bushwhackers" continued to occur, and acknowledged that the leading practitioners of this activity were Mosby's Rangers who knew the area well and struck where least expected. Moreover, he lamented that the guerillas were operating in such a way as "to defy their arrest."[21]

On May 25, the *Richmond Dispatch* republished a letter that had appeared in the May 18 edition of the New York *World* asserting that Hooker had exact information of the strength of Lee's forces before the battle of Chancellorsville, including the location and effective strength of every regiment. According to this letter, Lee had 49,800 men, composed of Jackson's corps with 35,100 and two of Longstreet's divisions totaling 14,700.[22]

The information cited in the letter, that was "obtained I know not how, but which General Hooker and General Butterfield insisted was reliable beyond question," was derived from reports that Sharpe's BMI, Hooker's intelligence staff, generated for him. The BMI order of battle for Lee's army dated April 28, 1863, listed the exact figures shown in the letter for Jackson's corps and Longstreet's divisions. Given the publication of this accurate, and therefore believable, information, Lee would have undoubtedly recognized that Hooker had an effective intelligence-gathering capability—especially in light of the tendency of previous Army of the Potomac commanders to wildly inflate the size of his army.[23]

Additional forewarning that the Rebel army would soon go on the offensive arrived in the war department from Winchester in the Shenandoah Valley in an apparently unsolicited letter dated May 26. A spy by the name of Michael Graham—a prominent citizen in the Winchester area and an entrepreneur in railroad construction who had previously worked for Maj. Gen. Nathaniel P. Banks—in the employ of Maj. Gen. Robert H. Milroy in

---

21 Ibid., 518.

22 Richmond *Dispatch*, May 25, 1863.

23 The New York *World* reporter undoubtedly had good connections within the Army of the Potomac. The Army of Northern Virginia order of battle dated April 28, 1863, is from the BMI files at the National Archives, RG393, and was published in Fishel, *The Secret War*, opposite page 369. Nonetheless, based on Letterman's report, Lee estimated Hooker's army to be 159,000, about 25,000 more than the actual number. However, in his preparation for invasion of the North, he used this inflated figure as leverage with the authorities in Richmond to reinforce his army. Lee to Seddon, May 10, 1863, *OR* 25, pt. 2, 790; Faust, *Historical Times Encyclopedia*, 128.

Winchester wrote to Stanton from Mount Jackson offering wide-ranging views on the "state of affairs in the Valley of Virginia."[24]

In his letter, sent most likely with the approval if not the urging of Milroy, Graham warned Stanton that the Valley could not be held unless he reinforced the Union forces there by "15,000 infantry, and 5,000 cavalry." He believed that a large force of cavalry and infantry would attack Milroy's outpost at Winchester "in less than ten days." (The attack actually came on June 14, several days after the spy's prediction.) Graham then proceeded to provide specific strategic and tactical advice within a geographic framework to counter a Rebel attack in the Valley. He also recommended proclamations be issued enticing Rebel soldiers to desert their army by offering "profitable employment in the North."[25]

In conjunction with this assault, Graham predicted that Stuart's cavalry would "steal a march" from Orange Court House or Culpeper. Further, he believed that, if "Hooker lies still," Stuart would move through Warrenton, Orleans, or Salem to Springfield or Markham where he will be joined by "guerrilla bands."[26]

Intelligence Confirms Rumors

> The Confederate army is under marching orders, and an order from General Lee was very lately read to the troops, announcing a campaign of long marches and hard fighting.
>
> Col. George H. Sharpe[27]

Five days after submitting his previous intelligence summary to the army commander, Sharpe followed up with a detailed BMI report about the location, composition, and intentions of Lee's army. He informed Hooker that deserters were saying that the Confederate army would soon be embarking on a movement "upon or above our right flank." In other words, Lee's army most likely would be marching west to the Blue Ridge Mountains or the Shenandoah Valley then northward. Although Union authorities were uncertain about Lee's

---

24 Graham to Stanton, May 26, 1863, OR 25, pt. 2. 525-27.

25 Ibid., 526.

26 Ibid.

27 Ibid., 528.

planned destination and intentions, they had already received indications that Washington and Baltimore could be the ultimate target.[28]

The essence of Sharpe's report, dated May 27, 1863, was as follows:

1: The enemy's line in front of us is much more contracted than during the winter. It extends from Banks' Ford, on a line parallel with the river, to near Moss Neck [a distance of about 17 miles]. Anderson's division is on their left. MeLaws' is next, and in rear of Fredericksburg. Early is massed about Hamilton's Crossing, and Trimble's is directly in the rear of Early. Rodes' (D. H. Hill's old division) is farther to the right, and back from the river, and A. P. Hill is the right of their line, resting nearly on Moss Neck. Each of these six divisions have five brigades.[29]

2: Pickett's division, of six brigades, has come up from Suffolk, and is at Taylorsville, near Hanover Junction.[30]

3: Hood's division, of four brigades, has also left from the front of Suffolk, and is between Louisa Court-House and Gordonsville.

4: Ten days ago there was in Richmond only the City Battalion, 2,700 strong, commanded by General Elzey.

5: There are three brigades of cavalry 3 miles from Culpeper Court House, toward Kelly's Ford. They can at present turn out only 4,700 men for duty, but have many dismounted men, and the horses are being constantly and rapidly recruited by the spring growth of grass. These are Fitz Lee's, William H. Fitzhugh [Rooney] Lee's, and Wade Hampton's brigades.

6: General Jones is still in the Valley, near New Market, with about 1,400 cavalry and 12 pieces of light artillery.

7: Mosby is above Warrenton, with 200 men.

8: The Confederate army is under marching orders, and an order from General Lee was very lately read to the troops, announcing a campaign of long marches and hard fighting, in a part of the country where they would have no railroad transportation.

9: All the deserters say that the idea is very prevalent in the ranks that they are about to move forward upon or above our right flank.

28 Ibid.

29 The positions of these divisions may have changed by June 3. See Bradley M. Gottfried, *The Maps of Gettysburg* (New York, 2007), 2-3.

30 Pickett's division had five brigades and not six. Two of his brigades did not accompany Pickett when his division rejoined Lee's army. Lee to Seddon, June 2, 1863, *OR* 25, pt. 2, 849.

The structure and composition of Sharpe's report would do credit to a modern-day intelligence summary. It focused on the location of enemy units supplemented by recently obtained data, provided a general description of the enemy's positions, and added specific unit locations. While the information still needed refinement, the report did provide a comprehensive representation of what was taking place on the other side of the Rappahannock. Sharpe wrapped up his report with evidence of Lee's intention to move his army a considerable distance from its present location.

After receiving Sharpe's report on the location and intentions of the enemy, Hooker notified Secretary Stanton of his belief that "the enemy will soon be in motion." In communicating directly with Lincoln and Stanton, Hooker did not follow the chain of command. From prewar days Halleck and Hooker did not get along, so the army commander often chose to bypass Halleck, and for the present Lincoln acquiesced in this arrangement. But on this occasion he had also notified Halleck earlier in the day taking care to mention Sharpe and the BMI, by way of refreshing his memory about the existence of the BMI and underscoring the reliability of the report.[31]

Hooker was concerned that the reason that Rebel cavalry were operating near Warrenton might be to screen an enemy movement north through the Shenandoah Valley. He ordered Pleasonton to have Buford make an all out effort to determine the meaning of this activity and to keep him informed by telegraph.[32]

Union Cavalry Expedition

Also on May 27, the 8th Illinois cavalry detachment that Hooker sent to sweep across the Northern Neck submitted a written report. The detachment, under the command of Lt. Col. David R. Clendenin, began operations on May 17 with orders to break up the contraband trade carried on in that area. Clendenin's force swept the area from north to south in three groups—one to the east along the Potomac, another west along the Rappahannock, and the third down the center along Ridge Road. The Union cavalry directed its efforts mainly against transportation facilities carrying contraband south to Richmond.

---

31 Ibid., 527-28. For details on the Hooker-Halleck relationship, see Hebert, *Fighting Joe Hooker*, 41,149, 151, 166, 170, 181, 227, 238-40, 242-45, 247.

32 Pleasonton to Buford, May 28, 1863, OR 25, pt. 2, 538.

Clendenin reported capturing 40 prisoners from the 9th and 15th Virginia Cavalry and the 40th Virginia Infantry, as well as a few conscripts and smugglers. At a cost of only three casualties, the cavalrymen had destroyed every ferryboat, sloop, scow, yawl, etc. they could locate, and about $50,000 worth of smuggled goods. They also brought back 810 "negroes," probably most, if not all, slaves, who were turned over to a Union quartermaster at Lower Belle Plain Landing. Along with his report, Clendenin submitted a list of men from sections of the Northern Neck where "a strong Union feeling prevailed," and "from whom valuable information was obtained."[33]

Though not mentioned in the official report, the 8th Illinois Cavalry regimental history records that some of the wealthiest citizens of the Northern Neck were supporting the rebellion and engaged in the smuggling business. These people paid dearly for these activities, since the Union cavalry liberated their slaves and confiscated large quantities of food, goods, and animals. But he also commended some very loyal citizens who rendered most valuable assistance.[34]

When Pleasonton forwarded Clendenin's report to army headquarters on May 28, he pointed out that only one ferry was still operating and capable of moving horses across the river. This would hamper the Rebels' ability to round up horses in the Northern Neck for use by the Confederate army.[35]

It is unclear whether Hooker was aware that the Confederate signal corps controlled part of the smuggling and blockade-running operations across the Potomac and through the Northern Neck. Signal corps commander, Maj. William Norris, had established this clandestine operation earlier in the war and ran it out of his war department office in Richmond. He kept this secret service activity separate from regular signal corps communications operations, and although the Yankees had temporarily disrupted its smuggling activities, it would continue them throughout the war.[36]

---

33 Quotes from Clendenin to Cohen, May 27, 1863, RG 393, NA; Ingalls to Butterfield, May 24, 1863, OR 25, pt. 2, 520; Abner Hard, *History of the Eighth Illinois Cavalry Regiment* (Dayton, OH, 1984), 239-41.

34 Hard, *Eighth Illinois Cavalry*, 240-41; Clendenin to Cohen, May 27, 1863, RG 393, NA.

35 Pleasonton's handwritten note on report from Clendenin to Cohen, May 27, 1863, RG 393, NA.

36 Taylor, *Signal and Secret Service*, 18-20; Tidwell, *Come Retribution*, 87-90, 95-96, 98.

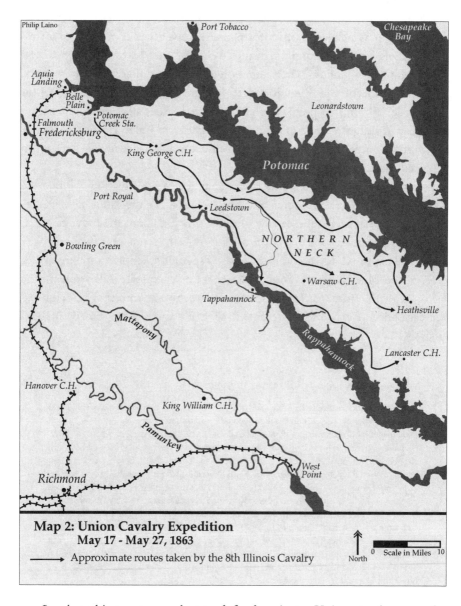

Philip Laino

Map 2: Union Cavalry Expedition
May 17 - May 27, 1863

→ Approximate routes taken by the 8th Illinois Cavalry

North   0   Scale in Miles   10

Lee kept his troops on alert to defend against a Union attack across the river. Longstreet instructed division commander Maj. Gen. Lafayette McLaws to have his pickets at Fredericksburg "communicate rapidly the earliest information" if the Union infantry pickets were relieved by cavalry—an indicator of an impending attack.[37]

On May 28, the Union spy Michael Graham sent a follow-up report to Stanton from Winchester with information received within the last two days that "rebels are collecting a heavy force of cavalry in Culpeper and Rappahannock Counties." Their intention in the spy's opinion was "to proceed along the foot of the Blue Ridge to the neighborhood of Piedmont or Upperville." From that point, Graham expected Stuart's cavalry to cross into the Valley through Ashby's Gap and coordinate with Jones' cavalry to pounce on Milroy's outpost at Winchester or conduct a major raid into Maryland to capture horses, or both.[38]

Also on May 28, Hooker summarized the situation along the Rappahannock River to Secretary Stanton based on the latest intelligence, complaining that he had no satisfactory information about the movements of the enemy, because scouts sent across the river had not returned and were presumed captured. It would be an act of desperation, Hooker thought, if Lee crossed the Blue Ridge and moved down the Shenandoah Valley toward the Potomac, with a force "no greater than we have reason to suppose." This had the earmarks of a realistic assessment of Lee's force, likely based on BMI analysis.[39]

---

37 Riely to McLaws, May 28, 1863, *OR* 51, pt. 2, 717.

38 Graham to Stanton, May 28, 1863, ibid., pt. 2, 25:540-41. As events played out over the next two weeks, the essence of Graham's report would prove to be accurate. He added ominously, "You may rely on what I say, for there will be stirring times between this and the first of July." Graham asserted that his information was reliable, since it came from deserters, exiles driven out by the rebels, and "from citizens of the South, who claim protection as foreigners," that Lee's army reinforced by Longstreet's force and by recent conscripts now numbered 100,000 men—erroneous, since Lee's May 1863 return showed a total of just over 68,000. The inflated estimate of a 100,000-strong Army of Northern Virginia would take on a life of its own in top Union commanders' thinking in the coming weeks, notwithstanding contrary evidence. Graham's assertion that "Grumble" Jones' force in western Virginia had grown to 8,000, more than two and half times its actual size, was an indication of his inflated estimates. Jones' force in Western Virginia at the time included Jenkins' cavalry brigade. The size of their two brigades on June 30 was about 1,745 for Jones and 1,330 for Jenkins, 3,075 total. Ibid., 540-41, 845-46; Busey and Martin, *Regimental Strengths and Losses at Gettysburg,* 169, 244.

39 Hooker to Stanton, May 28, 1863, *OR* 25, pt. 2, 542-43. For some reason, Hooker believed that Stuart had five cavalry brigades at Culpeper and Jefferson (there were actually four: Hampton, Fitz Lee, W. H. F. Lee, and Robertson, who had recently arrived from North Carolina; Jones' brigade was still in the Shenandoah Valley as Sharpe had reported on May 27). Robertson's demi-brigade of two regiments had reported to Stuart a few days prior to Hooker's

Hooker implied that but for the rundown condition of his horses (for which he blamed the now departed cavalry commander Stoneman), he would have sent an expedition across the river against Stuart to "pitch into him in his camps." Hooker recommended that Maj. Gen. Julius Stahel send an expedition from his Department of Washington cavalry division to the Shenandoah Valley "to see what is going on over there." When Stanton submitted this request to Halleck, however, the general in chief refused, citing the danger of attack on Alexandria and Washington if they were removed.[40]

As a result, on May 29, the BMI's Sharpe sent one of his civilian spies, John Howard Skinker, a prosperous slave owner in Stafford County, Virginia, who lived a few miles north of Union headquarters at Falmouth, across the Rappahannock to learn more about the location and activities of Lee's army.[41] Hooker also pressed Buford and Gregg to step up observance of enemy movements, especially around Waterloo and Sulphur Springs farther up the river. Concerned that the enemy would cross the river at the Rappahannock Bridge ford and stage an attack, he also wanted to know whether that would be "practicable for infantry at this time."[42]

That morning, May 29, Stahel sent a message to Heintzelman that one of his most reliable, trustworthy informants concurred with Stahel's cavalry's recent scouting reports that no strong force of the enemy was concentrated east

---

message to Halleck. Although Hooker's estimate of Lee's strength was generally on target at this stage, when the pressure of the invasion began building, he would lose touch and insist enemy strength superior to his own. Abstract of organization of the Cavalry Division, Army of Northern Virginia, May 25, 1863, *OR* 25, pt. 2, 825; Longacre, *Cavalry at Gettysburg*, 31-39.

40 Hooker to Stanton, May 28, 1863, Stanton to Hooker, May 29, 1863, *OR* 25, pt. 2, 542-43.

41 Skinker, whose brother Thomas was a Confederate cavalryman, led a small band of pro-Union residents in the area; he had been regularly providing information to the Union army since its arrival in the Fredericksburg area under Burnside in November 1862. Major General John Reynolds called him "the truest, boldest and most deserving Union man I have even known." Skinker left Sharpe's headquarters at 5:30 p.m. and proceeded to Grove Church some 15 miles north of Falmouth before moving on to the home of a Unionist friend near Germantown. Here, thwarted by nearby Confederate cavalry scouts, he would have to lay low for a couple of days. Skinker to Sharpe, June 3, 1863, RG 393; Fishel, *The Secret War*, 260-61, 425, 641n23.

42 At the same time in Washington, Halleck alerted Heintzelman to caution Stahel that enemy cavalry were reported collecting on the Upper Rappahannock, and Stahel should warn his outposts to maintain utmost vigilance to protect the Orange and Alexandria Railroad and the city of Alexandria. Williams to Buford, Pleasonton to Gregg, Halleck to Heintzelman, May 29, 1863, *OR* 25, pt. 2, 565-66.

of the Blue Ridge. (Only small parties of Mosby's Rangers were scouting in every direction. The informant added that Mosby was gathering men for mounting a raid to an undisclosed location. In fact, Mosby planned an attack on the Orange and Alexandria Railroad, a vital supply link for the Union army.)[43]

Stahel's spy also revealed that a relative of Maj. Gen. Richard Ewell who lived near Aldie, Virginia, was arranging with some of the local population to pasture a large number of cavalry horses, since it was believed Stuart would be arriving in the area within a week. This coincided with Sharpe's detailed report of May 27, as did the spy's revelation that:

> In Richmond last week it was discussed and determined that a forward movement should be made at once, as the Union Army is now weakened by a huge number of regiments who have gone home, whose places have not yet been filled, but will be in a short time. Consequently they regard the present as the best opportunity to make an attack upon our army.[44]

Given recent reports of a planned Rebel movement northward, Stanton told Milroy in Winchester to keep vigilant watch at all points, since his position in the Shenandoah Valley should enable him to gather information about any movement in that direction.[45]

By May 30, the war department had learned that Lee had a wagon train loaded with pontoon bridges, and that Longstreet's forces and units from the Carolinas had reinforced Lee. Halleck forwarded a copy of the report to Hooker, suggesting that logical use for this bridge material might be for the Rebel army to cross wide rivers such as the Potomac or the Susquehanna. Hooker, however, related it instead to a deserter's information that the Rebels

---

43 Stahel to Heintzelman, May 29, 1863, ibid., 566; Williamson, *Mosby's Rangers*, 63-64.

44 Stahel to Heintzelman, May 29, 1863, *OR* 25, pt. 2, 566-67. Stahel also told Heintzelman that his informant learned from paroled Union prisoners that "the rebel army is being concentrated on and near the Rappahannock for an immediate aggressive movement, and that Longstreet's division and Garnett's brigade are expected in the section of the country between the Blue Ridge and Bull Run."

45 Ibid., 567. Major General Schenck also contacted Milroy and Brig. Gen. Eliakim P. Scammon at Charleston that their forces at Harper's Ferry, the Shenandoah Valley, and West Virginia should be "alert and prepared for an attack." That night, Milroy telegraphed Schenck that "a secret rebel source entitled to some credit" reported that Lee had a seven-mile long pontoon train. According to the source, Lee meant to demonstrate up the Rappahannock River but turn back and use the pontoons to cross and "suddenly fall on Hooker, while the cavalry dash around his right and attack him in the rear." Milroy commented that he thought this was a pretty good theory.

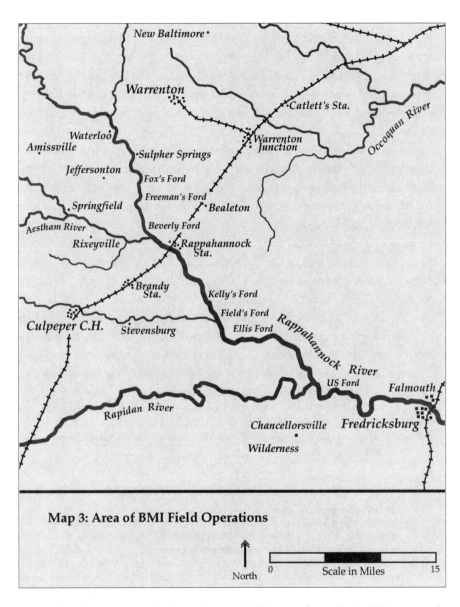

Map 3: Area of BMI Field Operations

North   0   Scale in Miles   15

were planning to cross the Rappahannock River and attack the Union supply base at Aquia.[46]

---

46 Hooker to His Excellency the President of the United States, April 21, 1863, *OR* 25, pt. 2, 238; Graham to Milroy, May 30, 1863, 570; Lee to Gilmer, April 11, 1863, 715; Luvass, "Intelligence in the Chancellorsville Campaign," 302; Nye, *Here Come the Rebels!*, 8. The spy

The Union spy Skinker, still looking for a safe route to the Rappahannock to cross to the south side, heard the sound of artillery fire as Mosby and his rangers attacked a Union supply train on the Orange and Alexandria Railroad near Catlett's Station. Well known in the area for his Unionist sentiments, Skinker could not move farther and arranged with a like-minded friend to cross the river.[47]

Also, on May 30, Lee informed Seddon in Richmond that two scouts from within the enemy's lines reported that Hooker was planning to turn Lee's flank to hold the Army of Northern Virginia in position while Union forces on the York River attempted to capture Richmond. Given this information, Lee told Stuart he was unable to discern the enemy's plans and intentions because of contradictory reports. So he instructed Stuart to find out whether the Union cavalry planned a raid across the Rappahannock or were just moving toward Fauquier County's ample grazing land. Although Lee felt the need "to punish them severely" if the enemy staged an attack within Confederate lines, he told Stuart to lay low and allow his cavalry to recuperate unless he saw "an opportunity for striking them a successful blow." Lee was obviously keeping his options open, and allowing Stuart to do the same.[48]

Edwin B. Coddington summed up the intelligence situation during this period in his classic work *The Gettysburg Campaign: A Study in Command*:

> At this time Lee's methods of obtaining news of the enemy were not as effective as those used by his opponent, and he found it hard to get reliable information. For one thing, Hooker had established strict security measures with the help of Colonel Sharpe,

---

Graham in Winchester sent this information to Milroy, identifying his source as Colonel Moore of Winchester. This was in all likelihood Lt. Col. Lewis Tilghman Moore of the 4th Virginia of the Stonewall Brigade who was severely wounded at Manassas in July 1861, discharged, and returned to his home in Winchester. Graham, Milroy's spy, apparently made his acquaintance there and convinced him of his loyalty to the Confederacy. The Rebel colonel claimed that Lee intended to cross the Rappahannock with his whole force and position his army between Hooker and Washington. Choosing his own ground, Lee would draw Hooker after him out of his present position. If Lee were to defeat Hooker in battle, the informant said, his plan was to "cross the Potomac, and once more try his fortunes in Maryland." Milroy passed this report to Stanton and Halleck in Washington. Krick, Robert K., *Lee's Colonels* (Dayton, OH, 1991), 277-79. As early as April 11, Lee had requested the Confederate Engineer Bureau to send a 350-foot pontoon train to Orange Court House, and to "keep the matter as quiet as practicable."

47 Skinker to Sharpe, June 3, 1863, RG 393, NA.

48 Lee to Seddon, May 30, 1863, *OR* 25, pt. 2, 834; Lee to Stuart, May 31, 1863, 844.

his new intelligence officer. The improved efficiency of the Union cavalry in forming a screen around the army also made it difficult for news to filter through the lines.[49]

BMI Field Operations

With the Union cavalry on the right flank of the army watching for enemy movements, BMI chief Sharpe sent Captain McEntee and a team of five scouts and a civilian spy from Virginia named George S. Smith to the area to help determine the location and intentions of Lee's forces. Sharpe's report of May 27 indicated the BMI had already learned that Stuart's cavalry brigades, under the command of "Rooney" Lee, Fitz Lee—Robert E. Lee's son and nephew respectively—and Wade Hampton, were located near Jeffersonton, about 13 miles north of Culpeper. McEntee sent scouts Henry M. Dodd and Anson B. Carney south toward Field's Ford; he dispatched Benjamin F. McCord and Edwin P. Hopkins, the best scout on his team, McEntee thought, north toward Jeffersonton. Their mission was to cross the Rappahannock and verify the location of the Rebel cavalry.[50]

In the meantime, McEntee learned potentially valuable information from an escaped slave he had recruited as a spy. The slave had run away a week earlier from Colston's brigade, at that time located at U.S. Ford on the Rappahannock. The escapee informed McEntee that no Confederate infantry were above U.S. Ford. When McEntee reported by courier to Sharpe, he told him that the slave said the Rebel brigade was under orders, and "the general rumor was that they intended to march to the [Shenandoah] valley and visit Maryland."[51]

Although attached to Pleasonton's cavalry command for logistical and security support, the BMI team operated semi-independently. The similarity in the intelligence-gathering missions generated some friction between the cavalry and the BMI. As a lowly captain, McEntee's lack of authority and influence with the cavalry command proved troublesome to his team's effectiveness,

---

49 Coddington, *The Gettysburg Campaign*, 50.

50 McEntee to Sharpe, May 30, June 5, 6, and 7, 1863, RG 393, NA; Boatner, *The Civil War Dictionary*, 475, 477. For the location of Fields Ford, see OR Atlas, Plate XLIV, No. 3.

51 McEntee to Sharpe, May 30, 1863, RG 393, NA. The runaway identified his brigade as Colston's. It had formerly been under Brig. Gen. Raleigh E. Colston, but now Brig. Gen. George H. Steuart was in command. The brigade was part of Maj. Gen. Edward Johnson's division in Ewell's corps. Coddington, *The Gettysburg Campaign*, 590; Faust, *Historical Times Illustrated Encyclopedia*, 52.

particularly since the cavalry was not inclined to cooperate with them anyway. Cavalry commander Pleasonton was especially reluctant to acknowledge the role of the BMI, an issue Hooker eventually had to address directly with him.[52]

Scouts Dodd and Carney returned to camp on Sunday, May 31, after being prevented from crossing the river by enemy infantry pickets that were in position up to Ellis Ford, about 10 miles farther north of U.S. Ford (the farthest point that four days earlier the escaped slave had reported the Rebel infantry to be), and by cavalry pickets above that point. These pickets were from the 4th Virginia—the parent organization of Stuart's scout Benjamin Franklin Stringfellow, which often supplied men for hazardous scouting assignments and for detached duty to perform covert missions. Stuart had left them behind to picket the lower Rappahannock when the cavalry moved to Culpeper on May 20.[53]

Up river, Hopkins and McCord managed to get across. They learned from local inhabitants that Hampton's cavalry brigade was between Rixeyville and Jeffersonton, and that it was the only Confederate force north of the Aestham (now Hazel) River. Contrabands and "several old ladies" provided the important information that Stuart's "main force" was located at Culpeper. Hopkins and McCord may have used cash to induce the contrabands and women to cooperate, since provost marshal Marsena Patrick provided confiscated Confederate currency to Sharpe for use by BMI scouts and spies to acquire information in enemy territory.[54]

About the same time, McEntee was forced to change his base of operations from Bealeton to Warrenton Junction because Mosby's Rangers attacked a

---

52 McEntee to Sharpe, June 11, 13, 19, 1863, RG 393, NA; Williams to Pleasonton, June 17, 1863, *OR* 27, pt. 3, 172.

53 McEntee to Sharpe, May 30, 31, 1863, RG 393, NA; Stiles, *4th Virginia Cavalry*, 27; Bakeless, *Spies of the Confederacy*, 90-91; Brown, *Stringfellow of the Fourth*, 11-22; *OR Atlas*, plate 22-5. .

54 McEntee to Sharpe, May 31, 1863, RG 393; Nye, *Here Come the Rebels!*, 16; Freeman, *Lee's Lieutenants*, 3:1; Sutherland, *Seasons of War*, 233; Sparks, *Inside Lincoln's Army*, 251. In his report to Sharpe, McEntee said that Hopkins and McCord "crossed the Hedgeman River." During the mid-nineteenth century, the area of the Rappahannock River forming the border between Culpeper and Fauquier Counties was called Hedgeman's River. Rixeyville and Jeffersonton were both located west of Bealeton across the Rappahannock. The Aestham River is now called the Hazel River. It runs east and west in Culpeper County two miles north of Rixeyville. See *OR Atlas*, plates 22, 5, 23, 4, and 43, 7; Culpeper County General Highway Map (Richmond, 1995). For the distance between Ellis Ford and U.S. Ford, see the *Official Military Atlas*, plates 23, 5 and 44, 3.

railroad train in the area, cut off McEntee's supplies, and damaged the telegraph lines. Buford reported to Pleasonton that Mosby's attack took place in Stahel's sector some five miles above his own area of responsibility, and that no Rebel activity was noted south of Waterloo Bridge over the Rappahannock—an indication that Lee's army had not yet moved that far north.[55]

Despite Mosby's successful attack on the supply train, Union cavalry pursued and captured a few of his men including Capt. R. P. Montjoy whom Lt. F. R. Havens of the 7th Michigan Cavalry described as a "Louisianian . . . with a reputation as a spy, scout, desperado, and an all-around bad man." Havens had drawn the unwelcome job of escorting the dangerous Montjoy to Fairfax Court House to be turned over to the Union provost marshal there. But Montjoy only spent a few days in Capitol Prison in Washington before inexplicably receiving a parole. He was back in the saddle with Mosby toward the latter part of June.[56]

Lee Finalizes His Invasion Plans

After obtaining approval from President Davis, Lee's invasion plans moved into high gear in early June. Since his ultimate destination was Pennsylvania and his large army had to travel long distances, Lee used a map that Jed Hotchkiss had prepared at Stonewall Jackson's request earlier in the year. This detailed 32 x 52" map included the names of residents, blacksmiths, mills, and landmarks from the Shenandoah Valley to Harrisburg, Pennsylvania,

---

55 McEntee to Sharpe, May 31, 1863, RG 393, NA; Buford to Alexander, May 31, 1863, *OR* 25, pt. 2, 571-72; John S. Mosby, *Stuart's Cavalry in the Gettysburg Campaign* (New York, 1908), 8. Waterloo was on the Rappahannock River some three miles north of Sulphur Springs. *OR Atlas*, plate 100-1.

56 F. R. Havens, "How Mosby Destroyed Our Train," in William O. Lee, *Seventh Regiment Michigan Volunteer Cavalry, 1862-1865* (Detroit, 1990), 90-95; Mosby, *Mosby's War Reminiscences*, 142-51; Williamson, *Mosby's Rangers*, 56-68, 78. Correspondence from Union cavalry headquarters reflected how effective bushwhackers, guerrillas, and scouts were in disrupting transportation routes, attacking isolated outposts, and gathering information about the disposition of Union forces. Mosby's Rangers were responsible for much of this activity. These attacks were meant to cut off Union supplies and create a diversion for Lee's invasion. But his main goal, as noted before, was to require Union commanders to leave behind an increasingly larger portion of their forces to protect their lines of communication. Taylor to Davis, May 17, 1863, *OR* 25, pt. 2, 499; Barstow to Pleasonton, May 21, 1863, 511; Brown to Gregg, May 23, 1863, 519; Jones, *Ranger Mosby*, 122-29; Russell, *Gray Ghost*, 151-53.

and on to Philadelphia. Hotchkiss, now assigned to Ewell's corps, also prepared operational maps of the routes Lee's army would follow.[57]

Since Lee lacked current details about the strength and leadership of his opponent, he relied on Stuart and his cavalry to gather this information. The absence of an intelligence staff at Lee's headquarters similar to the Army of the Potomac's BMI would prove to be detrimental to the Confederates during the upcoming campaign. For example, Lee had to ask Stuart about whether he knew how many enemy cavalry brigades there were and the names of their commanders. This order-of-battle data was information an intelligence staff would normally develop and provide.[58]

Lee did have Company A and C (6 officers and 85 men) of the 39th Battalion Virginia Cavalry attached to his headquarters to provide a variety of services, including as scouts, curriers, escorts, and guides. These units had done commendable work during the Chancellorsville campaign. And his First Corps commander, Lt. Gen. James Longstreet, had a scout named Henry Thomas Harrison working directly for him. As soon as Longstreet was certain that the advance northward would take place, he obtained gold coin from Richmond for the spy's expenses—something that required the express approval of the president—and instructed him to go to Washington and stay there until the latter part of June, and not to rejoin the army until he obtained "information of importance."[59]

In late May or early June, Stuart sent another scout, Thomas Nelson Conrad of the 3rd Virginia Cavalry, into Washington from his base on the Virginia side of the Potomac River. His mission was to report any information

---

57 Coddington, *The Gettysburg Campaign*, 7, 50. Regarding Hotchkiss' maps and their use during the Gettysburg campaign, see Archie P. McDonald, *Make Me a Map of the Valley: The Civil War Journal of Stonewall Jackson's Topographer* (Dallas, 1973), 116, 148-65. See also Alexander, *Military Memoirs of a Confederate*, 322; Nye, *Here Comes the Rebels!*, 8. A smaller version of the Hotchkiss map can be found in OR Atlas, plate 116, 2. Four selected details of Hotchkiss' map focusing on the areas surrounding Chambersburg, Gettysburg, Harrisburg, and Williamsport/ Shepherdstown are included in McElfresh, *Maps and Mapmakers*, 128-29.

58 Lee to Stuart, May 11, 1863, OR 25, pt. 2, 792.

59 Robert J. Driver, Jr. and Kevin C. Ruffner, *1st Battalion Virginia Infantry, 39th Battalion Virginia Cavalry, 24th Battalion Virginia Partisan Rangers* (Lynchburg, VA, 1996), 55; Tidwell, *Come Retribution*, 109-10, 212; Longstreet, "Lee's Invasion of Pennsylvania," 249-50; G. Moxley Sorrel, *Recollections of a Confederate Staff Officer* (Jackson, TN, 1958), 161. For a discussion of Harrison's identity, see James O. Hall, "The Spy Harrison," *Civil War Times Illustrated* (February 1986), 24:18-25.

Maj. Gen. Daniel Butterfield
Library of Congress

he obtained about Union military operations to Stuart's headquarters. According to Conrad, he made it to Washington by way of southern Maryland within three days, and set up operations at the Van Ness mansion, the home of a Confederate sympathizer located just two blocks from the U.S. war department.[60]

Stuart also ordered Mosby and his rangers into northwestern Virginia to gather intelligence and create a diversion for Lee's planned march northward through the Shenandoah Valley. In early June, Mosby officially organized his men as Company A, 43rd Battalion, Virginia Partisan Rangers, and immediately launched a diversionary raid across the Potomac at Rowser's Ford to Seneca, Maryland.[61]

Uneasiness in Both Commands

Chief of Staff Maj. Gen. Daniel Butterfield's message of June 1 reflected Hooker's desire for information about enemy activity. Butterfield instructed V Corps commander Maj. Gen. George Meade, whose troops were picketing the river as far north as Kelly's Ford, to exercise vigilance in watching the

---

60 Conrad, *The Rebel Scout*, 81. Thomas Green owned the Van Ness mansion located on the block bounded by C Street, Constitution Avenue, 17th Street, and 18th Street. He was married to Anne Lomax, a sister of Confederate Brig. Gen. Lindsay Lomax. He was reportedly a Confederate source in Washington and would be arrested on April 18, 1865, on suspicion of complicity in the Lincoln assassination. Tidwell, *Come Retribution*, 264.

61 Robert F. O'Neill, Jr., *The Cavalry Battles of Aldie, Middleburg and Upperville: Small But Important Riots, June 10-27, 1863* (Lynchburg, VA, 1993), 19-20; Jones, *Ranger Mosby*, 130-34. See also "Mosby, John Singleton" & "Mosby's Rangers" in Faust, *Historical Times Illustrated Encyclopedia of the Civil War*, 514-15.

movements of the enemy. Furthermore, units on duty along the river should be actively obtaining information and reporting it promptly to headquarters.[62]

Lee had his own concerns. Upon learning about Union troop movements along the lower Rappahannock River, he requested Stuart's signal officer, Capt. Richard E. Frazer (who was operating near Port Royal observing Union activity along the Potomac River) to contact 15th Virginia Cavalry commander Maj. Charles R. Collins by signal flag. Lee wanted to know "if there are any Yanks advancing further than [previously] reported [?]" Collins replied to Lee that about 100 cavalry and a regiment of infantry had approached within several miles of Tappahannock but had retreated to their base at Gloucester Point. Lee wanted to ensure that no major threat to the capital at Richmond existed before his invasion of the North got underway. Unknown to Lee, both his request for information and the reply ended up on Hooker's desk, since a Union signal station intercepted them and acting chief signal officer Capt. Charles S. Kendall sent verbatim copies to Union headquarters. This reflects the vulnerability of sending messages by signal flag without encrypting the contents.[63]

As the respective commanders continued to monitor their opponent's activities, Jones' cavalry brigade moved eastward out of the Shenandoah Valley toward Stuart's camp in Culpeper County. Jenkins' 1,250-man cavalry brigade remained in the Shenandoah Valley awaiting orders from Lee. Jones would join Stuart's other brigades of Hampton, Fitz Lee, Rooney Lee, and Robertson.[64]

Preparations for an invasion taking place on the south side of the river and efforts made on the river's north side to detect and intrude upon a movement northward did not go unnoticed in the Union ranks either. Captain James H. Kidd of the 6th Michigan Cavalry wrote to his parents on June 1 that "[r]eports are rife of a projected invasion . . . but we shall hear of it before[hand] . . . [s]couts are daily out on our front, so that the idea of the Rebel army reaching Washington without our knowledge is preposterous." Unfortunately, Kidd's

---

62 Butterfield to [Meade], *OR* 25, pt. 2, 593.

63 Chas. S. Kendall to [Hooker], June 1, 1863, RG 393, NA.

64 Richard L. Armstrong, *7th Virginia Cavalry* (Lynchburg, VA, 1992), 52; Michael P. Musick, *6th Virginia Cavalry* (Lynchburg, VA, 1990), 36; Festus P. Summers, *A Borderland Confederate: The Civil War Diaries and Letters of William L. Wilson* (Pittsburgh, PA, 1962), 67; Jack L. Dickinson, *16th Virginia Cavalry* (Lynchburg, VA, 1989), 20; Busey and Martin, *Regimental Strengths and Losses*, 244, Longacre, *The Cavalry at Gettysburg*, 17, 18.

optimism would prove to be only partially correct, because the Union cavalry would fail to detect Lee's invasion until it was well underway.[65]

In response to pressure from Sharpe for results by his team of scouts, McEntee called for patience and a realistic assessment of the difficulty involved in this process because he was "laboring under sundry disadvantages here which you do not seem to take into consideration." McEntee's base of operations was some distance from the river so that he could not access supplies and the telegraph, and his entire team included just five men and the spy Smith. Smith's home was only two-and-a-half miles from Field's Ford south of the river, but he could not cross because it was "strongly picketed all along there on our [north] side by infantry & on the other side by cavalry." Nor were McEntee and Smith able to find "a proper [pro-Union] man to send over the river," because "they have all left this country."[66]

Among the other "sundry disadvantages" were McEntee's doubts about Smith's loyalty, since "his affections he says are with the Southern people, but still he knows that they are wrong." Plus the ignorance of his five scouts who "know nothing about the other side of the river," and, even if they did, would be hindered and likely captured by Rebel cavalry. Another handicap was the sad condition of their horses, which were all old and used up.[67]

McEntee planned to send his scout Hopkins around the enemy flank, but that might require several days. He had not had access to a Rebel prisoner or an escaped slave for questioning since he had been there. As a result, McEntee recommended "the most certain and efficient way of ascertaining how they are situated would be to send a force of cavalry over [the river] to reconnoiter."[68]

On June 2, Hooker's Assistant Adjutant General Williams wired Buford that a report of unknown reliability stated that three brigades of enemy cavalry had gone to the Shenandoah Valley. Hooker wanted Buford to keep him fully advised about the enemy's presence and movements in his front. He also expected him to help determine the location and strength of the enemy's cavalry, "especially with a view to our future movements." This indicated that

65 Kidd, *Personal Recollections*, 105-06; Kidd to "Dear Mother and Father," cited in Wittenberg, *One of Custer's Wolverines*, 37.

66 McEntee to Sharpe, n.d. (probably early June, 1863), RG 393, NA.

67 Ibid.

68 Ibid.

Hooker was planning to stage an attack against Stuart's cavalry brigades south of the river. Hooker ordered Buford to keep scouting parties active and to send "all the news obtained by telegraph;" and, emphasizing a need for reliable intelligence, he added that the capture of "prisoners, contrabands, etc." was a good way to gather this information.[69]

The Richmond newspapers were either not aware of Lee's invasion plans or deliberately avoiding the mention of it. The *Dispatch* gave no hint of Lee's activities in the days before the march northward began. Peter W. Alexander, a Savannah *Republican* correspondent in Richmond on his way to rejoin Lee's army, did not know what to expect, yet speculated in his report, "Everything remains quiet on the Rappahannock, though there is reason to believe this quiet will be broken ere long."[70]

Union soldiers and officers were keenly interested in how events would play out in the near future. Captain Kidd of the 6th Michigan Cavalry wrote in a letter home his opinion, "Lee may make a rapid march through the Shenandoah Valley, and thence into Pennsylvania and Maryland, but nothing would please the Union army more than to have him make the attempt."[71]

Also on June 2, Maj. Gen. Erasmus D. Keyes in Yorktown alerted Hooker that persistent rumors had it "that an invasion of Maryland and Pennsylvania is soon to be made." On the same day, Maj. Gen. Robert H. Milroy informed his headquarters in Baltimore that reports he was receiving indicated the Rebels plan to attack him at Winchester with a force of 10,000. His commander, Maj. Gen. Robert C. Schenck, told Milroy to act with caution and fall back toward Harper's Ferry and Martinsburg if forced to do so. These reports would soon come to fruition: the invasion was about to be launched.[72]

---

69 Williams to Buford, June 2, 1863, *OR* 25, pt. 2, 595. By communicating directly with Buford, Hooker was bypassing cavalry commander Pleasonton as he had by-passed Halleck in communicating with Lincoln and Stanton. Hooker would soon discover that leaving superior or subordinate commanders out of the information loop could cause serious problems.

70 Richmond *Dispatch*, May 15-June 2, 1863; Styple, *Writing & Fighting the Confederate War*, 143.

71 Kidd, *Personal Recollections of a Cavalryman*, 106; Martha Gerber Stanford, *The Civil War Letters of Daniel Peck* (Freeman, SD, 1993), 49.

72 Keyes to Hooker, Piatt to Kelly, June 2, 1863, *OR* 25, pt. 2, 595-96. At the time, Keyes was assigned to the Department of Virginia under the command of Maj. Gen. John A. Dix. Faust, *Encyclopedia of the Civil War*, 416.

Chapter Five

Deciphering the Enemy's Movements:
June 3 to 7

The position occupied by the enemy opposite Fredericksburg being one in which he could not
be attacked to advantage, it was determined to draw him from it . . . and, if practicable, the
transfer of the scene of hostilities north of the Potomac.

Gen. Robert E. Lee[1]

So far as I was enabled to judge, from all my means of information . . . the enemy [plans] to
move up the river, with a view to . . . cross the Upper Potomac,
or to throw his army between mine and Washington.

Maj. Gen. Joseph Hooker[2]

June 3: The Campaign Begins: On to Culpeper Court House

In a dispatch to the Savannah *Republican*, Peter W. Alexander reported
his arrival in Richmond to join Lee's army as a correspondent and
offered his impressions about the current military situation. His comments
reflect how sensitive the Confederates were to hovering balloons watching over
their movements. It also indicated how much Lee and his commanders relied

---

1 Lee's post-action report, July 31, 1863, *OR* 27, pt. 2, 305.

2 Hooker to Lincoln, June 5, 1863, ibid., pt. 1, 30.

on Northern newspapers to reveal what the enemy knew about their plans and activities:

> The enemy persist in believing the Confederates contemplate a forward movement of some kind, and they very anxiously reconnoiter our position every morning from their safe and elevated perches in the balloons. Two balloons were up this morning—one just below Fredericksburg on the opposite side, and the other higher up the river. The [New York] *Herald* of Saturday [May 30] . . . says that these aerial reconnaissances have thus far developed no change in the position of the Confederate army around Fredericksburg. The opinion still prevails in Washington however, that Gen. Lee means mischief; and the *Herald* affirms that he even has designs upon Harrisburg and Philadelphia.[3]

Alexander's report about anticipation of a possible Rebel movement was timely, since that very day Lee's invasion of the North actually got underway: McLaws' and Hood's divisions of Longstreet's corps headed towards Culpeper Court House, the staging ground to the northwest of Fredericksburg. Major General Henry Heth of A. P. Hill's corps received orders for his division to picket the lines that Maj. Gen. Robert Rodes formerly held, since Rodes' division of Ewell's corps would be marching the following morning.[4]

As the campaign started, Lee announced the appointment of Maj. David B. Bridgford to his staff as provost marshal. Bridgford's command, the 1st Battalion Virginia Infantry, would travel north with Lee and the army as provost guards. This improved Lee's potential for gathering information about the enemy through interrogating Union prisoners and deserters and the submission of intelligence reports—a task this battalion had proven adept under Gen. Stonewall Jackson's command.[5]

Sharpe's civilian spy Howard Skinker arrived back in camp at Falmouth and reported that the man he sent across the Rappahannock had not returned. He could learn "nothing reliable" about the enemy's position, but, he stated, they, "beyond doubt," were concentrating cavalry "in the neighborhood" of Culpeper Court House, more than likely for "recruiting his horses." Skinker

---

3   Styple, *The Letters of Peter Wellington Alexander*, 5, 144. Alexander, who was an influential and admired war correspondent throughout the South, signed his dispatches with his initials P. W. A. The Savannah *Republican* published this dispatch on June 8, 1863.

4   Longstreet's and Rodes's post-action reports, OR 27, pt. 2, 357, 545; Coddington, *The Gettysburg Campaign*, 51.

5   Driver and Ruffner, *1st Battalion Virginia Infantry*, 32-33, 35-36.

also learned that Brig. Gen. William "Grumble" Jones had brought his cavalry brigade from the Shenandoah Valley, and his headquarters "was not very far distant from Culpeper C.H.—and that this information was obtained from some of his cavalry, whose homes were in Fauquier [County], and who had been over to see their friends." Without solid evidence, "except that derived from putting this & that together," Skinker speculated that a cavalry raid "of magnitude" would be made with Pennsylvania as the objective, and "if General Lee is making any moves, it is southward, with a part of his command, and not towards the Valley."[6]

Although designed to be helpful, this report could only serve to confuse the issue for Sharpe and Hooker. While there was an element of truth in the thought that Lee would move "southward," he would do so only to stay out of sight as he swung to the west and north. The report also helped center Hooker's attention on Culpeper Court House as to where Stuart's cavalry was, rather than Brandy Station where they were actually encamped.

Another spy's report arrived at army headquarter from Brig. Gen. John W. Geary through Maj. Gen. Henry Slocum of the XII Corps. Charles Whitlock, born in Connecticut but a resident of the Shenandoah Valley, had a brother in Aldie, Virginia, who told him that "the whole Rebel army about Richmond is in motion." According to the report, a large part of the Confederate forces in North Carolina had joined General Pickett at Hanover Court House, 20 miles north of Richmond, and Hood's division had occupied Culpeper Court House. Citizens in his area of Aldie were certain that Lee would strike somewhere soon, he continued and that the Rebel army's quartermaster department agents were "buying up all the supplies they can, and everything indicates a speedy move on the part of the Rebels."[7]

Although overstated and partly premature, the report correctly noted that some forces had arrived in the Richmond area from North Carolina, and Hood's division would soon march north to Culpeper Court House and arrive there on June 5. Geary endorsed this report to Slocum with the comment that previous intelligence from this source "had proven reliable," and that Whitlock had served him as an efficient "secret agent" during a number of operations in Virginia. Slocum immediately passed the report to Hooker. Undoubtedly, the

6   Skinker to Sharpe, June 3, 1863, RG 393, NA.

7   Charles Whitlock to John W. Geary, June 2, 1863, RG 393, NA.

information (although actually premature by a couple of days) that Hood's infantry division was as far north as Culpeper Court House proved particularly interesting to the Union commander.[8]

In his search for reinforcements to fill "a great need of troops in the Valley of Virginia," Lee requested Maj. Gen. Samuel Jones, commander of the Department of Southwestern Virginia at Dublin, to return to Brig. Gen. Albert Jenkins as many men previously detached from his command as possible. Jenkins was slated to lead a cavalry brigade in support of Ewell's corps, the vanguard of the invading army. Well aware that in future engagements with the Federal army he would be heavily outnumbered, Lee was scraping together as many men as possible for his campaign.[9]

Perhaps coincidentally, deserters came into the Union lines that evening with word that the Rebels would try to attack across the river the following morning. Whether these were genuine deserters or plants Lee sent to divert the opposition's attention away from his movements farther north and west was unclear.[10]

In the meantime, concern about Maj. Gen. Robert Milroy's isolated outpost at Winchester in the Valley and rumors of a possible attack there prompted Middle Department commander Maj. Gen. Robert Schenck in Baltimore to dispatch infantry and artillery reinforcements; he also ordered Milroy to be on the alert and fall back in the direction of Harper's Ferry or Martinsburg "as your better judgment may dictate." That night, Hooker also sent orders to the I, II, III, VI, XI, and XII corps, as well as the cavalry corps, reserve artillery, and the engineers to be ready by a half-hour after daylight the next day for "any movement that may be ordered."[11]

---

8 Ibid.

9 A. L. Long to Jones, June 3, 1863, OR 27, pt. 3, 858; Dickinson, *16th Virginia Cavalry*, 20. One handicap facing Lee was the lack of sufficient transportation. The army had a shortage of horses and wagons despite a previous reduction that Lee imposed on the allotment of wagons for each unit. To help alleviate this problem, he requested Jones to turn over some of the wagons his forces captured during recent raids in that area. Lee to Jones, June 3, 1863, OR 27, pt. 3, 858; General Orders No. 58, April 20, 1863, pt. 2, 25:739-40.

10 Butterfield to [Meade], June 3, 1863, OR 27, pt. 3, 3-4. Chief of Staff Butterfield sent word of the deserters' story to V Corps commander Major General Meade, and added, "We have no means of ascertaining the falsity of the report," but ordered Meade to send part of a division to Banks Ford as reinforcements just to be on the safe side.

11 Piatt to Milroy, Butterfield to Sedgwick, June 3, 1863, ibid., 4.

Near Frying Pan, five miles north of Chantilly, Virginia, Mosby's rangers attacked a patrol of Michigan cavalry, killing three, wounding several others, and capturing seven men and 10 horses. This type of encounter was commonplace in the Virginia countryside, and Mosby and his small band of guerrillas provided Lee with a constant threat that occupied thousands of Union soldiers defending military supply trains, facilities, and outposts. The presence and elusiveness of Mosby's rangers helped to offset the numerical advantage that the Federals normally enjoyed over the Confederates.[12]

June 4: Empty Campsites

On a day that started out cool then became clear and pleasant, observations by airborne balloons spotted empty Rebel camps and movement northward in the area opposite Bank's Ford, some three miles west of Fredericksburg. Another balloon aloft in the vicinity of the I Corps at White Oak Church reported seeing dust rising near Salem Church about four miles west of Fredericksburg, and wagons moving north on the Telegraph Road toward Fredericksburg—the latter perhaps arriving to remove the army's baggage and equipment. Captain Ulric Dahlgren, an energetic young member of Hooker's staff who would soon earn a reputation for daring exploits, made the rounds of signal stations along the river that were keeping watch on enemy movements. He reported that observers also discovered the camps of six enemy infantry regiments that had fires the previous night were missing.[13]

Given evidence that enemy campsites had been vacated the previous day, army headquarters ordered V Corps commander Meade, whose infantry was picketing the lower river fords, to "use all exertions" to keep both himself and Hooker informed about enemy movements. As a result, Meade ordered his Second Division commander George Sykes to reinforce his positions along the

---

12 Major John Scott, *Partisan Life with Col. John S. Mosby* (Lake Monticello, VA, 1989), 96. When Colonel Gray of the 5th Michigan led a detachment of three companies in pursuit of Mosby, he ended up losing eight of his troopers who were captured, while the Michiganders only captured one of Mosby's men. Longacre, *Custer and His Wolverines*, 117.

13 Dahlgren to Butterfield, June 4, 1863, OR 27, pt. 3, 5; Gottfried, *Maps of Gettysburg*, 5. Ulric Dahlgren was the son of Rear Admiral John Dahlgren, who at the time was commander of the Washington Navy Yard and chief of the Bureau of Ordnance, as well as a close personal friend of President Lincoln. Faust, *Encyclopedia of the Civil War*, 202; Robert J. Schneller, Jr., *A Quest for Glory: A Biography of Rear Admiral John A. Dahlgren* (Annapolis, MD, 1996), 183-89.

Rappahannock to prevent any river crossings at points he was defending. Meade sent Sykes a map of that section of the country, and instructed him to have his commanding officers "make themselves acquainted with the woods, paths, etc. leading from their posts up and down the river and back into the country." Sykes should consider his units on "advance picket duty, requiring the utmost vigilance and activity." Buford, whose cavalry were patrolling the right flank of the army in the vicinity of Bealeton and Warrenton, also received instructions to keep the country well scouted and advise headquarters of any indication of an enemy movement. Buford reported that his cavalry reconnoitered the country up river to Orleans, New Baltimore, and Thoroughfare Gap, but nothing "was seen or heard."[14]

Hooker passed Buford's report to Halleck in Washington, and added that "[t]he movements of the enemy in our front do not indicate what their purpose or object may be." Later chief of staff Butterfield alerted Halleck that information had been obtained from at least three different sources that Jones' cavalry had come from the Shenandoah Valley, and was located in the Culpeper area, thereby confirming McEntee's and Skinker's reports. The arrival of a cavalry brigade near Culpeper indicated that Lee planned to move his army in that direction northwest of his current position near Fredericksburg.[15]

Hooker, meanwhile, avoiding proper procedure again, communicated directly with Stanton about the reports of enemy camps being removed from their location south of the Rappahannock. Proper procedure would have been to pass this information to the general in chief and allow him to decide whether to send it on to Stanton. Hooker opted to bypass normal channels evidently to ignore Halleck as much as possible. Their relationship was on a downward spiral.[16]

14 Butterfield to Meade, Butterfield to Buford, June 4, 1863, *OR* 27, pt. 3, 4-5; Burford to Hooker, Locke to Sykes, June 4, 1863, *OR* 51, pt. 1, 29, 1044;

15 Hooker to Halleck, Butterfield to Halleck, June 4, 1863, *OR* 27, pt. 1, 29. Lee confirmed his planned destination in a request to Adjutant and Inspector General Samuel Cooper in Richmond to forward returning convalescents and other soldiers to Culpeper Court House rather than Fredericksburg. In further confirmation, mapmaker Jed Hotchkiss visited Col. William Proctor Smith, Lee's chief engineer, to gather material for preparation of maps of the routes toward Culpeper. Lee to Cooper, June 4, 1863, *OR* 27, pt. 3, 858-59; Hotchkiss, *Make Me A Map of the Valley*, 147.

16 Hooker to Stanton, June 4, 1863, *OR* 27, pt. 1, 29.

June 5: Stuart Ignores Need for Security

Given reports of possible enemy movements, Hooker became apprehensive. His mental meltdown at Chancellorsville was undoubtedly still fresh in his mind, as well as those of fellow officers and superiors in Washington. Late in the morning, Hooker addressed his concerns and uncertainties directly to President Lincoln. He informed the president that he had concluded from "all my means of information" that the Rebel forces were moving up river "with a view to the execution of a movement similar to that of Lee's last year"—implying that Lee planned to invade the Northern states.[17]

Hooker conjectured that Lee either would cross the Potomac River or get between the Union army and Washington. He thought Lee's route would be through Gordonsville or Culpeper. He further assumed that Lee "must have been greatly re-enforced . . . by the troops from Charleston." The only evidence he had of this was an unsubstantiated report from Maj. Gen. John A. Dix, commander of the Department of the East based at Fort Monroe in Virginia. The seed about a growing number of troops in Lee's army had been planted, however, and it would grow and blossom in Hooker's mind over the coming days despite evidence to the contrary.[18]

In something of a quandary about what he should do in response to the reported activity across the river, Hooker solicited Lincoln's views, especially in light of his orders of January 31 specifying the "importance of covering Washington and Harper's Ferry." If Lee moved northward with part of his forces, Hooker thought it was his duty "to pitch into his rear." Indeed, the issue of defending Harper's Ferry would soon become the focus of disagreement between Hooker and his superiors in Washington. Hooker also addressed the need for a single commander for all the troops in the region. Under the current system of independent armies, he complained, he was ignorant of the movement of the others. While denying that he desired the position of overall commander for himself, his comment could be construed to impugn Halleck for not exercising proper command of the Union armies in the region.[19]

17 Hooker to Lincoln, June 5, 1863, ibid., 30; Hebert, *Fighting Joe Hooker*, 91.

18 Hooker to Lincoln, *OR* 27, pt. 1, 30.

19 Ibid.

A mid-day report from George Meade fueled Hooker's concerns. The V Corps commander had learned from a deserter of the 10th Alabama, Brig. Gen. Cadmus M. Wilcox's brigade (Anderson's division, A. P. Hill's corps), "who swam the river [to our side] this morning before daylight," that the Rebels had artillery at Bank's Ford. The Alabama soldier further revealed that Wilcox defended the ford with his brigade of five regiments. In accordance with standing instructions, Meade sent the deserter to the "provost-marshal-general" at army headquarters for further interrogation by Sharpe and the BMI. Cavalry commander Pleasonton's report to army headquarters followed this one. He too cited a deserter—from the 55th Virginia, Brockenbrough's brigade of Heth's division—who said that his regiment and one other were directly across the river, but that Archer's brigade of his division was still some 15 miles to the south near Port Conway.[20]

In keeping with Hooker's plans, at noon Pleasonton sent instructions from his headquarters at Falmouth, Virginia, to Buford, the senior officer in charge of Union cavalry operating some 25 miles to the northwest near Catlett's Station, Virginia:

> You will make a strong demonstration without delay upon the enemy in your front toward Culpeper [Court House], and push them as far as possible without jeopardizing your command. The enemy are in motion in front of Fredericksburg; a portion have gone toward Orange Court House. Keep me fully advised."[21]

The wording of these orders would get this expedition off on the wrong foot, because Pleasonton had used ambiguous terminology and did not specify an objective. Although he had told Buford to "make a strong demonstration," the apparent intention was to conduct a reconnaissance in force toward the Culpeper area. A demonstration normally was an attack or show of force on one front designed to deceive the enemy where the main attack would take place. A reconnaissance in force, on the other hand, was an offensive thrust to ascertain

---

20 Meade to [Williams], June 5, 1863, *OR* 27, pt. 3, 9-10. In the estimate of Meade and one of his division commanders, Maj. Gen. George Sykes, the Rebels could force a crossing at this ford "owing to their artillery commanding the ground on this side in its immediate vicinity." Headquarters undoubtedly discounted the information about Archer's brigade, however, because there was no reason to believe that a unit of that size would be located so far from the Rebel's main defensive position. For the location of Port Conway, see *OR Atlas*, Plate 16.

21 Pleasonton to Buford, June 5, 1863, ibid., 10. It is not clear from the record whether Pleasonton sent these orders on his own initiative, or whether Hooker directed him to do so.

with certainty an opponent's position or strength. Clearly, Hooker sent cavalry across the river to gather information about the terrain around Culpeper Court House and the troops defending it, not to deceive the enemy regarding an attack in another location.[22]

However, Pleasonton did not address the objective of the mission at all. Was it to identify the type of enemy forces in the vicinity, determine their position and strength, learn their intentions, or engage them and take prisoners for interrogation? The orders were not specific. Nonetheless, according to Col. Alfred Duffié, Buford directed him to conduct a "demonstration on Culpeper Court-House" with his division of some 2,500 cavalry early the following morning.[23]

Pleasonton's orders to Buford undoubtedly engendered even further confusion, because he mentioned that the enemy at Fredericksburg was on the move, and "a portion have gone toward Orange Court House." What exactly, if anything, Buford was supposed to do about this reported enemy activity was left to his discretion, because Pleasonton offered no guidance. More importantly, the orders said nothing at all about the fact that Hooker was concerned about enemy cavalry activity in the vicinity of Culpeper Court House and wanted to find out exactly where they were located.[24]

Meanwhile, Hooker's telegraph message to Lincoln arrived in Washington in about three and a half hours. Lincoln replied almost immediately that his lack of military skill impelled him to refer Hooker's inquiry to Halleck for reply. Still, Lincoln suggested that if Lee was moving north of the Rappahannock, Hooker should not consider crossing to the south of it. Rather, he recommended that, depending on his estimate of the relative strength of the two armies, Hooker either fight Lee north of the river or go on the defensive.[25]

After the president passed Hooker's message to Halleck, the general in chief's reply was ready for transmission in less than an hour, reflecting

22 Ibid. For definitions of terminology, see "Demonstration," DOD Dictionary of Military Terms, http://www.dtic.mil/doctrine/dod_dictionary/?zoom_query=demonstration&zoom_sort=0&zoom_per_page=10&zoom_and=1, accessed June 12, 2014, and "Reconnaissance in force," Faust, *Encyclopedia of the Civil War*, 618.

23 Pleasonton to Buford, Duffie's report, June 5, 1863, *OR* 27, pt. 3, 10; pt. 1, 1049.

24 Pleasonton to Buford, June 5, 1863, *OR* 27, pt. 3, 10. While it is conceivable Pleasonton had expanded on his orders to Buford for this demonstration by other means, subsequent comments by the participants tend to render this possibility unlikely.

25 Ibid., pt. 1, 31.

Washington's high priority for all matters related to Lee's army and its potential to attack the capital city. In a demonstration of their mutual antipathy, Halleck curtly informed Hooker that the ball was squarely in his court. His original orders remained in effect: other than insuring the safety of Washington and Harper's Ferry, he was free to act as circumstances required.[26]

Halleck did advise that if Lee went north and left a part of his force at Fredericksburg, this might be a propitious opportunity to attack his flank. He also passed along his assessment that while troops in North Carolina had probably gone north to reinforce Lee, those from South Carolina and Georgia had likely gone to join Gen. Joseph Johnston in Mississippi. As for Hooker's desire for one commander over all the regional armies, Halleck dismissed it—and asserted his own authority— by instructing Hooker to forward any requests for assistance from Generals Dix at Fort Monroe, Heintzelman in Washington, and Schenck at Baltimore through his office.[27]

In an earlier message that afternoon, Halleck informed Hooker that interrogation of enemy prisoners and deserters revealed that Stuart was preparing to make a raid with a force of 15,000-20,000 cavalry and artillery, a highly inflated figure for the 10,000-man strength of Stuart's five brigades. Nonetheless, a communication from Buford to cavalry headquarters reinforced Halleck's report. Buford had just received what he considered to be reliable information from a refugee that Stuart had 20,000 cavalry under his command in Culpeper County. "Stuart, the two Lees, Robertson, Jenkins and Jones are all there," he said. Hooker decided to send this information directly to Secretary of War Stanton, once again bypassing his immediate commander, Halleck. But Buford did not account for Hampton's brigade, and the refugee's information about Jenkins was inaccurate, because that brigade remained in the Valley awaiting Lee's army to begin its march northward.[28]

In an apparent response to an inquiry from army headquarters, McEntee, whose BMI team was operating in the field from its base near Bealeton,

26 Halleck to Hooker, June 5, 1863, ibid., 31-32.

27 Ibid. Later, on July 2, a letter to Lee from President Davis that Union cavalry captured confirmed that troops were withdrawn from South Carolina and Georgia and sent to Johnston in Mississippi. See Davis to Lee, June 28, 1863, *OR* 27, pt. 1, 76.

28 Halleck to Hooker, Buford to Alexander, Hooker to Stanton, June 5, 1863, *OR* 27, pt. 1, pp. 31-32; pt. 3, 8. Army of Northern Virginia returns for May 31, 1863, show Stuart's cavalry with 10,292 officers and men. Walter H. Taylor, *Four Years with General Lee* (New York, 1962), 169.

telegraphed Sharpe that "I hear nothing of Jones movements," referring to "Grumble" Jones's cavalry brigade that had just arrived in the Culpeper area from the Valley. McEntee reiterated his previous estimate that the "whole force [totaled] about 1600" men. Given several exchanges regarding movement of Lee's army, Hooker reacted by issuing a circular to his commanders to hold their troops in readiness to move on "very short notice."[29]

Having gotten the army moving in a northerly direction, Lee awaited his opponent's reaction. Hooker would react. Lee told A. P. Hill to continue occupying the position near Fredericksburg and attempt to "deceive the enemy, and keep him in ignorance of any change in the disposition of the army." Lee wanted to keep the movement of his other two corps under wraps as long as possible, in order to gain a head start on the Union army moving northward.[30]

And he also ordered Hill to keep him informed about everything related to his corps and the enemy. Hill at once instructed Maj. Gen. Henry Heth to move his division up to within a mile of Hamilton's Crossing because the enemy "seem to be intent on another crossing [of the river]." Additionally, to prepare for joining the army's trek northward, Heth was to pack up everything and have his men prepare two days rations.[31]

Lee wanted to ensure that Hill had sufficient early warning of a potential attack on his position. The 4th Virginia Cavalry under Col. Williams C. Wickham would screen his left, while Maj. C. R. Collins and the 15th Virginia Cavalry would be on the right, and Frayser's signal party, presently about 20 miles downriver at Port Royal keeping watch on enemy movements, would provide a communication and observation capability.[32]

Displaying more assertiveness than earlier in the day, Hooker informed Lincoln that he had ordered a demonstration south of the river "to learn, if possible, what the enemy are about." A. P. Hill's troops reacted strongly to this probe and a number of Rebels had been captured. Interrogation of these prisoners, Hooker said, revealed that the reorganization of Lee's army had caused the recent changes in their camps; Longstreet's corps had rejoined Lee

---

29 McEntee to Sharpe, June 5, 1863, RG 393, NA; Williams to [commanding officers, II, XI, and XII Corps], ibid., pt. 3, 11. Jones' total force as of 30 June was 1,745. Busey and Martin, *Regimental Strengths and Losses*, 247, 251.

30 Lee to Hill, June 5, 1863, *OR* 27, pt. 3, 859.

31 Hill to Heth, ibid., pt. 2, 51:721.

32 Lee to Hill, ibid., pt. 3, 27:859.

from Suffolk, and, as Halleck had mentioned to Hooker earlier, no reinforcements had come up to Lee's army from the Charleston, South Carolina area. The prisoners also reported that Lee's infantry had gone no farther north than the junction of the Rappahannock and Rapidan Rivers; they also confirmed that the Rebel cavalry were at Culpeper, and that the threat of a Union attack across the river might cause the horsemen to return to the Fredericksburg area.[33]

Although accurate in some respects and confirming some of what Hooker had already learned about the status and disposition of Lee's army, key parts of this information were misleading or outdated. The Rebel army reorganization did not cause the change in campsites, given that elements of Longstreet's and Ewell's corps had already marched away from Fredericksburg on their way toward Culpeper. More importantly, Hood's division of Longstreet's corps arrived in Culpeper on this date and continued on to Brandy Station—meaning a large unit of Lee's infantry was much farther north than the prisoners had reported. Since the Confederate POWs were captured on June 5, they likely were unaware that Hood's division arrived in Culpeper and Brandy Station that day. The Union river crossing did prompt Lee to halt the march of Ewell's corps toward Culpeper. Even though he considered the maneuver a mere feint, he wanted to observe the enemy by daylight to be certain.[34]

With the buildup of his command to five brigades in anticipation of the invasion, the flamboyant Stuart decided to hold a grand review of the cavalry and horse artillery. Although a public spectacle of this nature was ill advised considering the need for security in preparation for an invasion, Stuart's pride in his expanded responsibilities led him to invite local citizens and guests from Richmond and Charlottesville to attend.[35]

33 Hooker to Lincoln, ibid., pt. 1, 32-33.

34 Ibid., pt. 2, 357, 459, 545-46; pt. 1, 32-33; Lee, *Recollections and Letters of General Lee*, 95; Gottfried, *Roads to Gettysburg*, 12-14; Longstreet, *From Manassas to Appomattox*, 337-38; McDonald, *Make Me A Map of the Valley*, 148.

35 Driver, *1st Virginia Cavalry*, 61; Howard, *2nd Virginia Cavalry*, 81; Nanzig, *3rd Virginia Cavalry*, 35; Musick, *6th Virginia Cavalry*, 37-38; Armstrong, *7th Virginia Cavalry*, 52; Stuart held the cavalry review on June 5 and another one on June 8 on the grounds of the John Minor Botts' farm between Culpeper and Brandy Station. For a drawing of the Botts' home, "Auburn," and property where the reviews took place, see Robert Knox Sneden, *Eye of the Storm: A Civil War Odyssey* (New York, 2000), 140.

Earlier in the day, Stuart instructed Frank Stringfellow, one of his most reliable scouts who operated in civilian garb, to leave that night on a hazardous assignment. He was to head northward behind enemy lines to scout the fords over the Potomac River east of Harper's Ferry. Stuart evidently wanted to learn at which fords his brigades would encounter the least resistance to their move across into Maryland. Since Lee's plan called for the cavalry to screen the movement of the army as the invasion got underway, Stuart arranged for Stringfellow to rendezvous with the cavalry somewhere in the vicinity of Salem (present day Marshall), 10 miles south of Upperville, after he had gathered the desired information.[36]

In mid-afternoon, Halleck again recommended that Hooker attack Lee if part of the Rebel army moved northward, and another part maintained a position at Fredericksburg. "[S]uch an operation would give you great advantages upon his flank to cut him in two, and fight his divided forces," he wrote. Nonetheless, Hooker must also consider "the safety of Washington and Harper's Ferry"—an important qualifier.[37]

June 6: "Feeling" the Enemy Along the Rappahannock

A refugee from Confederate-held territory came into Union lines with the information that two regiments of Rebel cavalry under Brig. Gen. Beverly H. Robertson had arrived from North Carolina—and that Stuart's reinforced division was lying between Brandy Station and Culpeper Court House.[38]

Hooker's reports of the previous day apparently aroused concerns for the Washington authorities. At 9:30 a.m. on July 6, Department of Washington headquarters ordered cavalry commander Stahel to send a strong reconnaissance into the Shenandoah Valley at once "to acquire any information which may be had of the enemy's whereabouts or intentions." Chief of Staff Lt. Col. J. H. Taylor informed Stahel: "There is little doubt that Lee has moved his army from Hooker's front," but his objectives were unknown. While there may

---

36 R. Shepard Brown, *Stringfellow of the Fourth* (New York, 1960), 197.

37 Halleck to Hooker, June 5, 1863, OR 27, pt. 1, 31-32.

38 McEntee to Sharpe, June 6, 1863, RG 393, NA.

Col. Alfred N. Duffié
Library of Congress

have been "little doubt" in Washington that Lee was on the move, Hooker still did not have the benefit of such clarity about Lee's activities and intentions.[39]

At 10:00 a.m. that morning, Hooker personally wrote to Buford at Bealeton: "Information has been communicated to me that three brigades of the enemy's cavalry are posted at Jefferson. . . . Can you tell me how this is?" This was an oddly phrased question, implying surprise that the enemy cavalry would be at that location, especially since Buford had reported the previous day that all of Stuart's cavalry was in Culpeper County. However, since Jefferson lay some 13 miles north of Culpeper Court House, the reported location of Stuart's cavalry, Hooker appears to have become apprehensive.[40]

Could Buford "shut off all communications for three days across the river as high up [the river] as Sulphur Springs[?]" Hooker inquired. For he was planning an attack towards Culpeper Court House, and wanted to ensure his force was not observed as approaching their launching points on the north side of the Rappahannock. Buford said he would attempt to comply, adding that Hooker's information about Rebel cavalry at Jefferson was inaccurate, since he had a large force reconnoitering in that area. After receiving Pleasonton's orders the previous day, Buford had sent "a very strong force to Culpeper Court House under the command of Col. Alfred N. Duffie."[41]

39 Taylor to Stahel, June 6, 1863, OR 27, pt. 3, 18.

40 Hooker to Buford, June 6, 1863, ibid., 12.

41 Hooker to Buford, Buford to Butterfield, Buford to Pleasonton, Stahel to Taylor, June 6, 1863, OR 27, pt. 3, 12, 14, 19. Sulphur Springs was some three miles northeast of Jefferson on

John Mosby's partisans posed the greatest threat to Buford's operations in the area. On June 4, Mosby had clashed with elements of Stahel's cavalry division near Frying Pan (present-day Floris) four miles north of Chantilly, and again on 6 June when they engaged a squadron of the 1st Michigan Cavalry just three miles upriver from Sulphur Springs at Waterloo Bridge. Mosby's area of operations also included the Shenandoah Valley where his men attacked lightly guarded wagon trains and outposts. In fact, this very day 75 partisans had attacked a train of six wagons coming from Winchester, soon to be the scene of a greater conflict between Union and Confederate forces.[42]

In the meantime, Butterfield contacted VI Corps commander Maj. Gen. John Sedgwick with orders from Hooker to conduct a reconnaissance to "ascertain the position and strength of the enemy" in front of the bridges he had placed on the south side of the river below Fredericksburg. Do it speedily and take "prisoners any citizens who could give any information." Butterfield explained that the absence of enemy pickets in Maj. Gen. Darius N. Couch's II Corps front near Falmouth indicated his "removal" from the area.[43]

Reports from signal officers observing the enemy across the river and from I Corps commander Maj. Gen. John F. Reynolds, Butterfield continued, indicated that one division would suffice to "ascertain the strength of the enemy." He also emphasized the desirability of securing as many escaped slaves, deserters, and prisoners as possible, and sending them at once to the provost marshal for examination by the BMI. Clearly, Hooker viewed the interrogation process as an effective means of gaining valuable information.[44]

The enemy position had been strengthened, Sedgwick responded, and he could not "move 200 yards without bringing on a general fight." Additionally, an escaped slave had reported that Lee and Longstreet were "at this place last night," and "all the prisoners confirm this information." Evidently Lee wanted to assess personally the seriousness of the Union river crossing, rather than relying on the reports of subordinates. At the same time, he had ordered Hood's division at Culpeper Court House to march to Ellis Ford on the Rappahannock

---

the north side of the Rappahannock River. OR *Atlas*, Plate 22, 7; Beach, *The First New York (Lincoln) Cavalry*, 228.

42 Mosby, *War Reminiscences*, 154-56; Longacre, *Custer and His Wolverines*, 117-18; *OR Atlas*, Plate 21, 13; Plate 7, 1.

43 Butterfield to Sedgwick, June 6, 1863, OR 27, pt. 3, 12; Gottfried, *Maps of Gettysburg*, 5.

44 Butterfield to Sedgwick, June 6, 1863, OR 27, pt. 3, 13.

Maj. Gen. John Sedgwick
Library of Congress

in preparation for an attack across the river the following morning. Although Lee was uncertain of the enemy's positions, this movement would place Hood on Hooker's right flank. It also allowed Hood to cooperate with Stuart's cavalry in fulfilling Lee's desire to "scatter Stoneman," as he had stated in an earlier message to Stuart, i.e., the Union cavalry now under Pleasonton's command.[45]

Lee's aide Walter Taylor confirmed that "after watching the enemy's operations the next day he became satisfied that A. P. Hill's command could manage the force on the south side." Lee knew he could not afford to allow a large part of his army to leave the area if a major threat of an attack existed. So he took the time to investigate the situation personally and informed President Davis that he "watched the enemy operations on Saturday [June 6]," and was satisfied they did not constitute a major threat. Thus he ordered Ewell to continue the march and sent word for Hood to cancel the attack across the river.[46]

A. P. Hill reacted to Sedgwick's crossing by shifting Heth's division closer to Fredericksburg and the major river crossings. Captain James S. Hall, a Union signal officer, reported from his observation station at the Phillips House, a high point on the north side of the river opposite Fredericksburg, that seven regiments had come up "from below" and taken position in rifle pits. The area between Marye's Heights and where Sedgwick made his crossing is "filled by these new troops." Hall also reported wagons heading south, and artillery and wagons moving north toward the railroad depot, the latter activity likely related

45 Sedgwick to Butterfield, ibid., 12-13, pt. 2, 25:792; Alexander, *Fighting for the Confederacy*, 221-22; Nesbitt, *35 Days to Gettysburg*, 37-38; Gottfried, *Roads to Gettysburg*, 13, 16.

46 Taylor, *General Lee*, 181; Dowdey, *Lee's Wartime Papers*, 503; Gallagher, *Fighting for the Confederacy*, 222; Nesbitt, *35 Days to Gettysburg*, 37-38; Gottfried, *Roads to Gettysburg*, 21.

to Lee's movement away from Fredericksburg. Hill had captured Union scouts sent out to ascertain Lee's movements and thus was having some success in limiting communications between the two sides of the river.[47]

Lee later acknowledged that Sedgwick's crossing caused him some concern, but he astutely concluded it was for observation not an attack. Therefore, Sedgwick's reconnaissance had not "arrested" his army's movements toward Culpeper Court House. Ewell's mapmaker Jed Hotchkiss noted that Ewell received approval from Lee to continue the march in mid-afternoon. To ensure the corps would be able to move expeditiously, the talented topographical engineer had worked during the delay preparing a map of Culpeper County and another one "on towards the [Blue Ridge] mountains."[48]

If Lee was not fooled by Hooker's maneuvers, apparently neither was John B. Jones from his observation point at the war department offices in Richmond. Jones noted in his diary rumors of "picket fighting" near Fredericksburg. He answered his own hypothetical question of whether another great battle would take place on the Rappahannock with the skeptical comment, "I think it is a ruse."[49]

Meanwhile, Hooker, feeling that he needed more time to organize an attack against Lee's forces that were gathering up river from Fredericksburg, instructed Pleasonton to suspend Buford's orders of the previous day to stage a strong demonstration toward Culpeper Court House. Buford responded that he had sent a courier to recall Duffié, who was leading a demonstration force of 2,500, but he correctly feared Duffié "has gone too far." He was unable to learn whether any enemy infantry were north of the Rapidan River, Buford added, but he was "certain there is a very heavy cavalry force on the grazing grounds in Culpeper County."[50]

47 James I. Robertson, Jr., *General A. P. Hill: The Story of a Confederate Warrior* (New York, 1987), 199, 346n12; *OR* 27, pt. 3, 14-15. For the location of the Phillips House and the Union signal station, see the map in Johnson and Buel, *B&L*, 3:74.

48 Lee's post-action report, *OR* 27, pt. 2, 305, 313; Jubal Anderson Early, *Jubal Early's Memoirs* (Baltimore, 1989), 237; Darrell L. Collins, *Major General Robert E. Rodes of the Army of Northern Virginia* (New York, 2008), 238; McDonald, *Hotchkiss Diary*, 148.

49 Jones, *A Rebel War Clerk's Diary*, 1:311-12.

50 Pleasonton to Buford, Buford to Pleasonton, Buford to Alexander, June 6, 1863, *OR* 27, pt. 3, 13-14.

Adding to Hooker's mix of information was a report dated June 2 sent from Capt. William Hogarth of the Maryland Purnell Legion at Frederick, Maryland. Hogarth wrote that he found a "bright mulatto boy" named Julius Hill in Hagerstown who claimed to be A. P. Hill's body servant, and he was on his way to Lancaster, Pennsylvania. The mulatto boy related what he said he overheard in Hill's tent: that the Rebels planned to place heavy guards at the Rappahannock River fords, while the army moved toward the Shenandoah Valley via Culpeper Court House. Also, Jeb Stuart would send cavalry detachments to threaten Winchester, Harper's Ferry, and Alexandria. Meanwhile his main body of cavalry would move north down the Valley via Strasburg and Hancock and then on to York or Lancaster, Pennsylvania, before joining Lee and the rest of the army at Harrisburg.[51]

Hooker had been piecing together information from a variety of sources, and he now decided it was time to take action. At 3 p.m., he alerted Halleck in Washington that he planned to break up a heavy Rebel cavalry force that was accumulating around Culpeper Court House. He would try to accomplish this by sending all of his cavalry "'stiffened' by some 3,000 infantry." He told Halleck the attack would not begin until the morning of the 9th, since it would require some time to get his forces into position.[52]

This was obviously a risky venture in Hooker's mind. More than one report numbered Stuart's cavalry division at 15,000 to 20,000 troopers, a 50 to 100 percent exaggeration of his actual strength. Pleasonton's 8,000 horsemen with 3,000 infantry in support would actually outnumber Stuart's command. But Hooker, believing his force outnumbered, requested Halleck to have Stahel's cavalry provide assistance by covering the river fords at Beverly and Sulphur Springs "during the forenoon of the 9th." This would help to relieve some of the burden on Pleasonton's cavalrymen. Stuart had received reinforcement, Hooker reminded Halleck, from Jones' brigade that had come in from the Valley and another brigade from North Carolina—Beverly Robertson's.[53]

---

51 Hogarth to Hooker, June 2, 1863, RG 393, NA. As with other reports of this type, some aspects of the story rang true, others did not. Although Hogarth did not make it clear, he implied that this person was an escaped slave trying to reach Lancaster. However, another possibility is that he was sent north by the Rebels to sow confusion in the minds of Northern authorities about their plans.

52 Hooker to Halleck, June 6, 1863, OR 27, pt. 1, 33.

53 Ibid.

Butterfield forwarded orders to Brig. Gen. Adelbert Ames, an XI Corps brigade commander assigned to lead 1,500 infantry in support of the cavalry in the planned attack across the river toward Culpeper Court House, to report to Pleasonton for further instructions. Demonstrating an awareness of counterintelligence requirements for the success of this mission, Butterfield specifically directed Ames to keep his command ignorant of their destination, and to pick up "any guerrillas, spies, or wanderers through the country which you traverse" to prevent them from communicating any information to the enemy.[54]

Meanwhile, Lee left Fredericksburg and arrived in Ewell's camp south of the Rapidan River that night. He had other concerns besides the possibility of an enemy attack across the river while his army was marching away from Fredericksburg. In the vicinity of Richmond to the south, Union Maj. Gen. John A. Dix's forces were maneuvering and stirring up anxiety among the Confederate authorities there. As a result, Pickett's division, which had already received orders to rejoin Lee's army, was being held in the Hanover Junction area until things got sorted out there.[55]

On the positive side, Davis had news for Lee: Gen. Joseph Davis' brigade was on its way (it had passed through Richmond that day), and should join Lee's army on the 7th. This was a mixed blessing for Lee, since Joseph Davis, the president's nephew and a lawyer before the war, had no prior military experience. And while two of Davis' four regiments had extensive experience, the other two had none. Davis' four regiments were 2nd, 11th, and 42nd Mississippi and the 55th North Carolina.[56]

Later in the evening, Hooker's adjutant Seth Williams alerted the II and XI corps commanders to prepare their units to move as soon as "early to-morrow." That night, Butterfield contacted Meade telling him that Hooker "would like to have you get him information." Butterfield elaborated: "Can you not feel the enemy, and cause him to develop his strength and position at various points along your front?" The chief of staff suggested that Meade allow

54 Butterfield to Ames, June 6, 1863, OR 27, pt. 3, 16-17.

55 Lee to Davis, June 7, 1863, OR 27, pt. 2, 293; McDonald, *Hotchkiss' Diary*, 149.

56 Davis to Lee, June 6, 1863, OR 51, pt. 2, 721; Gottfried, *Brigades of Gettysburg*, 613-14; Jones, *A Rebel War Clerk's Diary*, 1:341; Coddington, *The Gettysburg Campaign*, 593.

his pickets to chat with the enemy pickets across the river "to find out his regiments."[57]

Major General George Sykes, whose V Corps division was guarding United States and Banks Fords, reacted negatively to Butterfield's message. Sykes told Meade a crossing would be "exceedingly difficult," and a force could not get back "if the enemy chose to prevent it." Even though Sykes believed that only cavalry were picketing the other side, he could not be certain whether infantry lurked nearby. When Meade informed headquarters of Sykes' reaction to these orders, just before midnight Hooker reiterated to Meade "you are not to disregard the order to feel the enemy a little." Sykes also doubted that contact with the enemy would "determine a great deal about his strength." He did agree to have his pickets converse with their counterparts to see if any information could be gained. But even then he was skeptical of the reliability of such information.[58]

Ordered to make a "strong reconnaissance" into the Shenandoah Valley, Stahel asked for clarification regarding how strong the reconnaissance should be, since he only had 1,000 cavalrymen available. He also said that in response to a request from Buford, he had sent several detachments to Thoroughfare Gap, Salem, and toward the Blue Ridge. Lieutenant Colonel Taylor responded that a squadron would be sufficient to send to the Valley and requested that Stahel keep him informed of anything important related to Buford's reconnaissance toward Culpeper Court House.[59]

When some of Lee's units began arriving in Culpeper Court House, correspondent Peter W. Alexander, traveling with them, wrote to the Savannah *Republican* what he had heard about Sedgwick sending a small force across the Rappahannock "at the mouth of Deep Run, three miles below Fredericksburg." The reporter speculated that Hooker had learned "through his spies or balloonists" that the disposition of enemy forces had changed. Alexander, who obviously had good sources within the Army of Northern Virginia, also mentioned that Lee had learned that "a large number of transports" had been

---

57 Williams to [II & XI Corps commanders], June 6, 1863, *OR* 27, pt. 3, 17.

58 Sykes to Meade, Williams to Meade, June 6, 1863, ibid., 17-18.

59 Taylor to Stahel, Stahel to Taylor, ibid., 18-19.

sent to the Potomac in the vicinity of the Aquia Creek—a fact that suggested Hooker was "preparing for a retrograde movement."[60]

Captain Richard E. Frayser's signal party operating at a permanent post on a bluff overlooking the Potomac kept Lee informed via a line of signal stations to a telegraph office on the Fredericksburg railroad. He would have been the source about the Union transports at Aquia Creek. This strategic information about the enemy quickly filtered down through an army redeploying over a roundabout 40-mile route from Fredericksburg to Culpeper Court House.[61]

Lee planned to cross the Blue Ridge Mountains and move north into Maryland and Pennsylvania. Hill's corps would remain at Fredericksburg to keep the Yankees occupied until the march was well underway. Ewell's corps would lead the way north, followed by Longstreet, while Stuart's cavalry picketed along the Rappahannock and screened the infantry's movements. Sensing what was about to take place, William L. Wilson, a cavalryman in Jones's brigade, summed up the situation in his diary:

> Saturday June 6 – About midday we received orders to prepare three days rations and at 3 o'clk took up the line of march towards the Rappahannock—the whole command is in motion. Our brigade camped near Brandy Station. We anticipate an advance of our army.[62]

On this date, Lincoln approved the assignment of Brig. Gen. Daniel D. Tyler to the Middle Department under Schenck in Baltimore. Tyler was destined to play a key role in tracking Lee's army as it marched northward through the Shenandoah Valley into Maryland.[63]

Scouts and Spies in the Field

The BMI began to recruit civilians to serve as spies soon after its establishment in early 1863, and several Virginia Unionists agreed to cooperate with Sharpe's bureau. George Smith, a prosperous Virginian, was one of them, the civilian spy assigned to McEntee's BMI team. Smith had worked for the

---

60 Styple, *The Letters of Peter Wellington Alexander*, 145.

61 Taylor, *The Signal and Secret Service*, 8; *OR* 27, pt. 3, 859, 869.

62 Long, *Memoirs of Robert E. Lee*, 268-70; Summers, *A Borderland Confederate*, 71.

63 HQ Middle Dept., VIII Army Corps, General Orders, No. 37, *OR* 27, pt. 2, 37.

Union army for some time, including for Maj. Gen. John Pope, the commander during the Second Bull Run campaign in mid-1862. But despite Smith's claim he wanted to aid the Northern cause because he believed the South wrong to secede, many Union authorities had mixed emotions about his loyalty. McEntee, too, had been leery about Smith, but, after talking with him at some length, concluded his loyalty to the Union to be genuine. Smith complained that he had received little in the way of recognition for his work. Moreover, the Confederates had arrested him on suspicion of treason, and, according to Smith it had already cost him between $15-20,000 to purchase his freedom.[64]

McEntee sent an enciphered telegraph message to Sharpe from Warrenton Junction reporting that Stuart held a "grand review" of his cavalry the previous day near Culpeper Court House. This information further convinced Hooker that a concentration of such a large cavalry force meant that Stuart planned a raid. In a written report dated the same day, McEntee told Sharpe: "Smith with two of the men has gone to Fields ford to try & communicate with the other side. They may be there two or three days."[65]

In another enciphered telegraph message, McEntee told Sharpe that a refugee from Madison Court House had arrived with information that McEntee rated "reliable"—Hood's division formerly between Mountain Run and Raccoon Ford south of the Rapidan River had moved the previous Sunday, May 31, toward Fredericksburg; it had been seen near Chancellorsville on June 2 or 3. And Pickett's division was near Hanover Junction. Stuart's cavalry, some 20,000 strong, "were lying between Brandy Station & Culpeper, [and] has lately been reinforced by two cavalry brigades from North Carolina." Although the locations of Hood's and Pickett's divisions were accurate, the grossly inflated strength figure for the cavalry was repeated, and only two regiments, not brigades, had arrived from North Carolina.[66]

V Corps commander Major General Meade, who in a little more than three weeks would have the burden of army command thrust upon him, summarized

64 McEntee to Sharpe, June 6, 1863, RG 393, NA; Boatner, *The Civil War Dictionary*, 659, 743, 803; Fishel, *Secret War for the Union*, 195, 292-95, 427. Not all Yankees were suspicious of Smith. Lieutenant Colonel David H. Strother of the Topographical Engineer staff, for example, adjudged him honest.

65 McEntee to Sharpe, June 6, 1863, RG 393, NA; Hooker to Halleck, June 6, 1863, OR 27, pt. 1, 33; Fields Ford was located about three miles south of Kelly's Ford on the Rappahannock River. OR *Atlas*, Plate 44, No. 3.

66 McEntee to Sharpe, June 6, 1863, RG 393 NA.

the current status in a letter to his wife from his camp above Falmouth. Hooker "had received intelligence which induced him to believe Lee was about attempting a [flanking] manoeuvre similar to the one we tried last month [during the Chancellorsville campaign]," he wrote. Indicating that Hooker had expressed his concerns about Lee's army to his corps commanders, Meade added, "Hooker had reason to believe most of the enemy had left his immediate front on the heights back of Fredericksburg."[67]

Meade told his wife something he had believed for some time: "Lee would assume the offensive as soon as he was reinforced sufficiently to justify him in doing so; but whether he has yet commenced is, I think not positively settled." Meade worried that if Lee could get onto the flank and rear of the army and destroy or cripple it, "he will have no opposition to his progress of invasion." The current situation "makes me wonder at the supineness and apathy of the Government and people, leaving this army reduced as it has been by casualties of battle and expiration of service, and apparently making no effort to reinforce it." Meade's thinking now, and his tendency to inflate the strength of the enemy, mirrored his strained relationship with Washington authorities later, after he assumed command of the army.[68]

June 7: Tracking the Enemy's Movements

At 3 a.m., Buford forwarded Butterfield a dispatch from Duffié, indicating that he had returned from his expedition across the Rappahannock:

> I am safe with my command. The reconnaissance has been successful, and without any loss save 1 horse, which was shot in a skirmish. I went 4½ miles from Culpeper. The enemy has constantly run away from me, and did not show any idea of a fight. I shall forward my report to-morrow [June 8].[69]

Since this dispatch contained no substantive intelligence, the Union army command would have to await Duffié's full report. His use of the term "reconnaissance" rather than "demonstration," and his characterization of it as "successful" held out the possibility he had gathered some useful data. A

---

67 George Meade, *The Life and Letters of George Gordon Meade*, 2 vols. (New York, 1913), 1:382.

68 Ibid., 1:383.

69 Buford to Butterfield, June 7, 1863, *OR* 27, pt. 3, 24.

member of Hooker's staff, Capt. Ulric Dahlgren, told Pleasonton that Hooker was awaiting "the result of Duffié's reconnaissance yesterday." Hooker wanted to learn everything he could about the disposition of enemy forces below the river before finalizing his plan of attack.[70]

General Stahel's detachment left on its reconnaissance of the Valley at 3:00 a.m. About the same time, Hooker told Pleasonton he had not yet learned if the balance of Stahel's cavalry would be able to assist in the planned attack across the river.[71]

At 6:45 a.m., Union signal officer Capt. James S. Hall reported to Maj. Gen. Darius Couch, II Corps commander, that "reinforcements received yesterday by the enemy were one division or three brigades." True enough, but these were not reinforcements, rather the redeployment of Heth's division that A. P. Hill had moved into this area to fill the void created when Ewell's corps withdrew towards Culpeper.[72]

Later in the morning, Hall alerted Couch that a small camp of the enemy directly opposite Falmouth had been overlooked in his previous report, and that four pieces of artillery were positioned "30 degrees west of south from this point," just to the right of Hart's house—an indication of his use of a detailed map. Hall reported a few minutes later that the enemy was "constructing a new field work" opposite where Sedgwick's troops had crossed the river, and below two works already there. The Signal Corps was now collecting information normally acquired by airborne balloon program, now being steadily undermined by bureaucratic bungling. When the balloons deteriorated from lack of care over time and could not be flown safely, the program was allowed to fade into oblivion.[73]

Also, that morning, the New York *Times* headlined "A Daring Reconnaissance Made Below Fredericksburgh" by the Army of the Potomac and claimed "The Position and Intentions of Lee Ascertained." The dispatch, dated July 6 from reporter Lorenzo L. Crounse, described the previous day's action of the VI Corps constructing two bridges and crossing the river under

70 Dahlgren to [Pleasonton], June 7, 1863, ibid., 24-25.

71 Wittenberg, *Sixth Michigan Cavalry*, 39; ibid.

72 Hall to Couch, June 7, 1863, OR 27, pt. 3, 24-25; Gottfried, *Maps of Gettysburg*, 5; OR *Atlas*, Plate 31, 4.

73 Hall to Couch, June 7, 1863, OR 27, pt. 3, 26; Evans, *War of the Aeronauts*, 288-90; Fishel, *The Secret War*, 423, 442-43.

fire. "It is properly a reconnaissance," Crounse advised, whose purpose was "to obtain some positive information regarding the enemy's intentions." He went on to claim that "enough was ascertained to locate the greater portion of the enemy's force." He did not elaborate on what was learned about the "enemy's intentions," and for good reason. Evidently neither he nor his sources fully realized that the movement northward of Lee's army had already begun.[74]

Ewell and his staff crossed the Rapidan River at Summerville Ford that morning, while the infantry was crossing at Raccoon Ford three miles to the northeast. Lee and his headquarters contingent had crossed at Raccoon Ford earlier and traveled the 10 miles directly north to the town of Culpeper. Longstreet and Stuart were already in Culpeper, with their respective headquarters close by. With the exception of Hill, still with his corps in Fredericksburg, Lee had all his top commanders available for consultation.[75]

Pleasonton, who previously had his headquarters at Falmouth, announced his arrival at Warrenton Junction at 9 a.m. and wired Seth Williams that Duffié had returned, echoing Buford's report a few hours earlier that he had gotten within four miles of Culpeper. Pleasonton asked that his instructions for the upcoming attack against Stuart's cavalry be telegraphed to him "at an early moment," since his preparations would consume some time, and he wanted to get underway before the enemy knew of his whereabouts. Meanwhile, Halleck advised Hooker from Washington that Stahel would cooperate with Pleasonton in the attack, and that Hooker should coordinate with Maj. Gen. Samuel P. Heintzelman, Stahel's commander.[76]

At 11:45 a.m., Pleasonton informed Seth Williams that Duffié, who had returned in the early hours of the morning, "only reconnoitered the road from Sulphur Springs toward Culpeper [Court House]," and he did not know "what cavalry is on the Brandy Station or Stevensburg roads" farther to the east. In his history of the 3rd Pennsylvania Cavalry, Capt. William Brooke Rawle, succinctly described Duffié's mission:

---

74 *New York Times*, June 7, 1863.

75 McDonald, *Hotchkiss' Diary*, 149; Gottfried, *Roads to Gettysburg*, 22, 24; Neil Hunter Raiford, *The 4th North Carolina Cavalry* (Jefferson, NC, 2003), 4; Harrell, *The 2nd North Carolina Cavalry*, 110. For the location of Summerville and Raccoon Fords of the Rapidan River, see OR *Atlas*, Plate 100, 1.

76 Pleasonton to S. Williams, Halleck to Hooker, June 7, 1863, *OR* 27, pt. 3, 25-26.

At 4 o'clock on the morning of the 6th the Second Cavalry Division went on a reconnaissance in force, by way of Warrenton [and] Sulphur Springs, crossed the river there, and marched to Jefferson. After finding that the enemy was not there in force—Captain [Walter S.] Newhall's squadron in the advance only having had a little skirmish, capturing one man and losing one horse—we returned to camp, reaching there at 1:30 o'clock the same night.[77]

From this account and from what Duffié reported to Buford, evidently the reconnoitering force did not display enough initiative in searching the region for Stuart's cavalry brigades. Pleasonton, backhandedly criticizing Duffié, emphasized to army headquarters that the bulk of the enemy cavalry were reported to be on the Brandy Station and Stevensburg Roads. But if Pleasonton knew that the enemy was on those roads, it is curious why he did not instruct Duffié to observe those areas, rather than limiting his "demonstration" to the Sulphur Springs Road.[78]

Intelligence Officers Send Reports

Since Lee served as his own intelligence officer, and, unlike his counterpart Hooker, had no intermediary between him and the president, he wrote a lengthy summation of recent events to President Davis—much like Sharpe's reports to Union army headquarters. Lee described the activities of the armies on both sides of the river in detail. The enemy "appears to be extending up the Rappahannock from Fredericksburg," he said, and correctly noted the Union cavalry "massed along the line of the railway from Catlett's [Station] to Bealeton." He also located what he referred to as "Stoneman's" cavalry headquarters—Lee apparently was not aware that Pleasonton had replaced Stoneman—at Dr. Bailey Shumate's house on Cedar Run about a mile south of Catlett's Station.[79]

If he could create "apprehension for the safety of their right flank & the Potomac," Lee told Davis, this would force the enemy to bring up troops from

---

77 Ibid., 27; Rawle, *Third Pennsylvania Cavalry*, 245.

78 Pleasonton to S. Williams, June 7, 1863, *OR* 27, pt. 3, 27.

79 Lee to Davis, June 7, 1863, in Dowdey, *The Wartime Papers*, 502-03. The source of this information was undoubtedly Stuart's cavalry and Mosby's Rangers conducting forays into the countryside north of the river, and questioning captured enemy soldiers and local citizens about Union army activities.

the south as reinforcements. However, Lee believed that he could only gain the advantage if he had a large force, since "their army by all accounts is represented as very large." Lee was obviously lobbying the president for the transfer of troops from other regions to the Army of Northern Virginia.[80]

That same day, Sharpe wrote to Butterfield to call Hooker's "serious attention" to "the recent intelligence from the direction of Culpeper [Court House]." Having learned about the Confederate army's activities from a variety of sources, the BMI, just as Lee had updated the situation for President Davis that day, was prepared to proffer a follow-up to the extensive report it had submitted to Hooker on May 27.[81]

Sharpe reminded Hooker that he previously reported Stuart's "extraordinary exertions" to place his cavalry on a more effective footing. Sharpe believed that Stuart's original three brigades had been recruited from the previous estimate of 4,700 to a current figure of 7,500. The BMI chief went on to say that two brigades of cavalry "from the direction of North Carolina" perhaps numbering as many as 3,000, as well as Jones' brigade of at least 1,600, had reinforced Lee's cavalry division.[82]

Sharpe's estimates credited Stuart with a total force of 12,900 men, considerably lower than the previously reported and widely bruited-about 20,000 figure. However, Stuart's adjutant Henry McClellan listed a total of 9,536 for all five cavalry brigades based on returns for May 31, 1863—still an overestimate by the Union of nearly 3,400 men.[83]

Sharpe mentioned McEntee's report of Stuart's grand review near Culpeper Court House on June 5, and the observers' belief that 20,000 cavalrymen had participated, more than double the actual number. Stuart's chief engineer, W. W. Blackford, explained the tendency to inflate the number of cavalry. In effect, he said, appearances are deceiving: "It must be borne in

80 Ibid., 503. Lee specifically requested that two of his brigades (those under Cooke and Jenkins of Pickett's division) "be directed to follow me as soon as you think it safe for them to do so."

81 Sharpe to Butterfield, June 7, 1863, RG 393, NA. For Sharpe's report dated May 27, see *OR* 25, pt. 2, 528.

82 Ibid. It was two *regiments* that came from North Carolina, and they numbered less than 1,000. Sharpe reiterated inaccurately that some 800 infantry from Hood's division had been mounted and assigned to Stuart.

83 Ibid.; McClellan, *Stuart's Cavalry*, 293.

mind that cavalry show much larger than infantry, and . . . mounted men produced the effect of at least three times their number of infantry."[84]

Sharpe thought that Stuart holding a review "would seem to show that the preparations for the expedition on which the force is to be sent are near complete." The BMI chief further suggested "a force of the enemy's cavalry not less than 12,000 and possibly 15,000 men strong [were] on the eve of making the most important expedition ever attempted in this country."[85]

Sharpe conjectured that, upon the cavalry's departure, "there are strong indications that the enemy's entire infantry will fall back upon Richmond and thence reinforce their armies in the West." What the "strong indications" were, he did not say. Without specifying supporting data, he simply added that this information had been compiled from the "various sources of our Bureau of [Military] Information."[86]

Hooker added an endorsement and sent Sharpe's report, not to his immediate commander, Halleck, but directly to President Lincoln:

> The above is respectfully forwarded for information of Head Quarters. I need not say I consider it reliable, except perhaps in regard to the numbers of the force which may be overestimated.

> I have no doubt that an extended raid is in contemplation; for this reason it was my great desire to bust it up before it was fairly underway. All of my cavalry force will be in this vicinity tonight strengthened by as many infantry as I can spare.[87]

Sharpe's report overestimated the size of Stuart's force and cast doubt on his earlier report that Lee's army would be engaged in a "campaign of long marches and hard fighting," and were "about to move forward upon or above our right flank." It nonetheless reinforced Hooker's desire to attack Stuart's cavalry before it had the opportunity to leave the area and cause problems

---

84 Sharpe to Butterfield, June 7, 1863, RG 393, NA; Blackford, *War Years*, 212.

85 Sharpe to Butterfield, June 7, 1863, RG 393, NA.

86 Ibid. Sharpe may have been influenced by the scout John Skinker's conclusion in his report of June 3, not based on evidence but on his "impression," that Lee would move "southward" with a part of his army rather than towards the Shenandoah Valley. Skinker to Sharpe, June 3, 1863, RG 393, NA.

87 Sharpe to Butterfield, June 7, 1863, RG 393. Hooker added a hand-written note addressed to Lincoln at the end of Sharpe's report. Although this message was likely transmitted in some form to the White House, it is not included in the *Official Records*.

behind Union lines—even though Stuart's primary responsibility in Lee's overall plan was to screen the army during its march northward.[88]

A deserter from the 22nd North Carolina of A. P. Hill's corps who had recently arrived inside Union lines confirmed what the BMI believed to be the locations of Hill's three divisions on the south side of the Rappahannock. The deserter also alerted his inquisitors to the presence of a "masked" or hidden battery of 20 pieces near Hamilton's Crossing, which helped explain why the enemy had only one line of battle without reserves in that area.[89]

As promised, Sharpe augmented McEntee's BMI team with additional scouts. One was Ernest Yager, a civilian who had been the principal guide for Heintzelman and came highly recommended. McEntee sent Yager across the river to scout in the direction of Culpeper Court House; the spy George Smith was also attempting to get across.[90]

Gathering Information in Disguise

The back and forth between Meade and Butterfield about sending troops to the other side of the river continued. The chief of staff explained that Hooker wanted to find out what enemy troops were at Banks' Ford "by any stratagem" without bringing on a fight. At the same time, Hooker did not want Meade's "forces there known," implying he did not want the enemy to learn about Meade's presence, or anything about the size and location of his forces.[91]

In response to this request from army headquarters, officers of the 146th New York, a V Corps regiment, went to the river bank dressed as enlisted men and talked with a couple of Rebel pickets separately. Both said that Hill's "division" occupied the opposite bank, and five regiments of Fitz Lee's cavalry were serving as pickets. The chatty pickets placed Longstreet's corps "above Hill towards Kelly's Ford." But they may not have been aware or were disguising the fact that McLaws' division, the only one of Longstreet's corps in

---

88 For Sharpe's earlier report, see Sharpe to Williams, May 27, 1863, OR 25, pt. 2, 528.

89 Sharpe to [Hooker], June 7, 1863, RG 393, NA.

90 McEntee to Sharpe, July 7, 1863, ibid.; Fishel, *The Secret War*, 292. McEntee informed Sharpe that he had nothing new to report but was expecting to hear from one of his scouting parties soon.

91 OR 27, pt. 3, 24.

the area, had withdrawn from the river on June 3 and was marching toward Culpeper.

The Rebel pickets also told the disguised V Corps officers that they were anticipating the Union army to attack across the river, and that Lee's army was "stronger than at Chancellorsville," meaning it had been reinforced. The pickets declined to answer any questions about artillery positions but did say that General Lee was located "towards Fredericksburg"—another misleading bit of information, because Lee had arrived in Culpeper Court House that morning. The report continued: "If [the enemy] are sending any troops up the river, they did not know of it, & none had been sent to Vicksburgh." If anything, this report would have further confused army headquarters about Lee's intentions and the whereabouts of his army.[92]

Lee Instructs Valley Forces

Lee's first major objective, once the planned invasion got underway two days hence, was to have Ewell's corps move into the Shenandoah Valley as stealthily as possible and eliminate the strong Union outpost at Winchester. This would not only open Lee's lines of supply and communications through the Valley, but it would relieve the local populace from what Lee considered the draconian rule of the outpost's commander, Maj. Gen. Robert Milroy. In addition, the intelligence-minded army commander instructed Imboden's cavalry brigade to cooperate with Ewell's corps when it moved into the Valley, providing "him any information that you may deem important, and comply with any requisition on his part."[93]

Lee further ordered Imboden, located in Western Virginia, to "attract the enemy's attention" in order to detain Union forces located at New Creek, Cumberland, Cacapon, and other places in that area. He was to destroy bridges

---

92 Kenner Garrard to Fred T. Locke, June 7, 1863, RG 393, NA. The pickets correctly identified Fitz Lee's cavalry regiments as the 1st, 2nd, 3rd, 4th, and 5th Virginia. However, since four of these regiments were at that time with Stuart in the vicinity of Brandy Station (only the 4th Virginia was on picket duty in this area), these men were either ill-informed or deliberately misleading their questioners. Stiles, *4th Virginia Cavalry*, 27-28.

93 Lee to Imboden, June 7, 1863, *OR* 27, pt. 3, 865.

to prevent the transfer of Union forces to Martinsburg—another of Lee's targets.[94]

Albert Jenkins, commanding a cavalry brigade in the Shenandoah Valley, was next on the list to receive instructions. Lee ordered Jenkins to have his brigade prepared for active service and concentrated at or near Strasburg or Front Royal by June 10 to be able to cooperate "with a force of infantry"—which, although Lee did not specify, would be Ewell's corps marching northwestward to that place. Lee also emphasized that Jenkins was to send him "all the information you have about the position and strength of the enemy at Winchester, Martinsburg, Charlestown, Berryville, and any other point they may be."[95]

Lee was also concerned about securing his supply point at Staunton in the Valley, the closest location to the invasion route served by a railroad. So he wrote to Maj. Gen. Sam Jones, the commander of the department of West Virginia asking him to scout the area around Lewisburg and Huntonsville to ensure that the enemy was not planning a "hostile expedition" in Staunton's direction. The loss of that place would hamper Lee's ability to receive sick and wounded convalescents returning to the army by rail, and delay, if not prevent, receiving ammunition supplies for sustained operations in the North.[96]

Preparations for Surprise Attack

Butterfield informed Pleasonton that Brigadier Generals Ames and David A. Russell would each lead 1,500 infantry in support of the cavalry attack across the river. Later Butterfield sent Hooker's instructions that recommended, based on the "most reliable information at these headquarters," that the attack force cross the river at Beverly and Kelly's Fords and "march directly on Culpeper . . . to disperse and destroy the rebel force assembled in the vicinity . . . and destroy his trains and supplies . . . to the utmost of your ability." In fact, Stuart's five cavalry brigades were located a few miles to the northeast near Brandy Station,

---

94 Ibid.

95 Lee to Jenkins, ibid., 865-66. Since this information was to come directly to Lee, it would have to travel by courier or perhaps courier relay given the long distance involved. On this same date that Lee sent Jenkins his orders, Gen. Sam Jones informed Lee that he had no troops available to reinforce Jenkins. Lee to Jones, ibid., 866.

96 Lee to Jones, ibid., 866; ibid., pt. 2, 51:730-31; Coddington, *The Gettysburg Campaign*, 186-87.

which a more enterprising reconnaissance by Duffié would have revealed. In issuing these instructions, Hooker ignored Pleasonton's earlier request to allow him "discretion to cross at the best positions as determined by latest information." Pleasonton chose not to contest Hooker's recommendations, and the lack of flexibility would later prove costly to the Union forces.[97]

However, given Sharpe's BMI report plus the information acquired from Rebel pickets that day, Butterfield told Pleasonton that headquarters believed "the enemy has no infantry" at Culpeper. In reality, by June 7, all three of Ewell's divisions and two of Longstreet's divisions (Hood's and McLaws') had arrived in the Culpeper area, over 37,000 infantry.[98]

The undiscovered arrival of a sizable portion of Lee's army at Culpeper, the staging ground for the planned invasion, happened to coincide with a New York *Times* editorial sardonically engaged in a bout of self-criticism. It had been "Too Fast," the *Times* said, in previously publishing a Richmond *Examiner* article proclaiming "in very loud and ferocious language the rebel army was immediately going to assume the offensive." And further predicting that "within the next fortnight the campaign of 1863 will be pretty well decided." The *Times* added, "We have not heard that they have yet opened the campaign, much less closed it triumphantly."[99]

Meade notified Butterfield at 11:30 a.m. that Sykes reported all quiet along the lines. As Butterfield had done in his instructions to General Ames earlier, to maintain the secrecy of Union forces' movement toward the river for the June 9 attack, Adjutant Seth Williams sent instructions for the officers who would be leading infantry units. They would employ counterintelligence procedures by selecting routes that could not be observed by the enemy on the opposite side of the river. And they were to take into custody all citizens, guerrillas, spies, or "wanderers" they encountered along the way to "prevent them from informing against us." Further evidence of cautious security procedures came later in the

97 Butterfield to Pleasonton, June 7, 1863, OR 27, pt. 3, 27; pt. 2, 680; Gottfried, *Maps of Gettysburg*, 5, 7.

98 Butterfield to Pleasonton, June 7, 1863, OR 27, pt. 3, 28; McDonald, *Hotchkiss' Diary*, 149; Gottfried, *Roads to Gettysburg*, 24; Busey and Martin, *Strengths and Losses*, 169-70.

99 *New York Times*, June 7, 1863.

day when Williams sent instructions to Pleasonton by courier, because Hooker feared that the telegraph could too easily be tapped.[100]

By 2 p.m., Pleasonton telegraphed Williams that the "country people" were saying that the Rebels think that the Union army was planning to advance along the Orange and Alexandria Railroad. People were saying also that the enemy's "line of defense" would be at the Rapidan River. Although he did not comment on the credibility of this information, Pleasonton undoubtedly discounted it, since the Rapidan was 15-20 miles below Culpeper Court House, the suspected position of Stuart's cavalry.[101]

At 3 p.m., Hooker alerted Halleck in Washington of his plans to break up a heavy Rebel cavalry force around Culpeper Court House. He would accomplish this by sending all of his cavalry "stiffened" by some 3,000 infantry. He told Halleck the attack would not begin until morning of the 9th, since it required time to get his forces into position. Hooker notified Halleck that Jones' and Robertson's cavalry brigades had reinforced Stuart.[102]

All too aware of the history of Stuart's cavalry riding around McClellan's forces on more than one occasion the previous year, Hooker was concerned about protecting the left rear of his army—especially since he had shifted most, if not all, of his cavalry to his right flank to guard against a movement by Lee's troops in that direction. Hooker contacted Stahel directly at his Fairfax Court House headquarters told him the entire Army of the Potomac was located south of the Occoquan River, and wanted to know whether Stahel's cavalry picketed the Occoquan on both the north and south sides.[103]

Hooker had good cause for concern because Mosby's Rangers continually attacked isolated outposts, supply trains, and scouting parties sent out to capture them. Mosby and his 200 men were the only organized Rebel force operating north of the Rappahannock, and this tiny force tied down 3,400 men of Stahel's cavalry patrolling the roads and guarding facilities to protect the

---

100 Williams to Pleasonton, Williams to Reynolds, June 7, 1863, OR 27, pt. 3, 26, 29. Sykes also had reported that enemy pickets ominously informed V Corps officers that "they had been ordered to fire on all officers," but had not done so to date. Meade to Butterfield, June 7, 1863, ibid., 26.

101 Pleasonton to Williams, June 7, 1863, OR 27, pt. 3, 30; OR Atlas, Plate 43, 7.

102 Hooker to Halleck, June 6, 1863, OR 27, pt. 1, 33.

103 Hooker to Stahel, June 7, 1863, ibid., pt. 3, 29: OR Atlas, Plates 22, 5, 74, 1.

capital at Washington from attack—which inhibited Stahel's direct support to the Army of the Potomac during combat.[104]

That night, Stahel notified his headquarters he would start out the next day at 3 a.m. with 1,600-1,700 men and a battery. He did not mention the objective of his movement, although he had standing orders to reconnoiter the Shenandoah Valley.[105]

While all of this activity was taking place on the Union side of the river, Jeb Stuart established a new headquarters atop Fleetwood Hill overlooking the plain of Brandy Station and began actively planning yet another grand cavalry review. Since Lee had just arrived at Culpeper Court House, Stuart ordered the review in his honor and invited guests for the next day. For Stuart, pomp and circumstance for the moment prevailed over the need for concealment and security in expectation of the army's march northward on June 9.[106]

That evening, Col. Hugh Judson Kilpatrick, having returned from participating in Stoneman's raid through Virginia during the Chancellorsville campaign, socialized with the officers at his cavalry brigade headquarters regaling them with stories of incidents during the raid. As the evening lengthened, Kilpatrick told the men they better get some sleep, because the next day the cavalry corps would be preparing to cross the Rappahannock to "beard the lion in his den."[107]

As the two armies prepared to embark on a long and difficult campaign in which cavalry would play an increasingly important role, the extensive raid into Virginia the previous month had greatly boosted the confidence and perceived ability of the Union cavalrymen. Henry Pyne, 1st New Jersey Cavalry, expressed his fellow cavalrymen's desire for a more glorious role beyond the routine of their normal duties:

104 Mosby, *War Reminiscences*, 152, 157; Mosby, *Stuart's Cavalry*, 5-10. Meanwhile, Signal Officer Hall, still at the Phillips house on the north side of the Rappahannock observing enemy movements, updated the positions of the batteries across the river for II Corps commander Couch in a detailed report. Hall to Couch, June 7, 1863, *OR* 27, pt. 3, 30.

105 Stahel to Taylor, *OR* 27, pt. 3, 31.

106 McClellan, *Stuart's Cavalry*, 261; Blackford, *War Years*, 212; Trout, *In the Saddle with Stuart*, 52-53.

107 N. D. Preston, *History of the Tenth Regiment of Cavalry, New York State Volunteers* (New York, 1892), 82 (quoted); Tobie, *First Maine Cavalry*, 146.

[T]hat a great moral effect was produced by the independent manoeuvre of the mounted troops is undeniable. . . . . For the first time the cavalry found themselves made useful by their general, and treated as something better than military watchmen for the army. They saw that the long desired time had come when they would be permitted to gain honor and reputation, and . . . strike a blow for the cause of the nation and the credit of their commanders. It gave our troopers self-respect, and obliged the enemy to respect them; and was thus a fitting inauguration of that campaign.[108]

Coincidentally Lee and Hooker had chosen the same date, June 9, to launch an offensive. Lee's army was to begin its march northward, while a combined force of Federal cavalry and infantry was preparing to attack across the Rappahannock. Although operating with flawed information about the location and composition of Lee's forces, Hooker would have the advantage of surprise. On the other hand, Lee had successfully moved two of his three infantry corps to the invasion staging area at Culpeper Court House, and with effective picketing along the Rappahannock, had managed to do so undetected. The stage was set for a titanic clash.

---

108 Pyne, *1st New Jersey Cavalry*, 117.

Chapter Six

The Invasion Commences: Struggling to Outwit the Opponent, June 8 to 13

Lee wanted to conceal his march so that he could cross the Blue Ridge
and surprise Milroy in the Shenandoah Valley.

Charles Wells Russell[1]

June 8: Threshold of Invasion:
The Cat and Mouse Game Continues

Colonel Duffié only reconnoitered the road from Sulphur Springs toward Culpeper.
Does not know what cavalry is on the Brandy Station or Stevensburg Road.
Brig. Gen. Alfred Pleasonton[2]

Sharpe responded to McEntee's recent reports about Stuart's cavalry being reinforced that he believed the enemy was about to send out a heavy cavalry expedition, and McEntee should try to give advance notice of its movements—and that he soon would be sending him more men to help with the job. Lee's plan was for Jones' brigade to help Stuart's cavalry create a screen on the east side of the Blue Ridge as the army marched northward behind the mountains.[3]

1 Russell, *Gray Ghost*, 157. Lee confirmed this objective in his report. OR 27, pt. 2, 305-306.

2 Pleasonton to Williams, June 7, 1863, OR 27, pt. 3, 27.

3 OR 27, pt. 2, 687, pt. 3, 35; Mark Nesbitt, *35 Days to Gettysburg* (Mechanicsburg, PA, 1992), 25; Myers, *White's Battalion*, 180; Luvaas, *Lee: A General without Intelligence*, 120; McClellan, *Stuart's Cavalry*, 261; Blackford, *War Years*, 206.

On this morning described by one soldier as "fine" but "cool" for that time of year, the commanding generals of the two armies endeavored to learn more about the opposing forces. As Buford indicated in his message to Butterfield the previous day, Duffié submitted his report on the June 6 expedition south of the Rappahannock. Although he provided more detail than his preliminary account, the essence of his report had not changed. Encountering little opposition, Duffié had approached within four and a half miles of Culpeper Court House. After detachments returned from a brief reconnaissance to Springfield and Amissville, four miles south and five miles northeast of Jefferson respectively, Duffié led his entire division down the road toward Culpeper Court House. In other words, he had narrowly interpreted his orders to "make a strong demonstration . . . upon the enemy in your front toward Culpeper, and push them as far as possible."[4]

Since Pleasonton's orders lacked specificity, and Duffié did not employ sufficient initiative, this reconnaissance produced precious little useful intelligence. If Duffié had allowed the squadron scouting Springfield to go a few miles farther south, it would have found at least some of Stuart's cavalry brigades clustered around Brandy Station. Instead Duffié had the two Union cavalry squadrons on the flanks rejoin the main force for the trek down the road toward Culpeper Court House.[5]

Once this force passed Rixeyville and crossed the Aestham River, where they captured two Rebel pickets, it arrived at Muddy Run, some five miles north of Culpeper Court House. Here Duffié sent the 1st Massachusetts Cavalry to make a demonstration against Culpeper "in order to oblige the enemy to come out." However, as Duffié readily admitted, this regiment only moved forward about a mile "without meeting any force of the enemy." At this point, Duffié decided that it was getting late and his horses were tired, so he "was obliged to return to camp." Even though this expedition covered no more than 25 miles at its farthest point, Duffié, contrary to his orders, had made no strong demonstration against the Confederates. And because his instructions did not

4   Pleasonton to Buford (quoted), Buford to Butterfield, June 7, 1863, *OR* 27, pt. 3, 10, 24. The location of Springfield is found in Eugene M. Scheel, *Culpeper: A Virginia County's History through 1920* (Orange, VA, 1982), 82-83.

5   *OR* 27, pt. 3, 10, pt. 1, 1049-50.

specify that he was to pinpoint the location of Stuart's cavalry, no intelligence in support of the planned attack on June 9 was obtained.[6]

Duffié filed a report of his "demonstration on Culpeper Court House," stating that his reconnaissance had revealed "no enemy at all between Sulphur Springs and Aestham River." This was not new information, since Buford had already dispelled Hooker's understanding that three of Stuart's cavalry brigades were operating near Jefferson, across the river from Sulphur Springs.[7]

Duffié further reported, "The enemy is picketing Aestham River. His pickets do not allow any citizens to cross, motive for which I could not ascertain. There were two brigades of cavalry at Culpeper [Court House], commanded by Fitzhugh and W. H. F. Lee. Their regiments are very weak."[8]

Duffié provided no evidence to support his statement about the cavalry units at Culpeper Court House, and, in fact, it was inaccurate about the location and misleading about the strength of the units. The brigades of the two Lees had gone to Brandy Station with Stuart and were not at Culpeper Court House; moreover both were fast recruiting their strength as they obtained horses. At the time, Fitz Lee's brigade was picketing the area in which Duffié passed through, and in a minor clash the Yankee cavalry captured one of the Rebels. But Duffié did not identify the prisoner's unit in his report, or whether he was infantry or cavalry. Nor did he provide information about Stuart's other three brigades. BMI officer McEntee had sent another view of the situation on June 6 to Sharpe, stating that a civilian refugee, who came into Union lines from Confederate-held area, said that Stuart's cavalry "are lying between Brandy [Station] & Culpeper [Court House]."[9]

Duffié also reported "two companies of infantry" at Culpeper that "are expected to move in the Shenandoah Valley. The brigade of Fitzhugh Lee is composed as follows: First, Second, Third and Fifth Virginia Cavalry." The statement about the size of the infantry force at Culpeper was dangerously inaccurate, because two Confederate corps (Longstreet and Ewell) were at

6 Duffié to Cohen, n.d. June 1863, *OR* 27, pt. 1, 1050.

7 Ibid., pt. 3, 12.

8 Ibid., pt.1, 1050.

9 Driver, *1st Virginia Cavalry*, 50, 61; Driver, *2nd Virginia Cavalry*, 80-81; Nanzig, *3rd Virginia Cavalry*, 35; Stiles, *4th Virginia Cavalry*, 27, 29; Driver, *5th Virginia Cavalry*, 52; Musick, *6th Virginia Cavalry*, 37-38; Armstrong, *7th Virginia Cavalry*, 52; Robert K. Krick, *9th Virginia Cavalry*, (Lynchburg, VA, 1982), 18; Trout, *In the Saddle With Stuart*, 50-51; McEntee to Sharpe, June 6, 1863, RG 393, NA (quoted).

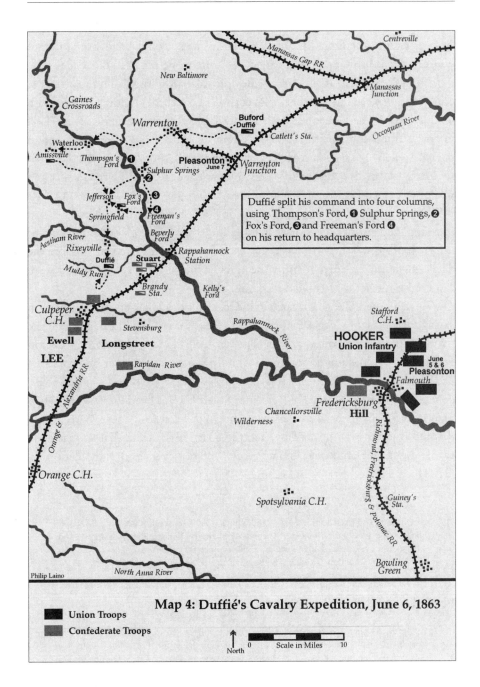

Duffié split his command into four columns, using Thompson's Ford, ❶ Sulphur Springs, ❷ Fox's Ford, ❸ and Freeman's Ford ❹ on his return to headquarters.

Map 4: Duffié's Cavalry Expedition, June 6, 1863

Union Troops

Confederate Troops

North   0   Scale in Miles   10

Culpeper. The mention of only two companies would have brought into question the information of an expected Confederate move to the Valley.[10]

"Jones' brigade is in the Valley at Harrisonburg," Duffié's report continued, "the Sixth, Seventh, Eleventh, and Twelfth Virginia Cavalry, with 400 infantry." The makeup given for Jones' brigade was accurate, if the "400 infantry" refers to the 35th Battalion Virginia Cavalry which often operated as guerrillas than as regular cavalry. However, as a number of sources had reported, Jones's brigade had moved from the Valley to join Stuart's cavalry and was now located near Brandy Station.[11]

Duffié closed by stating his division had sustained no losses and had captured "2 prisoners, 4 horses." Not only was a considerable amount of information in this report inaccurate, its lack of sources cited to support the data—including failure to identify the units from which the two prisoners were captured—further undermined its creditability.[12]

At 6:30 a.m., Pleasonton telegraphed army headquarters from Bealeton saying that the scout Yager had reported to Brig. Gen. David Gregg that "the two Lees [Fitz and Rooney] are at Culpeper [Court House]. Hampton's Legion and almost one thousand infantry at Brandy Station. Artillery at both places." That Fitz Lee and Rooney Lee's brigades were at Culpeper Court House coincides with Duffié's report, but, since Stuart had his headquarters at Brandy Station and none of his brigades were known to be at Culpeper Court House, this information was misleading. However, it did indicate that at least one cavalry brigade, Hampton's, and a force of infantry were at Brandy Station. In fact, Hood's entire division was there.[13]

---

10 Duffié to Cohen, n.d. June 1863, *OR* 27, pt. 1, 1050; Gottfried, *Roads to Gettysburg*, 27; Longacre, *The Cavalry at Gettysburg*, 17. The four regiments mentioned in Fitz Lee's brigade were accurate; however, the 4th Virginia was not included, on its way at the time to rejoin the brigade after being on picket duty farther down river. Stiles, *4th Virginia Cavalry*, 28.

11 Duffié to Cohen, n.d. June 1863, *OR* 27, pt. 1, 1050; Sharpe to Butterfield, June 7, 1863, RG 393, NA; Longacre, *The Cavalry at Gettysburg*, 18; Myers, *The Comanches*, 180; Armstrong, *7th Virginia Cavalry*, 52.

12 Duffié to Cohen, n.d. June 1863, *OR* 27, pt. 1, 1050. The record does not show whether Stuart's brigades or other Rebel units were aware that a large force of Union cavalry was operating behind their lines. Once Duffié approached Culpeper Court House, he was vulnerable to Stuart's circling behind him from his Brandy Station base. The Rebels either had an early-warning breakdown or deliberately ignored the intruders to avoid detection of Lee's infantry near Culpeper Court House. See *OR Atlas*, Plate 23, 4 and 5.

13 Pleasonton to Williams, June 8, 1863, *OR* 27, pt. 3, 32.

As a result of this "demonstration," as it was originally characterized, or "reconnaissance" as Duffié chose to label it in his report, the Union high command would continue to believe that Stuart's cavalry was located at the more distant Culpeper Court House, rather than near Brandy Station, which was closer to the Rappahannock and situated to prevent the two wings of the attacking Union forces from joining together south of the river. Hooker's orders regarding where the troops should cross the river ignored Pleasonton's warning about the limitations of Duffié's findings. Intelligence that the road from Sulpher Springs to within a few miles of Culpeper Court House was open and practically devoid of enemy troops was ignored, and the plan to approach Culpeper Court House from Beverly and Kelly's Fords was retained. This would ensure a surprise was in store for both the Union and Confederate forces on the south side of the Rappahannock.[14]

Continuing his report, Pleasonton added, "Yager says he has reliable information that infantry are being sent to the [Shenandoah] Valley from Lee's army, [and] that there is a force of infantry at Culpeper"—certainly timely and critical news given plans for a Union attack the next day across the river against Culpeper Court House. Pleasonton, however, confused matters by observing that the statement "may be incorrect in some of its particulars." He did not specify which facts he thought questionable.[15]

Hooker now had to digest information that one of Stuart's cavalry brigades was located at Brandy Station rather than Culpeper Court House, that Rebel infantry would be heading toward the Shenandoah Valley, and that an infantry force was at Culpeper Court House. Although the information about the location and intentions of the Rebel infantry was essentially accurate, one of Hooker's intelligence officers would soon challenge the overall credibility of Yager's report.[16]

Notwithstanding any doubts in Pleasonton's mind about the location of the enemy cavalry, he issued orders to Gregg to move his command toward Kelly's Ford in order to be ready to cross the Rappahannock "at daylight in the morning [June 9]." Gregg was instructed to make contact with Buford's command, which would be crossing the river upstream at Beverly Ford, in the

14 Wittenberg, *The Union Cavalry Comes of Age*, 253; Longacre, *The Cavalry at Gettysburg*, 63; OR 27, pt. 3, 27-28.

15 Pleasonton to Williams, June 8, 1863, OR 27, pt. 3, 32.

16 Ibid.

vicinity of Brandy Station, before jointly moving on to attack the cavalry forces believed to be at Culpeper Court House. Pleasonton told Gregg to take precautions not to reveal the presence of his cavalry to the enemy when it approached the river. Henry Pyne of the 1st New Jersey summarized this activity:

> It was on the eighth of June that Gregg's Division broke camp at Warrenton Junction, to march to Kelly's Ford. Arriving there after nightfall, the men, formed in column of battalions, holding their horses during the night, bivouacked without fires or sound of bugles [to maintain security].[17]

With both Ewell's and Longstreet's corps gone north, Lee informed A. P. Hill, whose corps was left behind at Fredericksburg to hold Hooker's forces in place, that he had not yet discovered the "exact position or intention" of the enemy—an indication that Hooker had successfully blocked Rebel civilian informers from crossing to the south side of the river, as well as prevented Lee's cavalry from penetrating Union lines. However, based on Hill's prior reports, Lee mistakenly thought that Hooker's army "cannot be very near Fredericksburg." In fact, except for the cavalry up river along with 3,000 infantry detached for the attack on Culpeper Court House, the entire Union army remained clustered across the Rappahannock from Fredericksburg. Hill's corps of 22,000 faced about 78,000 enemy troops. Greatly outnumbered with an extensive area to defend, Hill worried about protecting his right flank.[18]

He had not heard anything new about the enemy moving further up the Rappahannock, Lee told Hill. So he instructed him to contact Capt. Richard Frayser, operating with his signal party behind Union lines along the Potomac,

---

17 Pleasonton to Gregg, June 8, 1863, *OR* 51, pt. 1, 1047; Pyne, *First New Jersey Cavalry*, 117. The 1st Maine Cavalry's Edward Tobie later wrote "immense clouds of dust [could be seen] across the river, indicating that large forces of the enemy's troops were also in motion." Tobie, *First Maine Cavalry*, 147. Indeed, thousands of Stuart's cavalry were in motion. Colonel John Logan Black, 1st South Carolina, Hampton's brigade, recorded: "On the 8th of June was the memorable Review, 9,000 Calvary [sic] under Stuart were reviewed by Gen'l R.E. Lee . . . we passed in Review, in Columns of Squadrons." Eleanor D. McSwain, ed., *Crumbling Defenses or Memoirs and Reminiscences of John Logan Black* (Macon, GA, 1960), 18.

18 Nesbitt, *Campaign Diaries*, 45; *OR* 27, pt. 3, 369; Taylor, *General Lee*, 181; Busey and Martin, *Strengths and Losses*, 16, 22, 169. Hill ordered Heth to deploy Brig. Gen. J. Johnston Pettigrew's brigade south along the Port Royal Road down to the Massaponax River, a distance of about five miles. Pettigrew's 2,600 troops would constitute a thin shield over that lengthy distance. *OR* 51, pt. 2, 722; *OR Atlas*, Plate 16.

to obtain information about enemy activity in that area as well as at Aquia, the Union main supply base. Because of the earlier report of enemy transports arriving in Aquia Creek, Lee added that Hill should tell Frayser to keep a sharp lookout for them passing up and down the river.[19]

While Lee's operatives were gathering information on the north side of the river, at 9:23 a.m., Capt. John McEntee sent a summary report by telegraph, followed by a more detailed letter to Colonel Sharpe by courier. BMI's civilian spy, George Smith, and two scouts named Carney and Yaller, McEntee reported, had learned from an "intelligent contraband" just recently   at Culpeper Court House that there was a large cavalry force there and "in that neighborhood." The cavalry's horses were being shod and everything put in order to move; quantities of supplies, "shoes, clothing, subsistence and forage," were arriving daily. Also, the cavalry were holding "frequent reviews." The cooperative runaway slave also reported "no infantry in [the] neighborhood]" of the Fields' house, some 12 miles southeast of Culpeper Court House, and that the Rebel "inf[antr]y about Fredericksburg changed camp for sanitary reasons." While much of this information was accurate, two key pieces were not. Lee's infantry was moving away from Fredericksburg, but not for sanitary reasons. And the disposition of Stuart's cavalry had changed. It was now primarily based at Brandy Station, six miles southeast of Culpeper Court House, with detachments spread out farther north on picket duty.[20]

The 5th Virginia was picketing from Amissville on up to and beyond Warrenton. The 3rd Virginia, with their camp at Oak Shade Church, picketed the north side of the Hazel River. Part of the 1st Virginia camped at Rixeyville, and scouted toward Front Royal. Jones' brigade camped west of Beverly Ford with the 6th Virginia assigned to picket duty. Company A defended Beverly Ford.[21]

19 OR 27, pt. 3, 869; Styple, *The Letters of Peter Wellington Alexander*, 145. While Frayser kept watch on the Potomac, Hill's chief signal officer, Capt. Richard H. T. Adams and his party of signalmen, observed the movements of Hooker's army along the Rappahannock. Hill depended on Adams not only for surveillance of the enemy but also for maintaining reliable communications. Robertson, *General A. P. Hill*, 197.

20 McEntee to Sharpe, June 8, 1863, RG 393, NA. For the location of Field's Ford and the Field's house, see *OR Atlas*, Plate 44, 3.

21 Driver, *5th Virginia Cavalry*, 52; Nanzig, *3rd Virginia Cavalry*, 36; Driver, *1st Virginia Cavalry*, 61; Armstrong, *7th Virginia Cavalry*, 52; Musick, *6th Virginia Cavalry*, 38.

Site of the Battle of Brandy Station, overlooking Buford's Knoll
Photo by the author

McEntee was planning to move his base from Warrenton Junction six miles farther south to Bealeton, since the telegraph had been extended there. He reiterated to Sharpe that any additional men he would send to him should be "of a more venturesome character" than those already assigned. Reflecting his semi-independent operational status, McEntee asked Sharpe whether he should go with the Union cavalry if they moved. He had noticed the preparations for a Union cavalry expedition and intimated a move in the near future.[22]

As Pleasonton had also reported to headquarters, the scout Yager, after his reconnaissance across the river, said Lee planned to march to the Shenandoah Valley. However, McEntee had his doubts, because he concluded that Yager had not spent much time over the river. He told Shape he was sending Yager

---

22 McEntee to Sharpe, June 8, 1863, RG 393, NA. McEntee informed Sharpe that a 6th New York cavalryman named D. G. Otto had reported to him. Otto was a valuable addition to the BMI roster of scouts, since he had served as a schoolmaster in the South before the war. Fishel, *Secret War*, 315, 363.

back to headquarters, because "I think him perfectly worthless here." These negative comments could not have enhanced the credibility of Yager's report.[23]

After Jeb Stuart's cavalry review, Lee wrote his wife Mary that the men and horses looked well, and "Stuart was in all his glory." The recurring pomp and circumstance, however, took a toll on the cavalrymen and their mounts scheduled to depart the next day to screen the army's march northward. An unwelcome surprise in the morning would further compound their discomfort. Truth is Stuart had relaxed his vigilance while planning and conducting the review for Lee.[24]

Anticipating the invasion, Stuart sent one of his more daring scouts, Frank Stringfellow, to reconnoiter the fords over the Potomac River east of Harper's Ferry. Once he completed this mission, Stringfellow was to meet the cavalry by June 20 in the vicinity of Salem [now Marshall], Virginia, east of the Blue Ridge Mountains, some 30 miles north of Culpeper Court House. Salem was where Stuart expected to be at that time screening the army's march northward. Having the fords east of Harper's Ferry reconnoitered indicated that he planned crossing the river into Maryland at one of these points.[25]

Ewell's topographical engineer, Jed Hotchkiss, recorded in his journal that he "went to work on a map reaching to the mountains, towards Front Royal, as Gen. Ewell told me that was the route he wished the troops to take tomorrow [June 9]." Ewell's plan to get his corps moving early in the morning would not come off, however, because a Union cavalry attack across the river would take the Confederates by surprise.[26]

23 Fishel, *Secret War*, 430; McEntee to Sharpe, June 8, 1863, RG 393, NA.

24 Lee, *Recollections and Letters*, 95. When Lee attended the cavalry review on June 8, Stuart and his horse were bedecked in flowers. In what turned out to be a prophetically ominous comment, given that the battle of Brandy Station would occur the following day, Lee jocularly told Stuart: "Take care, General Stuart. That is the way [Union] General [John] Pope's horse was adorned when he went to the Battle of [Second] Manassas." Nye, *Here Come the Rebels!*, 49.

25 Brown, *Stringfellow of the Fourth*, 197; Bakeless, *Spies of the Confederacy*, 317. Marshall is 11 miles north of Warrenton on present-day Route 17. *OR Atlas*, plate 22, 5; Fauquier County General Highway Map, Virginia Department of Transportation, 1997.

26 McDonald, *Make Me a Map of the Valley*, 142, 145-46, 149 (quoted); Nesbitt, *35 Days to Gettysburg*, 45; Sparks, *Inside Lincoln's Army*, 256. When General Jackson died from his wounds on May 10, 1863, following the battle at Chancellorsville, Hotchkiss served on Ewell's staff after he took command of the Second Corps on June 1.

June 9: Brandy Station: A Security Breakdown

During the early morning hours, a combined Union cavalry and infantry force quietly crossed the Rappahannock River at Beverly Ford with the spy George Smith guiding the way. Although this force overwhelmed the unsuspecting Confederate pickets in the morning mist, it also aroused a Confederate artillery unit camped a short distance away. Thus was launched the battle of Brandy Station, the largest cavalry clash of the Civil War. After a late start, a second cavalry and infantry force crossed at Kelly's Ford a few miles to the south. After an all-day struggle in which some 18,000 horsemen clashed, Stuart managed to fend off the assault.[27]

Stuart would claim that the attack "was no surprise," and the "enemy's movements were known." But this was an obvious face-saving attempt, because the evidence clearly shows that the Union cavalry caught the Confederates completely off guard when they crossed the river. Major Henry McClellan and Capt. W. W. Blackford of Stuart's staff both confirmed that, in McClellan's words, they were "ignorant of any concentration of the enemy's cavalry" on the other side of the Rappahannock.[28]

Pleasonton knew beforehand from local "country people" that the Confederates suspected a Union advance along the route of the Orange and Alexandria Railroad. But Stuart, focused on the cavalry review for General Lee the previous day, undoubtedly had been distracted from picketing the river crossings effectively. A member of the 35th Battalion Virginia Cavalry made the same point more scornfully: "[W]hile the men, worried out by the military foppery and display (which was Stuart's greatest weakness) of the previous day's

---

27 McEntee to Sharpe, June 6, 1863, RG 393, NA; OR 27, pt. 3, 27-28, 35; Coddington, *The Gettysburg Campaign*, 56-57; Longacre, *The Cavalry at Gettysburg*, 64-66; Nesbitt, *35 Days to Gettysburg*, 49; OR 27, pt. 1, 949-50. McEntee to Sharpe, June 11, 1863, RG 393, NA. For a detailed account of the cavalry battle at Brandy Station, see Patrick Brennan, "Thunder on the Plains of Brandy" *North & South* (April 2002), 5:14-34; (May 2002), 5:32-51. Brennan also discusses intelligence efforts on both sides in connection with the battle.

28 Mitchell, *Stuart's Letters*, 323-25; McClellan, *Stuart's Campaigns*, 262; Blackford, *War Years with Jeb Stuart*, 213. A dispatch from a reporter traveling with the army bluntly stated that "Stuart's pickets were surprised or circumvented at every point where the enemy made the attempt." Styple, *The Letters of Peter Wellington Alexander*, 149.

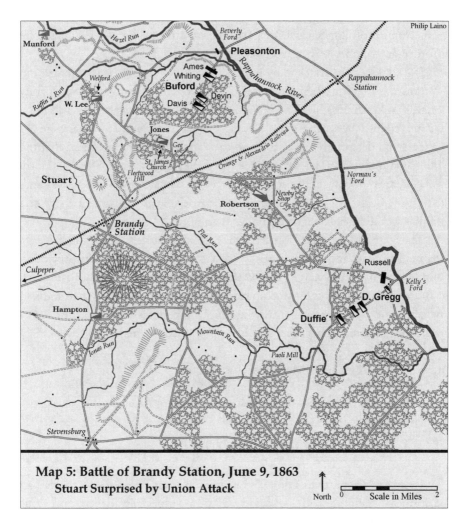

Map 5: Battle of Brandy Station, June 9, 1863
Stuart Surprised by Union Attack

North   0   Scale in Miles   2

review, were yet under their blankets, the enemy sounded for them the reveille from the smoking muzzles of carbines and revolvers."[29]

To maintain secrecy of the movement, Union army headquarters ordered the commanders of 3,000 infantry advancing toward their attack launching positions to implement tight security and counterintelligence procedures. Each commander was ordered to detain any citizen they might encounter "to prevent

29 OR 27, pt. 3, 30; Myers, *The Comanches*, 181.

them from informing against us." The enemy across the river was not to be afforded any opportunity to discover the movement.[30]

Lee adjudged the attack to be an armed reconnaissance to learn the size and position of his army, hence his desire to keep the infantry in the vicinity concealed if at all possible. Lee's assumption was logical since most of his army had moved into the area. He could not know that Pleasonton's orders were "to disperse and destroy the rebel force in the vicinity of Culpeper," and that the Union commander was operating under the belief there were few Rebel infantry in the area. So obviously Pleasonton's target was Stuart's cavalry brigades and, just as obviously, Hooker had accepted Sharpe's latest assessment that Lee's infantry would be heading south rather than north.[31]

The Southern press took Stuart to task after the battle for expending energy on grand reviews, and being surprised and strongly contested by the previously unimposing Yankee cavalry. The *Examiner* editorialized that the surprise attack at Brandy Station on his "puffed up cavalry" resulted from negligence and bad management. Not surprising, however, the Union attack on the day the Rebel invasion was slated to begin temporarily postponed the march northward.[32]

June 10: Ewell's Corps Marches Undetected

> General Ewell left Culpeper Court-House on the 10th. Crossing [the Blue Ridge Mountains and] the Shenandoah [River] near Front Royal, he . . . advanced directly upon Winchester.
>
> Gen. Robert E. Lee[33]

From the perspective of Stuart's cavalrymen, their Union counterparts had performed admirably at Brandy Station—especially given previous engagements. Stuart's adjutant general, Henry McClellan, thought the battle

---

30 *OR* 27, pt. 3, 27, 29.

31 Lee to Stuart, June 9, 1863, Butterfield to Pleasonton, June 7, 1863, *OR* 27, pt. 3, 876, 27-28; Pleasonton to Hooker, June 7, 1863, *OR* 27, pt. 1, 903; Sharpe to Butterfield, June 7, 1863, RG 393, NA.

32 Richmond *Examiner*, June 12, 1863, in Freeman, *Lee's Lieutenants*, 3:1, 19. "If any one asks you about the cavalry fight in Culpeper," sneered the Charleston *Mercury*, "tell [them] we . . . were not whipped, but were disgracefully surprised." And in the same vein several days later: "Officers under Stuart declare that the effort to give him a large command . . . is working great mischief to the cavalry service." Charleston *Mercury*, June 17, July 6, 1863.

33 *OR* 27, pt. 2, 305-06.

"had made the Federal cavalry," and his chief engineer, W. W. Blackford, noted that the previously ineffective Union cavalry "had become much more formidable."[34]

However, Charles Francis Adams, one of Pleasonton's officers, severely criticized his commander's performance at Brandy Station: "I am sure a good cavalry officer would have whipped Stuart out of his boots; but Pleasonton is not and never will be." Adams was right: Pleasonton's questionable performance at this battle was a harbinger of the problems he would cause in the days ahead.[35]

The Union cavalry's Brandy Station-enhanced reputation soon lost some of its luster when it bungled a reconnaissance mission that conceivably could have hindered or delayed, if not averted, Lee's invasion of the North. Pleasonton claimed that Brandy Station successfully broke up Stuart's planned "raid" into the North. Although not planning a raid, Stuart was prevented by the attack from screening Ewell's corps, the vanguard of the march northward, because the Rebel cavalry needed time to refit after the battle. Without a cavalry screen Ewell was left vulnerable to observation and attack en route to the Blue Ridge. Nonetheless, on the day after the battle Lee ordered Ewell's Second Corps to resume its march from the Culpeper Court House area toward the Blue Ridge Mountains and the Valley invasion route.[36]

As tighter enemy picketing began inhibiting the Union scouts and spies crossing the Rappahannock, escaped slaves brought information that Rebel infantry units were passing through Culpeper Court House. Although delayed by a day, Lee apparently was counting on disarray on the Union side of the river after Brandy Station to reduce the risk of Ewell's unprotected movement being discovered. So while Pleasonton's cavalry regrouped along the northern banks of the Rappahannock, Ewell began his march.[37]

Only Lt. Col. Elijah White's 35th Virginia Cavalry Battalion, detached from "Grumble" Jones' brigade, and an escort company of the 39th Battalion Virginia Cavalry accompanied Ewell's corps at the outset. The size of these units, about 250 and 30 men respectively, much too small to screen effectively,

34 McClellan, *Stuart's Cavalry*, 294; Blackford, *War Years*, 213.

35 Adams quoted in Starr, *The Union Cavalry*, I:391.

36 *OR* 27, pt. 1, 3, 49, 903-04, pt. 2, 313; Longacre, *The Cavalry at Gettysburg*, 93.

37 McEntee to Sharpe, June 11, 1863, RG 393, NA; *OR* 27, pt. 2, 305, 440.

Lt. Gen. Richard S. Ewell
Library of Congress

presented a narrow window of opportunity for the Union army, if Pleasonton could manage to exploit it. Jenkins' brigade and Maj. Harry Gilmor's 1st Maryland Cavalry Battalion, who would serve as Ewell's vanguard, awaited him at Cedarville in the Shenandoah Valley just above Front Royal. Lee instructed Jenkins to keep his scouts out to collect information about the strength and position of the enemy's forces at Winchester, Berryville, Martinsburg, and Harper's Ferry, and provide the latest intelligence to Ewell.[38]

Lee also alerted Imboden, who was moving from Romney in western Virginia, to help protect Ewell's left flank during the march by creating a diversion from planned Confederate movements in the Valley. He too was to provide Ewell any intelligence that might assist him.[39]

Lee saw the operations of his cavalry force and Jed Hotchkiss' maps as keys to success of his march northward. He depended on Rebel spies in the North for early warning of reinforcements for Hooker's army, and planned to use Imboden and Jenkins' irregulars to supplement information Stuart gathered. Meanwhile Mosby would maneuver in a way to confuse Union cavalry. Soon after officially organizing Company A, 43rd Battalion Partisan Rangers, Mosby led a force toward the Potomac to create havoc and draw Union troopers in pursuit.[40]

---

38 Myers, *The Comanches*, 187-88; Longacre, *The Cavalry at Gettysburg*, 94; Busey and Martin, *Strengths and Losses*, 251, 278; Dowdey, *The Wartime Papers*, 510; OR *Atlas*, Plate 44, 3.

39 OR 27, pt. 3, 865, 878; Longacre, *Lee's Cavalrymen*, 31, 94, 187. Imboden's biographer discusses the mission to guard Ewell's left but doesn't say anything about providing intelligence. Harold R. Woodward, Jr., *Defender of the Valley: Brigadier General John Daniel Imboden, C.S.A.* (Berryville, VA, 1996), 76, a perfect illustration of the propensity in Civil War historiography to underplay or neglect intelligence operations as critical to strategy and tactics.

40 Williamson, *Mosby's Rangers*, 69; John Scott, *Partisan Life with Col. John S. Mosby* (New York, 1867), 98-99.

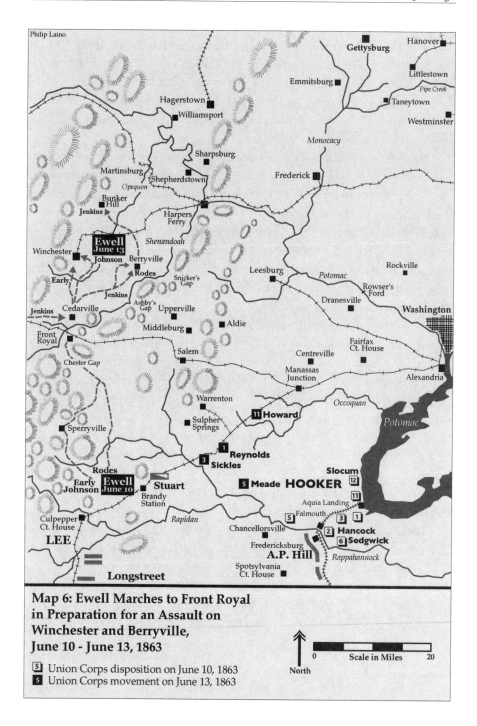

Philip Laino

Gettysburg

Hanover

Emmitsburg

Littlestown

Pipe Creek

Taneytown

Hagerstown

Williamsport

Westminster

Monocacy

Sharpsburg

Martinsburg

Shepherdstown

Frederick

Opequon

Bunker
Hill

Jenkins

Harpers
Ferry

Ewell
June 13

Johnson

Shenandoah

Winchester

Berryville

Leesburg

Potomac

Rockville

Rowser's
Ford

Early

Rodes

Snicker's
Gap

Dranesville

Washington

Jenkins

Ashby's
Gap

Upperville

Cedarville

Aldie

Jenkins

Middleburg

Fairfax
Ct. House

Front
Royal

Salem

Centreville

Alexandria

Chester Gap

Manassas
Junction

Warrenton

Occoquan

Sperryville

Sulpher
Springs

11 Howard

Potomac

1 Reynolds

3 Sickles

Rodes

Slocum **12**

Early
Johnson

Ewell
June 10

Stuart

5 Meade HOOKER

11

Brandy
Station

Aquia Landing

5 Falmouth

3 **1**

Culpepper
Ct. House

Rapidan

Chancellorsville

2 Hancock

LEE

Fredericksburg

6 Sedgwick

A.P. Hill

Rappahannock

Spotsylvania
Ct. House

Longstreet

Map 6: Ewell Marches to Front Royal in Preparation for an Assault on Winchester and Berryville, June 10 - June 13, 1863

5 Union Corps disposition on June 10, 1863
5 Union Corps movement on June 13, 1863

North

0   Scale in Miles   20

Pleasonton's responsibility to help defend against a Rebel crossing of the Rappahannock diverted his attention from discovering Ewell's march to the Valley. Nonetheless, this assignment was more to his liking, since it involved the potential for combat and the resulting recognition. "Have just reviewed my cavalry," he told Hooker enthusiastically. "They are in fine spirits and good condition for another fight."[41]

Meanwhile, Pleasonton learned potentially valuable information from the interrogation of two slaves captured at Brandy Station. One accurately placed Lee, Longstreet, and Ewell at Culpeper Court House, and A. P. Hill at Fredericksburg. He also predicted that Stuart would be unable to operate effectively for some time, because the cavalry's horses were broken down as a result of the Brandy Station battle. The other slave stated that Lee and other generals attended Stuart's cavalry review at Culpeper on June 8, and "said they were going to issue rations for three days, and after that they were to ration themselves up in Pennsylvania."[42]

Given these indicators, Pleasonton should have been on guard to patrol the region leading to the Blue Ridge. If he had carried out his reconnaissance duties properly, it is reasonable to expect he would have discovered Ewell's movement toward the Valley and notified Hooker. His specific orders were to "guard the river above Beverly Ford, and, if a raid is attempted northward, to check and thwart it by the energetic use of your whole force." Fortunately for the Rebels, however, Pleasonton approached his reconnaissance duties with ambivalence. That attitude, along with Stuart's continued presence across the Rappahannock River kept the Union cavalry commander from diligently searching the area. And this in turn decoyed Pleasonton into believing that the rest of the Rebel army remained in place.[43]

The replacement of an entire regiment, the 1st U.S. Cavalry, with only two 3rd Pennsylvania Cavalry companies to patrol the area up river between Warrenton and Sulphur Springs is a perfect example of Pleasonton's misunderstanding of the situation. When the Pennsylvanians spotted enemy cavalry across the Rappahannock, they did not pursue, evidently having no orders to do so. The only way to determine the accuracy of reports that Lee's

---

41 *OR* 27, pt. 3, 45-47, 58-59.

42 *OR* 27, pt. 3, 48-49.

43 Butterfield to Pleasonton, June 11, 1863, *OR* 27, pt. 3, 59; Longacre, *The Cavalry at Gettysburg,* 90.

army was on the move was to cross the river in force, capture prisoners, and question them to learn the enemy's intentions. A few days later, three companies of the 1st Pennsylvania Cavalry received orders to picket in the direction of Sulphur Springs and Waterloo, but nothing about moving on to scout the Shenandoah Valley. In the meantime, recently captured Rebel prisoners revealed to the BMI's McEntee that Jenkins' cavalry brigade was operating in the Shenandoah Valley, which was another indication of a possible Confederate movement in that direction.[44]

Once isolated, Ewell's corps, sandwiched between elements of Hooker's army and Union outposts in the Shenandoah Valley, would have been vulnerable. Halleck had previously advised Hooker to employ a similar strategy. He foresaw great advantages if Lee left part of his forces behind at Fredericksburg while the rest of the army moves toward the Potomac River. He advised Hooker to "cut him in two, and fight his divided forces.[45]

Despite the heightened prestige of the Union cavalry following Brandy Station the previous day, the Union forces had hardly achieved Hooker's objective to "disperse and destroy the rebel force assembled in the vicinity of Culpeper." With his usual posturing—since his casualties were nearly twice those of Stuart—and self-promotion, Pleasonton reported to army headquarters that he was "satisfied their cavalry was crippled yesterday, while mine was not." Pleasonton and his cavalrymen would soon discover how crippled his opponent was when the two forces soon met in Loudoun Valley.[46]

The Union "victory" had not been as much achieved on the battlefield as in the minds of the opposing forces. Brandy Station psychologically lifted the Yankee cavalrymen and upbraided the complacent Rebel horsemen, who had rarely been challenged up to this point in the war.[47]

Per Stuart's orders, Mosby conducted raids against Union communications in northwestern Virginia and across the border into Maryland, successfully

---

44 Rawle, *Third Pennsylvania Cavalry*, 249; Bayard, et. al., *First Regiment Pennsylvania Reserve Cavalry*, 56-57; McEntee to Sharpe, June 10, 1863, RG 393, NA.

45 Halleck to Hooker, June 5, 1863, *OR* 27, pt. 1, 31-32.

46 *OR* 27, pt. 3, 27-28; Longacre, *The Cavalry at Gettysburg*, 45-49, 87; Coddington, *The Gettysburg Campaign*, 65; Brennan, "Thunder on the Plains of Brandy (Part II)", 48-49; O'Neill, *The Cavalry Battles*, 18. Union casualties totaled more than 900, while the Confederates lost just over 500. Faust, *Historical Times Encyclopedia*, 76.

47 McClellan, *The Campaigns of Stuart's Cavalry*, 294. McEntee to Sharpe, June 10, 1863, RG 393, NA; Fishel, *Secret War for the Union*, 292, 430-31.

diverting Union attention while the Confederate army marched northward. Mosby operated with relative impunity despite desperate Union efforts to capture him and was able to send Stuart a continuous stream of information about Yankee activities.[48]

June 11: Pleasonton Ordered to Prevent Lee's Movement Northward

Sensing Pleasonton's reluctance to employ his cavalry in frequent reconnaissance that debilitated both men and horses, Butterfield told him he no longer had to picket the Rappahannock between Kelly and Beverly Fords. This change would free up Pleasonton's entire force to guard the river above Beverly Ford and "to check and thwart" any attempt by Lee's army to move northward.[49]

Pleasonton received orders at noon, specific instructions that should have left no doubt about the action to be taken, to send scouts to the Shenandoah Valley to see if the enemy was moving in that direction. Pleasonton's response, however, was obscure: "I have parties now out, gaining information."[50]

Simultaneously Pleasonton took time to issue orders reorganizing the cavalry into a corps with two divisions. And despite indications of a planned march by the enemy, Pleasonton chose to rest his troops back in their camps near Warrenton Junction, restructure the cavalry organization, make command reassignments, and bask in the glory of Brandy Station by conducting a cavalry review. This distraction, however well earned, prevented the general from concentrating on the job at hand, which was pinpointing the location of Lee's army.[51]

Since Pleasonton was having no success finding Lee, the Department of Washington notified its cavalry commander, Stahel, that doubtless Lee had, for some purpose, moved his army from Hooker's front. Stahel was given orders to

---

48 Mosby, *War Reminiscences*, 157-62; OR 27, pt. 3, 95; Jones, *Gray Ghosts and Rebel Raiders*, 177-80.

49 OR 27, pt. 3, 59-60.

50 Ibid., 59-61. Meade had underscored the need for aggressive reconnaissance in a note to Hooker: "It is very difficult to ascertain anything of the enemy's movements from this side [of the river], as he keeps his forces concealed."

51 OR 27, pt. 3, 58, 64; Longacre, *The Cavalry at Gettysburg*, 90-91; O'Neill, *The Cavalry Battles*, 15, 17.

find out why. "[P]ush a strong reconnaissance into the Shenandoah Valley at once, to acquire any information which may be had of the enemy's whereabouts or intentions."[52]

Aggressive reconnaissance was exactly what McEntee and his BMI scouts and spies were attempting to employ since they arrived in Bealeton, just north of the Rappahannock, from Union headquarters at the end of May. After returning with the Union cavalry from the Brandy Station battle, McEntee sent a steady stream of reports to Sharpe. Obviously something unusual was occurring. For the enemy had infantry pickets all along the river, and none of the scouts could work their way across. [53]

In fact Ewell's three divisions were marching northwestward on two parallel routes, one located just 10 miles south of Sulpher Springs, which sat on the Rappahannock's northern shore some 27 miles southeast of Chester Gap in the Blue Ridge. Fortuitously for Ewell, Mosby's raids across the Potomac into Maryland had generated such consternation in Union ranks that the Department of Washington ill-advisedly diverted Stahel's cavalry to search for Mosby. They would have been better employed helping Pleasonton to locate Lee's army.[54]

June 12: Where Pleasonton Fails, McEntee Succeeds

> Resuming the march on the 10th, we passed by Gaines' Cross-Roads, Flint Hill, and Front Royal, arriving at Cedarville [in the Shenandoah Valley] on the 12th.
> Lt. Gen. Richard Ewell[55]

While Pleasonton's cavalry was failing to discover Ewell's march toward the Blue Ridge, the Rebels closely monitored Hooker's army as it redeployed in a defensive array up river. "[On June 12] movements were discovered up the Rappahannock," Lee wrote the secretary of war, "& pickets report they continued all night."[56]

---

52 OR 27, pt. 3, 18.

53 McEntee to Sharpe, June 10-11, 1863, RG 393, NA.

54 OR 27, pt. 3, 64-66; Gottfried, Roads to Gettysburg, 33-41.

55 OR 27, pt. 2, 440.

56 Dowdey, The Wartime Papers, 513; Gottfried, Roads to Gettysburg, 41-42.

For the Yankees, searching for the enemy was a 24 hour a day job. At 3:00 a.m., Company H, 5th New York Cavalry of Stahel's division left Kettle Run east of Warrenton in the direction of Middleburg and Aldie above Hooker's right flank in pursuit of Mosby. Although they surprised and captured six of his Rangers including Capt. James William Foster, Mosby escaped the desperate grasp of the Union troopers once again.[57]

On this Friday morning, described in the 3rd Pennsylvania Cavalry journal as clear and warm, Hooker suspected that something significant was taking place below the Rappahannock, but was not sure what. At 7:00 a.m., he notified Halleck in Washington that observations made from an airborne balloon determined that "several new rebel camps have made their appearance this morning." Demonstrating his growing anxiety about confronting the enemy, Hooker said he had "no doubt" that "the enemy has been greatly re-enforced."[58]

An hour and a half later, Hooker exhibited his anxiety again in another message to Halleck. "I fear [Pleasonton] will not be able to prevent the rebel cavalry from turning his right." Hooker estimated the Union cavalry strength at 7,500, "while that of the enemy is certainly not less than 10,000." Pleasonton had pickets "beyond Sulphur Springs," Hooker continued and "will, however, do the best he can." Obviously lobbying Halleck for Stahel's division of some 3,500 cavalry to be placed under his command, Hooker failed. There was "no possibility of sending you more cavalry," Halleck told him.[59]

At 8:30 a.m., Hooker ordered Howard to move his XI Corps to Catlett's Station, over 30 miles northwest of its present position near Falmouth. Reynolds had received similar orders, and was already on the road with the I Corps to Bealeton. In view of what he believed to be a shortage of cavalry, the army commander was shifting infantry to the Orange and Alexandria Railroad to cover his right flank against potential enemy movements in that direction.[60]

The Union army commander now turned his attention to a summary report of the current situation he sent at 1:30 p.m. to Department of Virginia

---

57 Captain James Penfield, *The 1863-1864 Diary: 5th New York Volunteer Cavalry, Company H* (Ticonderoga, NY, 1999), 63; Jones, *Ranger Mosby*, 134-35.

58 Hooker to Halleck, June 12, 1863, OR 27, pt. 1, 36.

59 Ibid., 36-37

60 Ibid., pt. 3, 69.

commander Maj. Gen. John Adams Dix at Fort Monroe. Hooker's report further reflected the stress that was beginning to take its toll on him. Lee's army was extended along the Rappahannock from "Hamilton's Crossing to Culpeper," a distance of about 35 miles, Hooker explained. He described the location of Lee's three corps, with A. P. Hill on the right below Fredericksburg, Ewell's corps on Hill's left "reaching to the Rapidan [River]," and Longstreet "beyond that river." Hooker also noted that Stuart had "not less than 10,000 cavalry." While he had Hill's position on target, Hooker was badly informed about Ewell whose corps was, at that moment, passing through Chester Gap into the Shenandoah Valley. Also, Longstreet's entire corps was at Culpeper, not 15 miles farther south below the Rapidan. Hooker then launched into flights of hyperbolic fantasy: "These bodies [enemy corps] have been very much swollen in numbers of late, the enemy's divisions corresponding [in strength] to our corps." He also noted that "Several brigades of D. H. Hill's division in North Carolina are now with Lee." All of which added up to Hooker's decidedly exaggerated conclusion that Lee "has a numerical superiority over me."[61]

Like his predecessor Maj. Gen. George McClellan, Hooker mentally inflated the size of the enemy forces as the time for action drew near. He made these statements with little evidence to support them. On average, Lee's nine divisions had slightly more than half the number of men in each of the seven Union corps, and the BMI's order of battle for Lee's army should have confirmed this fact. While Brig. Gens. Joseph Davis and J. Johnston Pettigrew's brigades came north to join the ANV, two of Pickett's much more experienced brigades were held back to defend Richmond. In addition, Brig. Gen. Junius Daniels' untested brigade joined Lee in exchange for Brig. Gen. Alfred Colquitt's veteran brigade—thereby making the overall exchange more or less a wash, if not a net loss for Lee.[62]

That day, McEntee succinctly alerted Sharpe at BMI headquarters in Falmouth that a contraband captured at Brandy Station revealed that "Ewell's & Jackson's Corps" had passed through Culpeper Court House on June 8 "destined for the [Shenandoah] valley & Maryland." In addition, "Longstreet was then coming up [to Culpeper Court House]," and a "full division [was still]

---

61 *OR* 27, pt. 3, 70.

62 Ibid., pt. 2, 440, 459, 499, 546; Warner, *Generals in Gray*, 67, Gottfried, *Brigades of Gettysburg*, 517; Sears, *Gettysburg*, 49.

at Fredericksburg." Further confirmation came from BMI scout Martin Hogan who "saw another contraband who makes a similar statement." McEntee followed up with a message indicating that the captured contraband stated that Lee was at Culpeper on June 9 and that Ewell had arrived there on June 6. His corps cooked four days rations and "marched morning of 7th." In addition, Longstreet arrived on the 8th, cooked rations, and marched on the 9th. "I think statement reliable," McEntee added.[63]

Implying that he was having trouble getting cooperation from Pleasonton's cavalry, McEntee requested that Sharpe ask Hooker to send an order to Pleasonton to allow McEntee to interrogate deserters coming into the cavalry's lines. He complained that "two came in today, [and were] sent away before I knew of it." He also reassured his BMI chief that his "Scouts are all out [gathering information]."[64]

McEntee had accidentally found the captured slave, whose name was Charley Wright, working as a servant for the Union quartermaster who had "rescued" him from a group of Rebel prisoners. The fact that the man had not been interrogated when captured exemplified McEntee's concern about the cavalry's inefficiency. He had vital information that could have been made available at least two days earlier.[65]

McEntee was with the attacking force on June 9 at Brandy Station and later offered his insight into the problematic working relationship between the BMI and the cavalry. He told Sharpe that Buford only reluctantly agreed for him to accompany the cavalry, and doubted he would be of help. McEntee had to maintain good relations with the cavalry to ensure protection and support for his team. He wanted army headquarters to issue orders permitting him to interrogate all enemy prisoners and deserters, because he did not have enough leverage to garner this himself. He thought the cavalry leaders believed his operation detracted from their credit, especially since he reported to army headquarters through a separate channel.[66]

---

63 McEntee to Sharpe, June 12, 1863, RG 393, NA; Rawle, *Third Pennsylvania Cavalry*, 251; Fishel, *Secret War*, Gottfried, *Roads to Gettysburg*, 33, 40-44.

64 McEntee to Sharpe, June 12, 1863, RG 393, NA.

65 Ibid., June 12 and 13, 1863, RG 393, NA.

66 Ibid.

Pleasonton's message to Hooker as the Brandy Station battle raged is a prime example of this disconnect between the cavalry and the BMI: information from prisoners reported Stuart as having 30,000 cavalry—more than three times his actual strength. This wildly inaccurate figure undoubtedly resulted from questioning of the prisoners by cavalry, perhaps even Pleasonton himself. Typically, the cavalry commander reported this data to headquarters without placing it into more realistic context. Any credence lent to this inflated number would have been a needless restraining factor on Union offensive mindedness. An experienced interrogator would have recognized the absurdity of the figure and framed proper questions to elicit more accurate information.[67]

Given this latest BMI report, Butterfield wired Pleasonton at 3:20 p.m. that Hooker wanted any and all "possible information with regard to enemy's movements." The chief of staff emphasized, "He desires you to lose no opportunity and neglect nothing possible to be done to obtain it." In particular, "Look sharply to your right. By no means allow the enemy to turn it . . . Be watchful, vigilant, and let nothing escape you." Apparently still concerned about a possible cavalry raid rather than an infantry movement, Butterfield cautioned, "Though [Stuart] may be crippled by your gallant attack on the 9th, he will use the more exertion to get you or us at a disadvantage."[68]

At 6:00 p.m., while Ewell was completing his march unmolested through Chester Gap, Pleasonton replied to Butterfield's message, "There is no news of the enemy's movements. I have parties out to the right on the lookout." He then added in typical speculative and vague language: "The information I receive is that [the enemy] will play the defensive until we make a false step." Obviously Pleasonton had not assigned the desired priority to searching for the enemy. He was "inclined to believe" that Lee would not send his cavalry on a raid or make a move until he was certain what Hooker would do. Pleasonton offered no sources for this information. His reports since the battle at Brandy Station reflected offensive rather than defensive intent on the part of the Confederates. Despite his assurances that he would do everything to carry out his Hooker's orders and keep him advised, Pleasonton remained ambivalent about conducting aggressive reconnaissance.[69]

67 *OR* 27, pt. 1, 903.

68 Ibid., pt. 3, 70.

69 Ibid., pt. 2, 440; pt. 3, 70-71.

Since he neglected to say how far "to the right" his scouts were operating, at 7:45 p.m., Hooker told Butterfield to advise Pleasonton that he wanted to know how far beyond Sulphur Springs and in what area of the Shenandoah Valley his scouts were operating. Hooker also wanted Pleasonton to report to him "what you know positively regarding enemy's movements in that direction."[70]

Perhaps to divert attention from his unproductive performance, Pleasonton cooked up an incongruous plot to turn the Rebel partisan ranger John Mosby to the Union side. The cavalry commander queried army quartermaster Brig. Gen. Rufus Ingalls about the amount of money Hooker would be willing to allow as "a bribe to get Mosby's services." In his usual airy manner, Pleasonton elaborated that there "is a chance for him, and just now he could do valuable service in the way of information as well as humbugging the enemy." Army headquarters played it straight in its response. Ingalls wired Pleasonton, "If you think your *scheme* [emphasis added] can succeed in regard to Mosby, do not hesitate as to the matter of money." Pleasonton was advised to use his own judgment and do what is best "for the public interest." Not surprisingly, nothing further was heard from Pleasonton on this subject.[71]

At 10:00 p.m., Pleasonton responded to Butterfield that he had men picketing beyond Waterloo Bridge, a place a few miles above Sulpher Springs but more than 20 miles from Chester Gap leading into the Shenandoah Valley. Pleasonton said his scouts did not see any signs of the enemy, and that they were on the way to Luray and Chester Gaps. The scouts obviously had not penetrated very far on the other side of the Rappahannock, because for the entire day Ewell's corps had been marching through the gap from roads just south of the area the Union scouts were supposedly patrolling.[72]

Apparently frustrated with Pleasonton's inability to grasp the enormity of the situation and failure to provide specific information about the whereabouts of Lee's army, at 10:00 p.m. Hooker took action. He instructed Butterfield to alert I Corps commander Maj. Gen. John Reynolds that he was to assume command of the army's right wing, including the cavalry corps. Reynolds was to make every effort to gather information, especially in view of the absence of specifics about the intentions and movements of the enemy, and he was to

70 Ibid.

71 Ibid., pt. 2, 185; pt. 3, 72.

72 Ibid., pt. 3, 71; Longacre, *The Cavalry at Gettysburg*, 90; Gottfried, *Roads to Gettysburg*, 40; Nye, *Here Come the Rebels!*, 166.

gather this information from "all sources." Whether to attack the enemy and prevent him from crossing the river "to make his intended raid," was a matter Hooker left to Reynolds' own judgment.[73]

The desired information did not arrive in time, and Ewell's corps passed through Chester Gap into the Valley unmolested. The Union cavalry's failure to reconnoiter as far as the Blue Ridge proved detrimental. It permitted Ewell to reach the Shenandoah Valley and meet Jenkins' cavalry brigade at Cedarville. From there he could launch an attack on the unsuspecting Union outpost at Winchester—which Lee regarded as the only major obstacle along the invasion route to Maryland and Pennsylvania.[74]

Ewell's march from Culpeper to the Shenandoah Valley had been so uneventful, the battalion history of the accompanying 35th Virginia Cavalry ignored it completely. And the 16th Virginia Cavalry regimental historian reported the matter routinely: "On June 12 Ewell brought his corps across the mountains and was near Cedarville, three miles above Front Royal. Here Jenkins' [cavalry] brigade joined with Ewell and his II Corps."[75]

To his detriment, Pleasonton disregarded a valuable intelligence resource, virtually ignoring the BMI team operating informally under his command. Although McEntee's team was assigned to collect and interpret information about the disposition and intentions of Lee's forces, Pleasonton chose to treat the BMI operatives more as competitors than collaborators. McEntee complained of the Union cavalry's negligence in handling prisoners, because they sent them to Alexandria for processing without being searched, which gave them the opportunity to destroy important papers.[76]

With the invasion of the North underway and painfully aware of the enemy's greater strength, Lee continued to look for reinforcements. Even while on the march, he would doggedly elicit support from President Davis to

---

73 OR 27, pt. 3, 72-73. The right wing command consisted of the I, III, V, and XI corps of infantry and Pleasonton's cavalry corps.

74 Ibid., pt. 2, 440-42, 459-64; O'Neill, *The Cavalry Battles*, 20-21; Longacre, *The Cavalry at Gettysburg*, 90, 99.

75 Myers, *The Comanches*, 187-88; Dickinson, *16th Virginia Cavalry*, 22.

76 McEntee to Sharpe, June 11 and 12, 1863, RG 393, NA; Fishel, *The Secret War*, 435-36, 448-49. Meanwhile, indications that Lee's forces planned to march to the west and northward in the Shenandoah Valley prompted Halleck, army chief of staff in Washington, to instruct Maj. Gen. Robert H. Milroy, commander of Union forces at Winchester, Virginia, to "immediately take steps to remove your command . . . to Harper's Ferry." OR 27, pt.2, 50-51.

alleviate this disparity. Lee contacted Maj. Gen. Samuel Jones, commanding the Department of Southwestern Virginia, and requested that he provide "a good supply of beef cattle" and "any cavalry which you could spare."[77]

June 13: Pleasonton Falters While Ewell Reaches the Valley

I am directed by General Pleasonton . . . to say that there is no news, excepting rumors that the enemy are moving up to turn our right.
A. J. Alexander[78]

McEntee's report of the previous day that the enemy was marching toward the Blue Ridge, along with other indications, led Hooker to reposition part of his army along the Orange and Alexandria Railroad to defend his army's right flank. A follow-up BMI report on June 13 reinforced the belief the Rebels were moving, but Pleasonton had been unable to verify this by pinpointing the location of Ewell's forces.[79]

It was clear that army headquarters was relying on Pleasonton, however badly he was performing, to keep them informed about the movements of Lee's army. However, at 8:00 a.m., the cavalry commander sent another message to Hooker with outdated and misleading information from the Union spy, George Smith, who reported that morning: "Ewell left Culpeper last Sunday morning [June 7], and Longstreet on Monday [June 8] and Tuesday [June 9], for the [Shenandoah] Valley." Pleasonton claimed to "have [scouting] parties over the river, and expect to know more today." Despite having failed to follow direct orders to accomplish this task, he coolly inquired if it would not be a good idea "for General Stahel to send out [scouts] toward the Valley and see?"[80]

---

77 *OR* 27, pt. 3, 885-86.

78 Alexander to Howard, June 13, 2014, *OR* 27, pt. 3, 86. Alexander was Pleasonton's chief of staff and assistant adjutant general of the Cavalry Corps. The date of this message, June 13, was one day after Ewell's entire corps of over 20,000 men had passed safely through Chester Gap in the Blue Ridge Mountains undetected by Union cavalry. Ibid., pt. 2, 440.

79 McEntee to Sharpe, June 12-13, 1863, RG 393, NA; *OR* 27, pt. 3, 72-73, 87-89.

80 *OR* 27, pt. 2, 185. While it was true that Longstreet and Ewell's divisions had passed through Culpeper, both had halted their corps before moving off in opposite directions. Longstreet returned to his camp in the Culpeper area temporarily on the night of June 9 and early morning of June 10, while Ewell moved westward toward the mountains on June 10. *OR* 27, pt. 2, 440; Gottfried, *Roads to Gettysburg*, 21-22, 29-30.

Butterfield responded an hour later, directing Pleasonton to "[a]scertain speedily which roads the troops passing through Culpeper took—Sperryville, Madison, or Chester Gap." The chief of staff asked the cavalry commander whether he could "push a light reconnaissance or scout to Sperryville?" In a postscript, Butterfield said that it was important to know the truth of the contraband's story and wanted to know whether it was the contraband's story that "McEntee telegraphed to Sharpe?"[81]

At 9:00 a.m., with Ewell's men already across the Blue Ridge and in the Valley, Pleasonton informed Hooker that the "negroes say Ewell took the road to Sperryville," imprecisely adding, "They were all travelling the same way." Therefore, Pleasonton said he was "pushing reconnaissances in that direction." These efforts would bear no fruit, since Sperryville is located on the east side of the mountains while Ewell's corps was on the opposite side. Later in the day, Pleasonton continued to report the absence of any sightings of the enemy and notified headquarters that everything was quiet to the south and west.[82]

Butterfield fired off a question in response to Pleasonton's unhelpful missive. "When will you hear from your scouts?" He expectantly added, "We ought to hear from both routes from Culpeper to Thornton's Gap, Chester Gap, and New Baltimore." Unaware that it was already too late, the chief of staff ordered Pleasonton, "If their columns have passed through Culpeper in that direction, you must post us very quickly when and where they went."[83]

The lack of knowledge of the location and movements of the enemy prompted Hooker at 9:10 a.m. to have Butterfield alert and instruct wing-commander Reynolds that he should "[a]fter receiving all information you can from Pleasonton, post your command in the best position possible to accomplish prevention of enemy's movements, whatever they may be." It is probable, Butterfield added, "that a movement is on foot to turn our right or go into Maryland." The problem being, "When it is settled [regarding the enemy's plans], then we must concentrate at once, one way or the other; as it is, our line is necessarily extended and consequently weak." Butterfield proceeded to state the dilemma that Hooker found himself in at this juncture. "The general's instructions require him to cover Washington and Harper's Ferry; [but to] do

81 Ibid., pt. 3, 80.

82 Ibid., 81-82, 86, 92.

83 Ibid., 81.

this and hold the Fredericksburg line are impossibilities, if the enemy move as last year [into Maryland]." However, Hooker could not abandon this line "on any uncertainty." Thus Butterfield told Reynolds he needed to keep watching at his end of the line.[84]

Unknown to Pleasonton, Jenkins' cavalry, having joined Ewell's forces at Cedarville in the Valley, and infantry from Edward Johnson's division had already engaged Union pickets two miles from Winchester. Leaving little doubt about the direction Lee's army was heading, correspondent Peter W. Alexander wrote to the Savannah Republican, "My next letter may be dated from the top of the Blue Ridge or the lovely valley of the Shenandoah." Pleasonton's attention on this date, however, seemed to be more focused on administrative issues, such as issuing General Orders No. 19 announcing changes and assignments among the staff of his corps.[85]

While Pleasonton floundered in his efforts to determine the movements and objectives of Lee's army, the men in the ranks exuded confidence and anticipation. Captain James H. Kidd, 6th Michigan Cavalry, for example, wrote home: "Lee may make a rapid march up through the Shenandoah Valley, and thence into Pennsylvania or Maryland, but nothing would please the Union army more than to have him make the attempt."[86]

Actually, sending Ewell's corps without a substantial cavalry screen on its march to the mountains was a risky undertaking. Why did Lee do it? Because he had an uncanny ability to read his opponents. He told Seddon on the day after the cavalry battle at Brandy Station, that the Union forces "subsided" to their former lines. When Hooker's forces moved back across the river, Lee surmised that the Union army would be off guard for a sufficient amount of time to allow Ewell to reach the Blue Ridge safely.[87]

84 Ibid.

85 Dickinson, *16th Virginia Cavalry*, 22; Nelson Harris, *17th Virginia Cavalry* (Lynchburg, VA, 1994), 20; McDonald, *Make Me a Map of the Valley*, 151; Styple, *Writing and Fighting*, 150. For General Orders No. 19, see *OR 27*, pt. 3, 97-98.

86 Kidd, *Personal Recollections of a Cavalryman*, 106.

87 Lee to Seddon, June 13, 1863, in Dowdey, *The Wartime Papers*, 513; Luvaas, "Lee at Gettysburg," 122. Lee told Seddon he thought the enemy had been mystified as to the movements of his army until the publication of his dispatch to the War Department about the cavalry fight at Brandy Station on the 9th, along with "comments & assertions" of some of the Richmond newspapers. This reflects Lee's attention to intelligence matters and his concern that

Lee also exploited the significant advantage he held of greater familiarity with the terrain in that part of the country than his opponent. He assigned his topographical engineers the task of making maps of the march route to the Shenandoah Valley, and northward toward the Union outposts in the vicinity of Winchester—targeted, as Lee phrased it, for "the expulsion of the force under General [Robert H.] Milroy.[88]

McEntee had raised the issue of poor coordination between the cavalry and BMI personnel with Sharpe several times. Two deserters from Lee's army had come in the previous day, he reported, and were sent to Pleasonton and then on to Washington before McEntee had a chance to interrogate them. Given an opportunity to interrogate these deserters, McEntee could have corroborated the information derived from other contrabands that Ewell was marching toward the Blue Ridge. By the time Hooker addressed this problem, though, it was already too late.[89]

Lee's invasion plans would have certainly been disrupted, if not terminated, if Pleasonton had discovered Ewell's corps on its march to the Valley, cut it off from the rest of the Confederate forces, and called for infantry reinforcements. By conducting a cavalry review and focusing on administrative matters rather than urgently pursuing his reconnaissance duties, Pleasonton committed the same blunder after the battle of Brandy Station that Stuart was roundly criticized for before the fight. Just as Stuart's actions had consequences, Pleasonton's intelligence gaffe would likewise have devastating results for Union troops at outposts in the Valley.

After receiving additional details of McEntee's interrogations, Hooker ordered his commands to abandon their bases along the Rappahannock River and move the following day toward Washington. McEntee's information evidently was the catalyst that set these forces in motion to pursue Lee and defend the capital. Hooker's immediate objective was to shield Washington

---

Southern newspapers revealed important military information. Dowdey, *The Wartime Papers*, 513.

88 McDonald, *Make Me a Map of the Valley*, 149-51; *OR* 27, pt. 2, 313. Lee was correct about confusion in Union ranks concerning his activities, even though they had read in the Richmond papers that he was on the move. However, he showed no awareness of the intelligence resources operating against his army in the field, namely BMI scouts and spies who also reported his movements. *OR* 27, pt. 3, 42; Luvaas, "Lee at Gettysburg," 122.

89 McEntee to Sharpe, June 13, 1863, RG 393, NA; *OR* 27, pt. 3, 97-98; Longacre, *The Cavalry at Gettysburg*, 168.

from elements of the Rebel army being able to slip through the mountain gaps to attack the Federal capital. Since his principal assignment remained, however, to engage and crush Lee's army, he ordered his forces northward along the Orange and Alexandria Railroad. Slocum's XII Corps was to get on the road that night; the rest of the army would follow the next day.[90]

At 3:20 p.m., Butterfield notified Reynolds, in command of the army's right wing including the I, III, and XI corps, that orders were on the way for his command, as well as Meade's V Corps, to move to and hold the line of the Orange and Alexandria Railroad. Hooker laid out four possible scenarios regarding pursuit of Lee's army: (1) "Should the movement of the enemy develop itself to be toward Maryland, or the Upper Potomac, above Harper's Ferry, it will probably involve our marching on the inner circle [interior lines], and attack them, if opportunity offers." (2) "It is desired particularly to guard against their getting in advance of us, if their movement is that way, and coming in through Manassas Gap, and getting in a measure between this army and Washington." (3) "It may be that they have only intended a cavalry raid, and moved their infantry in the vicinity of Culpeper to support it." (4) "It may be also that they intended their cavalry raid should cover the movement of the bulk of their infantry around our right."[91]

As an indication of the confidence Hooker had in the BMI, he urged his corps commanders to take advantage of its support. Hooker told Reynolds that Colonel Sharpe's BMI assistant, Capt. John McEntee, was operating in the Bealeton-Warrenton vicinity. And Reynolds should have Pleasonton put him in touch with McEntee, because "Information is the thing most desirable, [and] you may act advisedly." Hooker also informed Reynolds that Meade of the V Corps, Birney of III Corps, and Pleasonton "will be directed to communicate all information received by them to you as well as [to army headquarters]."[92]

To ensure reliable communications between the right wing and army headquarters, Hooker ordered that a Signal Corps detachment be assigned to Reynolds, because, he explained, the field telegraph often failed when most

---

90 *OR* 27, pt. 1, 38, 42, pt. 3, 86-91; Fishel, *The Secret War for the Union*, 440-42.

91 Butterfield to Reynolds, Williams to Commanding Officer First Corps, June 13, 1863, *OR* 27, pt. 3, 86-87, 89.

92 Butterfield to Reynolds, June 13, 1863, *OR* 27, pt. 3, 87.

needed. Uncertain about the exact location and intended movements of Lee's army, Hooker, therefore, was preparing for any contingency.[93]

At 6:00 p.m., Pleasonton provided Reynolds with more useless information. "All quiet at Sulphur Springs and Waterloo at 10:30 a.m., when my scouts left. No enemy about," he said. The enemy, of course, would not be "about," since Ewell's corps had crossed the mountains the previous day. Since Sulphur Springs and Waterloo were above the Rappahannock River and well east of the Blue Ridge, it was obvious that Pleasonton had not responded to Hooker's orders to scout into the Shenandoah Valley.[94]

Lee's orders went out on the south side of the river as well for Stuart's cavalry to prepare to move northward and screen the infantry's march. To ensure the way was clear, Fitz Lee sent the 1st Virginia on a scout from Rixeyville up to Jefferson. The 5th Virginia camped near Amissville, while the 4th Virginia moved 10 miles farther northwest to Flint Hill. No one reported contact with the enemy: Pleasonton's patrols had not penetrated south or west of the river.[95]

Stuart planned to take the three brigades of Generals Fitz Lee, Robertson and Col. John R. Chambliss, Jr. (the latter replaced Rooney Lee who was severely wounded at Brandy Station) with him, while leaving Hampton's and Jones brigades behind to keep an eye on the enemy during the movement. Although the rank-and-file cavalrymen normally were not given details about operational plans, some 6th Virginia troopers realized something out of the ordinary was in the offing when they spotted a wagon train carrying pontoons. This was a strong indication that, in all likelihood, they soon would be crossing the Potomac River once again.[96]

Secretary Seddon expressed fears that Richmond would be left poorly defended during the army's invasion of the North and requested that Lee send a cavalry detachment to help defend the city. "I have not half as much [cavalry] as I require" to contend with the enemy's mounted force, Lee protested,

---

93 Ibid.

94 Ibid., 71, 89.

95 Driver, *1st Virginia Cavalry*, 62; Nanzig, *3rd Virginia Cavalry*, 36; Driver, *5th Virginia Cavalry*, 52; Stiles, *4th Virginia Cavalry*, 29.

96 *OR* 27, pt. 2, 687; Musick, *6th Virginia Cavalry*, 41. Stuart also instructed Fitz Lee to leave the 15th Virginia behind to cooperate with A. P. Hill's corps still in the area below Fredericksburg. *OR* 27, pt. 2, 687. For Rooney Lee's wounding at Brandy Station, see *OR* 27, pt. 2, 683.

exaggerating a good deal. If he released any of his cavalry for the protection of the capital, a greater "calamity may befall us than that we wish to avoid."[97]

In reality, Stuart now commanded five brigades of cavalry that outnumbered Pleasonton's force by about 1,000 men. In addition, Lee had some 2,700 cavalrymen available in two independent brigades. It is unlikely that Lee was unaware of his superiority in cavalry strength, since information on this score should have been available from the interrogation of Union cavalry captured during the battle at Brandy Station, and from spies operating in Washington.[98]

97 Lee to Seddon, June 13, 1863, *OR* 27, pt. 3, 886.

98 Busey and Martin, *Regimental Strengths and Losses*, 244. The estimated size of Stuart's five brigades was Fitz Lee, 2,200; Hampton, 2,000; Chambliss, 1,300; Robertson, 1,000; Jones, 1,700; and an artillery battalion, 700; for a total of 8,900. The independent brigades were Jenkins, 1,300, and Imboden, 1,400. The combined force numbered 11,600. French, Imboden's Brigade in the Gettysburg Campaign, 10. Pleasonton's cavalry corps numbered some 8,000. *OR* 27, pt. 1, 906. And he would soon gain about 3,900 additional cavalry from Stahel's former division, increasing his strength to about 11,900 and a slight advantage over Stuart. Longacre, *The Cavalry at Gettysburg*, 161-62; Busey and Martin, Strengths and Losses, 103. This advantage was enhanced to a certain extent by the fact that the Union horsemen were regular army, while the Confederates had a mix of regular and irregular cavalry. French, *Imboden's Brigade*, 9-10.

Chapter Seven

Searching for Lee: June 14 to 16

I was instructed by the commanding general to . . . move [north]
parallel to the Blue Ridge and on Longstreet's right flank.

Maj. Gen. Jeb Stuart[1]

It seems to disclose the intentions of the enemy to make an invasion, and, if so,
it is not in my power to prevent it.

Maj. Gen. Joseph Hooker[2]

June 14: Pleasonton's Lack of Effort Has Serious Consequences

It seemed strange that we should have been left at Winchester to be crushed by Lee's
army, without some word from headquarters . . . and somebody was to blame for such
a blunder.

Capt. James H. Stevenson[3]

With the Union army breaking camp and beginning to march northward, Pleasonton continued to be in the dark on the whereabouts of Lee's army. He sent word to Reynolds, the army's left wing commander, that he had not received any information from his scouts in the vicinity of Thoroughfare Gap in the Bull Run Mountains. He had not because

---

1   Stuart's post-action report, OR 27, pt. 2, 687.

2   Hooker to Lincoln, June 15, 1863, ibid., pt. 1, 43; Hebert, *Fighting Joe Hooker*, 238.

3   Jas. H. Stevenson, *A History of the First New York (Lincoln) Cavalry* (Harrisburg, PA, 1879),
188.

Ewell's corps, the vanguard of Lee's army, was marching beyond the Blue Ridge, about 15 miles farther west of the Bull Run Mountains. So as Hooker moved his headquarters from Falmouth to Dumfries, Virginia, he still knew little about Lee's movements and intentions, a fact that was reflected in his correspondence with Washington. At 1:14 p.m., Lincoln fired off a one-line message to Hooker, "Do you think it possible that 15,000 of Ewell's men can now be at Winchester?"[4]

In the meantime, Pleasonton messaged Stanton and Hooker that a "negro" who just arrived in camp had been at Gaines' Cross-Roads (10 miles southeast of Chester Gap in the Blue Ridge Mountains) the previous night told him that Lee's entire army had passed through that area on Friday, June 12, headed for Harper's Ferry by the following night. From there the plan was to cross into Maryland. While containing elements of truth, because Ewell's corps, not the entire army, had passed through that area on June 12, this information was misleading. Yet, Pleasonton believed it and said so, but he also provided no corroborating evidence.[5]

Pleasonton's message did not arrive at the War Department until 6:05 p.m. Having received a copy, Butterfield, who had arrived with Hooker at Dumfries, notified Reynolds at Warrenton Junction that Ewell's corps was reported to be in front of Winchester. "This is all we know of him."[6]

Late that afternoon, Lincoln sent a message to Hooker with an air of desperation and helplessness. "So far as we can make out here, the enemy have Milroy surrounded at Winchester and Tyler at Martinsburg." These were Union outposts in the Shenandoah Valley with a combined force of some 9,300 troops. "If they could hold out a few days, could you help them?" Lincoln asked. Echoing an earlier proposal to Hooker from Halleck that he consider attacking Lee's army if it was known to be strung out over long distances, Lincoln asked: "If the head of Lee's army is at Martinsburg and the tail of it on the Plank road between Fredericksburg and Chancellorsville, the animal must be very slim somewhere. Could you not break him?"[7]

---

4 Lincoln to Hooker, June 14, 1863, OR 27, pt. 1, 38; pt. 3, 99-100. Once the Army of the Potomac began its march north, the three corps under Reynolds became the left wing of the army.

5 Pleasonton to Stanton & Hooker, June 14, 1863, ibid., pt. 3, 101; OR *Atlas*, Plate 43, 7.

6 Butterfield to Reynolds, June 14, 1863, OR 27, pt. 3, 102.

7 Lincoln to Hooker, June 14, 1863, ibid., pt. 1, 39; pt. 3, 243.

At 7:10 p.m. Hooker unresponsively replied to Lincoln by referring him to Pleasonton's earlier dispatch containing information learned from a captured black. Hooker found himself in this awkward position, because his cavalry commander had disregarded his orders to send scouts into the Shenandoah Valley to search for Lee's army.[8]

Hooker also believed that Stuart's cavalry was with Lee's army, when in fact they were still refitting in the Brandy Station area. The enemy would "not think of crossing the Potomac with 15,000 artillery and infantry," Hooker believed, showing how completely Lee had deceived him by sending Ewell to the Shenandoah Valley without a sizable cavalry escort. But once Ewell crossed into the Valley, Lee had arranged for Jenkins' cavalry brigade to link up with him.[9]

Pleasonton's failure to gain firsthand information about the Rebel army prompted Reynolds to query army headquarters whether outposts in the Shenandoah Valley had sent them information pinpointing the enemy's location. Finally at 7:15 p.m., Pleasonton telegraphed the war office that his cavalry had returned from the Gaines' Crossroads area with information that the Rebels had in fact passed through Chester Gap on June 11-12, and that 15,000 infantry and artillery and a goodly number of cavalry—Longstreet's corps and Stuart's cavalry—still remained at Culpeper. His scouts reported seeing no signs of the enemy at Chester Gap, although they had heard shots fired some distance to the north.[10]

This information gathered by the Union scouts did not specify the enemy's location, and came some 48 hours too late to be of practical value, a critical delay. The shots heard on the 14th were undoubtedly from Ewell's attack on Milroy's outpost at Winchester, which would succumb the following day with great loss. Because Pleasonton did not provide timely information about Lee's movement, he had allowed the enemy to turn the Union right flank undetected, and now Hooker had to make up for lost time in order to protect the capital at Washington.[11]

---

8   Hooker to Lincoln, June 14, 1863, ibid., pt. 1, 39.

9   Butterfield to Pleasonton, June 14, 1863, ibid., pt. 3, 104, 879.

10   Ibid., 101-03. Apparently Pleasonton was responding to an inquiry from the war department; however, this inquiry does not appear in the records. Ewell's report on the campaign verified the route of march and dates the "negro" gave to Pleasonton. OR 27, pt. 2, 440.

11   Ibid., 440-42; Gottfried, *Roads to Gettysburg*, pp.56-59, 68-69.

Having a limited understanding of the primary role of cavalry, Pleasonton often injected unsubstantiated and cavalier statements into his reports. Learning from the "negro" he had reported on earlier the highly unlikely story that "rebel soldiers said they would not fight, except on their own soil," Pleasonton reached the dubious conclusion that the invasion "is not popular with their soldiers." And so he told Secretary Stanton, out of channels with no apparent permission to do so.[12]

It should have been axiomatic for a commander of the cavalry corps that the quickest and surest way to gather information about the enemy was to send a force across the river to capture a few prisoners to question. Doing so he would have certainly learned that Lee's army was on the march. This is exactly what occurred out in the Shenandoah Valley when the 1st New York (Lincoln) Cavalry, operating on the outskirts of Winchester, captured a number of prisoners who "informed us that we were fighting Ewell's Corps, of Lee's army, the whole of which was then on its way to invade Maryland and Pennsylvania." Although the Union cavalrymen found this information difficult to believe, because they had no forewarning, it was "confirmed by some [Rebel] deserters who came in shortly afterwards." But because Ewell's forces had isolated the Union garrison at Winchester, the 1st New York had no means of communicating this information to Washington or Hooker's headquarters.[13]

The men under attack in the Valley knew that someone had blundered in failing to track Lee's army. As a Union regimental historian later wrote: "It appeared that the authorities were not aware that Lee had made such progress in his movements, and supposed they would have plenty of time to notify Milroy before the enemy should make his appearance at the gaps of the Blue Ridge." The high price for this blunder topped 4,000 Union casualties plus the loss of 23 artillery pieces, 300 wagons, 300 horses, and large quantities of stores. Also, according to the Charleston *Mercury*, "About a thousand [contrabands or escaped slaves] were captured at Winchester," all of whom would be returned to slavery.[14]

---

12 Pleasonton to Stanton, June 14, 1863, *OR* 27, pt. 3, 105.

13 Stevenson, *First New York Cavalry*, 188; ibid., 108-09.

14 Stevenson, *First New York Cavalry*, 19. Union losses at Winchester were: 95 killed, 148 wounded, and nearly 4,000 captured. Faust, *Historical Times Encyclopedia*, 835; Charleston *Mercury*, June 23, 1863.

At 8:30 p.m., Hooker informed the president that his army was on the move northward, because he believed Lee's forces were on the march. Hooker acknowledged that "the head of the [enemy] column has had time to reach Winchester." In contrast to his earlier confidence that he had more than enough troops to contend with Lee's army, Hooker now waffled. He claimed that 70-80,000 of the enemy were on the march, while A. P. Hill's 30,000-strong corps remained south of the Rappahannock. Under mounting stress Hooker overestimated the opposition by 30,000 to 40,000 men. PMG Patrick observed that Hooker inflated the size of Lee's army because he was growing fearful of having to face him once again.[15]

As the Union march northward got underway and Hooker's headquarters relocated from Falmouth to Dumfries, some 20 miles to the northeast, signal corps parties deployed strategically along the route toward the capital to promote uniformity and facilitate communication among the seven Union infantry corps. These parties had orders to intercept enemy flag communications and get as close to Lee's army as possible to observe their movements. In addition, the Union cavalry marched north in advance and on the flanks of the army, on the line of the Orange and Alexandria Railroad to Manassas Junction.[16]

But for the surprise attack against Stuart's forces on June 9, Lee's plans for a northern invasion were progressing smoothly. All his intelligence resources—Stuart's cavalry, Mosby's rangers, agents Conrad and Stringfellow, and the espionage networks in the North—were in place and primed to perform their missions.[17]

Individual Confederate commanders also received daily reports of the Union army's activities, and they learned that the enemy had abandoned their position on Stafford Heights at Falmouth. At midnight, Longstreet alerted his three division commanders to prepare for movement "tomorrow." He later wrote, "we hear from day to day of the movements of Hooker's army . . . and [that he] was moving up the Potomac in the direction of Washington. Upon

---

15 Hooker to Lincoln, June 14, 1863, *OR* 27, pt. 1, 39; Busey and Martin, *Regimental Strengths and Losses*, 169; Sparks, *Inside Lincoln's Army*, 261.

16 Brown, *The Signal Corps, U.S.A.*, 357-58; Scheips, "Union Signal Communications," 2-3; Fishel, *Secret War*, 4; Nesbitt, *35 Days to Gettysburg*, 62; Hyndman, *History of a Cavalry Company*, 98.

17 *OR* 27, pt. 2, 321, 692-93; Brown, *Stringfellow of the Fourth*, 181; Russell, *Gray Ghost*, 163-67; Conrad, *A Confederate Spy*, 51; McPherson, *Battle Cry of Freedom*, 649.

receipt of that information, A. P. Hill was ordered to draw off from Fredericksburg and follow the movement of General Ewell [toward the Shenandoah Valley]."[18]

In preparation for screening the infantry's march, Fitz Lee's cavalry brigade moved toward the Rappahannock through Amissville, and made camp near Piedmont and Gaines Cross Roads. Details, including a squadron of the 4th Virginia, reconnoitered toward Jefferson and Waterloo to keep an eye on the enemy.[19]

Lee and his senior commanders considered secrecy to be paramount to the success of the mission, so the men in the ranks were told little about their destination and objectives. Nonetheless, camp scuttlebutt continuously circulated. For example, William L. Wilson, one of Brigadier General Jones' cavalrymen whose unit came from the Shenandoah Valley where Ewell's corps was operating, wrote in his diary: "We hear a great many rumors from the Valley—and our thoughts are always turned thither."[20]

Before beginning his march northward from the Rappahannock, Hill received information obtained from "examination" of a suspected Union spy who was captured coming into Confederate lines two days earlier. He related that the Federal capital was only lightly guarded. Brigadier General J. G. Martin's report stated only "three regiments of Pennsylvania drafted men in and near Washington," totaling some 2,500 men, and that three other Union prisoners confirmed this. If Hill credited this report and passed it on to Lee, who certainly would have considered attacking Washington if the opportunity availed itself, this information was highly misleading. While the figure for the "Pennsylvania drafted men," apparently a reference to the Pennsylvania Reserves stationed in Washington, approximated the actual number of around 2,900 troops, the entire garrison protecting the capital totaled almost 46,000.[21]

As Lee's army marched toward Pennsylvania, Hooker desperately wanted to pinpoint the location of these forces. Although Hooker had assigned Pleasonton this responsibility, he also had the BMI and the signal corps

---

18 OR 27, pt. 3, 888; Longstreet, "Lee's Invasion of Pennsylvania," in *B&L*, 3:249.

19 Driver, *1st Virginia Cavalry*, 62; Driver, *5th Virginia Cavalry*, 52; Stiles, *4th Virginia Cavalry*, 29.

20 Summers, *A Borderland Confederate*, 72.

21 Martin to Hill, June 14, 1863, OR 27, pt. 3, 889; Busey and Martin, *Strengths and Losses*, 57; OR 25, pt. 2, 586.

available to supplement the cavalry's intelligence collection efforts. In this regard, he had a distinct advantage over Lee. Lee, however, would benefit from the foresight of Longstreet who employed an "active, intelligent, enterprising scout" named Henry Thomas Harrison prior to departure from the Rappahannock. Harrison was destined to play a key role in the two armies eventually meeting in battle at Gettysburg and in rescuing Lee from a potentially dangerous situation.[22]

June 15: Pleasonton's Inept Reporting

> In order to mislead [Hooker] as to our intentions, and at the same time protect Hill's corps in its march up the Rappahannock, Longstreet left Culpeper Court-House on the 15th, and, advanced along the eastern side of the Blue Ridge.
> Gen. Robert E. Lee[23]

> I think Stuart will make for the mouth of the Monocacy.
> Brig. Gen. Alfred Pleasonton[24]

While Hooker's infantry headed northward, Pleasonton's cavalry continued to picket the Rappahannock River to defend against an assault on the rear of the withdrawing forces. Following his inability to detect Ewell's march, Pleasonton sent a confusing, inaccurate, and misleading report to army headquarters with a copy to the war department in Washington. A few minutes before 1:00 a.m., he informed Hooker that his scouts arrived back in camp from Chester and Ashby's Gaps, and reported Stuart at Upperville in the Loudoun Valley with 15,000 cavalry. People in that area, "both black and white," he continued, "state that Longstreet is supporting Stuart with 30,000 men." Stuart was moving slowly "in a direction to strike the Potomac between Leesburg and Harper's Ferry." The problem with this information was that Pleasonton had the locations and numbers wrong: although Longstreet's 23,350 (not 30,000) troops began their northward journey from the vicinity of Culpeper that

---

22 Longstreet, *From Manassas to Appomattox*, 324, 333; Longstreet, "Lee's Invasion," in *B&L*, 3:249.

23 Lee's post-action report, *OR* 27, pt. 2, 315.

24 Pleasonton to Butterfield, June 15, 1863, ibid., pt. 3, 117. The mouth of the Monocacy River was on the north side of the Potomac. At the time, Jeb Stuart and his cavalry were still below the Rappahannock River, yet another example of the inaccurate and speculative information that Pleasonton sent Hooker.

Lt. Gen. James Longstreet
Library of Congress

morning, they were still some 40 miles south of Upperville. Moreover, as we have seen, Stuart's cavalry, numbering just under 9,000 (not 15,000), was still in the general vicinity of Brandy Station and would not cross the Rappahannock to screen Longstreet's march until the following day. Also in his report, Pleasonton stated without further comment: "Heavy firing in the direction of Winchester all day long." Pleasonton either was unable to connect his cavalry's failure to detect Ewell's march to the Valley and the fighting at Winchester, or he chose to ignore it.[25]

Having set the stage with this alarmist information, Pleasonton stated that Ewell's corps, with 30,000 men (actually closer to 21,000), was "still south of the Rappahannock." Hooker and his staff must have been nonplussed by Pleasonton's inability to deduce that Ewell's corps was at that moment investing Milroy's outpost in the Valley.[26]

One accurate piece of information Pleasonton offered was that A. P. Hill's corps was still south of the Rappahannock. He added, however, that a prisoner reported "Hill [was] to cross in our rear at Banks' and United States Fords." Either the prisoner was misinformed—Hill's orders would take him along the

---

25 Ibid., 114; pt. 2, 357, 687; Philip Laino, *Gettysburg Campaign Atlas* (Dayton, OH, 2009), 42; Gottfried, *Roads to Gettysburg*, 67. It should be noted that one week earlier, on June 7, the BMI's Sharpe sent Hooker's headquarters a report that estimated Stuart's cavalry division to be 12,000-15,000 strong. Although the actual strength was fewer than 9,000, the combined reports of Pleasonton and Sharpe would have fortified the larger figure in Hooker's mind. Sharpe to Butterfield, June 7, 1863, RG 393, NA; Busey and Martin, *Regimental Strengths*, 244.

26 Pleasonton to Hooker, OR 27, pt. 3, 114; Busey and Martin, *Strengths and Losses*, 169. For Pleasonton's prior reporting on Confederate forces crossing the Blue Ridge into the Shenandoah Valley, see OR 27, pt. 3, 101-03.

same path to the Blue Ridge that Ewell's corps had followed—or he was sent into Union lines to spread false information.[27]

Meanwhile, Stuart ordered Col. Thomas T. Munford, temporarily in charge of Fitz Lee's cavalry brigade, to ride out in advance of Longstreet's corps. However, Longstreet's route would be along the eastern base of the Blue Ridge rather than into the Shenandoah Valley. Munford led Fitz Lee's regiments, that had been camped up river near Amissville, Gaines Cross-Roads, and Piedmont, northward across the Rappahannock. Robertson's and Chambliss' cavalry followed to the east of Longstreet in order to screen his movement, while Hampton's and Jones' brigades stayed behind to guard the Rappahannock and screen Hill marching west from Fredericksburg toward the mountains.[28]

About this time, Stuart reportedly instructed his scout Capt. Thomas Nelson Conrad at his outpost on the Potomac to go to the Federal capital and keep him posted on all the movements of the enemy during the planned invasion of Pennsylvania. Rumors among some Confederates said that a large portion of the forces around Washington had been sent to reinforce Hooker, leaving the capital almost defenseless. After going there, Conrad could verify the validity of this information and the condition of the capital's defenses.[29]

At 2:00 a.m., Major General Stahel, Department of Washington cavalry commander, informed Hooker that he "had sent a strong scouting party to Aldie and vicinity" with orders to report their findings to Howard whose XI Corps was at Centreville, the farthest north of the army. He followed up with another message that he had no further information from Chester Gap than what his cavalry had gathered on June 8. This was significant because Stahel's scouts had been in that vicinity before Ewell's corps marched through, and Pleasonton's scouts had arrived too late to discover this movement. Poor timing and coordination between the two cavalry forces had permitted Lee's vanguard to go unobserved.[30]

27 Pleasonton to Hooker, OR 27, pt. 3, 114. Pleasonton also stated that Hill had a 30,000-man corps, while his actual strength was about 23,000. Busey and Martin, *Strengths and Losses*, 169.

28 OR 27, pt. 3, 887-88; pt. 2, 306, 315, 357, 366, 687; McClellan, *Stuart's Cavalry*, 296; Blackford, *War Years*, 217; Driver, *1st Virginia Cavalry*, 62; Stiles, *4th Virginia Cavalry*, 29; Driver, *5th Virginia Cavalry*, 52; William N. McDonald, *A History of the Laurel Brigade* (Baltimore, MD, 1907), 148; Longacre, *Cavalry at Gettysburg*, 101.

29 Conrad, *A Confederate Spy*, 50-51; OR 25, pt. 2, 509-10.

30 Stahel to Hooker, June 15, 1863, OR 25, pt. 3, 114-15; Laino, *Gettysburg Campaign Atlas*, 42.

Unaware that Jenkins' cavalry, the lead elements of Ewell's corps in the Shenandoah Valley, would splash across the Potomac River into Maryland that morning, Pleasonton, at 6:00 a.m., sent separate messages from his headquarters at Warrenton Junction to Stanton and Hooker. Believing Stuart on his way to conduct a raid in the North, Pleasonton warned that artillery batteries should be placed at the mouth of the Monocacy River on the Potomac. He claimed Stuart would try to cross through the culvert under the canal but offered no evidence to support it. Halleck, thoroughly frustrated with Pleasonton's unsubstantiated reports, dismissed this suggestion since Washington had no batteries to send, and he believed them vulnerable to capture in any event.[31]

At 6:15 a.m., Pleasonton wired Stanton in Washington (with a copy to Hooker) that prisoners captured the previous night stated that "Lee's army has been reinforced from South Carolina, Georgia, and North Carolina," and repeated the erroneous information that Ewell's corps was still "south of the Rappahannock." No explanatory data placed this report into context. True, infantry and cavalry reinforcements had arrived from North Carolina, but in relatively insignificant numbers that were offset by unit detachments. No reinforcements had arrived from South Carolina and Georgia. Using McEntee's BMI personnel to interrogate these prisoners likely would have prevented this information going forward as stated. Pleasonton should also have been aware that planting the idea that troops had arrived from three different states could be interpreted (as indeed it would be) that Lee had been substantially reinforced.[32]

Pleasonton updated Hooker about the situation along the Rappahannock at 6:30 a.m. With his army withdrawing northward from the river, Hooker needed to be concerned about any potential threat to his rear. Reports from Union pickets along the river indicated the enemy in heavy force at Beverly Ford, including artillery, infantry, and cavalry. Only Rebel cavalry protected the other fords, however, and "their pickets are very light" below the Rappahannock Bridge.[33]

---

31 Pleasonton to Stanton, same to Hooker, June 15, 1863, *OR* 27, pt. 3, 115, 117; pt. 2, 442; Dickinson, *16th Virginia Cavalry*, 23.

32 Pleasonton to Stanton, June 15, 1863, *OR* 27, pt. 3, 115.

33 Ibid.

At 7:00 a.m., Lee sent a message to President Davis on Ewell's progress in the Shenandoah Valley, and told him Hill reported the enemy had "nearly all disappeared" across the Rappahannock and was moving northward. Lee's scouts had confirmed the movement, but he was proceeding with caution because "I have got no certain information on that point." Lee also alerted the president that "uncertainty of reports as to threatened expeditions of the enemy in southern Virginia and along the coast of North Carolina . . . has caused delay in the movements of [my] army." Not missing an opportunity to lobby for reinforcements, Lee added that "[t]wo of Pickett's brigades are [still] at Hanover Junction and Richmond, so I am quite weak."[34]

Somewhere between 8:00-9:00 a.m., Union V Corps commander Major General Meade wired right wing commander Reynolds from Manassas Junction that Pleasonton had told him the cavalry would be withdrawn that night from the Rappahannock River area and all but one regiment of the brigade currently at Thoroughfare Gap. It worried Meade that he would have no cavalry screen in his front toward the Rappahannock the next day, especially because Pleasonton believed "a large [enemy] force is left there." Therefore Meade told Reynolds he wanted cavalry "between me and the Rappahannock." Meade told Reynolds that Pleasonton thought the enemy force at and near Fredericksburg "will remain on the defensive." But he was not buying it totally. "Should [the enemy] choose to act otherwise," Meade requested Reynolds, "I would like to know it as soon as possible."[35]

While Stuart was still biding his time below the Rappahannock near Brandy Station, Pleasonton repeated to Butterfield his earlier claim that "Stuart will make for the mouth of the Monocacy [River]." He estimated that Stuart "will have 40 miles to make to-day," and that he (Pleasonton) "would have that [same] distance to-morrow to reach [the] same point." It is unclear how he reached this conclusion, and he provided no evidence.[36]

A message from Butterfield to Halleck in Washington at 10:20 a.m. reported more accurately than Pleasonton, by far. The previous morning, two

---

34 Lee to Davis, June 15, 1863, ibid., pt. 2, 295.

35 Meade to Reynolds, June 15, 1863, ibid., pt. 3, 117. Meade was making this request to Reynolds, the right wing commander, since, in its present location, Pleasonton's cavalry fell under Reynolds' jurisdiction. Butterfield instructed Pleasonton on June 13 to report to Reynolds. Butterfield to Pleasonton, ibid., 82, 85.

36 Pleasonton to Butterfield, June 15, 1863, OR 27, pt. 3, 117.

scouts returned from "the interior, above Fredericksburg," apparently meaning south of the Rappahannock and behind enemy lines. These scouts stated:

1. A. P. Hill with 60 guns and 20,000 men had been left on the heights around Fredericksburg. Also, on June 13, 4,000 men from Hill's corps moved toward Culpeper.

2. General Lee's headquarters was located on the Lacy farm between Brandy Station and Culpeper.

3. Citizens said that the cavalry expedition was intended for Alexandria, while Lee was to go up the (Shenandoah) Valley. However, the citizens now believe the cavalry raid is "now been given up," as the cavalry is divided, and a considerable part of it was still near Brandy Station.

4. The passage of the infantry is traced across the Hazel River.[37]

This report was remarkably on target. Although the number of Hill's guns and strength figures were somewhat understated (rather being vastly overstated as was the norm) and the movement toward Culpeper Court House of one of Hill's divisions (Anderson's) did not occur until the next day, June 14, this was a reasonably clear depiction of what was occurring with Hill's corps.[38]

Also, as the scouts reported, Lee was still in the Brandy Station/Culpeper Court House area at that time. And as they implied, Lee's plan was to use the cover of the Blue Ridge Mountains to march north through the Shenandoah Valley. They were right about the divided cavalry, too. Two brigades under Jenkins and Imboden were in the Shenandoah Valley, and Stuart with five brigades remained in the Brandy Station area. And Ewell's infantry corps, the vanguard of Lee's army, had indeed crossed the Hazel River moving westward toward the Blue Ridge.[39]

Because the message to Halleck came from Butterfield rather than Pleasonton, and the information so starkly contrasted with what the cavalry commander had reported, the scouts were undoubtedly part of Sharpe's BMI.

---

37 Butterfield to Halleck, June 15, 1863, ibid., pt. 1, 41.

38 Ibid.; Gottfried, *Roads to Gettysburg*, 59. Hill's strength was some 23,000, and his corps had about 80 guns. Anderson commanded a division of more than 7,000 men. Busey and Martin, *Strengths and Losses*, 220.

39 Butterfield to Halleck, June 15, 1863, OR 27, pt. 1, 41; pt. 2, 305-06, 440; OR Atlas, Plate 22, 5.

This was further illustration, if any were needed, of Pleasonton's folly in not properly employing McEntee's BMI team of trained intelligence operatives accompanying his horsemen. Evidently Pleasonton's ego did not permit a sharing of responsibility or credit for reports being sent to army headquarters.[40]

Pleasonton's failure to follow his reconnaissance orders and this latest venture in passing along confusing information made Hooker look even worse to the authorities in Washington. He seemed to be overlooking Pleasonton's misadventures in the field. Writing from Washington at 2 p.m., about the same time the Rebel cavalry under Jenkins were crossing the Pennsylvania line heading toward Greencastle, Halleck pointedly reminded Hooker that "Pleasonton's telegrams to you contain all the information we have on the enemy's movements. They are very contradictory." And he added "very unsatisfactory."[41]

From an operational perspective, Halleck accurately notified Hooker that enemy troops were believed to be crossing the Potomac, and "should be pursued." However, the size of the force he used for that purpose had to "depend upon information of the movements or position of the remainder of Lee's army." This was an imperative in Halleck's mind because, "Your army is entirely free to operate as you desire against Lee's army, so long as you *keep his main army from Washington.*"[42]

Further confirmation of Rebels crossing the Potomac arrived at the war department at 5:20 p.m. A report from Harper's Ferry said that Capt. Walker Personius of Schenck's VIII Corps had spotted from the Maryland side of the Potomac River a Confederate baggage train passing up river on the opposite side at Falling Waters sometime before 8:00 a.m. Petronius learned from a refugee that these trains had been passing for two hours. In just 20 minutes, he

---

40 Pleasonton's character flaws and unfitness of command did not go unnoticed by fellow officers. "Poor little pusillanimous Pleasonton," said a cavalry surgeon. "[H]e is about as fit for [cavalry corps commander] as any 2nd lieutenant in the command." Being under his command was "very demoralizing," he continued. Walter S. Newhall, 3rd Pennsylvania Cavalry, quoted in Petruzzi, "The fleeting fame of Alfred Pleasonton," 26.

41 Halleck to Hooker, June 15, 1863, OR 27, pt. 1, 42; pt. 3, 115; Dickinson, *16th Virginia Cavalry*, 23.

42 Halleck to Hooker, June 15, 1863, OR 27, pt. 1, 42. Emphasis added. Although Hooker did not replace Pleasonton, he would begin to monitor his cavalry commander more closely, and issue detailed instructions regarding his responsibilities. See ibid., pt. 3, 171-72, 176-77, 194-95, 210-11, 227-28, 287-88. This monitoring, however, would not bear much fruit in better performance of the cavalry in acquiring the information that Hooker desired.

counted 300 cavalry and 40 wagons, and estimated the advance of this train "must be in Williamsport [Maryland]." He was right: he was observing Jenkins' cavalry brigade that had begun crossing the Potomac via the fords at Williamsport into Maryland that morning.[43]

The Army of the Potomac's and the authorities' in Washington almost total reliance on Pleasonton's cavalry for information to counter Lee's army, and his repeated failures should have been grounds for replacing Pleasonton. Either of the two cavalry division commanders, Brigadier General Buford or Gregg, certainly qualified to take over this post. Yet, no evidence indicates Hooker even considered making a change. The army commander may have boxed himself in when he publicly criticized and essentially forced the ouster of the previous cavalry commander, Maj. Gen. George Stoneman, following the battle of Chancellorsville. According to Provost Marshal Patrick, "Pleasonton stands no higher in the opinion of Hooker than he does in mine." Yet, Hooker had warmly praised Pleasonton for his self-proclaimed heroic actions at Chancellorsville and assigned him to the corps commander's position when Stoneman left. It was a mistake Hooker would undoubtedly find it difficult to admit.[44]

Even though Hooker should have realized the sources that Pleasonton's scouts relied on for the estimates in his report were questionable at best, he latched onto the 100,000-plus figure and accepted it as Lee's strength despite contrary information. Employing the BMI personnel to conduct interrogations and prepare a more accurate enemy order of battle would have avoided this problem. Instead of trained intelligence operatives, Pleasonton forwarded the notoriously unreliable estimates of local inhabitants, which was often based on hearsay, and the word of a single prisoner.[45]

---

43 Woodhull to Schenck, June 15, 1863, ibid., 126; Dickinson, *16th Virginia Cavalry*, 23; Harris, *17th Virginia Cavalry*, 21; Longacre, *The Cavalry at Gettysburg*, 97.

44 For a detailed evaluation of Pleasonton's character and performance, see Petruzzi, "The fleeting fame of Alfred Pleasonton," 22-28. Pleasonton was among the few generals who publicly supported Hooker after Chancellorsville, and his bold, ambitious, and self-aggrandizing demeanor seemed to fit well with the similarly-constituted headquarters clique of Hooker, Butterfield, and Sickles. See Meade, *Life and Letters*, 1:351; Sparks, *Inside Lincoln's Army*, 209, 213, 216; Bill Hyde, ed., *The Union Generals Speak: The Meade Hearings on the Battle of Gettysburg* (Baton Rouge, LA, 2003), 30, 132-34, 239.

45 *OR* 27, pt. 1, 42; pt. 3, 114; McEntee to Sharpe, June 19, 1863, RG 393, NA.

That afternoon, Butterfield queried Hancock, whose corps remained near Aquia as rearguard, whether Pleasonton's cavalry picketing the river had news. Hancock's responded that everything was quiet. Maybe so, but, on the other side, Longstreet's corps was marching westward toward the Blue Ridge. And like Ewell's march five days earlier, this one would also go unobserved by Union eyes.[46]

At 7:30 p.m., Maj. Gen. Robert Schenck in Baltimore, commander of the Middle Department and VIII Corps, tried to disabuse Maj. Gen. Darius Couch, the commander of the Pennsylvania militia in Harrisburg of the idea that Rebels had arrived in Hagerstown. In fact, Jenkins' cavalry had arrived there around noon. Schenck insisted he had heard by telegraph from Frederick that "not a single Confederate soldier had appeared at Williamsport or Shepherdstown." Then he added unnecessarily: "I think your people are in a panic." Couch immediately replied that he had been told that the enemy were indeed in Hagerstown. Schenck, a political general, was again demonstrating the same insensitivity as when he ignored Halleck's directive to have Milroy abandon the outpost at Winchester before Ewell's attack.[47]

General Lee, who remained at Culpeper Court House, awaited additional information from his cavalry commander Jeb Stuart, but, as of 8:30 p.m., he had "received none." In fact there was not much to report. While awaiting orders, Stuart's cavalry performed the tedious job of picketing the Rappahannock River fords to prevent another enemy surprise attack.[48]

But Pleasonton's earlier false alarm about Stuart moving toward the Monococy River set off a rash of activity in the department of Washington. At 8:30 p.m., headquarters ordered the detachment at Poolesville to ensure that the aqueduct at the Monococy "must not be left unguarded." Not everyone was alarmed: a few minutes later, from his headquarters at Fairfax Court-House, Stahel threw more cold water on the claim that Stuart was moving toward the Potomac. If he were, he said, "I would be aware of it."[49]

46 Butterfield to Hancock, June 15, 1863, OR 27, pt. 3, 118.

47 Schenck to Couch, June 15, 1863, ibid., 130; Dickinson, *16th Virginia Cavalry*, 23; Longacre, *The Cavalry at Gettysburg*, 97; Nye, *Here Come the Rebels!*, 137.

48 Lee to Longstreet, June 15, 1863, OR 27, pt. 3, 890; Raiford, *The 4th North Carolina Cavalry*, 4; Musick, *6th Virginia Cavalry*, 41; Armstrong, *7th Virginia Cavalry*, 55.

49 Taylor to Jewett, Stahel to Taylor, June 15, 1863, OR 27, pt. 3, 121.

At 8:30 p.m., Schenck tried to cast further doubt on whether the vanguard of Lee's army actually had crossed the Potomac into Maryland. Schenck repeated what he told Couch, this time to Halleck in Washington, that he had learned that no Rebels had been seen at Williamsport or Shepherdstown. But the novice general failed to furnish a source for or corroboration of his report. Moreover, his information contradicted an earlier eyewitness account Schenck received from one of his officers that enemy cavalry were moving toward Williamsport early that morning. In fact, by 1:00 p.m., Jenkins' cavalry had already arrived in Hagerstown, Maryland.[50]

While Ewell's corps headed down the Shenandoah Valley toward the Potomac River, the new commander at Harper's Ferry, Brig. Gen. Daniel Tyler, decided to consolidate his forces across the Potomac River onto the more defensible Maryland Heights. At the time, Tyler reported he had available some 4,700 troops including nearly 1,000 cavalry. The information he sent to Hooker in the next several days about the movements of Lee's army would have a critical impact on the outcome of the battle that would eventually take place in Pennsylvania.[51]

At 10:50 p.m., Stanton received an alarming report from Couch in Harrisburg that elements of Lee's army had already reached Pennsylvania:

> The enemy are following my pickets 9 miles south of Chambersburg, and apparently moving north in three columns; one to Chambersburg, one to Gettysburg, and the other in the direction of the coal mines. Infantry reported with them.

The report of infantry being with the cavalry in Pennsylvania was incorrect; however, three of General Rodes' infantry brigades had crossed the Potomac near Williamsport late that morning.[52]

---

50 Schenck to Halleck, June 15, 1863, ibid., 126-27; Dickinson, *16th Virginia Cavalry*, 23; Longacre, *The Cavalry at Gettysburg*, 97; Nye, *Here Come the Rebels!*, 137.

51 Tyler's post-action report, OR 27, pt. 2, 21-22; Tyler to Eckert, June 15, 1863, pt. 3, 126; OR *Atlas*, Plate 42, 1. The Harper's Ferry forces were part of Schenck's VIII Corps. For Tyler's orders to assume command at Harper's Ferry, see Piatt to Tyler, June 15, 1863, OR 27, pt. 3, 123-24.

52 Couch to Stanton, June 15, 1863 27, pt. 3, 131. For the location of Rodes' brigades, see Ewell's post-action report, pt. 2, 442. The "enemy" in this case was Jenkins' cavalry that had crossed the Pennsylvania line in mid to late afternoon. Judging from this report, the Rebel cavalry apparently had fanned out in different directions. Jenkins' cavalry began arriving in Chambersburg between 11:00 p.m. and midnight. Dickinson, *16th Virginia Cavalry*, 23; Gottfried, *Roads to Gettysburg*, 69.

After 11:00 p.m., in response to Meade's earlier message of concern, Reynolds said he ordered Pleasonton to provide a cavalry screen for his corps. Aware of his record, Reynolds spelled out Pleasonton's responsibilities plainly: "You must leave pickets in Meade's front. . . . Have it done at once."[53]

June 16: Halleck Urges Hooker to Find Lee's Army

The Union cavalry commander was hardly covering himself in glory, for yet another opportunity to detect the movements of Lee's army was lost. Despite being in the immediate area, Pleasonton's cavalry failed to observe the movement of Longstreet's infantry and Stuart's cavalry. For the second time in less than a week, a major enemy expedition went undetected and unreported to Hooker's headquarters. Stuart later recorded his units crossed the Rappahannock uncontested, because the enemy had left their front during the night. Pleasonton had started moving his headquarters north from Warrenton Junction on the morning of June 15, and his cavalry picketing the river remained there until that night. That they did not observe the Confederate movements meant that they were not scouting far enough north along the river.[54]

That morning, Hooker suggested to Lincoln that it would be best to send nearly all the cavalry into Maryland at once by the most direct route to protect Harper's Ferry and to form a "direct line covering Baltimore and Philadelphia." Halleck threw cold water on the idea, citing lack of reliable information that the enemy had crossed the Potomac in force. The enemy's location was uncertain, he wrote, and the only way to find out was for Hooker to employ his cavalry, adding the little barb that they "should be kept near enough to the enemy to at least be able to tell where he is."[55]

At the same time, Hooker was complaining to Lincoln that his army would have difficulty discovering the enemy's location and intentions as long as Lee continued to deploy "a cloud of cavalry" to screen his army. Hooker concluded

---

53 Reynolds to Meade, June 15, 1863, *OR* 27, pt. 3, 119.

54 Stuart's post-action report, ibid., pt. 2, 687-88; Arnold Blumberg, "Rebel Sabres: Confederate Cavalry Leaders in the Gettysburg Campaign," in *Programs of the Seventh Annual Gettysburg Seminar, High Water Mark: The Army of Northern Virginia in the Gettysburg Campaign* (Gettysburg, PA, 1999), 20-21; Pleasonton to Butterfield, June 15, 1863, *OR* 27, pt. 3, 117.

55 Hooker to Lincoln, Halleck to Hooker, June 16, 1863, *OR* 27, pt. 1, 44-45.

the only way to find Lee was to break through that screen. As will be seen, Pleasonton continued to emphasize combat rather than reconnaissance to discover Lee's whereabouts. As a result, the BMI, by default, would assume the role as the Army of the Potomac's primary intelligence provider.[56]

The president decided to put an end to Hooker's predilection for bypassing Halleck and communicating directly with him. He placed Hooker in strict subordination to the "general-in-chief of all the armies." This move appeared to be a reaction to the dire nature of the enemy threat and a desire to avoid any misunderstanding of orders. But it also reflected Lincoln's own awareness of his lack of expertise as a military strategist as well as his preference for leaving these decisions in the hands of professionals. "I find that the understanding now is that Halleck is running the Marching and Hooker has the role of a Subordinate," Patrick noted in his diary on June 17. The new arrangement did not bode well for the future relationship between the proud Hooker and the stubborn Halleck.[57]

---

56 Hooker to Lincoln, ibid., 45. At the time, June 16, Hooker's cavalry totaled nearly 8,000, while Lee's enhanced cavalry of seven brigades totaled between 13,000 and 14,000. Ibid., pt. 1, 906; Blumberg, "Rebel Sabres," 20-21, 31; Longacre, *The Cavalry at Gettysburg*, 94n98.

57 Lincoln to Hooker, June 16, 1863, *OR* 27, pt. 1, 47; Sparks, *Inside Lincoln's Army*, 260. For Lincoln's views on the responsibility for military strategy, see *OR* 27, pt. 1, 31.

Chapter Eight

Screening the Army from Prying Eyes: June 17 to 21

The objective of the Union cavalry . . . was to penetrate the Confederate cavalry screen that protected the advance of Lee's army into Pennsylvania.

Samuel M. Blackwell, Jr.[1]

[Fitz. Lee's] brigade, moving to Aldie . . . were soon attacked by the enemy's cavalry.

Maj. Gen. Jeb Stuart[2]

June 17: Poor Union Cavalry and BMI Coordination

On searching the [enemy] officers captured yesterday, a quantity of letters and papers were found on their persons [by our cavalry, and, before I could examine them,] were allowed to be blown away as perfectly worthless.

Capt. John McEntee[3]

After initiating the BMI effort to gather information about Lee's movements from a base in Maryland, Hooker directed Pleasonton to determine the location of the Rebel army. He was instructed to place the main body of his command in the vicinity of Aldie, Virginia, and reconnoiter toward Winchester, Berryville, and Harper's Ferry in

---

1 Samuel L. Blackwell, Jr., *The 12th Illinois Cavalry* (Dekalb, IL, 2002), 88.

2 Stuart's post-action report, *OR* 27, pt. 2, 688.

3 McEntee to Sharpe, June 19, 1863, RG 393, NA.

the Shenandoah Valley. But, Hooker cautioned Pleasonton not to advance the main body of his cavalry beyond Leesburg. The commander wanted to ensure the cavalry provided sufficient security for the main army deployed in the area stretching about 15 miles from just south of Aldie on up to Leesburg.[4]

Hooker had planned to cross into Maryland in response to Halleck's message that Harper's Ferry was in danger, but he changed his mind after further consultation with Halleck. "[J]ust as we were striking Tents & preparing to load" for a move to Leesburg and across the river into Maryland, Patrick recorded in his diary on June 17, "we were directed to 'hold on' and not move until further Orders."[5]

Undoubtedly because Pleasonton had previously displayed a distaste for the grueling work of reconnaissance, the Union commander stressed the primary importance of providing information about "where the enemy is, his force, and his movements." Use his cavalry to drive in pickets, if necessary, he told Pleasonton, to acquire this information. In other words, better to suffer casualties, than to lack knowledge of the enemy "as we now seem to be." Hooker was taking no chances that Pleasonton would not receive this message by telegraph or not fully understand it. He also dispatched staff member Capt. Ulric Dahlgren with verbal orders directly to his cavalry chief.[6]

These orders addressed another issue of increasing concern to Hooker. He had learned from Sharpe that the cavalry was not cooperating with McEntee and his assigned scouts and spies. The situation had deteriorated to the point that McEntee sought Hooker's help. He wanted Hooker to order Pleasonton to allow McEntee to interrogate prisoners and deserters. That very day two deserters had arrived but were sent away before he had an opportunity to question them.[7]

Hooker had established the BMI earlier in the year to upgrade the quality of intelligence he needed for his planning. This and the critical nature of the problem at hand—learning the whereabouts of Lee's army—impelled Hooker to send specific guidelines about how the cavalry should work with the BMI. "Captain McEntee, of Colonel Sharpe's department, thoroughly understands

---

4   Williams to Pleasonton, June 17, 1863, *OR* 27, pt. 3, 172.

5   Hebert, *Fighting Joe Hooker*, 239-40; Sparks, *Inside Lincoln's Army*, 260.

6   Williams to Pleasonton, June 17, 1863, *OR* 27, pt. 3, 172.

7   McEntee to Sharpe, June 12, 1863, RG 393, NA.

the whole organization of the rebel army, and is sent out to join you," he wrote. As a result, after Pleasonton examined any prisoners, deserters, or contrabands, "you will give [McEntee] a chance to examine all of them." All information from these sources should be sent to Hooker right away. Nothing was to be left undone "to give the fullest information."[8]

Thus Hooker made it clear to Pleasonton that McEntee was privy to the results of the BMI's analysis of information about the Army of Northern Virginia from a variety of sources, with an emphasis on the interrogation of prisoners and deserters. Based on this analysis, the BMI constructed an organizational table of Lee's army complete with unit designations, subordination, strength, location, and identification of commanders.[9]

Hooker's message to Pleasonton suggests that no one outside the headquarters organization clearly understood the BMI's intelligence mission. Although secrecy was important to safeguard operational methods, the lack of understanding of the BMI's organizational purpose was causing antipathy, especially among the cavalry.[10]

Operational problems with the intelligence function at Army of the Potomac headquarters compounded the problems in the field. Patrick, who was administratively responsible for the BMI, noted that Hooker had treated Sharpe's "Secret Service Department" with indifference and even disrespect, even though it had furnished him with the most astonishingly correct information. He implied that Hooker was ignoring specific intelligence the BMI provided, because he "acts like a man without a plan and is entirely at a loss what to do, or how to match the enemy, or counteract his movements."[11]

Lee in the Shenandoah Valley

> I wish [A. P. Hill's] corps to follow Longstreet as closely as you can . . . take the Sperryville road as far as Woodville, and there turn off for Chester Gap to Front Royal,

8 Williams to Pleasonton, June 17, 1863, *OR* 27, pt. 3, 172. After the Army of the Potomac began moving away from the Rappahannock River on June 14, McEntee had apparently returned from the field to BMI headquarters.

9 For an example and order of battle compiled by the BMI, see Order of Battle of Pickett's Division, n.d. (c. July 3-4, 1863), RG 393, NA; Fishel, *The Secret War*, 318-22.

10 McEntee to Sharpe, June 11, 12, 1863, RG 393, NA; Fishel, *The Secret War*, 435-36, 438-39, 454-55.

11 Sparks, *Inside Lincoln's Army*, 260-61.

and so down the Valley.... *This road will tend to deceive the enemy as to our ultimate destination.*
(emphasis added)

Gen. R. E. Lee[12]

Although General Lee's plans for invasion of the North were unfolding exceptionally well, he took nothing for granted. He constantly reminded his corps commanders of the need to mislead the enemy regarding his operational objectives and to gain the advantage by ferreting out their intentions.

From his headquarters at Markham, Lee expressed concern to Longstreet that he had not heard about Hooker's movements from him or Stuart and could "form no opinion of the best move against him." If a part of the army could have operated east of the mountains, he lamented, it would have served more to confuse the enemy. Lee was obviously confused: he evidently believed that Longstreet's corps had crossed the mountains into the Shenandoah Valley. Longstreet, however, had not yet ordered his three divisions to cross over the Blue Ridge and would not do so until the next day. Lee also instructed Longstreet to circulate false information that the army's advance into Maryland was to attack Harper's Ferry.[13]

Since he left Culpeper, Lee had been traveling with staff members and support troops, including at least one company of Maj. John H. Richardson's 39th Battalion Virginia Cavalry, who served as couriers, scouts, escorts, and guides for the army. The battalion, some 120 officers and men, also had important information gathering duties: scouting enemy positions for proper routes for the army to travel along the line of march.[14]

---

12 Lee to Hill, June 16, 1863, *OR 27*, pt.3, 896.

13 Lee to Longstreet, June 17, 1863, ibid., 900. There is no record of a response to Lee's message from Longstreet, or a change in his operational plan as a result of it. In his report on the Gettysburg campaign, Lee does not refer to a miscommunication between himself and Longstreet but does say: "As [the demonstrations of Ewell in Maryland and Jenkins in Pennsylvania] did not have the effect of causing the Federal Army to leave Virginia, and as it did not seem disposed to advance upon the position held by Longstreet, the latter was withdrawn to the west side of the Shenandoah." Longstreet's campaign report sheds no further light either. Ibid., pt. 2, 306, 357. Nor does Longstreet make reference to Lee's message stating his concerns in his memoir. Longstreet, *From Manassas to Appomattox*, 340-41.

14 Robert J. Driver, Jr. and Kevin C. Ruffner, *1st Battalion Virginia Infantry, 39th Battalion Virginia Cavalry, 24th Battalion Virginia Partisan Rangers* (Lynchburg, VA, 1996), 51-52, 59-60, 67. Lee had assigned Richardson to his staff in June as he prepared to invade the North. The battalion included Capt. Augustus P. Pifer's Company A that probably was detailed to Hill's corps, Capt. William F. Randolph's Company B that served with Ewell's corps, Capt. Samuel B. Brown's Company C, known as "Lee's Body Guard," assigned to Army of Northern Virginia

Another unit Lee acquired prior to the invasion was the 1st Battalion Virginia Infantry, with about 250 officers and men that served as the army's provost guard. Major David B. Bridgford, whom Lee assigned to his staff as acting provost marshal, headed up this unit. Besides standard military police duties, this battalion also interrogated prisoners of war to obtain useful intelligence and submitted reports to Lee.[15]

Upon reaching the vicinity of Winchester, however, Lee assigned Bridgford as post commander and the 1st Battalion as provost guard for the city, relieving the 13th Virginia of Early's division of those duties. The decision to leave the 1st Battalion behind at Winchester now required Lee to rely on provost guard units at the brigade, division, and corps level to interrogate prisoners—meaning he would lack direct control over the process of deriving timely intelligence in a combat situation.[16]

Confusion within the Union High Command

> General Hooker followed [Lee's army] on an interior line . . . but the operations of both armies were so masked by the intervening mountains that neither could obtain positive information of the force and movements of the other.
>
> Maj. Gen. Henry W. Halleck [17]

> I have deemed it prudent to suspend any farther advance of the infantry until I have information that the enemy are in force in the Shenandoah Valley.
>
> Maj. Gen. Joseph Hooker [18]

At Union army headquarters, now located at Fairfax Court House, plans were on hold pending receipt of information regarding Lee's location. That

---

headquarters, and two detachments (later Company D) under Lt. John W. Jackson and Lt. William W. Page that possibly supported Longstreet's corps. Ibid., 51-52.

15 OR 51, pt. 2, 721; Driver, *1st Battalion Virginia Infantry*, 35-36.; Radley, *Rebel Watchdog*, 168, 258.

16 Driver, *1st Battalion Virginia Infantry*, 36; OR 27, pt. 2, 464; ibid., pt. 3, 915. Lee had intended to use troops of the 1st Maryland Infantry Battalion, Brig. Gen. George H. Steuart's brigade of Johnson's division, for provost guard duty but had lost track of them. Evidently there had been miscommunication between Lee and Ewell's corps, because Early had assigned the 13th Virginia as provost guard at Winchester. Coddington, *The Gettysburg Campaign*, 590; Radley, *Rebel Watchdog*, 158, 258.

17 Halleck's post-action report, OR 27, pt. 1, 15.

18 Hooker to Halleck, June 17, 1863, ibid., 50.

Munford came east through the town of Aldie on the Little River Turnpike and confronted
Kilpatrick on the other side of Aldie Gap, east of the Bull Run Mountains
Photo by the author.

night, Hooker informed Pleasonton, "If Lee's army is in rear of his cavalry, we shall move up by forced marches with the infantry." The implication was that Hooker was prepared to engage Lee's army once he had more definitive information.[19]

By this date, Jeb Stuart and three of his brigades had reached the Middleburg area. A detachment he sent to Aldie collided with Pleasonton's cavalry that was on its way to reconnoiter the Shenandoah Valley. Thus began a five-day running struggle between two powerful cavalry forces in the Loudoun Valley of Virginia—Pleasonton with orders to find Lee's army, and Stuart primed to deny him the opportunity.[20]

Earlier Hooker complained to Halleck about misleading information from Washington about the potential threat to Harper's Ferry; he wanted better data about activity north of the Potomac. Halleck responded that he had no reliable

19 Butterfield to Pleasonton, June 17, 1863, ibid., pt. 3, 177.

20 Ibid., pt. 1, 50, 142; pt. 3, 117, 173-74, 177.

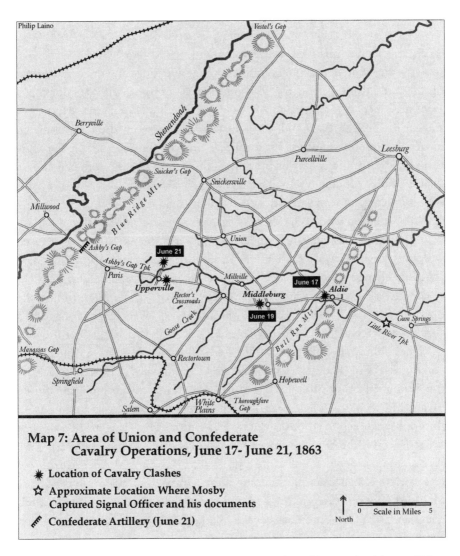

Map 7: Area of Union and Confederate Cavalry Operations, June 17- June 21, 1863

✳ **Location of Cavalry Clashes**

☆ **Approximate Location Where Mosby Captured Signal Officer and his documents**

🍂 **Confederate Artillery (June 21)**

0   Scale in Miles   5

North

information about Rebel movements in Maryland, and he was looking to Tyler, commanding the Harper's Ferry outpost, to use his cavalry to gain information. Halleck also informed Hooker that Schenck's Middle Department, including Tyler, had been placed under his control. But the wording left room for misinterpretation: he also told Hooker "that you will have control of any of his forces that are within the sphere of your operations."[21]

21 Hooker to Halleck, Halleck to Hooker, June 17, 1863, ibid., pt. 1, 48, 51.

The opposing cavalry commanders, Stuart and Pleasonton, both had received specific missions as two armies moved northward on parallel routes—the Confederates on both sides of the Blue Ridge and the Federals east of the Bull Run Mountains. Pleasonton was charged with conducting a reconnaissance of the Shenandoah Valley in search of Lee's army. His access route was through the Loudoun Valley located between the two mountain ranges. Stuart's mission was essentially to prevent this, i.e., screen the army from the eyes of the enemy by preventing the Union cavalry from penetrating the Blue Ridge Mountain gaps. The opposing cavalry forces, from their original starting points on opposite sides of the Rappahannock River, were moving toward a collision with each other in a large concentric circle.[22]

Pleasonton was operating under a misconception as his cavalry moved westward toward Aldie Gap in the Bull Run Mountains from Manassas Junction. He had concluded that Stuart was headed toward the Potomac River to conduct a raid in the North with Longstreet's corps in support. In fact, the opposite was true. Stuart was currently in the process of screening Longstreet's corps as it marched from Culpeper Court House north toward the Blue Ridge.[23]

That morning, Stuart sent Fitz Lee's brigade, temporarily under the command of Col. Thomas T. Munford, east toward Aldie in order to guard the gap in the Bull Run Mountains. Once there, Munford ran into Kilpatrick's cavalry brigade, the lead element of Gregg's division, which was arriving from the opposite direction accompanied by Pleasonton. The engagement cost both sides, especially the Yankees—over 300 Union and 119 Confederate casualties. When Stuart ordered Munford to pull back, Pleasonton decided to rest his troops rather than pursue. By doing so, he missed an opportunity to trap Munford between Gregg's division and a detached regiment under Duffié's command that Pleasonton had sent to Middleburg by a circuitous route to the south.[24]

At 11:00 a.m., Tyler sent an upbeat report from Maryland Heights: he was ready and had enough cavalry "to scour the country thoroughly," he said. But by early afternoon Hooker still had not gotten specific information and,

---

22 Stuart's post-action report, ibid., pt. 2, 687-88; pt. 3, 117; O'Neill, *The Cavalry Battles*, 31.

23 *OR 27*, pt. 3, 115-17, 173; Trudeau, *Gettysburg: A Testing of Courage*, 51.

24 *OR 27*, pt. 2, 688; pt. 1, 171, 906-08, 952-53; pt. 3, 173. Gregg had orders from Pleasonton to send a brigade through Aldie toward Front Royal in the Shenandoah Valley. Longacre, *Lee's Cavalrymen*, 190; Longacre, *The Cavalry at Gettysburg*, 109.

Brig. Gen. Daniel Tyler
Library of Congress

somewhat anxiously, inquired of Tyler: "Can you give me positive and correct information of any force of any kind and number of the enemy at any particular spot?"[25]

Pleasonton sent word to Hooker at 4:15 p.m. that one of McEntee's BMI scouts reported no Confederate infantry east of the Blue Ridge, adding that, according to the scouting report, they had confronted "all the cavalry" at Aldie that day. Given the situation as he understood it, the logical move for Pleasonton should have been to pursue, attack, and capture the Rebel cavalry brigade in his front, since that was "all the cavalry" in the area. Instead he decided to wait until the next morning to renew the pursuit.[26]

Still under the misapprehension that the enemy's objective was a cavalry raid into the North, Pleasonton surmised that the Rebel cavalry in his front showed that Stuart had not moved very far into Pennsylvania. Still not comprehending what was unfolding before him, Pleasonton told Hooker, that evening: "The fact of Fitzhugh Lee's cavalry being here does not speak well for Stuart's raid." Actually, in addition to Fitz Lee's brigade, Stuart had Robertson's and Chambliss' brigades with him in the Loudoun Valley. And two more brigades, Hampton's and Jones', were moving up to join Stuart from the Rappahannock River area, having been left behind to observe the Yankees until Hill's forces marched from Fredericksburg to the mountains safely.[27]

25 Tyler to Schenck, Hooker to Tyler, June 17, 1863, *OR* 27, pt. 3, 178, 181.

26 Pleasonton to Hooker, June 17, 1863, ibid., 173; pt. 1, 907, pt. 2, 687. Surprisingly, the usually reliable BMI scouts gave Hooker inaccurate information about Lee's infantry. Possibly Stuart's cavalry effectively screened the scouts from observing Longstreet's corps, and consequently they may have relied on not-always-reliable information from citizens.

27 Pleasonton to Hooker, June 17, 1863, ibid., 173; pt. 1, 907, pt. 2, 687.

Later, Pleasonton informed Hooker that he was certain there was no enemy infantry east of the Blue Ridge. Despite the capture of 50 Rebels during the fighting that day who could have clarified the situation if interrogated properly, this information was wrong. Longstreet's corps was east of the Blue Ridge behind Stuart's screen, and Hood's division would not clear Snicker's Gap into the Shenandoah Valley until the afternoon of June 20.[28]

Meanwhile, a Union signal corps detachment arrived to establish a station on Maryland Heights with orders to report enemy troop movements in the Shenandoah Valley. When the weather was clear, Tyler reported, the signal station could observe the entire area from Martinsburg to Williamsport and could see the ford at Shepherdstown perfectly. These were the points that Lee's army planned to use to cross the Potomac.[29]

At 5:00 p.m., Hooker finally received information about enemy whereabouts when Tyler reported that Rebel infantry and artillery had crossed the Potomac into Maryland by June 16, and that their strength was about "7,000 or 8,000 men of all arms at Williamsport." The "infantry and artillery are holding on in Maryland," he continued, "while the cavalry and light batteries are pushed into Pennsylvania." Tyler carefully stressed, however, that: "This is merely my opinion. I wish I could back it up by facts, but I can't"[30]

June 18: Lee Ponders Hooker's Movements

I wish [Stuart] to endeavor to ascertain the exact condition of things—whether this force is simply cavalry, or whether the enemy infantry is moving in that direction [toward the Shenandoah Valley].

R. E. Lee[31]

---

28 Pleasonton to Williams, ibid., 906; pt. 2, 315, 366. Gottfried, *Roads to Gettysburg*, 76, 88-89, 96-97, 102-104, 111. Pleasonton's faulty information about the location and intent of the Rebels was partly because he did not leave a detachment behind in the Rappahannock River area to keep watch on Rebel activities after the cavalry followed Hooker's infantry northward two days earlier.

29 Tyler's post-action report, June 17, 1863, Tyler to Hooker, June 19, 1863, *OR* 27, pt. 2, 22, 24.

30 Tyler to Hooker, June 17, 1863, ibid., 23.

31 Lee to Stuart, June 18, 1863, ibid., pt. 3, 1020.

Although Lee was receiving information about the Union army from cavalry scouts, Hooker's intentions were not clear. Lee notified President Davis that he believed the enemy was concentrating in the vicinity of Centreville, and that scouts were reporting that they were moving towards the upper Potomac. However, Lee could not decide whether they meant to proceed to Harper's Ferry, cross the Potomac River into Maryland, or advance through the mountains into the Shenandoah Valley.[32]

At 5:00 a.m., Pleasonton informed Hooker again that no enemy infantry "force of consequence" was operating east of the mountains. However, he had learned from prisoners that Stuart was present and directing the operations against Pleasonton's cavalry, and that more enemy cavalry had arrived in the area. Pleasonton's information about Stuart's whereabouts was wrong, once again, since Stuart and his staff remained in Middleburg taking their leisure while Munford moved toward Aldie. Stuart had to beat a hasty retreat and would barely escape capture when Duffié's regiment, which had taken a roundabout route, captured a Rebel scout who revealed his whereabouts.[33]

Further information from Tyler on Maryland Heights named three of Ewell's division commanders correctly—he only had three—and added "Walker and A. P. Hill." Tyler also reported that cavalry under Brig. Gens. John D. Imboden and Albert G. Jenkins had joined Ewell. This was only partially true also, because Imboden had not yet reached the army from Western Virginia.[34]

To get more help in the search for Lee's army, Hooker requested the Signal Corps commander Col. Alfred Myer to establish stations at Crampton's Gap and another South Mountain site (probably Turner's Gap). From these two locations, observers would be able to see the whole country north of the Potomac, and report enemy movements by telegraph. Hooker also asked

32 Lee to Davis, ibid., pt. 2, 295. Lee added that Longstreet's corps had moved east of the Blue Ridge to confuse the enemy regarding his own intentions. Note the contradiction between Lee's message to Davis and the previous one to Longstreet regarding the location of Longstreet's forces. Apparently the misapprehension had been cleared up in the interim.

33 Pleasonton to Williams, June 18, 1863, ibid., pt. 1, 907-08; Stuart's post-action report, ibid., pt. 2, 688; Raiford, *The 4th North Carolina Cavalry*, 46.

34 Tyler to Hooker, June 18, 1863, OR 27, pt. 2, 23. Obviously, word about changes in Confederate high command had not reached Tyler through the chain of command. Tyler was also misinformed about Jones' cavalry brigade being in this entourage: only White's 35th Battalion Virginia Cavalry of Jones' brigade accompanied Ewell's corps. The remainder of the brigade was serving under Stuart's direct command.

Halleck whether he could issue orders directly to Maj. Gen. Julius Stahel's cavalry division, which was under the jurisdiction of the Department of Washington. Halleck responded that Hooker could make direct contact with Gen. Samuel Heintzelman if he needed support from his forces.[35]

Early in the day, Pleasonton ordered a brigade toward Snicker's Gap to scout the Shenandoah Valley and to send parties to Winchester, Harper's Ferry, and Sperryville. This brigade pushed against light Rebel cavalry resistance until it got within two miles of Snicker's Gap, where fighting intensified. Lacking support, the brigade returned to the Aldie area without having achieved its objective. That morning Pleasonton also sent Gregg with two of his brigades and one of Buford's brigades toward Upperville and Ashby's Gap by way of the Little River Turnpike and Middleburg. This force did not get much beyond Middleburg before retreating in the face of a stout resistance from Confederate cavalry.[36]

Pleasonton just added to the confusion. He reported to Hooker claiming that none of Lee's infantry had moved north of the Rappahannock, thereby contradicting his earlier report that Longstreet's corps and Stuart's cavalry were operating in the vicinity of Upperville. In fact, by this time Longstreet's corps was marching north of the river through the Loudoun Valley behind Stuart's screen, and, of course, Ewell's corps had been north of the Rappahannock since June 12. Then he added, "Some negroes report that they heard Lee's forces were returning toward Culpeper [Court House]," and speculated this meant that Lee's objective was to send reinforcements from his army to Vicksburg. Pleasonton's ability as an intelligence provider, already questionable at headquarters, was sinking to new lows.[37]

But amazingly, Hooker recommended to Halleck that Pleasonton be promoted to major general and officially assigned as cavalry corps commander. It was justified, Hooker said, by "his gallant conduct at Chancellorsville . . . and his attack and surprise of Stuart's forces . . . on the Rappahannock on June 9."

35 Hooker to Halleck, Halleck to Hooker, June 18, 1863, ibid., pt. 1, 51. Regarding the South Mountain site, Hooker was probably referring to the Washington Monument near Turner's Gap on present day U.S. Alt Route 40: ideal for use by Signal Corps personnel. Bill Cameron, "Signal Corps at Gettysburg Part II," 104; Heidler and Heidler, *Encyclopedia of the American Civil War*, 4:1789.

36 Pleasonton to Williams, June 18, 1863, OR 27, pt. 1, 907-8; O'Neill, *The Cavalry Battles*, 97.

37 Pleasonton to Williams, June 18, 1863, OR 27, pt. 1, 908.

The Snickersville Turnpike where the 1st Massachusetts Cavalry suffered heavy casualties at the hands of Munford's cavalrymen on June 17.
Photo by the author

Hooker, perhaps inadvertently, was endorsing his cavalry commander's view that combat rated a higher priority than gathering intelligence.[38]

Mosby to Stuart's Rescue

> During all this period Mosby and his men kept us thoroughly informed of all movements of the enemy in that country.
>
> W. W. Blackford[39]

Whenever Jeb Stuart was in northern Virginia, he had valuable resources. Mosby and his partisan rangers, who often operated behind Union lines, provided vital information-gathering services. Indeed, Mosby struck gold on the night of the 18th by capturing Maj. William R. Sterling of Hooker's staff and Capt. Benjamin F. Fisher, acting chief signal officer of the Army of the Potomac. Sterling and Fisher were serving as couriers carrying dispatches from

38 Hooker to Halleck, June 18, 1863, ibid., 51.

39 Blackford, *War Years*, 218.

The town of Upperville—the scene of cavalry clashes as Pleasonton drove
Stuart towards the mountains on June 21.
Photo by the author

Hooker to Pleasonton. One of these messages revealed: the location of two
Union infantry corps, orders for Pleasonton to penetrate the Blue Ridge gaps,
and the deployment of Union infantry in support of the cavalry. The other was a
dispatch by Maj. Gen. Julius Stahel about a cavalry detachment from the
Department of Washington being sent to reconnoiter the Culpeper and
Warrenton areas. Mosby would claim that these captured documents were
"open sesame to all of Hooker's plans and secrets."[40]

From an intelligence perspective, however, it is noteworthy that, while
Hooker had a chief signal officer on his staff, Lee had none to coordinate signal
activities with the three corps-level signal officers. This shortcoming would
become evident as the campaign progressed.[41]

40 Stuart's post-action report, *OR* 27, pt. 2, 689; pt. 3, 172, 176-77, 192; Mosby's quote cited in
O'Neill, *The Cavalry Battles*, 94-95; Jones, *Ranger Mosby*, 138-39; McClellan, *The Life and
Campaigns*, 306, 312. Mosby's Rangers drove Union army headquarters crazy. Chief of staff
Butterfield flatly instructed Meade, commander of the V Corps, "Catch and kill any guerrillas,
then try them, will be a good method of treating them." Butterfield to Meade, June 18, 1863,
OR 27, pt. 3, 194.

41 Gaddy, "The Confederate Signal Corps at Gettysburg," 110-12.

June 19: The Search for the Enemy Continues

> Hood's division was sent yesterday from Upperville to replace Early's in order that you [Ewell] might have with you your whole corps to operate with in Maryland & Pennsylvania."
>
> Gen. R. E. Lee[42]

Lee, who had arrived at Millwood south of Berryville, updated Davis with a report that Stuart's cavalry had repulsed all attempts of the enemy to penetrate the mountains. He reiterated that it appeared the main body of Hooker's army was proceeding towards the Potomac. Lee also wrote Ewell that his strategy was for Longstreet's corps to operate in such a way so as to confuse the enemy regarding his army's movements. He intended to detain enemy forces east of the mountains until Hill's corps arrived to support Longstreet. However, if the enemy was able to force its way through the mountains, he told Ewell, his corps would be separated from the rest of the army. It was Longstreet's job to prevent this, if possible.[43]

At this stage of the invasion, Lee had a good fix on the location of Hooker's forces, but was uncertain of the Union commander's operational objectives. Hooker lacked specific information on both subjects about the Confederate army. And despite Hooker's desire for better intelligence, Provost Marshal Patrick criticized his handling of the information he did receive, and his lack of leadership as well. The BMI provided Hooker with accurate information about the size of Lee's army, Patrick wrote, but he refused to accept it. Hooker "has declared that the enemy are over 100,000 strong—it is his only salvation to make it appear that the enemy's forces are larger than his own, which is all false & he knows it." Hooker "knows that Lee is his master & is afraid to meet him in fair battle," he concluded. Hooker's actions in the next several days would lend plausibility to this assessment.[44]

At 10:20 a.m., Pleasonton reported Chester, Ashby's, and Snicker's Gaps well defended, and, he told Butterfield, it would require infantry to penetrate them. He still had no information about the location of Lee's army. And,

42 Lee to Ewell, June 19, 1863, *OR* 27, pt. 3, 905.

43 Lee to Davis, Lee to Ewell, ibid., pt. 2, 296; pt. 3, 905. Coordination between Lee and Longstreet still seemed to be out of kilter, since Longstreet began moving west of the mountains on June 18 and completed passage by the 20th. Gottfried, *Roads to Gettysburg*, 104.

44 Diary, June 19, 1863 in Sparks, *Inside Lincoln's Army*, 261.

despite strictures, he continued to employ his BMI personnel improperly. McEntee saw no reason to stay with the cavalry, because Pleasonton was using his scouts and spies as guides and couriers, not intelligence agents. Cavalry commanders would not allow them to examine papers taken from prisoners, which at times contained important information. Since the cavalry provost marshal did not understand the value of these papers, he allowed them to be lost or destroyed.[45]

Concerned about the security of his forces, Hooker had previously laid out guidelines to reporters and editors about the publication of military-related stories. He likely wondered what good they did when he received an abstract of the New York *Herald* from the previous day that described the recent movements of his army. As long as the newspapers continue to publicize its movements, he complained to Halleck, it would be difficult for his army to gain the advantage.[46]

Halleck chose to ignore Hooker's complaint about newspaper articles. Exemplifying the Union authorities' lack of accurate intelligence, he told Hooker: "No large body [of Lee's army] has appeared either in Maryland or Western Virginia." This was while Ewell's corps straddled the Potomac River in Maryland and Western Virginia preparing for a march into Pennsylvania.[47]

To attack the problem of acquiring reliable information in Maryland, Hooker ordered Sharpe to assign John Babcock, his most reliable agent, to go to Frederick, Maryland, as a forward area coordinator. Babcock's job was to recruit citizen scouts and direct them in searching for Lee in the northern end of the Shenandoah Valley and its Maryland extension, the Cumberland Valley.[48]

Meanwhile, Stuart was elated with the messages Mosby had captured from Hooker's aides that morning. For he now could make a substantive report about the enemy situation to his anxious commander. Stuart ordered one of his

45 Pleasonton to Butterfield, June 19, 1863, *OR* 27, pt. 1, 909; McEntee to Sharpe, June 19, 1863, RG 393, NA.

46 Hooker to Halleck, June 19, 1963, *OR* 27, pt. 1, 52. Hooker despaired of silencing the papers, because though he could suppress their circulation within his lines, he could not prevent the enemy from obtaining copies. For Hooker's guidelines to reporters and editors, see *OR* 25, pt. 2, 315-16; *OR* 27, pt. 3, 19.

47 Halleck to Hooker, June 19, 1863, ibid., pt. 1, 52-53; pt. 2, 442, 464, 503, 550-51; Gottfried, *Roads to Gettysburg*, 103-04.

48 Babcock to Sharpe, June 20, 1863, RG 393, NA.

staffers, Lt. Chiswell Dabney, to ride "regardless of horse flesh" with the dispatches to Lee, who was in the Valley near Millwood.[49]

The captured messages revealed the number of divisions in the Army of the Potomac, from which an estimate could be made of its approximate strength. Moreover, the captured correspondence prompted Stuart to revise his tactics, since Union infantry would be supporting their cavalry. He decided not to attack the enemy at Aldie, but assume the defensive and screen the movements of the main body of Lee's troops in the Shenandoah Valley by blocking the enemy's reconnaissance efforts and continually threatening to attack.[50]

Stuart undoubtedly was aware of the potential for criticism if he adopted defensive rather than aggressive tactics. The barbs in the Southern press directed at Stuart following Pleasonton's surprise attack at Brandy Station some 10 days earlier still rankled. And criticism for his actions in Loudoun Valley would not be long in coming either.[51]

Pleasonton Presses On Toward the Blue Ridge

> I directed . . . Gregg to . . . send a [cavalry] force on to Upperville and Ashby's Gap.
> Brig. Gen. Alfred Pleasonton [52]

That afternoon, Pleasonton finally reported evidence of Longstreet's movement northward to Hooker. His troopers captured a soldier with a pass from Maj. Gen. Richard B. Garnett's brigade of Longstreet's corps. And the following day, another prisoner provided information that Longstreet had been marching east of the Blue Ridge, and that his last unit had passed through Ashby's Gap into the Shenandoah Valley on the 19th.[53]

---

49 Stuart's post-action report, *OR* 27, pt. 2, 689; Williamson, *Mosby's Rangers*, 72; Trout, *With Pen and Saber*, 216.

50 Stuart's post-action report, *OR* 27, pt. 2, 689. If Stuart's statement is accurate about learning the strength of Hooker's army, the information was not contained in the orders from Hooker to Pleasonton signed by Butterfield. See *OR* 27, pt. 3, 176-77. It would have had to come from other documents the captured aides were carrying.

51 Richmond *Examiner*, June 12, 1863, cited in Freeman, *Lee's Lieutenants*, 3:19.

52 Pleasonton to Butterfield, June 19, 1863, *OR* 27, pt. 1, 909.

53 Ibid., 910-11. This report was not entirely correct, since Hood's division marched farther north and did not complete its passage through Snicker's Gap until the afternoon of June 20. Gottfried, *The Roads to Gettysburg*, 111.

Hooker faced a decision: to stay in a defensive array around the capital, or move into Maryland to shadow Lee's army. The decision of necessity had to be quick, decisive, and based on accurate information about the enemy's whereabouts. Hooker expressed his doubts to Halleck about whether Lee planned to send a considerable force across the river into Maryland. Pleasonton's impression, he continued, was that Lee's infantry was still on the west side of the Blue Ridge Mountains, and Lee meant to attack in the direction of Washington. Since he did not indicate what evidence Pleasonton had for his "impression," apparently the cavalryman was recklessly speculating once again.[54]

June 20: Babcock Operates Under Cover in Maryland

> Send me no information but that which you know to be authentic.
> Maj. Gen. Joseph Hooker[55]

Hooker dearly wanted Sharpe's agent to acquire "reliable and correct information concerning the enemy on the north side of the Potomac." Babcock planned to use Frederick, Maryland, as a base of operations— an area he knew well, having served as a member Pinkerton's intelligence staff during McClellan's Antietam campaign the previous year. On his way, he stopped by the war department in Washington to acquire funds for his secret service activities.[56]

Hooker wired detailed guidance about how the reconnaissance should be conducted. "Employ and send persons on to the heights of South Mountain," he told Babcock, "to overlook the valley beyond, and see if the enemy have camps there." Hooker's personal handling of this agent reflected the high priority he placed on gathering the needed intelligence to decide whether to cross the Potomac River in pursuit of Lee's army. He was precise:

---

54 Hooker to Halleck, ibid., 53.

55 Hooker to Babcock, ibid., pt. 3, 225.

56 Hooker to Halleck, June 17, 1863, ibid., pt. 1, 48; Babcock to Sharpe, June 20, 1863, RG 393, NA. The BMI drew funds from the secret service account maintained by the chief clerk of the war department. Fishel, *The Secret War*, 595-96.

Present day view of Winchester Hall (formerly Frederick Female Seminary)
that was used as a base of operations by John Babcock who was assisted by Hiram
Winchester, the principal and a Union sympathizer.
Photo by the author

Tell me whether it is infantry, cavalry or artillery they have seen. Direct them to avoid
the roads, and employ only such persons as can look upon a body of armed men
without being frightened out of their senses. If [your men] take a position in the forest,
they can even count them, as they pass on the road, with impunity.[57]

Babcock replied immediately that he had made arrangements exactly as
instructed and had hired capable men with a good telescope to observe enemy
movements from South Mountain. He told Hooker that he hoped to report
back quickly. Since the entire Union army remained below the Potomac,
Babcock's hazardous assignment was substantially on his own, and he would
have to keep his identity secret. Western Maryland, including Frederick County,
was about evenly divided between Union and Confederate sympathizers.[58]

57 Hooker to Babcock, June 20, 1863, OR 27, pt. 3, 225.

58 Ibid., 226. Babcock used the term "signal glass" for telescope, referring to a standard Signal
Corps, four-draw brass telescope that was about 30 power with a focal length of 26 inches. It
was sufficiently powerful to allow Babcock's operatives to observe the valley below from South

Hiram Winchester
Courtesy of Diversions Publications

That morning, Babcock sent one of his men to Martinsburg, West Virginia, to look for the enemy in the Shenandoah Valley. He also convinced the reluctant principal of the Frederick Female Seminary to permit him use of the school as a base of operations. Given Confederate forces nearby and a politically disparate community, aiding a Union secret agent was a dangerous undertaking.[59]

Babcock had learned that some 6,000 Confederate infantry had crossed the Potomac River into Maryland as of the morning of the 19th. Which only told part of the story, because by then both Johnson's and Rodes' divisions of Ewell's corps were in Maryland, about 15,000 infantry and 1,900 cavalry. Early's division remained on the south side of the Potomac near Shepherdstown with about 5,700 men.[60]

Babcock informed Sharpe that Jenkins' brigade, the vanguard of the Rebel invasion force, had already entered Pennsylvania and reached Chambersburg before falling back to Greencastle. With a little less conviction than when he wrote Hooker, he asked Sharpe to advise him about how to deploy his men to observe Lee's army. He also cautioned patience and reasonable expectations for the moment. Although he would not pretend to report on Lee's plans without

---

Mountain. Brown, *The Signal Corps*, 120; Clifford G. Manasco, *Signal Corps Camp of Instruction* (Fort Gordon, GA, n.d.), 16-17.

59 Babcock to Sharpe, June 20, 1863, RG 393. The Frederick Female Seminary building is currently occupied by the Frederick county government, which acquired and renamed the building Winchester Hall in 1931 in honor of the seminary's first principal, Hiram Winchester. Timothy L. Cannon, et al., *Pictorial History of Frederick, Maryland: The First 250 Years, 1745-1995* (Frederick, MD, 1995), 50.

60 Babcock to Sharpe, June 20, 1863, RG 393, NA; Gottfried, *Roads to Gettysburg*, 97, 103-05. The cavalry consisted of Jenkins' brigade (1,330), the 1st Maryland Battalion (350), and the 35th Virginia Battalion (262). Busey and Martin, *Regimental Strengths and Losses*, 194, 244, 247, 251-52.

solid information, he did want to mention that, according to the locals, Lee would exert every effort to hold the railroad from Chambersburg to the Potomac by fortifying the South Mountain passes. As soon as he heard of any undertaking, he would report it.[61]

Babcock told Sharpe on the 19th that the Rebels had entered Boonsboro, some 15 miles from Frederick, but then returned to Hagerstown. He feared the enemy would raid Frederick at any moment. "I am not overanxious to be [he drew a stick figure hanging from a gallows]," he drolly commented. And no help was near. With the exception of a small Signal Corps party, the nearest Union forces were cavalry detachments along the Potomac River fords and at Monocacy Junction, four miles southeast of Frederick.[62]

The personal danger that John Babcock alluded to materialized later that day when a small party of Confederate cavalry dashed into the city. (The raiders were members of Gilmor's 1st Maryland Cavalry, part of Jenkins' brigade. Although a newspaper account reported they were pursuing Signal Corps personnel from South Mountain, Ewell had also ordered them to destroy the "iron railroad bridge" at Monocacy near Frederick.) Caught off guard, Babcock was fortunate to escape. As he telegraphed to Sharpe, several "notorious Rebels" had followed him all day as if he were a suspicious character. When the cavalry arrived, he had incriminating papers on him that revealed his spying activities, so he destroyed them. To avoid being captured, he had to take refuge in a private home in a remote part of the town.[63]

Meanwhile, the raiders seized and destroyed supplies intended for the Federal army before being chased out of Frederick by Cole's Maryland Cavalry,

---

61 Babcock to Sharpe, June 20, 1863, RG 393, NA. Babcock identified Jenkins brigade as "mounted infantry;" however, the brigade was a hybrid of rifle-toting home guards, guerrillas, and regular cavalry. Faust, *Historical Times Encyclopedia*, 394. Jenkins cavalry arrived in Chambersburg on the night of June 15 and retreated the following day to Greencastle when spooked by a report that non-existent Union cavalry were approaching Chambersburg. Jacob Hoke, *The Great Invasion of 1863* (New York, 1959), 97-111; Nye, *Here come the Rebels!*, 141-47. In 1863, the Franklin Railroad (an extension of the Cumberland Valley Railroad from Chambersburg to Harrisburg) ran from Chambersburg as far south as Hagerstown, Maryland, but did not go all the way to the Potomac River. Paul J. Westhaeffer, *History of the Cumberland Valley Railroad, 1835-1919* (Washington, 1979), 40, 42.

62 Babcock to Sharpe, June 20, 1863, RG 393, NA; *OR Atlas*, Plate 81, 4.

63 Fishel, *The Secret War*, 463-68; Paul and Rita Gordon, *Never the Like Again: Frederick County, Maryland* (Frederick, 1995), 225; Driver, *First & Second Maryland Cavalry C.S.A.* (Charlottesville, VA, 1999), 50-51; Longacre, *The Cavalry at Gettysburg*, 139; *New York Times*, June 20, 21, 1863.

a unit operating under Tyler's command at Maryland Heights. Babcock slipped out of town during the excitement by commandeering a railroad handcar and reached a telegraph office, probably at Monocacy Junction, to alert Sharpe that his operation had been disrupted.[64]

Confederate cavalry east of South Mountain prevented Signal Corps personnel and Babcock's men from returning to the mountain to observe Lee's army. For assistance, Babcock asked Sharpe to send Sgt. Milton W. Cline to help locate the Rebels. One of the BMI's most daring and wily scouts, who in the past had successfully entered enemy camps along with his team disguised as Confederates, Cline was the "one man who won't run when there is nobody after him and is not frightened when he sees a greyback."[65]

Sharpe had a difficult task attempting to track Lee with his limited resources. Since the search for Lee would take place over an extensive area, Sharpe deployed small teams to obtain maximum coverage. But experienced scouts to penetrate enemy lines were in short supply. Hooker had highlighted these limitations a few days earlier when explaining his strategy to Lincoln. He emphasized his insufficient resources for gathering information across the enemy's wide area of operations.[66]

Increased Flow of (Good and Bad) Intelligence to Union Headquarters

> The commanding general is very anxious that you should ascertain, at the earliest possible moment, where the main body of the enemy's infantry are to be found at the present time, especially A. P. Hill's Corps.
>
> Maj. Gen. Daniel Butterfield[67]

---

64 Babcock to Sharpe, June 21, 1863, RG 393, NA. The Rebels returned with a larger cavalry force, about 200 men, and drove the Federal cavalry out of town; however, they were unable to destroy the bridge since it was protected by "a strong stockade at each end." Gordon, *Never the Like Again*, 224.

65 Babcock to Sharpe, June 20, 1863, RG 393; OR 27, pt. 3, 266; Fishel, *The Secret War*, 471. Babcock misspelled Sergeant Cline's name as "Kline." Cline was a 3rd Indiana cavalryman who transferred in early 1863 to the BMI as a scout. 292.

66 Fishel, *The Secret War*, 293, 456-57; Hooker to Lincoln, June 15, 1863, OR 27, pt. 1, 44.

67 Butterfield to Pleasonton, June 20, 1863, OR 27, pt. 3, 227-28.

Meanwhile, Tyler reported to Hooker that he learned from a reliable scout operating between Maryland Heights "and Hagerstown, that Ewell is at or near Williamsport, with his main force; [and] that Rodes and Johnson [infantry divisions] and Jones [cavalry] is about Sharpsburg, with not exceeding 8,000 men." He obviously had not yet learned that only White's battalion of Jones' brigade was with Ewell. "Imboden [cavalry brigade] has been out into Pennsylvania, stealing horses and plundering," he added. This information was generally accurate, because, on that date, Rodes was beyond Hagerstown, Johnson at Sharpsburg, and Early near Shepherdstown. Jenkins was operating in Pennsylvania. However, Imboden was still in what had become that day the new state of West Virginia. Only Jenkins' cavalry had been operating in Pennsylvania, but his brigade had returned to the Williamsport area.[68]

Tyler told Hooker that he believed Ewell's whole force had passed Winchester, and its strength did not exceed 30,000 men—about 12,000 of which had moved beyond Williamsport. Although his estimates were off— Ewell's corps high by about 8,000 men, and the force over the Potomac was low by some 3,000—the report still gave Hooker a general idea of the latest positions of Ewell's forces.[69]

Also that morning, Pleasonton informed Hooker that Stuart's cavalry force was numerous, and that Longstreet's infantry was supporting him by covering the gaps. He was accurate about Longstreet, since McLaws' division had moved to Ashby's Gap and Hood's division was covering Snicker's Gap within supporting distance of Stuart's cavalry. But because the Union cavalry was taking heavy losses in its skirmishes with Stuart's brigades, Pleasonton erroneously or perhaps disingenuously reported to Hooker: "Our cavalry is really fighting infantry behind stone walls." Stuart's tactics of employing his troops dismounted may indeed have caused that impression, but the Union cavalry chief obliviously contradicted himself by also reporting that "the Rebel infantry force which was on this side of the Blue Ridge . . . of Longstreet's corps,

68 Tyler to Hooker, ibid., pt. 2, 24-25, 442- 43; Gottfried, *Roads to Gettysburg*, 109; Faust, *Historical Times Encyclopedia*, 818. Imboden's cavalry reportedly did not move into Pennsylvania until June 25. Steve French, "Imboden's Advance to Gettysburg," *Gettysburg Magazine* (January 1999), no. 20, 12.

69 Tyler to Hooker, June 20, 1863, OR 27, pt. 2, 24-25; Myers, *The Comanches*, 187-88. This was the second report to Hooker that Ewell's corps could be as large as 30,000 men. The previous one came from Pleasonton. See OR 27, pt. 3, 114. Recent research credits Ewell's corps was 21,806. Busey and Martin, *Regimental Strengths and Losses*, 169, 194, 244.

passed through Ashby's Gap yesterday into the Shenandoah Valley, and that only Stuart's force is this side of the Blue Ridge." This information, which came from a "rebel infantry soldier," was correct, since by then Longstreet's corps had crossed from east to west side of the mountains but could still protect the gaps if Stuart's cavalry had to fall back to the Blue Ridge.[70]

Pleasonton requested permission from Hooker "to take my whole corps to-morrow morning, and throw it at once upon Stuart's whole force, and cripple it up . . . to do this effectively," he requested, "a couple of large brigades or a division of infantry" be sent to him as part of his force. Pleasonton's entire focus appeared to be on engaging in combat. He wanted to attack Stuart's cavalry with a large combined force of cavalry and infantry to "seriously impair the enemy's force for offensive operations." His plan of course omitted the primary duty assigned to him to provide "information of where the enemy is, his force, and his movements."[71]

Union army headquarters liked the idea. Pleasonton's message arrived there at 5:00 p.m., and 20 minutes later Butterfield replied that Hooker had authorized Pleasonton's proposed plan "to move to-morrow morning with your entire corps against the enemy's cavalry," and that V Corps commander Meade would be instructed to detach two infantry brigades in support. Nevertheless, Butterfield hastened to emphasize that Hooker desired the "earliest possible" information about Lee's army, especially the whereabouts of Hill's corps. Unfortunately, Pleasonton's plan did not account for supporting Rebel infantry in the mountain gaps, even if his forces did break through Stuart's cavalry screen. A successful attack would have gained little in pinpointing the location of Lee's infantry in the Valley—not to mention prospect of greater combat losses.[72]

Hooker approved Pleasonton's proposal after word from Babcock that he had learned from a civilian refugee that 3,000-5,000 of Rodes' infantry division and 1,200 of Jenkins' cavalry had crossed the river at Williamsport into Maryland. Rebel infantry were also reportedly crossing at Shepherdstown. But, the main body of Lee's army was not near the Potomac or in supporting

---

70 Pleasonton to Williams, June 20, 1863, *OR* 27, pt. 3, 223-24, pt. 1, 911; Longstreet's & Stuart's post-action reports, *OR* 27, pt. 2, 357, 691; Gottfried, *Roads to Gettysburg*, 96-97, 102-03, 110-11.

71 Pleasonton to Williams, June 20, 1863, *OR* 27, pt. 1, 911.

72 Butterfield to Pleasonton, June 20, 1863, ibid., pt. 3, 227-28.

distance of Ewell's troops. Together with Tyler's earlier reports from Maryland Heights, Hooker now had further confirmation of where Longstreet's and Ewell's corps were, but he did not know about Hill. This is what he needed Pleasonton to find out.[73]

In anticipation of conducting a full scale attack the following morning, that evening Pleasonton put in place security measures to deter Mosby's rangers from gaining information about the movement and plans of Hooker's forces. Pleasonton informed Gregg that he had information that all of the citizens of Middleburg "are implicated with Mosby." Pleasonton directed Gregg to arrest any men in the town, not permit women to leave their homes during the Union occupation, and search all houses along the line of march to check for "concealed soldiers."[74]

June 21: Pleasonton Provides Flawed Intelligence

A. P. Hill is not north of the Rappahannock, and is either guarding that river or is on his way up the [Shenandoah] Valley.
Brig. Gen. Alfred Pleasonton[75]

[Stuart's] cavalry . . . has hitherto prevented me from obtaining satisfactory information as to the whereabouts of the enemy.
Maj. Gen. Joseph Hooker [76]

The 1st New York Cavalry's Lt. F. G. Martindale and his scouts from Maryland Heights reconnoitered the Rebel camps around Sharpsburg, Maryland, and concluded they contained some 20,000 men. The actual number was closer to 15, 000, but Tyler, without explaining the basis for his figures, told Hooker that in his opinion the scout's figure was low by 7,000 to 10,000 men.

---

73 Babcock to Hooker, ibid., pt. 3, 227; Tyler to Hooker, ibid., pt. 2, 24-25.

74 Alexander to Gregg, ibid., pt. 3, 229; This was a wise precautionary move since Middleburg often served as Mosby's base of operations, and it provided safe haven for members of Mosby's unit. O'Neill, *The Cavalry Battles*, 100, 102; Williamson, *Mosby's Rangers*, 110-11.

75 Pleasonton to Williams, June 21, 1863, *OR* 27, pt. 3, 244.

76 Hooker to Lincoln, ibid., pt. 1, 54.

This was Tyler's second report that Ewell's corps could be as strong as 30,000 men. Like Pleasonton, Tyler tended to speculate.[77]

In the early morning hours, Pleasonton summarized for Hooker his latest assessment of the enemy's situation. He correctly placed Longstreet's corps in the Shenandoah Valley, but believed that Hill's corps were still below the Rappahannock—grossly mistaken since two divisions were already in the Shenandoah Valley and the third about to enter. He then accurately assessed Stuart's mission to screen Lee's army while it moved north toward the Potomac River. But then, without evidence, predicted "they will then turn westward toward Pittsburgh." People at headquarters must have wondered about his rationality.[78]

With some 3,500 infantry of Brig. Gen. James Barnes's division, Pleasonton launched an attempt to penetrate the Blue Ridge gaps. Following a daylong series of battles against four of Stuart's brigades totaling some 6,000 cavalrymen, Pleasonton drove the Rebels, who fought a stubborn delaying action, back toward Ashby's Gap. However, a part of McLaws' division of Longstreet's corps occupied the gap, and the Union cavalry leader chose to halt the pursuit at that point. "I have not been able to send to the top of the Blue Ridge," he explained. "Stuart has the Gap covered with heavy Blakelys and 10-pounder Parrotts." In other words, he had again failed to ascertain the location of Lee's army. He tried to put the best face on a bad situation by reporting "it was a most disastrous day to the rebel cavalry. I never saw the troops behave better or under more difficult circumstances. Very many charges were made, and the saber used freely, but always with great advantage to us."[79]

By withdrawing, Pleasonton missed an opportunity to draw the Rebel infantry defending the gaps into battle and capture prisoners for interrogation. This would have helped determine which units of Lee's army were in the vicinity. So Stuart's defensive strategy had succeeded in preventing Pleasonton

---

77 Tyler to Hooker, June 21, 22, 1863, ibid. pt. 2, 25-26; Busey and Martin, *Regimental Strengths and Losses*, 194, 244.

78 Pleasonton to Williams, June 21, 1863, OR 27, pt. 3, 244; Gottfried, *Roads to Gettysburg*, 104.

79 Barnes' post-action report, OR 27, pt. 1, 598-99; Pleasonton to Williams, June 21, 1863, 912; Busey and Martin, *Regimental Strengths and Losses*, 58, 244. Stuart's other brigade under Fitz Lee, 2,100 men, guarded Snicker's Gap and was not engaged in the cavalry battles of June 21. OR 27, pt. 2, 691; Busey and Martin, *Regimental Strengths*, 247.

from accomplishing his assigned mission: penetrate the mountain gaps and reconnoiter Winchester, Berryville, and Harper's Ferry in the Valley.[80]

Following the action at Upperville and Ashby's Gap, Pleasonton reported the unremarkable information that the enemy had no infantry in the Loudoun Valley. He also passed along more false information he learned from "negroes" in the area: that Ewell's corps had gone toward Winchester on June 17. In fact, by the 17th, Ewell had already captured Winchester and two of his divisions (Rodes' and Johnson's) had crossed the Potomac River into Maryland or were in the vicinity of Shepherdstown. As Pleasonton wrote this report, Ewell was preparing to march into Pennsylvania. The Union cavalry chief also reported that Longstreet had been moving toward Winchester on Friday, June 19, when in fact McLaws' and Pickett's divisions had not yet crossed the Blue Ridge Mountains, and Hood's division, that had crossed on June 18, was sent back to protect Snicker's Gap and support Stuart's cavalry that were engaged in a fight with the Federals.[81]

At the outset of the Gettysburg campaign, Hooker's main intelligence goal was to locate and learn the organization and intentions of the Army of Northern Virginia. He particularly wanted to find out if a Rebel invasion was in the offing, and whether the enemy intended to cross the Potomac River. He had a number of resources and a variety of methods to accomplish this. He relied primarily on his cavalry and Sharpe's BMI staff to gather the necessary information to formulate a plan for countering Lee's army while defending the Federal capital.

Hooker's task was complicated. His decisive defeat by Lee at Chancellorsville had lost him the confidence of some of his subordinate commanders and the authorities in Washington. So he needed to accomplish his current objectives while attempting to restore his reputation as a leader.

A confident Confederate commander who had convinced the authorities in Richmond of the efficacy of a Northern invasion confronted him. Lee's invasion rested on an intelligence plan that would be implemented primarily by Jeb Stuart's cavalry. Lee had two main objectives at the outset of the campaign: to screen his movements from the eyes of the enemy, and to be aware of the whereabouts of Hooker's army. Stuart's role, along with his intelligence

---

80 Stuart's post-action report, OR 27, pt. 2, 690-91; O'Neill, *The Cavalry Battles*, 100-58; Longacre, *The Cavalry at Gettysburg*, 119-33; Raiford, *The 4th North Carolina Cavalry*, 50-51.

81 Pleasonton to Williams, June 21, 1863, OR 27, pt. 1, 911-12; Ewell's post-action report, pt. 2, 442-43, 464; Gottfried, *Roads to Gettysburg*, 88-89, 96-97, 102-03, 110-11, 116-17.

resources, such as Mosby's Rangers and cavalry scouts, was to ensure these goals were met. Lee also looked to a network of spies operating in the North for information about the enemy's strategic plans and objectives.

During the early stages of the Gettysburg campaign, the Confederate cavalry outperformed the Union cavalry in intelligence and counterintelligence duties. For the most part, beginning on June 3 when the first Confederate units marched to the west from Fredericksburg, Lee had a good fix on the Union army. And notwithstanding the delay caused by the battle at Brandy Station, Stuart performed his screening and reconnaissance duties well.

Conversely, Pleasonton foundered in his most important mission—to discover the location of Lee's army. However, the BMI did provide army headquarters information gained by a team of scouts and spies that prompted Hooker's ordering the Union army northward on a track with the Confederates. But Pleasonton and the cavalry, who refused to cooperate with the BMI, were actually hampering its mission during the march north.

At this stage of the campaign, the upper hand seemed to be with Lee. Hooker was not getting timely or accurate information; he needed to solve this problem.

Chapter Nine

Absence of Coordination Undermines Lee's Objectives: June 22 to 25

If General Hooker's army remains inactive, you can withdraw with . . . three [cavalry brigades]. . . . You will . . . be able to judge whether you can pass around their army without hindrance.

General R. E. Lee[1]

The selection of the route through Hooker's army was based on the theory that the conditions would be maintained as they were until Stuart got through. The preservation of the status in Hooker's army depended on Lee.

John S. Mosby[2]

June 22: Intelligence Operatives at Work

Please inform me what the enemy are about in your vicinity [of Harper's Ferry] today. Have any of the infantry marched north from the Potomac?

Maj. Gen. Joseph Hooker[3]

While Hooker was not getting the desired information from his cavalry about the enemy, he was receiving a steady flow of reports from Tyler on Maryland Heights across the river from Harper's Ferry. Tyler's signal officer, Capt. Nahum Daniels, from a position near Sharpsburg, had observed the

---

1 Lee to Stuart, June 23, 1863, OR 27, pt. 3, 923.

2 Mosby, *Stuart's Cavalry*, 173.

3 Hooker to Tyler, June 22, 1863, OR 27, pt. 3, 261.

enemy crossing the river into Maryland all day, and he believed there were now as many as 30-40,000 troops in and around the town.[4]

That morning, after Pleasonton withdrew from the Blue Ridge to Aldie, two deserters from the 9th Georgia Regiment of Hood's division had arrived. They said that Lee was at Winchester; Longstreet's troops were on their way there; and Hill's corps was marching up from Culpeper on the west side of the mountains, but it had not yet reached the main army. In reporting this to Hooker, Pleasonton added that a Buford scouting party atop the Blue Ridge had spotted an infantry camp about two miles long on the Shenandoah River just below Ashby's Gap.[5]

Having been prevented by Stuart from penetrating the mountain gaps and obtaining information first hand, Pleasonton had to rely on more tentative sources: deserters and local blacks. Lee was not in Winchester as reported, but some 12 miles to the east in Berryville. Longstreet's corps was protecting the gaps before moving north toward the Potomac River, and not marching toward Winchester. The information about Hill was vague and for all practical purposes useless. By June 21, Hill's corps had reached the vicinity of White Post and Berryville in the Shenandoah Valley.[6]

Although Pleasonton did not identify the Rebel camp that Buford's men supposedly spotted in the Valley, it would have undoubtedly been McLaws infantry brought up to protect Ashby's Gap. But Pleasonton's claim that Buford sent a party to the top of the mountain is curious because neither Buford nor Col. William Gamble, 1st Brigade commander, mention this otherwise important incident in their post-action reports.[7]

For some reason Pleasonton failed to employ Capt. Samuel Means' Loudoun Rangers for scouting in the Loudoun Valley. This unit, normally

---

4 Tyler to Hooker, June 22, 1863, ibid., pt. 2, 26; Ewell's post-action report, n.d., 1863, 443. Daniels' estimate nearly doubled the actual number, since Ewell's entire corps including his cavalry support totaled less than 24,000. The Union signal officer had seen Early's division of Ewell's corps crossing the river. Ewell's other two divisions were already in Maryland moving northward. Gottfried, *Roads to Gettysburg*, 122-23. For the strength of Ewell's corps and its cavalry support, see Busey and Martin, *Regimental Strengths and Losses*, 169, 247, 251-52.

5 Pleasonton, to Williams, June 22, 1863, OR 27, pt. 1, 912.

6 Lee to Jones, June 20, 1863, in Dowdey, *The Wartime Papers*, 522-23; Walter Lord (ed.), *The Fremantle Diary: Being the Journal of Lieutenant Colonel Arthur James Lyon Fremantle* (Short Hills, NJ, 1954), 181; OR 27, pt. 2, 366, 613; Gottfried, *Roads to Gettysburg*, 104, 117.

7 Buford & Gamble post-action reports, OR 27, pt. 1, 920-21, 932-33.

based in the Berlin (Brunswick) and Point of Rocks area of Maryland just across the Potomac River from the Loudoun Valley, had been formed a year earlier from disaffected Virginians mostly from the Quaker community northwest of Leesburg. They were the natural enemy of Mosby's partisans and could have provided Pleasonton with a native Virginia force to help the Union cavalry maneuver around Stuart's screen. They had guided Union cavalry units through Northern Virginia in early 1862, and served as scouts and couriers during the Antietam campaign in September 1862.[8]

Although Munford's brigade blocked the roads leading out of Aldie toward Ashby's and Snicker's Gaps on June 17, conceivably Means might have recommended that Pleasonton bypass Munford by sending a party north to Vestal's Gap (present day Keyes Gap) which afforded a clear view of the Shenandoah Valley below and direct access to Berryville, the location of Lee's headquarters at the time.[9]

Pleasonton's orders from Hooker had been to "put the main body of your command in the vicinity of Aldie, and push out reconnaissances toward Winchester, Berryville, and Harper's Ferry [in the Shenandoah Valley]" in order to provide "information of where the enemy is, [the size of] his force, and his movements." Despite being unable to fulfill these requirements, Pleasonton stated in a message to Hooker, "Being satisfied I had accomplished all that the expedition designed, I returned to this place [Aldie]."[10]

Although the Army of Potomac command was dubious of Pleasonton's contention that he fulfilled his mission, a story in the New York *Herald* took him at his word: "General Pleasanton's [sic] official dispatch of the late cavalry fight at Aldie is dated from Upperville, near the eastern foot of the Blue Ridge. The battle of Sunday [June 21] . . . resulted in a decided success." Pleasonton's troopers drove Stuart's "for the entire day, until he reached Upperville, inflicting a severe loss." What this story does not reveal is that Pleasonton's five days of close encounters with Stuart's cavalry that reportedly inflicted "a severe

---

8   Gordon, *Never the Like Again*, 60-63.

9   Mumford to McClellan, June 22, 1863, *OR* 27, pt. 2, 739; Gordon, *Never the Like Again*, 63. The path around Munford's forces would have been north about 14 miles from Gilbert's Corner (just east of Aldie on present day U.S. 15) to Vestal's Gap Road (paralleling present day State Route 7) and west for some 15 miles to the gap in the Blue Ridge.

10   Pleasonton to General [Hooker], *OR* 27, pt. 1, 913; O'Neill, *The Cavalry Battles*, 168. For Hooker's original orders to Pleasonton, see Williams to Pleasonton, June 17, 1863, *OR* 27, pt. 3, 172.

loss" resulted in considerably more Union than Rebel casualties. Moreover, the Federals could not penetrate the Confederate screen to pinpoint the location of Lee's army. The line in this story reflects Pleasonton's own mindset—getting credit for fighting battles, at the expense of the actual objective of gathering useful information about the enemy. Stuart listed his losses during these operations as 65 killed, 279 wounded, and 166 missing, for a total of 510 casualties. The official Union count was 82 killed, 336 wounded, and 465 missing, for a total of 883.[11]

Stuart's adjutant, Maj. Henry McClellan, later observed that Pleasonton failed to achieve his objective, because Stuart had prevented it. Lieutenant Fitzhugh, 5th Virginia Cavalry, also noted Pleasonton's inability "to ascertain Lee's movements along the Potomac." In fact, this was the second failure on Pleasonton's part within a few days, since he did not follow orders to scout along the Rappahannock as far as the Blue Ridge, and thereby missed observing Ewell's corps before its attack on Winchester.[12]

Captain John Esten Cooke of Stuart's staff placed the cavalry battles that took place at Aldie, Middleburg, and Upperville from June 17-21 in proper perspective: "The enemy had accomplished their object, and they had not accomplished it. Stuart was forced to retire, but [Pleasonton's cavalry] had not succeeded in penetrating to the [Blue] Ridge."[13]

In the meantime, Sharpe had sent Sgt. Milton Cline and a team of BMI scouts out to search for Lee's forces. They discovered two regiments reportedly part of Longstreet's corps and found that the line of enemy infantry began between Piedmont and Rectortown and continued toward Front Royal where a "considerable" force was located. Pickett's and Hood's divisions were on the west side of Snicker's Gap. Cline had learned that Ewell was establishing a transportation line to move confiscated "stores" from Maryland and Pennsylvania back into Virginia, and Hill had reached the Shenandoah Valley.[14]

---

11 New York *Herald*, June 23, 1863; Stuart's post-action report, OR 27, pt. 2, 691; "General Return of Casualties in the Union Forces during the Gettysburg Campaign, June 3—August 1, 1863," pt. 1, 193. See also Trout, *In the Saddle with Stuart*, 73

12 McClellan, *The Life and Campaigns*, 312; Driver, *5th Virginia Cavalry*, 56.

13 John Esten Cooke, *Wearing of the Gray: being Personal Portraits, Scenes, and Adventures of the War* (Baton Rouge, 1959), 229.

14 Sharpe to Butterfield, June 23, 1863, OR 27, pt. 3, 266. Longstreet's regiments that Cline was referring to belonged to McLaws' division that on June 18 had marched from Mud Run in

Location in the center of Middleburg where Stuart's and Pleasonton's cavalry clashed.
Photo by the author

This timely and detailed report substantiated what Hooker knew about the location of Ewell and Longstreet, and added new, accurate information about Hill. It also confirmed Pleasonton's earlier report of Hill's corps being in the Shenandoah Valley, and therefore in position to support Longstreet. A message from Lee to Ewell confirmed that Hill arrived on June 21 in the vicinity of Berryville.[15]

That morning Stuart reported the results of his encounter with Pleasonton's cavalry to Lee, who was some 20 miles away on the west side of the mountains just outside Berryville. Lee thought the enemy was trying "to arrest our progress and ascertain our whereabouts." Lee was correct about Hooker's desire to pinpoint the location of his army, but Hooker had no

Fauquier County to Piedmont Station on the Manassas Gap Railroad. Longstreet's post-action report, ibid., pt. 2, 366.

15 Lee to Ewell, June 22, 1863, ibid., pt. 3, 914.

intention of penetrating the gaps with his infantry to engage Lee in battle "to arrest [his] progress."[16]

Notwithstanding Stuart's decision to use defensive tactics to prevent Pleasonton from penetrating the Blue Ridge gaps, Peter W. Alexander, a newspaper reporter accompanying Lee's army, continued his stream of criticism aimed at Stuart ever since Union forces had surprised him at Brandy Station. After praising Lee, Ewell, Longstreet, and Hill, Alexander went out of his way to censure Stuart, citing his subordinates as sources. The reporter's criticism was overblown and apparently was intended to damage Stuart's reputation. Although his officers and men may have questioned Stuart's decisions at the time, his close aides had none when later writing about the Loudoun County cavalry battles. Staff members H. B. McClellan, W. W. Blackford, John Esten Cooke, and Frank Smith Robertson agreed with Stuart that the confrontations called for a defensive strategy against Pleasonton. They also agreed that Stuart achieved his overall objective to deny the enemy information about the movements of Lee's army.[17]

Despite the dispatches Mosby had captured on June 17 that revealed Union army positions and immediate operational objectives, Lee continued to be anxious about the enemy's intentions. He inquired of Stuart whether he knew where the enemy was and what he was doing. Lee was rightly concerned that Hooker would "steal a march on us, and get across the Potomac before we are aware."[18]

16 Lee to Stuart, June 22, 1863, ibid., 913; Mosby, *Stuart's Cavalry*, 81; Gottfried, *Roads to Gettysburg*, 121-22. Lieutenant Colonel Fremantle, a British observer en route to catch up with the Confederate army, noted in his diary reaching Berryville at 9:00 a.m. on June 22 and that Lee's headquarters "were a few hundred yards beyond this place." Lord, *The Fremantle Diary*, 181. Lee remained in Berryville until the morning of June 24. Mosby, *Stuart's Cavalry*, 98.

17 Charleston *Mercury*, July 6, 1863; McClellan, *The Life and Campaigns*, 306-14; Blackford, *War Years with "Jeb" Stuart*, 221; Cooke, *Wearing of the Gray*, 228-29; Trout, *In the Saddle with Stuart*, 63-70. The dispatch was signed P. W. A., Alexander's initials. The Charleston *Mercury*, an arch critic of the Davis administration, had taken Stuart to task after Brandy Station. Charleston *Mercury*, June 17, 1863. In a letter to his wife, Stuart displayed no awareness of the reporter's criticism; rather he described the battle on June 21 as a success. Mitchell, *Stuart's Letters*, 325-26.

18 Lee to Stuart, June 22, 1863, OR 27, pt.3, 913; Mosby, *Stuart's Cavalry*, 64-67.

Road through Paris to Ashby's Gap. It was here that war correspondent
Peter W. Alexander filed his report criticizing Stuart as an ineffective cavalry commander.
Photo by the author

Stuart's Ill-fated Maneuver

> I submitted . . . the plan of . . . passing through [a] gap in Bull Run Mountains, attain the
> enemy's rear, passing between his main body and Washington, and cross into
> Maryland, joining our army north of the Potomac.
>
> Maj. Gen. J.E.B. Stuart[19]

> Stuart made to Lee a very unwise proposition, which Lee more unwisely entertained.
>
> Edward Porter Alexander[20]

Mosby's rangers had been hanging close to Hooker's forces observing
activity and capturing Union supply trains, horses, and mules. At Rector's
Crossroads, Mosby reported to Stuart that the Army of the Potomac was
stationary. At the time, the seven Federal infantry corps were sprawled across
the countryside defending Washington from attack. Stuart told Mosby that Lee
had instructed him that, if the enemy was not moving northward, he could leave

19 Stuart's post-action report, *OR* 27, pt. 2, 692.

20 Alexander, *Military Memoirs of a Confederate,* 374.

Location of Rector's Crossroads where Stuart made his headquarters and where
Mosby came to make his reports to Stuart.
Photo by the author

two brigades behind to guard the Blue Ridge Mountain gaps and protect his
rear, while he took the other three brigades into Maryland to screen the right
flank of Ewell's corps operating in Pennsylvania. Stuart was also ordered to
keep Ewell informed of the enemy's movements and gather supplies for the
army.[21]

Lee had previously written to Ewell, whose corps was strung out on both
sides of the Potomac, that he could not give "definite instructions" since he did
not know what Hooker's army was about. Meanwhile, Lee had given Imboden
similar instructions to those of Stuart: "advance north of the Potomac, and keep
on the left of [Ewell's] advance into Pennsylvania."[22]

---

21 Mosby, *Stuart's Cavalry*, 76; Jones, *Ranger Mosby*, 148-49; Lee to Stuart, June 22, 1863, *OR 27*,
pt. 3, 913, 915; Gottfried, *Roads to Gettysburg*, 129. The Union XII, XI, V and II corps stretched
from Leesburg south to Thoroughfare Gap in the Bull Run Mountains, a distance of about 20
miles. The I and III corps were 5-10 miles farther east at Guilford and Centreville, and the VI
Corps was about five miles even farther east at Fairfax Court House. Scott Bowden and Bill
Ward, *Last Chance for Victory: Robert E. Lee and the Gettysburg Campaign* (Cambridge, MA, 2001),
116-17.

22 Lee to Ewell, Lee to Imboden, June 19, 1863, *OR 27*, pt. 3, 905-06.

While meeting with Stuart at Rector's Crossroads, Mosby proposed a risky undertaking. He recommended taking a shortcut via Glasscock Gap in the Bull Run Mountains. By turning north after passing through the gap, Mosby believed Stuart could maneuver between the widely dispersed corps of the Union army and cross the Potomac at Seneca where Mosby had crossed several days before. Although hazardous, this route would be more direct and conceivably would save Stuart time in reaching Pennsylvania and Ewell's right flank.[23]

June 23: Working Hard To Get the Upper Hand: Lee's Plan of Deception

It looks as if Lee's movement is toward Hagerstown and in [to] Pennsylvania.
Brig. Gen. Daniel Tyler[24]

The season is now so far advanced as to render it improbable that the enemy will undertake active operations on the Carolina and Georgia coast. . . . This is confirmed by the Northern papers.
Gen. Robert E. Lee[25]

Lee's strategic invasion plan included a "diversion" that would siphon off part of the Army of the Potomac's forces. From his headquarters in West Virginia just across the Potomac from Williamsport, Maryland, Lee proposed the plan to President Davis. Based on information in Northern newspapers about Union forces along the coast of southern Virginia and North Carolina,

---

23 Jones, *Ranger Mosby*, 145; McClellan, *The Campaigns of Stuart's Cavalry*, 315; James A. Ramage, *Gray Ghost*, 93; O'Neill, *The Cavalry Battles*, 168-69. Mosby had also been the author of the plan that evolved into Stuart's successful expedition around McClellan's army during the Peninsula campaign in 1862. Mosby, *Gray Ghost*, 84-85. Since Stuart's scout Frank Stringfellow had not rejoined the cavalry at Salem on June 20 as expected with information about the Potomac River crossings, Stuart was uncertain about the most expeditious route northward. Bakeless, *Spies of the Confederacy*, 317-18.

24 Tyler to Hooker, June 23, 1863, *OR* 27, pt. 2, 27.

25 Lee to Davis, June 23, 1863, ibid., pt. 3, 924. Lee often relied on Northern newspapers for intelligence about Union army activities. Lee's access to Northern newspapers while he was moving through the Shenandoah Valley suggests they were delivered to him via the "Secret Line" operated by the Confederate Signal Corps, or by couriers from the forward elements of his invasion force in Pennsylvania. For more on the Secret Line, see Tidwell, *Come Retribution*, 87-91.

Lee thought the time propitious to transfer otherwise unengaged Confederate troops from those areas northward to threaten Washington. (He had already requested Brig. Gen. Samuel Jones, commanding the Department of Western Virginia, to harass Union troops there to prevent their being sent to "other points," i.e., to Hooker's army.)[26]

This, Lee believed, would cause Union authorities to divert units from Hooker's army in order to defend the capital city. In the event of a clash with Hooker, this maneuver would help Lee prevail. If Davis concurred with his suggestions, Lee suggested the story of a growing Rebel menace against Washington should be planted in the Richmond newspapers to mislead the enemy. Union troops might even be pulled out of southern Virginia and the Carolinas, Lee wrote, which "would, I think, relieve us of any apprehension of an attack upon Richmond during our absence."[27]

Lee's fertile and increasingly anxious mind was weighing the odds if a direct encounter with the enemy happened somewhere in the North. He knew Hooker outnumbered him, and he wanted to rectify that situation in any way possible. In this case, he attempted to accomplish this by deceiving the enemy.[28]

Signal Corps Tracks Lee's Movements into Maryland

> Thus, conjointly by flag signals and the signal telegraph, a complete line was established from a reliable station of observation on Maryland Heights direct to the commanding general at Fairfax Court House.
>
> Capt. Lemuel B. Norton[29]

That same day, Tyler provided important and detailed information to Hooker from Maryland Heights. Confederate troops at Sharpsburg the previous day had all left the area: the infantry and artillery moving northward toward Hagerstown and the cavalry eastward toward Frederick. Early's division

---

26 Lee to Jones, June 20, 1863, Lee to Davis, June 23, 1863, *OR* 27, pt. 3, 906, 924-25; Faust, *Historical Times Encyclopedia*, 404.

27 Lee to Davis, June 23, 1863, *OR* 27, pt. 3, 924-25.

28 Lee was able to keep tabs on the size of the opposing army through a combination of ready access to Northern newspapers, reports from spy networks in the North, and scouts that penetrated Union lines. Tidwell, *Come Retribution*, 80-102; Dowdey, *The Wartime Papers*, 502-50.

29 Norton's post-action report, *OR* 27, pt. 1, 200. Norton was Chief Signal Officer, Army of the Potomac.

of Ewell's corps with 34 pieces of artillery and about 15,000 infantry had the day before marched toward Hagerstown to join Rodes. Tyler concluded that Lee's army was moving into Pennsylvania via Hagerstown. However, Rebel cavalry moving east raised the possibility of a threat to Baltimore or Washington.[30]

This report, while providing vital information to Hooker, was mistaken about the troops and artillery belonging only to Early's division. Undoubtedly the signal corps team had observed both Johnson's and Early's divisions on the march. Attributing that large a force and number of guns to one division would have grossly inflated the size of Lee's army. In fact, Johnson's division had almost 6,800 troops and 16 guns. Adding them to Early's almost 5,800 troops and 16 guns would have accounted for the Signal Corps team's estimate of 15,000 troops and 34 guns.[31]

Still uncertain whether Lee's objective was Pennsylvania, Washington, or Baltimore, Hooker continued to hold his army south of the Potomac deployed roughly from Manassas north to Leesburg to shield the capital. He told Sharpe to instruct his agent Babcock, then at Monocacy Junction in Maryland, to send some men to the Turner's Gap area of South Mountain and scope out the Cumberland Valley to the west for enemy forces. Hooker also wanted to know whether the enemy controlled the National Road (present-day Route 40A) at Turner's Gap or Crampton's Gap in South Mountain. The vantage point atop South Mountain from these locations was some seven and 15 miles northeast of Maryland Heights respectively. From these three positions, Union observers had an excellent view of the routes Lee's army was traveling.[32]

---

30 Tyler to Hooker, June 23, 1863, ibid., pt. 2, 27.

31 Ibid.; Busey and Martin, *Regimental Strengths and Losses*, 194. Tyler also reported a clear atmosphere allowed observation of a line of troops 10 or 12 miles long moving from the Berryville area toward the ford at Shepherdstown. These troops belonged to Anderson's and possibly Heth's divisions of Hill's corps that were then marching toward the Potomac through Charlestown. Tyler to Hooker, June 23, 1863, OR 27, pt. 2, 27.

32 Sharpe to Babcock, ibid., pt. 3, 271; OR *Atlas*, Plate 62, 1; Plate 27, 1, 3. The next day, Col. Albert J. Myer, Union Signal Corps chief in Washington, sent a message to Norton, Chief Signal Officer of the Army of the Potomac, emphasizing the important intelligence aspects of controlling the mountain areas. If a considerable portion of the army was moving into Maryland, Myer wrote, he should suggest to Butterfield keeping the crest of South Mountain and Catoctin Ridge clear of enemy's scouts and signal officers by sending cavalry to these locations. Both were excellent platforms for observing movements in the valleys below. Myer to Norton, June 25, 1863, OR 27, pt. 3, 321.

Lee "Clarifies" Stuart's Orders

If General Hooker's army . . . [does] not appear to be moving northward, I think you
had better withdraw—this side of the mountain.

General R. E. Lee[33]

According to his staffer Maj. Charles Marshall, Lee worried about any misunderstanding, so he sent Stuart updated orders. However, these only confused matters. If Hooker's army remained inactive, Lee said, Stuart could withdraw with three of his brigades. In the event the Army of the Potomac should not appear to be moving northward, then Lee thought it better for Stuart to withdraw west of the mountains the following night, cross the Potomac at Shepherdstown, then move on to Frederick, Maryland. However, Lee added, Stuart would be able to judge whether he could "pass around their army without hindrance . . . and cross the river east of the mountains." In other words, Lee gave Stuart two distinct options regarding where to cross the Potomac—east or west of the mountains. As in the past, Lee authorized Stuart to use his best judgment how to act as circumstances dictated.[34]

After Stuart heard Mosby's plan for passing through the Union army, he ordered him to reconnoiter the Yankees once again to confirm that Hooker was still stationary. Mosby scouted within enemy lines, and found that Hooker's army had not moved. Reassured by Mosby's report, Stuart ordered him to reconnoiter the Potomac River approaches toward Dranesville and to rendezvous back with him near Gum Springs. That night, Stuart met with

33 Lee to Stuart, June 23, 1863, *OR* 27, pt. 3, 923.

34 Frederick Maurice, ed., Charles Marshall, *Lee's Aide-de-Camp* (Lincoln, NE, 2000), 201-02;
Lee to Stuart, June 23, 1863, *OR* 27, pt. 3, 923.

Road leading out of Burkittsville, Maryland, to Crampton's Gap in South Mountain. Hooker
instructed Babcock to find out if the gap was held by the enemy.
Photo by the author

Hampton's, Fitz Lee's, and W. H. F. Lee's brigades near Salem Depot
(present-day Marshall).[35]

June 24: Vital Information Arrives at Union Headquarters

> The students at St. James College Hagerstown came from there today. They report . . .
> no [Rebel] force between Hagerstown and Frederick. . . . No force at Boonsboro or . . .
> at South Mountain.
>
> John Babcock[36]

At Union headquarters, Hooker confirmed that Pleasonton had still not
discovered Lee's whereabouts when he asked him if it were possible to find a
local resident who was loyal to the cause to cross the Blue Ridge and "look into"
the Shenandoah Valley. Such a person, by avoiding regularly traveled roads,

35 Stuart's post-action report, *OR* 27, pt. 2, 691-92; Mosby, *Stuart's Cavalry*, 169; Jones, *Ranger Mosby*, 145-49.

36 Babcock to Sharpe, June 24, 1863, RG 393, NA.

would be able to perform this service for Pleasonton "with impunity," Hooker thought.[37]

Hooker was again instructing Pleasonton how to get better results. Not without reason: if Pleasonton had used the tactics Hooker suggested—avoiding the main roads to reach the Shenandoah Valley—earlier the likelihood of success would have been greater. Employing Means' Loudoun Rangers to do this mission would have further enhanced that possibility. But events would soon overtake any hope of rectifying this situation.[38]

The 1st New Jersey Cavalry's regimental history noted the purpose of the confrontation with Stuart's cavalry was to protect the Federal army's flank "and ensure the safety, rapidity and secrecy of the change of Hooker's position." So with this much disparity between what army headquarters expected (and what others understood) and what Pleasonton actually did, it's clear that he either misinterpreted his orders to reconnoiter the Shenandoah Valley to learn the location, strength, and intentions of the enemy, or he conveyed a different mission to his subordinates.[39]

Hooker told Halleck the situation had not changed much; however, as soon as he learned that the enemy troops at Shepherdstown had crossed the Potomac, he would begin moving northward by sending one or two corps to cut Ewell's forces off from the rest of Lee's army. If the enemy decided not to send additional forces across the river, he planned to make Washington secure with part of his army and use the rest to attack Lee's line of retreat. Whether the enemy decided to advance or retreat, Hooker promised, Halleck could expect "glorious results." This sounded a lot like the bravado before the disastrous outcome at Chancellorsville; it was likely greeted with considerable skepticism.[40]

37 Williams to [Pleasonton], June 24, 1863, OR 27, pt. 3, 288.

38 Ibid. In contrast to Pleasonton's fumblings, Capt. William H. Boyd, Company C, 1st New York Cavalry, operated in Pennsylvania with only 30-40 men. His instructions from General Couch, the Department of the Susquehanna commander, were to scout the lead elements of Ewell's corps and impede their movements. The experienced Boyd kept in contact with Brig. Gen. Albert Jenkins' cavalry brigade, delayed it, and kept tabs on the enemy's whereabouts and progress. Longacre, *The Cavalry at Gettysburg*, 96-97, 136-37; Beach, *The First New York (Lincoln) Cavalry*, 247-50.

39 Pyne, *First New Jersey Cavalry*, 126-27; General Orders, No. 47, April 30, 1863, OR 25, pt. 1, 171.

40 Hooker to Halleck, June 24, 1863, OR 27, pt.1, 55-56.

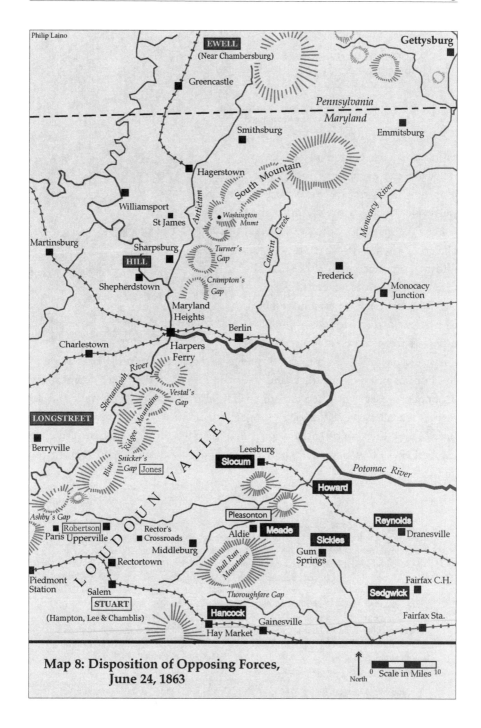

Map 8: Disposition of Opposing Forces,
June 24, 1863

Maj. Gen. Winfield S. Hancock
Library of Congress

Early that morning, Tyler reported to Halleck in Washington that a captured enemy courier placed Lee at Berryville the evening of June 23 and reported Longstreet's corps also at Berryville. That same courier had delivered a message routed to Ewell at Hagers- town. At that time, this information accurately located the three Confed- erate generals.[41]

John Babcock, having moved back to Frederick from Monocacy Junction, reported from there on June 24, that "beyond a doubt" Lee's entire army had passed through Martinsburg and on to the Potomac two days earlier, and the main body could be seen from South Mountain crossing at Shepherdstown. He also said that 9,000 men and 16 pieces of artillery passed through Greencastle, Pennsylvania. This would have been Rodes' division of Ewell's corps that marched through town on June 22, camped two miles beyond it, and requisitioned food and supplies from the citizenry on the 23rd.[42]

---

41 Tyler to Halleck, June 24, 1863, *OR* 27, pt. 2, 27, 28. Because of long distances involved, the Rebels used a courier relay system. Tyler sent this information to Halleck because he suspected the telegraph line to Hooker had been tampered with. Later, Tyler notified Halleck that the wagon train reported at Shepherdstown the previous night was now crossing the Potomac. These wagons doubtless belonged to Anderson's division of Hill's corps, which would cross the river the following day. The report also mentioned a large wagon train, extending as far as the eye could see on the Berryville road that was passing Charlestown toward Shepherdstown. Tyler believed this to be Longstreet's corps, but the wagons moving toward Shepherdstown undoubtedly belonged to Heth's and Pender's divisions of Hill's corps which Longstreet's corps had shielded from being spotted earlier. That morning, Longstreet's three divisions began marching northward, and ended the day in the vicinity of Summit Point, Darksville, and Berryville. Gottfried, *Roads to Gettysburg*, 133-34, 136.

42 [Babcock] to Hooker, June 14, 1863, *OR* 27, pt. 3, 285-86; Gottfried, *Roads to Gettysburg*, 123, 130. These figures were generally on target, since Rodes division had some 8,474 men and 16 guns. Busey and Martin, *Regimental Strengths and Losses*, 209. That afternoon Tyler notified

Later, Babcock informed Sharpe that student refugees from St. James College near Hagerstown had told him that Ewell's corps, including the general himself, with 70 pieces of artillery had passed through Hagerstown on the morning of June 23 towards Chambersburg. The students also reported rapid crossings of the Potomac by Longstreet's and Hill's corps and the presence of no Rebel forces at South Mountain or between Hagerstown and Frederick. This information was particularly important, especially in light of Tyler's report the previous day that Rebel cavalry had moved from Sharpsburg in the direction of Frederick. Except for Stuart's cavalry, Ewell's, Longstreet's, and Hill's corps constituted Lee's entire army. With most if not all of the Confederate forces said to be across the Potomac, a serious threat to Washington could now be discounted. And although the information about Longstreet's corps was premature—he would cross the following day—it triggered significant action at Union headquarters.[43]

Halleck that prisoner interrogations had revealed Longstreet's corps had crossed the ford at Shepherdstown: incorrect, because on that date Longstreet's three divisions were marching from Berryville toward Williamsport on the Potomac. The report also put Hill's corps still at Fredericksburg, clearly misinformation since Hill had reached the Valley by then. Tyler to Halleck, June 24, 1863, *OR* 27, pt. 2, 28; pt. 3, 266; Gottfried, *Roads to Gettysburg,* 133-34.

43 Babcock to Sharpe, June 24, 1863, RG 393, NA; Fishel, *Secret War,* 479. Hill's corps began crossing the Potomac at Shepherdstown on June 24 and was across by June 25. Longstreet's corps did not begin crossing the Potomac at Williamsport until June 25 and completed the following day. Longstreet's post-action report, *OR* 27, pt. 2, 358; Gottfried, *Roads to Gettysburg,* 136, 143. The South Mountain Gap refers to Turner's Gap on the National Pike (present day Alternate U.S. 40), since Reynolds' I Corps marched to Middletown, Maryland, located on the National Pike, then on to South Mountain. John W. Schildt, *Roads to Gettysburg* (Parsons, WV, 1978), 402-03. That evening, Hiram Winchester, Babcock's contact in Frederick, informed Halleck that a scout observed Ewell on June 23 with Johnson's and Rodes' divisions passing through Hagerstown from 1:00 to 5:00 p. m. towards Greencastle. This confirmed what the students had said except for time of day the movement took place. This report was only partially correct, because only Johnson's division was passing through Hagerstown. Rodes was already in Greencastle, Pennsylvania, on June 22. Winchester to Halleck, June 24, 1863, *OR* 27, pt. 3, 289; Gottfried, *The Roads to Gettysburg,* 123, 130; Early's post-action report, August 22, 1863, *OR* 27, pt. 2, 464. Early's division actually comprised 17 infantry regiments and did have 16 guns, but only one regiment of cavalry, the 17th Virginia of Jenkins brigade, supported them. However, Gordon's brigade of six regiments, about 1,900, traveled a separate route. Therefore, the total number of troops in Early's line of march totaled little more than 4,000. So the estimate of 8,000 was double the actuality. Busey and Martin, *Regimental Strengths and Losses,* 203, 251-52. The scout must have observed Johnson's four brigades, but the figure of 11,000 men (8,000 plus 3,000) was inflated since Johnson commanded a total of 7,300 troops including the cavalry units supporting him. Johnson's & Rodes' post-action reports, *OR* 27, pt. 2, 503, 545; Busey and Martin, *Regimental Strengths and Losses,* 195, 247, 251; Myers, *The Comanches,* 187-88; Gottfried, *The Roads to Gettysburg,* 123. The two cavalry "regiments" mentioned in Winchester's

June 25: Hooker's Decisive Action Disrupts Stuart's Plan

General Hancock reports that the enemy have appeared with a force estimated as from four regiments to 6,000 men, with one battery of artillery.

Brig. Gen. Seth Williams[44]

Assume command of the Third and XI Corps, with your own. They are all under orders to cross the river to-day.

Maj. Gen. Joseph Hooker[45]

About an hour after midnight, Stuart and his three brigades began a march that would take them through Glasscock's Gap in the Bull Run Mountains, then north toward Haymarket. To deceive the locals and maintain the secrecy of his mission, Stuart spread the rumor that the cavalry brigades were headed west toward the Shenandoah Valley rather than east across the Loudoun Valley. He also chose to leave in the dead of night to avoid enemy observation.[46]

Around the same time, Hooker, knowing now that most if not all of Lee's army had crossed the Potomac, ordered his forces to follow the enemy across the river. He ordered Reynolds to take charge of the III and XI corps in addition to his own I Corps, and "cross the river to-day." After reporting to Reynolds, a brigade of Stahel's cavalry, supported by a brigade and battery from the XI Corps, would "seize Crampton's Pass and . . . Turner's Gap" in South Mountain. Pleasonton's cavalry would cover the movement from the south side till all the wagon trains had cleared the Potomac, then he was to send one cavalry division ahead to Middletown, Maryland. At the same time, the BMI's

---

message probably were the 35th Virginia and 1st Maryland Battalions that were traveling with Ewell's corps. Longacre, *The Cavalry at Gettysburg*, 93-94. The scout said that Johnson had two brigades, plus two regiments of cavalry for a total of 8,000 men, and Rodes had two brigades totaling 3,000 men. In addition Ewell's corps was said to have 66 pieces of artillery, which was close to the figure of 70 the students had reported. Winchester to Halleck, June 24, 1863, *OR* 27, pt. 3, 289.

44 Williams to [Pleasonton], June 25, 1863, *OR* 27, pt. 3, 309.

45 Hooker to [Reynolds], June 25, 1863, ibid., 305.

46 Stuart's post-action report, August 20, 1863, ibid., pt. 2, 692; Cooke, *Wearing of the Gray*, 230; Harrell, *2nd North Carolina Cavalry*, 147.

Sharpe instructed Babcock to report to and remain with Reynolds' advance force sent to hold the mountain gaps.[47]

At 7:00 a.m., Hooker dispatched some timely orders to Maj. Gen. Winfield Scott Hancock, II Corps commander, to march toward Edward's Ferry on the Potomac via Sudley Springs and Gum Springs, the latter the exact location where Stuart planned to rendezvous with Mosby. Consequently Stuart's cavalry ran into Hancock's corps at Haymarket. The encounter obstructed their planned shortcut through the Union army to reach Ewell's corps in Pennsylvania. Given these unwelcome circumstances, Stuart withdrew about three miles to the southwest to Buckland Mills. Stuart later stated he did this "to deceive the enemy" about his intentions.[48]

Hancock alerted Hooker from his position near Thoroughfare Gap that an enemy force of from "four regiments to 6,000 men with one battery of artillery" had driven in his cavalry escort. Hancock's report triggered a message from army headquarters to cavalry commander Pleasonton ordering him to send a cavalry brigade to support Hancock. Accordingly, Pleasonton directed Gregg to comply with the request with a brigade from his division.[49]

---

47 Hooker to [Reynolds], Williams to Reynolds, Hooker to Hancock, Sharpe to Babcock, all June 25, 1863, *OR* 27, pt. 3, 305-06, 312, 314.

48 Hooker to Hancock, ibid., 306. After firing a few artillery rounds into the Union column, Stuart ordered Fitz Lee to reconnoiter toward Gainesville southeast of Haymarket and sent a dispatch to Lee informing him of Hancock's movements. Stuart's post-action report, ibid., August 20, 1863, *OR*, pt. 2, 692-93; Gottfried, *Roads to Gettysburg*, 143, 145, 149-52. About the same time, Hooker received a relayed message, sent from Couch in Harrisburg to Lincoln, with information from deserters who stated erroneously that Hill and Longstreet were both across the river. Couch put the size of their combined forces at 40,000, a figure slightly less than but reasonably close to the actual size of these two corps, which was almost 43,000. *OR* 27, pt. 2, 30; pt. 3, 295; Busey and Martin, *Strengths and Losses*, 169. Reynolds alerted army headquarters that the XI Corps signal station had not forwarded telegraphic orders to Pleasonton and V Corps commander Meade for their respective corps to march, because the station had already been "broken up" when XI Corps moved out. Reynolds underlined his concern that night in another message. Headquarters soon responded that the dispatches had been sent by messenger to both commanders in Aldie. Reynolds to Williams, Williams to Reynolds, June 25, 1863, *OR* 27, pt. 3, 314, 316, 320. For a discussion of how the Army of the Potomac conducted signal communications during the march northward in June 1863, see Brown, *The Signal Corps, U.S.A.*, 357-59.

49 Hancock to Butterfield, Alexander to Gregg, ibid., 309. The actual size of Stuart's force was about 4,800. Busey and Martin, *Strengths and Losses*, 244. Later, Hancock reported to Butterfield that two regiments of dismounted Rebel cavalry had driven in his cavalry. Hancock to Butterfield, June 25, 1863, *OR* 27, pt. 3, 318.

Pleasonton duly informed headquarters he had complied with the order to send a cavalry brigade to Hancock, but then oddly followed up with a message that he recalled the brigade "since it evidently was a mistake." He did not elaborate further on what this "mistake" was. Even though he had apparently missed an opportunity to confront Stuart and further impede his movements, there is no indication that Hancock or anyone from army headquarters protested Pleasonton's decision.[50]

Costly Lack of Coordination

The preservation of the status in Hooker's army depended on Lee. If Longstreet and Hill had rested one day longer in the Shenandoah Valley, Hooker would have done the same and Stuart would not have found the roads blockaded by his columns marching to the Potomac

John S. Mosby[51]

Because Hancock's corps blocked Stuart's route, his planned rendezvous with Mosby did not take place. When Mosby arrived at Gum Springs and heard artillery fire to the south, he surmised that Stuart had run into enemy forces and, as a result, would retreat toward the Blue Ridge. But when Mosby returned to the Loudoun Valley, he learned that Stuart had not turned back. Unsure of what to do now, Mosby dispersed his rangers and waited.[52]

Meanwhile, Lee, who was at the river crossing in West Virginia opposite Williamsport, informed President Davis that he had had to abandon his communications, because he lacked sufficient troops to defend them. Lee's inability to guard his lines of communications necessarily meant that couriers carrying messages between his army and Richmond would find the trip increasingly hazardous—a situation that would later prove to have serious consequences. The same lack of adequate forces also impelled Lee to pursue his plan to draw off troops from the Army of the Potomac.[53]

50 Pleasonton to Williams, June 25, 1863, *OR* 27, pt. 3, 321-22.

51 Mosby, *Stuart's Cavalry*, 173-79. Mosby, evidently not aware of the existence of the BMI, did not mention its role in setting the Union army in motion to track Lee's army northward.

52 Mosby, *Stuart's Cavalry*, 175, 177.

53 Lee to Davis, June 25, 1863, *OR* 27, pt. 3, 930-31. The route of Lee's lines of communication with Richmond can be traced in the movements of personnel from the signal bureau, the Confederate war department's intelligence organization, who escorted British observer Lt. Col. James Fremantle from the capital to the Confederate army in the Shenandoah

Lee took the opportunity in a letter to the president to reiterate his proposal that redeployment of Rebel forces from the southern Virginia and the Carolinas should be made to threaten the Union capital. He attempted to press the case that if the plan he had previously suggested to Davis—of organizing an army "even in effigy" at Culpeper Court House—could be put into effect, much relief would result for his army and beleaguered Confederate forces elsewhere.[54]

Later, after crossing the Potomac into Maryland, Lee allowed mounting anxiety to overcome his normal reserve in dealing with Davis. He wrote him yet another letter citing his strong conviction of the necessity of coordinated military activity to relieve all threatened localities in the South. Bringing troops north from Richmond and Carolina to the Culpeper area could do this, he believed. It would not only threaten Washington but would prevent the enemy from taking aggressive action. Moreover, he added what was likely his key consideration: "their assistance to this army in its operations would be very great."[55]

Lee had written four letters in the last two days about creating a deception. The closer Lee got to Pennsylvania, the more he became convinced of the necessity for such a stratagem. Although Lee technically had jurisdiction over the troops in the areas in question, he lacked the leverage to force compliance from local commanders. So he looked to Davis to overcome this basic weakness in the Confederate system in which the military prerogatives of individual states hindered and often preempted national requirements.[56]

After Stuart ran into Hancock's corps on June 25, he sent a dispatch to Lee to alert him that Hooker was on the march. Two days later, after detouring around the Union army, Stuart arrived at Fairfax Court House, the now vacated Union army headquarters, and sent a second message to Lee that the "main body" of Hooker's army had moved northward toward Leesburg. For reasons still not clear, Lee did not receive either message from Stuart. And even if he

---

Valley. They traveled through Culpeper, Woodville, Sperryville, and Chester Gap to Front Royal, across two branches of the Shenandoah River, and then north to Lee's headquarters at Berryville. Lord, *The Fremantle Diary*, 176-81.

54 Lee to Davis, June 25, 1863, *OR* 27, pt. 3, 930-31.

55 Ibid., 931-33.

56 Ibid. For Lee's assessment of the military situation throughout the Confederacy, see Lee to Davis, June 2, 1863, ibid., pt. 2, 25:848.

had, neither one reported that Hooker's army had crossed the Potomac—only that it was moving toward it.[57]

Hooker's decision to move his troops northward resulted from Babcock's and Tyler's intelligence reports that the enemy was crossing or preparing to cross the Potomac. Subsequently, Hooker's troops on the move blocked Stuart's passage through the Union positions, forcing his cavalry brigades to take a longer route around the Union forces. Stuart's lengthy delay in returning to the army severely limited Lee's ability to maneuver once the Army of the Potomac moved northward toward Pennsylvania.[58]

Lee did not foresee the necessity of maintaining the bulk of Hill's and Longstreet's corps below the Potomac until Stuart's cavalry was able to pass through the Union army. Nor did Stuart anticipate the need for the main army to remain stationary while he moved toward the Potomac. As a result, the enemy's timely intelligence reporting foiled their plans.

---

57 Stuart's post-action report, *OR* 27, pt.2, 692-94. Although Stuart makes no mention of this second message in his report, a copy of it was inexplicably delivered to the war department in Richmond. McClellan, *The Campaigns of Stuart's Cavalry*, 321-23; Jones, *A Rebel War Clerk's Diary*, 366; Douglas Craig Haines, "Jeb Stuart's Advance to Gettysburg," *Gettysburg Magazine* (July 2003), Issue 29. Charles Marshall says that Stuart later told him that he had sent another message to Lee from Rowser's Ford where he crossed the Potomac River. This would have been a third message from Stuart that never reached Lee. There is no other evidence that he actually sent this message, and Stuart makes no reference to it in his report. Haines, "Jeb Stuart's Advance to Gettysburg," 47.

58 For a detailed discussion of the sequence and accuracy of intelligence reports arriving at Hooker's headquarters during this critical period, see Fishel, *The Secret War*, 475-83.

Chapter Ten

Maneuvering for Advantage: June 26 to 27

General Stuart was directed to hold the mountain passes with part of his command as long as the enemy remained south of the Potomac, and, with the remainder, to cross into Maryland, and place himself on the right of General Ewell.

Gen. Robert E. Lee[1]

Of the troops that marched to the river at Shepherdstown yesterday, I cannot learn that any have crossed, and as soon as I do I shall commence moving.

Maj. Gen. Joseph Hooker [2]

June 26: Hard Traveling for Stuart's Cavalry

Reaching Fairfax Court-House . . . the information was conclusive that the enemy had left this front entirely, the mobilized army having the day previous moved over toward Leesburg.

Maj. Gen. J. E. B. Stuart[3]

[I]t must be acknowledged that the capture of the train of wagons was a misfortune . . . the delay caused to the subsequent march was serious at a time when minutes counted almost as hours.

Maj. Henry B. McClellan[4]

---

1 Lee's post-action report, January 1864, OR 27, pt. 2, 316.

2 Hooker to Maj. Gen. Henry Halleck, June 24, 1863, ibid., pt. 1, 55.

3 Stuart's post-action report, August 20, 1863, ibid., pt. 2, 693.

4 McClellan, *Stuart's Cavalry*, 325. McClellan was Stuart's adjutant general.

Having

been blocked from passing through the Union army, Stuart decided to maneuver his three cavalry brigades around the enemy rather than retreat westward toward the Blue Ridge Mountains. His route led him south and east and separated him from the main army for a number of critical days. Stuart's absence deprived Lee of his most important source of information about the enemy. This problem was only exacerbated when Stuart fell out of touch with Mosby, since Mosby had been successful in keeping watch on Hooker's army. After being delayed, Stuart finally arrived in Fairfax, Virginia. Although behind schedule, he still could reach Ewell's corps in Pennsylvania in a reasonably timely manner. However, recurring delays loomed ahead.[5]

Although Confederate intelligence collection functioned well at the outset of the campaign, it stumbled in adapting to the fluid operating conditions during the Northern invasion. This was largely due to the concentration of intelligence responsibility in Jeb Stuart and Lee. By contrast, the Union intelligence process centered on the BMI that Hooker had established earlier in the year. This agency provided a basis for the systematic acquisition and processing of all information about the enemy during the campaign.[6]

Confirming Babcock's report of June 24, Tyler informed Lt. Col. Donn Piatt, chief of staff of the Middle Department in Baltimore, that he believed Ewell's, Longstreet's, and Hill's corps had all crossed to the north side of the Potomac. The Union and Confederate armies were on a collision course that would throw them together in southern Pennsylvania.[7]

As Ewell's divided corps marched towards its target Harrisburg, mapmaker Jed Hotchkiss noted in his journal that General Lee had told Ewell he thought that a battle would eventually take place near Frederick, Maryland, or Gettysburg. Lee was well aware that the Union army might soon overtake his forces. The absence of specific information from Jeb Stuart about Hooker's location, however, lulled him into a false sense of security. Such was his reliance

---

5   Stuart's post-action report, August 20, 1863, OR 27, pt. 2, 693, 694-97; Williamson, *Mosby's Rangers*, 79-80; Jones, *Ranger Mosby*, 150-52; Alexander, "Gettysburg Cavalry Operations," 12-31.

6   Ryan, "A Battle of Wits: . . . Searching for Lee," *Gettysburg Magazine* (July 2004), Issue 31, 6:37-38. The BMI and other information collection elements, such as the Signal Corps, served as alternate suppliers of intelligence, especially when the Union cavalry was unsuccessful in fulfilling its reconnaissance mission.

7   Tyler to Piatt, June 26, 1863, OR 27, pt. 2, 32.

on Jeb Stuart, Lee thought that if the Federal army had crossed the Potomac, he would have definitely heard from him. Silence from Stuart meant that Hooker was still in Virginia.[8]

Pleasonton's main job at this juncture was to guard the rear of the Union army while it crossed the pontoon bridges over the Potomac. At 1:00 a.m., he informed Gregg, whose division was guarding the roads from Aldie and Gum Springs, that he wanted to know as early as possible if he encountered any enemy force in his front.[9]

After returning to Aldie, Pleasonton moved to Leesburg and informed Butterfield that his cavalry were covering the army as it moved north across the pontoon bridges at Edward's Ferry into Maryland. The telegraph operator of Hancock's corps reported "a body of several thousand cavalry at Gainesville, from the direction of New Baltimore." And, while a force of this size posed a major threat, Pleasonton smugly downplayed it, giving every indication he had the situation under control. Unknown to Pleasonton, this threatening body of cavalry was Stuart and his three brigades.[10]

After the main Confederate army completed crossing the Potomac River into Maryland, it continued on into Pennsylvania without serious incident. Lee and his headquarters contingent, after fording the river the previous day at Williamsport, continued on to the Maryland-Pennsylvania border. Meanwhile, Ewell's corps had moved on to Carlisle and York.[11]

Keeping Pace with the Enemy

> So far as the general [Stahel] has been able to ascertain, there is no force of the enemy in the neighborhood of any of the [South Mountain] gaps, nor do they appear to have any intention of coming this side.
>
> Maj. H. Baldwin, Jr.[12]

---

8 McDonald, *Make Me a Map of the Valley*, 155; Lee's post-action report, January 1864, *OR* 27, pt. 2, 316; Early's post-action report, August 22, 1863, 465.

9 HQ Army of the Potomac Orders, June 25, 1863, *OR* 27, pt. 3, 314; Alexander to Gregg, June 26, 1863, 333.

10 Pleasonton to Butterfield, June 26, 1863, ibid.

11 Lee to Davis, July 4, 1863, ibid., pt. 2, 298; Driver and Ruffner, *1st Battalion Virginia Infantry, 39th Battalion Virginia Cavalry, 24th Battalion Virginia Partisan Rangers*, 56.

12 Baldwin, Jr. to Williams, June 26, 1863, *OR* 27, pt. 3, 337. Baldwin was AAG of Stahel's cavalry division.

Brig. Gen. H. Judson Kilpatrick
Library of Congress

Hooker had instructed Stahel's cavalry division to report to Reynolds and his three-corps vanguard as it crossed the river into Maryland and moved towards South Mountain. Upon his arrival, Reynolds sent Stahel ahead to protect the mountain gaps from an advance by Lee's forces. Stahel found no enemy activity in the area of Crampton's and South Mountain [Turner's] Gaps. From what he was able to learn, he told Reynolds, the "whole Rebel army was marching toward Harrisburg."[13]

Besides covering the mountain gaps, Stahel deployed a brigade north of Frederick to reconnoiter into Pennsylvania. He assured Reynolds that he had sent out reliable scouting parties to penetrate the enemy's lines and learn their strength and plans. Local organizations were also actively snooping around, including civilian volunteers under the leadership of Gettysburg lawyer David McConaughy.[14]

Stahel would not be afforded the opportunity to oversee completion of this mission, however. For Hooker arranged for his cavalry division to be transferred officially from the Department of Washington to the Army of the Potomac, and then orchestrated Stahel's reassignment to the Department of the Susquehanna. Stahel had too much seniority, and Hooker wrote, his "presence here as senior major-general will much embarrass me and retard my movements." Thus Stahel's cavalry was folded as a division into Pleasonton's

---

13 Hooker to Slocum, June 25, 1863, ibid., 312; Stahel to Reynolds, June 27, 1863, 334. Longacre, *The Cavalry at Gettysburg*, 162-63. BMI's Colonel Sharpe sent both civilian agent Babcock and Captain McEntee to Reynolds' support, greatly enhancing his intelligence capability. Fishel, *The Secret War*, 486.

14 Stahel to Reynolds, June 26, 1863, *OR* 27, pt. 3, 335; Longacre, *The Cavalry at Gettysburg*, 163; Eric J. Wittenberg, "John Buford and the Gettysburg Campaign," *Gettysburg Magazine* (July 1994), no. 11, 37; Fishel, *The Secret War*, 456-57.

corps, and newly promoted Brig. Gen. Hugh Judson Kilpatrick assumed command of it. Though he could not have known it at the time, Hooker's ham-handed method of undercutting Stahel foreshadowed his own imminent demise.[15]

Just after noon, Pleasonton again informed Butterfield and Stanton that he had learned the night before that several thousand Rebel cavalry were currently at Gainesville. Since he had Gregg's and Buford's divisions guarding the roads to the west and south, he reassured them that his "dispositions cover that." In other words, don't worry, I am on top of the threat.[16]

Pleasonton offered no details, however, as to how his "dispositions" were going to blunt "several thousand" enemy cavalry that posed a threat to the Union army. No evidence indicates that Pleasonton ordered a reconnaissance of this large, and, at the time, unidentified force. Obviously he had foregone yet another opportunity to pinpoint the location of Stuart's brigades and possibly track their movements as they circled around the Union army. Pleasonton's lack of perceptiveness and enterprise in this situation raises serious questions about his judgment and reliability. His job was to protect the rear of the marching army, yet he could not be stirred to investigate a force of reportedly up to 6,000 mounted Rebels operating close to Union lines. In addition to his own cavalry, Pleasonton could have requested help from BMI chief Sharpe to have his scouts check on the threat. He did not do so.[17]

It appears Pleasonton took no action to learn more about the nature of this force, nor did anyone at Hooker's headquarters ensure that he did. Pleasonton's behavior at this period of the campaign, as indeed at others, is virtually inexplicable. Was it simple whimsy? Did he decide that doing nothing was something he had the liberty to do with impunity as a member of the army headquarters cronyism crowd? And did this membership shield him from

15 Hooker to Stanton, July 26, 1863, Halleck to Hooker, July 27, 1863, *OR* 27, pt. 1, 58-60; Longacre, *The Cavalry at Gettysburg*, 163-64. Reynolds also helped pile on Stahel by expressing dissatisfaction with the performance of his cavalry to Hooker. Reynolds to Butterfield, June 27, 1863, *OR* 27, pt. 3, 350-51; Reynolds to Butterfield, June 27, 1863, 351-52.

16 Pleasonton to Butterfield & Stanton, July 27, 1863, *OR* 27, pt. 3, 333.

17 Ibid., 333. Sharpe had previously assigned McEntee and a team of scouts to Pleasonton's cavalry to collect information and produce intelligence. However, since Pleasonton had employed these BMI personnel improperly, Sharpe reassigned them to Reynolds during his march northward. Williams to Pleasonton, June 17, 1863, *OR* 27, pt. 3, 172; Ryan, "A Battle of Wits . . . Searching for Lee," 15-16; Fishel, *The Secret War*, 486.

criticism of his inaction by Hooker? Whatever the explanation, the Army of the Potomac would soon pay a steep price for this inattention to a looming threat in the rear of the army.[18]

June 27: Linchpin of a Battle Lost

In another confusion of orders, [Robertson's and Jones'] cavalry remained for days staring at the empty passes in the Blue Ridge long after Lee had crossed the Potomac.
Clifford Dowdey[19]

Stuart's brigades continued northward and crossed the Potomac the night of June 27 about the same time the tail end of Hooker's forces were crossing the river some eight miles upstream. Lee, who had arrived in Chambersburg along with Hill's and Longstreet's corps, was orchestrating the movement of his army across Pennsylvania unaware that Hooker's army cautiously, but steadily, pursued them.[20]

With the Union army to his west between him and Lee, Stuart's task of informing Lee about enemy activities fell to Robertson who commanded the two brigades (one of them Brig. Gen. William "Grumble" Jones's) that remained at the Blue Ridge gaps. Stuart's instructions were to operate on the "usual" front around Middleburg and observe the enemy. And in case the enemy withdrew from the area, both brigades were to rejoin the main army.[21]

The mission Stuart assigned Robertson involved standard cavalry duty, yet, in this case, if not implemented correctly, it had the potential to disrupt Lee's Northern invasion. Robertson's written instructions from Stuart were specific: he was "to watch the enemy; deceive him as to our designs, and harass his rear if you find he is retiring." After the enemy had moved away from the area, Robertson was to withdraw to the west of the mountains and the Shenandoah

18 Coddington, *The Gettysburg Campaign*, 198, 228; Rummel, *Cavalry on the Roads to Gettysburg*, 145.

19 Clifford Dowdey, *Lee*, 364-65.

20 Lee's post-action report, January, 1863, *OR* 27, pt. 2, 316, Longstreet's post-action report, July 27, 1863, 358; Stuart's post-action report, August, 20, 1863, 693-94; Blackford, *War Years With Jeb Stuart*, 223.

21 Stuart's post-action report, August 20, 1863, *OR* 27, pt. 2, 692. For background on Stuart's troubled relationship with Robertson and Jones, see McClellan, *The Campaigns of Stuart's Cavalry*, 319-21; Longacre, *Lee's Cavalrymen*, 34, 54, 73, 204, 224, 241, 246.

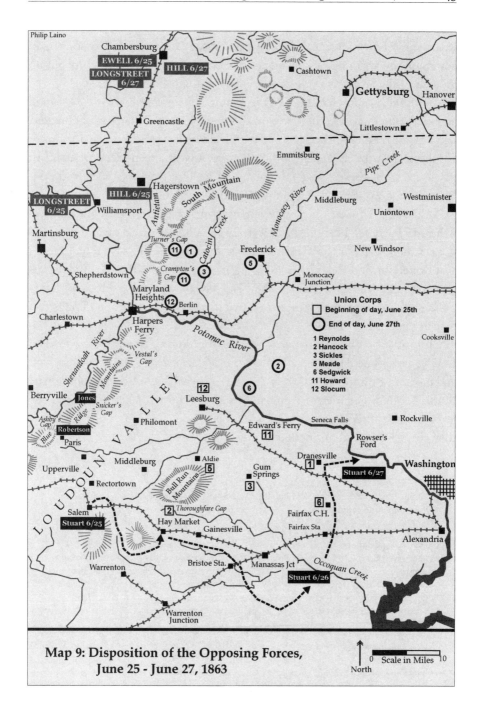

Map 9: Disposition of the Opposing Forces, June 25 - June 27, 1863

Philip Laino

Chambersburg
EWELL 6/25
LONGSTREET 6/27
HILL 6/27
Cashtown
Gettysburg
Hanover
Greencastle
Littlestown
Emmitsburg
Pipe Creek
Hagerstown
South Mountain
HILL 6/25
Middleburg
Westminister
LONGSTREET 6/25
Williamsport
Antietam
Catocin Creek
Monocacy River
Uniontown
Martinsburg
Turner's Gap
11 1
Frederick
5
New Windsor
Shepherdstown
Crampton's Gap
11 3
Maryland Heights
12 Berlin
Monocacy Junction
Charlestown
Harpers Ferry
Cooksville
Shenandoah River
Vestal's Gap
Potomac River
2
6
Berryville
Jones
Snicker's Gap
Leesburg
12
Rockville
Ashby's Gap
Robertson
Paris
Blue Ridge
Philomont
Edward's Ferry
11
Seneca Falls
Rowser's Ford
Upperville
Middleburg
Aldie
5
Gum Springs
Dranesville
1
Stuart 6/27
Washington
Rectortown
Bull Run Mountains
3
6
Salem
Stuart 6/25
Thoroughfare Gap
2
Hay Market
Gainesville
Fairfax C.H.
Fairfax Sta
Alexandria
Warrenton
Bristoe Sta.
Manassas Jct
Occoquan Creek
Stuart 6/26
Warrenton Junction

Union Corps
☐ Beginning of day, June 25th
○ End of day, June 27th

1 Reynolds
2 Hancock
3 Sickles
5 Meade
6 Sedgwick
11 Howard
12 Slocum

0   Scale in Miles   10
North

River, and follow the army while keeping to its right and rear. Robertson was to communicate anything of importance to Longstreet, whose corps brought up the rear of the army, by using cavalry relays through Charlestown.[22]

With Stuart completely out of the picture insofar as gathering information and screening the army, these responsibilities fell upon Robertson's shoulders. Lee now depended on Robertson for critical intelligence. Not only that, once Hooker's army moved northward, Robertson was to screen the movements of the army from the eyes of the enemy by keeping to Lee's right and rear. Robertson, however, failed to implement these orders.[23]

Although Hooker's army began crossing the river into Maryland at Edward's Ferry on the morning of June 25 and the rear-guard cavalry corps did not clear it until the night of June 27, it was not until two days later, on June 29, that Robertson and Jones began to move northward from the Blue Ridge gaps to rejoin Lee in Pennsylvania. They had failed to observe Hooker's army crossing the Potomac; and, therefore, had not alerted Lee through Longstreet that this had taken place.[24]

Information about this period—from the time of Stuart's departure on June 25 until June 29 when Robertson finally decided to abandon his position and move northward—is minimal. Neither Robertson nor his two subordinate North Carolina regimental commanders filed reports. While Jones and the leaders of his three regiments did write reports on the Gettysburg campaign, they virtually ignored this period of time.[25]

22 Stuart to Robertson, June 24, 1863, OR 27, pt. 3, 927. Robertson was also to hold the Blue Ridge Mountain gaps as long as the enemy remained in his front.

23 See Patrick A. Bowmaster, "Confederate Brig. Gen. B. H. Robertson and the 1863 Gettysburg Campaign" (M.A. thesis, Virginia Polytechnic Institute and State University, 1995), 61-94 (copy in GNMP library), for Robertson's role and responsibilities during the Gettysburg campaign. It is possible that neither Lee nor Longstreet were aware that Stuart chose Robertson to command the detachment until after Stuart left on his march to the east. See, for example, Longstreet's message to Stuart on June 22 citing an expectation that Brig. Gen. Wade Hampton would command the two brigades. OR 27, pt. 3, 915.

24 Itinerary of the Army of the Potomac and co-operating forces, June 5-July 31, 1862, ibid., pt. 1, 143; Buford's post-action report, August 27, 1863, 926: Jones' post-action report, July 30, 1863, pt. 2, 751-52; Marshall's post-action report, August 9, 1863, 760; Williams to Howard, June 24, 1863; pt. 3, 290-91, Hooker to Commanding Officer First Corps, June 25, 1863, 305-06; Benham to Williams, June 27, 1863, 353-54.

25 Jones post-action report, July 30, 1863, ibid., pt. 2, 751-52; Flournoy post-action report, July 18, 1863, 756; Marshall post-action report, August 9, 1863, 760.

This seeming lack of activity made it appear that the two brigades had stood down from contact with the enemy following the hard fought battles in the Loudoun Valley that had concluded on June 21. Under ordinary circumstances, a breather to refit after battle would have been justified; however, the urgency of the moment—amidst a monumental invasion of foreign territory—dictated heightened diligence and vigilance. The perfunctory report of Lt. Col. Thomas Marshall, 7th Virginia Cavalry, Jones' brigade, exemplifies instead Confederate lassitude. Here is Marshall's report of June 23: "Moved to Snicker's Gap, and relieved in part the pickets of General Fitzhugh Lee." He goes on to dismiss the following six days, June 24-29, thus: "June 24—Still on picket, and until June 29, upon which day moved in rear of the brigade to camp near Berryville, Clarke County [Virginia]."[26]

The absence of any substantive reporting lends credence to the idea that these brigades basically ignored their mission. The Union army marched for almost three full days within 15-20 miles of the Rebel cavalry's Middleburg and Philomont area of operations, and proceeded northward undiscovered and undisturbed. It was as if Robertson had received no instructions to be always on alert, observe everything, and report anything of importance.[27]

Union cavalry commander Pleasonton reported the inactivity of the two Rebel brigades to Hooker's headquarters. On the second day of Hooker's army crossing the river into Maryland, Pleasonton noted that very few Confederate cavalry pickets had been seen near Middleburg (Robertson's area of operations) that morning, and none in the Snicker's Gap pike area where Philomont was located (Jones' area of operations).[28]

These events were taking place in what has become known as "Mosby's Confederacy," the Loudoun Valley area, yet the partisan leader John Mosby was also uncharacteristically quiescent during the Army of the Potomac's river crossing. He had become separated from Stuart on June 25 and returned to his normal area of operations around Middleburg. Mosby's activities for the next three days while the Union army completed its crossing of the Potomac are

26 Ibid.

27 Longacre, *Lee's Cavalrymen*, 224. Robertson and Jones' bases for operations were Ashby's and Snicker's Gaps in the Blue Ridge, respectively. Stuart to Robertson, June 24, 1863, *OR* 27, pt. 3, 927; Sears, *Gettysburg*, 139-41. One of Robertson's men would later record that they had not seen or made contact with the enemy during this time. Trudeau, *Gettysburg*, 77.

28 Pleasonton to Butterfield, June 26, 1863, *OR* 27, pt. 3, 333.

unknown. Nor is there evidence of any exchange between Mosby and Confederate cavalry when the partisans passed through Snicker's Gap on their way to Pennsylvania on June 28. Coordination might have prevented Mosby's taking a roundabout route northward, rather than following the route the army had taken, and eventually failing to join Lee in Pennsylvania.[29]

Robertson's inaction not to mention his visits to "Oakley," the nearby Dulaney family manor house, plainly indicated that he failed to understand the gravity of the situation and his mission. Despite evidence he did not follow instructions. Robertson claimed in an article published in the *Philadelphia Weekly Times* after the war that, during the latter part of June 1863, he had obeyed Stuart's orders "exactly." He defended himself similarly in a friendly interview in the Memphis *Weekly Appeal* in 1877. In both the article and interview, however, Robertson ignored his failure to follow his chief's orders, exactly or any other way. He carried out no observations of the Yankees, reported nothing to Longstreet, harassed not a soul on the enemy's rear. He maintained that his only duty was to hold Ashby's and Snicker's Gaps, and then withdraw to follow Lee northward.[30]

Mosby later claimed that if Robertson had complied with Stuart's instructions and promptly followed on the right of the army when the enemy crossed the Potomac, Lee's forces would have been able to concentrate sooner and been ready for an attack. Had Robertson acted differently, Lee may have been able to fight a defensive battle, and the outcome at Gettysburg might well have been different.[31]

Robertson should have been observing the Union army as it began crossing the Potomac on the morning of June 25 and sent a message by the cavalry relay system to Longstreet and Lee. The message likely would have arrived in

---

29 Russell, *Gray Ghost*, 94, 156-98; Williamson, *Mosby's Rangers*, 79-80. For a discussion of Mosby's activities after he became separated from Stuart, see Ryan, "A Battle of Wits," pt. 3, 32, 34.

30 Bowmaster, *Robertson and the 1863 Gettysburg Campaign*, 69; Patrick A. Bowmaster, ed., "Confederate Brig. Gen. B. H. 'Bev' Robertson Interviewed on the Gettysburg Campaign," *Gettysburg Magazine* (January 1999), Issue 20, 19-26, 69; Beverly H. Robertson, "The Confederate Cavalry in the Gettysburg Campaign," in Johnson and Buel, eds., *B&L*, 3:253.

31 Mosby, "The Confederate Cavalry in the Gettysburg Campaign," in Johnson and Buel, eds., *B&L*, 3:252. Mosby later recanted his criticism of Robertson in this situation, but his reasoning raises more questions. Mosby, *Stuart's Cavalry*, 195-201.

Chambersburg no later than the end of the day on June 26, which would have been ample warning to give Lee time to concentrate his army.[32]

As it turned out, Stuart's separation from the main army, from the early morning hours of June 25 until the afternoon of July 2, had thrust upon Robertson the primary responsibility for Army of Northern Virginia's information gathering and screening operations. His performance would be a significant factor for continued success of the Northern invasion, and his failure to fulfill this mission placed Lee's army in grave danger as it marched across Pennsylvania.[33]

Anxiety Overtakes Hooker's Better Judgment

> I am fatigued [and] feel very much disgusted and satisfied that there is great want of a [new] Commander.
>
> Provost Marshal General Marsena Patrick[34]

> Maryland Heights have always been regarded as an important point to be held by us . . .
> I cannot approve their abandonment.
>
> Maj. Gen. H. W. Halleck[35]

Hooker instructed his chief of staff Butterfield to send a cavalry force north from Frederick toward Gettysburg and Emmitsburg to see what they could find out about enemy movements. He sent this message from Point of Rocks while on his way to Harper's Ferry and Maryland Heights. The previous day, Stahel had already dispatched the 5th and 6th Michigan Cavalry in that direction.

32 See *OR* 27, pt. 2, 28, for the Confederate courier relay process. Robertson's unexceptional record (Stuart previously rated him poorly, particularly on outpost duty) might have presaged his lack of energy during the campaign. The same cannot be said for "Grumble" Jones, who was considered one of the best outpost officers in the Confederate army. And Jones had separate orders from Stuart, sent through Robertson, that should have made his duties explicit. Stuart to Robertson, June 24, 1863, ibid., pt. 3, 927; Bowmaster, *Robertson and the Gettysburg Campaign*, 65.

33 One writer maintains that Lee instructed Robertson and Jones to stay in place in the Blue Ridge gaps. See Patrick Brennan, "It Wasn't Stuart's Fault," *North & South* (July 2003), 6:34. Another believes that Lee did this in order to protect shipments of cattle and supplies to the South. See David Powell, "Stuart's Ride: Lee, Stuart, and the Confederate Cavalry in the Gettysburg Campaign," *Gettysburg Magazine* (January 1999), Issue 20, 41. Although these ideas are plausible, little evidence can be found to support them.

34 Sparks, *Inside Lincoln's Army*, 261.

35 Halleck to Hooker, June 27, 1863, *OR* 27, pt. 1, 59.

When they arrived in Gettysburg, citizen spies and a captured Confederate courier informed them that Lee's headquarters was at Chambersburg and Ewell's troops were marching toward Carlisle and York.[36]

At Maryland Heights, Hooker found a force of some 10,000 men that, in his opinion, were in condition to take the field, so he requested that they be released for duty with his army. Maryland Heights could not be abandoned, Halleck peremptorily informed him. In that case without these additional troops, Hooker asserted, he was no longer able to meet the requirements of the mission to cover both Harper's Ferry and Washington. He was facing "an enemy in my front of more than my number." Hooker had convinced himself, despite reliable intelligence to the contrary, that the enemy outnumbered him, when the actuality was precisely the opposite. He had had enough: "I am unable to comply with this condition with the means at my disposal," he informed Washington, "and earnestly request that I may at once be relieved from the position I occupy." The army commander's request could not have come at a less propitious time.[37]

36 Hooker to Butterfield, June 27, 1863, ibid., pt. 3, 349, 370; Longacre, *The Cavalry at Gettysburg*, 163-64. On the Gettysburg civilian spies, see Jim Slade and John Alexander, *Firestorm at Gettysburg: Civilian Voices* (Atglen, PA, 1998), 6; Fishel, *The Secret War*, 679n24.

37 Hooker to Halleck, June 26, 1863, OR 27, pt. 1, 58; Halleck to Hooker, June 27, 1863, 59; Hooker to Halleck, June 27, 1863, 60. For PMG Patrick's view of Hooker's claim that his army was outnumbered, see Sparks, *Inside Lincoln's Army*, 261. When the two armies eventually met on the battlefield, Union forces numbered about 94,000 of all arms to Lee's nearly 72,000. Busey and Martin, *Regimental Strengths and Losses*, 16, 169.

Chapter Eleven

A Spy Brings News of the Enemy: June 28 to 29

General Lee heard, through a scout at Chambersburg, of Hooker's advance. As no information of it had come from the cavalry he left in Hooker's front in Virginia, he thought that Hooker was still there.

John S. Mosby[1]

June 28: New Leadership, New Approach

I tell you I think a great deal of that fine fellow Meade . . . [he] will fight well on his own dunghill."

President Abraham Lincoln[2]

[Lee] was of the opinion that the difficulties which would beset Meade in taking command of an army in the midst of a campaign would more than counterbalance his superiority as a general over the previous commander.

Col. A. L. Long[3]

---

1   Mosby, "The Confederate Cavalry in the Gettysburg Campaign," in Johnson & Buel, *B&L*, 3:252.

2   Quoted in Freeman Cleaves, *Meade of Gettysburg* (Norman, OK, 1960), 126.

3   Long, *Memoirs of Lee*, 274.

Washington

acted quickly on Hooker's request to be relieved. In the early morning hours of June 28 near Frederick, Maryland, V Corps commander Meade was astounded to learn of his selection to replace Hooker to lead the Army of the Potomac in pursuit of the invading forces. Lincoln had chosen Meade at this critical stage because he believed Hooker was manifesting some of the same undesirable characteristics that McClellan had in the past when forced to confront Lee.[4]

Meade, a graduate of the 1835 class at West Point and a veteran of the Mexican War, was 48 years old in 1863. After the outbreak of hostilities in 1861, he served with considerable distinction as a brigade, division, and corps commander in the Army of the Potomac during the Peninsula and Seven Days campaigns and at Second Bull Run, Antietam, Fredericksburg, and Chancellorsville.

Lincoln had been "studying" Meade for some time and was aware he had the support of fellow generals as a replacement for Hooker. After deciding on Meade and to ensure that he accepted the assignment, Lincoln made his orders mandatory rather than optional. Given the political considerations inherent in the position, especially because the Army of the Potomac operated close to the seat of power in Washington, Meade had mixed emotions about the appointment. The pride of being chosen army commander was tempered by the proximity of authorities in Washington and their potential to intervene in military decisions and operations. "[Y]ou know how reluctant we both have been to see me placed in this position," Meade explained to his wife, but "as a soldier, I had nothing to do but accept and exert my utmost abilities to command success."[5]

Meade and his opponent, Robert E. Lee, had similar backgrounds in certain ways. Both came from prosperous, aristocratic families that had fallen on hard times. Both had lost their fathers at a young age, Lee through abandonment and Meade through death. As a result, both sought appointments to the Military Academy at West Point because their families could not afford the cost of an education at a private school. Also, though Meade and Lee shared an abiding

---

4   Halleck to Meade, June 27, 1863, OR 27, pt. 1, 61; Meade, *Life and Letters*, 2:11-12; Doris Kearns Goodwin, *Team of Rivals: The Political Genius of Abraham Lincoln* (New York, 2005), 531.

5   Boritt, *Lincoln's Generals*, 85; Warner, *Generals in Blue*, 315-16; Meade, *Life and Letters*, 1:373; 2:11-12.

Maj. Gen. George G. Meade
Library of Congress

interest in and dedication to family and friends, they both had a sense of duty that superseded all other considerations. One difference, however, was that while both wrote frequent letters to their wives while on assignment, Meade invariably wrote in detail about his military plans, strategy, and tactics, while Lee rarely mentioned military matters at all. Meade, like Lee, had acquired knowledge and skills in the field of engineering that would shape his approach to combat. But Lee, older than Meade by almost nine years, had considerably more experience as a military commander. While Lee had already demonstrated audacity and aggressiveness, Meade's style of leadership was less well defined. It remained to be seen how he would perform in his new role as army commander.[6]

Meade avidly avoided the infighting and politics that routinely took place in the military, yet did everything possible to advance his career. His wife, a member of a prominent family, was active in ensuring that the decision makers in Washington did not overlook her husband when it came to approving promotions. But the general's rapid rise in the military had been well earned. Early in the war, at least two of his commanders and one fellow officer praised Meade for his "intelligence" and "gallantry" and as one who fought bravely and commanded with distinction. He was wounded in the arm and side on June 30, 1862, during the battle of White Oak Swamp (Glendale) but quickly recovered and returned to lead his brigade during the Antietam campaign. He was soon elevated to division command to replace Brig. Gen. John Reynolds who was reassigned, and then assumed temporary command of I Corps when Major General Hooker was wounded at Antietam. He took charge of V Corps following the battle of Fredericksburg.[7]

After Lincoln appointed Meade to take the reins of the army from Hooker, another former army commander, Maj. Gen. Ambrose Burnside, sent him best wishes. You are "quite equal to the position you are called to fill," he told Meade, and was "regarded by all who know you as an honest, skillful and unselfish officer, and a true, disinterested patriot." Burnside no doubt recalled how well Meade had fought at Fredericksburg, while other Union commanders greatly disappointed him. "General Meade and his troops deserve great credit for the skill and heroism displayed on this occasion," Burnside had written.

---

6   Meade, *Life and Letters*, 1:1-389; 2:1-8; Lee, *Recollections and Letters of General Robert E. Lee*, 3-96; Long, *Memoirs of Lee*, 17-274.

7   Meade, *Life and Letters*, 1:241, 298-301, 308, 311, 312, 338; Richard A. Sauers, *Meade: Victor at Gettysburg* (Washington, DC, 2003), 16; McCall's report, August 12, 1862, OR 11, pt. 2, 392; Seymour's report, 404; Fremont's report, pt. 1, 12:320; Irvin McDowell statement, February 9, 1863, pt. 2, 343, 345; McClellan report, October 15, 1862, pt. 1, 19:57; Hooker's report, November 7, 1862, pt. 1, 19:216; Meade's report, September 24, 1862, pt. 1, 19:266, 270; V Army Corps, General Orders, No. 5, December 26, 1862, 21:887. Meade had received the approbation of his commander Gen. William J. Worth during the Mexican War too, who wrote that the young officer had performed his duties with "intelligent zeal and gallantry." Cleaves, *Meade of Gettysburg*, 37.

"Their brave efforts deserved better success, which, doubtless, would have attended them had he been well supported." It was a measure of the confidence his superior officers had in Meade that his division, despite being one of the smallest in the army, was chosen to lead the fighting at Fredericksburg,[8]

Meade had a reputation for having a volatile temper, yet it flared mainly when others performed their duty improperly or when someone cast unjust aspersions on Meade or his units. Still his demeanor did tend to get him into trouble on occasion. Although respected as a commander, he was not universally popular. Meade sometimes made vengeful enemies, such as Major Generals Daniel Sickles, Butterfield, and Pleasonton.[9]

He also had the reputation as a stern disciplinarian. On the subject of stragglers, for example, he said: "Nothing, in my judgment, short of taking of life will have any effect." And when he assumed command of the army, he issued a circular authorizing commanders "to order the instant death of any soldier who fails in his duty at this hour." Perhaps well intentioned and necessary, this order clearly was not designed to endear him to his men.[10]

Lieutenant Colonel James F. Rusling, quartermaster of the III Corps, offered this candid observation of the newly-appointed army commander:

> General Meade was then tall and slender, gaunt and sad of visage, with iron gray hair and beard, ensconced behind a pair of spectacles, and with few popular traits about him, but with a keen and well-disciplined intellect, a cool and sound judgment, and by both education and temperament was every inch a soldier.

Meade had keenly observed previous army commanders. He had mixed emotions about the imperious McClellan. Though admiring his "talents and mental organization," he thought that McClellan "never studied or practiced

---

8 Burnside to Meade, June 29, 1863, OR 27, pt. 3, 410; Burnside's report, January 23, 1863, OR 21, 92-93.

9 Dana, *Recollections of the Civil War*, 189; Hyde, *The Union Generals Speak*, 28-98, 132-62, 238-75.

10 Williams to Gibbon, April 30, 1862, OR 25, pt. 2, 302 (quoted); Meade to Marcy, September 23, 1862, OR 19, pt. 2, 348; HQ Army of the Potomac Circular, June 30, 1863, pt. 3, 27:415. Meade did not get along with the press either. During the Overland campaign, for example, he disciplined and humiliated a Philadelphia *Inquirer* correspondent whose story about Meade's operations displeased him. The "Bohemian Brigade," as the reporters sometimes referred to themselves, extracted retribution by avoiding the mention of Meade's name in print except in a negative light. Meade, *Life and Letters*, 2:202-03; Sauers, *Meade*, 81-82; Starr, *Bohemian Brigade*, 278.

the art of pleasing [others]" and feared that he lacked "moral courage, without which no man can be a great commander." Following the battle of Antietam, Meade commented that McClellan "errs on the side of prudence and caution, and that a little more rashness on his part would improve his generalship." McClellan "was always waiting to have everything just as he wanted before he would attack, and, before he could get things arranged as he wanted them, the enemy pounced on him and thwarted all his plans."[11]

When Lincoln chose Burnside to replace McClellan, a distressed Burnside adjudged himself, accurately, as "not fit for the position." The disastrous battle of Fredericksburg and the subsequent humiliating "Mud March" up the Rappahannock River quickly proved him right. Having lost the confidence of his officers as well as the government, Burnside also lost his job to the ambitious Hooker. Meade agreed with Burnside's self-assessment: although he had "respect and I may almost say affection" for him, "he was not equal to the command of so large an army." Though he "had some very positive qualifications, such as determination and nerve," Burnside lacked "knowledge and judgment, and . . . that enlarged mental capacity . . . essential in a commander."[12]

When Hooker took command, Meade thought he was over his head, without "qualifications to command a large army." He was skeptical of Hooker's ability for "carrying on a campaign." Meade also questioned his "judgment and prudence, as he is apt to think the only thing to be done is to pitch in and fight." He had accurately discerned Hooker's shortcomings, some of which became evident during the battle of Chancellorsville. After that disaster, Meade noted that Hooker, who had been exceedingly critical of Burnside's leadership, was "more cautious . . . even than McClellan." "[A] man may talk big when he has no responsibility," he observed, "but that it is quite a different thing, acting when you are responsible and talking when others are." Having taken over as army commander from Hooker, Meade now had the opportunity to demonstrate the qualities he found lacking in his predecessors. He had set a pretty high bar high for himself.[13]

---

11 Meade, *Life and Letters*, 1:232, 253, 319, 345.

12 Ibid., 325, 351.

13 Ibid., 318-19, 372.

The Mansion at Prospect Hall in Frederick, Maryland. This was Hooker's headquarters
where Meade met with Hooker to take command of the Army of the Potomac
in the early morning of June 28, 1863.
Photo by the author

Meade and Intelligence Operations

[General Meade was a] thorough soldier, and a mighty clear-headed man; and one who
does not move unless he knows where and how many his men are; where and how
many his enemy's men are; and what sort of country he has to go through.

Col. Theodore Lyman[14]

I had no information concerning the enemy beyond the fact that a large force under
General Lee, estimated at about 110,000 men, had passed through Hagerstown, and
had marched upon the Cumberland valley; and through information derived from the
public journals.

Maj. Gen. George G. Meade[15]

Meade's combat experience during the Mexican War and the first two years
of the current conflict provided rudimentary experience in intelligence-related

14 Quoted in Coddington, *The Gettysburg Campaign*, 211. Lyman was a member of Meade's
staff.

15 Hyde, *The Union Generals Speak*, 101-02.

operations. He served as a topographical engineer during the Mexican War as a member of Maj. Gens. Zachary Taylor's and Winfield Scott's staffs. He conducted reconnaissance in unfamiliar and dangerous territory, sketched maps of these areas for the use of his commander, and performed various combat staff duties.[16]

As a Civil War commander, Meade had to acquire information about the enemy's strength and location. To do this during the fighting at Second Bull Run, South Mountain, and Antietam in 1862, Meade assigned the 13th Pennsylvania Reserves or 1st Rifles (Bucktails) under Col. Hugh W. McNeil as skirmishers to make contact with the enemy. After South Mountain, Meade acknowledged his debt to McNeil and his regiment "for ascertaining the exact position of the enemy."[17]

In February 1863, after Fredericksburg, while briefly in charge of the army's Center Grand Division (III and V corps), Meade issued precise instructions for cavalry and infantry units serving on picket duty along the Rappahannock River. The objective was "to watch the enemy," provide "timely notice of any attempt on the part of the enemy to cross a body of troops at any point," while, at the same time, "not to let them know of our movement." These cavalry and infantry units were to communicate with each other, remain hidden, and "take measures to prevent citizens communicating intelligence" to the enemy.[18]

As commander of the V Corps at Chancellorsville in April and May 1863, Meade had the 6th New York Cavalry assigned to him for guiding, reconnaissance, and skirmishing duties. He employed them to locate the enemy, drive in their pickets, capture prisoners, and clear the marching route for his corps. Meade also used infantry brigades to reconnoiter and "feel for the enemy." Providing them with maps, he instructed them to operate with "vigilance and activity," become acquainted with area roads, paths, etc., ascertain if the enemy was in their front, and "give timely warning of their

---

16 Meade, *Life and Letters*, 2:19-195; Cleaves, *Meade of Gettysburg*, 25-47.

17 Meade's post-action report, September 5 & 22, 1862, OR 12, pt. 2, 397-99; pt. 1, 19:270. Following the battle of Antietam, Meade sadly reported the mortal wounding of McNeil whom he had grown to depend on for providing information.

18 [Meade] to Carr, February 4, 1863, OR 25, pt. 2, 48.

approach." Meade was experienced with information gathering and counterintelligence operations.[19]

Meade Pursues the Army of Northern Virginia

> I am moving at once against Lee...a battle will decide the fate of our country and our cause.
>
> Maj. Gen. George G. Meade[20]

> The cavalry will guard the right and left flanks and the rear, and give the commanding general information of the movements, etc., of the enemy in front.
>
> HQ Army of the Potomac Orders, June 28, 1863[21]

After taking command in the early morning hours of June 28, Meade began gathering information about the enemy's whereabouts, strength, and intentions using the BMI, the intelligence bureau at headquarters, and a variety of other information-gathering resources. Late that afternoon he made a decision and wired Halleck: "I propose to move this army to-morrow in the direction of York."[22]

Upon assuming command, Meade told Halleck that he did not know the enemy's exact position. (The reason was because Hooker kept his corps commanders "in total ignorance of [his plans] until they are developed in the execution of orders.") He did know, however, that Lee's army was marching across Pennsylvania toward the Susquehanna River, and he would therefore move his forces in that general direction.[23]

---

19 Meade's post-action report, May 12, 1863, ibid., pt. 1, 505-06.

20 Meade to his wife, June 29, 1863, in Meade, *Life and Letters*, 2:12.

21 *OR* 27, pt. 3, 375.

22 Meade to Halleck, June 28, 1863, ibid., pt. 1, 65; Fishel, *The Secret War*, 495-97. For details about Meade's strategy for confronting Lee, see Coddington, *The Gettysburg Campaign*, 209-41; Cleaves, *Meade of Gettysburg*, 127-40; George Gordon Meade, *The Battle of Gettysburg* (Gettysburg, PA, 1988), 7-46. The author of the latter source is Meade's son who was a captain in the Union army and his father's aide-de-camp at Gettysburg.

23 General Orders No., 194, June 27, 1863, *OR* 27, pt. 3, 369; Meade, *Life and Letters*, 1:389 (quoted). See also Halleck to Hooker, Halleck to Meade, June 27, 1863, pt. 1, 60-61. For background on Hooker's decision to resign and Meade's replacing him, see Sears, "Meade Takes Command," 12-20.

Not only was he uncertain of the enemy's specific location, but Meade was also under the impression that Lee's army had a force of about 110,000, almost a third more than it actually had. Right before Meade took command, he told his wife that Lee had a large army numerically superior to the Federal army. "[U]nless his forces have been very much exaggerated," he said, Lee had "over ninety thousand infantry and fifteen thousand cavalry, with a large amount of artillery"—while Hooker's army had "at present no such force to oppose him." Meade later told a Congressional investigating committee that when he replaced Hooker, Lee's army was "estimated at over 100,000"—undoubtedly inflated figures from Hooker and Butterfield.[24]

On the day he took command, however, Meade received information that contradicted what he knew or suspected about the strength of Lee's army: a report of intelligence acquired from Thomas McCammon, "a good man, from Hagerstown." The report said that a number of reliable local citizens had individually counted the Rebels as they marched through town, and after meeting at night to compare figures, they determined that Lee's entire army did not exceed 80,000. According to the report, some regiments had only 150-175 men, and the average regiment did not exceed 400. Based on this information, together with the BMI's existing record of Lee's order of battle, and the fact that citizen headcounts of enemy troops were notoriously overstated, the correct conclusion would have been Lee's army numbered between 70,000-80,000, which in fact was an accurate number. For unknown reasons, Meade chose not to accept these figures.[25]

McCammon also reported that a Confederate sympathizer in Hagerstown had been overheard saying he learned from Lee's officers that the army had 100,000 men. Scuttlebutt of this type was common during the war, and Lee and his officers routinely spread disinformation to deceive the enemy. A few days before Meade took command, Lee instructed Longstreet and Ewell to give out erroneous information to cloud Rebel operations around Harper's Ferry. He

---

24 Meade, *Life and Letters*, 1:386, 388; 2:34, 355; Meade's post-action report, October 1, 1863, *OR* 27, pt. 1, 114.

25 Meade to Halleck, June 28, 1863, *OR* 27, pt. 1, 65. The 80,000 estimate was still inflated by about 14,000, since only some 66,000 Rebels had passed through Hagerstown. Another 9,600 Rebel cavalry were operating elsewhere: Stuart's 5,500, Robertson's two brigades of 2,700, and Imboden's independent brigade of some 1,400 were already in Pennsylvania. Lee's post-action report, January 1864, pt. 2, 316; Stuart's post-action report, August 20, 1863, 692-94; Busey and Martin, *Regimental Strengths and Losses*, 169, 244.

also encouraged President Davis to arrange with Southern newspapers to abstain from printing certain facts about troop movements hoping to create a false impression in the minds of the enemy.[26]

Meanwhile, Maj. Gen. Darius Couch, commander of the Department of the Susquehanna at Harrisburg, informed Stanton "15,000 [of the enemy] are in or near Carlisle, and 4,000 or 8,000 from Gettysburg to York and Hanover." The forces at Carlisle Couch referred to included Rodes' and Johnson's divisions of Ewell's corps and Jenkins's cavalry brigade along with the 1st Maryland Cavalry Battalion, about 15,600 men who had arrived in Carlisle on June 27. The enemy troops in the Gettysburg-York-Hanover area were Early's division of Ewell's corps and its cavalry escort, of some 5,900. Couch's total estimate of 19,000-23,000 came pretty close to Ewell's actual strength of about 22,200.[27]

In early evening that same day, Brig. Gen. William F. "Baldy" Smith, commanding forces at Bridgeport, Pennsylvania, across the Susquehanna River from Harrisburg informed Couch that a citizen from Carlisle reported "the enemy, with thirty-five pieces of artillery, 2,000 cavalry, and 14,000 infantry, entered [Carlisle] last evening at 7 o'clock." With this further confirmation of the strength of enemy forces, Couch responded to an anxious query from Lincoln that "Probably 15,000 men [were] within a short distance of my front."[28]

In Search of Lee

At 1:00 p.m., Meade informed Halleck he had "reliable intelligence" that Stuart had crossed the Potomac at Williamsport in the rear of Lee's army. Before receiving this erroneous information, Halleck had telegraphed Meade to warn him that, in fact, a brigade of Stuart's cavalry had crossed the Potomac near Seneca Falls in Meade's rear rather than Lee's, and was moving toward the railroad to cut off his supplies. Halleck also wrote that another Rebel cavalry brigade still lurked south of the Potomac, which was not so since all three

---

26 Ibid.; Meade, *Life and Letters*, 1:386, 388; 2:3, 8, 14, 135; Hyde, *Union Generals Speak*, 101-02, 119. Lee to Ewell, June 17, 1863, *OR* 27, pt. 3, 900-01; Lee to Davis, June 23, 1863, 925.

27 Couch to Stanton, June 28, 1863, *OR* 27, pt. 1, 390; Ewell's post-action report, (n.d.), 1863, *OR* 27, pt. 2, 443; Busey and Martin, *Regimental Strengths and Losses*, 194, 217, 247, 251-52.

28 Couch to [Lincoln], Reno to Couch, June 28, 1863, *OR* 27, pt. 3, 385, 387-88.

brigades with Stuart had crossed the river early that morning. If Pleasonton had followed through when alerted to the nearby presence of a large cavalry force on June 25, this confusion about the location and composition of enemy cavalry would have been avoided.[29]

Meade responded by ordering Gregg to send two of his cavalry brigades and a battery in pursuit of the enemy cavalry operating in the army's rear. Were some of the enemy still south of the Potomac? he asked Halleck, because his information indicated that Lee's entire army had passed through Hagerstown by the morning of June 27.[30]

Halleck replied it was doubtful that aside from a few thousand cavalry, there were many Confederates south of the river. But he did not know the actual location of Stuart's three brigades that already crossed into Maryland since the early morning hours of June 28. Nor did he know that Robertson's and Jones' cavalry brigades were still in Virginia guarding the Blue Ridge Mountain gaps.[31]

While Meade was chasing Lee, Stuart's forces had become an untimely distraction in his rear. Concerned about his communications, Meade requested "reliable information" from the war department telegraph office about which direction the Rebel cavalry force in the area of Rockville, Maryland, had taken. What time had they left? What were the names of any generals or colonels, and the designation of any regiments? Did they go south back across the river? Or North? On which road? When? This was all vital information for Meade about enemies to his rear.[32]

The hurried efforts to locate and check the enemy cavalry operating behind the lines were not quick enough to prevent the capture of a large wagon train of supplies destined for Meade's forces.[33]

---

29 Halleck to Meade, Meade to Halleck, June 28, 1863, ibid., pt. 1, 62. Williams to [Pleasonton], June 25, 1863, ibid., 309; Pleasonton to Butterfield, June 26, 1863, ibid., 333.

30 Meade to Halleck, Halleck to Meade, ibid., pt. 1, 62-64; pt. 3, 376-77.

31 Halleck to Meade, ibid., pt. 1, 64; Stuart's post-action report, August 20, 1863, pt. 2, 692-93.

32 Meade to Halleck, Butterfield to Eckert, June 28, 1863, OR 27, pt. 1, 64.

33 Stuart's post-action report, August 20, 1863, OR 27, pt. 2, 693-94; Blackford, *War Years With Jeb Stuart*, 223.

The Search Moves into Pennsylvania

> Rodes and Jenkins were at Chambersburg last night. Have been advancing all day. I
> shall not at present with my force be able to drive them from the Valley.
> Maj. Gen. Darius N. Couch[34]

While Stuart worked his way northward on the Union army's right flank, the main Confederate force moved with deliberate yet steady speed toward the Susquehanna River. Until Meade could close the gap between the two forces, Pennsylvania Governor Andrew Curtin, Couch, and a variety of military and civilian scouts and observers had the responsibility to track and confront Lee's army. Curtin issued proclamations calling for volunteers to defend the state, and established military departments in eastern and western Pennsylvania.[35]

Couch marshalled scratch groups of regular military, militia, and untrained volunteers trying to slow the progress of the Rebels' march across the state. He was actively fortifying Harrisburg against attack and ordered Col. Jacob G. Frick of the 27th Pennsylvania Volunteer Militia to Columbia to guard the important bridge across the Susquehanna connecting Wrightsville, just east of York, with Columbia. Word had already arrived from Maj. Granville Haller that the Rebel advance guard had chased his small militia detachment through Gettysburg. And word circulated that Confederate units had arrived in Carlisle and that York had surrendered to Early's troops.[36]

As this was taking place, a Union signal station at Turner's Gap on South Mountain in Maryland just west of Frederick reported to Brig. Gen. Adolph von Steinwehr, commander of the Second Division, XI Corps, that only small groups of cavalry and pickets could be seen west of the mountain. Since several important points such as Shepherdstown, Hagerstown, and Sharpsburg, among

---

34 Couch to Stanton, June 24, 1863, OR 27, pt. 3, 297. Couch referred to Maj. Gen. Robert Rodes, a division commander in Ewell's corps.

35 Gov. A .G. Curtin, A Proclamation, [June 12], June 16 and [June 26], 1863, ibid., pt. 1, 79, 169, 347. For details about the military and civilian information-gathering activities underway in support of the Union army, see Fishel, *The Secret War*, 471-72.

36 Couch to Milroy, June 24, 1863, OR 27, pt. 3, 296; HQ Dept. of the Susquehanna, Special Orders, No. 14, June 24, 1863, 297-98; Haller to Couch, June 26, 1863, 344; Cameron to Lincoln, June 27, 1863, 364; Scott to Black, June 27, 1863, 367.

others, could be easily seen from the mountain, this was proof positive that Lee's entire main force had moved into Pennsylvania.[37]

A Spy Changes Lee's Plans

> A young man had been arrested by our outlying pickets under suspicious circumstances . . . he proved to be Harrison, the valued scout.
>   Lt. Gen. James Longstreet[38]

> The advance against Harrisburg was arrested by intelligence received from a scout on the night of the 28th.
>   Gen. Robert E. Lee.[39]

That evening, two days before Ewell's planned attack on Harrisburg, the scout Harrison arrived at Longstreet's camp near Chambersburg reporting that Hooker's army had crossed the Potomac on June 25 and 26. Harrison did his job well. Soon after Hooker began moving the Union forces north across the Potomac on June 25, Harrison got word of it, left the capital, and fell in with the Union army on June 27 and 28. He gathered valuable information and headed toward Longstreet's camp on the Gettysburg turnpike just outside of Chambersburg, arriving late on June 28. He was able to report the location of five of the seven Union corps, three in the vicinity of Frederick and two more to the west near South Mountain.[40]

According to Lee's AAG Walter Taylor, when Longstreet sent Harrison to Lee with this critical information, Lee was surprised and annoyed that he had gotten no word from cavalry commander Stuart about Hooker's movements. According to Longstreet, because of Lee's "want of faith in reports of scouts," especially those personally unfamiliar to him, the commanding general was reluctant to modify his operational plans. However, as Lee's aide Charles Marshall pointed out, though lacking corroborating information from Stuart and concerned that the information might be true, the general immediately saw the need to protect his communications with Virginia. He ordered Hill and

---

37 Buchwalter to Steinwehr, June 27, 1863, ibid., 372.

38 Longstreet, *From Manassas to Appomattox*, 346-47.

39 Lee's post-action report, *OR* 27, pt. 2, 316.

40 Longstreet, *From Manassas to Appomattox*, 347.

Longstreet to move east across the mountains to Cashtown, and sent word to Ewell to change course and move south from the Carlisle area to Cashtown—which he soon changed to Gettysburg.[41]

Lee lamented the fact that the absence of the cavalry made it impossible to determine the enemy's intentions. Historians have criticized Stuart on Lee's behalf for not being aware of Hooker's approach earlier. But as discussed previously, Robertson bears some blame for Lee's predicament, because he was ordered to watch the Union army and screen Lee's army in Stuart's absence. Neither of which did he do.[42]

At the outset of the invasion, Stuart ordered his scout Conrad to Washington on a spying mission evidently independent of the scout Harrison's assignment. Conrad discovered that many of the units defending the capital had been sent to reinforce Hooker's army. Armed with this information and learning that Stuart was operating in the city's outskirts, Conrad attempted to contact him but failed because Stuart had already moved on. If Conrad had reached him, Stuart, though sorely tempted, likely would have rejected the risky and time-consuming venture of a raid on Washington. Ironically, Conrad's base of operations while in Washington was Southern sympathizer Thomas Green's stately home two blocks from the White House and war department.[43]

Stuart's captured supply train proved to be a burden during their march northward and slowed it considerably. The necessity to parole captured prisoners, frequent stops to feed and graze the animals, and skirmishes with small Union cavalry detachments at Cooksville and Westminster, Maryland, also impeded Stuart's progress.[44]

---

41 Taylor, *General Lee: His Campaigns in Virginia*, 184; ibid.; Marshall, *Lee's Aide-de-Camp*, 218-20; Longstreet's & Ewell's post-action reports, July 27, 1863, and n.d., 1863, *OR* 27, pt. 2, 358, 443. For Longstreet's comment, see Longstreet, *From Manassas to Appomattox*, 347.

42 Lee's post-action report, January 1863, 316; Stuart to Robertson, June 24, 1863, pt. 3, 927-28. For the historical controversy surrounding Stuart's role in the intelligence failure at Gettysburg, see Wittenberg and Petruzzi, *Plenty of Blame to go Around*, 179-298.

43 Conrad, *The Rebel Scout*, 81-87; Tidwell, *Come Retribution*, 72-73. On Washington, D.C., during the war, see Benjamin Franklin Cooling III, "Civil War Deterrent: The Defenses of Washington," *Military Affairs*, (Winter 1966), no. 4, 24:164-78, and David S. Heidler and Jeanne T. Heidler, *Encyclopedia of the American Civil War: A Political, Social, and Military History*, 5 vols. (Santa Barbara, 2000), 5:2068-71.

44 Stuart's post-action report, *OR* 27, pt. 2, 694-95; McClellan, *The Campaigns of Stuart's Cavalry*, 323-26.

After Harrison informed Longstreet and Lee about the enemy's movements across the Potomac to the vicinity of Frederick, Lee attempted to verify and expand this information. At the time, the seven cavalry brigades accompanying the army were deployed at some distance from Lee's headquarters. Hampton, Lee, and Chambliss were with Stuart; Robertson and Jones were en route to rejoin Lee; and Imboden and Jenkins were supporting Ewell's corps.[45]

Lee did have available Capt. Augustus P. Pifer's Company A and Capt. Samuel B. Brown's Company C of Maj. John H. Richardson's 39th Virginia Cavalry Battalion—a total of about 90 men. Company C served as Lee's escort. Although organized and trained essentially for intelligence-related activities, Lee employed the 39th Battalion in a variety of ways: accompanying engineers on reconnaissance missions, serving as couriers and scouts, performing provost duty, and guarding wagon trains.[46]

June 29: Intelligence Opportunities Missed by Both Sides

As soon as it was known that the enemy had crossed into Maryland . . . it was expected that General Stuart, with the remainder of his command, would soon arrive.

Gen. Robert E. Lee[47]

In the absence of the cavalry, it was impossible to ascertain the purpose of the enemy.

Walter H. Taylor [48]

45 Ewell's post-action report, n.d., 1863, OR 27, pt. 2, 440; Stuart's post-action report, August 20, 1863, 692; pt. 3, 924. After the spy Harrison arrived on June 28, Lee ordered Robertson and Jones to rejoin the army. Lee's post action report, January 1863, pt. 2, 321. These brigades did not arrive until the morning of July 3. Bowmaster, *Robertson and the Gettysburg Campaign*, 76; Longacre, *Cavalry at Gettysburg*, 233.

46 Driver, *39th Battalion Virginia Cavalry*, 51-52, 55-57, 59; Busey and Martin, *Regimental Strengths and Losses*, 169, 194; Tidwell, *Come Retribution*, 109-10. The 31 men of Capt. William F. Randolph's Company B were assigned to Ewell's corps. Richardson organized the companies into the 39th Battalion in late 1862. Two other detachments that later became Company D and served with Longstreet's corps may not have accompanied the battalion during the campaign. Company A had accompanied Ewell's corps on the march northward as far as Winchester, and then traveled with Lee as well as Hill's and Longstreet's corps into Maryland and Pennsylvania. Company C was specifically assigned to Lee's headquarters.

47 Lee's post-action report, January 1863, OR 27, pt. 2, 321.

48 Taylor, *General Lee*, 187.

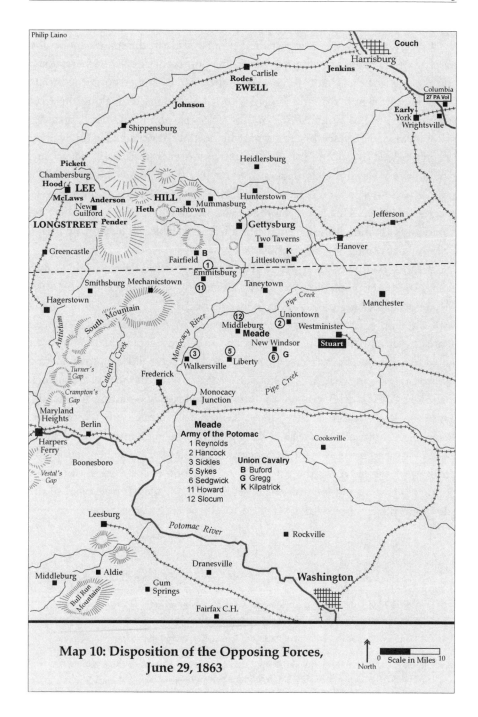

Map 10: Disposition of the Opposing Forces,
June 29, 1863

Once Lee knew the Army of the Potomac was on the march and in the absence of his regular cavalry, he sent scouts out to check on the whereabouts and progress of the Union forces. After they left Chambersburg, the scouts could have run into Buford's brigades moving northeasterly along the road from Boonsboro to Emmitsburg, but for some reason this did not happen.[49]

Knowledge of Buford's cavalry moving northward would have forewarned Lee of the need to gain control of Gettysburg as soon as possible. Which in turn would have allowed the Confederates to occupy the high ground and make a stand there. Meade would have been forced to give battle, or withdraw to another position. This is yet another example of why Lee relied heavily on Stuart for gathering information: had he been available, he likely would have discovered Buford's march northward.[50]

As they continued their trek, Stuart's cavalry cut the Baltimore and Ohio railroad and telegraph lines, seriously disrupting communications between Meade and Washington—another consequence of Pleasonton's not dealing with the Confederate cavalry threat earlier in Virginia. Stuart had also been spared a major confrontation in Maryland at Westminster when Pleasonton failed to heed a warning from Hancock. Local residents in Uniontown alerted him to Stuart's presence in Westminster just seven miles to the east. Hancock informed Meade who passed the information to Pleasonton for action. Thinking that Union cavalry under Gregg had arrived in Westminster, Pleasonton surmised that the local citizens had mistaken them as Confederates. Based on that unsubstantiated conclusion, he took no further action. By sending scouts to verify the information, Pleasonton could have ordered a combined cavalry and infantry attack on Stuart's brigades. But he misread the situation and compounded his failure to act when Stuart's cavalry ran into

---

49 Coddington, *The Gettysburg Campaign*, 264; Sears, *Gettysburg*, 153. Although Lee's scouts did not make contact with Buford, on June 30 Buford ran into two Mississippi regiments at Fairfield. Rather than delay his mission to Gettysburg, Buford reversed course and took another road. Buford's post-action report, August, 27, 1863, *OR* 27, pt. 1, 926.

50 Lee's post action report, January 1863, *OR* 27, pt. 2, 321. Buford reached Gettysburg in the late morning or afternoon of June 30. Buford to Pleasonton, June 30, 1863, *OR* 27, pt. 1, 923; Buford's post-action report, August 27, 1863, 926. Lee's scouts reported the Union army to be in Middleburg, Maryland. In order to travel from Chambersburg to Middleburg on June 29 and return to Greenwood (Lee's camp) on June 30, the scouts would twice have had to cross over the roads Buford was traveling from Middletown, Maryland, to Gettysburg. Sears, *Gettysburg*, 153; *OR Atlas*, Plate 136.

Hancock's corps in Northern Virginia on June 25. Stuart continued his ride toward Pennsylvania unmolested.[51]

The Strength of Enemy Forces in the Mind's Eye

From Harrisburg, Couch informed Meade, "Twenty-five thousand men are between Baltimore and here." Meade was aware these troops belonged to Ewell's corps marching in the vanguard of Lee's army toward Harrisburg. In calculating the strength of the enemy he was confronting, the information about the size of Ewell's forces was useful for Meade to know—especially because 25,000 for Ewell's corps challenged Meade's belief that the enemy had 110,000 to 115,000 troops. For this to be true, Lee's three infantry corps would have to average at least 33,000 men (considering the cavalry numbered about 12,500). The figure of 25,000 reported for Ewell's forces applied to the strength of Lee's other two corps would roughly equate to the estimate the Hagerstown citizens provided of not more than 80,000.[52]

Even though Meade had at first credited the Hagerstown report, he had a change of heart and concluded that Lee's army was "over 100,000 strong." The consequence was a misapprehension on Meade's part that became a restraint on his combat operations during the remainder of the campaign.[53]

Despite PMG Patrick's assessment that the BMI's estimate of Lee's order of battle was "accurate information," Meade apparently did not take this data

---

51 Halleck to Meade, June 28, 1863, Meade to Halleck, June 29, 1863, OR 27, pt. 1, 63, 67-68; Stuart's post-action report, August 20, 1863, pt. 2, 694; Williams to [Hancock], June 30, 1863, pt. 3, 1084; Coddington, The Gettysburg Campaign, 228.

52 Couch to Meade, June 29, 1863, OR 27, pt. 3, 407-08; Meade to Halleck, June 30, 1863, pt. 1, 68-69. It is unclear why Couch used Baltimore rather than Carlisle as a reference point, since Baltimore was to the south and the enemy soldiers were marching from the west. For the Hagerstown report, see Meade to Halleck, June 28, 1863, ibid., 65.

53 For Meade's estimate of at least 100,000 for Lee's army, see Meade's post-action report, October 1, 1863, ibid., pt. 1, 114. Meade testified to a joint congressional committee in March 1864 that when he assumed command he "had no information concerning the enemy beyond the fact that a large force under General Lee, estimated at about 110,000, had passed through Hagerstown. He also said the only other information available was 'derived from the public journals,' i.e., newspapers. He elaborated that while his army numbered about 95,000, Lee's army was about 10,000 to 15,000 my superior. Lee had about 90,000 infantry, from 4,000-5,000 artillery, and about 10,000 cavalry." Hyde, The Union Generals Speak, 101-02, 119. Lee's army in fact numbered about 80,000 of which 71,600 were engaged during the fighting at Gettysburg. Busey and Martin, Regimental Strengths and Losses, 169.

into consideration in his calculation of Lee's strength. The BMI had earned credibility during the Chancellorsville campaign with estimates of the opposing army within a minute margin of error. Despite this, the new commander chose to ignore their reports, which perhaps reflected his unfamiliarity with the BMI and his view of their role—especially regarding "all-source" reporting.[54]

News of the Enemy's Whereabouts

Union left wing commander Reynolds, riding ahead of his corps, informed Butterfield from Emmitsburg that one of Sharpe's BMI scouts named Hopkins had just returned from Gettysburg with information that Early's division of Ewell's corps had passed there towards York. Another division of Ewell's was moving through the Cumberland Valley (this was Johnson's), and that Rodes' division was near Carlisle. In addition, the scout said that Hill's corps was reportedly moving from Greencastle to Chambersburg. In fact, Hill's corps had passed through Chambersburg on June 27, and camped nearby at Fayetteville.[55]

The BMI scout also learned that citizens sympathetic to the Southern cause had left Frederick for Hagerstown to alert the Rebels that four Union corps were at Frederick the day before and were believed to be moving on parallel routes toward the Emmitsburg area. In fact, the four Union corps in the Frederick area received orders to travel north the next day on separate roads. The citizens' information, substantiating the spy Harrison's report about the Union army's movements, undoubtedly would have been forwarded to Lee's headquarters at Chambersburg immediately.[56]

---

54 For Patrick's view of the BMI's reporting, see Sparks, *Inside Lincoln's Army*, 261. For the BMI's accurate reporting during the Chancellorsville campaign, see Fishel, *The Secret War*, order of battle chart facing page 369. Two of Meade's predecessors, McClellan and Hooker, notoriously inflated the strength of opposing forces. Although, as their subordinate, Meade criticized these men, he adopted similar questionable practices after he took command. Over time the BMI's name would change along with its methods of intelligence gathering and reporting. For a discussion of Meade's differing views about the role of the BMI, see Fishel, *The Secret War*, 540-41; Feis, *Grant's Secret Service*, 235, 268.

55 Reynolds to Butterfield, June 29, 1863, *OR* 27, pt. 3, 397; Anderson's post-action report, August 7, 1863, pt. 2, 613; Wilcox's post-action report, July 17, 1863, 616; Gottfried, *Roads to Gettysburg*, 169. Meade's headquarters affirmed Reynolds' previous assignment under Hooker as left wing commander of the I, III, and XI corps in a message dated June 30, 1863. Williams to [Reynolds], June 28, 1863, *OR* 27, pt. 3, 372, Williams to Reynolds, June 30, 1863, 414-15.

56 HQ Army of the Potomac Orders, June 28, 1863, Reynolds to Butterfield, June 29, 1863, *OR* 27, pt. 3, 375, 397.

Orders indeed went out from Meade to all seven corps, including the four Union corps in the Frederick area (I, III, V, and XI), to depart beginning at 4 a.m. and continuing at 8 a.m. Meade directed the corps commanders to send out scouts before them to gather information about the enemy. He instructed Pleasonton to guard both flanks and the rear of the army and also gather information about enemy movements.[57]

The commanders of the three cavalry divisions, Buford, Gregg, and Kilpatrick, received special orders that morning. Buford would leave immediately with two of his brigades for Emmitsburg and continue on to Gettysburg on June 30. He was to cover the main army's left front, and communicate quickly any information about the enemy. Buford's other brigade would move to Mechanicstown (Thurmont) to protect the army's rear. Lieutenant Aaron B. Jerome's signal party accompanied Buford to observe the enemy and communicate with other units of the army.[58]

Kilpatrick's two brigades were to leave Frederick at 8:00 a.m. and reach Littlestown, Pennsylvania, that night. Their unstipulated mission was to serve as the point of the army. Gregg's three brigades would move north to Westminster and New Windsor the next day to protect the right flank and front of the army. Two of the three brigades and a battery had already gotten underway on June 28 to pursue Rebel cavalry reported to have crossed the Potomac. They were delayed in reaching their destination, however, because the Union army marching north blocked the route.[59]

Notwithstanding his skepticism about their estimates of the enemy's strength, Meade was relying on the BMI in addition to the cavalry to learn more about Lee's intentions. He ordered Sharpe to send scouts to Pennsylvania towns and villages—Gettysburg, Hanover, Greencastle, Chambersburg, and

---

57 HQ Army of the Potomac Orders, ibid., 375-76; Gottfried, *Roads to Gettysburg*, 190.

58 HQ Cavalry Corps Special Orders No. 98, ibid., 376. These orders reorganized the cavalry corps into three divisions and a brigade of horse artillery. HQ Cavalry Corps Special Orders No. 99, June 29, 1863, ibid., 400-01. These orders directed the cavalry units to move to specific destinations. See also, Buford's post-action report, August 27, 1863, pt. 1, 926; Devin's post-action report, August 6, 1863, 938; Brown, *The Signal Corps, U.S.A.*, 359; Cameron, "The Signal Corps at Gettysburg," 9.

59 HQ Cavalry Corps Special Orders No. 99, June 29, 1863, OR 27, pt. 3, 400-01.

Jefferson—that night to acquire as much information as possible about the strength, location, and movements of the enemy.[60]

BMI operative Cline, already out mixing with the enemy in disguise, reported from Hagerstown to I Corps that Lee, Ewell, Longstreet, Hill, and other generals had gone beyond Hagerstown, and that the Rebel rear guard had passed through late the previous night. This confirmed the previous day's report from the signal station on South Mountain that Lee's army had moved into Pennsylvania. Cline also said that a large wagon train would be coming through Hagerstown that evening.[61]

Cline also alerted Doubleday that if he sent a small cavalry force, it "could secure [capture] some of the rebel spies [in Hagerstown] if sent soon." Since the main Rebel army had reportedly passed on into Pennsylvania, the information about the wagon train was important. It implied it would not be heavily guarded. Yet no evidence indicates that Union commanders sent troops to intercept this train that likely was carrying ammunition and provisions. It is possible that by the time Cline's message got to Meade's headquarters, the wagon train had already cleared Hagerstown.[62]

Organizationally, Meade decided that Pleasonton's corps headquarters should be collocated with army headquarters, currently at Middleburg, Maryland. This meant that the cavalry divisions would operate in the field semi-independently, and the quality of reports to army headquarters would likely improve. For they would emanate from the cavalry division commanders, not Pleasonton, whose record of shoddy reporting thus far in the campaign spoke for itself.[63]

---

60 Butterfield to Sharpe, June 29, 1863, ibid., pt. 3, 399.

61 Cline to Doubleday, June 29, 1863, RG 393, NA. Cline sent this message through Maj. Gen. Abner Doubleday, a division commander, because he believed it to be the closest Union headquarters to Hagerstown at the time.

62 Ibid.

63 HQ Cavalry Corps, Special Orders, No. 99, June 29, 1863, OR 27, pt. 3, 401. These orders locate Pleasonton's headquarters at Middleburg.

Chapter Twelve

All Signs Point to Gettysburg: June 30 to July 1

June 30: Union Cavalry Locates Lee's Army

That morning, Meade had sized up the enemy situation sufficiently and was prepared to press further ahead. To encourage him to stand firm at Harrisburg, Meade acknowledged in a message to Couch his uncertainty about the enemy's exact location. But he reassured him the army was moving with all possible speed either to his relief or to engage the enemy as circumstances and new information might indicate. Could Couch keep the enemy from crossing the Susquehanna River? Meade asked, as yet unaware Lee had recalled Ewell from his planned operations against Harrisburg—a turn of events that would allow Meade to focus exclusively on Lee's army.[1]

At 5:30 a.m., Buford, while moving toward Gettysburg from Fairfield with two of his brigades, dashed off a brief note with timely information to Reynolds whose I Corps occupied the heights just north of Emmitsburg, about 10 miles

---

1 Meade to Couch, June 30, 1863, OR 27, pt. 1, 67-68; Lee's post-action report, pt. 2, 316. An effort by Brig. Gen. John B. Gordon's brigade (Early's division) to capture the bridge over the Susquehanna River at Wrightsville was foiled when Union militia set fire to the bridge and destroyed it. Early's post-action report, August 22, 1863, pt. 2, 466-67; Couch to Meade, June 29, 1863, pt. 3, 407-08.

southwest of Gettysburg. Buford reported that the enemy was strongly positioned eight to 10 miles west of Gettysburg just behind Cashtown, and that his scouts ran into "a superior force, strongly posted" toward Mummasburg, five miles northwest of Gettysburg. Other scouts went "up the road due north [probably Carlisle Road] 3 miles out" from Gettysburg, and "met a strong picket, had a skirmish, and captured a prisoner of Rodes' division" of Ewell's corps. This was a model intelligence report: succinct, to the point, factual, and absent speculation. It alerted Reynolds of the close proximity of the enemy both to the west and north of Gettysburg. Meade's assignment of Pleasonton to his headquarters which kept him out of the field had already paid dividends. Buford also updated Pleasonton:

> This morning at 4:30 a.m. at Millersburg [Millerstown], I found two regts of Mississippi In[fan]try (1,400 strong). I drove their pickets to camp. Being out of position assigned me and fearing I might interfere with other plans, I did not attack them, but endeavored to get into my proper place. My column is now in motion towards Gettysburg. I have seen Genl Reynolds and posted him. Do get me some maps. I can get no information from the inhabitants. Everyone seems frightened to death. Yesterday I marched 38 miles, and encamped within 2 miles of the Reb force. I heard nothing of them until I found them. Had the people a spark of enterprise, I could have captured the whole.[2]

Around 11:00 a.m., Buford arrived at Gettysburg and reported to Pleasonton at army headquarters that a regiment (actually Brig. Gen. James J. Pettigrew's brigade, Heth's division, Hill's corps) had been advancing on the town from the west, but it retired when Buford made his presence known. Buford also learned that Maj. Gen. Richard H. Anderson's division of Hill's corps was moving between Mummasburg and East Berlin, 15 miles northwest of Gettysburg. Pleasonton, however, tended to discount this since that route would have taken Anderson away from Gettysburg toward York. To verify and gather as much information as possible, Buford dispatched scouting parties toward Cashtown, Mummasburg, Hunterstown, and Littlestown on roads that spiked out eight to 10 miles in all directions from Gettysburg—then notified

---

2 Buford to Reynolds, June 30, 1863, *OR* 27, pt. 1, 922; Doubleday's post-action report, December 1, 1863, 243; Buford's post-action report, August 27, 1863, 926; Gottfried, *Roads to Gettysburg*, 205; Buford to [Pleasonton], June 30, 1863, RG 393, NA.

Maj. Gen. John F. Reynolds
Library of Congress

Reynolds who scribbled on the dispatch "received and forwarded [probably to Meade], June 30, 4:00 p.m:"

Your [message] has just been received ... I have pushed the pickets or rather the rear guard of the Rebs 6 miles towards Cashville [Cashtown]. I am satisfied that the force that came here this morning was the same that I found at Fairfield. I have parties on all of the approaches to town. Have heard nothing more than what I have already sent. I can do nothing more at present, or will be on foot.[3]

Buford instructed signal officer Jerome to occupy the Pennsylvania (now Gettysburg) College cupola to keep an eye out for the enemy and communicate anything important by signal flag. He also ordered Second Brigade commander Col. Thomas C. Devin to send scouting parties to observe the roads from Carlisle, Harrisburg, and York. The moves soon bore fruit: Buford forwarded a message to Pleasonton that Devin's men captured from an enemy courier on the road to (New) Oxford seven miles west of Gettysburg. Jubal Early had written this message to an unidentified "Colonel:"

Get between Gettysburg and Heidlersburg [10 miles to the north] and picket at Mummasburg and Hunterstown [five miles northwest of Gettysburg]. Send [scouts] in the direction of Gettysburg and see what is there, and report to General Ewell at Heidlersburg. A small body of Yankee cavalry has made its appearance between Gettysburg and Heidlersburg. See what it is.

3 Buford to Pleasonton, June 30, 1863, OR 27, pt. 1, 923; Reynolds to Howard, pt. 3, 417; Lee's post-action report, January 1864, pt. 2, 317; Buford to Reynolds, June 30, 1863, RG 393, NA.

Col. Thomas C. Devin
Library of Congress

This provided further evidence that Ewell's corps no longer threatened Harrisburg but had turned its attention to the area around Gettysburg. It also told the Yankees that the Rebels knew they were there.[4]

Buford's report confirmed that Lee's army was marching on Gettysburg, and it prompted Meade to take more definitive action. Meanwhile, Buford lamented the townspeople's lack of energy in obtaining grain from the countryside for his horses. And he could not shoe his horses either: Early had confiscated "every shoe and nail" when he passed through Gettysburg a few days earlier.[5]

Shortly after his arrival at Gettysburg, Buford learned additional vital information from his scouts about the location and probable destination of Lee's forces. At 11:30 a.m., he dispatched a courier and informed Reynolds, now located only six miles south at Moritz Tavern:

> Anderson's division is camped last night [June 29] 9 miles west of Gettysburg on Chambersburg Pike at [the] base of S[outh] Mountain 1 mile beyond Cashtown. One regiment of infantry came near Gettysburg at 11 am and retired as I advanced. The main force is believed to be marching north of Gettysburg through Mummasburg and Hunterstown. Hampton['s cavalry brigade] is towards Berlin & York. I will send parties out on roads towards the supposed position of the enemy.

---

4   Cameron, "The Signal Corps at Gettysburg," 9; Devin's post action report, August 6, 1863, *OR* 27, pt. 1, 938. The unidentified Rebel colonel was probably Col. William H. French, commander of the 17th Virginia Cavalry that Ewell had assigned to accompany Early's division during the march. Early's post-action report, August 22, 1863, *OR* 27, pt. 2, 464. For Early's captured message, see Buford to Pleasonton, June 30, 1863, *OR* 27, pt. 1, 922.

5   Buford to Pleasonton, June 30, 1863, *OR* 27, pt. 1, 923.

Reynolds immediately forwarded this information to Howard at Emmitsburg and Meade, headquartered near Middleburg, Maryland.[6]

Late in the morning, Meade alerted Reynolds that Gregg had reported the presence of a large Rebel cavalry force at Westminster yesterday; the enemy force was believed to be headed toward Littlestown, just across the Pennsylvania border. This was Jeb Stuart and his three brigades. But Stuart had actually changed course from Littlestown, where his scouts had discovered a Union presence, to Hanover.[7]

After receiving Buford's information, Meade alerted the corps commanders that the enemy was advancing on Gettysburg, probably in strong force. Meade decided to hold the seven corps in place where they were until the enemy's plans "have been more fully developed." The Union forces were deployed thusly: on the west at Emmitsburg (III Corps) and Manchester (VI Corps); on the east, at Taneytown (II Corps), Hanover (V Corps), and Two Taverns (XII Corps); and in between, the I and XI corps near Gettysburg. Meade instructed the corps to be ready to march at a moment's notice, but while awaiting orders the commanders should familiarize themselves with roads connecting themselves with their counterparts so as to be prepared to support each other.[8]

When Stuart's cavalrymen finally arrived in Pennsylvania on the morning of June 30, they unexpectedly ran into Kilpatrick's cavalry division that was passing through Hanover. Stuart's attack on the 18th Pennsylvania marching in the rear of the column precipitated a series of clashes that continued throughout the day, and again blocking Stuart's passage northward. During the night an increasingly pressed Stuart stealthily withdrew to the east around Hanover to continue his march. He had suffered yet another lengthy delay in reaching the main Confederate army. Kilpatrick, a proud newly-minted brigadier, reported his clash with Stuart to Pleasonton with considerable

---

6 Buford to Reynolds, [June 30, 1863], RG 393, NA; Reynolds to Howard, June 30, 1863, *OR* 27, pt. 3, 417.

7 Williams to Reynolds, June 30, 1863, *OR* 27, pt. 3, 417; Stuart's post-action report, August 20, 1863, pt. 2, 695; Buford to Reynolds, June 30, 1863, pt. 1, 922.

8 HQ Army of the Potomac Orders and Circular (quoted), ibid., pt. 3, 416-17. V Corps would not arrive at Hanover until Stuart's brigades had already passed around the town. *OR* 27, pt. 3, 424. See below.

bravado—"we do not fear Stuart's whole cavalry," he said—and remained overnight near Hanover.[9]

While these events were unfolding, Meade had the ground west to the Emmitsburg area reconnoitered for a good location to concentrate his army given its present dispersal. His study resulted in a potential position along Pipe Creek, a few miles below the Pennsylvania border that corps commanders were ordered to occupy if contingencies dictated. The so-called Pipe Creek line became a subject of controversy and contention in the aftermath of Gettysburg.[10]

Meade had been elevated to command of the Army of the Potomac because Hooker had succumbed to pressure generated by his belief that the enemy had a larger army. To his detriment, however, Meade also discounted information that demonstrated that the Army of Northern Virginia was much weaker than his own. Apparently, being new to the job in a time of crisis and not yet having confidence in his intelligence staff, he was not prepared to trust the BMI's enemy order of battle estimates and relied instead on citizen eye-witness and newspaper accounts.[11]

Information Leads the Armies to Gettysburg

> This was the first intimation that General Lee had that the enemy had moved from the point he supposed him to occupy, possibly thirty miles distant.
>
> Maj. Gen. Henry Heth[12]

9 Stuart's post-action report, August 20, 1863, ibid., pt. 2, 695-96; 986-87; Kilpatrick's post-action report, August 10, 1863, pt. 1, 992; Kilpatrick to Pleasonton, June 30, 1863, pt. 1, 987 (quoted).

10 Meade, *Life and Letters*, 29-30. On the Pipe Creek Line, see Frederic Shriver Klein, "Meade's Pipe Creek Line, 1863," a pamphlet reprinted from the June 1962 issue of *Maryland Historical Magazine*, 1-17.

11 Hooker to Halleck, Halleck to Meade, June 27, 1863, OR 27, pt. 1, 60-61; Hyde, *The Union Generals Speak*, 101-02.

12 Maj. Gen. Henry Heth, "Letter," *Southern Historical Society Papers*, 52 vols. (Richmond, VA, 1876-1943), 4:158, CD-ROM. Hereinafter cited as *SHSP*.

General Ewell was . . . directed to join the army at Cashtown or Gettysburg, as circumstances might require. The advance of the enemy to the latter place was unknown.

Gen. Robert E. Lee[13]

As the opposing armies slowly converged on Gettysburg, the Rebels from the west, north, and east and the Yankees mainly from the south, it became increasingly likely this little farming community would witness a major conflict. By nighttime, all three Confederate infantry corps were within a 25 mile radius of Gettysburg, with two of Hill's divisions (Heth's and Pender's), just eight miles away at Cashtown. Earlier in the day, Pettigrew's brigade of Heth's division had ventured toward Gettysburg to search for supplies only to find it occupied by enemy forces. Lacking cavalry to conduct reconnaissance, Pettigrew believed he was facing cavalry supported by infantry and therefore withdrew.[14]

Lee, meanwhile, along with Hill, sent scouts to determine the enemy's current position. They reported Meade's army still in the vicinity of Middleburg, Maryland, 15 miles south of Gettysburg. So Lee was surprised when he learned that Pettigrew's brigade had discovered an unidentified Union force occupying Gettysburg. This was not welcome news.[15]

Now that Meade apprehended a battle with Lee's army all but inevitable, he had important business to tend to. As V Corps commander during the earlier part of the march northward, Meade had observed cavalry commander Pleasonton in action against Stuart's forces in the Loudoun Valley; he knew of his proclivity for engaging the enemy in preference to giving information gathering priority. Although Halleck had given him carte blanche to "remove from command . . . any officer . . . you may deem proper," to his later regret, Meade chose to retain Pleasonton as cavalry commander. To forestall any

13 Lee's post-action report, January 1864, *OR* 27, pt. 2, 317.

14 Longstreet's post-action report, ibid., July 27, 1863, 358; Ewell's post-action report, ibid., n.d., 1863, 444; Hill's post-action report, November 1863, ibid., 607; Heth's post-action report, September 13, 1863, ibid., 637.

15 Lee's post-action report, January 1864, *OR* 27, pt. 2, 317; Heth, "Letter," *SHSP*, 4:157; Sears, *Gettysburg*, 153; Coddington, *The Gettysburg Campaign*, 264. Heth recalled that Hill advised him on June 30: "I am just from General Lee, and the information he has from his scouts corroborates that I have received from mine—that is, the enemy are still at Middleburg, and have not yet struck their tents."

misunderstandings, however, Meade issued Pleasonton written instructions: "it was of utmost importance that he received reliable information" on the enemy's location, strength, and movements. Because the people in the countryside were too frightened to be helpful, Meade told Pleasonton he depended solely on the cavalry, and it must be "vigilant and active." His choice of the term "solely" signaled again that Meade had not yet taken the BMI into his confidence.[16]

"[R]eports must be those gained by the cavalry themselves, and information sent in should be reliable," Meade lectured Pleasonton. "The duty you have to perform is of a most important and sacred character. Cavalry battles must be secondary to this object." Meade left nothing to chance, however, and assigned Pleasonton to his staff so that he could monitor and maintain tighter control over cavalry operations.[17]

Not that Meade's move solved all of the problems. From his position near Emmitsburg in support of Reynolds' I Corps that had moved up to Marsh Creek, Maj. Gen. O. O. Howard, XI Corps commander, requested Meade assign the 3rd West Virginia cavalry of Buford's division to his corps. Howard's existing cavalry detachment, the 59 men of Company I and K of the 1st Indiana, were too few to gather a sufficient quantity of information and, as might be expected, "very much worn out with scouting."[18]

Already delayed in its movement toward Pennsylvania, Gregg's cavalry division received the first of a series of conflicting orders from Pleasonton on June 30. Because of delays and confusion, Gregg's brigades would not arrive on the battlefield at Gettysburg until around noon July 2.[19]

16 Halleck to Meade, June 27, 1863, *OR* 27, pt. 1, 61; Meade to Pleasonton, June 30, 1863, pt. 3, 421.

17 Meade to Pleasonton, June 30, 1863, *OR* 27, pt. 3, 421; Longacre, *Lincoln's Cavalrymen*, 178.

18 Howard to Williams, June 30, 1863, *OR* 27, pt. 3, 423; Busey and Martin, *Strengths and Losses at Gettysburg*, 83, 107. It appears that Howard's request was denied, since the 3rd West Virginia fought with Devin's brigade on July 1. Devin's post-action report, August 6, 1863, *OR* 27, pt. 1, 942-43; Longacre, *Cavalry at Gettysburg*, 183.

19 Pleasonton to Gregg, June 30, 1863, *OR* 27, pt. 3, 425; Gregg's preliminary post-action report, July 25, 1863, pt. 1, 956; Alexander, "Gettysburg Cavalry Operations," 28; Longacre, *The Cavalry at Gettysburg*, 203-04.

July 1: Lee Stumbles into a Fight

I cannot think of what has happened to Stuart . . . In the absence of reports from him, I am in ignorance as to what we have in front of us here. It may be the whole Federal army, or it may be only a detachment.

Gen. Robert E. Lee[20]

Ewell is massing at Heidlersburg. A. P. Hill is massed behind the mountains at Cashtown. Longstreet somewhere between Chambersburg and the mountains. The news proves my advance has answered its purpose.

Maj. Gen. George G. Meade[21]

This battle was precipitated by the absence of information which could only be obtained by an active cavalry.

Col. A. L. Long[22]

At 7:00 a.m., in his headquarters nine miles east of Middleburg, Maryland, Meade knew enemy cavalry to be on his right and Hill's corps at Cashtown on his left, but he was uncertain of Ewell's and Longstreet's exact whereabouts. Still, Meade had a better understanding than Lee about the enemy's location. Newly received information from Couch in Harrisburg, however, reinforced his belief that Lee's army had about 100,000 troops. Recent scholarship places the figure closer to 72,000, and, according to Lee's aide Walter Taylor, Rebel strength at Gettysburg was 67,000 of all arms. In short, Lee had about 30,000 fewer troops than Meade believed.[23]

20 Longstreet, "Lee in Pennsylvania," 420. Longstreet wrote that Lee made these comments to Maj. Gen. Richard Anderson sometime after 10:00 a.m. on July 1 upon hearing heavy firing along Hill's front.

21 Meade to Halleck, July 1, 1863, OR 27, pt. 1, 70.

22 Long, Memoirs of Robert E. Lee, 277. Colonel A. L. Long served on Lee's staff as his military secretary during the Gettysburg campaign and also assisted in the deployment of artillery batteries. Faust, Historical Times Encyclopedia, 444.

23 Meade to Halleck, June 30, 1863, OR 27, pt. 1, 69-70; Williams to Reynolds, July 1, 1863, pt. 3, 460; Haupt to Halleck, July 1, 1863, pt. 3, 476-77; Lee's post-action report, January 1864, pt. 2, 317; Meade, Life and Letters, 2:34; Fishel, The Secret War, 520; Taylor, Lee's Campaigns, 211, 303. A more recent calculation for the strength of Lee's army engaged at Gettysburg was 71,699. Busey and Martin, Strengths and Losses, 169.

Capt. Lemuel Norton, chief signal officer for
the Army of the Potomac.
Library of Congress

Meade formulated his general plan based on the reconnaissance he ordered the previous day along Pipe Creek and disseminated it in a circular. In sharp contrast to his predecessor Hooker, he kept his subordinates informed as the situation evolved. Meade ordered his chief signal officer to ensure that his headquarters was linked telegraphically to all units. He directed that the "true Union people" in the local population be advised to send in information what "regiments by number of colors, number of guns, generals' names, etc." He also stressed the importance of gaining knowledge of the terrain to conceal the army's movements and location from the Rebels, which in their hands "would be fatal to our success." Meade was obviously aware of the imperative to provide specific guidance to his subordinates about effective communications, timely intelligence, and importance of counterintelligence measures against disclosure of the army's location and movements.[24]

When Meade moved his headquarters to Taneytown, Maryland, his newly-appointed chief signal officer, Capt. Lemuel B. Norton, had by mid-afternoon established a signal station in the spire of the Trinity Lutheran Church and observation points at several nearby locations. Norton's availability gave Meade an advantage over Lee, whose signal capabilities were dispersed to the three corps and who had no chief signal officer on his staff to coordinate overall army operations. Lee's lack of a headquarters signal officer contributed to poor communications between Lee and his commanders once battle was joined. Stuart's absence limited Lee's strategic and tactical options, as would

24 HQ Army of the Potomac Circular, July 1, 1863, *OR* 27, pt. 3, 458-60.

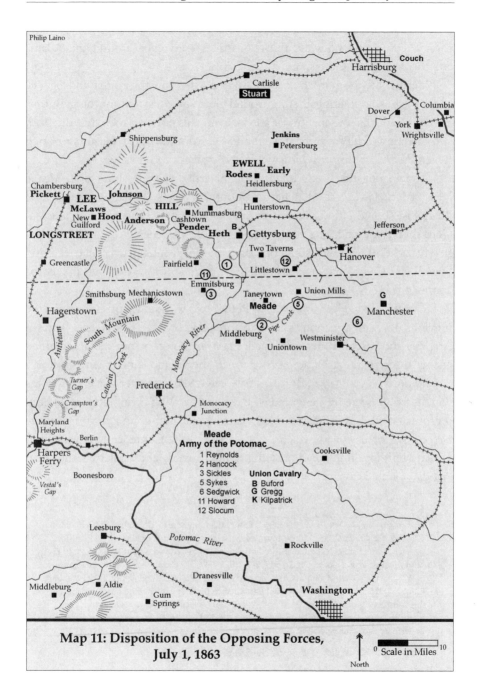

Philip Laino

Couch
Harrisburg

Carlisle
Stuart

Dover   Columbia
York
Wrightsville

Shippensburg

Jenkins
Petersburg

EWELL **Early**
Chambersburg   Rodes
Pickett **LEE** **Johnson**   Heidlersburg
McLaws   Hunterstown
New **Hood** **Anderson** **HILL**
Guilford   Cashtown **Mummasburg**   Jefferson
LONGSTREET   **Pender** **Heth** B
Greencastle   Fairfield   **Gettysburg**
                Two Taverns   K
            (11)   (12) Hanover
Emmitsburg (1) Littlestown
            (3)
Smithsburg Mechanicstown   Taneytown Union Mills G
Hagerstown   **Meade** (5)   Manchester
                (2)   (6)
        Middleburg Pipe Creek
                Uniontown Westminister

Frederick

Monocacy
Junction
Turner's
Gap
Crampton's   **Meade**
Gap   **Army of the Potomac**
Maryland   Cooksville
Heights Berlin   1 Reynolds
Harpers   2 Hancock
Ferry   3 Sickles   **Union Cavalry**
        Boonesboro   5 Sykes   B Buford
Vestal's   6 Sedgwick G Gregg
Gap   11 Howard   K Kilpatrick
            12 Slocum

Leesburg
            Potomac River
                Rockville
Middleburg Aldie   Dranesville
        Gum   **Washington**
        Springs

Map 11: Disposition of the Opposing Forces,
July 1, 1863

0   10
Scale in Miles
North

soon become evident when the two armies converged around the Adams county borough of Gettysburg.[25]

Meanwhile, the burden was on Buford's division to provide intelligence about the hostile clouds gathering around Gettysburg. At mid-morning, Buford alerted Meade that the enemy was advancing on his position at Gettysburg from two directions, Hill from the west and Ewell from the north. He also reported Reynolds' I Corps approaching within three miles of Gettysburg.[26]

Anticipating that Lee's infantry might arrive at Gettysburg first, Meade informed Sedgwick at Manchester about his plans in that eventuality. If Reynolds should "find himself in the presence of a superior force" at Gettysburg," he said, "he is instructed to hold the enemy in check, and fall slowly back." If Reynolds could pull this off, Meade intended to fall back upon "the [Pipe Creek] line indicated in the circular of to-day" to the corps commanders.[27]

That morning, Heth followed up Pettigrew's withdrawal from the town the previous day with a reconnaissance-in-force. He ordered Brig. Gens. James J. Archer's and Joseph R. Davis' brigades forward to scope out the unidentified enemy force there. A battle erupted when they made contact with Buford's cavalry northwest of town. Buford immediately sent a courier to alert Reynolds that his troops were fully engaged with the enemy. With no infantry to fall back on for support, Buford dismounted his troopers and put up a stout resistance backed by horse artillery which not only stifled the Confederate advance but misled Heth into thinking he faced infantry, cavalry, and artillery, rather than just dismounted cavalry.[28]

---

25 Brown, *Signal Corps, U.S.A.*, 359; Louise Miller interview, December 2000, Trinity Episcopal Lutheran Church, Taneytown, MD. Norton replaced Capt. Benjamin F. Fisher, whom Mosby's Rangers captured near Aldie on June 18, 1863. Brown, *Signal Corps, U.S.A.*, 358; Norton's post-action report, OR 27, pt. 1, 200; Mosby, *Stuart's Cavalry in the Gettysburg Campaign*, 64-67. On Lee's lack of options, see Sears, *Gettysburg*, 226-240; Coddington, *The Gettysburg Campaign*, 315-22; Bowden and Ward, "Last Chance for Victory," 76-85. Some, but not all, division commanders had signal officers as well. Each signal detachment had an officer and sergeant assigned, with about 12-18 enlisted men detailed to them from other parts of the army to perform signal duties; Gaddy, "The Confederate Signal Corps at Gettysburg," 110-11.

26 Buford to Meade, July 1, 1863, OR 27, pt. 1, 924.

27 Ibid., pt. 3, 462.

28 Buford to Meade, July 1, 1863, pt. 1, 924; Buford's post-action report, 927; Heth's post-action report, September 13, 1863, pt. 2, 637; Wadsworth's post-action report, July 4, 1863, pt. 1, 265.

The widow Lydia Leister's house along Taneytown Road south of Gettysburg
where General Meade met with his commanders on the night of July 2.
Photo by the author

After Reynolds' and later Howard's corps arrived on the field, sustained
fighting took place with heavy casualties on both sides, including Reynolds'
death early in the initial fighting. With Ewell's arrival in the afternoon, the
Rebels gained the upper hand and forced the withdrawal of both Federal corps.
The beleaguered Union troops sought refuge on Cemetery Hill and Cemetery
Ridge south of town.[29]

According to AAG Taylor, Lee wanted to press forward without delay to
exploit the advantage already gained. Vague information about the strength of
the surviving enemy forces and location of possible supporting units, however,
factored into the decision not to continue the assault on the injured foe until the
next day. Although the 17th Virginia Cavalry and the 35th Battalion Virginia
Cavalry accompanied Early's division and were available to Lee on July 1, they
were not used to advantage in scouting the battlefield or surrounding territory
to determine the enemy's dispositions. Given Stuart's absence, neither Lee nor

29 Howard's & Doubleday's post-action reports, August 31 & December 14, 1863, ibid.,
701-04, 253-63.

anyone on his staff assumed the initiative in directing cavalry operations with the resources on hand.[30]

Not only did Lee not employ available cavalry resources for reconnoitering purposes, neither did Ewell put them to use on a tactical level after Union forces retreated to Cemetery Hill. Rather than performing scouting duty, the 17th Virginia guarded some 5,000 prisoners during the latter part of July 1 and all day on July 2. Upon arrival at Gettysburg, Ewell sent the 35th Battalion to the left flank where they observed the fighting on the field from high ground. Apparently receiving no orders to scout the enemy positions, the troops went into camp at dark. Ewell's lack of assertiveness reflected Lee's being of two minds on whether to renew the attack. He instructed Ewell "to carry the hill occupied by the enemy, if he found it practicable, but to avoid a general engagement until the arrival of the other divisions of the army." After evaluating the inherent complications of nighttime operations, Ewell was unsuccessful in mounting an attack on Cemetery Hill or occupying Culp's Hill—two strategic points.[31]

Stuart, still wandering through the Pennsylvania countryside, reached Carlisle at mid-day after failing to locate the Confederate army. That night a courier from Lee found him and delivered orders to come to Gettysburg.[32]

In the meantime, upon hearing of Reynolds's death and disarray on the battlefield, Meade ordered II Corps commander Hancock to Gettysburg to take charge of all the troops on the field. Meade's selection of Hancock was based on his record of solid performance throughout his career in the army. Previous commanders considered him a superb officer. The 1844 West Point graduate was known for his military bearing and professional attitude. Meade had "full

---

30 Taylor, *General Lee*, 193; Lee's post-action report, January 1864, OR 27, pt. 2, 317; Heth's post-action report, September 13, 1863, 637. For details of the July 1 fighting at Gettysburg, including the decision by Lee and his commanders not to press the attack, see Harry W. Pfanz, *Gettysburg—The First Day* (Chapel Hill, NC, 2001), esp. 342-49; Lee's post-action report, January 1864, OR 27, pt. 2, 354-56.

31 Harris, *17th Virginia Cavalry*, 24; Myers, *The Comanches*, 196-99; Lee's & Ewell's post-action reports, January 1864 & n.d., 1863, OR 27, pt. 2, 318, 445-46; Phanz, *Gettysburg—The First Day*, 343-49.

32 Stuart's post-action report, August 20, 1863, OR 27, pt. 2, 696-97.

confidence in his ability" to assess the situation and use good judgment in submitting his recommendations.[33]

Upon his arrival on Cemetery Hill around 3:00 or 4:00 p.m. on July 1, Hancock assumed command and, along with Howard, worked to restore order among the shaken Union troops and fortify the heights against attack. He reportedly told Howard that this place was the strongest natural position upon which to fight a battle he had ever seen. When Meade received Hancock's assessment, he ordered the rest of the army to Gettysburg and moved his headquarters there by midnight to take command.[34]

Lee's army had stumbled into a battle at a time and place not of its choosing. The absence of Stuart's cavalry had left Lee in the lurch. "The eyes of the giant were out," Heth later observed, "he knew not where to strike, a move in any direction might prove a disastrous blunder." Lee evidently did not consider his small headquarters cavalry detachment a viable back-up information gathering capability and was not aggressive in employing other cavalry units that had arrived with Ewell's corps. Yet, despite these problems, Lee's army had won a clear victory on the first day of battle.[35]

Meade, on the other hand, had reliable information about the location and movements of the enemy. He would steadfastly maintain, however, that the strength of Lee's army was about 40 percent larger than it actually was. Consequently Meade proceeded cautiously. Nonetheless, his intelligence at this stage of the confrontation surpassed Lee's. Despite the adverse outcome of the first day, the Union army was in a strong position to continue the fight.

33 Butterfield to Hancock, July 1, 1863, ibid., pt. 3, 461; Glenn Tucker, *Hancock the Superb* (Dayton, OH, 1980), 13-28; Faust, *Historical Times Encyclopedia*, 337; Meade, *Life and Letters*, 2:36.

34 Hancock's post-action report, n.d., 1863, *OR* 27, pt. 1, 367-69; Meade, *Life and Letters*, 2:36-37, 54-55, 62; E. P. Halstead, "Incidents of the First Day at Gettysburg," in *B&L*, 3:285. Halstead was AAG of I Corps.

35 Heth, "Letter," *SHSP*, 4:156.

Chapter Thirteen

Intense Effort to Gain the Intelligence Advantage: July 2

[T]o get intelligence . . . you have to look for it. Intelligence never comes by itself.

Napoleon Bonaparte[1]

The Intelligence Posture

By the word "information" we denote all the knowledge which we have of the enemy and his country; therefore, in fact, the foundation of all our ideas and actions.

Carl Von Clausewitz[2]

In preparing for what was to come on July 2, Meade had more intelligence resources available and used them with greater efficiency than Lee. While the Union cavalry protected the army's flanks and rear and defended its supply base at Westminster, the BMI, the signal corps, and an elite brigade known as Berdan's Sharpshooters were available to support tactical operations.

As discussed earlier, in January 1863, the commander of the Army of the Potomac, Maj. Gen. Joseph Hooker, formed an intelligence staff that became known as the bureau of military information. Administratively subordinate to PMG Marsena Patrick, the BMI operated semi-independently and reported

---

1   John R. Elting, *Swords Around a Throne: Napoleon's Grande Armée* (New York, 1988), 103.

2   Carl Von Clausewitz, *On War* (New York, 1968), 162.

directly to the army commander. Its mission was to gather information about the enemy from a variety of sources and distill this data into useable intelligence. A team of scouts and spies recruited from the army and local population constituted the bulk of BMI's personnel.

By the time of the battle of Chancellorsville in May, Colonel Sharpe's bureau had provided data on the size, location, and leadership of Lee's army. One observer believed that the "secret service [i.e., BMI] . . . is far superior to anything that has ever been here before." The accuracy of the bureau's estimates about the Army of Northern Virginia's strength and disposition provided Hooker with reliable information. When Meade took over the reins from Hooker on June 28, he inherited this intelligence staff.[3]

With about 700 Rebels captured during the fighting on July 1, the provost marshal established a prisoner-processing depot in Taneytown, Maryland. The next day, he selected other prisoner holding areas behind the lines at Gettysburg, most likely in the area east of Lydia Leister farmhouse on Taneytown Road, Meade's headquarters. Provost and BMI personnel interrogated the prisoners to gather military information and update their order-of-battle records of the enemy for Meade's use in operational planning. Some BMI personnel, including Capt. John McEntee and his team of scouts and spies and civilian John Babcock, who had arrived along with the I Corps on July 1, were already on the field in Gettysburg for immediate interrogation of prisoners.[4]

Several months after the battle, Colonel Sharpe described the interrogation process which was always aimed at extracting the most "valuable information" for the army commander. BMI examined as many captured soldiers, deserters, refugees, and escaped slaves as possible, extensively if time permitted. A lawyer in civilian life, Sharpe used the language of his trade in describing how

---

3 Fishel, *Secret War for the Union*, 318-22, 375-76; Sears, *Chancellorsville*, 68-70, 101-02, 130-32, 151. Luvas and Nelson argue that Lee had a decided advantage in intelligence over Hooker at Chancellorsville; however, their research did not include material from the BMI files at the National Archives. See Luvas & Nelson, "Intelligence in the Chancellorsville Campaign," 300-13.

4 Longacre, *The Cavalry at Gettysburg*, 208; Sharpe to Butterfield, July 3, 1863, RG 393, NA; Sparks, *Inside Lincoln's Army*, 266-67; Gregory A. Coco, *A Strange and Blighted Land: Gettysburg, The Aftermath of Battle* (Gettysburg, PA, 1995), 271, 294; Fishel, *The Secret War*, 526. Since Lee had left his headquarters provost guard behind in Winchester, it is unclear what process the Southerners used to examine prisoners. In all likelihood, the provost marshal at corps, division, and brigade level did it. Driver, *1st Battalion Virginia Infantry*, 36.

incentives were offered interviewees for "speedy liberation" in exchange for "their making full discovery of their knowledge of the enemy."[5]

"Speedy liberation" evidently included release from captivity to seek work in the North, or return to their homes in areas under Union control. According to Sharpe, the most cooperative prisoners were Southerners who had been born and raised in the North or pro-Union Southerners coerced or conscripted into the Confederate army. Sharpe contended that, as a result of its interrogation methods, the BMI was "entirely familiar with the organization of the rebel forces . . . with each regiment, brigade and division, with the changes therein, and in their [commanding] officers and locations." This afforded Union commanders a significant advantage over their opponents.[6]

The newly appointed chief signal officer of the army, Capt. Lemuel Norton, had assigned signal parties to each of the seven Union infantry corps. He also had on hand a reserve of eight officers and a number of noncommissioned officers and enlisted men to use as needed. The signal corps personnel were not only trained to provide communications between headquarters and its field units, but they also performed observation and reconnaissance duties. The army's previous engagements in the Eastern theater from the Peninsula campaign to Chancellorsville had honed them into a skillful specialized resource.[7]

Since Early's cavalry had cut the telegraph between Gettysburg, Hanover, and Hanover Junction, and Stuart's riders had severed telegraph connections with Washington, Meade could only maintain communications with the capital by the more roundabout and slower combination of courier to Westminster, Maryland, train from there to Baltimore, and telegraph from Baltimore to Washington. Although builders and operators from the Military Telegraph Service had the required material and were prepared to establish direct lines to the army at Gettysburg, Meade, leery of the hazardous conditions in the area, did not believe it expedient to do so. He also chose not to use the telegraph wire on hand at Gettysburg to link army and corps headquarters. He decided to rely on flag communications instead. This departed from Hooker's practice during the Chancellorsville campaign. Hooker thought flag communications more

5   Sharpe to Martindale, December 12, 1863, RG 393, NA.

6   Ibid.

7   Cameron, "The Signal Corps at Gettysburg," 10; Brown, *The Signal Corps*, 289-357.

vulnerable to intercept by the enemy, and preferred to rely on telegraph. Meade evidently had no such qualms.[8]

Another method of acquiring information about the enemy for both sides was using skirmishers deployed beyond the army's position on the field to make contact with the enemy. Their job was to find the enemy's location, determine its strength, and provide early warning of an attack. While skirmish duty was common to all units on the field, the Army of the Potomac had troops especially suited for this duty, Berdan's Sharpshooters.[9]

Berdan's 1st and 2nd U.S. Regiments (Ward's brigade, Birney's division, III Corps), all expert marksmen, were a powerful force for the enemy to contend with. At times, the sharpshooters led the army while on the march; they also performed reconnaissance to pinpoint the enemy's location and inhibited the enemy's ability to determine the Union army's location.[10]

Lee had a number of intelligence-related issues to deal with. The absence of Stuart and his cavalry brigades which normally conducted reconnaissance for the army inhibited his consideration of tactical options for the critical second day of battle. Stuart would not rejoin the army until late in the day.[11]

Stuart had established a reputation for reliability in gathering information about the enemy and in denying him access to information about Lee's forces. If there was a weakness in the disposition of the opposition, Stuart was certain to discover it. He proved this on a number of occasions, particularly during the Peninsula campaign in 1862, and the more recent Chancellorsville campaign. As we have seen, Stuart and his men had honed their skills in reconnoitering, scouting, screening, maintaining communications, and deceiving the enemy since early in the war. Not having these resources available placed Lee at a major disadvantage.[12]

---

8 Haupt's post-action report, July 7, 1863, *OR* 27, pt. 1, 22; Butterfield to Sedgwick, May 3, 1863, *OR* 25, pt. 2, 384-85; Plum, *The Military Telegraph*, 2, 17; Brown, *The Signal Corps*, 348-57; Sears, *Chancellorsville*, 396.

9 Murray, *Berdan's Sharpshooters*, 1-2.

10 Coddington, *The Gettysburg Campaign*, 579; Murray, *Berdan's Sharpshooters*, 60-78.

11 Lee's post-action report, January 1864, *OR* 27, pt. 2, 321-22; Stuart's post-action report, August 20, 1863, 692-97.

12 Thomas J. Ryan, "Stuart a vital force as Rebel leader" & "Stuart's intelligence role invaluable," *Washington Times*, August 26, December 8, 2007.

Lee did not have a dedicated staff or even a single individual monitoring the collection and processing of information—nothing on the order of Meade's BMI. Moreover, while the Army of Northern Virginia had signal corps parties assigned to all three corps and selected divisions, they operated independently of any centralized headquarters function. And even these intelligence activities among Confederate units at Gettysburg remain a mystery, since the record of them has been either lost or destroyed. David W. Gaddy's research has found that Lee handled intelligence in an "informal" or "ad hoc" manner, and that he basically served as his own intelligence officer. Nonetheless Lee performed the task well and had a history of being attentive to intelligence and security requirements.[13]

In order to "feel" the enemy and determine their location and strength, the Confederates used skirmishers as the Union army did. At Gettysburg, although it had sharpshooters integrated within various units, the Confederates did not have a specialized, experienced group like Berdan's Sharpshooters. A relatively new unit of marksmen under Maj. Eugene Blackford in Rodes' division, directly involved in the July 1 action, would begin establishing a reputation during the Gettysburg campaign. A difficulty Confederate sharpshooter units encountered was their unfamiliarity with the terrain.[14]

Lee's excursion into Union territory resulted in little or no help from the generally hostile local population. Lee had expected to be able to gain recruits for his army upon entering the slave state of Maryland still within the Union, but he had limited success. Most civilians in Maryland and Pennsylvania assisted the Federal army during Lee's invasion, or remained neutral fearing reprisals from either side.[15]

---

13 Lee's post-action report, January 1864, *OR* 27, pt. 2, 318, 321; Luvas, "Lee at Gettysburg," 132-34; Gaddy, "The Confederate Signal Corps," 110-11; David W. Gaddy, unpublished lecture to the Museum of American History, "Lee's Use of Intelligence," November 21, 1994. Quoted with author's permission.

14 Ray, *Shock Troops of the Confederacy*, xi, 62-72.

15 For examples of civilians aiding Union forces, see Meade to Halleck, June 28, 1863, *OR* 27, pt. 1, 65; Winchester to Halleck, June 24, 1863, pt. 3, 289.

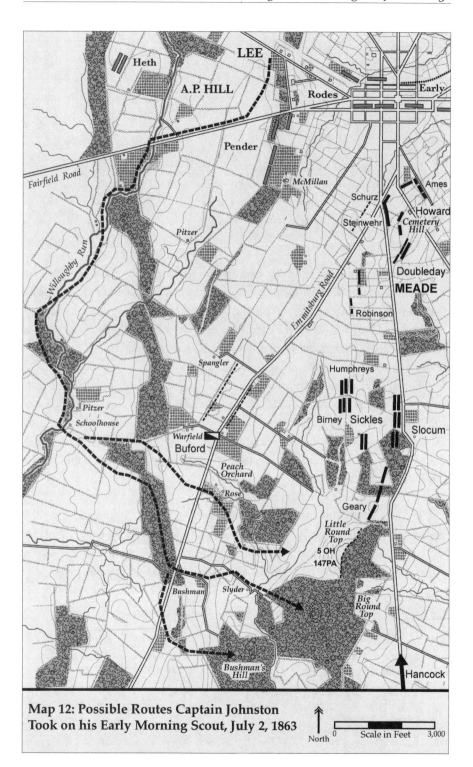

Map 12: Possible Routes Captain Johnston Took on his Early Morning Scout, July 2, 1863

North   0   Scale in Feet   3,000

Assessing the Combat Situation

The general commanding the [XII] corps wishes that you would pay particular attention to your right and keep skirmishers well out and to the front, so that the first movement of the enemy may be known at once and communicated.

Capt. William W. Moseley[16]

I surveyed the enemy's position toward some estimate of the ground and the best mode of attack. So far as judgment could be formed from such a view, assault on the enemy's left by our extreme right might succeed, should the [Little Round Top] mountain there offer no insuperable obstacle.

Brig. Gen. William N. Pendleton[17]

Lee was considering an attack on the enemy's left with Longstreet's First Corps on his right. Before forming his operational plan for the day, he needed better intelligence about the terrain and his opponent's strength in that area of the battlefield. From prisoners captured the previous day, he learned that the Union I and XI corps were on the field, and "that the remainder of that army, under General Meade, was approaching Gettysburg."[18]

The dilemma Lee faced now, however, was that lacking "information as to its proximity, the strong position which the enemy had assumed could not be attacked without danger of exposing the four divisions present." An enemy dispatch captured that night revealed the XII Corps near Culp's Hill and V Corps only some five miles away. This accounted for four of the Union corps, but Lee still did know the whereabouts of the other three corps except that they were thought to be approaching Gettysburg.[19]

To dispel these uncertainties, in early morning, before daylight, Lee sent his artillery chief, Brig. Gen. W. L. Pendleton, along with his aide, Col. A. L. Long and chief engineer, Capt. Samuel R. Johnston to reconnoiter the Union positions on Cemetery Ridge on the right front of the Confederate lines. After

---

16 Moseley to Williams, July 1, 1863, ibid., pt. 3, 466-67. Moseley was Slocum's aide-de-camp.

17 Pendleton's post-action report, September 12, 1863, ibid., pt. 2, 350.

18 Ibid., 317; McDonald, *Make Me a Map of the Valley*, 157; Gary W. Gallagher, "If the Enemy is There, We Must Attack Him': R. E. Lee and the Second Day at Gettysburg," in Gary W. Gallagher, ed. *The Second Day at Gettysburg* (Kent, OH, 1993), 26.

19 Lee's post-action report, January, 1864, *OR* 27, pt. 2, 317; Longstreet, *From Manassas to Appomattox*, 359, 362.

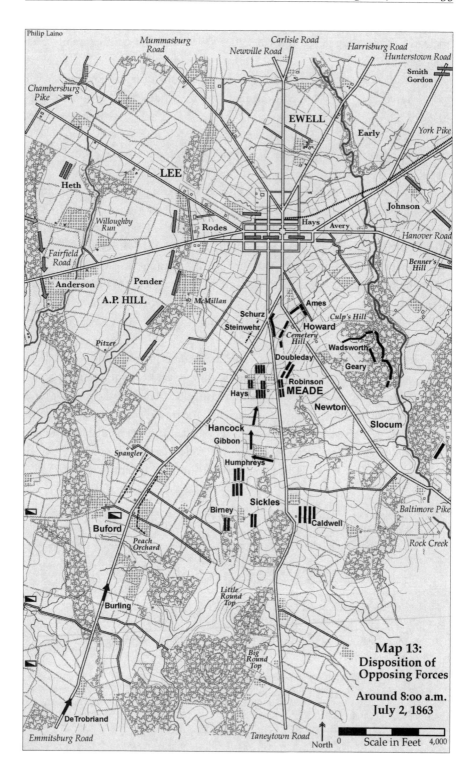

Philip Laino

Mummasburg
Road

Carlisle Road

Newville Road

Harrisburg Road

Hunterstown Road

Smith
Gordon

Chambersburg
Pike

EWELL

Early

York Pike

Heth

LEE

Johnson

Willoughby
Run

Rodes

Hays

Avery

Hanover Road

Fairfield
Road

Benner's
Hill

Anderson

Pender

McMillan

A.P. HILL

Ames

Schurz

Culp's Hill

Steinwehr

Howard

Cemetery
Hill

Wadsworth

Pitzer

Doubleday

Geary

Robinson

Hays

MEADE

Newton

Slocum

Hancock

Gibbon

Spangler

Humphreys

Sickles

Baltimore Pike

Birney

Caldwell

Buford

Peach
Orchard

Rock Creek

Little
Round
Top

Burling

**Map 13:
Disposition of
Opposing Forces**

**Around 8:00 a.m.
July 2, 1863**

Big
Round
Top

DeTrobriand

Emmitsburg Road

Taneytown Road

North   0   Scale in Feet   4,000

their inspection, Pendleton informed Lee that an assault on the enemy's left might succeed.[20]

Lee followed up this initial foray by sending Johnston and a small party to gather additional information about the Union left flank. This group included Maj. John J. Clarke, an engineer on Longstreet's staff, and a number of enlisted men, probably from the 39th Battalion Virginia Cavalry, horsemen attached to Lee's headquarters and trained to accompany engineers on such scouting missions.[21]

Meanwhile Lt. Gen. Richard Ewell was preparing his corps to mount a diversion on the Union right, "to be converted into a real attack, if an opportunity offered," in support of Longstreet on the left. Union commander Meade likewise contemplated taking the offensive. He ordered XII Corps commander Maj. Gen. Henry W. Slocum to "examine the ground in your front" to determine the feasibility of an attack on the enemy in that area. Meade desired "a strong and decisive attack" with Slocum's corps supported by the V Corps as well as the VI Corps that he apparently expected to arrive on the field soon.[22]

That morning before dawn, Meade had taken an inspection ride along Cemetery Ridge with Generals Howard and Hunt and topographical engineer Capt. William Paine, who sketched the terrain. Later Meade noted on the sketch where he wanted each Union corps placed. Paine traced copies of this map and supplied them to the corps commanders who had already arrived at Gettysburg. Only Sedgwick's VI Corps had not yet fully reached the battlefield by mid-afternoon, but the bulk of it had arrived about 6:00 p.m.[23]

20 Lee's post-action report, January, 1864, *OR* 27, pt. 2, 308, 318; Pendleton's post-action report, September 18, 1863, 349-50; Longstreet's post-action report, July 27, 1863, 358.

21 Bill Hyde, "Did You Get There? Capt. Samuel Johnston's Reconnaissance at Gettysburg," *Gettysburg Magazine* (July 2003), 86-93; David A. Powell, "A Reconnaissance Gone Awry: Capt. Samuel R. Johnston's Fateful Trip to Little Round Top," *Gettysburg Magazine* (January 2002), 88-99; Driver, *39th Battalion Virginia Cavalry*, 59.

22 Ewell's post-action report, n.d., 1863, *OR* 27, pt. 2, 446; Butterfield to Slocum, July 2, 1863, pt. 3, 486.

23 Meade, *The Life and Letters of George Gordon Meade*, 2:62-63; *OR*, 27, pt. 1, 663, 665, 671, 673, 680, 686, 688, 690. Using translucent paper to trace copies of a sketch or map was far more practical and quicker than using the superior lithographing method. McElfresh, *Maps and Mapmakers*, 69-71.

Lydia Leister farmhouse and barn where Meade made his headquarters at Gettysburg. The Bureau of Military Information would have set up their operations in these fields.
Photo by the author

Also about 8:00 a.m., the BMI reported to Meade's chief of staff, Butterfield, about newly-arrived prisoners from all three divisions of Ewell's corps. The report listed the number of prisoners captured from what regiments. The report included a postscript: "further examination shows that Ewell's whole corps was on our right yesterday, [and] is now attacking." The latter perhaps referred to Rebel skirmishers advancing on the right from Walker's and Jones' brigades of Johnson's division "for the purpose of feeling the enemy" and determining its position. This succinct yet detailed report reflected a timely and thorough examination of prisoners and demonstrated that the excellence of the BMI interrogation process.[24]

Having no cavalry unit assigned to his headquarters, Major General Slocum sent half a dozen volunteers from the 10th Maine, a unit serving as provost guard for the corps, to reconnoiter the ground upon which the Union attack on the right would be made. Slocum also wanted "to learn if the enemy was attempting to flank the right of Meade's army." Slocum's own observations, with the assistance of Meade's chief engineer, Brig. Gen. Gouverneur K. Warren, convinced him the ground was not suitable to launch an attack. With

---

24 Sharpe to Butterfield, July 2, 1863, RG 393, NA; Johnson's post-action report, September 30, 1863, *OR* 27, pt. 2, 504. The prisoners from Ewell's corps were three each from the 7th Louisiana and 57th North Carolina and one each from the 6th and 21st Louisiana of Early's division; three from the 4th Georgia and one each from the 3rd and 10th Alabama and the 12th and 44th Georgia of Rodes' division; and one from the 21st Virginia of Johnson's division. All these were part of Ewell's order of battle, except the 10th Alabama that may have been a mistake for the 12th Alabama.

this report and in a strong defensive position, Meade decided to wait and see what move Lee would make.[25]

Lee faced some weighty imponderables. While uncertain whether he faced all seven corps of the Federal army, the BMI's John Babcock was able to advise Meade that "all prisoners now agree" that Lee's entire army had arrived at Gettysburg, and that A. P. Hill's and Longstreet's forces had been badly hurt during the previous day's fighting, with several general officers "injured." (Mentioning Longstreet obviously was a slip of Babcock's pen, since he undoubtedly knew that only Hill's and Ewell's corps were involved in the July 1 fight.) The knowledge that Lee's entire army was on the field, however, was of dubious help to a Union army commander who still believed Lee's army had about 30,000 troops more than it actually did, a figure that existed only in his imagination.[26]

The Information Collection Process

On the morning of July 2, Lee rode to Ewell's headquarters to discuss operational plans for the day, and he took time to make a personal reconnaissance of Cemetery Ridge. His observations convinced him that an attack should be launched expeditiously, since Union positions were visibly gaining strength. Based on a dispatch captured during the night that placed the V and XII corps nearby, Lee must have thought he was watching these two corps. In fact, what he was actually witnessing was the arrival of the II Corps and elements of the III Corps, and the relief and repositioning of troops that had fought the previous day. Although Lee, confident of success, chafed to get operations underway, he knew it would require "a great sacrifice of life."[27]

When Captain Johnston returned from his reconnaissance of the Union left flank around 9 a.m. or earlier, he mistakenly reported to Lee that the two

25 Slocum to Meade, July 2, 1863, OR 27, pt. 3, 487; Harry W. Pfanz, *Gettysburg: Culp's Hill & Cemetery Hill* (Chapel Hill, NC, 1993), 117-19 (quoted); Meade, *Life and Letters*, 2:72.

26 Sedgwick's post-action report, August 8, 1863, OR 27, pt. 1, 663; Sharpe to Butterfield, July 2, 1863, RG 393, NA; Hyde, *The Union Generals Speak*, 101-02, 119.

27 Long, *Memoirs of Robert E. Lee*, 281; Longstreet, *From Manassas to Appomattox*, 362-63; Meade, *Life and Letters*, 2:63-64; Harry W. Phanz, *Gettysburg: The Second Day* (Chapel Hill, NC, 1987), 61-62; Coddington, *The Gettysburg Campaign*, 373-74; Freeman, *Lee's Lieutenants*, 3:111-12; Hancock's post-action report, n.d., 1863, OR 27, pt. 1, 369; Birney's post-action report, August 7, 1863, 482; McDonald, *Hotchkiss' Diary*, 157.

Little Round Top, the scene of battle of Day Two.
Photo by the author

hills at the south end of the Union position—Little and Big Round Tops—and the ground around them were undefended. If, in fact, Johnston was actually there and not another location, an unusual set of circumstances apparently prevented Johnston and his small party from observing the III Corps units in the vicinity to the north, and Buford's cavalry brigades to the south. Moreover, the II Corps was camped just east and south of Little Round Top near a portion of the encamped army's artillery reserve. Elements of the XII Corps also were preparing to leave or had just left the area. Nonetheless, as a result of Johnston's report, Lee, apparently convinced the Union left flank was unprotected, reiterated to Longstreet that he should make an assault there with selected forces from his and A. P. Hill's corps.[28]

Johnston's reconnaissance was destined to become one of the most controversial issues related to the battle of Gettysburg. A 30-year-old Virginian, he had worked as a civil engineer before the war. In December 1861, he volunteered to serve on Jeb Stuart's staff and soon received an appointment as a

28 Coddington, *The Gettysburg Campaign*, 374; Phanz, *Gettysburg: The Second Day*, 106-07; Freeman, *Lee's Lieutenants*, 3:113-14; OR 27, pt. 2, 482, 493, 531; Hyde, "Did You Get There?," 86.

second lieutenant. With his "remarkable qualifications as a military engineer" he rose to first lieutenant and then captain in the engineer corps." Johnston had demonstrated special talent for reconnoitering enemy positions, one of the most common duties of an engineering officer.[29]

D. H. Mahan, a professor at West Point during the Civil War era, taught that a reconnaissance officer must "ascertain precisely the duty required of him" and provide "clear and specific information" to his commander so that he "makes his dispositions with confidence." However the results of Johnston's reconnaissance on the morning of July 2 led Lee to a misunderstanding of troop disposition on the enemy's left flank around Little Round Top, which reinforced his thinking that an attack northward guiding up the Emmitsburg Road was indeed operable. Lee aimed to drive the enemy from ground where "our artillery could be used to advantage in assailing the more elevated ground beyond, and thus enable us to reach the crest of the ridge." The position for placing artillery was "the high ground along the Emmitsburg Road," now referred to as the Peach Orchard.[30]

Based on Johnston's reconnaissance, Lee believed that the left flank of Meade's line extended along the Emmitsburg Road some distance north of the Peach Orchard, and that Little Round Top was unoccupied. Although there are differing accounts about the sequence of events, it was probably around 10:00 a.m., after Johnston's return from his reconnaissance, when Lee ordered Longstreet to prepare for an attack. According to the plan, McLaws' and Hood's divisions would make the assault supported by Anderson's division of Hill's corps.

Since his division would lead the attack, Lee ordered McLaws to reconnoiter the ground with Captain Johnston, who was now supposedly

29 Hyde, "Did You Get There?," 86; Karlton D. Smith, "'To Consider Every Contingency': Lt. Gen James Longstreet, Capt. Samuel R. Johnston, and the factors that affect the reconnaissance and countermarch, July 2, 1863," in Karlton D. Smith, ed., *The Most Shocking Battle I have Ever Witnessed: The Second Day at Gettysburg* (Gettysburg, PA, 2008), 99, 103. Recognition for Johnston's work from a variety of high-ranking Confederate officers led to his promotion to captain in August 1862 and an assignment to Lee's staff. Johnston earned mention for meritorious service in both Lee and Longstreet's reports at Fredericksburg and in Maj. Gen. Richard Anderson's report on Chancellorsville. Hyde, "Did You Get There?," 86-87; *OR* 21, 552, 569; *OR* 25, pt. 1, 852; *OR* 27, pt. 2, 308, 318.

30 D. H. Mahan, *Advanced-Guard, Out-Post, and Detachment Service of Troops Service of Troops*, 105-06; Lee's post-action report, July 31, 1863, *OR* 27, pt. 2, 308; Lee's post-action report, January 1864, 318-19; Longstreet's post-action report, 358; Smith, "Reconnaissance and Countermarch," 103-04.

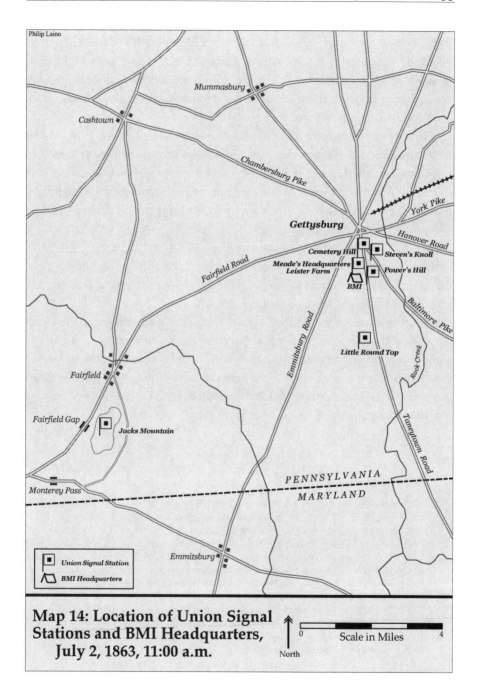

Philip Laino

Mummasburg

Cashtown

Chambersburg Pike

York Pike

Gettysburg

Hanover Road

Cemetery Hill

Steven's Knoll

Fairfield Road

Meade's Headquarters
Leister Farm

Power's Hill

BMI

Little Round Top

Rock Creek

Baltimore Pike

Emmitsburg Road

Fairfield

Fairfield Gap

Jacks Mountain

Taneytown Road

Monterey Pass

PENNSYLVANIA

MARYLAND

Emmitsburg

■ Union Signal Station

⌂ BMI Headquarters

Map 14: Location of Union Signal Stations and BMI Headquarters, July 2, 1863, 11:00 a.m.

North

0   Scale in Miles   4

familiar with the target area. According to McLaws, however, Longstreet objected to his leaving his division at that point, nor did he want McLaws to send his chief engineer, Lt. Thomas J. Moncure, to check out the ground. Longstreet may have thought additional reconnaissance unnecessary, since Johnston had already scouted the area.[31]

While this activity took place on the Confederate side of the field, around 9:00 a.m., Union cavalry commander Pleasonton incomprehensibly agreed to Brigadier General Buford's request for relief. Confusion at headquarters about this led to Meade's allowing Buford to depart with his two brigades that were protecting the Union left flank and move to Westminster, Maryland—to refit and guard the army's supply trains. Since neither Gregg's nor Kilpatrick's cavalry divisions had yet arrived at Gettysburg, this inexplicable and costly error impaired Meade's defensive and early warning capability. With Buford gone, the army had no cavalry at all for several hours to screen and reconnoiter the area on the far left of the Union line.[32]

Because most of the Federal cavalry were deployed elsewhere, the signal corps took on a heavier burden for detecting enemy movements. Late in the night of July 1 after the bulk of the army had arrived on the field, the signalmen set up flag and torch communications between Little Round Top and the rear of the army at Indian Lookout behind Emmitsburg. This station served as a communications relay to Union headquarters at Taneytown.

---

31 McLaws, "Gettysburg," *SHSP*, 7:68; Hyde, "Did You Get There?," 86-93; Powell, "A Reconnaissance Gone Awry," 88-99.

32 Pleasonton's post-action report, August 31, 1863, *OR* 27, pt. 1, 914; Buford's post-action report, August 27, 1863, 927-28; Butterfield to Pleasonton, July 2, 1863, pt. 3, 490; Eric Wittenberg, "The Truth About the Withdrawal of Brig. Gen. John Buford's Cavalry, July 2, 1863," *Gettysburg Magazine* (July 2007), Issue 37, 71-82; Longacre, *The Cavalry at Gettysburg*, 204-07. When he approved Pleasonton's request to allow Buford's division to depart from the battlefield, Meade did not realize the other cavalry divisions had not yet arrived. Gregg's cavalry finally arrived about noon, and at 1:45 p.m., Pleasonton ordered him to detail a regiment to cover the area Buford's division had occupied. Receiving the order in Gregg's absence, Col. John B. McIntosh detached Lt. Col. William E. Doster's 4th Pennsylvania Cavalry for the task. By this time, however, the damage of uncovering the Union left had already been done. When Doster reported to Pleasonton, he was told to return to Gregg's division, since there was no need of exposing the cavalry in the front lines. After receiving orders from Pleasonton, Kilpatrick's division began moving toward Gettysburg from north of Hanover; it would clash with Hampton's cavalry brigade at Hunterstown early in the afternoon of July 2. *OR* 27, pt. 1, 956, 992, 1058-59, pt. 3, 490; Wittenberg, "Buford's Withdrawal," 77; Hyde, *The Union Generals Speak*, 138; Longacre, *The Cavalry at Gettysburg*, 207; William E. Doster, *Lincoln and Episodes of the Civil War* (New York, 1915), 217.

By 11:00 a.m. on July 2, chief signal officer Norton had the commander's new headquarters at Gettysburg, where the general had moved during the night, in communication by visual signals with every corps commander on the field. Signal corps teams manned major strategic points: Cemetery Hill, the spur of Culp's Hill (Steven's Knoll), Power's Hill, and Little Round Top. All of these stations provided communications, but they also served as observation posts on enemy activity.[33]

Longstreet, skeptical about the wisdom of Lee's plan, required considerable time to get his troops into position for the attack. He assigned young Col. Edward Porter Alexander to "act as director of artillery" rather than Col. James B. Walton, the senior corps artillery officer, and sent him to "get an idea of the ground." Fearing his forces too weak to make the assault without Maj. Gen. George Pickett's division, then marching toward Gettysburg after protecting the Confederate rear at Chambersburg, Longstreet requested and received Lee's permission to delay the attack until Brig. Gen. Evander M. Law's brigade of Hood's division arrived. Left behind on picket duty at New Guilford, it departed there in the morning and joined its division around noon. Considering his desire to get underway as soon as possible and that the attack was behind schedule, it must have taken some effort on Lee's part to agree to Longstreet's request, but he deferred to his most trusted corps commander. Awaiting Law's arrival postponed the attack about another hour, and more serious delays were already pending.[34]

In the morning, Colonel Alexander, under instructions from Longstreet, examined all the roads leading to the right and front of the Confederate lines, and reconnoitered the enemy's left to determine the best approaches to make an attack. Pendleton, who had scouted the enemy earlier, guided Alexander to the

33 Norton's post-action report, September 18, 1863, *OR* 27, pt. 1, 202; Bill Cameron, "The Signal Corps at Gettysburg," *Gettysburg Magazine*, July 1, 1990, Issue 3, 10. There was another Union signal station behind enemy lines on Jack's Mountain beyond Fairfield, but even though the Gettysburg battlefield and the signal flags on Little Round Top were visible, the distant station could not establish communications with the station on Little Round Top. Cameron, "The Signal Corps at Gettysburg, Part II," January 1, 1991, Issue 4, 102. When Hancock arrived on the battlefield on July 1, he gave Chief Signal Officer Norton the information needed to formulate a signal operations plan. Brown, *The Signal Corps*, 360.

34 Alexander, *Military Memoirs*, 391-92; Gallagher, *The Personal Recollections of General Edward Porter Alexander*, 235; Longstreet's post-action report, July 27, 1863, *OR* 27, pt. 2, 358; Longstreet, *From Manassas to Appomattox*, 365; Law, "The Struggle for 'Round Top," in *B&L*, 3:319. For a discussion of Lee's expectations and Longstreet's deliberate response to them, see Coddington, *The Gettysburg Campaign*, 371-78.

Right: Brig. Gen. William N. Pendleton
Library of Congress
Below: Brig. Gen. Edward Porter Alexander
Library of Congress

location he had previously used for observation, probably in the vicinity of Spangler Woods. But the Confederates took special precautions because enemy sharpshooters were active in that area.[35]

While Pendleton and Alexander reconnoitered the enemy position, a "sharp contest" broke out to their right and rear in a wooded area. This was a skirmish between a detachment of Berdan's Sharpshooters, who were conducting a reconnaissance of Pitzer's Woods, and the Alabama regiments of Brig. Gen. Cadmus Wilcox's brigade of Anderson's division, A. P. Hill's corps.[36]

---

35 Alexander, *Military Memoirs*, 391-92; Gallagher, *Fighting for the Confederacy*, 235-36; Pendleton's post-action report, September 12, 1863, *OR* 27, pt. 2, 350; Alexander's post-action report, August 3, 1863, 429; Longstreet, *From Manassas to Appomattox*, 365. Although there is no record of a report from Alexander to Longstreet, he had couriers with him during his reconnaissance in the late morning and it makes sense that Alexander would have appraised his commander of the enemy situation along the Emmitsburg Road.

36 Pendleton's post-action report, September 12, 1863, *OR* 27, pt. 1, 350. Although Walton's title was chief of artillery for the corps, Longstreet looked more to Alexander to command the artillery in tactical situations, a situation that naturally caused Walton considerable consternation. Longstreet addressed this issue in Longstreet, "The Mistakes of Gettysburg," *The Annals of the Civil War*, 631-32.

When the Alabamians drove Berdan's men out of the woods, Pendleton decided to survey the area "much further to the right that had yet been examined." Along the way, he met General Lee himself "en route to survey the ground." Since Wilcox had already been to the right beyond Pitzer's Woods in his pursuit of the retreating Union sharpshooters, he volunteered to lead Pendleton and Lee's aide, Colonel Long, to a farmhouse on Millerstown Road near Emmitsburg Road (most likely either the Snyder or Warfield farmhouse). Pendleton observed the field and the enemy's batteries before returning to Longstreet to help conduct his attack force to this location.[37]

The Union signal corps' operational plan paid dividends as stations tracked enemy movements during the hours before Longstreet's attack on the Union left. Just before noon, Jerome from the station on Little Round Top reported a firefight occurring about a mile to the west—the clash between Berdan's sharpshooters, supported by the 3rd Maine, and the 10th and 11th Alabama regiments of Wilcox's brigade near Pitzer's Woods. In absence of a cavalry screen in that area after Buford's departure, Maj. Gen. David B. Birney, who commanded a division in the III Corps, received permission from corps commander Sickles to order Berdan to deploy skirmishers "to feel the enemy and discover their movements."[38]

Jerome alerted Butterfield that the Union skirmishers gave way under pressure, and the woods were full of the enemy. Birney credited Berdan's reconnaissance for providing information about the strength of the enemy in Pitzer's Woods and that "three columns of [the enemy] . . . marching to our left"—probably the other three regiments of Wilcox's brigade. This report triggered Sickles' decision to move his III Corps forward to the Emmitsburg Road "to meet the attack." He may have been considering this move for some time, for he alleged he was uncertain exactly where Meade had assigned the III Corps on the left flank of the Union line along Cemetery Ridge.[39]

37 Pendleton's post-action report, September 12, 1863, OR 27, pt. 1, 350. Apparently Pendleton did not arrange to establish a permanent lookout point at this farmhouse.

38 Jerome to Butterfield, July 2, 1863, ibid., pt. 3, 488; Birney's post-action report, August 7, 1863, pt. 1, 482; Berdan's post-action report, July 29, 1863, 515; Wilcox's post-action report, July 17, 1863, pt. 2, 617; Brown, The Signal Corps, 360; Murray, Berdan's Sharpshooters in Combat, 60-70.

39 Jerome to Butterfield, see note above; Birney's post-action report, August 7, 1863, pt. 1, 482-83, 515; Wilcox's post-action report, see note above; Coddington, The Gettysburg Campaign, 592. Before entering Pitzer's Woods, Berdan's men unwisely ignored a local young man's

Maj. Gen. Daniel E. Sickles
Library of Congress

Fear of Disclosure Hinders the Attack

That wretched little signal station upon [Little] Round Top [on July 2] caused one of our divisions to lose over two hours and probably delayed our assault nearly that long.

Col. E. Alexander[40]

There is nothing in your front; you will be entirely on the flank of the enemy.

Lt. Gen. James Longstreet[41]

Despite Alexander's reconnaissance of the roads, Longstreet's forces still encountered delays as they moved into position for the attack. Early that morning Lee had assigned Col. John Logan Black and some 250 cavalry to Longstreet. Black had arrived at Gettysburg late with a number of his 1st South Carolina and miscellaneous other cavalry after having been slightly wounded on June 21 in the clash with Pleasonton's cavalry at Upperville, Virginia.[42]

Longstreet could employ this cavalry detachment to guide the march to the point of attack if he so desired. Instead he deployed Black's contingent to explore roads and guard the bridge over Marsh Creek and a nearby road (probably Black Horse Tavern Road) in the area where he had his headquarters.

---

warning that "lots of rebels" were concealed in the woods. Murray, *Berdan's Sharpshooters*, 63-64. For a discussion of Sickles' concern about his position, see Coddington, *The Gettysburg Campaign*, 343-55.

40 Alexander's post-war (1887) response to an inquiry from J. Willard Brown. Brown, *The Signal Corps*, 367-68.

41 Longstreet to McLaws. LaFayette McLaws, "Gettysburg," *SHSP*, 7:69-70.

42 Black to Bachelder, March 22, 1886, Ladd, David L. and Audrey J. Ladd, *The Bachelder Papers: Gettysburg in Their Own Words*, 3 vols. (Dayton, OH, 1994), 2:1240. Black said that Lee assigned him "to command Hart's battery and some cut off detachment of [Wade] Hampton's brigade, to which was added one or two organized detachments of Virginia Cavalry."

Lee assigned Col. John Logan Black and about 250 cavalrymen to assist Longstreet in preparation for the attack on July 2.
Confederate Veteran, 1927

Around noon, Longstreet sent two of Black's officers, Lts. Fred Horsey and J. Wilson Marshall to conduct a reconnaissance for some three or four miles—Horsey south along Seminary Ridge, and Wilson probably to the southwest. Horsey returned in about an hour and reported seeing no enemy. Oddly, because several Union regiments—the 99th Pennsylvania, the 3rd Maine supported by the 63rd Pennsylvania, and the 4th Maine—had been deployed as skirmishers west of Emmitsburg Road beyond the Sherfy peach orchard that morning.[43]

Longstreet claimed that Lee assigned Captain Johnston, who had conducted the early morning reconnaissance, to lead McLaws' and Hood's divisions to the point of attack. Johnston denied receiving such orders. Adding to the confusion, Longstreet chose to ride "in the middle of the line" with Hood's division during the march, rather than at the front with McLaws where he would have been in position to render guidance and direction if needed.[44]

43 Ibid.; Phanz, *Gettysburg: The Second Day*, 116; Birney's post-action report, August, 7, 1863, OR 27, pt. 1, 482; Danks' post-action report, July 10, 1863, 498; Sawyer's post-action report, July 27, 1863, 509. Since Horsey did not observe any Union activities, he must have reached Seminary Ridge from his starting point on Herr's Ridge somewhere south of the peach orchard on a route that likely took him to the vicinity of Warfield Ridge opposite Big Round Top. The circumstances of this recon were eerily reminiscent of Captain Johnston's earlier one when he also observed no enemy.

44 Longstreet, *From Manassas to Appomattox*, 365-66; Phanz, *Gettysburg: The Second Day*, 489-90n45; Paul Clark Cooksey, "Around the Flank: Longstreet's July 2 Attack at Gettysburg," *Gettysburg Magazine*, (July 2003), Issue 29, 95. Lee had two companies of scouts and guides of the 39th Virginia Cavalry Battalion available to help guide Longstreet's divisions, and he could also have drawn on Albert Jenkins' cavalry brigade, which had arrived at Gettysburg on July 1, to serve as guides. However, he had assigned Jenkins' brigade to support Ewell's operations against Cemetery and Culp's Hills on the Confederate left. Driver, *39th Battalion Virginia Cavalry*,

As Johnston rode with McLaws, they came to a clearing visible from the Union signal corps station on Little Round Top. So, when McLaws informed his commander of this problem, Longstreet, aware that Lee wanted him to move his forces into position unobserved, told McLaws to countermarch his division to avoid being seen. He agreed to allow them to retrace their steps and follow a route to the jump off point that McLaws and Johnston discovered after a brief exploration.[45]

At 1:30 p.m., signal officer Hall reported from the station on Little Round Top, "A heavy column of enemy's infantry, about 10,000 strong, is moving from opposite our extreme left toward our right." Forty minutes later, he added, "Those troops were passing on a by-road from Dr. [Samuel E.] Hall's house to Herr's tavern, on the Chambersburg pike. A train of ambulances is following them." The signal station had apparently spotted Hood's division of over 7,000 troops marching on Herr's Ridge Road and a farm lane of Dr. Hall's property. Rather than continuing to march toward the right, however, the column would change course via the Willoughby Run Road toward the area of attack. During the countermarch, Longstreet permitted Hood, his other division commander, to send scouts ahead to reconnoiter the field. This information tended to confuse the issue for Meade, who remained uncertain

---

56-59; Paul M. Shevchuk, "The Wounding of Albert Jenkins, July 2, 1863," *Gettysburg Magazine* (July 1990), Issue 3, 59. McLaws supported Longstreet's contention that Lee assigned Johnston to guide the forces to the battlefield: "Major [Captain] Johnston, of General Lee's staff, came to me and said he was ordered to conduct me on the march." McLaws stated in postwar remarks that Longstreet did not permit him to reconnoiter the ground upon which his and Hood's divisions would fight prior to deployment. McLaws later recorded that he took it upon himself to scout the position and "was soon convinced that by crossing the ridge where I then was, my command could reach the point indicated by General Lee, in a half hour, without being seen." At the time, McLaws was around Herr's Ridge near the Black Horse Tavern and Fairfield Road. McLaws, "Gettysburg," *SHSP*, 7:68-69; Lafayette McLaws, "The Second Day at Gettysburg: General Sickles Answered by the Commander of the Opposing Forces—The Federal Disaster on the Left," *Gettysburg Sources*, 3 vols. (Baltimore, MD, 1990), 3:140-41.

45 Longstreet, *From Manassas to Appomattox*, 365-67; Sears, *Gettysburg*, 258; John L. Black to John Bachelder, *The Bachelder Papers*, March 22, 1886, 2:1240. McLaws, "The Second Day at Gettysburg," 140; McLaws, "Gettysburg," *SHSP*, 69; Roger J. Greezicki, "Humbugging the Historian: A Reappraisal of Longstreet at Gettysburg," *Gettysburg Magazine* (January 1992), no. 6, 62-67; J. B. Hood, *Advance and Retreat: Personal Experiences in the United States and Confederate Armies* (Edison, NJ, 1985), 57.

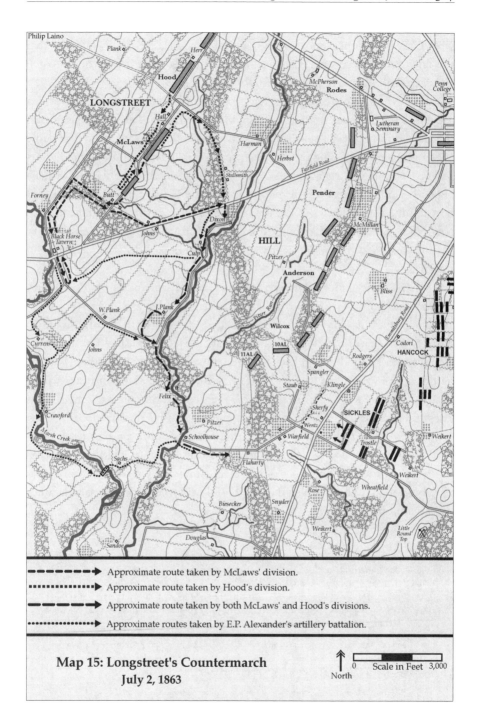

- ► Approximate route taken by McLaws' division.
- ► Approximate route taken by Hood's division.
- ► Approximate route taken by both McLaws' and Hood's divisions.
- ► Approximate routes taken by E.P. Alexander's artillery battalion.

Map 15: Longstreet's Countermarch
July 2, 1863

North   0   Scale in Feet   3,000

what Lee's intentions were.[46] Meade later informed Halleck in Washington that the enemy had been operating on both his flanks, "but it is difficult to tell exactly [what] his movements [signify]."

Meanwhile, Confederate cavalry commander Stuart, who had been separated from the army since June 25, finally arrived at Lee's headquarters in the afternoon of July 2, apparently to a frosty reception. Although he reportedly chastised Stuart for being out of touch for several days, Lee undoubtedly was relieved to have his cavalry leader back with him. Although Lee normally depended upon Stuart for information about the enemy, in this case he assigned him and the four brigades of cavalry that had thus far arrived at Gettysburg to cover the York and Heidlersburg Roads on the army's left flank, and to defend against an attack by Union cavalry, elements of Gregg's division, operating in that area.[47]

When scouts Hood had sent ahead returned with news of the country around the Round Tops and the good possibility that the enemy could be assaulted in flank and rear, Hood requested Longstreet's permission to maneuver in that direction. Nothing could be accomplished by marching straight ahead, Hood thought, since the enemy had formed "a concave line" of battle between Emmitsburg Road and Little Round Top. Such an attack would cost his division a "fearful sacrifice," he feared. Sickles had created an unexpected obstacle as well as an inviting target after he advanced his two divisions to the Emmitsburg Road in mid-afternoon, exactly on the line that Lee had ordered Longstreet's forces to follow during its planned attack. Sickles' position had forced Longstreet to make adjustments by moving Hood to the right of McLaws. This doubled the length of the line of attack and essentially cut its power in half.[48]

46 Hall to Butterfield, July 2, 1863, *OR* 27, pt. 3, 488; Longstreet's post-action report, July 27, 1863, pt. 2, 358; Busey and Martin, *Strengths and Losses*, 171. Meade to Halleck, July 2, 1863, pt. 1, 72. Local citizen Daniel H. Klingle who had been brought to the hilltop may have aided the signalmen by pointing out places, distances, and the names of roads and where they led. Smith, "The Reconnaissance and Countermarch," 111.

47 Lee's post-action report, January 1864, *OR* 27, pt. 2, 322; Stuart's post-action report, August 20, 1863, 697; Longacre, The Cavalry at Gettysburg, 198, 202; Alexander, *Military Memoirs of a Confederate*, 376-77; Gregg's post-action report, July 25, 1863, *OR* 27, pt. 1, 956 .

48 J.B. Hood, *Advance and Retreat*, 57-58; Gallagher, *The Personal Recollection of General Edward Porter Alexander*, 237; Longstreet's post-action report, July 27, 1863, *OR* 27, pt. 1, 358, 482-83; Longstreet, *From Manassas to Appomattox*, 367.

Flawed Reconnaissance Undermines Lee's Plan

As preparations for an assault against the Union left had evolved, a more timely and thorough reconnaissance would have alerted Lee and Longstreet to the initial movements of Sickles troops, and with it the necessity of launching the attack expeditiously. But for the information Hood's scouts had gathered, all other reconnaissance occurred before Sickles' move forward between 2:00 and 3:00 p.m. A window of opportunity had existed to strike before the III Corps had solidified its position along the Emmitsburg Road. An earlier assault would have also left open an alternative strategy of having Hood's troops occupy and fortify Little Round Top and harass the Union rear before the Union VI Corps began arriving around 3:00 p.m. The desire for secrecy during the march and the resultant countermarch had inadvertently prevented a more expeditious movement to the point of attack.[49]

Although Alexander had discovered a route to move his artillery forward to the battlefield unobserved, the assignment of Lee and Longstreet's engineers, Johnston and Clark, to lead Longstreet's forces to the point of attack created problems. If Alexander had been used to guide the movement, he would have likely been able to get Hood and McLaws to the battlefield unseen. Alexander met Longstreet's forces as they prepared to countermarch, but since Longstreet's had decided to stay to the rear during the march, neither Alexander nor any of the other officers present took responsibility for sending the troops along the protected route Alexander had taken earlier. Longstreet's decision not to march at the head of his forces compounded an already disordered situation.[50]

---

49 Hewitt, "The Confederate Deliberate Attack," 1-38; Meade, *Life and Letters*, 2:71, 87. When Hancock arrived on the field on July 1, he recognized Little Round Top's commanding control of Emmitsburg Road to the front and Taneytown Road to the rear. So he ordered Brig. Gen. John Geary to occupy it with units of his Second Division, XII Corps. The key height became uncovered when Geary's units were repositioned after Sickle's III Corps relieved them in the early morning of July 2. Sickles, however, failed to occupy the hill. Geary's post-action report, July 29, 1863, OR 27, pt. 1, 825; Tucker, *Hancock the Superb*, 138-39; Coddington, *The Gettysburg Campaign*, 299; Meade, *Life and Letters*, 2:62-84; .David A. Ward, "'Sedgwick's Foot Cavalry': The March of the VI Corps to Gettysburg," *Gettysburg Magazine* (January 2000), Issue 22, 64. On the critical nature of Little Round Top, see Phanz, *Gettysburg: The Second Day*, 205-06; Sears, *Gettysburg*, 269-71.

50 Longstreet's post-action report, July 27, 1863, OR 27, pt. 2, 358; Cameron, "The Signal Corps at Gettysburg," 10; Mahan, *Advanced-Guard, Outpost, and Detachment Service*, 114-16; Gallagher, *Alexander's Recollections*, 236; Longstreet, *From Manassas to Appomattox*, 366.

When the attack finally got underway, delays in getting units into position and the Confederates' spotty knowledge of both the terrain and disposition of Union forces contributed to the stalemate that ensued after both sides suffered staggering casualties. With Lee and Longstreet in mind, Peter W. Alexander, a reporter traveling with Lee's army, voiced the sentiments of many Confederate officers and men after the bloodbath of July 2:

> But little disposition was shown to undertake a proper reconnaissance of the ground—an omission which every man in the army now deeply regrets. It was well known that Meade had chosen a formidable position, but the extent and strength of his line [that] bore to the mountain spurs on the right, were but little understood.[51]

While these remarks encapsulate Confederate shortcomings on July 2, Lee and Longstreet had sent out a number of aides to scout the enemy positions and had done so themselves. All these previews took place, however, before Sickle's advance to the Emmitsburg Road. Apparently because of the sloping lay of the land on both sides of the Emmitsburg Road, no Confederates were in position to observe the change in the Union position. Certainly no such observation was reported up the chain of command. Nonetheless the considerable number of Union skirmishers west of that road might have alerted the Rebels to the presence of a larger body of Federal troops out of sight behind them. And what

---

Apparently Johnston and Clark had not observed a signal station in action on Little Round Top during their morning reconnaissance, since the XII Corps signal party that had originally occupied it had likely already abandoned the station. Jerome of Buford's cavalry reoccupied the site early in the morning of July 2 but probably arrived after Johnston and Clark had left the area, otherwise the Rebel officers would have spotted the signal flags on top of the mountain. And surely they would have known an enemy signal station along the route of march must be avoided, since all their reconnaissance training taught that "the enemy must be seen but not encountered." The countermarch was further delayed because of McLaws' desire to have his division remain in the lead, instead of giving way to Hood. Thus Hood's division had to postpone its march until McLaws retraced his steps.

51 Styple, *Writing & Fighting the Confederate War*, 162-63. Alexander wrote this report on July 4 while the armies still occupied the field. He had the reputation as a capable and objective reporter who offered praise and criticism impartially. Freeman attributed the lack of a thorough reconnaissance of the Federal left to the absence of Stuart's cavalry. Freeman, *Lee's Lieutenants*, 3:175.

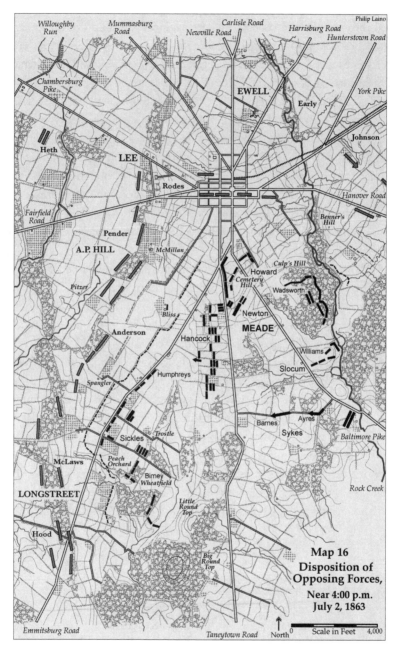

Map 16
**Disposition of
Opposing Forces,**
Near 4:00 p.m.
July 2, 1863

about Wilcox's brigade on the far right of the Confederate line? It may or should have been in position to observe the III Corps' movement, but for reasons that remain as yet unexplained, word never reached Hill or Lee, much less Longstreet, or Pendleton who, sometime in the afternoon prior to the attack, scouted the area of the crossroads where McLaws' division eventually arrived, and, as Pendleton reported, he observed the field and the enemy's batteries.[52]

A letter McLaws sent to his wife a few days after the battle reveals what was actually known about Union forces present in the area of Sherfy's Peach Orchard. Longstreet's attack, he wrote, was intended "to get in rear of the enemy who were supposed to be stationed principally in rear of Gettysburg or near it. The report being that the enemy had but two regiments of infantry and one battery at the Peach orchard." A likely source of this report was Col. E. P. Alexander after he had conducted a reconnaissance of the Union lines around noon in accordance with Longstreet's, or Pendleton who, sometime in the afternoon prior to the attack, scouted the area of the crossroads where McLaws' division eventually arrived, and, as Pendleton reported, he observed the field and the enemy's batteries.[53]

As Alexander readily admitted, the presence of a signal station on Little Round Top played a key role in the repulse of Longstreet's assault: by causing him to order a countermarch, his attack got delayed until later in the day. By then the strength and disposition of Union forces had changed, and this derailed Lee's plan. The resultant heavy Union casualties would likely have been reduced, however, if Sickles' corps had held its position on Cemetery Ridge as directed, instead of creating a salient by moving forward to the Emmitsburg road. Sickles justified his action by citing what he believed to be an imminent threat of attack as a result of information obtained during Berdan's reconnaissance, and the removal of Buford's cavalry which had been guarding his flank. The Union army paid a high price for Sickles' bravado.[54]

Soon after the battle started on the Union left, Ewell's corps began bombarding the Union right between 4:00-5:00 p.m., before launching an attack "about dusk." The lateness of the hour, however, soon brought a halt to

---

52 Longstreet's post-action report, July 27, 1863, OR 27, pt. 2, 358; Wilcox's post-action report, July 17, 1863, 617-18. Neither Longstreet nor Wilcox address the movement of Sickles' corps forward to the Emmitsburg Road.

53 McLaws to "My Dear Wife," July 7, 1863, in John C. Oeffinger, ed., *A Soldier's General: The Civil War Letters of Major General Lafayette McLaws* (Chapel Hill, NC, 2001), 195-97: Pendleton's post-action report, OR 27, pt. 2, 350.

54 Longstreet's post-action report, July 27, 1863, OR 27, pt. 2, 358; Birney's post-action report, August 7, 1863, pt. 1, 482-83; Hyde, *The Union Generals Speak*, 42, 138; Hewitt, "The Confederate Deliberate Attack," 26-27.

Maj. Gen. George E. Pickett
Library of Congress

this fighting, with no significant change of position by either side, just thousands more casualties.[55]

The day's battles produced hundreds of Rebel prisoners—600 on July 2 alone—all potential sources for the BMI to increase its knowledge of important aspects of Lee's army. BMI's Babcock, who signed Sharpe's name to the report, sent Meade a summary of prisoner interrogations in the late afternoon of July 2. Prisoners had been taken from every brigade in Lee's army "excepting the four brigades of Pickett's Division," and from nearly a hundred different regiments. The lack of prisoners from Pickett's division kept Babcock from learning only three brigades and not four, as he stated, had accompanied Pickett to Gettysburg. However, the BMI's timely intelligence and the arrival of the VI Corps that afternoon should have assured Meade his army would be in greater strength and better prepared for battle than the enemy on July 3.[56]

Meade's and his chief of staff Butterfield's understanding of the enemy's strength was distorted, as we have seen. Clearly they lacked confidence in the BMI's calculations of the enemy order of battle. This perhaps was more understandable in Meade's case because of his recent assumption of command. Butterfield, on the other hand, had been directly involved with Colonel Sharpe

---

55 Ewell's post-action report, n.d., 1863, *OR* 27, pt. 2, 446-47; Johnson's post-action report, September 30, 1863, 504. For details of fighting on the Union right on July 2, see Pfanz, *Gettysburg: Culp's Hill & Cemetery Hill*, 1-283.

56 Sharpe to Butterfield, July 3, 1863, RG 393, NA; [Babcock] to Butterfield, July 2, 1863, RG 393, NA; Fishel, *The Secret War*, 527; Sedgwick's post-action report, August 8, 1863, *OR* 27, pt. 1, 663. Pickett's division normally comprised five brigades not four as cited in Babcock's report, but only three (Garnett, Kemper, and Armistead) went to Gettysburg; the other two (Corse and Jenkins) had been assigned to Maj. Gen. D. H. Hill's command in North Carolina. Sears, *Gettysburg*, 52. The BMI estimated 5,220 troops in three brigades of Pickett's division present at the battle. Order of Battle, Pickett's division, [July 3 or 4, 1863], RG 393, NA.

and the BMI for months, and he should have been aware that it was reliable and based its reports on well-tested methods of analysis of a variety of solid sources rather than citizen observations and press reports.[57]

At the end of the fighting on July 2, Meade called a commanders' meeting to discuss his army's condition and the next day's action plan. Before the meeting, he questioned Sharpe to verify the accuracy of the BMI's prisoner interrogation summary. With minor corrections, Sharpe substantiated that Lee had used all of his units in battle except for Pickett's division. Those troops, he said, were now up and ready for deployment. This information, depending upon the weight the Union commanders gave it—and there's no clear way of knowing that—may have been an important factor in the their opting to stay in position and await a Rebel attack on the following day.[58]

Timely Intelligence is the Key to Success

In preparation for combat on July 2, Meade had received a steady flow of information from his intelligence resources. The BMI, assisted by provost personnel, conducted prisoner examinations that produced accurate, up-to-date information about the strength, leadership, and disposition of Lee's forces. In addition, the signal corps kept watch from its various perches around the battlefield and reported enemy movements as they occurred. The combination of their observations along with BMI's prisoner interrogation and information analysis provided the Union high command excellent data for operational planning.[59]

In addition, Berdan's Sharpshooters had furnished forewarning of an impending attack to Sickles by reporting movements of enemy forces toward the left of the Union line. They also screened the left flank of the Union army before Longstreet's assault. A detachment of Union cavalry made a significant contribution to the Union cause when it captured letters from President Davis

---

57 Meade, *Life and Letters*, 2:34, 355; Hyde, *The Union Generals Speak*, 101-02, 247. For an assessment of the BMI's performance prior to Gettysburg, see Fishel, *The Secret War*, 275-411.

58 John Gibbon, "The Council of War on the Second Day," in *B&L*, 3:313-14; Butterfield, "Minutes of Council, July 2, 1863," *OR* 27, pt. 1, 73; Meade, *Life and Letters*, 2:94-96; Fishel, *The Secret War*, 527-28.

59 Sparks, *Inside Lincoln's Army*, 267.

and Adjutant General Cooper to Lee that revealed important strategic information.

In contrast, the unavailability of Stuart's cavalry, his primary information-gathering resource laid considerable constraint on Lee. In Stuart's absence, Lee received inaccurate information about enemy presence around Little Round Top early on July 2. The reconnaissance party under Captain Johnston failed to find the left flank of the Union army or find a suitable route for Longstreet's attack force, since the one Johnston provided was under observation of a Union signal station, necessitating a time-consuming and wearying counter-march for two divisions. That Johnston was largely a victim of unfortunate circumstance—the signal station on Little Round Top was not operating during his inspection—did not diminish the harm it inflicted on Confederate plans.[60]

Nor does evidence indicate that Longstreet used the cavalry Lee provided him to full advantage. He could have deployed Colonel Black's detachment to reconnoiter and provide early warning of enemy activity in the area where the attack would take place. Longstreet also sent Alexander to reconnoiter the roads leading to the attack area. And despite his artilleryman's success in getting his guns to the field undetected, Longstreet did not take advantage of his knowledge to guide his forces to the point of attack.

Almost complete lack of documentation limits any evaluation of Confederate signal corps operations at Gettysburg. It appears that commanders primarily relied on time-consuming courier communication. David W. Gaddy, who has studied this subject carefully, says that "reading the reports and personal accounts [of the battle], one is struck repeatedly with references to written or oral messages, directly or via couriers . . . which indicates that signal communications were not available, or not used."[61]

Lee's desire for his orders to be expedited and Longstreet's skepticism about Lee's plan of operations militated against a thorough, proper reconnaissance of the ground where the assault would take place. Although both generals conducted their own personal observation of enemy positions, and had sent emissaries to do so at various times in the morning and early afternoon, evidently no personnel were assigned to keep watch on the Union

---

60 Lee's post-action report, January 1864, OR 27, pt. 2, 321; Hyde, "Johnston's Reconnaissance," 87; Smith, "The Reconnaissance and Countermarch," 102-04.

61 Gaddy, "Confederate Signal Corps at Gettysburg," 111-12.

left on a sustained basis. When Pendleton discovered an excellent place for viewing the area of Emmitsburg Road at the Sherfy's peach orchard from a farmhouse on Millerstown Road just to the west, he abandoned it without assigning a team for continued observation.[62]

In addition, even after Maj. Gen. J. B. Kershaw, who commanded a brigade in McLaws' division, saw "a large body of troops" of the Union army moving along the Emmitsburg Road on the morning of July 2 from his vantage point just off the Fairfield Road, apparently no surveillance posts were established at this location to keep watch on the enemy. McLaws was also aware of this vantage point, because he ordered Kershaw to move his brigade to the rear "under the cover of the hill" out of view of enemy observers.[63]

McLaws had little doubt about the cause of the heavy Confederate losses during the July 2 assault, including "many of the most valuable officers in the whole service . . . killed." McLaws claimed he was misled regarding the strength of the enemy at the point of attack. He faulted Longstreet for the inaccurate information:

> In place of there being but two regiments of infantry and one battery, the enemy were in very great force, very strongly posted and aided by very numerous arty. I think the attack was unnecessary and the whole plan of battle a very bad one. Genl Longstreet is to blame for not reconnoitering the ground and for persisting in ordering the assault when his errors were discovered.[64]

The apparent inability of Rebel units in the field to observe Sickles corps moving forward to the Emmitsburg Road, precluded vital adjustments to Lee's

---

62 Pendleton post-action report, September 12, 1863, *OR* 27, pt. 2, 350. After conducting this reconnaissance, Pendleton returned to "an elevated point on the Fairfield road," which furnished a "very extensive view" from which he could see "the enemy's cavalry in considerable force" as well as "bodies of infantry and artillery, accompanied by their trains" that were moving up the Emmitsburg Road "toward the enemy's main position." Yet evidently neither Pendleton nor anyone else saw to it that a signal party received orders to occupy this location to observe the enemy and provide information to Lee. Had someone done so, observers should have been able to see the III Corps as it moved out onto the Emmitsburg Road taking up positions. Clearly, early observation should have alerted Longstreet and Lee that the Union line extended much farther south before McLaws division arrived at that intersection to discover it under entirely different circumstances.

63 Kershaw to Bachelder, March 20, 1876, Ladd and Ladd, *The Bachelder Papers*, 1, 453; E. B. Kershaw, "Kershaw's Brigade at Gettysburg," in *B&L*, 3:331.

64 Oeffinger, *A Soldier's General*, 197.

operational plan. Although Anderson's division of Hill's corps was in position on the west side of Emmitsburg Road and could see the enemy line "plainly in view, about 1,200 yards" to his front, the line he referred to was doubtless on the higher ground of the Cemetery Ridge. Brigadier General Cadmus Wilcox, whose brigade held the right flank of Anderson's division, would have been in the best location to observe the forward movement of Sickles' corps to the Emmitsburg Road. Yet Wilcox makes no mention of this movement in his report on the battle. This was clearly a missed opportunity to alert Lee and Longstreet to the changed disposition of enemy troops in the area of the planned attack.[65]

An undated Gettysburg National Park study likely conducted in the 1950s sheds some light on this situation. The study concluded that the only place on the battlefield the Rebels could have observed Sickles' move forward to the Emmitsburg Road from the ground level was from a point along the Emmitsburg road from the Klingle house south to the Peach Orchard; however, Union skirmishers prevented them from getting that far forward. This study was limited to ground-level reconnaissance on the battlefield and did not address observation of Union positions east of Emmitsburg Road in the vicinity of the Peach Orchard from elevated locations off the battlefield such as the cupola of the Lutheran Seminary building and vantage points along Herr's Ridge. As noted previously, no observation posts are known to have been established in these elevated locations. The combination of these limitations certainly handicapped Lee and the units of his army that fought on July 2.[66]

After the fighting on the battle's second day, Lee realized that his options were limited and the following day might be his last opportunity to achieve his objectives. The partial success of Wright's brigade of Anderson's division that penetrated Union defenses toward the right center of the Union line along Cemetery Ridge during Longstreet's assault provided a glimmer of hope for Lee. Even though Wright eventually had to withdraw for lack of support, Lee saw it as a partial success. As far as he was concerned, "The general plan of attack was unchanged." Although this plan was to dislodge Union forces from

65 Anderson's post-action report, August 7, 1863, *OR* 27, pt. 2, 614; Wilcox's post-action report, July 17, 1863, 617.

66 Frederick Tilberg and J. Walter Coleman, "Reconnaissance of the Confederate Right, July 2, 1863," in Freeman, *Lee's Lieutenants*, 3:755-56.

Cemetery Ridge, the success these forces had in resisting Longstreet and the heavy losses they inflicted during his assault portended things to come.[67]

Porter Alexander would later look back on these events and observe: "Thus ended the second day, and one is tempted to say that thus ended the battle of Gettysburg." Alexander acknowledged the signal station on Little Round Top for its role in disrupting Longstreet's assault on July 2 when he half-jokingly referred to this event in a letter to Lt. J. Willard Brown of the Union signal corps when he said, "I have forgiven all my enemies now, and . . . you fellows there [on Little Round Top] were about the last that I did forgive."[68]

---

67 Lee's post-action reports, July 31, 1863, and January 1864, OR 27, pt. 2, 308, 320.

68 Ibid., 308, 319-20; Alexander, *Military Memoirs*, 412; Brown, *The Signal Corps*, 368.

Chapter Fourteen

Lee's Flawed Assumptions: July 3

The result of operations [on July 2] induced the belief that, with proper concert of action . . . we should ultimately succeed, and it was accordingly determined to continue the attack.

Gen. Robert E. Lee[1]

. . . the point selected and the method of the attack would certainly have been chosen for us by the enemy had they had the choice.

Edward Porter Alexander[2]

Lee's Strategy of Deception

If an army could be organized . . . and pushed forward to Culpeper Court-House, threatening Washington from that direction, it would not only effect a diversion most favorable for this army, but would, I think, relieve us of any apprehension of an attack upon Richmond during our absence.

Gen. Robert E. Lee[3]

[D]ispatches [from President Davis and Adjutant General Cooper to General Lee] have been intercepted by our scouts.

Maj. Gen. George G. Meade[4]

---

1   Lee's post-action report, January 1864, OR 27, pt. 2, 320.

2   Alexander, *Military Memoirs*, 416-17.

3   Lee to Davis, June 23, 1863, OR 27, pt. 3, 925. Deception and disinformation were important aspects of Lee's intelligence arsenal. He directed his subordinates to mislead the enemy through faulty information given out to the public that would make its way to the other side. The Confederate army employed deception as a standard practice, an example being Stonewall Jackson's troops waving an American flag during the battle of Chancellorsville to entice a Union cavalry officer into their lines. Hard, *8th Illinois Cavalry*, 235.

4   Meade to Halleck, July 3, 1863, OR 27, pt. 1, 75.

Apart of Lee's strategy was to siphon troops from the enemy by deception, and he proposed a plan to President Davis and Adjutant General Samuel Cooper while marching toward Pennsylvania. He wanted the president to shift troops from southern Virginia and the Carolinas to the Culpeper Court House area to pose a threat to Washington. Lee believed the Northern authorities, reacting true to form, would detach troops from the Army of the Potomac to defend the capital. He was confident this maneuver would succeed, having orchestrated a similar ruse a year earlier that helped defeat McClellan's Peninsula campaign. Lee, uncharacteristically insistent, brought up the matter with Davis three times.[5]

Longstreet later recollected that Lee's "plan of campaign" included an effort to deceive the enemy:

> General Beauregard was to be called from his post, in the South, with such brigades as could be pulled away temporarily from their Southern service, and thrown forward . . . along the Orange and Alexandria Railroad in threatening attitude towards Washington City.[6]

Longstreet described Lee's circumspect manner of negotiating with Davis: "[Lee's] experience with Richmond authorities taught him to deal cautiously with them in disclosing his views . . . he did not mention the part left open for Beauregard until he had their approval of the march."[7]

However, in a gloomy synopsis of the state of affairs, Davis told Lee that he was unable to approve his plan, because not enough troops were available. Lee's failure to take the president into his confidence factored into Davis' rejection. Davis was "embarrassed," Cooper explained, to learn of the "plan of assembling an army at Culpeper Court-House," because he had heard nothing about it.[8]

---

5   Lee to Davis, Lee to Cooper, June 23, 1863, ibid., pt. 3, 924-26; Lee to Davis, June 25, 1863, 930-33; Sears, *The Peninsula Campaign*, 157-58. Cooper, the highest-ranking general in the Confederate army, was a Northerner by birth and 1815 West Point graduate who married a Virginia woman and settled in the Old Dominion. In 1861, he resigned his commission as Adjutant General of the United States Army and cast his lot with the South. Warner, *Generals in Gray*, 62-63.

6   Longstreet, *From Manassas to Appomattox*, 335-37.

7   Ibid., 336-37.

8   Butterfield to Halleck, July 3, 1863, *OR* 27, pt. 1, 75-76; See the Appendix for Lee's letters to Davis, and Davis' and Cooper's responses to Lee.

Adjutant General Samuel Cooper warned
Lee to protect his lines of communications
as he moved north.
Miller's Photographic History

In seeking Davis' approval of his plan, Lee had contended he lacked enough troops to safeguard his lines of communication—so he had to abandon them. Cooper advised Lee "to spare a portion of your force to protect your line of communication against attempted raids by the enemy," warning him about Yankee cavalry roaming the countryside destroying railroads and inflicting other damage designed to break Lee's commun- ications with Richmond. Cooper emphasized the paucity of forces on hand to combat these raids. And of course none could be spared to support Lee's plan "because we must look chiefly to the protection of the capital." Lee would be abandoning protection of the line along which dispatches and supplies would travel—as well as his line of retreat, the adjutant general warned, and as Cooper feared, Lee's decision would bring serious consequences.[9]

Lee's first letter to Davis on this subject dated June 23, sent from a location near Williamsport, Maryland, arrived in Richmond on the evening of June 28. Davis' response that same night along with Cooper's accompanying letter the following day took only three days to reach Pennsylvania. Lee never received either reply, however, since, according to the *Philadelphia Press*, Capt. Ulric Dahlgren, Captain Cline of the 3rd Indiana Cavalry, and a small party of Union horsemen and scouts operating behind Confederate lines captured the courier carrying these letters—"Lee's private orderly and his entire escort,"—at Greencastle on July 2. "Captain" Cline was actually the BMI's Sgt. Milton Cline who accompanied Dahlgren on this mission. Dahlgren received valuable assistance from Thomas Pawling and a band of Greencastle citizens who

---

9 Ibid.; Longacre, *The Cavalry at Gettysburg*, 208-10.

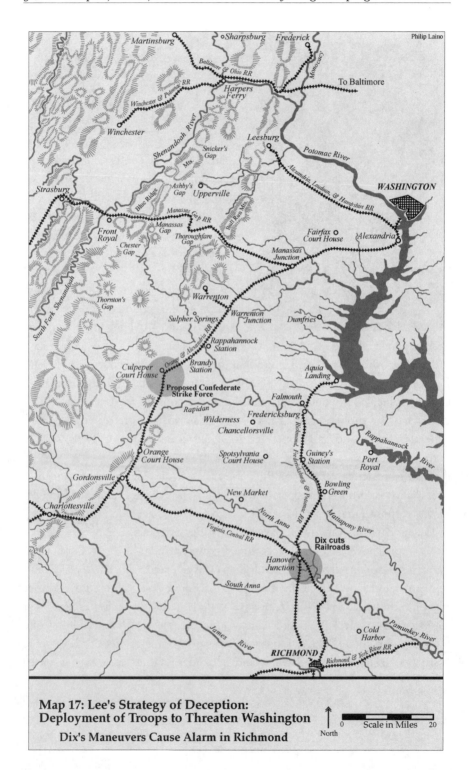

**Map 17: Lee's Strategy of Deception:
Deployment of Troops to Threaten Washington**

Dix's Maneuvers Cause Alarm in Richmond

Imboden's wagon train traveled through the "diamond" or square in Greencastle on July 5. This is also the location where on July 2 Capt. Ulric Dahlgren captured a message from President Davis informing Lee that no reinforcements were available to his army.

Photo by the author

guided the party by generally unknown routes through mountain passes and forests.[10]

Dahlgren immediately sent Davis' and Cooper's responses to Lee to Gettysburg, and as Friday, July 3, dawned, they were in Meade's possession. The Rebel dispatches had fallen victim to Lee's unprotected communications lines as Cooper had warned. Moreover, as Colonel Alexander of Longstreet's corps lamented, "the immense blunder was made of sending that letter by a courier & not putting it in cipher." Given this timely information that Lee would not be supported or reinforced, Meade had reason to be reassured about

10 Philadelphia *Press*, July 10, 1863; W. P. Conrad and Ted Alexander, *When War Passed This Way* (Shippensburg, PA, 1982), 173-75; Longacre, *The Cavalry at Gettysburg*, 208. Thomas Pawling of Greencastle organized a band of local citizens who operated as guerrillas against Rebel forces as they moved through the area. The *Press* account leaves the impression that reporter J. F. McDevitt interviewed "Captain" Cline, which is unlikely because Cline, an experienced BMI operative who frequently worked behind enemy lines, would know to remain out of the limelight. More likely, someone briefed the reporter without Cline's knowledge. Wittenberg, *One Continuous Fight*, 16-17, 386.

Edward M. Stanton
Library of Congress

the tactical situation at Gettysburg. He had the advantage of being aware of the Confederate government's response to Lee's plan, while Lee awaited a reply.[11]

With no word from the president, Lee could only guess whether the Federal government had withdrawn or withheld troops from Meade's army to protect Washington. In the meantime, Lee tried to spread the rumor that Confederate forces were massing to attack Washington. It did get some traction: Brig. Gen. Lorenzo Thomas, Couch's adjutant in Harrisburg, alerted Stanton and Meade that a civilian who had been in Chambersburg while Lee's forces were there had reported: "a belief in the rebel army that [Gen. P. G. T.] Beauregard, with 40,000 men, is in the vicinity of Manassas." Stanton recognized the deception and dismissed it out of hand: "The story about Beauregard coming, no doubt, has been told by Lee to keep up the spirits of his men. Davis' [captured] dispatch is the best view we have ever had of the rebels' condition. . . . Lee must fight his way through alone, if he can."[12]

In a propitious move while Lee's army was on the march and before he floated his proposal in Richmond to threaten Washington, Halleck pursued a

11 Fishel, *The Secret War*, 531; Sears, *Gettysburg*, 354; Longacre, T*he Cavalry at Gettysburg*, 208; Gallagher, *Alexander's Recollections*, 247. Davis and Cooper's letters to Lee are in BMI files at the National Archives RG 393. Dahlgren reportedly had targeted the courier based on information acquired by the BMI's Sgt. Milton Cline while mixing in disguise with Stuart's cavalry while it was leaving Salem, Virginia, to ride through the Union army. Longacre, *The Cavalry at Gettysburg*, 208. While Cline may have learned about the courier route and perhaps the courier schedule between Richmond and Lee's headquarters, he could not have known about these specific letters. There is no possibility that Stuart or his forces could have known about these letters at the time.

12 Thomas to Stanton, Stanton to Thomas, July 4, 1863, OR 27, pt. 3, 525-26.

similar objective. He ordered Maj. Gen. John A. Dix, Department of Virginia commander at Fort Monroe, to concentrate all available forces to threaten Richmond. Dix's subsequent demonstration near Richmond gave Davis pause, hence his negative reply to Lee.[13]

The BMI's Timely Intelligence

> A further examination shows that Ewell's whole corps was on our right yesterday.
> Col. George H. Sharpe[14]

Lee's tactical plan for July 3, substantially unchanged from the previous day, was to remain on the offensive. Since Lee had no dedicated intelligence staff to support his operations and Stuart had just arrived the previous day, it is uncertain what Lee actually knew about the strength, disposition, and intentions of the opposing forces. Thousands of prisoners captured the previous two days were a potential source of information, yet no evidence suggests extensive interrogation of these prisoners.[15]

The previous night, Lee ordered Ewell and Longstreet to be prepared early in the morning to launch a coordinated attack against the right flank and the left center of the Union line respectively. Ewell designated Johnson's division to open the fighting on Culp's Hill supported by other units. Johnson lost the initiative, however, when the enemy attacked first.[16]

Fortuitously, Meade had decided to assault the enemy left flank to recapture positions lost on Culp's Hill the previous day. At 3:30 a.m., elements of Slocum's XII Corps attacked with artillery and infantry before Johnson had gotten underway. Moreover, at 6:00 a.m. Pleasonton told Gregg that Meade wanted him to occupy a ridge near the Baltimore Pike to protect the army's right

---

13 Halleck to Dix, June 14, 1863, OR 27, pt. 3, 111; Dix to Halleck, June 29, 1863, 412; Davis to Lee, June 28, 1863, pt. 1, 77.

14 Sharpe to Butterfield, July 2, 1863, RG 393, NA.

15 Lee's post-action report, January 1863, OR 27, pt. 2, 320, 322; Stuart's post-action report, August 20, 1863, 697; Longstreet to Louis T. Wigfall, August 2, 1863, cited in Sears, *Gettysburg*, 501. Lee lacked an interrogation capability partly because his provost guard, the 1st Battalion Virginia Infantry, had been left behind to guard the base at Winchester. Driver, *1st Battalion Virginia Infantry*, 36.

16 Lee's post-action report, January 1863, ibid., 320; Ewell's post-action report, n.d., 1863, 447.

rear from attack. "This point is so important that it must be held at all hazards," he emphasized. Just how important would soon be apparent.[17]

At 7:00 a.m., Butterfield asked Sharpe whether he was "satisfied that there are only two divisions of Ewell in front of Slocum, & how strong do you think they are." If Meade "was pretty sure of this he would make an attack there." Since an attack to regain lost positions on Culp's Hill was already underway, this implied that Meade wanted to expand it into a full-scale assault.[18]

The BMI had already reported on July 2 that prisoners had been captured from all three of Ewell's divisions, and that "Ewell's whole corps was on our right yesterday." Responding to Butterfield, the BMI reiterated, "We have prisoners from all three Divisions of Ewell's Corps. There is little doubt of their all being here on their left." The report, derived from prisoner interrogations over the past two days and written by BMI order of battle analyst Babcock, listed the names of Ewell's division and brigade commanders, and estimated strength of each brigade as contained in the list on the following page.

The BMI's order of battle statistics compares reasonably well with Busey and Martin's *Regimental Strengths and Losses at Gettysburg*, a reliable source that lists 6,755 for Johnson's division, 5,743 for Early, and 8,474 for Rodes. Despite the absence of Daniel's brigade and the differences in the size of each division, the BMI's total estimate of 21,200 is remarkably close to Busey and Martin's total of 21,806 for Ewell's corps not counting casualties. The report provided Meade a realistic sense of the enemy force on his right. It concluded: "This is an over estimate." Very likely Ewell's 3,800 casualties on July 1 were not factored in, because the prisoners would have had no way of knowing about them. Despite accurate intelligence, Meade cautiously continued to perceive Lee's army to be much stronger.[19]

Although the BMI had confirmed that all three divisions of Ewell's corps were on the field and had estimated their strength, it did not specify which of Ewell's divisions were at Slocum's front. Nonetheless, the battle on Culp's Hill

---

17 Meade's post-action report, ibid., pt. 1, 117; Slocum's post-action report, August 23, 1863, 761; Geary's post-action report, July 29, 1863, 828; Ewell's post-action report, n.d., 1863, pt. 2, 447, Pleasonton to Gregg, July 3, 1863, pt. 3, 502.

18 Butterfield to Sharpe, July 3, 1863, RG 393, NA.

19 Sharpe to Butterfield, [July 3], 1863, RG 393, NA. Daniel's brigade was not listed with Rodes' division; evidently none of the prisoners were from that unit. Daniel's brigade of over 2,100 joined Lee's army just before the campaign, so it would not have been carried on the BMI's previous order of battle.

Johnston's [Johnson's] Division

Colston [Steuart]	2,000
Nichol[l]s [Williams]	1,800
Jones	1,200
Walker	2,000
[Johnston's Division Total]	7,000

Early's Division

Hayes [Hays]	1,600
Hoake [Hoke]	1,800
Smith	1,600
Gordon	2,000
[Early's Division Total]	7,000

Rodes' Division

Ramseur	2,000
Iverson	2,000
Doles	1,200
O'Neil [O'Neal]	2,000
[Rodes' Division Total]	7,200

[Ewell's Corps Total]   21,200[22]

raged on for several hours, and Meade sent in reinforcements. When it concluded late in the morning, Ewell's forces had been defeated and the Union had reoccupied positions lost the previous day. The Rebels suffered heavy casualties, including over 500 taken prisoner. The BMI would of course interrogate these men to gain additional information for Meade's use.[20]

With his right flank secured, Meade turned his attention back toward the center. Brigadier General John Gibbon, who commanded the Second Division, II Corps, later recalled that Meade, after he met with his corps commanders at army headquarters on the night of July 2, commented to him that, if Lee continued on the offensive the next day, he would strike the Union center. While this may have been true at the time, it is instructive to note that Meade later had a different recollection: "The strong attack of the enemy on my left

---

20 Ibid.; Post-action reports: Meade's, August 4, 1863, *OR* 27, pt. 1, 117; Slocum's, August 23, 1863, 761; Geary's, July 29, 1863, 828-33; Ewell's, n.d., 1863, pt. 2, 447-48; Johnson's, September 30, 1863, 504-05.

flank [on July 2] . . . induced the supposition that [on July 3] a movement, upon their part, to my left and rear might be made." This was a reflection of Meade's fear that his left flank was vulnerable, a situation that would not go unnoticed by Longstreet in his planning that morning.[21]

In addition to operational concerns, Meade had to deal with a vexing bureaucratic issue. He learned that enciphered communications from Halleck in Washington were unintelligible because the civilian telegraph operator, A. H. Caldwell, had gone to Westminster without notification. Since only civilian operators were authorized to hold the cipher key, Meade instructed Seth Williams to notify Caldwell that his immediate presence was required at Gettysburg. Butterfield contacted Maj. Thomas T. Eckert in Washington inquiring who controlled the telegraph operators. Although no reply is on record, Meade would have learned that the owners of civilian telegraph companies now directing the Military Telegraph Service had received Stanton's approval to maintain control of the telegraph rather than commanders in the field. Anyway, with cipher communication between Meade and Halleck reestablished, it appeared that Caldwell was back on the job.[22]

Reading the Tea Leaves Differently

> Generals Lee and Longstreet's staff . . . were reconnoitering and making preparations for renewing the attack.
>
> Lt. Col. Arthur Fremantle[23]

As the struggle on Culp's Hill raged in the early morning, Lee anticipated that Ewell and Longstreet would coordinate on a strike against Union defenses. Longstreet, however, had something else in mind. After sending out "scouting parties . . . in search of a way by which we might strike the enemy's left, and push

---

21 Slocum's post-action report, August 23, 1863, OR 27, pt. 1, 761; Meade's post-action report, August 4, 1863, 117; Gibbon, "The Council of War," in B&L, 3:314. Meade's quote from Hyde, *The Union Generals Speak*, 127. For details of the July 3 fighting on Culp's Hill, see Phanz, *Culp's Hill and Cemetery Hill*, 284-352; Coddington, *The Gettysburg Campaign*, 465-92; Sears, *Gettysburg*, 360-71.

22 Meade to Halleck, July 3, 1863, OR 27, pt. 1, 74; Williams to Caldwell, July 3, 1863, pt. 3, 1088; Butterfield to Eckert, July 3, 1863, pt. 1, 78. For Civil War military telegraph operations, see Plum, *The Military Telegraph*; Greely, "The Military-Telegraph Service," *The Photographic History of the Civil War*, 4:342-68.

23 Lord, *The Fremantle Diary*, 209-10.

it down towards the center," he planned to send troops around the rear of the enemy in the vicinity of the Round Tops. Concerned about the delay, Lee rode south and learned what Longstreet had in mind. He ordered him to follow his instructions to attack the Union left center. Apparently Longstreet and Lee were not on the same page about the action plan for the day. Despite evidence to the contrary, Longstreet later claimed he had not received orders from Lee for an early morning attack in coordination with Ewell's corps.[24]

Longstreet resisted Lee's approach. "I have had my scouts out all night," he said, "and I find that you still have an excellent opportunity to move around to the right of Meade's army, and maneuvre him into attacking us." As we have seen, Meade considered this move to be "sound military sense" and feared that Lee would make it. But Longstreet pleaded to no avail. To continue the previous day's attack would be suicidal, but Lee would not be moved. He was adamant. According to Longstreet, the commander pointed his fist at Cemetery Hill and declared: "The enemy is there, and I am going to strike him."[25]

Lee's mind was closed on this issue because he had already considered the options. As he had done the previous day, that morning he sent members of his staff to reconnoiter Union positions on the right from the ground won by Longstreet's assault the previous day. Lee also personally made a "careful examination . . . of the ground," which convinced him that the original plan of attack should go forward.[26]

After Lee completed his reconnaissance, he adjusted his plan to focus the attack upon where Cemetery Ridge slopes to the west forming a depression. This looked like a weak point offering "a reasonable prospect of success." After "forcing the Federal lines at that point," the attack was to turn toward Cemetery Hill. Lee ordered an extensive artillery bombardment before the offensive was launched.[27]

---

24 Longstreet's post-action report, July 27, 1863, OR 27, pt. 2, 359; Longstreet, *From Manassas to Appomattox*, 385-86; Gallagher, *Fighting for the Confederacy*, 244.

25 Longstreet, "Lee in Pennsylvania," *The Annals of the Civil War*, 429; Meade, *Life and Letters*, 2, 105. Lee's statement echoed his response to Longstreet in the late afternoon of July 1 when Longstreet questioned the wisdom of attacking the enemy rather than fighting on the defensive. Longstreet quoted Lee, "If the enemy is there to-morrow, we must attack him." Longstreet, "Lee in Pennsylvania," 421.

26 Lee's post-action report, January 1864, OR 27, pt. 2, 320; Lord, *The Fremantle Diary*, 210.

27 Long, *Memoirs of Lee*, 287.

Lee directed Stuart, who was positioned on Ewell's left flank along the York and Heidlersburg Roads after arriving the previous afternoon, to move his four cavalry brigades, about 5-6,000 troopers (with Jenkins' brigade under command of Lt. Col. Vincent Witcher), "forward to a position . . . where a commanding ridge completely controlled a wide plain of cultivated fields stretching toward Hanover, on the left, and reaching to the base of the mountain spurs, among which the enemy held position." This was Cress Ridge about two to three miles beyond Gettysburg out the York Road. Lee, in effect, had ordered Stuart to conduct a reconnaissance-in-force to discover a vulnerable point in the Union rear, and to be prepared to cooperate with the planned attack against Cemetery Ridge and Cemetery Hill.[28]

Stuart moved his command "secretly through the woods" to "effect a surprise" on the enemy. Lee instructed him to be in "such a position as not only to render Ewell's left entirely secure . . . but [one that] commanded a view of the routes leading to the enemy's rear." Stuart explained, "Had the enemy's main body been dislodged . . . I was in precisely the right position to discover it and improve the opportunity." In other words, Stuart was to be prepared to attack if the assault on the Union center succeeded and the enemy tried to retreat down the Baltimore Pike.[29]

After reaching Crest Ridge, Stuart lamented that the element of surprise was lost when, around noon, units of his cavalry "debouched into the open ground, disclosing their presence, and causing a corresponding reaction by a large force of the enemy's cavalry." Stuart was unaware that XI Corps commander Howard on Cemetery Hill had observed his movements out the York Road and alerted Gregg, whom Pleasonton had posted out on Hanover Road, to "large columns of the enemy's cavalry" moving to the right.[30]

---

28 Lee's post-action report, January 1864, *OR* 27, pt. 2, 308, 322; Stuart's post-action report, August 20, 1863, 697; Eric J. Wittenberg, *Protecting the Flank: The Battles for Brinkerhoff's Ridge and East Cavalry Field, Battle of Gettysburg, July 2-3, 1863* (Celina, OH, 2002), 36-46, 55-56; Longacre, *The Cavalry at Gettysburg*, 220; Busey and Martin, *Strengths and Losses*, 244-45. Colonel Milton Ferguson had taken command of Jenkins' brigade after Jenkins was wounded on July 2. However, Ferguson and a detachment of Jenkins' cavalry were on prisoner guard duty on July 3, so Witcher was in command of the remaining brigade forces that accompanied Stuart.

29   Stuart's post-action report, August 20, 1863, *OR* 27, pt. 2, 697, 699.

30 Gregg's post-action report, July 25, 1863, ibid., pt. 1, 956-57; Lee's post-action report, January 1864, pt. 2, 322; Stuart's post-action report, August 20, 1863, 697-98; Wittenberg, *East Cavalry Field*, 163; Marshall D. Krolick, "Forgotten Field: The Cavalry Battle East of Gettysburg on July 3, 1863," *Gettysburg Magazine* (January 1991), Issue 4, 75-88.

Maj. Gen. Oliver O. Howard
Library of Congress

Gregg shortly received an order from Pleasonton to send Custer's brigade, also located nearby, to rejoin Kilpatrick's division then operating on the Union left flank. Fearing serious consequences if he weakened the forces on hand given the impending threat before his eyes, Gregg wisely ignored the order and kept Custer's regiments with him. Gregg's and Custer's combined force of some 3,400 troopers clashed with Stuart's cavalry during the day, and prevented the Rebels from gaining the army's rear. Howard's timely warning to Gregg played a key role in this outcome.[31]

Confirmation that Lee would renew the attack in the vicinity of the Union center arrived early in the morning from Howard on the right and Warren on the left who both reported Confederate troop movements. This information convinced Meade that the Rebels would "make the attempt to pierce our center." So at 8:00 a.m., Meade strengthened his defenses in the center of the line by ordering VI Corps commander John Sedgwick to deploy whatever troops he had available "in a central position," to support the units in that area.[32]

During the day, BMI's Sharpe received a note from Lt. John V. Bouvier, aide to PMG Patrick: "Genl Butterfield says he wants you to send what information you have gathered from the latest prisoners. They wish to know something in order to operate." Though unsophisticated to say the least—a

---

31 Gregg's & Stuart's post-action reports, 698-99, see note above; Wittenberg, *East Cavalry Field*, 163.

32 Butterfield to Sedgwick, July 3, 1863, OR 51, pt. 1, 1068. Sedgwick sent at least four brigades—Torbert's, Russell's, Eustis', and Shaler's. Sedgwick's post-action report, August 8, 1863, OR 27, pt. 1, 663; Richard Rollins, "George Gordon Meade and the Defense of Cemetery Ridge," *Gettysburg Magazine* (July 1998), Issue 19, 82.

specific list of the army commander's information needs would have been helpful—the request obviously indicated a growing acceptance in the army's top leadership of BMI's intelligence products.[33]

Although there is no record of the BMI reply, the "latest prisoners" would have been the 500 or so captured during the morning combat on the Union right flank against Ewell's corps. Certain Rebel soldiers, for a variety of reasons, were antagonistic to the Confederacy and inclined to cooperate with interrogators, so it is not unlikely that the BMI questioners learned about the planned coordinated attack against the Union right and left center. Since Ewell's movement on the right had already materialized, this would have been another indication an attack on the Union center, however delayed, was in the offing.[34]

The BMI had reported on July 2 that all of Lee's forces had seen action the first two days except Pickett's division. Its order of battle for Picket listed four brigades with five regiments in each brigade, the names of unit commanders, and estimated strength of each regiment. Only three of Pickett's five brigades—Armistead's, Kemper's, and Garnett's—were actually at Gettysburg, so the inclusion of Brig. Gen. Montgomery Corse's brigade was erroneous, and probably derived from Davis' and Cooper's captured letters informing Lee Corse's brigade was en route to rejoin the army. However, since it had not yet arrived,

Brig. Gen. George A. Custer
Library of Congress

33 Bouvier to Sharpe, July 3, 1863, RG 393, NA.

34 Sharpe to Martindale, December 12, 1863, RG 393, NA; Ella Lonn, *Desertion During the Civil War* (Lincoln, NE, 1998), 102-05.

Meade would have understood Pickett's force to be around 7,000 instead of 5,200.[35]

In mid-afternoon, an estimated 12,500 troops under Longstreet's overall command charged the Union lines with Pickett, Pettigrew, and Maj. Gen. Isaac R. Trimble leading the way. The attackers, their approach blanketed by artillery and small arms fire, faced a daunting task, and sustained casualties of more than 50 percent—making the earlier battles on the right pale in comparison. The assault known as Pickett's Charge crested on Cemetery Ridge before melting away in a firestorm, signaling the end of major combat at Gettysburg. The disaster that unfolded poses the question whether Lee should have deferred to Longstreet's plan to move around the Union left flank. Longstreet later wrote that several months after Gettysburg, Lee sent him an apologetic letter, "If I only had taken your counsel even on the 3d, and had moved around the Federal left, how different all might have been."[36]

Alexander, Longstreet's artillery officer, also critiqued Lee's generalship on this day. The "point selected for Pickett's attack was very badly chosen," he maintained. "Lee's most promising attack from first to last was upon Cemetery Hill by concentrated artillery fire from the north and assaults from the nearest sheltered ground between the west and northeast." Although his objective Cemetery Hill was the same as Lee's, Alexander differed on the approach to the target. Lee and his commanders did not recognize this because the army did not have enough "trained staff and reconnoitering officers," and the ground of the attack had not been "carefully examined." The apparent absence of thorough examination of the terrain in preparation for the attack lends credence to Alexander's contention. Lee relied on the sketchy evidence of partial success in

35 BMI report, n.d., RG 393, NA; Lee to Davis, June 9, 1863, *OR* 27, pt. 3, 874; Gottfried, *Brigades of Gettysburg*, 463. Pickett's fifth brigade under Brig. Gen. Micah Jenkins was left in Virginia to guard the approaches to Richmond. The BMI estimated a total of 7,020 troops in four brigades of Pickett's division: Armistead 2,000, Kemper 1,950, Garnett 1,270, and Corse 1,800. The BMI and Busey and Martin figures for the three brigades at Gettysburg were remarkably close (5,220 vs. 5,474). Busey and Martin, *Strengths and Losses*, 170. Corse's brigade did not rejoin Lee's army until the latter part of July. Army of Northern Virginia organization chart, July 31, 1863, *OR* 27, pt. 3, 1058.

36 Wayne E. Motts, "Pickett's Charge Revisited: 'A Brave and Resolute Force,'" *North & South* (June 1999), 2:28-34; Longstreet, "Lee's Right Wing at Gettysburg," in *B&L*, 3:349. Two members of Longstreet's staff, Maj. Thomas Goree and Capt. Erasmus Taylor, corroborated Longstreet's statement about Lee's apology. Wert, *General James Longstreet*, 296-97. For details on Pickett's Charge, see Jeffry D. Wert, *Gettysburg: Day Three* (New York, 2001), 94-285; Sears, *Gettysburg*, 354-458; Coddington, *The Gettysburg Campaign*, 465-534.

penetrating the Union positions the previous day. In other words, Lee's plan failed because of poor intelligence resources and insufficient reconnaissance. Equipped with better information and more receptiveness to advice, Lee may well have sought an alternative such as Longstreet suggested to the disastrous frontal assault.[37]

In addition to lack of intelligence, Lee's questionable decision also played a part in the July 3 catastrophe for Confederate arms. Given the majority of the attack force being from Hill's corps, placing Longstreet in command, despite his having little faith in its potential success, created a vacuum when timely support was required. Under the circumstances, Lee should have retained overall command to ensure Longstreet, Hill, as well as Ewell cooperated in maintaining pressure at the point of attack with supplemental forces. Even though Lee was on the scene during the assault, he remained oddly detached from the events around him. When the charge had been repulsed, everything seemed to come clear for him. "Never mind," he consoled his retreating soldiers, "all this has been my fault—it is I that have lost this fight, and you must help me out of it in the best way you can."[38]

Among the numerous Confederate casualties on July 3 were nearly 2,000 prisoners captured during the day's fighting. The BMI's Babcock compiled a list of high-ranking Confederate officers that fell victim in the fighting: Pickett, slightly wounded, and his three brigade commanders, Lewis A. Armistead, Richard B. Garnett, and James L. Kemper, killed. (Actually the latter sustained what should have been a mortal wound, but he later recovered). Four regimental commanders were listed by name as killed, and two others wounded.[39]

In his report of the fighting on July 3, after mentioning the Confederate artillery bombardment and the appearance of the infantry from the woods

37 Alexander, *Military Memoirs*, 417-18; Lee's post-action report, January 1864.

38 Longstreet, *From Manassas to Appomattox*, 385-86, 399-401; Lord, *The Fremantle Diary*, 214-15 (quoted); Earl J. Hess, *Pickett's Charge—The Last Attack at Gettysburg* (Chapel Hill, NC, 2001), 5-9; George R. Stewart, *Pickett's Charge: A microhistory of the final attack at Gettysburg, July 3, 1863* (Boston, MA, 1959), 109.

39 Sharpe to Butterfield, July 3, 1863, RG 393. The BMI reported 1,788 "privates" and 64 officers captured thus far, and that prisoners were "coming in yet." The high-ranking casualty list included Colonels Hodges and Edmonds of Armistead's brigade and Carrington and [Stuart] of Garnett's brigade killed, and Hunton and Gantt of Garnett's brigade "badly wounded." Report, n.d., BMI files, RG 393, NA.

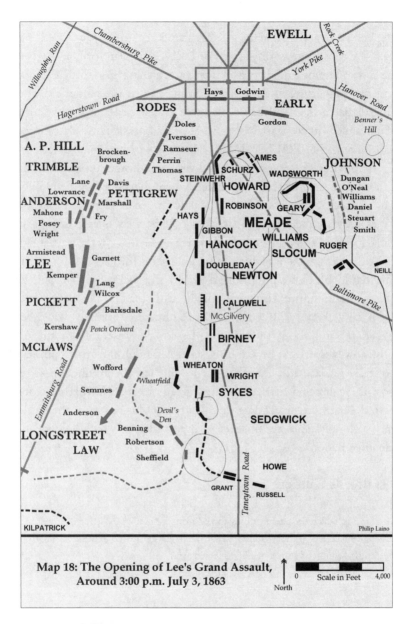

Map 18: The Opening of Lee's Grand Assault, Around 3:00 p.m. July 3, 1863

0   Scale in Feet   4,000

North

Philip Laino

"forming for an assault against our left and center," Meade succinctly described the results of the Pickett-Pettigrew-Trimble Charge. He said the assault was directed primarily against II Corps which repelled the attack with help from troops of I Corps. He did not mention the vital information his intelligence staff provided, a less tangible instrument of success than soldiers, but just as real.[40]

40 *OR* 27, pt. 1, 117.

Stephen W. Sears filled in the intelligence scorecard for July 3 perceptively, "Perhaps the most noteworthy aspect of Lee's battle plan for Day Three . . . is how barren and uninformed it was." It was astonishing "how little General Lee knew of his own army, of the enemy's army, and of the battlefield when he announced that his general battle plan was unchanged and threat the attack would continue." In contrast, "General Meade's knowledge at that moment is striking. From the B.M.I., Meade had trustworthy intelligence on his enemy—about Lee's reserves (Pickett's division) and, since he was known to be part of Longstreet's corps, approximately where Pickett might be employed." Lee, on the other hand, "knew little of Meade's forces, except that they seemed to be massed just where he had attacked." Sears' view is emblematic of Sun Tzu's maxim that "foreknowledge" is the key to victory on the battlefield, and Meade held a substantial information advantage on July 3.[41]

The battle of Gettysburg was over. In the estimation of one Union eyewitness, "This entire army has fought with terrible obstinacy, and has covered itself with glory." Recognition of this bravery for many would be seen in detailed reports about the conflict. Essentially absent from the official citations, however, would be the BMI staff. Although the army commanders had not fully realized it, behind-the-scenes intelligence production at several stages of the campaign had contributed greatly to the Northern victory and Southern defeat. Conversely, Lee would lament in his report of the battle that his army suffered due to the absence of the cavalry on which he depended to provide information.[42]

Success Breeds Caution

A victory, by which the enemy is only forced from the battle-field is for the most part but a half success, as the losses under fire are but small compared to those arising from the demoralization of a broken and dispersed army.

D. H. Mahan[43]

---

41 Sears, *Gettysburg*, 348; Clavell, *The Art of War by Sun Tzu*, 77.

42 Ingalls to Meigs, July 3, 1863, *OR* 27, pt. 3, 502-03; Lee's post-action report, January 1864, pt. 2, 321.

43 Mahan, *Advanced-Guard, Out-post and Detachment Service of Troops*, 210.

Following the victorious defensive stand on July 3, Meade carefully weighed his options while assessing Lee's intentions. Lieutenant Frank A. Haskell of II Corps met Meade as he rode up to front lines to check on the progress of the fighting. When Haskell informed him the enemy had been repulsed, Meade was incredulous but gratified that the assault had been driven back so quickly. He surveyed the field observing both his celebrating soldiers and the surviving enemy troops racing toward Seminary Ridge and safety. His initial reaction was not to go on the offensive, but to prepare for another attack: he ordered his troops to reestablish their defensive positions.[44]

Pleasonton claimed that after the repulse, he rode with Meade up to Little Round Top and urged him to advance the entire army—believing the Rebels demoralized and nearly out of ammunition. Pleasonton thought the enemy could easily be defeated and routed and offered to cooperate in a counterattack by sending his cavalry into the rear of Lee's army. While these recollections smack of more Pleasonton self-aggrandizement, other Union generals concurred. Chief engineer Warren went on record, "I think we should have advanced on the evening of the 3rd of July, after the enemy were repulsed at Gettysburg, with all the force we had on our left." I Corps division commander Wadsworth opined that "the spirit of the troops was unimpaired," and they "were in good condition to have taken the offensive, and they would have taken it with alacrity." He thought that Meade "did not, perhaps, appreciate fully the completeness of his victory." Butterfield favored a countercharge, but found Meade concerned that Lee wanted to induce him to attack a strong position. III Corps division commander Humphries said he had great difficulty keeping his men from advancing without orders.[45]

In an opinion he later tempered, Meade's artillery chief, Hunt, initially thought a counterattack could have been made by troops on the right who had moved out beyond their lines and were ready to join in an attack. He agreed with Pleasonton that the cavalry should have been employed to cut off the enemy's retreat, because "We must risk to win." Meade, too, held similar aggressive sentiments when commenting on his predecessors as commanders of the Army

44 Frank A. Haskell, *The Battle of Gettysburg* (New York, 1992), 229-39.

45 Hyde, *Union Generals Speak*, 111, 139-40, 179, 195, 233, 259.

of the Potomac failing to lead the army with more vigor, but since assuming command himself, he had adopted a more cautious approach[46]

Hancock, who sustained a serious wound on July 3, vociferously lamented a lost opportunity to stage a counterattack, "[O]ur lines should have advanced immediately." Meade had assured Hancock that if the enemy attacked II Corps' position on July 3, he would place the V and VI Corps on their flank. Hancock sent a note to Meade from his ambulance that if he followed through with his promise, "I believed he would win a great victory."[47] Meade, however, delayed taking action until he could learn more about the status of his troops. By the time he received a report, it was "so late in the evening as to induce me to abandon the assault I had contemplated." Instead, Meade ordered Pleasonton to send the cavalry to the rear of Lee's army, not to block their escape or attack them, but to learn if they were really retreating. Meade's conservative approach inevitably relinquished the initiative to an opponent like Lee.[48]

Longstreet's artillerist E. P. Alexander adjudged that Meade made a "colossal mistake" because he:

> did not organize a counter-stroke as soon as he discovered that the Confederate attack had been repulsed. . . . Our ammunition was so low and our diminished forces were, at the moment, so widely dispersed along our unwisely extended line, an advance by a single fresh corps, the 6th, for instance, could have cut us in two.[49]

While Alexander, Pleasonton, and others thought that Meade should have taken immediate action following the repulse of the Confederate attack on July 3, premier historian of the battle Edwin B. Coddington adopted a more conservative view of the situation. He believed it would have been difficult for Meade to organize a cohesive counterattack given the disorganization in many units once the fighting ceased and the dispersal of reserve troops to various positions on the battlefield to fill gaps in the defense. He did point out,

---

46 Ibid., 313-15; Henry L. Hunt, "The Third Day at Gettysburg," in *B&L*, 3:376; Meade, *Life and Letters*, 1:345.

47 Hyde, *Union Generals Speak*, 218.

48 Ibid., 111, 140, 325. Another top general who agreed with Meade on the inexpediency of going on the offensive was the ever-cautious Sedgwick. His VI Corps was only minimally engaged at Gettysburg, and he did not seem well tuned-in to events. He believed the enemy "held a very strong position . . . with equal force to our own."

49 Alexander, *Military Memoirs*, 432.

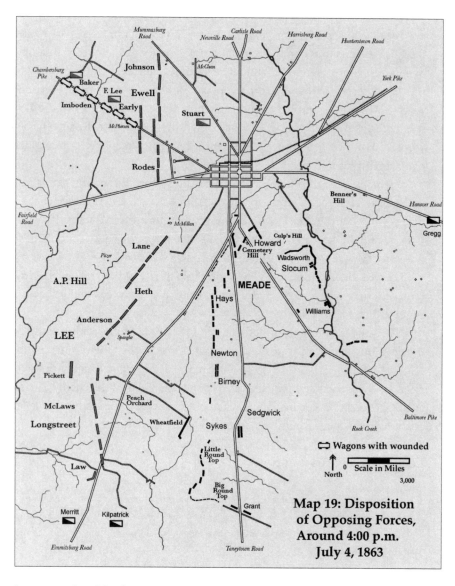

Map 19: Disposition of Opposing Forces, Around 4:00 p.m. July 4, 1863

however, that Meade apparently gave no orders to Sykes and Sedgwick, the commanders of the primary reserve units, V and VI corps, to prepare their troops for a counteroffensive as he had earlier intimated to Hancock he would do.[50]

50 Coddington, *The Gettysburg Campaign*, 532-34; Hyde, *The Union Generals Speak*, 218.

Meade's decision not to stage a counterattack stemmed in part from the fact that since taking command he had not changed his clothes, had a regular night's rest or regular food, and all at all times had been "in a great state of mental anxiety." A Boston Journal reporter on the scene wrote of a "stooping, weary" Meade who moved his headquarters during the night from the Leister farmhouse southeast a short distance down the Taneytown Road. The signal corps established a station at the new location to keep the commander in contact with his army.[51]

The repulse of the enemy assault probably occurred sometime after 3 p.m., with plenty of daylight left to organize a counterattack. Given intelligence from the previous day that Lee had used almost his entire army in the first two days of fighting and the strength of the third day's attack was the equivalent of only two divisions, Meade very well could have concluded that Lee's army was much weaker than he had previously thought. His surprise at how quickly his troops repulsed the assault that had been totally unsupported might have also suggested the same thing.

That night, Meade informed Halleck that Lee might be withdrawing from the field, but when "an armed reconnaissance was pushed forward from the left . . . the enemy [was] found to be in force." Meade rightly highly praised his cavalry, which had been "engaged all day on both flanks of the enemy, harassing and vigorously attacking him with great success, notwithstanding they encountered superior numbers, both of cavalry and infantry."[52]

Lee Relies on Stuart in Retreat

> After the failure of the attack . . . [t]here was danger of the line of communications being cut by the enemy. . . . Under these circumstances General Lee determined upon a retreat, but not such an immediate or hasty one as would present the appearance of flight.
>
> Col. A. L. Long [53]

---

51 Charles Carleton Coffin, *The Boys of '61: Four Years of Fighting* (Boston, MA, 1896), 319-20; Isaac R. Pennypacker, *General Meade* (New York, 1901), 200-01; W. C. Storrick, *Gettysburg* (Harrisburg, PA, 1932), 64; Brown, *The Signal Corps*, 369. This move was necessary since his original headquarters was now serving as a field hospital "filled with the wounded and dying." Meade, *The Life and Letters*, 2:132.

52 Meade to Halleck, July 3, 1863, OR 27, pt. 1, 75.

53 Long, *Memoirs of Robert E. Lee*, 295.

As the three-day battle at Gettysburg closed, Lee was painfully aware that a paucity of information about the disposition, strength, and intentions of Meade's army had been a key element in his army's defeat. The basis for this intelligence and counterintelligence failure, the absence of Stuart and his cavalry during a critical part of the march toward Pennsylvania, and the battle itself had been rectified as Lee prepared to order a withdrawal. Stuart was now prepared to perform his primary mission: to screen the army's withdrawal from observation and attack and provide information about the enemy's movements and intentions. His command had expanded with the arrival of Robertson's and Jones' brigades together with the brigades of Jenkins (Ferguson), Hampton (Col. Laurence Baker), Fitz Lee, and Chambliss, to a total of about 8,700 men. A seventh cavalry brigade, Imboden's, reported directly to Lee.[54]

Lee had little opportunity to mull the disastrous assault on the Union positions that day. His immediate tasks were to encourage his troops and deploy them to meet a counterattack. When Meade chose to remain on the defensive, Lee was able to focus on the arduous task of withdrawing from the battlefield. He reformed his lines west of Gettysburg along Seminary Ridge and Oak Ridge, and had the infantry fortify their positions. Behind this shield, the army would gradually withdraw. Retreating with a large army, thousands of wounded soldiers and prisoners of war, herds of livestock, and wagon trains stretched out over many miles would require careful selection of routes, agile movement, and prudent deployment of his cavalry, as Lee well knew. But he could feel more confident about the retreat, however, because Jeb Stuart and his men were with him to protect his army en route.[55]

54 Lee's post-action report, January 1864, OR 27, pt. 2, 305, 307, 311, 322; Stuart's post-action report, August 20, 1863, 697-99; Busey and Martin, Regimental Strengths and Losses, 244, 315; Longacre, The Cavalry at Gettysburg, 202, 220; Wittenberg and Petruzzi, Plenty of Blame to go Around, 156. Jenkins was wounded on July 2 and Hampton the next day.

55 Lord, The Fremantle Diary, 213-15; McDonald, Make Me a Map of the Valley, 157-58; Lee's post-action report, January 1864, OR 27, pt. 2, 322; Stuart's post-action report, August 20, 1863, 699; Taylor, General Lee, 212; Kent Masterson Brown, Retreat from Gettysburg: Lee, Logistics, and the Pennsylvania Campaign (Chapel Hill, NC, 2005), 67-92.

Chapter Fifteen

Lee Retreats as Meade Deliberates:
July 4 to 5

General Orders No. 74:

Hdqrs. Army of Northern Virginia, July 4, 1863.

The army will vacate its position this evening. . . . The commanding general earnestly exhorts each corps commander to see that every officer exerts the utmost vigilance, steadiness, and boldness during the whole march.

R. E. Lee[1]

I fear that while Meade rests to refresh his men and collect supplies, Lee will be off so far that he cannot intercept him. A good force on the line of the Potomac to prevent Lee from crossing would, I think, insure his destruction."

Brig. Gen. Herman Haupt[2]

July 4: Observers Report Enemy Withdrawal

Hill's corps will commence the movement . . . Longstreet's corps will follow, and . . . Ewell's corps [will] bring up the rear . . . General Stuart [and his] cavalry command will. . . precede and follow the army . . . guarding [its] right and rear . . . [and] left and rear.

R. E. Lee[3]

---

1   OR 27, pt. 2, 311.

2   Haupt to Halleck & Haupt to Stanton, July 4, 1863, ibid., pt. 3, 521-22, 523. Haupt, who was in charge of U.S. military railroads, was working to improve and restore railroads that were supporting the Army of the Potomac. Faust, *Historical Times Illustrated Encyclopedia*, 351.

3   See note 1.

At 6:45 a.m., 1st Lts. J. Calvin Wiggins and Norman Henry Camp at the VI Corps signal station reported evidence to Meade's headquarters that Lee had begun to retire from the field. The message reported enemy wagon trains moving toward Millerstown (Fairfield), on the road leading from Gettysburg to the Fairfield road. In addition, the enemy had a very heavy line of skirmishers, "extending from our extreme left to the brick house [probably the Codori house] on our right."[4]

Meade informed Halleck at 7:00 a.m. that he had deployed pickets to "ascertain the nature and extent of the enemy's movement." He had insufficient information, he said, to determine whether Lee was planning to "retreat or maneuver for other purposes." He was clearly undecided about whether to move with caution or haste. "The general only desires to know where the enemy are," Butterfield told I Corps commander John Newton, "and not by any means to bring on an action [against them]."[5]

With indications that Lee may have been withdrawing from the battlefield, Meade, who had moved his headquarters again to the Baltimore Pike near Rock Creek, wanted to find out whether the Rebels were retreating or had other objectives in mind. Meade deployed his cavalry and BMI scouts to gather specifics on Lee's intentions and to capture or destroy his wagon trains. He also planned to send chief engineer Warren along with Sedgwick's VI Corps to conduct a reconnaissance-in-force. All the signal stations, meanwhile, remained on watch at the battlefield and in town.[6]

While in process of breaking off contact with the Army of the Potomac, Lee sent an interim report to President Davis explaining that the final assault on the enemy at Gettysburg had failed, and "our troops were compelled to relinquish their advantage and retire" from contact with the enemy. Lee would begin withdrawing from the battlefield that night.[7]

---

4   Wiggins & Camp to Norton, July 4, 1863, ibid., pt. 3, 514; Brown, *The Signal Corps, U.S.A.*, 364-65, 896.

5   Meade to Halleck, July 4, 1863, *OR* 27, pt. 1, 78; Butterfield to Newton, July 4, 1863, pt. 3, 513.

6   Meade, Life and Letters, 2:115; Meade to Halleck, July 4, 1863, *OR* 27, pt. 1, 78; Post-action reports: Meade's, October 1, 1863, 117; Pleasonton's, August 31, 1863, 916; Buford's, August 27, 1863, 928; Gregg's, August 22, 1863, 958-59; , Kilpatrick's, August 10, 1863, 993;Williams to Sedgwick, July 4, 1863, pt. 3, 517; Brown, *The Signal Corps*, 739, 896.

7   Lee to Davis, July 4, 1863, *OR* 27, pt. 2, 298, Lee's post action report, July 31, 1863, 309.

The intelligence produced by both sides over the next several days would establish a basis for action by the two commanders. Meade used his resources to determine Confederate movements, while maintaining a position between the Army of Northern Virginia and the capital at Washington. In order to arrive safely back in Virginia without significant damage to his forces, Lee needed to conduct a vigilant, expeditious, and orderly retreat toward the Potomac. The Savannah *Republican* correspondent Peter Wellington Alexander summed up the situation in a dispatch to his paper:

> Today all has been quiet along the lines. Gen. Lee has endeavored to provoke the enemy to make an assault upon his position, by throwing his skirmishers forward; but Gen. Meade, who has displayed much skill and judgement, [sic] is too well aware of the strength of his own position and the madness of attacking Lee.[8]

Lee decided to send his forces toward the Potomac along two routes. He assigned Imboden's cavalry brigade of about 1,300 men to guard the wagon train some 17 miles long that included ambulances carrying thousands of wounded troops, as well as quartermaster, subsistence, and ordnance wagons. Although Lee had mixed emotions about the dependability of this cavalry brigade, fearing at least some of its men "unsteady" and "inefficient," he had little choice but to trust Imboden, and hope for the best. The immense train got underway in late afternoon.[9]

Dangers to this lightly-defended column lurked from both Maj. Gen. Darius Couch's forces to the north as well as from Meade's cavalry. Lee therefore directed Stuart to have two cavalry brigades guard the right flank of the army during the withdrawal. Couch had ordered Brig. Gen. William F. "Baldy" Smith's mixed force of some 4,500 (later increased to about 6,000) infantry, cavalry, and artillery to move south from Carlisle toward Cashtown. His advance reached Mount Holly (then called Papertown), some 24 miles northeast of Cashtown, by the early evening. Although mainly inexperienced

---

8   Styple, *Writing & Fighting the Confederate War*, 165.

9   Lee to Imboden, July 4, 1863, *OR* 27, pt. 3, 966; Lee to Stuart, July 9, 1863, 985 (quoted); Imboden, "The Confederate Retreat from Gettysburg," in *B&L*, 3:420-23. Although Busey and Martin list a strength of 2,359 for Imboden's brigade, Lee stated that it was about 1,300. Busey and Martin, *Regimental Strengths and Losses*, 244; Lee to Jones, June 7, 1863, *OR* 27, pt. 3, 866. Recent scholarship places the number between 1,300-1,400. See French, *Imboden's Brigade in the Gettysburg Campaign*, 10.

militia, these troops nonetheless posed a threat to Lee's lightly guarded wagon trains. The question was whether they would move quickly enough to be of any consequence.[10]

Lee was counting on speed of movement to enhance security of the train. He impressed upon Imboden not to halt along the way for any cause whatever. Using maps prepared by mapmaker Jed Hotchkiss, Lee provided Imboden with detailed guidance. The total distance from Gettysburg to Williamsport, Maryland, along this route was about 50 miles. Once at Williamsport, Imboden was instructed to send scouts out toward Hagerstown, Boonsborough, and other directions as well, to keep a watch for potential danger. Lee urged him to preserve order in his train, and maintain a secrecy of movement and a high state of vigilance. Imboden had to understand just how hazardous this expedition would be, so he was given precise orders about when and where to dispatch scouting parties along his route to the Potomac.[11]

Lee also gave Imboden a message for the commanding officer at Winchester instructing him to inform the regiments from Ewell's corps, which had been left behind to protect that important supply point, to proceed northward to Falling Waters, where they would guard the pontoon bridge there and the ford at Williamsport.[12]

About four miles south of Williamsport, Falling Waters was where Lee had expected that the pontoon bridge his army used to cross the river on the way north remained in place. However, Major General French sent a detachment of Union cavalry from Frederick under Maj. Shadrack Foley of the 14th Pennsylvania Cavalry to destroy this bridge. He also dispatched Maj. H. A. Cole with another cavalry detachment farther south to Harper's Ferry to destroy trestle-work on each side of the railroad bridge as well as the nearby bridge over the Chesapeake and Ohio Canal. (The enemy had floored the railroad bridge and was crossing the river in small detachments.) French apparently ordered these actions on his own initiative, once he heard the cannon fire at Gettysburg on July 3, to hamper Lee's ability to retreat back to Virginia after the battle. This

---

10 Lee, General Orders, No. 74, July 4, 1863, *OR* 27, pt. 2, 311; Williams to Smith, July 4, 1863, 517; Couch to Meade, July 4, 1863, 518; Thomas to Stanton, Couch to Stanton, July 4, 1863, 526-27; Report on Smith's division, July 11, 1863, 642-43.

11 Imboden, "The Confederate Retreat," in *B&L*, 3:424; Lee to Imboden, July 4, 1863, *OR* 27, pt. 3, 966-67; French, *Imboden's Brigade*, 82.

12 Lee to Imboden, July 4, 1863, *OR* 27, pt. 3, 967.

Lower Marsh Creek Church on the Fairfield Road about six miles from Gettysburg.
General Ewell used the church as a hospital for badly wounded men during the retreat.
Those that died were buried along the road.
Photo by the author

was an alert and assertive action on the part of a general with a reputation for being cautious and slow to react.[13]

Lee had another assignment for Imboden. He gave him a sealed package for President Davis, which Imboden was to retain in his possession until he crossed the Potomac. Then Lee instructed him to have a reliable commissioned officer take the package to Richmond "with all possible dispatch" and deliver it personally to the president. He emphasized that it "must not fall into the hands of the enemy." This package likely contained a report to Davis that summarized the campaign from the time the Army of Northern Virginia crossed the Potomac near the end of June until after the repulse of the Pickett-Pettigrew-Trimble charge on July 3. The report probably also listed senior Confederate officers killed, wounded, or missing in battle, hence Lee's desire for special precautions.[14]

13 French's post-action report, ibid., pt. 1, 488-89; French to Halleck, July 4, 1863, pt. 3, 524.

14 Imboden, "The Confederate Retreat," 422; Lee to Davis, July 4, 1863, ibid., pt. 2, 298.

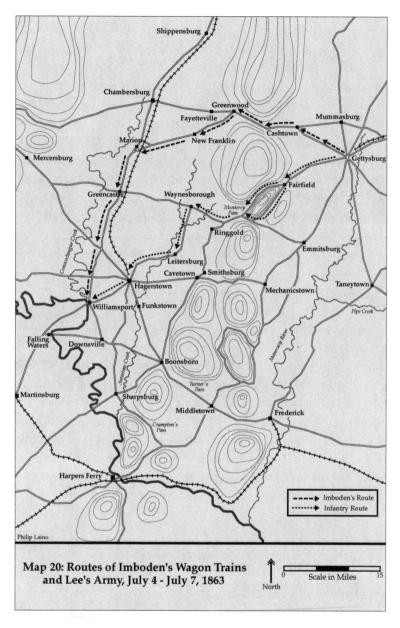

**Map 20: Routes of Imboden's Wagon Trains
and Lee's Army, July 4 - July 7, 1863**

Scale in Miles

North

In the meantime, at 11:00 a.m., Halleck informed Brig. Gen. Benjamin F. Kelley in Clarksburg, West Virginia, that captured dispatches from Jefferson Davis show that the country between Lee's army and Richmond was entirely stripped of troops. Therefore Brig. Gen. E. Scammon's planned expedition aimed at cutting Lee's vital supply line, the Virginia Central Railroad, should move ahead post haste. Moreover, Kelley should concentrate forces at Hancock, Maryland, to be "in a position to attack Lee's flanks, should he be compelled to recross the Potomac."[15]

Lee's second line of march during the retreat involved the army itself. A train that included all the wagons of Ewell's corps plus the reserve wagon train of booty collected throughout the Pennsylvania countryside led the way. Longstreet would stay in the center position and escort thousands of Union prisoners. Hill and Ewell would take turns occupying the vanguard and rear positions. Other wagons not part of the lead train moved in the middle of the column for protection. The army took a more southern and slightly shorter route than Imboden: from Fairfield through Monterey Gap in South Mountain to Waynesboro, Leitersburg, Hagerstown, and on to Williamsport, a distance of about 43 miles. Ewell's experienced and trusted quartermaster, Maj. John A. Harman, was in charge of this enormous wagon train expedition that moved toward Fairfield, followed by in order: Hill's, Longstreet's, and then Ewell's corps.[16]

Lee instructed Stuart to detach not more than two squadrons to lead and follow the army. Fitz Lee and Hampton's brigades were to go to Cashtown that afternoon to hold that town until the rear of the army had passed Fairfield, then move on toward Greencastle to guard the right and rear of the army on its march to Hagerstown and Williamsport. Additionally, Stuart ordered Robertson's and Jones' brigades at Fairfield to "hold the Jack['s] Mountain passes" that led to Monterey Gap. Stuart himself would lead the remaining cavalry, Jenkins' and Chambliss' brigades, that evening to Emmitsburg, Cavetown, and Boonsborough to guard the left and rear of the army.[17]

---

15 Halleck to Kelley, July 4, 1863, *OR* 27, pt. 3, 528. A later message specified Scammon's expedition as being aimed at cutting the Virginia Central Railroad, a vital supply line for Lee's army. On July 22, 1863, T. B. A. David told Col. Anson Stager, Superintendent of the U.S. military telegraph corps, that Scammon's party sent to cut the railroad had been repulsed. *OR* 27, pt. 3, 750.

16 Ibid., pt. 2, 311; Ted Alexander, "Ten Days in July: The Pursuit to the Potomac," *North & South* (August 1999), 2:15. The order of march did not always follow Lee's original plan. On July 6, Lee ordered Longstreet to take the lead while Hill's corps occupied the middle position. Brown, *Retreat from Gettysburg*, 263.

17 Post-action reports: Lee's, July 31, 1863, & January 1864, *OR* 27, pt. 2, 309, 322; Longstreet's, July 27, 1863, 360-61; Ewell's, n.d. 1863, 448; Hill's, November 1863, 608; Stuart's, August 20, 1863, 699. Lee's General Orders, No. 74, July 4, 1863, 311.

It is clear from his instructions to Stuart that Lee expected the greatest threat from Meade to be against the left and rear of his army, since that is where he assigned the bulk of the cavalry. He expected Meade to move south and follow his army on a parallel route southwestward toward the Potomac River. Lee was aware that Meade would be limited in his options, since the defense of Washington had to be factored into his deployment.[18]

Lee planned to vacate his position under the cover of darkness and fortify the South Mountain passes on the strongest ground facing east until his forces safely passed through the gaps to the other side. Lee lightened the army's burden by leaving behind numerous Confederate and captured Union soldiers too badly wounded to survive the arduous trip south. After an attempt to arrange an exchange of prisoners with Meade failed, Lee was still able to divest himself of some 2,000 prisoners who personally agreed to be paroled and sent back to Union lines.[19]

Meade Cautiously Orders Reconnaissance

I shall require some time to get up supplies, ammunition, etc., rest the army, worn out by long marches and three days' hard fighting.

Maj. Gen. George G. Meade[20]

Our army is waiting for supplies to come up before following [Lee's army]—a little of the old lagging infirmity.

Secretary of the Navy Gideon Welles[21]

While Lee was engrossed in planning and implementing a secure withdrawal of his defeated army, several issues demanded the attention of his counterpart Meade. In particular, the Union commander wanted time to look to the rest and provisioning of his own forces and to consider how to follow-up his advantage against the enemy. Having received indications from the VI

---

18 OR 27, pt. 1, 61.

19 Lee's post-action report, July 31, 1863, OR 27, pt. 2, 309, 311; Meade to Halleck, July 4, 1863, pt. 1, 78.

20 Meade to Halleck, see note above.

21 Gideon Welles, *Diary of Gideon Welles: Secretary of the Navy Under Lincoln and Johnson*, 3 vols. (Boston, 1911), 1:357. Diary entry is for July 4, 1863.

Corps signal station that Lee's army might be withdrawing, on the morning of July 4, Meade ordered the V, XI, and XII corps to send units forward to reconnoiter the enemy positions on the battlefield. He assigned chief engineer Warren the task of pinpointing Lee's location and movements. Sedgwick also received orders to have his VI Corps ready at 4:30 a.m. on July 5 to support Warren's reconnaissance.[22]

Meade instructed Pleasonton to send Kilpatrick's Third Cavalry Division to Emmitsburg and rendezvous there with Col. Pennock Huey's brigade of Gregg's division—the combined force about 5,300 men—to pursue Ewell's command, reported to be in the mountains near Monterey. Kilpatrick "was expected to . . . destroy [Ewell's wagon] train, and operate on the enemy's rear and flanks." Notably absent, however, were orders for Kilpatrick to block the mountain passes and prevent Lee's army from passing through them.[23]

Pleasonton directed the Union cavalry to follow the enemy and "gain his rear and line of communication, and harass and annoy him as much as possible in his retreat." These orders, however, lacked specificity, and they were unlikely to inspire a wholehearted effort to impede and damage the Rebel army. Particularly striking about them, especially in view of Meade's concern about the paucity of information, was the absence of instructions to determine and immediately report the movements and intentions of the enemy. Although downplaying reconnaissance in favor of combat had been Pleasonton's pattern since the outset of the campaign, in this case, the orders most likely came directly from Meade through Pleasonton.[24]

These directives caused the cavalry to be widely dispersed rather than concentrated for action. When McIntosh moved with his brigade of Gregg's division to Emmitsburg, he learned from the local population that Stuart had already passed through the town. He captured a courier with a dispatch showing the location of Longstreet's and Ewell's corps in the vicinity of Fairfield, and sent this information to headquarters. He then received orders to join Brig.

22 Wiggins & Camp to Norton, July 4, 1863, *OR* 27, pt. 3, 514; Meade to Halleck, see note 19; Williams to Sedgwick, July 4, 1863, pt. 3, 517.

23 Post-action reports: Pleasonton's, August 31, 1863, *OR* 27, pt. 1, 917; Huey's, August 6, 1863, 970; Kilpatrick's, August 10, 1863, 993; A. Wilson Greene, "From Gettysburg to Falling Waters: Meade's Pursuit of Lee," in Gary W. Gallagher, ed., *The Third Day at Gettysburg & Beyond* (Chapel Hill, NC, 1994), 164; Busey and Martin, *Strengths and Losses*, 104-05.

24 Pleasonton's post-action report, see note above.

Gen. Thomas H. Neill and his VI Corps brigade that Sedgwick would detach after his reconnaissance in the mountains to watch the rear guard of the enemy and send frequent reports to Meade about their activities.[25]

Stuart had dispatched his cavalry on July 4 to screen the army's retreat in accordance with Lee's directive. The poor weather conditions and difficult terrain, as well as Kilpatrick's attack after dark, assisted Stuart. Kilpatrick met with limited success in interrupting Lee's retreat, breaking off contact with Stuart's forces prematurely and leaving the route to Williamsport open for the Army of Northern Virginia.[26]

Not everyone believed that Lee was retreating. Brigadier General Francis C. Barlow, commander First Division, XI Corps, sent word from inside the town of Gettysburg that he believed "the movement of the enemy to be a mere feint." Barlow had been wounded on July 1, captured, and left behind when the Rebels withdrew. Although Barlow provided no evidence for his comments, Meade gave them some credence. "Barlow's opportunities for judging [the situation] are good," he said. Events would soon prove Barlow quite mistaken. His captors may well have fed him misinformation about their intentions, a common practice for the Rebels. In any event, incidents like these reinforced Meade's cautious approach to following Lee's army.[27]

Meade wrote a congratulatory message to his army for their "heroic courage and gallantry" in defeating the enemy at Gettysburg and forcing them to withdraw. Part of his message to the troops, however, would come back to haunt him. Their task was not yet completed, he told his men, and he looked "for greater efforts to drive from our soil every vestige of the presence of the invaders." While this may have seemed like an aggressive stance to Meade, the idea of driving the enemy from "our soil" rather than intercepting and attacking

---

25 Post-action reports: McIntosh's, August 20, 1863, OR 27, pt. 1, 967; Longstreet's, July 27, 1863, pt. 2, 361; Ewell's, n.d. 1863, 448; Meade's, October 1, 1863, pt. 1, 117-18; Neill's, July 17, 1863, 678-80; Peter C. Vermilyea, "Maj. Gen. John Sedgwick and the Pursuit of Lee's Army After Gettysburg," *Gettysburg Magazine* (January 2000), no. 22, 120.

26 Post-action reports: Stuart's, August 20, 1863, OR 27, pt. 2, 11, 700-01; Kilpatrick's, pt. 1, 993-95; McClellan, *The Life and Campaigns of Major-General J. E. B. Stuart*, 349-56; Eric J. Wittenberg, "'This was a night never to be forgotten': The Midnight Fight in the Monterey Pass, July 4-5, 1863," *North & South* (August 1999), 2:44-54; John W. Schildt, *Roads from Gettysburg* (Shippensburg, PA, 1998), 18-19.

27 Meade to Halleck, July 4, 1863, OR 27, pt. 1, 75; Butterfield to Newton, July 4, 1863, pt. 3, 513; Meade, *The Life and Letters*, 2:118. On Barlow's wounding and capture, see Sears, *Gettysburg*, 470.

them would soon draw Lincoln's attention. It also may have reflected the thinking of some of his subordinate commanders. Brigadier General John Geary wrote his wife: "Our prospects to drive out speedily the rebels is very good and I think in another week there will not be a rebel in the state."[28]

Meade's hesitant approach to Lee's army was certainly reflected in a circular that AAG Seth Williams issued from army headquarters. It instructed the corps commanders: "The intention of the major-general commanding is not to make any present move, but to refit and rest for to-day." Furthermore, the "lines as held are not to be changed without orders, the skirmishers being simply advanced, according to instructions given, to find and report the position and lines of the enemy."[29]

Meade had myriad duties, and found little time to rest. He had observed the Rebels as they reformed their lines west of Gettysburg, withdrew their skirmishers, and left their dead and wounded on the field. Based on what he knew about the enemy at this point, Meade might well have concluded that he had a sizable advantage in forces over Lee. Yet, even with reliable reports in hand of Lee's beginning strength of approximately 75,000, Meade still believed Lee's army to be as strong if not stronger than his after three days of ferocious battle with horrendous losses on both sides. It was an opinion he continued to hold despite credible information to the contrary. Instead of responding like a shark with blood in the water and going on the offensive, Meade adopted a cautious approach, remained where he was, rested his army, and assessed its condition. Upon learning that Meade did not intend to pursue Lee immediately, Brig. Gen. Hermann Haupt, in charge of the Military Railway Department, told Halleck, "I fear that while Meade rests to refresh his men and collect supplies, Lee will be off so far that he cannot intercept him."[30]

Late in the day under the mixed blessing of a violent rainstorm, the Confederate army began its retreat. Lee and Longstreet stood conferring in the pouring rain while a roaring bonfire, kept alive with continuous replenishment of fresh wood, lighted the scene. The severity of the weather slowed the withdrawal of the wagon trains and the troops, but also hampered Meade's cavalry in their effort to harass the retreating columns. The success of Lee's

---

28 General Orders, No. 68, July 4, 1863, *OR* 27, pt. 3, 519; William Alan Blair, *A Politician Goes to War: The Civil War Letters of John White Geary* (University Park, PA, 1995), 98.

29 HQ Army of the Potomac Circular, July 4, 1863, *OR* 27, pt. 3, 520.

30 Thomas to Stanton, July 4, 1863, ibid., 525; Haupt to Halleck, July 4, 1863, 523.

strategy, however, depended heavily upon how quickly his opponent organized his army to pursue the Rebel forces.[31]

Uncertainly Prevails in Union Camp

> I make a reconnaissance to-morrow [July 5], to ascertain what the intention of the enemy is.
>
> Maj. Gen. George G. Meade[32]

Around noon on July 4, Couch in Harrisburg reported, mistakenly, to Meade that the Rebels had fortified the passes in South Mountain. As a result, Buford received orders while guarding the army's supply trains at Westminster to move to South Mountain (Turner's) Pass and prevent the enemy from occupying it. Buford and two of his brigades thus moved toward Frederick. Meade followed up with additional orders for Buford to overtake Imboden's wagon train headed in that direction. Meanwhile, Imboden, with only minor damage to his train, had managed to fend off attacks by detachments of Couch's forces and citizens along the route. Colonel J. Irvin Gregg's brigade could have inflicted serious injury on the train, but it pursued tentatively and avoided a full-scale confrontation.[33]

In addition to Huey, who was serving with Kilpatrick, the other brigades of Gregg's division received special assignments. J. Irvin Gregg's brigade operated independently moving to Hunterstown, about seven miles northeast of Gettysburg, to contest the enemy's cavalry pickets. The next day, Gregg swept along Chambersburg Pike as far as Fayetteville, some seven miles from Chambersburg, reportedly capturing some 4-5,000 Rebel stragglers attempting to reach safety. Confirmation soon arrived from Couch that Gregg had indeed captured 4,000 Rebel prisoners near Fayetteville. Lee later acknowledged that 5,000 of his "well men" had straggled away from the army and started out on

---

31 Lee's post-action report, January 1864, OR 27, pt. 2, 322; Ross, *Cities and Camps*, 65; Wittenberg, "'This was a night never to be forgotten,'" 44-54. For an assessment of Meade's initial reaction to reports of the enemy retreating, see Keith Poulter, "Errors That Doomed a Campaign," *North & South* (August 1999), 2:83-88.

32 Meade to Halleck. July 4, 1863, OR 27, pt. 1, 78.

33 Couch to Meade, July 4, 1863, ibid., pt. 3, 515; post-action reports: Pleasonton's, pt. 1, 916; Buford's, 928; Imboden, "The Confederate Retreat," in B&L, 3:425; Longacre, *The Cavalry at Gettysburg*, 250-51.

their own initiative to overtake the wagon train of wounded. Lee correctly feared that most of these men were captured by Union cavalry. Although an unmistakable indicator of disenchantment within Lee's ranks, there is no indication it influenced any of Meade's calculations.[34]

Pleasonton ordered McIntosh's brigade to picket the roads on the extreme left of the Union army and observe the movements of the enemy. While the Union cavalry deployed in search of the enemy, Sharpe ordered his BMI scouts to reconnoiter both the Sharpsburg and Williamsport areas and track the movements of Lee's army. James W. Greenwood, a civilian, went to Sharpsburg and a man named Browning to Williamsport, while Sgt. Milton Cline and four scouts apparently in Confederate uniforms or partisan garb went to mix in with the retreating enemy forces.[35]

The Signal Corps continued to observe Confederates in the area of Seminary Ridge and beyond. In the late afternoon and early evening of July 4, 1st Lt. Peter A. Taylor, the II Corps signal officer, from a station in the Court House steeple in Gettysburg, and 1st Lts. William H. Hill and Isaac S. Lyon, manning the V Corps signal station on Little Round Top, reported continual movement of wagons and cavalry toward the Chambersburg and Fairfield Roads, the two main arteries of Lee's withdrawal.[36]

At 5:15 p.m., Taylor notified Meade that three enemy cavalry regiments and four wagons "passed along our front, 2½ miles out from town, halted on the hills northwest from the [Pennsylvania] college building, and were there joined by two more regiments, a battery of artillery, and two ambulances coming from behind the hills." This "column is now moving toward the Chambersburg Road." Taylor was apparently observing part of Fitz Lee's and Hampton's brigades that Stuart, by Lee's orders, had sent to Cashtown to protect the army's right flank until it safely moved past Fairfield. These brigades were to protect

---

34 Post-action reports: Gregg's, August 22, 1863, OR 27, pt. 1, 958-59; McIntosh's, August 20, 1863, 967; J. Irvin Gregg's, August 17, 1863, 977-78; Avery's, August 13, 1863, 981-82; Couch to Halleck, July 6, 1863, pt. 3, 582; Lee to Davis, July 29, 1863, pt. 3, 1048.

35 Sharpe to Williams, July 9 & 10, 1863, RG 393, NA. Greenwood lived in Martinsburg, West Virginia, and had worked with the BMI's Babcock during the Antietam campaign in 1862 and again during Babcock's BMI assignment in Maryland in June 1863. Fishel, *The Secret War*, 153, 464, 467.

36 Taylor to Meade, Hill & Lyon to Meade, July 4 1863, *OR* 27, pt. 3, 516, Brown, *The Signal Corps, U.S.A.*, 365; Cameron, "The Signal Corps at Gettysburg Part II," 101.

the army's "right and rear" by following it to Williamsport via the road through Greenwood.[37]

"Dense smokes have been seen all day behind the hills in the direction of Cashtown," Taylor concluded. Samuel Pickens of the 5th Alabama explained the smoke in his diary: his regiment "didn't travel more than two or three miles before they were stopped due to the road being blocked by the wagon trains. There, they were drenched by a cold rain, but when it subsided they made fires and made themselves as comfortable as possible under the circumstances." Building fires to ward off the chill and dampness was undoubtedly a common practice throughout the slowly retreating army. Major Eugene Blackford of the 5th Alabama added to the smoky atmosphere when he ignited hay stored inside a house Union skirmishers had been using to fire upon the retreating Rebels.[38]

Two hours later, Taylor sent another message to Meade: "A train of thirty-three wagons just passed from near Herr's tavern [on Chambersburg Road] toward the Fairfield road." Also, "Several smaller trains have been seen during the day in the same direction." The wagons near Herr's Tavern probably were part of Hill's corps that withdrew on the night of the 4th, and the ones seen during the day belonged to one of the other two corps that withdrew earlier. Taylor updated Meade about the cavalry reported previously moving along the Chambersburg Road; they had "halted behind the woods north of the [Lutheran Theological] seminary" with the "head of the column resting on the Tapeworm road"—a reference to the unimproved railroad cut that ran just north of and parallel to the Chambersburg Road that was sometimes used as an alternate route. The cavalry was "still there at this hour; horses grazing," an indication how slowly the retreat was progressing.[39]

At 7:40 p.m., the signal officers on Little Round Top informed Meade, "All quiet in front. Enemy just relieved their outer pickets." These pickets, however, were screening Lee's retreating forces. "[F]or the past twenty-five minutes," the report continued, there was movement out the Fairfield Road, including "a steady stream of heavy wagons, ambulances, cavalry, and what seems to be

37 Taylor to Meade, July 4, 1863, OR 27, pt. 3, 516; Lee's General Order, No. 74, July 4, 1863, pt. 2, 311; Stuart's post-action report, 699.

38 Taylor to Meade, see note above; Noah Andre Trudeau, ed., "5th Alabama Sharpshooters Taking Aim at Cemetery Hill," *America's Civil War* (July 2001), 52.

39 Taylor to Meade, July 4, 1863, OR 27, pt. 3, 516; Hill's post-action report, pt. 2, 608.

artillery, or else flying artillery, and no cavalry." This succinct but detailed message closed with: "They move slowly and to our left."[40]

That evening, Meade called his commanders together to discuss possible courses of action. The majority wanted to keep the army in place until a reconnaissance could determine Lee's movements and intentions. According to Warren, some generals were concerned that premature departure of the army from the battlefield would allow Lee to claim victory, and the prevailing mood was "we had saved the country for the time," so caution was called for so as not to jeopardize that success. As word of the decision to delay pursuit of the Rebel army filtered back to the administration in Washington, perceptive, candid Gideon Welles, the secretary of the navy, discerned the army leadership's mood and feared that "Lee and the Rebels may escape as a consequence" of it. Halleck would be satisfied with just driving Lee's army away, Welles thought, because "That has been his great anxiety, and too many of our officers think it sufficient if the Rebels quit and go off,—that it is unnecessary to capture, disperse and annihilate them." Welles fretted about the president's decision to defer to Halleck in all military matters; he thought Lincoln had better instincts than Halleck, who in his opinion was "incapable of originating or directing military operations."[41]

Meade reiterated his plans in a message to Baldy Smith informing him that he intended to remain at Gettysburg the following day burying the dead, and "determining by a reconnaissance the nature of the movements and intentions of the enemy." Meade had decided to conform to the sentiments of his subordinates not to take the initiative or act aggressively until he learned more about Lee's intentions. Meade thought the enemy was retreating via Fairfield and Cashtown, yet he was not certain of it. Should the enemy be retreating, however, he planned to pursue them "by the way of Emmitsburg and Middletown, on his flank," the route Lee had anticipated Meade would take.

---

40 Hill & Lyon to Meade, ibid., pt. 3, 516. Union pickets in position out in front of the army on the right sent similar reports. XI Corps chief of staff Charles W. Asmussen told his boss Major General Howard that pickets thought they were hearing artillery or wagon trains moving "in a western direction" out the Cashtown (Chambersburg) Road.

41 Meade, *Life and Letters*, 2:116; Cleaves, *Meade of Gettysburg*, 174; Hyde, *The Union Generals Speak*, 128, 153-56, 172; Welles, *Diary of Gideon Welles*, 1:358, 364.

Because his army suffered a substantial number of casualties, Meade informed Smith he "would be glad to have you join" us.[42]

July 5: Meade Hesitates for Lack of "reliable information"

> The most difficult part of my work is acting without correct information on which to predicate action.
>
> Maj. Gen. George G. Meade[43]

> The march was continued during [July 5] without interruption from the enemy, excepting an unimportant demonstration upon our rear in the afternoon when near Fairfield, which was easily checked.
>
> Gen. Robert E. Lee[44]

At 5:30 a.m. on July 5, Butterfield informed Smith again that Meade was holding on at Gettysburg, still uncertain about the enemy's movements and intentions. He was thus relying on reconnaissance and scouts to furnish the information he needed. "Should the enemy be retreating," Butterfield added, "the general will move rapidly through the Valley toward Frederick." As of "last night," Butterfield stated, the enemy stood "with his left near Hunterstown and his right across the Emmitsburg road, forming a semi-circle around Gettysburg." Since Meade was concerned that Smith's untested militia units would be vulnerable against enemy regulars, he warned him away from Cashtown: "your position is precarious in the direction in which you are coming, as you are out of reach of support." Yet, with a quick move from Carlisle to Cashtown, Smith might be able to interfere with Lee's retreat, especially by delaying Imboden's wagon train.[45]

Ten minutes later, signal officer Hall, from his vantage point at the Pennsylvania College, alerted Meade that the enemy had evacuated their position of the previous day. Nothing indicated an enemy anywhere except out on the Chambersburg road, and then only in small force. In addition, enemy

---

42 Williams to Smith, July 4, 1863, *OR* 27, pt. 3, 517.

43 Meade to his wife, July 5, 1863, Meade, *Life and Letters*, 2:125.

44 Lee's post-action report, July 31, 1863, *OR* 27, pt. 2, 309.

45 Butterfield to Smith, July 5, 1863, ibid., pt. 3, 531.

batteries had disappeared from the hills near the seminary, and captured Rebels said "that the enemy have gone to Hagerstown."[46]

Also, early that morning, Butterfield emphasized to Sedgwick the "orders for the reconnaissance" meant to ascertain "the position and movement of the enemy," and that Meade did not intend to engage them in battle at this time. Butterfield instructed Sedgwick not to take his ammunition train with him, and he was to return to Gettysburg once he got the necessary information in order to join in a general pursuit of Lee across the mountains. One has to wonder about the temper of Meade's intent to pursue Lee's army expeditiously and aggressively. Assigning an entire infantry corps to do what a cavalry detachment could accomplish much faster and efficiently certainly raises the question.[47]

Major General Herman Haupt made a point of coming to Gettysburg that morning to exhort Meade to get his forces underway in pursuit of Lee. Meade insisted however, "that a period of rest was necessary." Thoroughly frustrated by this inaction, Haupt took a train to Washington to encourage more weighty authorities—Halleck, Stanton, and Lincoln—to urge Meade onward.[48]

Meade told Halleck that he had 55,000 effective troops, not counting cavalry and requested all available reinforcements be sent to him without delay. This indicated that he was preparing to do battle again, once he felt his forces strong enough to contend with Lee. In his planning, Meade had to consider not only the heavy casualties his army had sustained during the three-day battle, but also the loss of experienced, trusted corps commanders such as Reynolds, killed on the first day of battle, and Hancock, seriously wounded during the Confederate assault on July 3. Of the seven corps commanders, four (Newton, Brig. Gen. Alexander Hays, Sykes, and French) were new to the job, while the remaining three (Sedgwick, Howard, and Slocum) had more experience.[49]

Later in the morning, Capt. Edwin Pierce from the signal station on Little Round Top reported "no signs of the enemy on our left front . . . a heavy body

---

46 Ibid., 532; Brown, *The Signal Corps, U.S.A.*, 369; Cameron, "The Signal Corps at Gettysburg II," 101.

47 *OR 27*, pt. 3, 530-31.

48 Herman Haupt, *Reminiscences of General Herman Haupt* (Milwaukee, WI, 1901), 221, 224, 227.

49 Meade to Halleck, July 5, 1863, *OR 27*, pt. 1, 79. For a discussion of Meade and his generals during Lee's retreat, see Coddington, *The Gettysburg Campaign*, 550-67; Sears, *Gettysburg*, 477-90. Sykes had replaced Meade as V Corps commander when Meade took over command of the army.

of troops . . . is now moving to the left, [from the Chambersburg road] toward the Fairfield road." Signal officers Hill and Lyon on Little Round Top underscored these observations: "At these points not a single object can be seen moving on either line, which leads to the belief that the enemy have left our front." To obscure his army's movements from the probing eyes of the enemy, Lee had ordered his defensive fortifications set on fire. This tactic only partially succeeded, however, because Hill and Lyon reported, that even through the smoke "many of the points which yesterday composed the enemy's front and reserve lines can be distinctly seen."[50]

French's report to Halleck about destruction of Lee's pontoon bridge on the Potomac prompted a response from Lincoln who was gathering his own intelligence about the progress of the Gettysburg battle from incoming messages in the war department telegraph office. Since the president earnestly desired that Lee should not be allowed to escape without further damage, he pressed to know whether the enemy was able to ford the river. The river was too high for Lee's forces to cross at the Williamsport ford, French replied, allaying Lincoln's fears for the time being.[51]

Meade instructed Butterfield to prepare orders to move the army to Middletown, Maryland, and the South Mountain Pass (Turner's Gap) pending the results of Warren's and Sedgwick's findings. At 8:30 a.m., Meade informed Halleck that the "enemy retired, under cover of the night and heavy rain, in the direction of Fairfield and Cashtown." All his available cavalry were pursuing, he continued, staying on the enemy's left and rear. He planned on pursuing with the army on Lee's flank "via Middletown and South Mountain Pass." Butterfield elaborated on these plans, informing Smith that army headquarters would move at 6:30 the next morning with Frederick as its destination. "We move, to turn the enemy, via South Mountain passes." For all intents, it appeared that Meade meant to block the enemy's escape route and engage them. All the intelligence indicated that Lee's army was marching toward Fairfield. The obvious and logical conclusion for the Union army's high

---

50 Hill and Lyon to Sykes, Pierce to Norton, July 5, 1863, OR 27, pt. 3 532; Brown, *Retreat from Gettysburg*, 171, 175, 178.

51 Lincoln to French, July 5, 1863, OR 27, pt. 3 544; French to Halleck, July 5, 1863, 546; Bates, *Lincoln in the Telegraph Office*, 155; Tom Wheeler, *Mr. Lincoln's T-Mails: the Untold Story of how Abraham Lincoln Used the Telegraph to Win the Civil War* (New York, 2006), 120, 126.

command would have been that the enemy was retreating southwest towards Maryland rather than back into Pennsylvania.

In the meantime, without checking with Meade, Butterfield issued movement orders to the corps commanders. It's unclear whether he had misunderstood Meade's intentions; however, upon learning what had occurred, Meade halted the III and V corps in case Sedgwick might need support. After Sedgwick reported later that day that the enemy appeared in force in his front, Meade thought that Lee could be making a stand in the mountains. He halted the other corps until Lee's intentions could be discerned.[52]

Pleasonton sent McIntosh's command to Emmitsburg to check on a report that some of the enemy's cavalry were seen moving towards that place. The report of Rebel troops evidently was of Jeb Stuart leading Jenkins and Chambliss' brigades moving in "column four hours in passing—from 1 to 5 o'clock this morning" to guard the left and rear of Lee's army. If the enemy should attempt to attack the rear of the Union army, Pleasonton told McIntosh to "follow them up to prevent it."[53]

Meanwhile, the BMI's Sharpe learned more about the Confederate retreat from a detailed report from Lt. Col. Charles E. Livingston, the adjutant of Third Division, I Corps. Livingston told Sharpe that he had collected information "from prisoners and others" that day and learned many details about the enemy's activities from an unidentified colonel of his division who had been "wounded and taken prisoner and held near the battle-field of I Corps." The report accurately described Lee's plans to retreat via two routes, sending the wounded one way and the army another. It also discussed the direction they were heading, and the strength, condition and morale of the forces.[54]

In a vivid and detailed description, the colonel related, on July 4, Lee sent a wagon train of wounded, consisting of about 500 wagons, ambulances, hay

52 HQ Army of the Potomac Circular, ibid., pt. 3, 532-33; Hyde, *The Union Generals Speak*, 114; Cleaves, *Meade of Gettysburg*, 175-77; Meade, *Life and Letters*, 2:123; Coddington, *The Gettysburg Campaign*, 495, 558.

53 Post-action reports: McIntosh's, August 20, 1863, OR 27, pt. 1, 967, Stuart's, August 20, 1863, 699; Lee's General Orders, No. 74, July 4, 1863, pt. 2, 311;

54 Livingston to Sharpe, July 5, 1863, ibid., pt. 3, 541-42; Huidekoper's post-action report, n.d. 1863, pt. 1, 346-47; John F. Krumwiede, "A July Afternoon on McPherson's Ridge," *Gettysburg Magazine* (July 1999), Issue 21, 21-44; Gregory A. Coco, *A Vast Sea of Misery* (Gettysburg, PA, 1988), 16. Lieutenant Colonel Henry S. Huidekoper, 150th Pennsylvania, was the likely information provider. He was wounded on July 1, captured, and left in Gettysburg when the Rebels retreated.

wagons, etc., out the Chambersburg Road with "crowds" of walking wounded accompanying the train who told him their destination was Winchester, Virginia. In a reference to Imboden's brigade, he said two cavalry regiments and one full battery, along with many damaged "caissons, limbers, and guns," guarded the wagon train, and no provision train accompanied them—an indication that they intended to move with great speed. And indeed a perceptive observation, given that Lee had instructed Imboden not to allow the train to stop en route to Williamsport for any reason whatsoever. The description and destination of the train and the size of its escort was timely information for Meade in assigning forces to pursue the retreating enemy. A large number of the wagons were marked U.S. property, and were "said to have been captured near Washington by Hampton," undoubtedly the 125 wagons Stuart's horsemen had captured outside of Rockville, Maryland, the week before.

In his report, the colonel added, about 6 a.m. that morning, "two more regiments of cavalry, several squads of cavalry, and one battery, with a large lot of stragglers took the [Chambersburg] road, saying they were going to Millerstown [Fairfield]." These stragglers likely contributed to the large number of prisoners that fell prey to Irvin Gregg's pursuing cavalry. He also reported that Lee's army was "very short of food," but well supplied with ammunition. The Rebels, apparently with soldierly bravado, "seemed to be in no great hurry to get away," he continued, "saying, that if we followed them, they were ready for us, and, if we did not molest them, they would cross [the river] quietly." This report closely reflected how events actually evolved as Lee's army withdrew from the battlefield.[55]

Despite the observation that the Rebels had an ample supply of ammunition, Lee wrote that he could not continue the fight following the Pickett-Pettigrew-Trimble Charge on July 3, because he lacked ammunition. Foreign observers Fremantle and Fitzgerald Ross both noted in their diaries the lack of ammunition, especially for small arms—only enough left for one more day of fighting—made Lee's retreat imperative.[56]

Livingston then related what the released colonel had to say about Lee's forces. The "main body, trains, and artillery [of the Rebel army] marched for

---

55 Livingston to Sharpe, July 5, 1863, *OR* 27, pt. 3, 541-42; Stuart's post-action report, August 20, 1863, pt. 2, 694; Imboden, "The Confederate Retreat from Gettysburg," in *B&L*, 3:424.

56 Lee's post-action report, January 1864, *OR* 27, pt. 2, 322; Lord, *Fremantle's Diary*, 218; Ross, *Cities and Camps*, 78.

[Fairfield]." He estimated the strength of their "left wing and part of their center" at "about 40,000 men" from the best calculation possible at the time. This implied that he had an opportunity to actually observe Ewell's corps on the Confederate left and part of Hill's corps in the center. However, in real terms the figure of 40,000 is practically meaningless, since he related it to forces in only a general sense. Nonetheless, this figure could have been interpreted at Meade's headquarters as showing Lee's army stronger than it actually was, especially if they drew the implication that it represented only half of their forces.

The colonel reported that the enemy is "thought to have taken 5,000 of our prisoners," a figure closely corresponding to the Union army's official casualty report of 5,182 prisoners captured during the battle, and Busey and Martin's calculation of 5,369 Union prisoners captured there. The report closed by noting that "A rebel colonel said their loss in all was probably from 20,000 to 25,000," an accurate estimate in light of recent scholarship's estimate of 23,231.[57]

From this report and others, Confederate officers evidently interacted readily with captured Union officers, and, at times, the prisoners enjoyed a certain amount of freedom of movement in camp and in the town. The experience of Col. Henry A. Morrow of the 24th Michigan, 1st Brigade, First Division, I Corps, who also was wounded and captured on July 1, bears this out. While he was a prisoner, Morrow said: "I conversed freely with distinguished rebel officers" about the July 1 battle. A major on A. P. Hill's staff provided him with information about the battle and allowed him to observe the assault on July 3 from the courthouse steeple in Gettysburg. This Rebel officer told Morrow that Lee's "army present at Gettysburg was about 90,000 strong, and that their line of battle was estimated to be 8 miles long." The inflated figure of 90,000 was either an attempt to mislead Morrow about Lee's real strength, or it reflects the basic ignorance of lower-ranking officers about the army's actual strength of closer to 70,000.[58]

57 Livingston to Sharpe, July 5, 1863, *OR* 27, pt. 3, 541-42; Busey and Martin, *Regimental Strengths and Losses*, 125, 260. It is doubtful that Sharpe would have sent this report with its inflated troop estimate to headquarters verbatim. Instead, he more likely followed his normal practice: summarized the information for Meade and commented on its accuracy.

58 Morrow's post-action report, February 22, 1864, *OR* 27, pt. 1, 272-73; Busey and Martin, *Regimental Strengths and Losses*, 169.

Having spent two full days in Confederate hands during the fighting at Gettysburg, Morrow had an opportunity to assess their attitude and morale, and despite some inaccuracies he pretty well got it right:

> At first the [Rebel] officers seemed very sanguine of their ability to dislodge the Army of the Potomac from its position, and the capture of Washington and Baltimore was considered a thing almost accomplished, and this feeling was fully shared by the private soldiers; but the admirable means taken by General Meade to meet every attack, and the successful manner in which he repulsed them, seemed to have a powerful influence in abating their confidence before the final order was received for the evacuation of the town.[59]

Buford arrived in Frederick where his other brigade under Brig. Gen. Wesley Merritt joined him. Since Meade had subsequently instructed French's detached division at Frederick to seize and hold the South Mountain passes, Buford stayed overnight before continuing on to Williamsport "to destroy the enemy's trains." The report from the wounded colonel, abandoned when the Rebels retreated, that a wagon train of wounded underway from Gettysburg to Winchester may have prompted these orders.[60]

But the wagon train of wounded was making good its escape. Imboden's mostly intact wagon train began arriving at Williamsport on the swollen, impassable Potomac River in the afternoon. After concentrating the wagons as much as possible near the river, his brigade strengthened the small force already in place to protect the train and its valuable cargo.[61]

While Meade adopted a more cautious wait-and-see attitude about the significance of enemy movements, others did not. Brigadier General Rufus

---

59 Morrow's post-action report, February 22, 1864, *OR* 27, pt.1, 272-73. Although Morrow's report was not submitted until February 1864, his commanders undoubtedly debriefed him at Gettysburg. The misleading information it contained about the enemy's strength would have reinforced Meade's mistaken belief on this subject. But the report was instructive about Lee's objectives to "dislodge the Army of the Potomac from its position" on Cemetery Ridge and Cemetery Hill, and to capture Washington and Baltimore.

60 Post-action reports: Pleasonton's, August 31, 1863, ibid., 916; Buford's, August 27, 1863, 928; Merritt's, July 18, 1863, 943; Butterfield to French, July 4, 1863, pt. 3, 517-18.

61 Imboden, "The Confederate Retreat from Gettysburg," in *B&L*, 3:425; post-action reports: Murchison's, August 5, 1863, ibid., pt. 2, 488; Stuart's, August 20, 1863, 701; Steve French, "Hurry Was the Order of the Day: Imboden and the Wagon Train of the Wounded," *North & South* (August 1999), 2:35-39; Brown, *Retreat from Gettysburg*, 191-93; Gallagher, *The Personal Recollections of General Edward Porter Alexander*, 269.

Ingalls, Meade's chief quartermaster, informed his boss in Washington, Brig. Gen. Montgomery C. Meigs: "The enemy is in full retreat. We shall follow via Frederick." Which was, in fact, correct. But Meade's troops would need the means of crossing rivers and creeks in their pursuit. Sometime during the day, Butterfield instructed Brig. Gen. Henry W. Benham at the Washington Navy Yard to send his pontoon bridge wagon trains to Harper's Ferry. Butterfield told Benham, who was in charge of Meade's Engineer Brigade, that he would telegraph further orders from Frederick to Poolesville or Rockville where he expected Benham to be the next day. Employment of pontoon bridges loomed large in the planning about how best to engage Lee's army.[62]

Indeed, the push was on to mobilize all the Federal forces in the area to go after Lee. Responding to orders from Washington to move his forces to Hancock, Maryland, Kelley, in Clarksburg, West Virginia, notified Halleck's office that it would be impossible to concentrate his forces there promptly since Brig. Gen. William W. Averell and his cavalry units were away and would not return for "some days." Should he wait for Averell, or move the 4,500 men he had at New Creek and Cumberland to Hancock immediately? This hesitancy prompted a sharp response from Stanton: Kelley should have already been underway, he wrote, "by rapid and vigorous motion" in order to "inflict a heavy blow upon the enemy . . . There should be no rest, night or day." At 10 p.m. Halleck informed Kelley unequivocally that Lee's army "is in full retreat" and ordered him to do everything in his power to capture or destroy his wagon trains, which would try to cross the Potomac at Williamsport or Falling Waters.[63]

A severe storm had greatly hampered his movements, Lee reported later, and the rear of his army did not abandon its position near Gettysburg until after daylight. However, he noted that the march continued unimpeded despite an enemy force (the VI Corps) staging an ineffectual demonstration at Fairfield. Longstreet confirmed that heavy rains and bad roads delayed the march, and his corps did not reach the top of South Mountain until that night. Ewell, whose corps was the last to depart the battlefield, noted that enemy units threatening his rear were easily repulsed. Jubal Early, whose division was last in line, was also the first to learn of Union harassment from the rear from White's 35th

---

62 Ingalls to Meigs, Butterfield to Benham, July 5, 1863, *OR* 27, pt. 3, 543, 547.

63 Kelley to Townsend, Stanton to Kelley, Halleck to Kelley, July 5, 1863, ibid., 550.

Virginia Cavalry Battalion, part of Ewell's rear guard. Early deployed a regiment of Gordon's brigade, the 26th Georgia, to contain it.[64]

Stuart Screens the Army and Gathers Information

For two days, Stuart's brigades moving toward the Cumberland Valley had skirmished with enemy cavalry while traversing the mountains. A citizen informed him that he had been engaged with Kilpatrick, who had captured "not more than 40 wagons" rather than the much larger number Kilpatrick had claimed. Stuart decided it incumbent to open communication with the main army, because "I was led to believe that a portion of this [enemy cavalry] force might still be hovering on its flanks." He therefore sent one of his most reliable scouts, Pvt. Robert W. Goode, to advise Lee that he repulsed the enemy cavalry and to see what else he might be able to learn en route. Goode took the most direct route across the country and found Lee on the Hagerstown Road west of Fairfield. He filled Lee in on Stuart's activities, and advised him what to expect along the withdrawal route. Stuart later cited Goode and another scout in his report on the campaign for rendering "distinguished service" with "rare intelligence, great daring, and heroism." Stuart's honoring privates in a report showed his reliance on specially talented individuals to fulfill critical intelligence missions.[65]

Lee, who was traveling in the middle of the army that was marching behind the cavalry, acknowledged Stuart's message and later expressed his appreciation for his service in guarding the army's flanks during what he labeled the "retrograde movement." Lee had other concerns, however, because continual heavy rains had rendered the Potomac impassable at the Williamsport ford, and Union cavalry had virtually destroyed his pontoon bridge at Falling Waters, the alternate crossing point a few miles downstream. Lee had asserted to his subordinates that he was "determined to fight the enemy if they came on to a place he should select." And he had hoped Meade would attack his lines the previous day, but absent that, he would look for other opportunities to extract retribution as the withdrawal progressed. In the meantime, Stuart ably fulfilled

---

64 Post-action reports: Lee's, July 31, 1863, ibid., pt. 2, 309; Longstreet's, July 27, 1863, 361; Ewell's, n.d. 1863, 448; Early's, August 22, 1863, 471; Myers, *The Comanches*, 204-05.

65 Stuart's post-action report, August 20, 1863, *OR* 27, pt. 2, 700-01, 710, 718. For a description of the hazardous life of a scout, see Cooke, *Wearing of the Gray*, 467-70.

the key intelligence and counterintelligence roles that his commander relied upon him to do, especially while the army was in motion.[66]

---

66 Lee's post-action report, January 1864, ibid., 322; French to Halleck, July 4, 1863, pt. 3, 524; McDonald, *Make Me a Map of the Valley*, 158.

Chapter Sixteen

A Battle of Wits and a Test of Wills:
July 6 to 11

In a lost battle the power of an Army is broken, the moral to a greater degree than the physical. A second battle unless fresh favorable circumstances come into play, would lead to a complete defeat, perhaps, to destruction.

Carl Von Clausewitz[1]

It is the business of cavalry to follow up the victory, and to prevent the beaten army from rallying.

When a retiring army is pursued, it is more especially upon the flanks that the weight of cavalry should fall if you are strong enough in that arm to cut off his retreat.

Napoleon Bonaparte[2]

A retreat . . . always gives an advantage to the pursuing army; and this is particularly the case after a defeat and when the source of supplies and reinforcements is at a great distance; for a retreat then becomes more difficult . . . in proportion to the skill exhibited by the enemy in conducting the pursuit.

Baron De Jomini[3]

---

1   Von Clausewitz, *On War*, 359.

2   Cairnes, *Napoleon's Military Maxims*, 58.

3   De Jomini, *The Art of War*, 193.

July 6: A Cautious Meade Proceeds Methodically

[Meade's actions] all appear to me to be connected with a purpose to cover Baltimore and Washington, and to get the enemy across the river again.

Abraham Lincoln[4]

Early on the morning of the 6th, I received intelligence of the approach [to Williamsport] from Frederick of a large body of cavalry.... These were the divisions of Generals Buford and Kilpatrick, and Huey's brigade of Gregg's division ... about 7000 men.

Brig. Gen. John D. Imboden[5]

After receiving a dispatch the previous day from Meade's headquarters to ship his pontoon bridge wagon trains to Harper's Ferry, engineer brigade commander Brig. Gen. Henry Benham responded from Washington at 1:00 a.m. His land transportation capability was insufficient at the moment, so he planned to ship two bridges as soon as the quartermaster made transportation available—or he would send them via the Chesapeake and Ohio Canal, which Stuart's cavalry had damaged on its way northward on June 28, if it were repaired in time.[6]

At 2:00 a.m., based on a conversation with Warren who had accompanied Sedgwick's VI Corps toward Fairfield to conduct a reconnaissance of Lee's army and returned, Meade advised Sedgwick to "push your reconnaissance, so as to ascertain, if practicable, how far the enemy has retreated." He wanted Sedgwick to determine "the character of the gap and practicability of carrying the same, in case I should determine to advance on that line." Meade was leaving open the possibility of pursuing Lee's army into the mountains. He also instructed Sedgwick to keep watch on his right and rear, since there was reason to believe that the enemy was in force in the Cashtown area, and to report back to him every two or three hours. He was not going to move from his present

---

4   Lincoln to Halleck, July 6, 1863, in Basler, *Collected Works of Abraham Lincoln*, 6: 318.

5   Imboden, "The Confederate Retreat from Gettysburg," in *B&L*, 3:426.

6   Butterfield to Benham, July 5, 1863, *OR* 27, pt. 3, 547; Benham to Williams, July 6, 1863, 564; Stuart's post-action report, August 20, 1863, pt. 2, 694.

position, Meade said, "until I am better satisfied the enemy are evacuating the Cumberland Valley."[7]

Sometime later in the morning, Sedgwick reported that he was still in the same position near Fairfield where Warren had left him. Cautious because of "the character of the country and density of the fog," he sent cavalry and infantry forward to scout the enemy, but he could not determine whether they had taken the Hagerstown Road or Emmitsburg Road or both. Citizens reported that they had used both roads, but he still was not certain. Based on the large number of campfires, he speculated the presence of a strong enemy rear guard. He also relayed information from a "recaptured prisoner (a civilian)" who reported that Lee had sent an infantry division out the Cashtown Road to counter a Union force "supposed to be 40,000 strong" advancing south from Carlisle. Obviously a reference to the small force under Baldy Smith of some 4,500 men moving toward Cashtown, the wildly inflated figure illustrated how panicked observers could overestimate the strength of marching armies.[8]

At 3:00 a.m., Sedgwick informed I Corps commander Newton that he wanted both supporting corps, the I and III, to proceed to Emmitsburg, and Meade approved this movement. A little over an hour later, Howard notified Butterfield that scouts in the field reported the "enemy moving from Fairfield, through Jack's Mountain." The enemy could head in the direction of Mechanicstown (Thurmont) or Hagerstown, Howard noted, but, in either case, he thought it best for his XI Corps to move to Emmitsburg as quickly as possible. A few minutes later, Sykes informed Howard that he had been ordered to halt his V Corps where he was: at Marsh Creek between Gettysburg and Emmitsburg.[9]

A message from French at Frederick to Halleck in Washington arrived at 8:20 a.m. with the critically important information that the Potomac River was too high to be forded at either Shepherdstown or Williamsport. Consequently, the enemy was sending their wounded across in flat boats. Although he did not identify the source of this information, it likely came from his cavalry reconnoitering the enemy and questioning local citizens.[10]

---

7   Meade to Sedgwick, July 6, 1863, ibid., pt. 3, 554.

8   Sedgwick to Williams, July 6, 1863, ibid., 555.

9   Williams to Newton, Howard to Butterfield, Sykes to Howard, July 6, ibid, 556-57.

10 French to Halleck, July 6, 1863, ibid., 564.

Despite knowing that the swollen river would prevent Lee's army from reaching safety beyond the Potomac, uncertainty and indecision set in as Meade coordinated deployment of the various corps. By 9:00 a.m., signal officers alerted Norton at Meade's headquarters that the enemy column reported moving out the Fairfield Road had passed, and the road had been empty for the last half hour. Meade, however, not yet convinced that Lee was in retreat, told Sedgwick to continue his reconnaissance of Lee's army but to avoid an engagement. "All evidence seems to show a movement to Hagerstown and the Potomac," he conceded. "No doubt the principal force is between Fairfield and Hagerstown; but I apprehend they will be likely to let you alone, if you let them alone." Given this tentative approach to pursuit of the enemy, Meade decided he would suspend his flanking movement of Lee's army until "satisfied that the main body is retiring from the mountains." He, therefore, disapproved Sedgwick's proposal to move his corps to Emmitsburg and instead issued time-consuming instructions to deploy his "pickets well on your left flank; reconnoiter in all directions, and let me know the result." Up to this point, the Union army commander had chosen a wary approach, displaying little ingenuity pursuing Lee's army, blocking his retreat, or confronting his defeated army.[11]

With so many balls in the air, Meade's juggling act was taking a toll mentally. He had sent the VI corps without its ammunition train, with I and III in support, to reconnoiter Lee's army, but told Sedgwick not to bring on an engagement—the only sure way to capture prisoners and learn the enemy's plans. Within the hour after issuing these ambiguous instructions to Sedgwick, he complained to Couch in Harrisburg: "I cannot get very reliable intelligence of the enemy's movements," yet, despite this, he correctly stated, "they are in retreat for the Potomac." He knew this based on hard intelligence gained from a "captured dispatch [addressed] to a Rebel cavalry officer, dated July 6, [that] says Longstreet is moving through Jack's Mountain, and orders him to picket roads to Emmitsburg, and to report to Longstreet, at Jack's Mountain, and Ewell, at Fairfield." Meade seemingly had all the intelligence he needed, but he was not yet ready or willing to act.[12]

---

11 P[ierce] and C[amp] to Norton, Meade to Sedgwick, ibid., 557.

12 Meade to Couch, Pleasonton to Sedgwick, ibid., 559; McIntosh's post-action report, 967.

Meanwhile, cavalry commander Pleasonton ordered McIntosh's brigade to communicate with Sedgwick and send scouts out "to feel for the enemy." At 11:00 a.m., Pleasonton, who, along with Warren, was serving as chief of staff following Butterfield's sustaining a slight wound, informed French at Frederick that Meade had "suspended his operations for the present," since it had not been "positively ascertained" that Lee intended to evacuate the Cumberland Valley. Pleasonton reassured French that Lee's army "is very much crippled," and Meade did not believe the enemy would attack French's position. By mid-afternoon, McIntosh passed along the information from his position near Emmitsburg that the bulk of Lee's army had headed out the Waynesboro Pike from Fairfield after passing through the mountains at Fountain Dale and Monterey on July 5, headed, he thought, to Hagerstown. The enemy's force was reported to be 80,000 strong, he said, but since that information came from a citizen, it "must be taken for what it is worth."[13]

Although they had gotten under way the previous day, Meade halted the army, because, as he explained to Halleck, he "deemed it prudent to suspend the movement to Middletown until I could be certain the enemy were evacuating the Cumberland Valley." He did not elaborate on how he would reach this conclusion, but he told Halleck that Sedgwick had reported a "very formidable" gap at Fairfield that "would enable a small force to hold my column in check for a long time." But by the same logic, which Meade failed to mention, if Lee could hold his army in check with a small force on the eastern end of the gap, his army could employ a relatively small force to prevent Lee's escape by blocking the western side of the gap.[14]

Meade also complained to Halleck about his "great difficulty in getting reliable information." In light of the many reports from signal stations observing enemy movements, the interrogation of prisoners, debriefing of released Union prisoners about the withdrawal of Lee's army, as well as reconnaissance activity, this complaint seems curious at the least.[15]

Earlier Benham updated AAG Seth Williams on the status of the pontoons. One of the bridges destined for Harper's Ferry was on its way to the canal at Georgetown, and another was being loaded onto wagon trains. At 3:45 p.m.,

13 Pleasonton to French, McIntosh to Alexander July 6, 1863, 559, 561.

14 Meade to Halleck, July 6, 1863, OR 27, pt. 1, 80.

15 Ibid., pt. 1, 663, 832. Examples of reconnaissance activity include the VI Corps' reconnaissance-in-force on July 5 and 6, and the 7th Ohio of II Corps on July 5.

Benham reported the railroad to Harper's Ferry open, and said he would arrange to send one of the pontoon bridges by that route. If all went well, the bridge would arrive at Harper's Ferry early the next day—which would facilitate Meade's sending cavalry across the Potomac.[16]

By mid-afternoon on July 6, Meade, finally satisfied that the enemy was retreating, informed Halleck that he had restarted his army toward Middletown, Maryland, in pursuit of Lee. He planned to cooperate with Couch, whom he instructed to move down the Cumberland Valley and communicate with his army. "[I]f the enemy has not crossed the river, I shall give him battle," Meade promised, "trusting, should misfortune overtake me, that a sufficient number of my force, in connection with what you have in Washington, would reach that place so as to render it secure." Meade decided to detach an infantry and a cavalry brigade to track Lee's movements, after Sedgwick suspended his reconnaissance of Lee's withdrawal in the mountains. Whether Lee's two-day head start along a shorter route could be overcome, or whether the swollen Potomac would prevent his crossing the river, remained to be seen.[17]

Once Meade started out after Lee in earnest, he kept Halleck well informed of his destination, progress, and intentions. In return, Meade received encouragement and advice, a mixture of Lincoln's and Halleck's thinking that was not always harmonious. Although he told Halleck, "My cavalry have been attacking the enemy on both flanks, inflicting as much injury as possible," he did not elaborate on the objective of these operations—i.e., whether they were intended to bring Lee's retreat to a halt in order to attack him, or whether Meade had something else in mind.[18]

In the afternoon, as Lee's army marched toward Hagerstown with Hill's corps bringing up the rear, Union cavalry suddenly appeared. In anticipation of the enemy's arrival, Rodes, a division commander in Hill's corps, put Maj. Eugene Blackford in charge of all five of the division's sharpshooter battalions to serve as the army's rear guard. Forming two long skirmish lines and alternating their positions, Blackford deployed his sharpshooters for maximum use of their firepower and kept the Union cavalry at bay.[19]

16 Benham to Williams, July 6, 1863, ibid., 565.

17 Meade to Halleck, July 6, 1863, ibid., pt. 1, 80-81; Warren to Sedgwick, pt. 3, 561-62.

18 Meade to Halleck, see note above.

19 Ray, *Shock Troops of the Confederacy*, 71.

That day, communications between Little Round Top and Taneytown and Emmitsburg and Taneytown were discontinued. This was because the signal parties assigned to each of Meade's corps traveled with them during the pursuit. Chief signal officer Norton ensured that each of the corps maintained communications between it and headquarters by positioning teams at various locations along the route. Once they reached South Mountain, the I Corps signal officers would occupy stations at Turner's Gap and the nearby Washington Monument where they could observe Hagerstown and its vicinity.[20]

In addition, in response to special orders no. 106, Capt. W. J. L. Nicodemus arrived from Washington with a signal detachment of 12 officers and 27 enlisted men to work with the existing signal corps personnel, but to operate independently of them directly under Meade's command. Meade ordered Nicodemus to the front to "open communication between Frederick City and South Mountain Pass [Turner's Gap], and establish observation stations to command the Boonsboro Valley." He also sent signal parties to Maryland Heights and Crampton's Pass. Other stations operated on a hill overlooking Boonsboro and at Elk Ridge, as well as on Hagerstown Pike near Boonsboro.[21]

Meanwhile, that morning at Williamsport, Imboden had placed Co. F, 21st Virginia, into position guarding two roads that led into town. A "fine looking" young lady with a boy on horseback smiled and bowed as she rode past the picket into town and an hour or two later as she passed on her way out. The guards, with orders that no one should be allowed to pass, stopped her. Her appeal to officers almost succeeded until a soldier, overhearing the conversation, fingered her as a spy who had "come in here to find out all she can, and now she is going back to tell the Yankees." The Co. F regimental history noted, without elaboration, the men learned that "it was well she did not [receive permission to] pass." Although this woman is not identified, the BMI sent civilian spies behind enemy lines to obtain information about the location and disposition of Lee's forces during the retreat and pursuit.[22]

20 Norton's post-action report, September 18, 1863, OR 27, pt. 1, 203; Cameron, "The Signal Corps at Gettysburg, Part II," 101.

21 Nicodemus's post-action report, July 21, 1863, OR 27, pt. 1, 207; Cameron, "Signal Corps at Gettysburg, Part II," 102, 104; Brown, *Signal Corps U.S.A*, 372-73.

22 Worsham, *One of Jackson's Foot Cavalry, a History of Co. F, 21st Virginia*, 168-69; Sharpe to Williams, July 9-11, 1863, RG 393, NA.

Having pushed Kilpatrick out of the mountains and learning from "Grumble" Jones of a threat by Buford to the wagon trains that had arrived at Williamsport, Stuart began moving in that direction. Buford arrived in front of Williamsport in late afternoon and fought his way to within a half-mile of the town. When Kilpatrick learned of Buford's presence in the area, the two met and decided that Kilpatrick should confront Stuart's cavalry at Hagerstown. At about 5:00 p.m. near Saint James College, Buford encountered enemy pickets, drove them in, and prepared to capture the town. Steadfast resistance by Imboden's cavalry brigade, supported by two infantry regiments, invalids, and teamsters in impromptu defensive positions with an array of artillery, successfully repulsed the Union cavalrymen. By boldly advancing his thin line of troops, Imboden had decoyed Buford into believing the Confederate defenses were deep and strong. Buford requested help from Kilpatrick, who left a brigade behind at Hagerstown to keep Stuart in check, and marched rapidly with two brigades to Williamsport to lend Buford assistance.[23]

However, the lateness of the hour forced Buford's and Kilpatrick's combined body of troops to retire to avoid being cut off by newly-arrived Confederate infantry. Imboden thankfully acknowledged, "A bold charge at any time . . . would have broken our feeble lines, and then we should all have fallen as easy prey to the Federals." If Buford and Kilpatrick had been able to destroy the ordnance, quartermaster, and subsistence trains, Lee's army would have been hard-pressed to defend against an attack by Meade's forces. But for the inadequacy of the Union cavalry's tactics and timing, Buford might have reprised the heroic role he played on July 1 at Gettysburg.[24]

By 7:30 p.m., AAG Seth Williams had received Benham's messages about the pontoon bridges and responded that Benham "must have material for two bridges at Berlin [near Harper's Ferry] by the 10th." If Lee were able to cross the Potomac, Meade wanted to insure he had the means to pursue him.[25]

---

23 Stuart's post-action report, August 20, 1863, *OR* 27, pt. 2, 701, 753-54; Buford's post-action report, August 27, 1863, pt. 1, 928; Kilpatrick's post-action report, August 10, 1863, 995; Imboden, "The Confederate Retreat," 427-28; French, "Hurry Was the Order of the Day," 40-42; McClellan, *The Campaigns of Stuart's Cavalry*, 357-61.

24 Buford's post-action report, August 27, 1863, *OR* 27, pt. 1, 928; Kilpatrick's post-action report, August 10, 1863, 995-96; Imboden, "The Confederate Retreat," in *B&L*, 3:428; Brown, *Retreat from Gettysburg*, 254. About 700 sick and wounded Rebel soldiers, teamsters, and wagoners participated in the defense of Williamsport. Brown, *Retreat from Gettysburg*, 226, 241.

25 Williams to Benham, July 6, 1863, *OR* 27, pt. 3, 566.

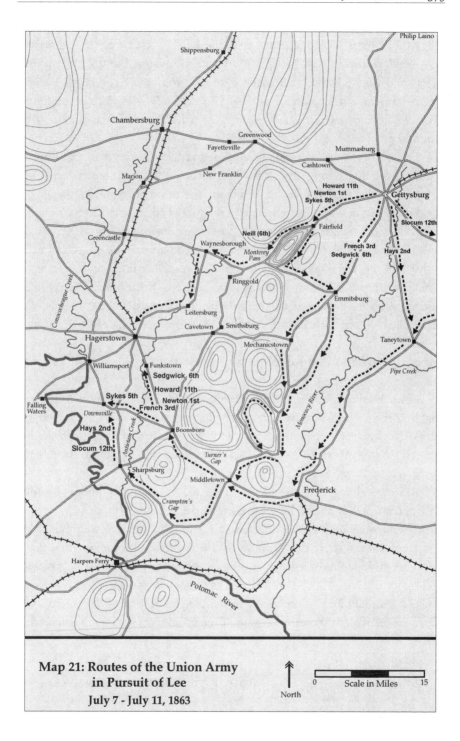

Map 21: Routes of the Union Army in Pursuit of Lee

July 7 - July 11, 1863

North

0   Scale in Miles   15

At 9:30 p.m., Kelley reported to Halleck and Meade that he had arrived with 4,500 troops in Cumberland, Maryland. He planned to leave during the night, and his "advance will reach Hancock tomorrow evening." Kelley's original mission "to capture or destroy Lee's trains," however, was no longer possible, since the wagons had already reached Williamsport and were safely behind Lee's lines.[26]

Except for cavalry harassing the wagon trains, Lee's army made the difficult journey from Gettysburg to Williamsport without "serious interruption." The troops arrived in the Hagerstown area in the afternoon of July 6 and morning of the 7th. That evening from Leitersburg, Maryland, Stuart sent a dispatch evidently with an updated situation report on the enemy to Lee with a courier and a 10-man escort, but they returned at 3:00 a.m. without finding Lee to deliver the message—an example of the extraordinary difficulty operating in unfamiliar territory, and at night at that. Learning from Stuart the pontoon bridge at Falling Waters had been partially destroyed by the enemy, Lee immediately ordered the construction of a new bridge.[27]

July 7: Information on Rebel Activities Arrives

From Frederick at 10:30 a.m., Meade sent Halleck the unwelcome news that Buford attacked the wagon train at Williamsport but had been repulsed by a supposedly "large force of infantry and artillery," which as we have seen was not the case. Meade informed Halleck his army would assemble at Middletown the next day, and "I will immediately move on Williamsport."[28]

After receiving the president's message of concern about Meade's congratulatory message to his troops citing the remaining task to drive Lee's army from "our soil," Halleck directed Meade to follow up his "stunning blow" at Gettysburg and strike Lee again before he reached the Potomac. Halleck did not reiterate Lincoln's uncompromising language "to prevent [Lee's] crossing and to destroy him," but he advised of "strong evidence that [Lee] is short of artillery ammunition,"—probably from the interrogation of Gettysburg prisoners arriving in the capital—and "if vigorously pressed, he must suffer."

26 Kelley to Townsend, ibid., 576.

27 Lee's post-action report, January 1864, ibid., pt. 2, 322; Stuart's post-action report, August 20, 1863, 700-01; Beale, *Ninth Virginia Cavalry*, 90-91.

28 Meade to Halleck, Buford to French, July 7, 1863, OR 27, pt. 2, 81-82, 925.

Maj. Gen. Gouverneur K. Warren
Library of Congress

Halleck opined that Maryland Heights seemed to be a most important point, and asked what force had Meade sent there. The enemy should be prevented from occupying it, he said, because if "his crossing above [that point] be impossible, he will probably attempt to take and hold that position until he can make the passage [over the river]."[29]

Without explaining the objective, chief engineer Warren alerted Benham that Meade wanted to be able to cross cavalry to the south side of the Potomac, but that the Harper's Ferry railroad bridge was impassable. Warren wanted to know how soon Benham could have one pontoon bridge at Harper's Ferry. Obviously both Lee and Meade were on the same wave length about bridging the swollen Potomac, each for his own purposes.[30]

July 8: Inaccurate Information Prompts Call for Immediate Action

Be assured I most earnestly desire to try the fortunes of war with the enemy this side of the [Potomac] river . . . [however] I wish in advance to moderate the expectations of those who, in ignorance of the difficulties to be encountered, may expect too much.

Maj. Gen. George G. Meade[31]

I think we shall have another battle before Lee can cross the river, though from all accounts he is making great efforts to do so.

Maj. Gen. George G. Meade[32]

29 Halleck to Meade, July 7, 1863, *OR* 27, pt. 1, 82-83.

30 Warren to Benham, July 7, 1863, ibid., pt. 3, 585-86.

31 Meade to Halleck, July 8, 1863, ibid., pt. 1, 84. Meade did not specify to whom he was referring, but the underlying implication was President Lincoln.

32 Meade to his wife, July 8, 1863, in Meade, *The Life and Letters*, 2:132.

Lee learned from Imboden of reinforcements on their way to Meade from West Virginia via Hancock, Maryland: Kelley's advance brigades that had apparently arrived at Hancock. Even with Williamsport fewer than 20 miles away, Kelley cautiously made no further movement southward in an attempt to capture Lee's wagons or engage his troops. Had Meade decided to collaborate with Kelley, it would not have been a simple task. He would have to do so by telegraph through Washington or possibly Frederick, or try to reach him by courier. All communication with Kelley had come from Washington.[33]

To go on the offensive, Meade needed information. A lot of it was forthcoming. In the late afternoon, he heard from Couch that scouts reported the Rebels slowly crossing wagons over the swift-moving Potomac on flat boats. Neill, whose small force was tailing Lee's army, sent regular updates about the enemy's progress. And Meade had already learned from his cavalry about the Rebels' occupation of Hagerstown and Williamsport.[34]

Benham informed Williams that the pontoon bridges Meade ordered would likely require two days before they arrived at Harper's Ferry. In the meantime, army engineer Lt. John R. Meigs requested permission from Meade to repair the Harper's Ferry railroad bridge to facilitate Union troops crossing over. For some unexplained reason, Meade did not respond to this request. Whatever his thinking was on this issue, he did not order Meigs to repair the bridge.[35]

In response to Halleck's inquiry and advice the previous day, Meade informed him that he ordered Brig. Gen. H. M. Naglee and his eight regiments to reinforce and take command from Brig. Gen. John R. Kenly, already in place on Maryland Heights overlooking Harper's Ferry—increasing the total force there to 6-7,000 men. Meade had ordered Naglee "to hold his command in readiness to move forward to my support if required." Meade also told Halleck

33 Lee to Imboden, July 9, 1863, *OR* 27, pt. 3, 987-88; Kelley to Townsend, July 6, 1863, 576; Kelley to Townsend, Stanton to Kelley, Halleck to Kelley, July 5, 1863, 550; Brown, *Retreat from Gettysburg*, 277.

34 Meade to Halleck, July 8, 1863, *OR* 27, pt. 1, 84; Brown, *Retreat from Gettysburg*, 271.

35 Benham to Williams, July 8, 1863, *OR* 27, pt. 3, 603; Meigs to Meade, July 8, 1863, 607. One possible reason Meade did not respond to Meigs was a message sent him by J.W. Garrett, president of the B&O Railroad, warning him that an attempt to repair the bridge may provoke Rebels on the opposite side of the river to burn the bridge. Garrett to Stanton, July 9, 1863, 626. Garrett forwarded the message he sent to Meade to Stanton "for your information and any action you may deem judicious."

that he had a bridge train along with an engineer party at Harper's Ferry, but that the bridge would be "thrown over [the Potomac River] only when any command, cavalry or other, should arrive there to cross." In fact, the bridge train had not yet arrived, but once again Meade implied he planned to send troops across the river for some as yet unidentified purpose.[36]

At 12:30 p.m., Halleck alerted Meade, without providing a source, of reliable information that the enemy was crossing the Potomac at Williamsport. The opportunity to attack Lee's divided forces should not be lost, he urged. "The President is urgent and anxious that your army should move against him by forced marches." Later that afternoon, Meade informed Halleck that his information about Lee's army crossing the river "does not agree" with what Meade understood about the situation. Lee's "whole force is in position between Funkstown and Williamsport," he explained. "I have just received information that he has driven my cavalry force in front of Boonsborough." Addressing the president's apparent anxiety, Meade pointedly commented that his army was making forced marches while "short of rations, and barefooted." He cited one corps marching more than 30 miles the previous night. Meade emphasized, somewhat ambiguously, to his superiors, "I take occasion to repeat that I will use my utmost efforts to push forward this army."[37]

Meade's task, a difficult one, was to balance his preference for a more measured response to Lee's movements with demands from Washington for swift direct action. At the same time, Halleck, the man in the middle between Lincoln and Meade, attempted to mollify both:

> Do not understand me as expressing any dissatisfaction; on the contrary . . . I only wish to give you opinions. . . . If Lee's army is so divided by the river, the importance of attacking the part on this side is incalculable. . . . If, on the contrary, he has massed his whole force on the Antietam, time must be taken to also concentrate your forces. . . . my only fear now is that the enemy may escape by crossing the river.[38]

---

36 Meade to Halleck, July 8, 1863, ibid., pt. 1, 83-84. While Meade did not clarify the purpose for certain forces crossing the river, this likely was preparation related to his earlier stated concern for instructions on what route to take in pursuit of Lee's army in Virginia if it successfully crossed the river prior to another engagement between the combatants—rather than a planned attempt to send forces over to get behind Lee and impede his army from crossing of the river.

37 Halleck to Meade, Meade to Halleck, July 8, 1863, ibid., pt. 1, 84-85.

38 Halleck to Meade, July 8, 1863, ibid., 85.

With this exchange between Washington authorities and their commander in the field in the background, Meade took the unusual step of including both in a circular to his corps and division commanders. He identified Halleck's comments as "from the President," and informed his commanders that he was circulating this message and his response "in the earnest hope that they will use their best efforts to assist the commanding general in meeting the wishes of the President." Whatever Meade's intent in circulating these exchanges, either to stimulate backing from his subordinates for his position regarding the Washington authorities or toward aggressive confrontation with the enemy, the former resulted. Noah Brooks, a Sacramento *Union* reporter and a friend and confidant of Lincoln who followed the army and caught up with Meade's headquarters near Boonsboro, observed that "Meade's staff officers were considerably disgruntled by the so-called Washington 'interference'," and that Meade's response to the urgings of Halleck and the president "had scored a good point on the Washington authorities from the President downward."[39]

What caused the president to press Meade to engage Lee? Brooks recalled:

> [T]he anxiety, almost anguish, with which Lincoln had said before I left Washington that he was afraid that 'something would happen' to prevent that annihilation of Lee's army, which, as he thought, was then certainly within the bounds of possibility.

Nonetheless, optimism abounded within the Union ranks. Lieutenant Colonel James F. Rusling of the III Corps wrote in a letter that day, "The news here is all good. We have won a great and important victory. We shall give Lee battle again at Antietam or Williamsport, within forty-eight hours." With inadvertent prescience he added, "if he escapes, will chase him through Virginia."[40]

While Meade was correct that the bulk of Lee's army had been unable to cross the swollen river, Lee had ordered Imboden to send two infantry regiments and a battery across from Williamsport to "the south side of the river . . . for the defense of the [army's] crossing." Imboden assigned this task to Maj. Benjamin F. Eshleman who was to take his Washington Artillery troops across

39 HQ Army of the Potomac Circular, July 8, 1863, ibid., pt. 3, 605; Noah Brooks, *Washington in Lincoln's Time* (New York, 1895), 87-88; Starr, Bohemian Brigade, 157-58; Carl Sandburg, *Abraham Lincoln: The War Years*, 4 vols. (New York, 1939), 4:115, 255.

40 Brooks, *Washington in Lincoln's Time*, 94; Gen. James F. Rusling, *Men and Things I Saw in Civil War Days* (Cincinnati, OH, 1899), 307.

by swimming his horses, while his guns, caissons, and the infantry crossed by flat boat. Evidently, Lee anticipated Meade would send troops across the river to try to block his escape.[41]

From his headquarters located just south of Hagerstown, Lee also instructed Pickett to employ the remnants of his battered division (about 2,700 men) to guard the wagon trains and the large contingent of Union prisoners at Williamsport; as soon as they could cross the swollen Potomac River on flat boats, he was to escort them to Winchester.[42]

Pickett protested indignantly about the menial duty of guarding prisoners, so Lee changed his plans and gave Imboden's cavalry the responsibility for the prisoners after they crossed the river on flat boats. One of Imboden's regiments under his brother, Col. George W. Imboden, was already assigned to picket northwards toward Hancock gathering information on the Union forces, i.e., Kelley's troops, known to be in that area.[43]

July 9: BMI Scouts Gain Important Information

> Although the information respecting the position of the enemy is not very definite, yet he is believed not to have crossed any large part of it over the Potomac, but to be concentrating it between Hagerstown and Williamsport.
>
> AAG Seth Williams[44]

At 9:00 a.m., Sharpe provided Meade with the first of a series of reports over the next three days from BMI scouts operating near and behind enemy lines. He informed Meade that Sgt. Milton Cline, with a team of four scouts posing as Confederates, reported from Beaver Run (probably Beaver Creek between Smithsburg and Boonsboro) that he "fell in with a train of 9 wagons, with a guard of 30 [Rebel] infantry," and learned that Lee's army had a large

41 Imboden to Eshleman, July 8, 1863, OR 51, pt. 2, 735.

42 Lee's post-action report, January 1864, ibid., pt. 2, 27:322; Lee to Pickett, July 8, 1863, pt. 3, 983, 986-88, McDonald, *Make Me a Map of the Valley*, 159; Busey and Martin, *Strengths and Losses*, 271.

43 Lee to Pickett, Lee to Imboden, July 9, 1863, ibid., 986-88.

44 Williams to Smith. July 9, 1863, OR 27, pt. 3, 621-22. Imboden later wrote that only the 62nd Virginia Regiment of his brigade guarded the Union prisoners on their trek to Staunton for shipment by rail to Richmond. Imboden, "The Confederate Retreat from Gettysburg," in *B&L*, 3:428-29.

force at Hagerstown and Williamsport, were fortifying in the Hagerstown area, and were confiscating all the flour and horses in the vicinity. Cline advised Sharpe to send cavalry to Smoketown southwest of Boonsboro to attack the wagon train. At the same time Sharpe reported information gained by Greenwood, a scout who had gone to Sharpsburg first, then three or four miles up the road to Keedysville, and finally about five miles towards Downsville (12 miles northwest) on the Williamsport Road. Although he saw no enemy in his travels, he heard that their pickets were posted one mile east of Downsville. He also learned that a man who had been in Williamsport that morning reported the Rebels making poor progress crossing their wounded on flat boats, but that the level of the river was falling. Other BMI scouts, Sharpe added, had cut loose the ferry at Shepherdstown, a potential alternate crossing route for the Rebels.[45]

That morning, Neill, still bird-dogging Lee's infantry northeast of Hagerstown, provided additional information to Meade from a scout who confirmed "Lee has one corps intrenched on the Williamsport pike from Hagerstown; another on Boonsborough pike; and Early is said to be up toward Middleburg (quien sabe?) between Newcastle [probably Greencastle] and Hagerstown." Neill also reported that Baldy Smith had joined him with his "mixed command" of national guard and militia troops.[46]

At 10:30 a.m. Kelley reported to Halleck from Hancock: a citizen, who had been in Hagerstown the previous day, had informed him that "Lee's army is all in that neighborhood; that Longstreet has pushed through town toward Sharpsburg; Ewell is toward Williamsport, and that General Hill was encamped north of [Hagerstown]." Although Kelley added, "Don't know that this is reliable," the citizen's report was in fact accurate, and Lee's army would remain in these positions until July 11 or 12 while entrenchments were being prepared in the Williamsport/Falling Waters area. Meade's delayed and slow-paced pursuit from Gettysburg allowed Lee's forces time to rest, recuperate, and prepare fortifications.[47]

Sharpe's, Neil's, and Kelley's reporting summarized where Lee's army was located (Hagerstown and Williamsport) and was not located (Sharpsburg), plus

---

45 Sharpe to Williams, July 9, 1863, RG 393, NA. For the location of Smoketown, see *OR Atlas* Plate 27, 1, Plate 29, 1 and 2; and for the town of Beaver Creek, see *OR Atlas* Plate 136, D7.

46 Neill to Williams, ibid., 87; pt. 3.

47 Kelley to Townsend, July 9, 1863, OR 27, pt. 3, 624-25; post-action reports of Lee, Longstreet, Ewell and Hill, pt. 2, 323, 361, 448, 609.

the important information they were entrenching and using flat boats for transportation, however slow, across the river. Yet, at 11:00 a.m. from Middletown, Meade told Halleck that he had sent his cavalry to gather more information, because, as he again complained, "It is with the greatest difficulty that I can obtain any reliable intelligence of the enemy." He did not elaborate on what information he felt was lacking. Contrary to what he was telling Washington, Meade was in fact receiving a steady stream of intelligence reports from a variety of sources. His comments otherwise seemed to reflect a growing level of anxiety, similar to what his predecessor Hooker had experienced when confrontation with Lee was in the offing. "I think the decisive battle of the war will be fought in a few days," Meade told Halleck. "In view of its momentous consequences, I desire to adopt such measures as in my judgment will tend to insure success, even though these may be deemed tardy." He was trying to make his position clear, but Meade's "deemed tardy" remark without further explanation simply gave Lincoln and Halleck yet another reason to be apprehensive about his action plan and commitment to engaging Lee again.[48]

By noon, Sharpe informed Meade that one of his scouts, probably Greenwood, who had first given his information to Major General Sykes, had returned from Sharpsburg and reported no enemy infantry at or near Sharpsburg or between there and the Potomac. The main body of Lee's troops were between Boonsboro and Hagerstown. The enemy was still crossing wagons at Williamsport on a flat boat, he continued, which required two hours to make the round trip. And as for the earlier mention of the river falling, this scout said the Potomac had already risen about eight feet and was running rapidly. In short, under present conditions Lee would be forced to remain on the north side of the river, at least for the time being.[49]

Meanwhile, a considerable clash of cavalry forces had occurred on July 8, when Stuart's men attacked Buford's near Boonesboro. Howard told Meade's newly installed chief of staff, Brig. Gen. Andrew A. Humphries, that a Rebel deserter from Fitz Lee's cavalry brigade came into his lines with the information that the Rebel attack against Buford's cavalry the previous day had been a mounted reconnaissance for the purpose of "feeling our strength." But when Howard sent Maj. Gen. Carl Schurz's division forward in response to Buford's

48 Meade to Halleck, July 9, 1863, *OR* 27, pt. 1, 86.

49 Sharpe to Williams, 12 noon, July 9, 1863, RG 393, NA; Sykes to [Humphreys], ibid., pt. 3, 615.

call for support, the deserter said the Rebel mounted attack "retired as soon as they saw the (infantry) re-enforcements approaching."[50]

According to Stuart his intention was to mount "a bold demonstration, to threaten an advance upon the enemy, and thus cover the retrograde of the main body." He was, in other words, screening the retreat of Lee's army. And although he claimed this movement successful, it had been costly. Lee told his cavalry chief that he regretted "very much to learn your loss was so great yesterday." But both men knew the situation to be dire and the price required to protect the retreating army. "I hope your parties that you have sent out may gain us information of the enemy," Lee told Stuart. "It is much needed"—confirming the deserter's explanation of the cavalry sortie.[51]

While the confrontation was underway, Stuart learned from captured prisoners that "the main cavalry force of the enemy was in our front." When he received word of heavy Yankee reinforcements, he decided to retire since he had achieved his objective of screening Lee's army. Besides, he had other tasks to do. Lee also requested that Stuart gather "all the flour and forage on Beaver Creek," because the enemy in the nearby Clear Spring Valley (Kelley's troops) were attacking and capturing their foraging parties. In a rare display of open criticism, Lee implied that this was happening because the regiment of Imboden's cavalry—the one under his brother's command—supposedly protecting that area "are unsteady, and, I fear, inefficient."[52]

Lee had instructed Imboden to have his brother "sift the reports [about enemy movements] that may reach him, and report only such as he has reason to believe to be correct." Fearing his northern flank vulnerable, Lee issued guidelines for Colonel Imboden to "throw his pickets well out, keep his men on the alert, and not suffer them to be surprised or taken." Lee thought it would be unwise for this particular enemy force, Kelley's troopers, to try to link up with Meade's main army, which he believed "is certainly [still] beyond South

---

50 Howard to Williams, July 8, 1863, ibid., pt. 3, 604; Howard to Humphreys, July 9, 1863, 615; Howard's post-action report, September 9, 1863, pt. 1, 708; Stuart's post-action report, August 20, 1863, pt. 2, 703; Wittenberg, *One Continuous Fight*, 184; Oliver Otis Howard, *Autobiography*, 2 vols. (New York, 1908), 1:444.

51 Stuart's post-action report, August 20, 1863, OR 27, pt. 2, 703; Lee to Stuart, July 9, 1863, pt. 3, 985; Howard to Williams, Meade to Howard, July 8, 1863, pt. 3, 604; Howard to Humphreys, July 9, 1863, pt. 3, 615.

52 Stuart's post-action report, August 20, 1863, OR 27, pt. 2, 703; Lee to Stuart, July 9, 1863, pt. 3, 985.

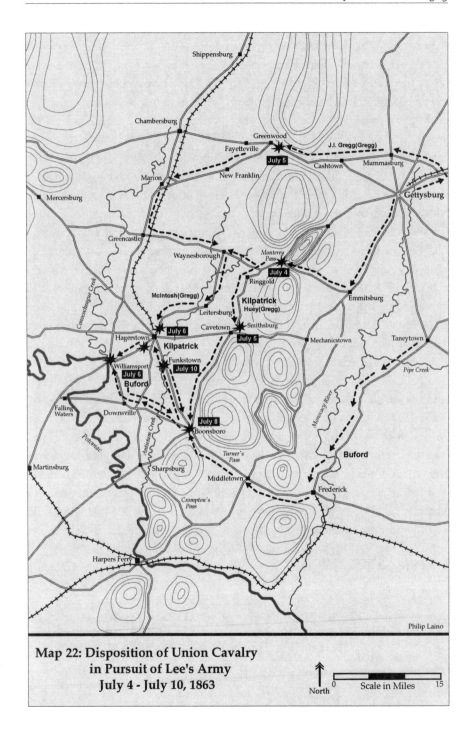

**Map 22: Disposition of Union Cavalry
in Pursuit of Lee's Army
July 4 - July 10, 1863**

North   Scale in Miles

Mountain." What Lee didn't know, however, was that by the end of the day, all or part of the seven Union infantry corps had crossed west of the mountains.[53]

The deserter from Fitz Lee's cavalry had also revealed to Howard that a pontoon bridge had been brought from Winchester to the Williamsport area and "put down." He located "the whole [Rebel] army . . . on this side of the Potomac . . . between Funkstown and Williamsport," and "thinks they have taken position beyond [west of] the Antietam [Creek], their right resting some distance south of Funkstown." Howard sent the deserter, a valuable intelligence asset, to army headquarters for further interrogation. There he provided insight into the morale of the Confederates, commenting that "the men are in good spirits; expect a battle, and think if they can once get us agoing, they can recover all." Still, he admitted that Lee's men had not been given the demoralizing news that Vicksburg had surrendered. This timely information certainly provided a rationale for Meade to send cavalry across the river to investigate and, if possible, destroy Lee's pontoon bridge, foul up his communications, and intercept his supplies. Despite its possession of this intelligence, however, Union army headquarters issued no orders to take action.[54]

Meanwhile in Richmond, Davis wrote to Lee that he had ordered Maj. Gen. Samuel Jones in western Virginia to proceed to Winchester with 3,000 troops and two artillery batteries "to cover your communication [in the Shenandoah Valley]." Davis, who had earlier denied Lee's proposal to support his invasion of the North by posing a threat to Washington with troops from Virginia and North Carolina, clearly worried now about the fate of Lee and his army during the retreat. Jones immediately complied with these orders, dispatching the men and batteries to Winchester by rail, even though he informed Richmond of the unstable tactical situation in his own area. Major General D. H. Hill in North Carolina underscored Davis' apprehension, warning Seddon that if the Yankees captured Lee's lightly guarded supply base at Winchester, it might "starve his army to death." Reports from a Rebel scout named Carroll heightened concern

---

53 Lee to Imboden, July 9, 1863, ibid., pt. 3, 987-88; Laino, *Gettysburg Campaign Atlas*, 404. Providing insight into how the Union forces communicated in a mobile environment, Meade told Howard that he requested Pleasonton to telegraph Buford asking whether he required infantry support. Also he related that a telegraph operator was located at Boonsboro, and "one on the mountain, so that you can, through the latter, communicate with Schurz or myself." The mountain operator likely referred to a signal party with a capability to send and receive messages by flag or telegraph.

54 Howard to Humphreys, July 9, 1863, *OR* 27, pt. 3, 615; Howard, *Autobiography*, 444.

for the welfare of Lee's army. Dix's Union troops that had been threatening the Rebel capital "were rapidly falling back" and "are ordered to Yorktown . . . on their way to join" Meade's army.[55]

Meanwhile, Capt. F. C. Roberts, the Confederate commander at Martinsburg sent President Davis a succinct yet detailed report:

> General Lee's headquarters are at Hagerstown. He is said to be waiting there for ammunition, which has just passed this place. I cannot tell whether he intends to recross the river or to advance. No news from the enemy's army. The Yankees have reoccupied Maryland Heights at Harper's Ferry, it is supposed with a brigade. The rear cavalry skirmishing every day. The [Union] prisoners not paroled are at the river. River falling.

In other words, a shipment of ammunition in horse or mule-drawn wagons intended for Lee's army was in transit over a distance of some eight miles from Martinsburg to the Potomac River, a trip requiring several hours. If Meade had ordered cavalry to cross the river, this would have been a possible target, and one critical to the outcome of a battle looming at Williamsport.[56]

Also at noon, Slocum notified Meade that his XII Corps had crossed South Mountain to Rohrersville, and the II Corps was still "way back, say 8 or 10 miles." He got "no information of the enemy whatever," he continued, meaning Lee's army was not in that immediate vicinity. He also reporting finding "a good map of the county;" a prized resource for commanders about to go into battle. At the same time, Sykes informed Slocum his V Corps was located north of him at the junction of Rohrersville and Boonsborough Road with Old Sharpsburg Road (about halfway between Rohrersville and Boonsborough). One of Howard's divisions, Sykes continued, was at Boonsboro the previous day. Thus a healthy portion of Meade's army had crossed South Mountain and was closing the gap with Lee's forces.[57]

By 12:30, Col. Thomas Devin, a brigade commander in Buford's cavalry division, alerted Howard that at least a division of enemy infantry was advancing on the Harristown Road. Operating in the vicinity of Funkstown,

55 Davis to Lee, July 9, 1863, OR 27, pt. 3, 986; Cooper to Jones, Jones to Cooper, Jones to Seddon, July 9, 1863, 986, 989, 991; Hill to Seddon, July 9, 1863, 990.

56 Roberts to Davis, ibid., 988.

57 Slocum to Williams, Sykes to Slocum, July 9, 1863, ibid., 616, 618.

Devin may have observed Longstreet's troops. "[A]lso a line [of troops] in plain sight [is] on our right," he continued, "and working to our right front."[58]

At 2:45 p.m., Meade issued a circular summing up the intelligence he had available at that point: "Information received from reconnoitering parties and scouts indicates that the enemy is concentrating in our front to meet our attack." He therefore ordered the infantry commanders to "move up your corps to the immediate vicinity of the corps in your front on the same road." Although these instructions suggested preparation for an assault on Lee's position, Meade gave no indication he recognized a window of opportunity to cut Lee's army off from the river crossings at Williamsport and Falling Waters by swiftly moving forward. In fact, his statement appeared to be a misreading of the intelligence received about the location of Lee's army. Reports from a deserter, a citizen, and scouts all placed Lee's army in the vicinity of Hagerstown, Funkstown, and Boonsboro, which were all to the north and not directly in front of Meade's army. In other words, a sizable gap still existed between Lee's position and the Potomac River. But, at the same time, there may have been poor communication between Halleck and Meade. While Meade had the information from a deserter and his scouts about the location of Lee's army, it is not clear whether Halleck forwarded the message from Kelley that a citizen reported Lee's entire army in the Hagerstown area.[59]

At 3:00 p.m., Halleck sent word, "The evidence that Lee's army will fight north of the Potomac seems reliable." He did not explain what this evidence was, but advised, "In that case you will want all your forces in hand." In effect, this gave Meade a reason to delay a confrontation with Lee until conditions were ideal. Moreover, Halleck offered additional mollifying words that would have certainly distressed Lincoln: "Do not be influenced by any dispatch from here against your own judgment. Regard them as suggestions only. Our information here is not always correct."[60] These mixed signals from Washington only complicated Meade's burden. At the same time Halleck was confusing the issue with the Union army's commander, he was also assembling thousands of reinforcements, sending them on to Meade, and informing him of the gathering of Kelley's troops at Hancock. With the addition of French's

---

58 Devin to Howard, ibid., 617.

59 HQ Army of the Potomac Circular, ibid; Kelley to Townsend, July 9, 1863, 624-25.

60 Halleck to Meade, July 9, 1863, *OR* 27, pt. 1, 88.

division, Meade already had nearly 30,000 more troops than Lee, with Kelley's 4,500 nearby in Maryland and another nearly 22,000 mostly emergency militia within a reasonable distance in Pennsylvania. This numerical advantage, though considerable, was mitigated by several other key factors: Meade's belief that Lee's forces were at least equal to his and his realization that his army was responsible for covering Washington. There were also supply shortages in the army, as well as its exhausting march through the mountains in pursuit of Lee's army. Finally, and, perhaps most importantly, was the fact of Meade's inexperience as army commander; he had been in command since June 28.[61]

July 10: A Flood of Intelligence for Meade

> Up to now, the enemy pursued us as a mule goes on the chase of a grizzly bear—as if catching up with us was the last thing he wanted to do.
>
> Col. E. P. Alexander[62]

> Corps commanders . . . will study with care the ground held by them, and in advance, in order that their reports upon it may convey all the information desired by the major-general commanding.
>
> HQ Army of the Potomac circular[63]

In the early morning hours, after learning from Lt. Thomas L. Norwood, wounded, captured, and escaped at Gettysburg, about "a division" of reinforcements for Meade on their way from Couch's command, Lee acknowledged information Stuart sent from his scouts and spoke with urgent concern: "We must prepare for a vigorous battle, and trust in the mercy of God and the valor of our troops. Get your men in hand, and have everything ready."

---

61 Ibid.; Keith Poulter, "Errors that Doomed a Campaign," *North & South* (August 1999), 2:87. The Army of the Potomac had an engaged strength at Gettysburg of 93,921 less 23,055 casualties equaling 69,866. Plus French's division (less Lockwood's brigade already with the Meade at Gettysburg) of 9,101 for a total of 78,967. For Lockwood's brigade, see OR 27, pt. 3, 444. The engaged figure for the Army of Northern Virginia was 71,699 less 23,231 casualties, equals 48,468. Plus 1,266 cavalry not engaged for a total of 49,734. Busey and Martin, *Strengths and Losses*, 16, 125, 169, 244, 260; French, *Imboden's Brigade*, 10. Using these figures, the Union advantage was 29,233 troops. Coddington places Meade's advantage at about 30,000 troops as of July 10. Coddington, *The Gettysburg Campaign*, 569.

62 Gallagher, *Fighting for the Confederacy*, 270-71.

63 HQ Army of the Potomac Circular, July 10, 1863, OR 27, pt. 3, 627.

Stuart took Lee's words to heart. He dashed off a note to his pregnant wife Flora, at home in Lynchburg, that the army was on "the eve of another battle," and implored her to "Pray without ceasing, that God will grant us the victory." Adding a basis for optimism, he confirmed that Lee's army had just received "a fresh supply of ammunition."[64]

Another glimpse of the expectations in the Rebel camp came from the pen of war correspondent Peter W. Alexander. He sent this astute assessment of the situation to the Savannah *Republican* and in the process perfectly surmised Lincoln's objective:

> The opinion is prevalent [here in camp] that Gen. Meade intends to cross swords with Gen. Lee again. Knowing that there is a freshet in the Potomac that would render escape impossible in the event of a disaster to our arms . . . [Meade] may hope, with the aid of fresh reinforcements . . . by one fell blow to end [Lee]. Whether the trial will come to-morrow or next day, or whether, finding that the river is falling, and Lee prepared to receive him, the Federal commander may not reconsider the matter, remains to be seen. . . . Under such unequal [manpower] conditions [between the two sides], Mr. Lincoln may hope by rapid and repeated blows so far to disable us as to place us at his mercy.[65]

Acutely aware of his vulnerability with the swollen river at his back, Lee labored mightily to get his army safely over the river. He assigned his engineers to designing and constructing a trestle bridge over the Chesapeake and Ohio Canal and a pontoon bridge across the Potomac down river at Falling Waters. The only question was whether this work could be completed in time.[66]

As noted, Lee's army had arrived around Hagerstown during the afternoon of July 6 and morning of July 7. Longstreet's corps remained there until July 10 before moving into a defensive position in front of Williamsport and was within 24 hours securely entrenched. Ewell moved his corps the following day "into line between Hagerstown and Williamsport . . . and began fortifying, and in a short time" they too "were well protected." Hill, less detailed and precise about

---

64 Lee to Stuart, July 10, 1863, ibid., 991; Mitchell, *Stuart's Letters*, 326-27. Lee identified Norwood's unit as the 37th North Carolina.

65 Styple, *Writing & Fighting the Confederate War*, 171; Savannah *Republican*, July 21, 1863.

66 Lee's post-action report, January 1864, OR 27, pt. 2, 323; Alexander, *Military Memoirs*, 439-40; Brown, *Retreat from Gettysburg*, 321.

his situation, simply stated that his corps "lay in line of battle from the 7th to the night of the 13th" at Hagerstown.[67]

Porter Alexander penned a good overall description the situation:

> [T]he engineers selected and fortified a line of battle upon which we would make a last stand. A fairly good line was found with its right flank on the Potomac near Downsville, passing by St. James College and resting its left on the Conococheague [Creek] . . . [and] spent three full & busy days on this work, the enemy not following us nearly as closely as we expected. . . . but, at last, on Friday morning the 10th, the whole of Meade's army drew near.[68]

But the Yankees came up softly. At 10:30 a.m., Warren alerted Col. Ira Spaulding, his chief engineer at Harper's Ferry, "Events are yet to determine where we shall want the bridge across the Potomac, and when." However, he did order 200 feet of bridging to be loaded and held ready for use on the Antietam Creek if required. Again, no explanation why Meade held off sending troops across the river, despite intelligence that the Rebels were busily reconstructing their pontoon bridge.[69]

Notwithstanding the BMI scout's report earlier that Lee's army was situated between Hagerstown and Boonsboro, with abiding caution, Meade issued orders for his army to go forward the following day. If it had advanced immediately, it may have intercepted at least part of the Confederate force moving into entrenchments prepared on a line from Hagerstown south to Downsville. It appears the intelligence that reported Lee's army had not yet moved into the entrenchments had been overlooked or not given sufficient weight.[70]

In early afternoon, Meade informed Halleck "information received today indicates that the enemy occupy positions extending from the Potomac, near Falling Waters, through Downsville to Funkstown, and to the northeast of Hagerstown." He then specified the locations of Lee's three corps: "Ewell's . . .

---

67 Post-action reports: Lee's, January 1864, OR 27, pt. 2, 322; Longstreet's, July 27, 1863, 361; Ewell's, n.d. 1863, 448; Hill's, November 1863, 609.

68 Alexander, *Military Memoirs*, 439; Gallagher, *Fighting for the Confederacy*, 269-71.

69 Warren to Spaulding, Warren to Palmer, July 10, 1863, OR 27, pt. 3, 628.

70 Sharpe to Williams, July 9, 1863, RG 393, NA; HQ Army of the Potomac Circular, July 10, 1863, OR 27, pt. 3, 626-27.

northeast of Hagerstown, Longstreet at Funkstown, and Hill on their right [north of Hagerstown]." Therein, however, lay a puzzling misapprehension, because it should have been obvious that given the locations cited for the three corps clustered around Hagerstown, the Rebels could not be occupying "positions extending from the Potomac, near Falling Waters, through Downsville." So if he moved quickly, Meade could take control of Downsville and the road leading to Falling Waters where Lee's pontoon bridge was under reconstruction.[71]

Meade told Halleck that he was advancing "on a line perpendicular to the line from Hagerstown to Williamsport, and the army will this evening occupy a position extending from the Boonsborough and Hagerstown road, at a point 1 mile beyond Beaver Creek, to Bakersville, near the Potomac." Since Bakersville lay just three miles southeast of Downsville, a quick thrust up the road connecting the two towns could have secured Downsville and ceded control of the critical road leading from Williamsport to Falling Waters to the Union. But Meade dithered: "I shall advance cautiously on the same line to-morrow until I can develop more fully the enemy's force and position, upon which my future operations will depend." If the bulk of Lee's army was six to eight miles northeast of Downsville near Funkstown and Hagerstown, as he had stated, Meade's strategy was far too restrained.[72]

Meanwhile Buford was contending with three Rebel cavalry brigades near Funkstown, and he drove "them back upon Longstreet's whole corps, which occupies the crest beyond the Antietam." He also passed on valuable intelligence: "My information is the whole of Lee's army is in the vicinity of Hagerstown, Jones' Cross-Roads, and extending toward Williamsport. . . . His line will be along the Antietam." He continued, "He has a large force in front of a bridge a mile below Funkstown." Buford said he had sent his staff officers all over the area "examining ground and measuring distances." Devin, too, confirmed that Longstreet's corps held Funkstown.[73]

Colonel William Gamble, one of Buford's brigade commanders, complained that despite his brigade's occupying the heights above Funkstown and keeping the enemy at bay, Major General Sedgwick had refused requests to

---

71 Meade to Halleck, June 10, 1863, *OR* 27, pt. 1, 89.

72 Ibid.

73 Buford to [Pleasonton], July 10, 1863, ibid., 925-26. Devin's post-action report, August 6, 1863, 942.

move units of his VI Corps forward in support. Instead, they "pitched their shelter-tents, and commenced cooking and eating, in spite of repeated and urgent requests to the commanding officer . . . to occupy our excellent position and relieve us." The cavalry's frustration at taking casualties on the front lines was understandable, but Sedgwick was simply following Meade's instructions to the letter to remain in place pending further orders. Certainly no Reynolds or Hancock, Sedgwick was as cautious and conservative as Meade, so his rigid interpretation of his instructions was perfectly in character. Later in the day, when he joined Buford in clearing the Rebels out of Funkstown and opening a path for Meade's army all the way to the Potomac, Sedgwick would advance only so far. A Union officer observed: "Had the Sixth Corps been pushed in on Lee's flank . . . and properly supported, some serious trouble might have been made for the Army of Northern Virginia."[74]

Meanwhile, Brig. Gen. David Gregg, whose cavalry division was based at Boonsboro, ordered Col. Pennock Huey's brigade to operate toward Williamsport in front of V and XII corps. Huey took the Williamsburg Road to Jones' Cross-Roads "where we met the enemy, and, after a severe skirmish, drove him about 1 mile." Gregg sent the 13th Pennsylvania Cavalry along with "Scott's 900" (11th New York Cavalry), two regiments he had received as reinforcements, to Smoketown east of Boonsborough in order to "throw out pickets to Cavetown and Smithsburg." Their mission was to "closely observe the movements of the enemy in that direction, and report anything of interest at once to [Gregg's] headquarters." In addition, a detachment of Kilpatrick's cavalry moved farther south toward Bakersville to reconnoiter that area.[75]

---

74 Gamble's post-action report, August 24, 1863, ibid., 936; Wittenberg, *One Continuous Fight*, 224 (quoted). Kilpatrick credited the signal corps with the Union victory at Funkstown, which "was fought and won by the aid of signals; every move of the enemy was seen by the signal officers occupying an elevated position and quickly transmitted." Wittenberg, *One Continuous Fight*, 214.

75 Post-action reports: Gregg's, August 22, 1863, *OR* 27, pt. 1, 959; Huey's, August 6, 1863, 971; Fuller's, July 28, 1863, 1036; Gregg to Kerwin, July 10, 1863, pt. 3, 627-28. The 13th Pennsylvania Cavalry had been assigned to Milroy's outpost in Winchester before Ewell attacked it in mid-June. The regiment evacuated to Harper's Ferry and then to Frederick with French's division before receiving an assignment to Gregg's brigade at Boonsborough. Samuel Bates, *History of the Pennsylvania Volunteers, 1861-1865*, 5 vols. (Harrisburg, PA, 1870), 3:1267-71. The Department of Washington sent the 11th NY to the Army of the Potomac as reinforcements, and it was assigned to Gregg's division. Thomas West Smith, *The Story of a Cavalry Regiment: "Scott's 900," The Eleventh New York Cavalry* (Chicago, n.d.), 108.

Farther to the north, McIntosh's brigade of Gregg's division, supporting Neill's brigade in close observance of Lee's army, received orders from Baldy Smith, whose division of local troops had joined Neill at Waynesboro, to reconnoiter the area of Smithsburg and Cavetown "to ascertain if any enemy was in that locality." Having located the enemy, McIntosh withdrew to Waynesboro to report his findings. According to Neill, this action took place "between 3 and 4 miles from Hagerstown, on the north side." Finding no enemy there, McIntosh stumbled over more evidence that the Confederates were still in the Hagerstown area. He

> retraced [his] steps toward Leitersburg, and three miles to the west of it, and about a mile from Antietam Creek, met the enemy's cavalry, which I drove across that stream, and which I found strongly guarded with cavalry, infantry, and artillery.

In addition, the signal officer attached to Neill's brigade observed the enemy from Franklin's Cliff on South Mountain near Leitersburg and "discovered the numbers and position of the enemy in and around Hagerstown." He sent the information to Neill and also to Meade by courier. Neill sent couriers to Meade on a daily basis updating him on the enemy's position.[76]

From Meade's headquarters near Beaver Creek crossing, west of Boonsborough, the signal corps opened communication via the station on Washington Monument with the signal party established at each of the corps' headquarters: II and XII near Bakersville, III and V near Antietam Bridge, and I and VI near Beaver Creek crossing. Apparently communication with the XI Corps was direct.[77]

At 6:00 p.m., the signal officer at Boonsboro, Capt. C. F. Stone, sent a message "By order of Major-General French" to Meade: "I have been informed by the citizens that it is reported a large amount of ammunition is expected by the rebs to-day from Richmond." A half hour later, Sharpe confirmed the ammunition shipment when he informed Williams that the BMI scout Browning, just back from Downsville near the Potomac, learned from

---

76 Post-action reports: Neill's, July 17, 1863, *OR* 27, pt. 1, 679; McIntosh's, August 20, 1863, 968; Norton's, September 18, 1863, 204; Neill's post-action report, July 13, 1863, *OR* 51, pt. 1, 196-97.

77 Norton's post-action report, September 18, 1863, *OR* 27, pt. 1, 203-04.

Smithsburg: McIntosh's cavalry brigade received orders to reconnoiter
this area "to ascertain if any enemy was in that locality."
Photo by the author

informants that sick and wounded were crossing the river by flat boat, with ammunition coming back on the return trip. This report coincided with the one from Martinsburg to Davis the previous day that an ammunition train had passed through that town toward the Potomac. There is no record of Meade's reaction to this news, despite earlier indications he planned to send cavalry across the river. Knowledge of an ammunition train's arrival on the south side of the Potomac should have motivated him to take some action to capture or destroy it.[78]

Sharpe also reported that scout Browning placed the enemy's line as extending from Downsville at least to Hagerstown. Jenkins' brigade with Ferguson in charge had about 2,000 cavalry at Dam No. 4 on the Chesapeake and Ohio Canal two-and-a-half miles above Mercersville, and batteries positioned to the east of Downsville. The scout also reported that a pontoon

---

78 Stone to Meade, July 10, 1863, ibid., 219; Sharpe to Williams, July 10, 1863, RG 393, NA.

bridge was at Williamsport, and enemy forces in position on the other side of Conocoheague Creek.[79]

"The water has fallen about a foot in the Potomac," Sharpe added, "but must fall three feet more before it is fordable. Informant learned that Lee's intention was to cover his retreat toward Hancock." This information, which Sharpe highlighted, clearly reflected Lee's contingency plan to cross at fords upriver as far as Cumberland, if he were forced to abandon the Williamsport area. The intelligence he was receiving helped clarify the picture Meade was developing of Lee's positions, and his plans for the continued withdrawal of his army. It was a continually shifting picture. Lee's forces changed their deployment late into the night when Longstreet shifted his corps to the south on the right flank, and Hill took the center position opposite Funkstown. Ewell remained on the left near Hagerstown.[80]

At 9:00 p.m., Halleck responded to Meade's early afternoon status report saying he would advance cautiously the next day "to develop more fully the enemy's force and position." Although Lincoln deferred to Halleck's judgment on military matters, he hardly would have concurred when Halleck reinforced Meade's caution by advising him "to postpone a general battle till you can concentrate all your forces and get up your reserves and reinforcements." As if to underscore the point, Halleck added, "Beware of partial combats." There is evidence that Lincoln, fretful about Meade's commitment to attacking Lee and fearing the inevitable after seeing Halleck's equivocating correspondence with the army's commander, sent an order to Meade by special messenger exhorting him to "attack Lee as soon as possible before he can cross the river."[81]

---

79 Sharpe to Williams, see note above.

80 Sharpe to Williams, July 10, 1863, RG 393, NA; Kent Masterson Brown, "A Golden Bridge: Lee's Williamsport Defense Lines and His Escape Across the Potomac," *North & South* (August 1999), 2:59, 61. Imboden, who was intimately knowledgeable with these fords, briefed Lee in detail about them on July 9. For a discussion of Lee's contingency escape plan, see Imboden, "The Confederate Retreat From Gettysburg," in *B&L*, 3:428-29.

81 Halleck to Meade, July 10, 1863, OR 27, pt. 1, 89; Stephen E. Ambrose, *Halleck: Lincoln's Chief of Staff* (Baton Rouge, LA, 1962), 142. For Lincoln's message to Meade, see Gabor S. Boritt, "'Unfinished Work': Lincoln, Meade, and Gettysburg" in Gabor S. Boritt, ed., *Lincoln's Generals* (New York, 1994), 98-101.

July 11: BMI Reports on Lee's Ammunition and Pontoons

[O]n the night of July 11, [t]he troops were not in position: we had got no very definite information of the enemy, and we had not heard of the [Union] columns on our right.

Maj. Gen. Gouverneur K. Warren[82]

Early in the morning, Sharpe alerted Meade that his scout James Greenwood had arrived during the night from Sharpsburg and corroborated earlier reports "that the enemy's ammunition train was expected to reach the river last night." Greenwood obtained this information from a Rebel soldier who was visiting his home in Shepherdstown the day before. In addition, the scout reported "a pontoon train was on its way between Winchester & Martinsburg yesterday morning." In fact, Lee's engineers got work underway at dawn reconstructing the pontoon bridge Union cavalry had damaged at Falling Waters. Construction would be quickened, because a number of pontoons strewn along the riverbank downstream had been recovered. Greenwood's information, Sharpe observed "agrees that the enemy has crossed nothing except wounded." While generally correct about the Confederates at Williamsport, Sharpe's report showed him unaware that Union prisoners had been ferried across the river and were being held on the West Virginia shore pending movement to Staunton, Virginia.[83]

Meanwhile, Kelley moved from Hancock to Indian Springs on the west base of North Mountain within about 12 miles of Williamsport. His cavalry scouts had skirmished with the enemy's cavalry near Clear Spring the previous day—likely Colonel Imboden's cavalry protecting Lee's flank in that direction. Kelley was "blockading with fallen timber all the roads between the turnpike and the river, so as to prevent any detachments [of Lee's army] making their escape to fords above." He planned to move his units across the mountain to the east side. Despite reports of the pontoon and ammunition trains arriving in support of Lee, neither Halleck nor Meade urged Kelley to cross south of the Potomac with his 4,500 troops, and destroy the supply trains headed for Williamsport and Falling Waters. Meade's chances of success in his planned

82 Hyde, *The Union Generals Speak*, 173.

83 Sharpe to Williams, July 11, 1863, RG 393, NA; Brown, *Retreat from Gettysburg*, 321; Alexander, *Military Memoirs of a Confederate*, 439; Coco, *A Strange and Blighted Land*, 300.

attack on Lee would be enhanced considerably if the Rebels ammunition supply could be interrupted.[84]

Having advanced cautiously that morning, by 4:00 p.m. the Army of the Potomac reached Antietam Creek with its right on the Smoketown to Funkstown Road about two miles from the latter town. From there the line crossed the Antietam passing south through Jones Cross-Roads, to the left flank near Marsh Run—roughly a distance of five miles running slightly northeast to southwest. Meade informed Halleck, "Everything indicates that the enemy is massing between Hagerstown and Williamsport, and from various sources it is stated they are intrenching." He let Halleck know he sent a strong infantry force on reconnaissance toward Funkstown on both sides of the Antietam, and sent cavalry out on the left on the Boonsborough and Williamsport Road and to the right toward Hagerstown from Chewsville some three miles to the west and Leitersburg about six miles to the north. Still in the information gathering mode, Meade had yet to exhibit a disposition toward offensive action.[85]

Command Pressures Generate Anxiety

That evening Lee still awaited the river level to drop, while at the same time anticipating that Meade would attack. He directed Stuart to keep sufficient cavalry in front of the defensive positions running approximately from Hagerstown south to Downsville, at least until they were driven back upon the infantry. At that point, Stuart was to take a position on the left. An uncharacteristically antsy Lee had lost some of his ardor for another confrontation with Meade. Porter Alexander commented, "I never before, and never afterward, saw him as I thought visibly anxious over an approaching action; but I did on this occasion." Lee's personal attention to the placement of his troops into entrenched positions reflected his concern. As he later acknowledged, he was pleasantly surprised that enemy forces arrived belatedly while "manifesting no disposition to attack."[86]

---

84 Kelley to Townsend, July 11, 1863, *OR* 27, pt. 3, 652.

85 Meade to Halleck, ibid., pt. 1, 90-91.

86 Lee's post-action report, January 1864, *OR* 27, pt. 2, 323; Alexander, *Military Memoirs*, 439.

Meade was also cumulatively assessing the current situation. He believed another battle would take place before Lee could cross the river, and his preference was to fight in Maryland rather than pursue Lee back to Virginia. He, too, was anxious, as an update letter to his wife the previous day revealed:

> Lee has not crossed and does not intend to cross the river, and I expect in a few days, if not sooner, again to hazard the fortune of war. I know so well that this is a fortune and that accidents, etc., turn the tide of victory, that, until the question is settled, I cannot but be very anxious.

Moreover, he considered himself misjudged and beleaguered in recent exchanges with Washington about the pace of his pursuit of Lee's army:

> I also see that my success at Gettysburg has deluded the people and the Government with the idea that I must always be victorious, that Lee is demoralized and disorganized, etc., and other delusions which will not only be dissipated by any reverse that I should meet with, but would react in proportion against me.

Having described the situation on a decidedly personal level, he ironically concluded, "I make but little account of myself, and think only of the country." The state of the army commander's psyche did not bode well for coherent and assertive decision making in planning an attack on the enemy to his immediate front.[87]

Meade also had to contend with his troops' state of mind in the wake of his congratulatory message following the victory at Gettysburg urging them "to drive out from our soil every vestige of the presence of the invader," rather than "the literal or substantial destruction of Lee's army" that Lincoln urged. Brigadier General John Geary, a division commander, believed, "Our prospects to drive out [of our territory] speedily the rebels is very good." Now Meade had to convince his army and its leaders that the real mission was to confront Lee and defeat him. Not everyone needed convincing. Warren, who distinguished himself on July 2 at Gettysburg, observed that "The enemy is cornered, and we shall have another battle." XI Corps commander Howard echoed Warren's

---

87 Meade to his wife, July 8 & 10, 1863, in Meade, *Life and Letters*, 2:132-34.

thoughts, "We are near the enemy. Lee has not yet crossed the Potomac and we must have one more trial."[88]

Lee, however, was not anxious to fight. The critical question for him was could he escape with his army essentially intact in order to fight another day, or be forced to withstand an attack from a force he correctly understood to be much superior in strength to his own. So far he had reason to be hopeful, because the enemy displayed little eagerness to confront him again. If Meade delayed one or two more days, the Falling Waters bridge would be repaired, perhaps allowing Lee's army to slip away into the night.

On the other hand, Meade had received reports about the arrival of ammunition trains and bridge-building pontoons on the south side of the river, and that Lee had deployed a force to the north to secure an alternate escape route to the upper fords. He was also aware of thousands of Union prisoners in Lee's hands facing incarceration in toxic Confederate prisons, if they survived the long march south.

Meade's engineers had bridging materials available at Harper's Ferry for crossing troops over the river when Meade gave the word. A host of potential objectives beckoned on the south side of the Potomac, including capture of ammunition supply trains, destruction of the pontoon bridge under reconstruction, and liberating the hapless prisoners, not to mention simply sowing fear and confusion in the enemy's rear. Meade's task, an increasingly burdensome one to him, was to set priorities and implement a strategy to accomplish them.

---

88 HQ Army of the Potomac, General Orders, No. 68, July 4, 1863, *OR* 27, pt. 3, 519; Lincoln to Halleck, [July 7, 1863], pt. 1, 88; Geary to his wife, July 4, 1863, William Allen Blair, ed., *A Politician Goes to War: The Civil War Letters of John White Geary* (University Park, PA, 1995), 98; Warren to "Emily," July 9, 1863, quoted in Emerson Gifford Taylor, *Gouverneur Kemble Warren: The Life and Letters of An American Soldier, 1830-1882* (Boston, 1932), 133; Howard, *Autobiography*, 1:444.

Chapter Seventeen

The Controversial Escape: July 12 to 14

As long as General Meade remains in command, he will receive the cordial support of the Department, but since the world began no man ever missed so great an opportunity of serving his country as was lost by his neglecting to strike his adversary [at Williamsport].

Secretary of War Edwin M. Stanton[1]

If ... any successful commander was ever justified in disregarding ... Bonaparte's [maxim about pursuing a defeated army], General Meade was that commander; for a considerable portion of Lee's army ... was still in excellent fighting trim, and ... would have responded with alacrity to Lee's call to ... deliver battle.

Maj. Gen. John B. Gordon[2]

July 12: Rebel Positions Located and Observed

[T]he army moved through South Mountain, and by July 12 was in front of the enemy.
Maj. Gen. George G. Meade[3]

[A]n attack was awaited during that ... day [July 12]. This did not take place, though the two armies were in close proximity, the enemy being occupied in fortifying his own lines.

Gen. Robert E. Lee[4]

---

1   Benjamin P. Thomas and Harold M. Hyman, *Stanton: The Life and Times of Lincoln's Secretary of War* (New York, 1962), 275.

2   John B. Gordon, *Reminiscences of the Civil War* (New York, 1903), 159.

3   Meade's post-action report, August 4, 1863, *OR* 27, pt. 1, 118.

4   Lee's post-action report, July 31, 1863, ibid., pt. 2, 309.

At 6:30 a.m., Howard of XI Corps notified Meade that his reconnaissance that morning of the northern end of the Confederate position had gone within two miles of Hagerstown with no enemy in sight, and no firing heard at Funkstown. However, Howard reported that pickets had heard artillery moving southwesterly from these two areas during the night, indicating that Lee was moving his troops into the prepared trenches to the south. At 7 a.m., Buford informed Pleasonton that down at the southern end he had located the enemy "line" on a height "this side of Downsville" extending south to the Potomac River about a mile and three quarters to the southwest. Buford had "pushed pickets to within 800 yards of the enemy's entrenchments at Downsville," where, he reported, one of Longstreet's divisions was further "intrenching themselves." He added the unwelcome news that Lee's position occupied "a very rugged country, with many stone walls parallel to their front;" the area near the river, he judged, "is impracticable for any considerable force to advance." Buford also reported that although the fog hampered visibility, there "seems to be but a few [enemy] cavalrymen between [Bakersville] and Downsville," some three miles to the northeast.[5]

Abner Hard, 8th Illinois Cavalry, described the conditions at Bakersville:

Sunday, the 12th, was one of the warmest days of the season, and . . . there came up one of the hardest rain-storms I ever witnessed. In five minutes the water came down the hills . . . and stood over a foot deep in camp. . . . Little fighting was done, and only two prisoners brought in, though the pickets exchanged shots, and kept the camp alarmed.[6]

After maneuvering between Hagerstown and Williamsport to screen the Rebel infantry's movements, Fitz Lee's cavalry brigade returned to Downsville. Once Lee's army occupied the fortifications their engineers had designed and constructed, Stuart ordered Fitz Lee to move his brigade north to the Hagerstown area to be in position in the event the army could cross the river the following day. The brigade spent a miserable night holding the reins of their

---

5 Howard to Humphreys, Buford to Pleasonton, July 12, 1863, ibid., 656-57; Buford's post-action report, pt. 1, 929. For the map dated October 1, 1863, that accompanied Meade's report, see *OR Atlas*, Plate 42-5.

6 Hard, *8th Illinois Cavalry*, 264.

horses while rain poured down. Meanwhile, the First Maryland Cavalry remained on picket almost as far north as Greencastle.[7]

Also at 7 a.m., signal officer Capt. Nahum Daniels, from his station near Funkstown, alerted Meade that "the enemy is intrenching himself on the crest of a hill one-half mile east of Funkstown, and has batteries, supported by infantry, on the hills north of Funkstown." Daniels was probably observing Johnson's or Lane's divisions of Ewell's corps. Ewell's topographical engineer, Jed Hotchkiss, noted in his diary, "Our line was very well fortified this morning."[8]

At around the same time, Brig. Gen. Horatio G. Wright's division of VI Corps took control of the heights beyond Funkstown with little opposition from Lee's troops. Wright deployed skirmishers "well out toward Hagerstown." Chief of staff Humphreys characterized Wright's movement as "a strong reconnaissance . . . being made on Hagerstown."[9]

Early in the day, Union cavalry took possession of Hagerstown, and the signal corps moved in to establish stations in different parts of the town by mid-morning. The Union cavalry drove Chambliss' and Robertson's cavalry brigades, which were screening Ewell's infantry, out of town and captured prisoners, but they could proceed no further immediately. Rebel resistance stiffened outside of town. Sergeant James H. Avery, 5th Michigan Cavalry, described some of the action at Hagerstown:

> [W]e advanced . . . on the rebel lines at Hagerstown . . . made a dash, driving them back toward the city, when we mounted and charged the town, driving them out, and beyond. We . . . moved . . . in advance of the Williamsport Pike . . . just out of town . . . when the rebels rose in heavy force, from behind a stone wall . . . and gave us a volley. . . . Returning the fire, and finding them too strong, we returned and halted for the night.

Kilpatrick then ordered Custer to send a regiment to clear out the Rebels behind the stone wall, but Custer hesitated because a battery and cavalry were pummeling his men. Kilpatrick then turned to his headquarters guard, the 1st

---

7   Stiles, *4th Virginia Cavalry*, 34; Driver, *1st Virginia Cavalry*, 68; Driver, *First & Second Maryland Cavalry*, 62.

8   McDonald, *Make Me a Map of the Valley*, 60. Bill Cameron, "The Signal Corps at Gettysburg Part II: Support of Meade's Pursuit," *Gettysburg Magazine* (January 1991), Issue 4, 108.

9   Humpreys to Couch; Sedgwick to Howard, July 12, 1863, OR 27, pt. 3, 657.

Ohio Cavalry, who used their pistols to engage the enemy near the stone wall and captured a company of 26 men. A 1st Ohio historian later wrote that this was "the second time we had charged where Custer and his Michigan men refused to go."[10]

Custer then placed his cavalry about a mile and a half south of Hagerstown where he could observe nearby enemy lines and reconnoiter the Falling Waters area where Lee had a pontoon bridge under reconstruction. Farther south and closer to the river, a member of Devin's brigade swam his horse across and also got a look at the bridge building activity at Falling Waters. Farther up river he spotted wagons, artillery, and limbers crossing by flatboats in the vicinity of Williamsport. He reported his findings to Devin, who undoubtedly passed the results of this daring reconnaissance to army headquarters. With an eyewitness account of the pontoon bridge still under construction in hand, Meade should have been motivated to dispatch forces across the river to destroy it. But he did not. And his lack of aggressiveness did not go unnoticed in the ranks: "The boys wonder why Meade has not attacked Lee."[11]

The Federals had a good fix on where their enemy was. Howard alerted Meade that "Stuart, with his cavalry and some infantry, is reported massed on the other side of [Hagerstown]" and that the enemy "has thrown up earthworks about 1½ miles southwest of [Hagerstown]; has got infantry there . . . [and] appears to be in considerable force." Signal officer Capt. William Nicodemus later confirmed enemy entrenchments "west and southwest of Hagerstown."[12]

From a signal station near Hagerstown, Lt. Julius M. Swain reported that he made a reconnaissance "circuit" within sight of the enemy's left and placed his signal party in a hollow and watched the enemy over the hill in front. "Their left is advancing slowly but surely," he reported, "and now occupies ground which I left within half an hour. . . . From what I can see I think the rebels are in considerable force over the crest of the hill. We can see them there with the naked eye." Swain sent word of his observations to Capt. David Oliphant of the 5th Michigan Cavalry that was serving as the outer vedettes. He explained that

10 Avery, *Under Custer's Command,* 41-43; Gillespie, *Company A, First Ohio Cavalry,* 164.

11 Longacre, *Custer and His Wolverines,* 162; Wittenberg, *One Continuous Fight,* 254 (quoted); Brown, *Retreat From Gettysburg,* 316.

12 Howard to Humphreys & Howard to Meade, July 12, 1863, OR 27, pt. 3, 658; Nicodemus's post-action report, July 21, 1863, pt. 1, 207; Brown, *The Signal Corps,* 375.

he could send this message without fear of enemy observation, because "My flag is behind the hill, though in plain sight of you."[13]

Once Stuart withdrew his brigades from Hagerstown, he "massed on the left of the main body [of infantry]" and established a line of "heavy outposts" out the National Road (present day Route 40) to the Conococheague Creek—a distance of five and a half miles—in accordance with Lee's orders. Stuart's mission was to protect the northern or left flank of the army, a formidable task given the length of the line and the weakened condition of his men and horses after continuous engagement with the enemy since leaving Gettysburg some eight days ago. Jenkins' brigade received orders to move to the left between Hagerstown and Williamsport, Chambliss' brigade took a position blocking the Greencastle Road coming in from northwest of Hagerstown, and Jones' brigade was positioned to operate between the Cavetown and Funkstown Roads.[14]

A little after 9:00 a.m. from Bakersville, Buford confirmed for Pleasonton the significant information that the river remained unfordable and the enemy was not crossing. Only sick and wounded were being sent over via a flat-boat attached to a wire rope. At 10 a.m., Huey received orders to move out from Jones' Cross-Roads into the Williamsport Road to reconnoiter the area.[15]

Meade learned from a number of sources that Hill's Corps had moved from Hagerstown towards Downsville the previous afternoon. Acting upon this latest data about the position of enemy forces, Meade redeployed his army forward along a line roughly paralleling the Hagerstown-Downsville Road, within one-half mile to a mile at different points of the enemy's fortifications.[16]

In response to Meade's request for a reconnaissance of his current vicinity, Slocum reported that a "Virginia refugee" had provided information that Longstreet's force occupied a line from Dam No. 4 on the Potomac to Downsville, and Ewell's troops from that point up to the heights toward Saint

---

13 Swain to Nicodemus, July 12, 1863, *OR* 27, pt. 1, 219; Cameron, "In Support of Meade's Pursuit," 108.

14 Stuart's post-action report, August 20, 1863, *OR* 27, pt. 2, 704-05; Jack L. Dickinson, *16th Virginia Cavalry* (Lynchburg, VA, 1989), 31; Norton, *Eighth New York Cavalry*, 181; *OR Atlas*, Plate 42. For the cavalry battles from July 4 to July 12, see Wittenberg, Petruzzi, and Nugent, *One Continuous Fight*, 249-62.

15 Buford to Pleasonton, July 12, 1863, *OR* 27, pt. 3, 657-58; Buford's post-action report, August 27, 1863, pt. 1, 929; *OR Atlas*, Plate 42.

16 Humphreys to Sykes, et al., July 12, 1863, *OR* 27, pt. 3, 658-59; *OR Atlas*, Plate 42.

Kemp Hall at St. James College. Lee's defensive positions near Williamsport ran
north and south immediately in front of the college grounds.
Photo by the author

James College. However, this informant was uncertain whether all of
Longstreet's corps was there, but he estimated the number to be about 7,000.
(If Longstreet's entire corps was in place as indicated, it would have numbered
just under 13,300.) Anchoring the left of the Union army, Slocum assured
Meade that his current position was strong, stronger than the previous one, and
if he were reinforced he thought he could hold it.[17]

Given the changing positions of the army, Chief Signal Officer Norton
arranged for signal telegraph wire to be extended from Meade's headquarters to
Sedgwick's new VI Corps headquarters at Funkstown and some two and a half
miles to Slocum's XII Corps headquarters near Four Corners. Both V and XI
corps communicated with Meade by flag signals. In addition to flag and wire
communications between army and corps headquarters, the signalmen
continued to maintain observation stations at strategic locations such as
Maryland Heights, Crampton's Pass, Fairview, and Washington Monument,
and they would open a new station on Elk Mountain. Thick fog and an

17 Humphreys to Slocum, Slocum to Humphreys, July 12, 1863, *OR* 27, pt. 3, 659-60; Busey
and Martin, *Strengths and Losses*, 260.

excessively smoky atmosphere hampered signal flag communications all day, so communication from Black Rock on South Mountain proved impossible.[18]

Army headquarters continued to receive excellent intelligence. Howard informed Meade about what he had learned from local Union sympathizers:

> The best news . . . is that the enemy has taken position, his right resting on the Potomac, near Williamsport, his left within 1½ miles from [Hagers]town, Longstreet commanding the right, Hill the center, Ewell the left, Stuart's cavalry covering the flank. All agree that no ammunition has been received by the rebels, and the way they received our attack [today] shows that they are saving their powder.

This critical information, along with what had been learned earlier about the pontoon bridge still under reconstruction at Falling Waters, constituted prima facie evidence that a Federal sortie across the river would reap dividends by disrupting or destroying the ammunition shipment and the bridge that would allow Lee's army to escape. It became increasingly apparent, however, that Meade had taken this option off the table. Beyond the initial indication from Warren on July 7, no evidence indicates that the army's high command was even considering sending a force across the river. This raises the possibility Meade would have been equally, if not more content to see Lee and his army hightail it back to Virginia, as he had indicated in his message to the troops following the battle.[19]

At 10:20 a.m., Meade, displaying his utter confidence in his engineer chief's judgment, informed his corps commanders that he had directed Warren to "examine the position of the enemy." In accordance with this inspection, the corps commanders were to be prepared to "conform the disposition of their troops to such changes in the line as General Warren may deem necessary."[20]

All along the line, Union movements in response to Warren's reconnaissance occasioned clashes with the Rebels. Brigadier General Adelbert

---

18   Post-action reports: Norton's, September 18, 1863, OR 27, pt. 1, 204; Fisher's, July 18, 1863, 214; Briggs's, July 19, 1863, 216; Cameron, "In Support of Meade's Pursuit," 108. Artist Edwin Forbes of *Frank Leslie's Illustrated Newspaper* who was traveling with the Union army captured an image of a Union signal station in a house along Marsh Run overlooking the Confederate defense line east of Williamsport. Brown, *Retreat from Gettysburg*, 318; Starr, *Bohemian Brigade*, 210.

19   Howard to Meade, July 12, 1863, OR 27, pt. 3, 661; Warren to Benham, July 7, 1863, 585-86.

20   HQ Army of the Potomac Circular, July 12, 1863, ibid., 669.

Ames' First Division of XI Corps moved into Hagerstown in support of Kilpatrick's cavalry and captured about 100 prisoners. At 10:30 a.m., Howard reported:

> The enemy had two pieces of artillery near [Hagerstown], which they withdrew after firing a few shots. They have a battery of 20-pounder Parrotts in position on the Williamsport road, about 1½ miles from town, which fired a few shots. The battery is supported by infantry, and the road is lined with skirmishers.

At 11:00 a.m., the remainder of the XI Corps marched through Funkstown, crossed Antietam Creek, and took position on the right of the I Corps, about a mile south of Hagerstown. Geary informed Meade his division of the XII Corps was engaged in skirmishing, and had captured 110 prisoners.[21]

As to the Rebel position at Saint James College, Huey reported a large force with a strong line of skirmishers in his front. After driving them from their first position, he discovered a long line of rifle-pits just back of the college. Some of the enemy, he said, had taken refuge in the college buildings, and he found that with his extended line he could go no further without infantry support. Huey's position was only about 150 yards from "the first line of the enemy breastworks, which they were busily engaged in extending." Rather than being told to hold that line and prepare to assault the enemy, Huey received orders "to retire," so he led his brigade back to Jones' Cross-Roads. Longstreet acknowledged how close the enemy had approached his lines: their "sharpshooters came up the Boonsborough road, and to within long range of our picket line."[22]

At noon, Ranald S. MacKenzie, a lieutenant of engineers at Sandy Hook, Maryland, notified Warren that the Potomac has fallen 18 inches in the last twenty-four hours. This report countered what Buford had said three hours earlier, and other observers seemed to agree. A citizen familiar with the river, MacKenzie said "judges . . . that the fords near Shepherdstown and

---

21 Howard's post-action report, September 9, 1863, OR 27, pt. 1, 709; Howard to Meade, July 12, 1863, pt. 3, 661-62; Elliott W. Hoffman (ed.), *A Vermont Cavalryman in War and Love: The Civil War Letters of Brevet Major General William Wells and Anna Richardson* (Lynchburg, VA, 2007), 186; Howard's post-action report, September 9, 1863, OR 27, pt. 3, 662; pt. 1, 709; Geary to Meade, July 12, 1863, pt. 3, 663.

22 Huey to Pleasonton, July 12, 1863, ibid., 660; Huey's post-action report, August 6, 1863, pt. 1, 971; Longstreet's post-action report, July 27, 1863, pt. 2, 361.

Top: Fields in front of St. James College where rifle pits were part of Lee's defensive line.

Bottom: Jones' Crossroads where Buford and Kilpatrick met on the night of July 6 after being repulsed by Imboden at Williamsport.

Photos by the author

Williamsport are now practicable for infantry [to cross]." If it were possible for infantry to cross, cavalry apparently had no problem at all since Jones' 7th Virginia left the Hagerstown area and crossed the river at Williamsport. News about falling waters in the Potomac should have been a red flag at army headquarters that any successful attack to prevent Lee's army from escaping across the river had to been launched quickly.[23]

Couch, now in Chambersburg, alerted Meade at 12:30 p.m. that "rebels crossed a good many horses yesterday at Williamsport, swimming the river, and that fourteen [flatboats] were nearly completed yesterday." Obviously the Confederates were demonstrating greater capacity to cross the river. Couch said his Second Division, about 7,000 mainly Pennsylvania militia and New York National Guard units, would be joining Meade's army "as soon as my provisions are up." Couch also related that he could not "find out that any large force of the enemy is at Fairview [Maryland]," located some eight miles south of Greencastle just below the Pennsylvania border. Meade, anxious to receive Couch's reinforcements, quickly replied that his troops could use the now-open road to Hagerstown to come up. Meanwhile, the 6th Pennsylvania Cavalry of Merritt's brigade, having crossed South Mountain in the heavy rainstorm, moved from Middletown to Boonsboro and bivouacked in front of the town.[24]

There was little doubt that the Rebels were preparing well to thwart any Union attack. At 2 p.m., signal officer James Hall confirmed earlier information that the enemy occupied and were entrenching on the heights behind Saint James College. They were visible for at least a mile on the crest of a hill.[25]

Meade: Speaking Offensively; Acting Defensively

PMG Patrick noted in his diary the intense heat that day until 2:00 or 3:00 in the afternoon, when a heavy, soaking rain began. He also reflected the Union camp's mounting frustration with inaction. It was, he wrote, "A most painful day. Nothing going on—not any movement of Troops. Our Troops simply watching the enemy." Word circulating about the enemy's efforts to escape across the swollen Potomac only fueled the frustration. A member of the 2nd U.S. Sharpshooters recorded in his diary: "We have all kinds of reports as

23 Mackenzie to Warren, July 12, 1863, ibid., pt. 3, 669; Armstrong, *7th Virginia Cavalry*, 58.

24 Couch to Warren & Meade to Couch, July 12, 1863, OR 27, pt. 3, 663-64. Although no record can be found of the Second Division's strength, it was probably similar in size to 7,159-man First Division. Department of the Susquehanna return, July 10, 1863, OR 27, pt. 3, 643; Gracey, *Sixth Pennsylvania Cavalry*, 192.

25 Hall to Meade, July 12, 1863, OR 27, pt. 3, 664.

regards the enemy's means of crossing the Potomac," including their efforts to "construct bridges, etc."[26]

Meanwhile, in Washington, Heintzelman wrote in his journal that: "We have reports of [Confederate] General Beauregard's being at Culpeper in force. We don't believe it." This rumor undoubtedly stemmed from Lee's disinformation efforts designed to discombobulate the authorities in Washington.[27]

Meade sought III Corps commander French's opinion about how to obtain information about the enemy, an indication he lacked confidence in the intelligence he was receiving. "Good topographical maps, spies, prisoners, deserters, well-affected citizens, reconnoitering parties, and preparatory attacks," French replied—"these are the means absolutely within our power." One of two possibilities loomed, French thought. Either Lee had hunkered down in a position to await the Union attack, or we will "stumble on him" in our present advance. In either case, he ventured:

> Whichever has the advantage of a previous study of the configuration of the country, water-courses, roads, bridges, extension of roads, etc., with the best order for marching, and the best routes of direction, will have so far the advantage. Should your attack be unexpected by Lee, I do not fear the result.

While French offered sound advice about intelligence gathering and cited two logical scenarios that could happen, his last statement must not have encouraged Meade. It was inconceivable that Lee would not be expecting an attack.[28]

At 3:15 p.m., Meade ordered his corps commanders to advance their line of pickets until they encountered the enemy's pickets. He also wanted the commanders "to report the character of the country in front." Displaying his wariness in approaching Lee and his army, Meade issued a circular to his corps commanders that reflected his defensive state of mind:

> Intelligence having been received which satisfies the commanding general that the enemy are taking position behind Marsh Run, extending from Downsville to the

---

26 Sparks, *Inside Lincoln's Army*, 27; Wittenberg, *One Continuous Fight*, 249 (quoted).

27 Heintzelman's post-action report, n.d., *OR* Supplement, pt. 1, 5:41.

28 French to Meade, July 12, 1863, ibid., pt. 3, 668.

vicinity of Hagerstown, he directs that corps commanders will move their commands with the utmost celerity into the positions heretofore designated, and be prepared to *meet an attack from the enemy* [emphasis added].[29]

As a result of his operational maneuvering and reconnaissance of the enemy's positions, Meade sent a situation report to Halleck in Washington at 4:30 p.m. Lee's forces had abandoned both Funkstown and Hagerstown, he said, and his own line now extended from Hagerstown south to Fair Play. Eight and a half miles separated Hagerstown and Fair Play, but according to the map accompanying Meade's report, the Union lines began about a mile south of Hagerstown and ended almost a mile north of Fair Play, about five and a half miles. Meade provided details about the enemy's positions, and said they were entrenching and had established batteries on high ground. Nonetheless, Meade averred, "It is my intention to attack them to-morrow," but he carefully added "unless something intervenes to prevent it." As in his earlier assertions of offensive intentions, Meade left himself a loophole.[30]

Before assuming sole responsibility of army command, Meade had been aggressive about taking the offensive against Lee's army. He criticized his former commanders who he believed unwilling to encounter risks in warfare. Quoting Shakespeare's Macbeth, he counseled speedy action: "if it were done, then 'twere well it were done quickly." However, his "fire-eater" mentality, as he labeled it, morphed into a cautious wait-and-see attitude now that he bore singular responsibility for the fate of the army.[31]

While Meade kept the authorities in Washington apprised of the situation on the Potomac, the Confederate high command in Richmond, out of direct communication with Lee, had only speculation and wishful thinking to rely on. Word of Lee's defeat and withdrawal from Gettysburg had not yet reached the capital. War department clerk John B. Jones noted rumors that "Lee's account of the battle of Gettysburg will be published to-morrow, showing that it was the 'most brilliant and successful battle of the war.'" At least that was the hope, especially if Lee reported it.[32]

---

29 HQ Army of the Potomac Circular, July 12, 1863, ibid., 669-70. Only the southern half of Lee's fortifications was behind Marsh Run. OR *Atlas*, Plate 42.

30 Meade to Halleck, *OR* 27, pt. 1, 91; *OR Atlas*, Plate 42.

31 Meade, *Life and Letters*, 1:344-45, 49.

32 Jones, *A Rebel War Clerk's Diary*, 1:377.

Despite Meade's belief the two armies were equal in strength, Lee realized the danger he faced being greatly outnumbered with enemy reinforcements continuing to arrive. Given his desperate situation, Lee directed Maj. Gen. Sam Jones in Dublin, Virginia, to gather up "men . . . improperly absent from this army, who may be arrested, together with all convalescents and other soldiers en route to join the army, to be organized into parties under charge of such officers and with such arms as are available, and sent on to Williamsport." So while Meade was accruing entire units, Lee was scraping the bottom of the barrel for help. Moreover, he wasn't even aware that a response to his earlier appeal to Davis for assistance from forces in southern Virginia and North Carolina, intercepted by Union cavalry, would never arrive.[33]

By 5:00 p.m., Meade's entire army had crossed Antietam Creek and stood "in front of the enemy" in position along the Sharpsburg-Hagerstown Pike. Hunt had orders to move the artillery reserve to a suitable location in the vicinity of Jones' Cross-Roads, about a mile to the east behind Union lines. The Union line ran roughly five miles directly facing Lee's army which was stretched to the maximum over some nine miles. Meade's right flank anchored on Antietam Creek, while his left flank hung "in the air," except for the protection of high ground and a cavalry screen. The Confederate left flank was also "in the air," except for a cavalry screen. A five and a half-mile gap existed between the left flank and Conococheague Creek. To cover that extensive area, Jeb Stuart set up heavy cavalry outposts along this line. "The two armies are directly in front of each other," Union III Corps quartermaster, Lt. Col. James F. Rusling, observed, "and a collision will not long be delayed."[34]

Hostile activity between the two sides began increasing. After its initial screening of the army's defensive position, the 9th Virginia Cavalry moved northward to help screen the left flank, crossing Antietam Creek at Funkstown and moving northeast of Hagerstown. There it fought a sharp firefight with Union forces and sustained a number of casualties. C. W. Bardeen, a 1st Massachusetts fifer, recorded the III Corps took up a position within a half mile

---

33 Lee to Jones, July 12, 1863, OR 27, pt. 3, 999; Butterfield to Halleck, July 3, 1863, pt. 1, 75-77.

34 Humphreys to Hunt, July 12, 1863, ibid., pt. 3, 666; Oliver Wilson Davis, *Life of David Bell Birney* (Whitefish, MT, 2010), 195; Stuart's post-action report, August 20, 1863, OR 27, pt. 2, 704-05; Rusling, *Men and Things that I Saw*, 308; OR *Atlas*, Plate 42.

of the front as a reserve. On the other side of the field, Pvt. Louis Leon, 1st North Carolina, noted heavy skirmishing on the left and center of the line.[35]

Once Meade's army confronted him, Lee anticipated an attack would soon come. Doubtless pleased and surprised, however, he watched the enemy preparing defensive positions. Meade, with his army now directly confronting the enemy, decided it prudent to entrench in case Lee decided to go on the offensive. Lee's staffer Taylor later recollected the events:

> On the 12th the enemy appeared in our front, and a line of defense having been selected [by us], covering the Potomac from Williamsport to Falling Waters, our army took position, ready and anxious for attack . . . [but] the enemy in front manifesting no disposition to attack, but steadily engaged in throwing up earthworks for defense.[36]

Douglas Southall Freeman summed up the anticlimactic scene similarly:

> That day, the Federal infantry approached. Lee's ragged veterans steeled themselves for another Antietam, but to Southern eyes the enemy appeared more anxious to cover himself with entrenchments of Maryland earth than to prepare for attack.[37]

Collecting Information for Combat Purposes

> Colonel Long has returned from a survey of our position occupied by the corps of Longstreet and Hill.
>
> Gen. R. E. Lee[38]

At 5:30 p.m., Lee passed the results of a recent recon by a trusted member of his staff of the Union lines on to cavalry commander Stuart. Colonel Armistead L. Long had "discovered the enemy massing their troops in their front, and thinks the principal attack on our lines will be between the Williamsport and Boonsborough road and the Frederick road." Long had not

---

35 Krick, *9th Virginia Cavalry*, 26-27; Charles Wilson Bardeen, *A Little Fifer's War Diary* (Charleston, SC, 2011), 243; Louis Leon, *Diary of a Tar Heel Confederate Soldier* (Charleston, SC, 2008), 40.

36 Taylor, *General Lee*, 212-13.

37 Lee's post-action reports, July 31, 1863 & January 1864, OR 27, pt. 2, 309, 323; Freeman, *Lee's Lieutenants*, 3:166-67.

38 Lee to Stuart, OR 27, pt. 3, 998.

yet checked out the area in front of Ewell's corps, but based on Stuart's and Ewell's earlier reports, Lee surmised that "there seems to be no enemy in that quarter."[39]

Expecting Meade to attack the following morning, Lee told Stuart, in that event he should "bear down on the enemy's right, endeavoring to select good positions for your horse artillery, to harass and retard him." And he should also be keeping "a good lookout on the Chambersburg and Greencastle road, and not leave our left uncovered."[40]

While the two armies stared at each other across a grassy no-man's land, thousands of Union prisoners continued to be herded southward toward Staunton. Trudging along on foot with little food and water, many died or fell out and were paroled along the way. One of the prisoners, an 8th Pennsylvania Cavalry officer, later wrote that they were hoping to be rescued by Union forces that could cross the river via Harper's Ferry. Those hopes were dashed once they moved as far south as Winchester.[41]

Meade understood that Lee's army occupied a strong position on the heights of Marsh Run in front of Williamsport. Probes of the enemy's lines had confirmed it. After the Union army arrived on the scene, the cavalry and troops of the XI and VI corps engaged in skirmishes with the Rebels; Longstreet confirmed in the evening that a skirmish took place with Union sharpshooters at Saint James College.[42]

Meade Defers to His Reluctant Commanders

The same consequences which have uniformly attended . . . councils of war will follow at all times. They will terminate in the adoption of the worst course . . . the most timid. . . . The only true wisdom in a general is determined courage.

Napoleon Bonaparte[43]

39 Lee to Stuart, July 12, 1863, *OR* 27, pt. 3, 998.

40 Ibid.

41 Penfield, *Civil War Diary*, 73-74; John L. Collins, "A Prisoner's March from Gettysburg to Staunton," *B&L*, 3:432.

42 Meade's post-action report, October 1, 1863, *OR* 27, pt. 1, 118; Longstreet's post-action report, July 27, 1863, pt. 2, 361.

43 www.worldfuturefund.org/wffmaster/reading/quotes/totalitquotes.htm accessed October 11, 2014.

Earlier in the day, Meade told Humphreys he intended to attack Lee's fortifications. He planned "to move the army forward and feel the enemy, and to attack them at such points as he should find it best to attack." But he grew hesitant about his decision, however, and called his commanders together around 8:00 p.m. to dispense instructions and learn what they knew about the strength of Lee's fortifications. Perhaps reflecting sentiments of the more reluctant officers, reporters traveling with the army reported Meade plans to attack the Rebel position, but also said there was little hope he would damage the enemy to any great extent.[44]

With his commanders Meade stated his understanding about the strength of Lee's position and the enemy's determination to give battle and defend it if attacked. And there was no time to expand their knowledge of the ground and conduct a reconnaissance of Lee's fortifications. Wadsworth recalled that Meade briefly stated the condition of the army, an estimate of the army's strength, including figures he had on the strength of the enemy. As Wadsworth remembered, Meade said his army was superior in numbers.[45]

Although Meade did not specify the size of Lee's army, newspaper dispatches citing the "best sources" in Washington placed the figure at 50,000.[46] Meade's post-Gettysburg army numbered about 70,900, not counting the some 16,000 regulars who arrived as reinforcements from various locations, and six additional artillery batteries. Another 25,000 mostly emergency and militia troops of indeterminate value were posted nearby, if Meade chose to use them. Thus Meade's advantage over Lee was nearly 37,000 plus the six fresh batteries, not counting the militia troops and granting Lee's strength to be a questionable 50,000 (44,000-45,000 a more realistic figure).[47]

---

44 Hyde, *The Union Generals Speak*, 199; Henry Greenleaf Pearson, *James S. Wadsworth of Geneseo* (New York, 1913), 232; Sacramento *Union*, July 14, 1863.

45 Hyde, *Union Generals Speak*, 234.

46 The 50,000 figure for the Confederates was generous, since about 48,500 of Lee's army marched away from Gettysburg, and another 5-6,000 were lost through straggling or in skirmishes along the way—leaving 42,500-43,500 of all arms. Some infantry, perhaps 1,000, that did not accompany Lee to Gettysburg rejoined the army at Williamsport, bringing the net total to 43,500-44,500. Busey and Martin, *Strengths and Losses*, 260.

47 Sacramento *Union*, July 14, 1863; Busey and Martin, *Strengths and Losses*, 125. For a detailed discussion of the number and quality of Meade's reinforcements, see Coddington, *The Gettysburg Campaign*, 559-61.

Meade presented his plan to conduct a reconnaissance-in-force the following morning to obtain a better idea of the location and strength of the enemy positions. This recon would be converted into a full-scale attack if feasible. Most of his corps commanders opposed the plan, and rather than order them to carry it out, Meade, much to the chagrin of those supporting an attack, chose to postpone the offensive so as to conduct a personal reconnaissance of the Rebel positions the next day. The main reasons dissenters from the attack idea advanced were that another battle might jeopardize Meade's great victory at Gettysburg. Moreover, a loss at Williamsport would leave Baltimore and Washington open to attack. Howard, who favored an attack, remembered:

> We had present, I think, nine corps commanders [actually eight]; six [five: Hays, French, Sykes, Sedgwick and Slocum] were of the opinion that we had better not assault Lee there. The other three, Wadsworth, Pleasonton, and I, pleaded for an immediate attack.

In the opinion of Meade's chief engineer Warren, however, if Meade had decided to attack the enemy position at Williamsport, he would have been successful. Wadsworth agreed: months later, in response to a question from the chairman of the Joint Congressional Committee on the Conduct of the War whether a vigorous attack would have been destructive to Lee's army, he said, "I believe almost everybody in the army admits that now."[48]

One resource that Meade did not employ during this meeting was his intelligence chief. A briefing from Sharpe about the disposition and strength of enemy forces would have helped dispel some commanders' beliefs that Lee's army was equivalent in size. While Meade may not have been acquainted with Sharpe and the BMI sufficiently to consider their reports trustworthy, it is more likely he chose to rely on his own interpretation of the intelligence—a practice he would continue while eventually eliminating the BMI's all-source reporting function.[49]

---

48 Meade's, Wadsworth's & Warren's Joint Congressional Committee on the Conduct of the War (JCCCW) testimony, March 5, March 23, & March 9, 1964, Hyde, *The Union Generals Speak*, 117, 170, 234-35; Howard's post-action report, August 31, 1863, OR 27, pt. 1, 709; Howard, *Autobiography*, 444-45; Schildt, *Roads from Gettysburg*, 95.

49 Meade's opinion about the strength of Lee's army is reflected in Sedgwick's comments that after Gettysburg the enemy "was with equal force to our own . . . [and] I think that was pretty

At 9:00 p.m., Lee provided evidence he was not exclusively defensive-minded in this situation. He instructed Stuart, "should an opportunity occur . . . advance upon the enemy's right and rear with your horse artillery, to shake him in his position or attack," adding, "Should we be fortunate enough to break him, you will then have an opportunity to pursue" his retreating forces. Reflecting his concern about unexpected enemy movements, however, Lee exhorted Stuart to "Keep your eye over the field, use good judgment, and give assistance where necessary."[50]

Despite the bold front Lee exhibited and the later assertion by one of his staff officers that the army "stood in an attitude of defiance . . . hoping to be attacked," Lee confessed his mixed feelings in a letter to his wife that night. Rumors of success at Gettysburg were inaccurate, he wrote, "we failed to drive the enemy from his position, and . . . our army withdrew to the Potomac . . . had the river not unexpectedly risen, all would have been well with us," he added. In other words, he had no intention to stand and fight again after Gettysburg, but rather to cross the river and return to Virginia. He prayed that the waters would recede and his communications would open up to allow his army to escape; however, "I trust that a merciful God, our only hope and refuge, will not desert us in this hour of need, and will deliver us by His almighty hand."[51]

July 13: Lee Waits No Longer

> On the forenoon of the 13th, General Lee sent for me, and announced that the river was fordable and the bridge repaired, that the trains would be started at once, and the troops would follow when night could conceal the move.
>
> Lt. Gen. James Longstreet[52]

---

much the opinion of most of the general officers present there." Sedgwick's JCCCW testimony, April 8, 1864, Hyde, *The Union Generals Speak*, 32. For a discussion of Meade's preference to rely on his own interpretation of intelligence about the enemy rather than that of the BMI, and his elimination of all-source reporting, see Fishel, *Secret War*, 540-41.

50 Lee to Stuart, July 12, 1863, *OR* 27, pt. 3, 998.

51 Taylor, *Four Years With General Lee*, 110; Lee, *Recollections and Letters*, 101-02.

52 Longstreet, *From Manassas to Appomattox*, 429.

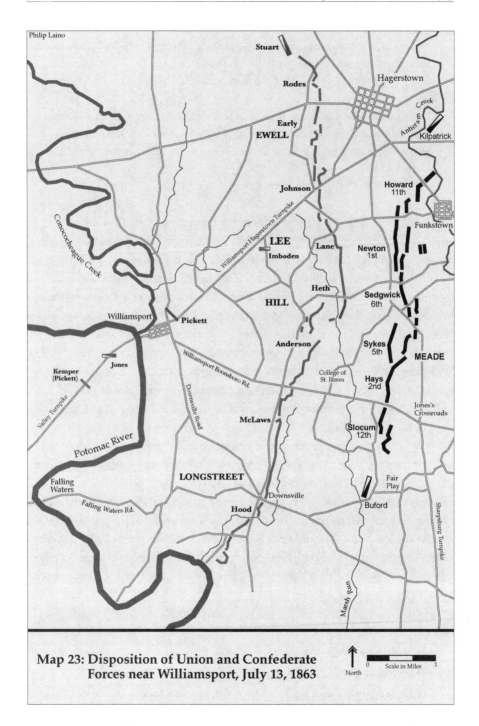

Philip Laino

Map 23: Disposition of Union and Confederate
Forces near Williamsport, July 13, 1863

0   Scale in Miles   1

North

The Rebels, it is now certain, have a Bridge across the Potomac at Falling Waters. . . . should not be surprised if they cross the River tonight.

PMG Marsena Patrick[53]

I wish you to place your cavalry in position before night, so as to relieve the infantry along the whole extent of their lines when they retire [tonight]. . . . Direct your men to be very vigilant and bold, and not let the enemy discover that our lines have been vacated.

Gen. Robert E. Lee[54]

While Meade and his commanders were examining the Confederate lines, signal officer McCreary alerted Meade: "The enemy are reported by a citizen from within their lines to have broken up their camps, and to be moving all their wagon trains toward Falling Waters." This development obviously called for immediate action. Meanwhile, signal officer Daniels pinpointed the locations of both Lee's and Longstreet's headquarters, as well as the headquarters of Hood's, Anderson's, and Heth's divisions. The enemy had a line of rifle pits from the National pike near Hagerstown south to the Potomac River below Williamsport, Daniels added, with artillery emplacements in "circular redoubts" to the rear. Despite these timely, significant reports, Meade would later inexplicably claim "not much information was obtained" from his examination of enemy lines that day.[55]

PMG Patrick, the administrative head of the BMI, disagreed with Meade's assessment. He noted the enemy short of supplies that day, and prisoners admitting Confederate losses at about 40,000 men. Nonetheless, Patrick thought that Lee's strongly entrenched army would repulse any Union attack. He also learned that reconstruction of the pontoon bridge at Falling Waters had been completed, and "I should not be surprised if they cross the River tonight." Oddly, Patrick, who should have known, made no reference to Meade's either being aware of or placing a priority on learning about the bridge completion, or

---

53 Sparks, *Inside Lincoln's Army*, 271.

54 Lee to Stuart, July 13, 1863, *OR* 27, pt. 3, 1001.

55 McCreary to Nicodemus, July 13, 1863, *OR*, ibid., pt. 1, 213; Daniels to Meade, [July 13, 1863], Cameron, "The Signal Corps at Gettysburg," *Gettysburg Magazine*, Issue 4, 108-09; Meade's JCCCW testimony, March 5, 1863, Hyde, *The Union Generals Speak*, 118.

if any action was under consideration to interrupt an escape across a completed bridge.

After a reconnaissance on his front and "the information I could collect," Howard also concluded the Rebels prepared to retreat without giving battle. Because of his concerns, he requested Meade's approval to make a reconnaissance the next morning at 3:00 a.m. hoping "to make a lodgment on the enemy's left." Without explaining the later time, Meade responded with orders for a 7:00 a.m. start time for a reconnaissance-in-force in combination with other corps the next morning.[56]

Late in the afternoon, Meade finally notified Halleck, who along with Lincoln urgently awaited word about the attack, that "something intervened to prevent it:"

> Upon calling my corps commanders together and submitting the question to them, five out of six were unqualifiedly opposed to it. Under these circumstances, in view of the momentous consequences attendant upon a failure to succeed, I did not feel myself authorized to attack until after I had made more careful examination of the enemy's position, strength, and defensive works.

Meade went on to explain that examination being made showed "the enemy to be strongly intrenched on a ridge running from the rear of Hagerstown past Downsville to the Potomac." He would "hazard an attack," if he should discover a weak point in the enemy's line. He complained about the poor condition and short terms of service of the reinforcements sent him. He did not mention, however, the critical information that the reconstruction of the pontoon bridge at Falling Waters reportedly was completed, and the river water level had dropped to a level very likely fordable.[57]

After consulting with Lincoln and Stanton, Halleck responded immediately and plainly:

> You are strong enough to attack and defeat the enemy before he can effect a crossing. Act upon your own judgment and make your generals execute your orders. Call no

---

56 Howard's post-action report, OR 27, pt. 1, 709; Howard, *Autobiography*, 445.

57 Meade to Halleck, July 13, 1863, OR 27, pt. 1, 91-92.

Falling Waters road leading to the Potomac River. Its present-day appearance is much like it would have been during the Civil War.
Author's collection

council of war. It is proverbial that councils of war never fight. Re-enforcements are pushed on as rapidly as possible. Do not let the enemy escape.[58]

By this time, the river had indeed become fordable, and Lee decided that any further delay would only enable the enemy to obtain additional reinforcements. And because of the difficulty in getting "a sufficient supply of flour for the troops," he would await an attack from Meade no longer. With the cavalry screening the movement on that dark and rainy night, wagons, artillery, and soldiers crossed over the pontoon bridge at Falling Waters and forded the river at Williamsport.[59]

While the withdrawal was underway, Jeb Stuart took time to write his wife a lengthy letter that he was "all right thus far" and that all of his staff had escaped across the river. Perhaps reflecting a considerable easing of tension, he engaged in small talk about making a number of purchases in the North his wife had requested, but "no black silk could be had." He summarized his accomplishments during the campaign, delightedly reporting that he "had a grand time in Pennsylvania" while adding imprecisely "we return without defeat." He implied that the onus for Lee's lack of success should be put on the authorities in Richmond: "If they had only sent 10,000 reinforcements and plenty of ammunition to join him here our recrossing would have been with banners of peace." Ignoring the long ordeal the army had just endured, Stuart

58 Halleck to Meade, ibid., 92.

59 Lee's post-action report, January 1864, *OR* 27, pt. 2, 323.

claimed it was crossing the river only to "recuperate and reinforce," because "We must invade again—it is the only path of peace."[60]

July 14: The Great Escape

> Orders were accordingly given to cross the Potomac. . . . no interruption was offered [on the 14th] by the enemy . . . [and they] made no effort to follow excepting with his cavalry.
>
> Gen. Robert E. Lee[61]

> July 14 . . . when the Union troops, so long held back, moved forward, they found the Confederate pickets withdrawn; the intrenchments behind which Lee's worn and wasted veterans had made such an imposing show of strength were empty.
>
> Brig. Gen. James S. Wadsworth[62]

Because of the inevitable delays, day had dawned before much of the infantry started across the river. The Yankees offered no interruption, Lee later reported, "until about 11:00 a.m., when his cavalry, supported by artillery, appeared in front of General Heth." By then it was too late to do any serious damage to Lee's army. His forces replaced artillery with "Quaker guns" (wooden logs painted to resemble cannon) and flew flags over their former emplacements to deceive the enemy that troops remained in the bunkers. In addition, the smoke from thousands of campfires left burning obscured the Rebel movements.[63]

Although Meade would later testify to the JCCCW that "on the night of the 13th I directed that the next morning at daylight the whole army should move forward with a view to attacking the enemy," his orders actually called for a reconnaissance in force, not an attack, by at least one division of the II, V, VI, and XII corps, not the whole army, to begin at 7:00 a.m., not daylight, on July 14 to gain information about the enemy's "position, defensive works, force, and its arrangements." These orders said nothing about attacking the enemy and only instructed the corps commanders to be prepared in the event the enemy should

---

60 Mitchell, *Stuart's Letters*, 327-28.

61 Lee's post-action report, January 1864, *OR* 27, pt. 2, 323-24.

62 Pearson, *James S. Wadsworth*, 235.

63 Ibid., 323; Brown, *Retreat from Gettysburg*, 329.

The Donnelly House along Falling Waters Road. Confederate Brig. Gen. James J. Pettigrew was mortally wounded during fighting in this area on July 14.
Photo by the author

offer a general engagement. Under the circumstances, these orders were remarkably conservative. If these troops had moved out at dawn, they would have encountered the enemy, because Ewell's corps was not completely across until 8:00 a.m. and Hill's and Longstreet's corps did not begin crossing until daylight—delayed by rain, darkness, and the slow passage of artillery, ammunition wagons, and ambulances across the pontoon bridge. Before the Union troops got underway, however, Howard informed Meade at 6:35 a.m., "My brigade commander in Hagerstown reports the works in his front evacuated."[64]

Lincoln's Expectations vs. Meade's Reality

[A] magnificent success was within [Meade's] grasp. But the commanding general called a council of war—which it is said, never fights.

Augustus Woodbury, 2nd Rhode Island[65]

64 Meade's JCCCW testimony, March 5, 1864, Hyde, *The Union Generals Speak*, 118; HQ Army of the Potomac Circular, July 13, 1863, *OR* 27, pt. 3, 675; Lee's post-action report, January 1864, pt. 2, 323; Wright's post-action report, August 21, 1863, pt. 1, 667; Coddington, *The Gettysburg Campaign*, 570; Howard to Humphreys, July 14, 1863, *OR* 27, pt. 3, 683.

65 Quoted in Peter C. Vermilyea, "Maj. Gen. John Sedgwick and the Pursuit of Lee's Army after Gettysburg," *Gettysburg Magazine*, Issue 22, 126.

The Battle of Gettysburg in its results was a great victory for the Federal cause, but
Lee's army did not feel at all like a beaten one. There was no rout or confusion; not
even pursuit to remind us that our invasion had come to an end.

W. W. Blackford, Stuart's Chief Engineer[66]

From the outset, the Union effort to pursue the Rebels' withdrawal from
Gettysburg was undertaken with great caution. Meade received indications early
on from signal corps observations, testimony from prisoners, deserters, and
captured Union troops left behind by the enemy that the enemy was retreating.
Infantry reconnaissance, cavalry, and BMI scouting reports provided additional
knowledge of the Confederate withdrawal. Meade should have known that
Rebel forces were seriously reduced in numbers. The BMI's order of battle data,
thousands of casualties left on the field, captured prisoners, and wounded
soldiers abandoned in makeshift hospitals near the battlefield all indicated as
much. Yet Meade was concerned that Lee might fortify a position in the
mountains or choose to stay in the Cumberland Valley. If Meade had gotten the
army underway on July 4, he would have arrived in the vicinity of Williamsport
with more time to reconnoiter and attack Lee's positions. And if Lee had
decided to take a stand in the mountains, Meade's tracking force under Neill
would have informed him. The Union army, by then south of its enemy, could
have marched northward to confront him.

The performance of the Union cavalry lacked cohesion. There was no
overall plan, clear direction, or sustained effort. The absence of Pleasonton
personally commanding cavalry operations in the field proved a drawback.
Although he had not performed well in his role as information provider during
the march northward under Hooker's command, he was still an aggressive
fighter. Since Meade was employing the cavalry as a combat unit as well as
gathering intelligence during his pursuit of Lee, he needed Pleasonton in the
field to coordinate the work of disrupting Lee's withdrawal.

Concerning an attack on Lee's fortifications: risk required

Union generals, including Sedgwick, Humphreys, and Howard, later
observed that Lee's defense line was a strongly fortified position. PMG Patrick

---

66 Blackford, *War Years with Jeb Stuart*, 234.

noted, "Their lines were strongly entrenched—too strongly to be forced by us." Colonel Charles S. Wainwright, artillery chief of Howard's corps, declared Lee's works to be "the strongest I have seen yet . . . [t]he parapet was a good six feet wide on top, and the guns . . . were all placed so as to get a perfect cross fire and to sweep their whole front." Captain Stephen Weld, of Maj. Gen. John Newton's I Corps staff, offered an even more emphatic assessment: "The enemy occupied a strong natural position here, made almost impregnable to our small force by fortifications." Weld's characterization of "our small force," however, indicated his ignorance of the actual facts.[67]

From a Confederate perspective, Col. Bradley T. Johnson, one of Ewell's brigade commanders, commented while the fortifications were "rude [i.e., makeshift]," they "materially strengthened the position." Ewell recorded, after moving into line, his corps began fortifying, and "in a short time my men were well protected." Longstreet noted his "troops were put to work, and, in twenty-four hours, our line was comfortably intrenched." Colonel E. P. Alexander succinctly described Lee's defensive posture:

> A fairly good line was found with its right flank on the Potomac near Downsville, passing by St. James College and resting its left on the Conococheague [Creek]. Longstreet's corps held its right flank, Hill the center, and Ewell the left.[68]

The Rebel works' merits, however, lay in the eye of the beholder. A 1st Ohio cavalryman considered the enemy fortifications beyond Hagerstown and stretching "away to the river" to be "hastily constructed earthworks." Colonel Rusling of French's III Corps evidently was not impressed either, since he concluded upon inspection of the works that "Meade here missed a great and golden opportunity." Sacramento Union reporter, Noah Brooks, while visiting Meade's headquarters beforehand, heard that Lee's positions were of "great strategic strength." But when he later surveyed the abandoned Rebel lines, he

---

67 JCCCW testimony: Hunt's, April 4, Humphreys, March 21, & Sedgwick's, April 8, 1864, Hyde, *The Union Generals Speak*, 316, 201, 328; Howard, *Autobiography*, 446; Sparks, *Inside Lincoln's Army*, 271; Charles S. Wainwright, *A Diary of Battle: The Personal Journals of Colonel Charles Wainwright, 1861-1865* (New York, 1962), 261; Stephen Weld, *War Diary and Letters of Stephen Minot Weld, 1861-1865* (Cambridge, MA, 1912), 129.

68 Longstreet's, Ewell's, & Johnson's post-action reports, *OR* 27, pt. 2, 361, 448, 534; Alexander, *Military Memoirs*, 439.

depicted them as "rifle pits and other hastily constructed earthworks."[69]

These descriptions lead to the conclusion that the Confederate entrenchments at Williamsport were of varying quality: strongly constructed in some areas but more vulnerable in others. It is doubtful that these fortifications were impenetrable by a strong and determined force, especially considering the indisputable fact that the L-shaped defensive position stretched out over a distance of 16 miles (a 10-and-a-half mile front and five-mile left flank). It is highly unlikely Lee had enough troops to defend a line of this length. Meade's engineering chief Warren may have summed it up best when he was asked what would have been the result of a general assault upon the enemy's position: "I think," Warren said unhesitatingly, "we should have cut them all to pieces; that was my opinion."[70]

Among Meade's close advisers at the time, Warren was not alone in his desire to go on the offensive against Lee's fortifications. Chief of staff Humphreys supported an aggressive approach:

> Subsequent information showed that the enemy had a very strong position, and indicated that had we made an attack we should have suffered very severely. But it was proper that we should have made an attack at that time—that is, a reconnaissance in force, converting it into a battle upon circumstances warranting it.[71]

Cavalry commander Pleasonton also believed an attack should have been made, because probes revealed the vulnerability of certain points along the lines, and "I was satisfied that their army was short of ammunition." Pleasonton was referring to Huey's cavalry that drove the enemy into their defenses and took up a position close to their breastworks. They had to retire, however, because the infantry of Slocum's XII Corps, under orders not to engage the enemy, did not come to their support.[72]

Meade's artillery chief, Hunt, thought that a direct attack against the Confederate fortifications could have been avoided by "by moving up to our

---

69 Gillespie, *Company A, First Ohio*, 164; Rusling, *Men and Things I Saw in Civil War Days*, 72; Sacramento *Union*, July 14, 1863; Brooks, *Washington in Lincoln's Time*, 89.

70 Warren's JCCCW testimony, March 9, 1864, Hyde, *The Union Generals Speak*, 176. OR *Atlas*, Plate 42.

71 Humphreys' JCCCW testimony, March 21, 1864, Hyde, *The Union Generals Speak*, 201.

72 Pleasonton's JCCCW testimony, March 7, 1864, ibid., 142.

right . . . and moving down upon the [left flank of the] enemy from that direction," since that area was not entrenched and defended by cavalry only. As to the advisability of attacking the enemy after Gettysburg, Hunt concluded, "We must risk to win." Brigadier General Albion Howe, Second Division, VI Corps, expressed astonishment that we should remain [in front of the enemy's position] without attacking, with the river so high that the rebel army could not cross it, and were almost without ammunition, while our men were in good fighting trim, and the rebels dispirited and demoralized.

Howe based his reasoning on a report from Neill, his brigade commander who tracked Lee's army during the retreat, about the mountains being full of rebels who had fallen out and were going in every direction. They were so many of them, Neill could not stop to pick them up.[73]

Reflecting on how the enemy responded to Lee's entrenched position, E. P. Alexander concluded:

> Gen. Meade showed no disposition to attack us. If he had he would not have had any easy task, though his superior resources & forces, & the rare chance of ruining us which success would have given he certainly should have tried it for all he was worth. Or—if from Gettysburg he had marched hard & fast for Harpers Ferry, he might there have crossed the river & opposed us from the south bank & compelled us to again attack him in position.[74]

On Alexander's latter point, Henry Hunt echoed these sentiments from a Union perspective:

> I thought then, and I have seen no reason since to change my opinion, that a comparatively small force, which might have consisted mostly of cavalry, with some infantry, could, if thrown across the river, whether from that army, or pushed up from Frederick or from Washington, [could] have prevented their crossing, and have shut them up on the north side of the river, where they would have been compelled to stand an attack from us . . . or, from all I heard of the character of the roads behind them, they would have been compelled to abandon the most of their material, in order to escape up the river, by the Hancock road, and cross above.

---

73 Howe's & Hunt's JCCCW testimony, March 3, April 4, 1864, ibid., 91, 316.

74 Gallagher, *Fighting for the Confederacy*, 269-71; Alexander, *Military Memoirs*, 439.

Hunt ended his statement by emphasizing, "I was then under the impression that we should have made an attack."[75]

While it is not surprising that Meade was cautious about a frontal attack against Lee's fortified positions at Williamsport, he did not take advantage of an opportunity to gain control of the south bank of the Potomac at Lee's expected crossing points. Even though French had burned the bridge at Harper's Ferry, Meade had ordered a pontoon bridge placed there to allow troops to cross the river, and he had already deployed some 7,000 troops to Maryland Heights directly across the river from Harper's Ferry. According to Warren, although the means and men were on hand to accomplish it, Meade never gave the order for troops to cross the river to destroy Lee's ordnance trains and prevent reconstruction of the pontoon bridge at Falling Waters. Troops positioned on the south bank could have bombarded and impeded Lee's crossing on July 13-14, forcing him to seek other locations to cross upriver toward Hancock—a plan the Confederate commander already laid out as a contingency. Had Lee been forced to make such a move, Meade would have been given an opportunity to catch him in the open while vulnerable to attack. The Union commander should have been alert to this strategy especially after learning that Lee would be receiving no reinforcements.[76]

JCCCW member Representative Daniel Gooch had this issue on his mind when he asked Sedgwick during his testimony before the committee why Meade did not place troops on the south side of the Potomac to impede the enemy's crossing while the main body of the Union army attacked Lee's forces. Sedgwick, seemingly nonplussed by this line of questioning, tersely rationalized that he thought there were not enough troops available for that purpose. Yet Meade's plan did not take the south side of the river into consideration at all. An attack on the ordnance train arriving there would have added substance to Lee's concern about a shortage of ammunition.[77]

Meade's caution reflected his fear of tactical error and apprehension about suffering extensive casualties. He did not want to undermine his triumph at Gettysburg by experiencing a disaster elsewhere. In his testimony before the JCCCW the following year, Meade explained that he really desired to attack Lee

---

75 Hunt's JCCCW testimony, April 4, 1864, Hyde, *The Union Generals Speak*, 317.

76 Warren to Benham, July 7, 1863, *OR* 27, pt. 3, 585-86; Gallagher, *Fighting for the Confederacy*, 271; Meade to Halleck, July 8, 1863, *OR* 27, pt. 1, 83-84.

77 Sedgwick's JCCCW testimony, April 8, 1864, Hyde, *The Union Generals Speak*, 329-30.

at Williamsport. But having been in command only a brief time and understanding the issues involved, including the potential for the victory at Gettysburg being dissipated, however, he "did not feel that I would be right in assuming the responsibility of blindly attacking the enemy without any knowledge of his position. I therefore called a council of my corps commanders." Twice during the post-battle period, July 4 and 12, Meade acceded to the recommendations of his generals not to assume the offensive. On both these occasions, although BMI intelligence experts were available to brief the commanders and enlighten them about the enemy's relative strength, disposition, and probable intentions, Meade unwisely let them go unheard.[78]

Lieutenant Colonel Rusling often had an opportunity to observe Meade while he was considering an attack on Lee at Williamsport, and he thought Meade "greatly anxious and troubled over what to do and how to do it." Although one of his admirers, Rusling concluded:

> I think history will hold as due proof that [Meade] ought to have attacked immediately, when he found Lee in such desperate straits, with a defeated and depleted army, and the unfordable Potomac at his back, and had he done so the chances are he would have covered himself and the army with imperishable renown.[79]

Meade was ambivalent about the task of confronting Lee again following the battle at Gettysburg, and this is reflected in letters to his wife. On July 8, he explained that his mission was to pursue and fight the retreating Confederates, and he "would rather do it at once and in Maryland than to follow [Lee's army] into Virginia." Two days later he wrote that he expected "to hazard the fortune of war" soon against the Rebel army, but once they escaped across the river, however, Meade's true feelings about this issue became evident:

> The proper policy of the Government would have been to be contented with driving Lee out of Maryland, and not to have advanced till this army was largely reinforced and reorganized, and put on such a footing that its advance was sure to be successful.[80]

---

78 Meade's JCCCW testimony, March 5, 1864, ibid., 116.

79 Rusling, *Men and Things I Saw in Civil War Days*, 70-71.

80 Meade to his wife, July 8, 10, and 18, Meade, *Life and Letters*, 2, 132-33, 136.

Despite his uneasiness and the hesitancy of his generals, Meade sent his forces forward to reconnoiter Lee's positions on July 14. As it turned out, the timing could hardly have been worse, because the water level of the river had dropped sufficiently to permit Lee's army to cross safely. But for this eventuality, the town of Williamsport may have witnessed a battle as historic as the one that took place at Gettysburg.

In reality, Lincoln's expectations about destroying Lee's army were greater than they should have been under the circumstances. Winning a decisive victory at Gettysburg, Meade had performed a great service to the government of the United States. A loss there could have led to independence for the South. Given Meade's recent elevation to a job no other general had mastered to that point, he performed better than most thought possible. Lincoln was anxious for the war to end, and Lee appeared to be within Meade's grasp—why not reach out and destroy him? It came down to what appeared to be achievable from Lincoln's perspective in Washington versus the personal limitations of the commander in the field. Other key factors, including timely and accurate intelligence, could not alter this reality.

While Coddington wrote of his conviction that "Meade set out after Lee for the express purpose of battling him again, the sooner the better," the Union commander's words and actions proved otherwise. An examination of the evidence reveals Meade hesitant from the start to pursue Lee and reluctant to engage him again when the opportunity presented itself. He, along with several of his corps commanders, preferred not to jeopardize their victory at Gettysburg with a potential defeat along the escape route. Stephen W. Sears gives Meade credit where credit is due: "The fact of the matter is that George G. Meade, unexpectedly and against the odds, thoroughly outgeneraled Robert E. Lee at Gettysburg." Washington was greatly chagrined, however, that Lee was allowed to escape before another confrontation took place.[81]

Fallout from the Escape

[I]ntelligent negroes who have escaped from the Rebel army on its retreat from Pa. & Md. & came inside our lines . . . told me that the Rebels were badly whipped at

---

81 Coddington, *The Gettysburg Campaign*, 547; Sears, *Gettysburg*, 506; Halleck to Meade, July 14, 1863, *OR* 27, pt. 1, 92.

> Gettysburg & if Meade had only attacked Lee when he couldn't cross the [Potomac] river we could have captured his entire army.
>
> Sgt. John B. Kay, 6th Michigan Cavalry[82]

But the Army of Northern Virginia was able to cross the Potomac relatively unscathed, with the result that attention shifted from the decisive Union victory and Confederate defeat at Gettysburg to Lee's daring escape under dire circumstances. The reactions of those who counted most, Abraham Lincoln and Jefferson Davis, told the story. Taylor, Lee's aide, recorded when Lee tendered his resignation after the loss at Gettysburg, Davis reassured him by insisting that the overall campaign was a success despite the defeat in battle. Davis philosophically concluded:

> To ask of me to substitute you by some one in my judgment more fit to command, or who would possess more the confidence of the army, or of the reflecting men of the country, is to demand an impossibility.[83]

By contrast, after Lee and his army escaped across the river, Lincoln was inconsolable. He penned a letter to Meade that expressed, in his eyes, the enormity of his failure to attack. But upon reconsideration, the president judiciously decided against either signing or sending it. It would have been quite a blow to a man who had been in command less than a month:

> Again, my dear general, I do not believe you appreciate the magnitude of the misfortune involved in Lee's escape. . . . as it is, the war will be prolonged indefinitely. . . . Your golden opportunity is gone, and I am distressed immeasurably because of it.[84]

While the escape was a victory for Lee, one of his officers may have captured the mood of the Confederate army best when he compared the great confidence it had during the march northward with being chased by the enemy during the retreat: "True we are not whipped. . . . But . . . the contrast is a sad one." Wadsworth may have summed up the reaction of the Union troops best

82 Kay to "My Dear Brother Ricky," August 6, 1863, Bentley Historical Library.

83 Taylor, *General Lee*, 220-21; Douglas Southall Freeman, *R.E. Lee: A Biography*, 4 vols. (New York, 1935), 3:156-58; Hattaway and Jones, *How the North Won*, 413-14.

84 Lincoln to Meade, July 14, 1863, Williams, *Selected Writings and Speeches of Abraham Lincoln*, 219; Donald, *Lincoln*, 446.

when asked why Lee escaped. He succinctly replied, "Because nobody stopped him."[85]

While the battle of Gettysburg was a decisive victory for Meade, realistically speaking the overall campaign was a draw between the two armies. Lee could claim success in his ability to retreat across the Potomac with his army still intact, and he would remain in the field for the better part of two more years. Despite Lincoln's disappointment, after the clamor in Washington over Lee's escape had abated, Halleck took it upon himself to unofficially place the matter into perspective in a letter to Meade:

> Your fight at Gettysburg met with universal approbation of all military men here. . . . You should not have been surprised or vexed at the President's disappointment at the escape of Lee's army . . . [because he] thought that Lee's defeat was so certain. . . . [Your victory at Gettysburg] has proved your superior generalship, and you merit, as you will receive, the confidence of the Government and the gratitude of the country.[86]

At Gettysburg, Meade's generalship was largely based on the intelligence advantage he enjoyed over Lee, and for the most part his recognition and use of that intelligence. The absence of his cavalry commander Jeb Stuart and the superior intelligence he normally provided proved a considerable handicap to Lee. And the result was a victory for the Northern army and a crushing defeat for the Confederates.

During Lee's retreat from Gettysburg and Meade's pursuit, Meade received a multitude of intelligence reports about the vulnerability of Lee's position in front of Williamsport and Falling Waters from a variety of sources. Unlike his performance at Gettysburg, however, he chose to overlook or disregard much of the intelligence he received.

Lee, on the other hand, profited from Stuart's screening of his army during the hazardous withdrawal from Gettysburg, as well as the information he gathered about the enemy's movements. At Williamsport, however, even though information about the enemy's strength and intentions proved hard to come by for Lee, he still won the battle of wits and the contest of wills, and safely ushered his army across the river to fight another day.

---

85 Confederate officer quoted in Brown, *Retreat from Gettysburg*, 297; Pearson, *Wadsworth*, 236.

86 Halleck to Meade, July 28, 1863, *OR* 27, pt. 1, 104-05.

Chapter Eighteen

The Intelligence Battle: An Appraisal

[O]ne of the most important of all truths about the role of intelligence in warfare [is] that however good the intelligence before an encounter may appear to be, the outcome, given equality of force, will still be decided by the fight; and in a fight, determination . . . will be the paramount factor.

John Keegan[1]

The Gettysburg campaign comprised two distinct but related stages. The first stage, June 3-July 3, 1863, involved the long march from Fredericksburg, Virginia, the starting point of Lee's invasion, to south central Pennsylvania that led to the three-day battle at Gettysburg. The second encompassed Lee's withdrawal from the battlefield, and Meade's pursuit culminating near Williamsport, Maryland, July 4-14, 1863. From an intelligence standpoint, each of these stages took on a character of its own.

The March Northward and the Battle of Gettysburg

The imperturbable Meade deserves much credit for directing the perilous battle to its spectacular conclusion. . . . Never again would the main Confederate army be so potent; never again could its commander take the initiative offensively.
Herman Hattaway[2]

---

1 John Keegan, *Intelligence in War: Knowledge of the Enemy from Napoleon to Al-Qaeda* (New York, 2003), 324.

2 Herman Hattaway Foreword in Cleaves, *Meade of Gettysburg*, xiii.

The failure to crush the Federal army in Pennsylvania in 1863, in the opinion of almost all the officers of the Army of Northern Virginia can be expressed in five words—the absence of the cavalry.

Maj. Gen. Henry Heth[3]

Sharpe's Bureau of Military Information . . . had thwarted Lee's final effort to take the war into the North.

G. J. A. O'Toole[4]

During the march northward from Culpeper beginning on June 10, Lee and his army benefited both from the ineptness of Union cavalry commander Pleasonton in carrying out Hooker's orders to pinpoint their location and the effectiveness of Stuart's cavalry screening their movements from the eyes of the enemy. The Rebels moved virtually unobserved until they crossed the Potomac into Maryland. At that point, however, the BMI and signal corps alerted Hooker that Lee had crossed the river and was moving toward Pennsylvania. This information spurred Hooker to start his army northward, which led directly to the separation of Stuart's horsemen from the main army, and significantly changed Lee's fortunes for the worse.

Lee's problems began when Stuart delegated responsibility for intelligence operations to support the invading army to Robertson's two-brigade cavalry detachment. The unreliable Robertson did not follow orders to watch the enemy, and he failed to alert Lee after Hooker's forces crossed the Potomac. He then exacerbated these errors by not promptly rejoining Lee's army to guard its flank and rear. Diligence rather than indifference on Robertson's part would have mitigated Stuart's absence from the army. The unavailability of Stuart's cavalry disadvantaged Lee when the armies met in combat in south central Pennsylvania in early July. Lee's military secretary A. L. Long confirmed that Stuart's absence hampered Lee's movements and foiled his plan to engage the enemy in the vicinity of Gettysburg at a time and location of his own choosing.[5]

The ultimate responsibility for inadequate intelligence before and during the battle of Gettysburg, however, was Lee's. The unexpected arrival of the

3   "Letter from Major General Heth of A. P. Hill's Corps, A.N.V.," *SHSP* (October 1877), 4:155.

4   O'Toole, *Honorable Treachery*, 171.

5   Long, *Memoirs of Lee*, 272, 277.

scout Harrison confirming that the Union army had crossed the Potomac and arrived at Frederick was a stroke of luck for Lee. It permitted him time to concentrate his forces before the Federals arrived. With both Stuart's and Robertson's cavalry absent, it would seem to be imperative that he use other cavalry resources for reconnaissance on July 1-2. But he did not, and his almost exclusive dependence on Stuart for intelligence accounts for this lapse.[6]

The lack of a dedicated staff to help manage the intelligence process also hurt Lee's operational planning. The task fell principally upon a man with already more than enough to do. Availability of intelligence specialists collating information from various sources, such as his opponent had, would have permitted him to concentrate on strategy and tactics. Lee had to assume the offensive against formidable Union positions because his cavalry's absence limited his maneuverability.[7]

Nonetheless, Lee could have gained the upper hand during the first two days of fighting at Gettysburg. More aggressive action on his and his commanders' parts on July 1 may have enabled them to secure Cemetery Hill and Culp's Hill. Better use of reconnaissance resources would have alerted them to these possibilities. If Longstreet's attack had been organized earlier on July 2, his forces likely would have occupied the Peach Orchard high ground with minimal fighting, and Little Round Top with virtually no opposition—a far better combat result that included the possibility of dislodging the enemy

---

6 These resources included Col. William H. French's 17th Virginia of Jenkins' brigade, Lt. Col. Elijah V. White's 35th Battalion Virginia Cavalry, and Capt. William F. Randolph's Company B of the 39th Battalion Virginia Cavalry that arrived at Gettysburg along with Ewell's corps on July 1. Jenkins added significantly to this number when the rest of his brigade reached the area by late in the afternoon on July 1. Lee also had on hand as part of his headquarters contingent Capt. Augustus P. Pifer's Company A and Capt. Samuel B. Brown's Company C of the 39th Battalion that he could have used more aggressively. Myers, *The Comanches*, 196; OR 27, pt. 2, 443, 464; Shevchuk, "The Wounding of Albert Jenkins," 57-58; Driver, *39th Virginia Cavalry*, 51. In addition to these mounted resources, Lee also had available on July 1 the 1st Maryland Battalion that had been assigned to Ewell's corps for the campaign. The other cavalry brigade assigned to Ewell's corps, Imboden's, as well as Robertson's and Jones' brigades did not report for duty in the Gettysburg area until July 3. Longacre, *The Cavalry at Gettysburg*, 31, 234-35.

7 Aide de camps Majs. Charles Marshall and Charles S. Venable at times performed intelligence-related duties on Lee's staff, however, no evidence indicates that either did this at Gettysburg. Tidwell, *Come Retribution*, 107-08. On the lack of information available to Lee, see Jay Luvaas, "Lee at Gettysburg: A General Without Intelligence," in Michael I. Handel, *Intelligence and Military Operations* (London, 1990), 116-35.

from Cemetery Ridge. At the very least, Lee's troops would have been in an advantageous position to launch a powerful strike on July 3.

Delays in getting Longstreet's divisions in place earlier for the attack on July 2 were in part due to unfamiliarity with the terrain, a deficiency which availability of Stuart's cavalry could have alleviated. Nonetheless, Hood's scouts had observed a potential weak link in the Union defenses before the attack. But Lee was not present to approve a change in plans. The history of the battle might have been changed because of this, Col. E. P. Alexander later lamented. Still, it is questionable Lee would have approved such a move.[8]

Unlike their opponents, the Army of Northern Virginia had no chief signal officer and no apparent signal communications plan. Command and control was effected mostly by time-consuming personal contact or courier. The absence of Lee's detachment of his headquarters provost guard, the 1st Battalion Virginia Infantry, left behind at Winchester, also hurt. They could have been used to interrogate thousands of prisoners at Gettysburg for vital information on the location, strength, and intentions of Meade's army. Instead, Lee used them to replace a regiment of combat troops, a bargain he could ill afford.[9]

Another factor leading to Lee's defeat at Gettysburg was his failure to secure Davis' approval to lure troops from the Army of the Potomac for Washington's defense by staging a threat of an attack on the capital with forces redeployed from Virginia and the Carolinas to Culpeper. A timely movement of Union troops threatening Richmond foiled this plan. Davis rejected a deception plan that might have tipped the balance of power at Gettysburg.

On the Union side, Pleasonton's unclear orders and Duffié's poorly conducted "demonstration" toward Culpeper before the cavalry clash at Brandy Station on June 9 led to problems for Union forces and helped Stuart avoid sustaining serious damage to his forces. The BMI's timely reporting based on interrogation of escaped slaves, refugees, prisoners, and deserters and their observation of Lee's marching army offset Pleasonton's inability to locate Lee's army marching northward from Culpeper. The signal corps kept Federal units

---

8 Hood, *Advance and Retreat*, 57; Alexander, *Military Memoirs of a Confederate*, 394.

9 Confederate Signal Corps historian David W. Gaddy concluded, in the absence of information to the contrary, that at Gettysburg "Lee, the traditionalist, [preferred] a trusted courier or staff officer [rather than sending a message by signal] even when speed was of the essence." Gaddy, "The Confederate Signal Corps at Gettysburg," 112; Gallagher, *The Personal Recollection of General Edward Porter Alexander*, 242; Driver, *1st Battalion Virginia Infantry*, 36.

in communication with each other with flag signals and by telegraph and kept watch from observation posts. Union commanders also received information from loyal civilians who actively tracked Rebel movements. The BMI's Sharpe personally thanked Gettysburg civilian David McConaughy for the valuable information he and his band of partisans provided.

Competent intelligence support benefited the Union army; it did not so benefit the Confederates. Meade, who replaced Hooker as army commander on June 28, received a steady flow of information about the enemy, and he assigned cavalry leader Pleasonton to his staff rather than as a field commander. As a result, with Buford sending reports from Gettysburg on June 30 instead of Pleasonton, clear, concise, and accurate (rather than speculative and inconsistent) information flowed to headquarters. It helped enable Meade to maneuver his forces into an advantageous defensive position at Gettysburg.

Meade encouraged all of his army units, line or staff, to gather information about the enemy. Primarily through prisoner interrogation, during the heat of battle the BMI generated timely tactical intelligence on the strength, leadership, and disposition of the opposing forces. It also immediately responded to Meade's ad hoc intelligence requirements. Sharpe provided a detailed report on the condition and strength of Lee's forces prior to Meade's meeting with his corps commanders on the evening of July 2. It proved an important element in the decision to remain in position at Gettysburg and fight another day.

The signal corps did yeoman work maintaining reliable field communications between combat units and Meade's headquarters and producing timely intelligence through observation of enemy activities. As Confederate artillery commander Alexander acknowledged, the mere presence of the signal corps station on Little Round Top played a key role in delaying Longstreet's attack on July 2 during which Union forces deployed newly arrived forces to counter an attack.[10]

The capture of Davis' letter rejecting Lee's plan to divert Union forces to defend the capital and its receipt early in the day on July 3 assured Meade he would continue to have the upper hand over his opponent. The BMI's information about the size, location, and leadership of Ewell's corps assisted Meade in the struggle for Culp's Hill on the morning of July 3. The BMI's report that the enemy had a shortage of fresh troops before the

---

10 Brown, *The Signal Corps*, 367-68.

Pickett-Pettigrew-Trimble assault on July 3 boosted confidence that the troops could repulse an attack.

Timely information from these intelligence sources allowed Meade to make rapid and informed tactical decisions while undermining the enemy's prospects of victory on the battlefield. While Lee lamented that the battle had commenced in the absence of correct intelligence, Meade could well have claimed the battle was won because of the timeliness and accuracy of intelligence he received.[11]

Although the fighting at Gettysburg had ended, the campaign itself had not yet played out. Lee had to extract his forces from Northern soil, a difficult and hazardous endeavor. This time, however, Stuart's cavalry, his primary source of intelligence, would be on hand to play a key role in the outcome of this phase of the campaign.

Retreat and Pursuit

> Meade, it must be confessed, was not a great general . . . [he] was extremely cautious, too cautious to be apt to win a great victory like the capture or annihilation of the army opposed to him.
>
> Capt. Robert Beecham[12]

> As commander, Meade seemed to me to lack the boldness that was necessary to bring the war to a close. He lacked self-confidence and tenacity of purpose.
>
> Charles A. Dana
> Assistant Secretary of War[13]

After their defeat during the three-day battle, the Confederates retreated toward the safety of the Potomac River crossings. During the retreat, the two armies resumed the cat and mouse game that took place earlier in the invasion. Meade was ordered to overtake and attack the Army of Northern Virginia before it crossed the Potomac into its home territory. Meade, however, pursued cautiously, while Lee withdrew with dispatch.[14]

---

11 Lee, *Recollections and Letters*, 102.

12 R. K. Beecham, *Gettysburg: The Pivotal Battle of the Civil War* (Chicago, 1911), 128, 144.

13 Charles A. Dana, *Recollections of the Civil War: With the Leaders at Washington and in the Field in the Sixties* (Lincoln, NE, 1996), 189-90.

14 *OR* 27, pt. 1, 82-83; pt. 2, 311.

Stuart's cavalry, reunited with the army on July 2, conducted efficient intelligence and counterintelligence operations during Lee's withdrawal. The Union cavalry, however, maneuvered erratically, thereby allowing the Confederates to reach the Potomac relatively unscathed. Lee, who had suffered his first major defeat at Gettysburg, maintained an aggressive attitude during the retreat. The victor Meade, however, was ambivalent about another encounter with Lee and his army. He operated hesitantly and ceded the initiative to his enemy who otherwise faced a dire situation when high waters choked off crossing points at the Potomac. Ironically Meade, who won a great victory over Lee at Gettysburg, would subsequently fade from history's spotlight. The meritorious reputation he earned at the battle got considerably tarnished when he did not reengage nor attempt to impede Lee's army before its escape across the Potomac River ten days after the battle.

When the two armies clashed at Gettysburg, Lee repeatedly attacked Meade's army over a three-day period. Meade wisely chose to fight on the defensive, but he hesitated to stage a counteroffensive after handing Lee's army a crushing defeat on July 3. Given knowledge of the weakened condition of the enemy, a more aggressive general would have vigorously pursued and inflicted further damage on the enemy's retreating forces.

Meade's inclination to remain on the defensive deprived him of a more complete victory at Gettysburg, and it virtually negated his stated purpose to reengage Lee's army during the pursuit after the battle. His decision to entrench his army in the face of the enemy at Williamsport, rather than ordering an attack against a weakened and vulnerable opponent, as well as his refusal to send troops across the river to block Lee's retreat, reflected the character of a man more inclined to safety than risk. As Lincoln observed, Meade would never again have more ideal conditions to engage the enemy with the odds so much in his favor.[15]

Meade displayed uneasiness in his new role as army commander in other ways: he hesitated to accept a considerable amount of intelligence about the location, strength, condition, and morale of Lee's army following the battle. He neglected opportunities to go on the offensive and even directed his commanders not to engage the enemy. Moreover, Meade's orders for a four-division reconnaissance-in-force on the morning of July 14 was aimed at

---

15 Roy P. Basler, *Abraham Lincoln: His Speeches and Writings* (Cleveland, OH, 2001), 711-12.

gathering information about the enemy's position, not directing the entire army to attack the enemy as he would later claim.[16]

Before Lee's army crossed the Potomac, some Union officers and men recognized that the enemy was abandoning their position and moving toward the river. It was known for certain that the Rebels had a bridge across the Potomac and likely would cross the river the night of the 13th. Yet, Meade kept his own counsel, and paid no heed to these reports. Meade had also received several reports, including an eye-witness observation, that Lee had a pontoon bridge under reconstruction at Falling Waters to facilitate his army's escape. Inexplicably, he chose not to send cavalry across the river at Harper's Ferry to impede construction or destroy Lee's bridge. When informed that Lee sent troops to hold open an alternate escape route up river, Meade took no action to cut off that route despite the presence of thousands of Union troops nearby.

On a number of occasions, Meade complained he lacked information about the enemy, but he did not specify what was lacking. In reality, he received a steady flow of intelligence about the location, strength, and intentions of the enemy. From July 9-11, Sharpe furnished Meade with seven separate reports on Lee's activities from BMI scouts operating near and behind enemy lines. The cavalry also provided a steady supply of information about the location and strength of enemy positions. Inundated with a plethora of details about the enemy from several sources, Meade was still slow to absorb it and take action.

Meade bowed to the will of his corps commanders on July 12 not to stage an attack the following day instead of ordering them to follow his direction. He did not feel "authorized to attack," he told an infuriated Halleck until he learned more about the enemy's position and strength. The new army commander clearly lacked self-confidence, and this would continue to hamper his ability to lead.[17]

Meade eventually revealed his privately-held beliefs about the enemy prior to their crossing the river. When Meade wrote to his wife, he was free to express his real feelings. Though he had stated his intention to engage Lee's army before it crossed the Potomac, on July 14, he loathed admitting that the enemy had done just that during the night, and that the Washington authorities had censured him for allowing it. Meade vented his frustration that his superiors

16 HQ Army of the Potomac Circular, July 13, 1863, OR 27, pt. 3, 675.

17 Meade to Halleck, July 13, 1863, OR 27, pt. 1, 91-92.

expected him to do the impossible and then refused to accept his resignation. He expected Washington criticism; his predecessors had received the same. But he thought Washington should have been content with his driving Lee out of Maryland and not prodded him to engage Lee again until his army had been reinforced and reorganized.

The Gettysburg campaign ended when Lee's army crossed the Potomac River on July 14. It had played out over a period of six weeks and had provided an outstanding example of how military leaders rely on information resources to support operational planning. At Gettysburg, the Union army gathered and applied intelligence about the enemy to advantage and thereby gained a victory. While the intelligence and counterintelligence operatives on both sides carried out their missions during the retreat, the outcome of that phase of the campaign depended on the commitment and steadfastness of the respective army commanders. And in this area the Confederates prevailed. Timely and accurate intelligence cannot affect the outcome of a conflict unless it is coupled with resolute leadership. As historian John Keegan maintains, wise opinion holds that "in combat willpower always counts for more than foreknowledge."[18]

Other factors helped limit Meade's ability to contest Lee's safe crossing of the Potomac. Stuart's horsemen played a key role in keeping Meade's pursuing forces at bay and providing Lee timely information. And without his success in screening the Rebel army during the retreat, the outcome might have been different. By contrast, the Union cavalry performed much less effectively against Lee's retreating army largely because Meade and Pleasonton failed to provide it clear and purposeful direction.

Two distinct concepts of intelligence operations competed during the Gettysburg campaign. While Stuart demonstrated considerable effectiveness at gathering intelligence and in counterintelligence operations on the march northward and during the retreat, Lee discovered that without Stuart on hand for a period leading up to and partially during the battle, his invincible army had become vulnerable. Conversely, the BMI's concept of producing all-source intelligence by a dedicated staff, though unique at the time, proved more effective than Lee's method of personally analyzing information mainly collected by the cavalry.

Lee's invasion of the North that led to the battle of Gettysburg is considered one of the Civil War's decisive campaigns. Although both sides

18 Keegan, *Intelligence in War*, 25.

claimed a degree of success, the character of the war gradually changed in favor of the North after the two armies returned to Virginia. Many individuals and units earned recognition for their important contributions during the campaign. Less attention is paid, however, to the role of gathering, evaluating, and reporting information for the use of army commanders. Hopefully, this study has rectified that oversight.

Appendix

Lee-Davis-Cooper Correspondence on Lee's Deception Plan

Gen. Robert E. Lee sent three letters, one dated June 23 and two dated June 25, 1863, to President Jefferson Davis proposing moving Confederate troops from the Carolinas and Virginia to threaten Washington. Pertinent extracts of these messages follow:

Headquarters Army of Northern Virginia, June 23, 1863
His Excellency President Davis, Richmond

Mr. President: The season is now so far advanced as to render it improbable that the enemy will undertake active operations on the Carolina and Georgia coast before the return of frost. If an army could be organized under the command of General Beauregard, and pushed forward to Culpeper Court-House, threatening Washington from that direction, it would not only effect a diversion most favorable for this army, but would, I think relieve us of any apprehension of an attack upon Richmond during our absence. The well known anxiety of the Northern Government for the safety of its capital would induce it to retain a large force for its defense and thus sensibly relieve the opposition to our advance. Last summer, you will remember, that troops were recalled from Hilton Head, North Carolina, and Western Virginia for the protection of Washington, and there can be little doubt that if our present movements northward are accompanied by a demonstration on the south side of the Potomac, the coast would be again relieved, and troops now on the Peninsula and south of the Potomac be withdrawn.

If success should attend the operations of this army, and what I now suggest would greatly increase the probability of that result, we might even hope to compel the recall of some of the enemy's troops from the west.

Very respectfully, your obedient servant,
R. E. Lee, General.[1]

Opposite Williamsport, [Maryland], June 25, 1863

His Excellency President Davis, Richmond

Mr. President: If the plan that I suggested the other day, of organizing an army, even in effigy, under General Beauregard at Culpeper Court-House, can be carried into effect, much relief will be afforded. If even the brigades in Virginia and North Carolina, which Generals [D.H.] Hill and [Arnold] Elzey think cannot be spared, were ordered there at once, and General Beauregard were sent there, if he had to return to South Carolina, it would do more to protect both States from marauding expeditions of the enemy than anything else.

With great respect, your obedient servant,
R. E. Lee, General.[2]

Williamsport, June 25, 1863

His Excellency President Davis, Richmond

Mr. President: So strong is my conviction of the necessity of activity on our part in military affairs, that you will excuse my adverting to the subject again, notwithstanding what I have said in my previous letter of to-day.

I feel sure, therefore, that the best use that can be made of the troops in Carolina, and those in Virginia now guarding Richmond, would be the prompt assembling of the main body of them, leaving sufficient to prevent raids, together with as many as can be drawn from the army of General Beauregard, at Culpeper Court-House, under command of that officer. I do not think they could more effectually prevent aggressive movements on the part of the enemy in any other way, while their assistance to this army in its operations would be very great.

1   Lee to Davis, June 23, 1863, OR 27, pt. 3, 924-25.

2   Ibid., June 25, 930-31.

I am, with great respect, your obedient servant,

R. E. Lee, General.[3]

Both Adjutant General Samuel Cooper and President Davis responded to the plan Lee proposed on June 23, but neither letter reached Lee. On July 2, 1863, a Union cavalry detachment operating behind Confederate lines at Greencastle, PA, captured these letters, and delivered them to Maj. Gen. George G. Meade at Gettysburg by early morning on July 3. Meade's chief of staff, Maj. Gen. Daniel Butterfield, telegraphed the text of the letters to general-in-chief Henry Halleck in Washington.[4] Pertinent extracts follow.

Near Gettysburg, Pa., July 3, 1863. (Received [in Washington] July 4, 4.10 a.m.)

Major-General Halleck, General-in-Chief:

The following dispatches have been intercepted by our scouts.

DANL. BUTTERFIELD, Major-General, Chief of Staff.

[Inclosure No. 1.]

Adjutant-General's Office, Richmond, Va., June 29, 1863

General R. E. Lee, Comdg. Army Northern Virginia, Winchester, Va.

General: While with the President last night, I received your letter of the 23d instant. After reading it, the President was embarrassed to understand that part of it which refers to the plan of assembling an army at Culpeper Court-House under General Beauregard. This is the first intimation that he has had that such a plan was ever in contemplation, and, taking all things into consideration, he cannot see how it can by any possibility be carried into effect. You will doubtless learn before this reaches you that the enemy has again assembled in force on the Peninsula, estimated between 20,000 and 30,000 men.

Every effort is being made here to be prepared for the enemy at all points, but we must look chiefly to the protection of the capital. In doing this, we may be obliged to hazard

3   Ibid., 931-33.

4   Ibid., pt. 1, 75-77.

something at other points. You can easily estimate your strength here, and I would suggest for your consideration whether, in this state of things, you might not be able to spare a portion of your force to protect your line of communication against attempted raids by the enemy.

Very respectfully, your obedient servant,
S. COOPER, Adjutant-General

(Inclosure No. 2)

RICHMOND, VA., June 28, 1863
General R. E. LEE, Commanding, &c

General:
Yours of the 23d received this evening, and hasten to reply to the point presented in relation to the forces on the coast of South Carolina and Georgia.

Grant reached the river, got re-enforcements, made intrenchments, and General Johnston continues to call for re-enforcements, though his first requisition was more than filled by withdrawing troops from Generals Beauregard and Bragg. General Bragg is threatened with attack, has fallen back to his intrenched position at Tullahoma, and called on Buckner for aid. General Beauregard says that no troops have been withdrawn by the enemy from his point [front] since those returned to New Berne, and that his whole force is necessary to cover his line . . . and communicating the fear that Vicksburg would fall unless Johnston was strongly and promptly re-enforced. D. H. Hill has a small force, part of which has been brought here. Clingman's brigade is near Wilmington; Colquitt's, Kinston; Martin's, nominally on railroad (Weldon, &c.). Cooke's, Ransom's, and Jenkins' have been brought here, the last two temporarily from the defense of Petersburg and country thereabouts. Wise's brigade is, as you left it, engaged in the defense of Richmond, and serving in the country to the east of the city. The enemy have been reported in large force at White House, with indications of an advance on Richmond. We are organizing companies for home defense, and the spirit of resistance is increasing. Corse's brigade, in accordance with your orders, left Hanover Junction. All the artillery, I am informed, was taken away, and the single regiment of infantry which constituted the guard for the bridges proved unequal to the duty, as you have no doubt learned. Re-enforcements were ordered to go up, but some delay occurred, and they arrived too late to save the bridge or the brave guard which had unsuccessfully defended it. The Yankees, reported to be three regiments of cavalry, returned from the Central road in the direction of Hanover (Old Town), and nothing has been heard of them since.

The advance of your army increases our want of cavalry on the north and east of the city, but, excepting one regiment from North Carolina, I do not know of any which we can expect soon to be available to us.

In yours of the 20th, you say, " . . . if any of the brigades that I have left behind for the protection of Richmond can . . . be spared, I should like them to be sent to me." It has been an effort with me to answer the clamor to have troops stopped or recalled, to protect the city and the railroads communicating with your army. Corse's brigade has gone, and Wise's is the only other left by you. Cooke's was in North Carolina, and Davis' brigade was sent to complete Heth's division in place of Cooke's. Ransom's and Jenkins' constitute the defense of the south side as far as Weldon, and are relied on for service elsewhere, from Wilmington to Richmond. General Elzey is positive that the enemy intend to attack here, and his scouts bring intelligence which, if I believed it, would render me no more anxious for the city than at any former time. I do not believe the Yankees have such force as is stated, but that they have enough to render it necessary to keep some troops within reach, and some at Petersburg, at least, until Suffolk is truly evacuated.

Do not understand me as balancing accounts in the matter of brigades; I only repeat that I have not many to send you, and enough to form an army to threaten, if not capture, Washington as soon it is uncovered by Hooker's army. My purpose was to show you that the force here and in North Carolina is very small, and I may add that the brigades are claimed as properly of their command. Our information as to the enemy may be more full and reliable hereafter. It now is materially greater than when you were here.

Very respectfully and truly yours,
JEFFERSON DAVIS.

Bibliography

Primary Sources

Manuscripts

Babcock, John C. Papers. Library of Congress, Washington, DC
Duvall, Eli. Message Book. Museum of the Confederacy. Richmond, VA
Fishel, Edwin C. Collection, Georgetown University Library, Washington, DC
Hooker, Joseph Collection. Huntington Library, San Marino, CA
Kay, John B. Papers. University of Michigan. Bentley Historical Library, Ann Arbor, MI
Kidd, James H. Collection. University of Michigan. Bentley Historical Library, Ann Arbor, MI
Pleasonton, Alfred Papers. Library of Congress, Washington, DC
Records of the Bureau of Military Information. Record Group 393. National Archives, Washington, DC
Sharpe, George H. Collection. Senate House State Historic Site, Kingston, NY
Venable, Charles Collection. University of North Carolina, Chapel Hill, NC

Newspapers

Charleston Mercury
New York *Times*
Philadelphia Press
Richmond *Dispatch*
Richmond *Examiner*
Sacramento Daily Union

Books

Alexander, Edward Porter. *Military Memoirs of a Confederate: A Critical Narrative*. New York: Da Capo Press, 1993.
Baker, L. C. *The Secret Service in the Late War*. Philadelphia, PA: John E. Potter & Company, 1874.
Basler, Roy P. *Collected Works of Abraham Lincoln*, 9 Vols. . New Brunswick, NJ: Rutgers University Press. 1953.
Bates, David Homer. *Lincoln in the Telegraph Office: Recollections of the United States Military Telegraph Corps During the Civil War*. Lincoln, NE: University of Nebraska Press, 1995.
Bates, Samuel. *History of the Pennsylvania Volunteers, 1861-1865*. 5 Vols. Harrisburg, PA: B. Singerly, State Printer, 1870.
Blackford, W. W. *War Years with Jeb Stuart*. Baton Rouge, LA: Louisiana State University Press, 1993.
Brooks, Noah. *Washington in Lincoln's Time*. New York: The Century Co., 1895.

Brown, J. Willard. *The Signal Corps, U.S.A. in the War of the Rebellion*. Baltimore, MD: Butternut and Blue, 1996.

Brown, R. Shepard. *Stringfellow of the Fourth*. New York: Crown Publishers, Inc., 1960.

Caren, Eric C. *Civil War Extra: A Newspaper History of the Civil War From 1863 to 1865*. 2 Vols. Edison, NJ: Castle Books, 1999.

Coffin, Charles Carleton, *The Boys of '61: Four Years of Fighting*. Boston, MA: Estes and Lauriat, 1896.

Conrad, Thomas N. *A Confederate Spy: A Story of the Civil War*. New York: J. S. Ogilvie Publishing Company, 1892.

———. *The Rebel Scout: A Thrilling History of Scouting Life in the Southern Army*. Washington, DC: The National Publishing Co., 1904.

Cooke, John Esten. *Wearing of the Gray: being Personal Portraits, Scenes, and Adventures of the War*. Baton Rouge, LA: Louisiana State University Press, 1959.

Doster, William E. *Lincoln and Episodes of the Civil War*. New York: G. P. Putnam's Sons, 1915.

Douglas, Henry Kyd. *I Rode With Stonewall*. Chapel Hill, NC: The University of North Carolina Press, 1968.

Dowdey, Clifford and Louis H. Manarin, eds. *The Wartime Papers of Robert E. Lee*. New York: Bramhall House, 1961.

Early, Jubal Anderson. *Jubal Early's Memoirs*. Baltimore, MD: The Nautical & Aviation Publishing Company of America, 1989.

Eby, Cecil D., Jr. *The Diaries of David Hunter Strother: A Virginia Yankee in the Civil War*. Chapel Hill, NC: The University of North Carolina Press, 1989.

Gallagher, Gary W., ed. *Fighting for the Confederacy: The Personal Recollections of General Edward Porter Alexander*. Chapel Hill, NC: University of North Carolina Press, 1989.

Haskell, Frank A. *The Battle of Gettysburg*. New York: Bantam Books, 1992.

Haupt, Herman. *Reminiscences of General Herman Haupt*. Milwaukee, WI: Wright & Joys, 1901.

Hoffman, Elliott W., ed. *A Vermont Cavalryman in War and Love: The Civil War Letters of Brevet Major General William Wells and Anna Richardson*. Lynchburg, VA: Schroeder Publications, 2007.

Hood, J. B. *Advance and Retreat*. Edison, NJ: Blue and Grey Press, 1985.

Howard, Oliver Otis. *Autobiography*. 2 Vols. New York: Baker & Taylor Company, 1908.

Jones, J. B. *A Rebel War Clerk's Diary at the Confederate States Capital*. 2 Vols. Philadelphia, PA: J. B. Lippincott & Co., 1866.

Jones, John William, Robert Alonzo Brock and James Power Smith, eds. *Southern Historical Society Papers*. 52 Vols. Richmond, VA: Southern Historical Society, 1899-1959.

Kidd, J. H. *Personal Recollections of a Cavalryman with Custer's Michigan Cavalry Brigade in the Civil War*. Grand Rapids, MI: The Black Letter Press, 1969.

Ladd, David L. and Audrey J. Ladd. *The Bachelder Papers: Gettysburg in Their Own Words*. 3 Vols. Dayton, OH: Morningside Books, 1994.

Lee, Robert E. *Recollections and Letters of General Robert E. Lee*. Garden City, NY: Garden City Publishing Co., 1924.

Long, A. L. *Memoirs of Robert E. Lee: His Military and Personal History*. Edison, NJ: The Blue and Grey Press, 1983.

Longstreet, James. *From Manassas to Appomattox: Memoirs of the Civil War in America*. New York: Smithmark Publishers, 1994 reprint.

Lord, Walter. *The Fremantle Diary: Being the Journal of Lieutenant Colonel Arthur James Lyon Fremantle, Coldstream Guards, on his three Months in the Southern States*. Short Hills, NJ: Burford Books, 1954.

Mahan, D. H. *Advanced-Guard, Out-Post, and Detachment Service of Troops, with the Essential Principles of Strategy, and Grand Tactics for the use of Officers of the Militia and Volunteers*. New York: John Wiley, 1863.

McClellan, H. B. *The Campaigns of Stuart's Cavalry*. Edison, NJ: The Blue and Grey Press, 1993.

McDonald, Archie P., ed. *Make Me a Map of the Valley: The Civil War Journal of Stonewall Jackson's Topographer*. Dallas, TX: Southern Methodist University Press, 1973.

McLean, James L. Jr. and Judy W. McLean. *Gettysburg Sources*. 3 Vols. Baltimore, MD: Butternut and Blue, 1986-90.

McSwain, Eleanor D., ed. *Crumbling Defenses or Memoirs and Reminiscences of John Logan Black*. Macon, GA: J. W. Burke Company, 1960.

Meade, George. *The Life and Letters of George Gordon Meade*. 2 Vols. New York: Charles Scribner's Sons, 1913.

Mitchell, Adele H., ed. *The Letters of Major General James E. B. Stuart*. Centreville, VA: Stuart-Mosby Historical Society, 1990.

Mosby, John S. *War Reminiscences and Stuart's Cavalry Campaigns*. New York: Dodd, Mead & Company, 1887.

——. *Stuart's Cavalry in the Gettysburg Campaign*, New York: Moffat, Yard & Company, 1908.

Oeffinger, John C., ed. *A Soldier's General: The Civil War Letters of Major General Lafayette McLaws*. Chapel Hill, NC: University of North Carolina Press, 2001.

Penfield, Captain James. *1863-64 Civil War Diary*. Ticonderoga, NY: The Penfield Foundation, Inc., 1999.

Pennypacker, Isaac R. *General Meade*. New York: D. Appleton and Company, 1901.

Pinkerton, Allan. *The Spy of the Rebellion*. Lincoln, NE: University of Nebraska Press, 1989.

Plum, William R. *The Military Telegraph during the Civil War in the United States*. 2 Vols. Chicago, IL: Jansen, McClurg & Company, 1882.

Ross, FitzGerald. *Cities and Camps of the Confederate States*. Urbana: University of Illinois Press, 1997.

Rusling, Gen. James F. *Men and Things I Saw in Civil War Days*. Cincinnati, OH: Easton & Mains, 1899.

Russell, Charles Wells, ed. *Gray Ghost: The Memoirs of Colonel John S. Mosby*. New York, Bantam Books, 1992.

Scott, John. *Partisan Life with Col. John S. Mosby*. Lake Monticello, VA: Old Soldier Books. 1989.

Sneden, Robert Knox. *Eye of the Storm: A Civil War Odyssey*. New York: The Free Press, 2000.

Sparks, David S., ed. *Inside Lincoln's Army: The Diary of General Marsena Rudolph Patrick, Provost Marshal General, Army of the Potomac*. New York: Thomas Yoseloff, 1964.

Sorrell, G. Moxley. *At the Right Hand of Longstreet: Recollections of a Confederate Staff Officer*. Lincoln, NE: University of Nebraska Press, 1999.

Stanford, Martha Gerber. *The Civil War Letters of Daniel Peck*, Freeman, SD: Pine Hill Press, Inc., 1993.

Styple, William B., ed. *Writing & Fighting the Confederate War: The Letters of Peter Wellington Alexander, Confederate War Correspondent*. Kearny, NJ: Belle Grove Publishing, 2002.

Summers, Festus P. *A Borderland Confederate: The Civil War Diaries and Letters of William L. Wilson*. Pittsburgh, PA: University of Pittsburgh Press, 1962.

Taylor, Chas. E. *The Signal and Secret Service of the Confederate States*. Harmans, MD: Toomey Press, 1986.

Taylor, Walter H. *General Lee: His Campaigns in Virginia, 1861-1865*. Lincoln, NE: University of Nebraska Press, 1994.

——. *Four Years with General Lee*, New York: Bonanza Books, 1962.

Trout, Robert J. *With Pen and Saber: The Letters and Diaries of J.E.B. Stuart's Staff Officers*. Mechanicsburg, PA: Stackpole Books, 1995.

——. ed. *In The Saddle With Stuart: The Story of Frank Smith Robertson of Jeb Stuart's Staff*. Gettysburg, PA: Thomas Publications, 1998.

Wainwright, Charles S. *A Diary of Battle: The Personal Journals of Colonel Charles Wainwright*, 1861-1865. New York: Harcourt, Brace & World, 1962.

War of the Rebellion: A Compilation of the Official Records of the Union and Confederate Armies, 128 Vols., Washington, D.C., 1880-1901.

Weld, Stephen. *War Diary and Letters of Stephen Minot Weld, 1861-1865.* Cambridge, MA: The Riverside Press, 1912.

Welles, Gideon. *Diary of Gideon Welles: Secretary of the Navy Under Lincoln and Johnson.* 3 Vols. Boston, MA: Houghton Mifflin Company, 1911.

Williams, T. Harry, ed. *Selected Writings and Speeches of Abraham Lincoln.* Chicago, IL: Packard and Company, 1943.

Williamson, James J. *Mosby's Rangers: A Record of the Operations of the Forty-third Battalion Virginia Cavalry.* New York: Ralph B. Kenyon, 1896.

Wittenberg, Eric, ed. *One of Custer's Wolverines: The Civil War Letters of Brevet Brigadier General James H. Kidd, 6th Michigan Cavalry.* Kent, OH: Kent State University Press, 2000.

Wittenberg, Eric J. *Under Custer's Command: The Civil War Journal of James Henry Avery.* Washington, DC: Brassey's, 2000.

Worsham, John H. *One of Jackson's Foot Cavalry: His Experience and What He Saw during the War, 1861-1865.* New York: The Neale Publishing Company, 1912.

Articles

Gibbon, John. "The Council of War on the Second Day." Johnson and Buel, eds. *Battles and Leaders of the Civil War.* 4 Vols. New York: Thomas Yoseloff, 1956. Vol. 3, 313-14.

Greely, A. W. "The Signal Corps." *The Photographic History of the Civil War*, 10 Vols. Secaucus, NJ: The Blue & Grey Press, 1987. Vol 4, 312-340.

Hall, James O. "The Spy Harrison," *Civil War Times Illustrated* (February 1986). Vol. 24, no. 10, 19-25.

Halstead, E. P. "Incidents of the First Day at Gettysburg." Johnson and Buel, eds. *Battles and Leaders of the Civil War.* 4 Vols. New York: Thomas Yoseloff, 1956. Vol. 3, 284-85.

Havens, Lieutenant F. R. "How Mosby Destroyed Our Train." William O. Lee, *Seventh Regiment Michigan Volunteer Cavalry, 1862-1865.* Detroit, MI: Detroit Book Press, 1990, 90-95.

Imboden, John D. "The Confederate Retreat From Gettysburg," Johnson and Buel, eds. *Battles and Leaders of the Civil War,* 4 Vols. New York: Thomas Yoseloff, 1956. Vol. 3, 420-29.

Kershaw, E.B. "Kershaw's Brigade at Gettysburg." Johnson and Buel, eds. *Battles and Leaders of the Civil War.* 4 Vols. New York: Thomas Yoseloff, 1956. vol 3, 31-38.

Longstreet, James. "Lee's Invasion of Pennsylvania." Johnson and Buel, eds. *Battles and Leaders of the Civil War.* 4 Vols. New York: Thomas Yoseloff, 1956. vol 3, 244-51.

——. "Lee in Pennsylvania." Alexander Kelly McClure, ed. *The Annals of the Civil War Written by Leading Participants North and South.* New York: Da Capo Press, 1994. 414-46.

——. "The Mistakes of Gettysburg." Alexander Kelly McClure, ed. *The Annals of the Civil War Written by Leading Participants North and South.* New York: Da Capo Press, 1994, 619-33.

McLaws, LaFayette. "Gettysburg." *Southern Historical Society Papers.* 52 Vols. Richmond, VA, 1876-1959. Vol. 7 (February 1879), 64-90.

——, "The Second Day at Gettysburg: General Sickles Answered by the Commander of the Opposing Forces—The Federal Disaster on the Left." *Gettysburg Sources.* 3 Vols. Baltimore, MD: Butternut and Blue, 1990. Vol. 3, 132-44.

Mosby, John S., "The Confederate Cavalry in the Gettysburg Campaign, Part I." Johnson and Buel, eds. *Battles and Leaders of the Civil War.* 4 Vols. New York: Thomas Yoseloff, 1956. Vol. 3, 251-53.

Power, J. Tracy. "The Confederate as Gallant Knight: The Life and Death of William Downs Farley." *Civil War History.* 1991. Vol. 37, No. 3.

Price, Channing. "Stuart's Chambersburg Raid: an Eyewitness Account," *Civil War Times Illustrated* (January 1966), 9-15.

Robertson, Beverly H., "The Confederate Cavalry in the Gettysburg Campaign." Johnson and Buel, eds. *In Battles and Leaders of the Civil War.* 4 Vols. New York: Thomas Yoseloff, 1956. Vol 3, 253.

Taylor, Colonel W. H. "The Campaign in Pennsylvania." Alexander Kelly McClure, ed. *The Annals of the Civil War Written by Leading Participants North and South.* New York: Da Capo Press, 1994. 305-18.

Online Sources

Greely, A.W. *Military-Telegraph Service,* http://www.civilwarsignals.org/pages/tele/telegreely/telegreely.html

"3rd Regiment Indiana Cavalry (45th Regiment Volunteers)." *Union Army Regimental History Index.* http://www.civilwararchive.com/Unreghst/unincav.htm#3rd

Tortorelli, Susan (transcriber). *Illinois Sturgis Rifles Regiment History.* http://civilwar.illinoisgenweb.org/history/misc-003.html

Secondary Sources

Books

Allen,Thomas B. George Washington, *Spymaster: How the Americans Outspied the British and Won the Revolutionary War.* Washington, DC: National Geographic, 2004.

Ambrose, Stephen E. *Halleck: Lincoln's Chief of Staff.* Baton Rouge, LA: Louisiana State University Press, 1962.

Bakeless, John. *Spies of the Confederacy.* Mineola, NY: Dover Publications, Inc., 1970.

Bartholomees, Boone Jr. *Buff Facings and Gilt Buttons: Staff and headquarters Operation in the Army of Northern Virginia, 1861-1865.* Columbia, SC: University of South Carolina Press, 1998.

Beatie, Russel H. *Army of the Potomac: Birth of Command, November 1860-September 1861.* Cambridge, MA: Da Capo Press, 2002.

——. *Army of the Potomac: McClellan Takes Command,* Cambridge, MA: Da Capo Press, 2004.

Beringer, Richard E., Herman Hattaway, Archer Jones, William N. Still, Jr. *Why the South Lost the Civil War.* Athens, GA: The University of Georgia Press, 1986.

Blair, William Alan. *A Politician Goes to War: The Civil War Letters of John White Geary.* University Park, PA: The Pennsylvania State University Press, 1995.

Boatner, Mark M. III. *The Civil War Dictionary.* New York: David McKay Company, Inc., 1959.

Boritt, Gabor S. *Lincoln's Generals.* New York: Oxford University Press, 1994.

Bowden, Scott and Bill Ward. *Last Chance for Victory: Robert E. Lee and the Gettysburg Campaign.* Da Capo Press: Cambridge, MA, 2001.

Bowmaster, Patrick A. "Confederate Brig. Gen. B. H. Robertson and the 1863 Gettysburg Campaign". M.A. thesis. Blacksburg, VA: Virginia Polytechnic Institute and State University, 1995.

Brown, Kent Masterson. *Retreat from Gettysburg: Lee, Logistics, and the Pennsylvania Campaign.* Chapel Hill, NC: University of North Carolina Press, 2005.

Brown, R., Shepard. *Stringfellow of the Fourth.* New York: Crown Publishers, Inc., 1960.

———. *The Amazing Career of the most successful Confederate Spy.* New York: Crown Publishers, 1960.

Busey, John W. and David G. Martin. *Regimental Strengths and Losses at Gettysburg.* Hightstown, NJ: Longstreet House, 2005.

Cannon, Timothy L. Tom Gorsline, and Nancy F. Whitmore. *Pictorial History of Frederick, Maryland: The First 250 Years, 1745-1995.* Frederick, MD: Key Publishing Group, 1995.

Cleaves, Freeman. *Meade of Gettysburg.* Norman, OK: University of Oklahoma Press, 1960.

Coco, Gregory A. *A Strange and Blighted Land: Gettysburg, The Aftermath of a Battle.* Gettysburg, PA: Thomas Publications, 1995.

———, *A Vast Sea of Misery,* Gettysburg, PA: Thomas Publications, 1988.

Coddington, Edwin B. *The Gettysburg Campaign.* New York: Charles Scribner's Sons, 1968.

Collins, Darrell L. *Major General Robert E. Rodes of the Army of Northern Virginia.* New York: Savas Beatie, 2008.

Conrad, W.P. and Ted Alexander. *When War Passed This Way.* Shippensburg, PA: Beidel Printing House, Inc., 1982.

Davis, Oliver Wilson. *Life of David Bell Birney.* Whitefish, MT: Kessinger Publishing, 2010.

Davis, William C. "Join the Cavalry," *Rebels & Yankees: The Fighting Men of the Civil War.* London: Salamander Books, 1999.

"Department of Defense Dictionary of Military and Associated Terms." *Joint Publication 1-02,* October 16, 2006.

Donald, David Herbert. *Lincoln.* New York: Simon & Schuster, 1995.

Dowdey, Clifford. *Lee.* New York: Bonanza Books, 1965.

Evans, Charles M. *War of the Aeronauts: A History of Ballooning in the Civil War.* Mechanicsburg, PA: Stackpole Books, 2002.

Faust, Patricia L., ed. *Historical Times Illustrated Encyclopedia of the Civil War.* New York: Harper & Row, Publishers, 1986.

Fellman, Michael, ed. *Memoirs of General W. T. Sherman.* New York: Penguin Books, 2000.

Ferguson, Ernest B. *Chancellorsville 1863: The Souls of the Brave.* New York: Alfred A. Knopf, 1992.

Fishel, Edwin C. *The Secret War for the Union: The Untold Story of Military Intelligence in the Civil War.* Boston, MA: Houghton Mifflin Company, 1996.

Foote, Shelby. *The Civil War: A Narrative: Fredericksburg to Meridian.* New York: Vintage Books, 1986.

Fordney, Ben F. *Stoneman at Chancellorsville: The Coming of Age of Union Cavalry.* Shippensburg, PA, White Mane Press, 1998.

Fox, William F. *Regimental Losses in the American Civil War, 1861-1865.* New York: Albany Publishing Company, 1889.

Freeman Douglas Southall. *R. E. Lee: A Biography.* 4 Vols. New York: Charles Scribner's Sons, 1935.

———. *Lee's Lieutenants.* 3 Vols. New York: Charles Scribner's Sons, 1971.

French, Steve. *Imboden's Brigade in the Gettysburg Campaign.* Berkeley Springs, WV: Morgan Messenger, 2008.

Gallagher, Gary W. ed. *The Second Day at Gettysburg.* Kent, OH: Kent State University Press, 1993.

Goodhart, Briscoe. *History of the Independent Loudoun Virginia Rangers, U.S. Vol. Cav. (SCOUTS), 1862-65.* Washington, DC: Press of McGill & Wallace, 1896.

Goodwin, Doris Kearns. *Team of Rivals: The Political Genius of Abraham Lincoln.* New York: Simon & Schuster, 2005.

Gordon, Paul and Rita. *Never the Like Again: Frederick County, Maryland.* Frederick, MD: The Heritage Partnership, 1995.

Gottfried, Bradley M. *Brigades of Gettysburg: The Union and Confederate Brigades at the Battle of Gettysburg.* Cambridge, MA: Da Capo Press, 2002.

——. *The Maps of Gettysburg.* New York: Savas Beatie, 2007.

Harris, Brayton. *Blue & Gray in Black & White: Newspapers in the Civil War.* Washington, DC: Brassey's, 2000.

Harsh, Joseph L. *Confederate Tide Rising: Robert E. Lee and the Making of Southern Strategy, 1861-1862.* Kent, Ohio: Kent State University Press, 1998.

——. *Taken at the Flood: Robert E. Lee and Confederate Strategy in the Maryland Campaign of 1862.* Kent, OH: Kent State University Press, 1999.

Hattaway, Herman and Archer Jones. *How the North Won: A Military History of the Civil War.* Urbana: University of Illinois Press, 1991.

Hebert, Walter H. *Fighting Joe Hooker.* Lincoln, NE: University of Nebraska Press, 1999.

Hennessy, John J. *Return to Bull Run: The Campaign and Battle of Second Manassas.* New York, Simon and Schuster, 1993.

Hoke, Jacob. *The Great Invasion of 1863.* New York: Thomas Yoseloff, 1959.

Hyde, Bill, ed. *The Union Generals Speak: The Meade Hearings on the Battle of Gettysburg.* Baton Rouge, LA: Louisiana State University Press, 2003.

Jomini, Baron De. *The Art of War.* El Paso, TX: El Paso Norte Press, 2005.

Jones, Virgil Carrington. *Ranger Mosby.* Chapel Hill, NC: University of North Carolina Press, 1944.

——. *Gray Ghosts and Rebel Raiders.* New York: Galahad Books, 1956.

Katcher, Philip. *Sharpshooters of the Civil War.* Oxford, UK: Osprey Publishing, 2002.

Kegel, James A. *North with Lee and Jackson: The Lost Story of Gettysburg.* Mechanicsburg, PA: Stackpole Books, 1996.

Krick, Robert E. L. *Staff Officers in Gray: A Biographical Register of the Staff Officers in the Army of Northern Virginia.* Chapel Hill, NC: University of North Carolina Press, 2003.

Krick, Robert K. *Lee's Colonels.* Dayton, OH: Morningside Press, 1991.

Laino, Philip. *Gettysburg Campaign Atlas.* Dayton, OH: Gatehouse Press, 2009.

Larson, Rebecca D. *Blue and Gray Roses of Intrigue.* Gettysburg, PA: Thomas Publications, 1993.

Leech, Margaret. *Reveille in Washington.* New York: Carroll & Graf Publishers, Inc, 1969.

Longacre, Edward G. *Lincoln's Cavalrymen: A History of the Mounted Forces of The Army of the Potomac, 1861-1865.* Mechanicsburg, PA: Stackpole Books, 2000.

——. *Custer and His Wolverines: The Michigan Cavalry Brigade, 1861-1865.* Conshohocken, PA: Combined Publishing, 1997.

——. *The Cavalry at Gettysburg: A Tactical Study of Mounted Operations during the Civil War's Pivotal Campaign, 9 June-14 July 1863.* Lincoln, NE: University of Nebraska Press, 1986.

——. *Lee's Cavalrymen: A History of the Mounted Forces of the Army of Northern Virginia, 1861-1865.* Mechanicsburg, PA: Stackpole Books, 2002.

Lord, Francis A. *They Fought for the Union.* New York: Bonanza Books, 1960.

Manasco, Clifford G. *Signal Corps Camp of Instruction.* Fort Gordon, GA: United States Army Signal Corps Museum, n.d.

Martin, David G. *Gettysburg July 1.* Cambridge, MA: DaCapo Press, 1995.

Martin, Samuel J. *Kill-Cavalry: The Life of Union General Hugh Judson Kilpatrick.* Mechanicsburg, PA: Stackpole Books, 2000.

McDonald, Archie P. *Make Me a Map of the Valley: The Civil War Journal of Stonewall Jackson's Topographer.* Dallas, TX: Southern Methodist University Press, 1973.

McElfresh, Earl B. *Maps and Mapmakers of the Civil War.* New York: Harry N. Abrams, Inc., 1999.

McPherson, James M. *Battle Cry of Freedom: The Civil War Era.* New York: Ballantine Books, 1988.

Miller, Francis Trevelyan, ed. "Soldier Life and Secret Service." *The Photographic History of the Civil War.* 5 Vols. Secaucus, NJ: The Blue & Grey Press, 1987.

Miller, William J. *Mapping for Stonewall: The Civil War Service of Jed Hotchkiss.* Washington, DC: Elliott & Clark Publishing, 1993.

Milton, George Fort. *Abraham Lincoln and The Fifth Column*. Washington, DC: The Infantry Journal, 1943.

Murray, R. L. *Berdan's Sharpshooters in Combat: The Peninsula Campaign and Gettysburg*. Wolcott, NY: Benedum Books, 2005.

Nesbitt, Mark. *35 Days to Gettysburg*. Mechanicsburg, PA: Stackpole Books, 1992.

——. *Saber and Scapegoat: J. E. B. Stuart and the Gettysburg Controversy*. Mechanicsburg, PA: Stackpole Books, 2002.

Nye, Wilbur Sturtevant. *Here Come the Rebels!* Dayton, OH: Morningside Bookshop,1988.

O'Neill, Robert F., Jr. *The Cavalry Battles of Aldie, Middleburg and Upperville: Small But Important Riots, June 10-27, 1863*. Lynchburg, VA: H. E. Howard, Inc., 1993.

O'Toole, G. J. A. *Honorable Treachery: A History of U. S. Intelligence, Espionage, and Covert Action from the American Revolution to the CIA*. New York: Atlantic Monthly Press, 1991.

——. *The Encyclopedia of American Intelligence and Espionage: From the Revolutionary War to the Present*. New York: Facts on File, 1988.

Pfanz, Donald C. *Richard S. Ewell: A Soldier's Life*. Chapel Hill, NC: The University of North Carolina Press, 1998.

Pfanz, Harry W. *Gettysburg: Culp's Hill & Cemetery Hill*. Chapel Hill, NC: University of North Carolina Press, 1993.

——. *Gettysburg—The First Day*. Chapel Hill, NC: The University of North Carolina Press, 2001.

——. *Gettysburg: The Second Day*. Chapel Hill, NC: The University of North Carolina Press, 1987.

Pryor, Elizabeth Brown. *Reading the Man: A Portrait of Robert E. Lee through His Private Letters*. New York: Penguin Group, 2007.

Radley, Kenneth. *Rebel Watchdog: The Confederate States Army Provost Guard*. Baton Rouge, LA: Louisiana State University Press, 1989.

Raines, Rebecca Robbins. *Getting the Message Through: A Branch History of the U.S. Army Signal Corps*. Washington, DC: Center of Military History, 1999.

Ramage, James A. *Gray Ghost: The Life of Col. John Singleton Mosby*. Lexington, KY: The University Press of Kentucky, 1999.

Ray, Fred L. *Shock Troops of the Confederacy: The Sharpshooter Battalions of the Army of Northern Virginia*. Asheville, NC: CFS Press, 2006.

Reardon, Carol. *Pickett's Charge in History & Memory*. Chapel Hill, NC: The University of North Carolina Press, 1997.

Rister, Carl Coke. *Robert E. Lee in Texas*. Norman, OK: University of Oklahoma Press, 2004.

Robertson, James I., Jr. *General A.P. Hill: The Story of a Confederate Warrior*. New York: Random House, 1987.

——. *Stonewall Jackson: The Man, the Soldier, the Legend*. New York: Simon & Schuster Macmillan, 1997.

Rose, Alexander. *Washington's Spies: The Story of America's First Spy Ring*. New York: Bantam Dell, 2006.

Rummel, George A., III. *Cavalry on the Roads to Gettysburg: Kilpatrick at Hanover and Hunterstown*. Shippensburg, PA: White Mane Books, 2000.

Russell, Charles Wells. *Gray Ghost: The Memoirs of Colonel John S. Mosby*. New York: Bantam Books, 1992.

Sandburg, Carl. *Abraham Lincoln: The War Years*. 4 vols, New York: Harcourt, Brace & Company, 1939.

Schildt, John W. *Roads to Gettysburg*. Parsons, WV: McClain Printing Company, 1978.

——. *Roads from Gettysburg*. Shippensburg, PA: Burd Street Press, 1998.

Schneller, Robert J. Jr. *A Quest for Glory: A Biography of Rear Admiral John A. Dahlgren*. Annapolis, MD: Naval Institute Press, 1996.

Scott, Major John. *Partisan Life with Col. John S. Mosby*. New York: Harper and Brothers, 1867.

Sears, Stephen W. *Chancellorsville*. Boston: Houghton Mifflin Company, 1996.

———. *Landscape Turned Red: The Battle of Antietam*. New York, Popular Library, 1983.

———. *To the Gates of Richmond: The Peninsula Campaign*. Boston, MA: Houghton Mifflin, 1992.

Singer, Jane. *The Confederate Dirty War: Arson, Bombings, Assassination and Plots for Chemical and Germ Attacks on the Union*. Jefferson, NC: McFarland & Co., 2005.

Slade, Jim and John Alexander. *Firestorm at Gettysburg: Civilian Voices*. Atglen, PA: Schiffer Military/Aviation History, 1998.

Smith, Thomas T. *The Old Army in Texas: A Research Guide to the U. S. Army in Nineteenth-Century Texas*. Austin, TX: Texas State Historical Association, 2000.

Starr, Louis M. *Bohemian Brigade: Civil War Newsmen in Action*. Madison, WI: University of Wisconsin Press, 1987.

Starr, Stephen Z. *The Union Cavalry in the Civil War*. 3 Vols. Baton Rouge, LA: Louisiana State University Press, 1979.

Stevens, C. A. *Berdan's United States Sharpshooters in the Army of the Potomac, 1861-1865*. Dayton, OH: Morningside Bookshop, 1972.

Storrick, W. C. *Gettysburg*. Harrisburg, PA: Mount Pleasant Press, 1932.

Sun Tzu. *The Art of War*. New York: Dell Publishing, 1988.

Sutherland, Daniel E. *Seasons of War: The Ordeal of a Confederate Community, 1861-1865*. Baton Rouge, LA: Louisiana State University Press, 1995.

———. *A Savage Conflict: The Decisive Role of Guerrillas in the American Civil War*. Chapel Hill, NC: University of North Carolina Press, 2009.

Thomas, Benjamin P. and Harold M. Hyman. *Stanton: The Life and Times of Lincoln's Secretary of War*. New York: Alfred A. Knopf, 1962.

Thomas, Emory M. *Bold Dragoon: The Life of J.E.B. Stuart*. New York: Vintage Books, 1988.

Thomason, John W. Jr. *Jeb Stuart*. New York: Charles Scribner's Sons, 1930.

Thompson, John W., IV. *Horses, Hostages, and Apple Cider: J. E. B. Stuart's 1862 Pennsylvania Raid*. Mercersburg, PA: Mercersburg Printing, 2002.

Tidwell, William A., James O. Hall, and David Winfred Gaddy. *Come Retribution: The Confederate Secret Service and the Assassination of Lincoln*. Jackson, MS: University Press of Mississippi, 1988.

Tidwell, William A. *April '65: Confederate Covert Action in the American Civil War*. Kent, OH: Kent State University Press, 1995.

Trudeau, Noah Andre. *Gettysburg: A Testing of Courage*. New York: Harper Collins Publishers, 2002.

Tucker, Glenn. *Hancock the Superb*. Dayton, OH: Morningside Bookshop, 1980.

Varon, Elizabeth R. *Southern Lady, Yankee Spy: The True Story of Elizabeth Van Lew, A Union Agent in the Heart of the Confederacy*. Oxford, UK: Oxford University Press, 2003.

Wagner, Arthur L. *The Service of Security and Information*. Washington, DC: James J. Chapman, 1893.

Warner, Ezra J. *Generals in Gray: Lives of Confederate Commanders*. Baton Rouge, LA: Louisiana State University Press, 1959.

———. *Generals in Blue: Lives of Union Commanders*. Baton Rouge, LA: Louisiana State University Press, 1964.

Wert, Jeffry D. *General James Longstreet: The Confederacy's Most Controversial Soldier*. New York: Simon & Schuster, 1993.

———. *Gettysburg: Day Three*. New York: Simon & Schuster, 2001.

———. *Mosby's Rangers*. New York: Simon and Schuster, 1990.

Westhaeffer, Paul J. *History of the Cumberland Valley Railroad, 1835-1919*. Washington, DC: National Railway Historical Society, 1979.

Wheelan, Joseph. *Libby Prison Breakout: The Daring Escape from the Notorious Civil War Prison*. New York: Public Affairs, 2010.

Wheeler, Tom. *Mr. Lincoln's T-Mails: the Untold Story of how Abraham Lincoln Used the Telegraph to Win the Civil War.* New York: Harper Collins, 2006.

Williams, T. Harry. *Lincoln and His Generals.* New York: Vintage Books, 1952.

Wittenberg, Eric J. and J. David Petruzzi. *Plenty of Blame to Go Around: Jeb Stuart's Controversial Ride to Gettysburg.* New York: Savas Beatie, 2006.

Wittenberg, Eric J. *Protecting the Flank: The Battles for Brinkerhoff's Ridge and East Cavalry Field, Battle of Gettysburg, July 2-3, 1863.* Celina, OH: Ironclad Publishing, 2002.

——. *The Union Cavalry Comes of Age.* Washington, DC: Potomac Books, Inc., 2003.

Woodward, Harold R., Jr. *Defender of the Valley: Brigadier General John Daniel Imboden, C.S.A.* Berryville, VA: Rockbridge Publishing Company, 1996.

Wright, Robert K., Jr. *Military Police.* Washington, DC: Center of Military History, U.S. Army.

Regimental Histories

Armstrong, Richard L. *7th Virginia Cavalry.* Lynchburg, VA: H. E. Howard, Inc., 1992.

Bayard, George D., Owen Jones and John P. Taylor. *History of the First Reg't Pennsylvania Reserve Cavalry.* Philadelphia, PA: King and Baird Printers, 1864.

Beach, William H. *The First New York (Lincoln) Cavalry.* Milwaukee, WI: Burdick & Allen, 1902.

Blackwell, Samuel L., Jr. *The 12th Illinois Cavalry.* Dekalb, IL: Northern Illinois University Press, 2002.

Boudrye, Louis N. *Fifth New York Cavalry.* Albany, NY: S. R. Gray, 1865.

Dickinson, Jack L. *16th Virginia Cavalry.* Lynchburg, VA: H. E. Howard, Inc., 1989.

Driver, Robert J. Jr. *1st Virginia Cavalry.* Lynchburg, VA: H. E. Howard, Inc., 1991.

——. *5th Virginia Cavalry.* Lynchburg, VA: H. E. Howard, Inc., 1997.

——. *First & Second Maryland Cavalry C.S.A.* Charlottesville, VA: Rockbridge Publishing, 1999.

——. and H. E. Howard, *2nd Virginia Cavalry.* Lynchburg, VA: H.E. Howard, Inc., 1995.

——. and Kevin C. Ruffner. *1st Battalion Virginia Infantry, 39th Battalion Virginia Cavalry, 24th Battalion Virginia Partisan Rangers.* Lynchburg, VA: H. E. Howard, Inc., 1996.

Gillespie, Samuel L. *A History of Company A, First Ohio Cavalry, 1861-1865.* Washington, OH: Ohio State Register, 1898.

Gracey, Rev. S. L. *Annals of the Sixth Pennsylvania Cavalry.* Philadelphia, PA: E. H. Butler & Co., 1868.

Hard, Abner M.D. *History of the Eighth Cavalry Regiment Illinois Volunteers.* Dayton, OH: Morningside Bookshop, 1984.

Harrell, Roger H. *The 2nd North Carolina Cavalry.* Jefferson, NC: McFarland & Company, 2004.

Harris, Nelson. *17th Virginia Cavalry.* Lynchburg. VA: H. E. Howard, Inc., 1994.

Hyndman, Capt. William. *History of a Cavalry Company: A Complete Record of Company "A," 4th Penn's Cavalry.* Philadelphia, PA: Jas. B. Rodgers Co., 1870.

Krick, Robert K. *9th Virginia Cavalry.* Lynchburg, VA: H.E. Howard, Inc., 1982.

Lee, William O. *Seventh Regiment Michigan Volunteer Cavalry, 1862-1865.* Detroit, MI: Detroit Book Press, 1990.

McDonald, William N. *A History of the Laurel Brigade.* Kate S. McDonald, 1907.

Myers, Frank K. *The Comanches: A History of White's Battalion, Virginia Cavalry.* Marietta, GA: Continental Book Company, 1956.

Musick, Michael P. *6th Virginia Cavalry.* Lynchburg, VA: H. E. Howard, Inc., 1990.

Nanzig, Thomas P. *3rd Virginia Cavalry.* Lynchburg, VA: H. E. Howard, Inc., 1989.

Norton, Henry. *Eighth New York Volunteer Cavalry.* New York: Chenango Telegraph Printing House, 1889.

Penfield, Captain James. *The 1863-1864 Diary: 5th New York Volunteer Cavalry, Company H.* Ticonderoga, NY: Press of America, Inc., 1999.

Preston, N. D. *History of the Tenth Regiment of Cavalry, New York State Volunteers.* New York: D. Appleton and Company, 1892.

Pyne, Henry R. *The History of the First New Jersey Cavalry.* New Brunswick, NJ: Rutgers University Press, 1961.

Raiford, Neil Hunter. *The 4th North Carolina Cavalry.* Jefferson, NC: McFarland & Company, 2003.

Rawle, William Brooke. *History of the Third Pennsylvania Cavalry.* Philadelphia, PA: Franklin Printing Company, 1905.

Stevenson, Jas. H. *A History of the First New York (Lincoln) Cavalry.* Harrisburg, PA: Patriot Publishing Company, 1879.

Stiles, Kenneth L. *4th Virginia Cavalry.* Lynchburg, VA: H. E. Howard, Inc., 1985.

Tobie, Edward P. *History of the First Maine Cavalry, 1861-1865.* Boston, MA: Press of Emery & Hughes, 1887.

Articles

Alexander, Ted. "Gettysburg Cavalry Operations, June 27-July 3, 1863." *Blue & Gray Magazine* (October 1988). Vol. 6, no. 8, 8-60.

——. "Ten Days in July: The Pursuit to the Potomac." *North & South* (August 1999). Vol. 2, no. 6, 10-34.

Anthony, William. "Reminiscences Told by Robert E. Spangler," *Battle of Hanover*, Hanover, PA: William Anthony, 1945, 143-46.

Bauer, Daniel. "Did a Food Shortage Force Lee to Fight?" *Columbiad* (Winter 1998). Vol. 1, no. 4, 57-74.

Bean, Theo. W., "General Buford at Gettysburg—The Cavalry Ride into Pennsylvania and the Choice of the Field of Battle—The First Day on the Outposts Before the Arrival of the Infantry," *Gettysburg Sources.* 3 Vols. Baltimore, MD, Butternut and Blue, 1990. Vol. 3, 73-80.

Becker, Bernie. "A Man Called Harrison," *America's Civil War* (November 2004), 46-52.

Blumberg, Arnold. "Rebel Sabres: Confederate Cavalry Leaders in the Gettysburg Campaign." *High Water Mark: The Army of Northern Virginia in the Gettysburg Campaign.* Gettysburg: Gettysburg National Military Park, 1999, 19-35.

Boritt, Gabor S.. "'Unfinished Work': Lincoln, Meade, and Gettysburg." In Gabor S. Boritt, ed. *Lincoln's Generals.* New York: Oxford University Press, 1994, 79-120.

Bowmaster, Patrick A., ed. "Confederate Brig. Gen. B. H. 'Bev' Robertson Interviewed on the Gettysburg Campaign." *Gettysburg Magazine* (January 1999), Issue 20, 19-26.

Brennan, Patrick. "Thunder on the Plains of Brandy." *North & South* (April 2002). Vol. 5, no. 3, 14-34.

——. "Thunder on the Plains of Brandy" Part II. *North & South* (May 2002). Vol. 5, no. 4, 32-57.

——. "It Wasn't Stuart's Fault." *North & South* (July 2003). Vol. 6, no.5, 22-39.

Brown, Kent Masterson. "A Golden Bridge: Lee's Williamsport Defense Lines and His Escape Across the Potomac." *North & South* (August 1999). Vol. 2, no. 6, 56-65.

Cameron, Bill. "Signal Corps," *Encyclopedia of the American Civil War: A Political, Social, and Military History.* In David Stephen Heidler and Jeanne T. Heidler, eds. 5 Vols. New York: W. W. Norton & Company, 2002. Vol. 4, 1788-89.

——. "The Signal Corps at Gettysburg." *Gettysburg Magazine.* (July 1990), no. 3, 9-16 .

——. "The Signal Corps at Gettysburg Part II: In Support of Meade's Pursuit." *The Gettysburg Magazine* (January 1991), no. 4, 101-109.

Cooksey, Paul Clark. "Around the Flank: Longstreet's July 2 Attack at Gettysburg." *Gettysburg Magazine* (July 2003), Issue 29, 94-105.

de Peyster, John Watts. "The Third Corps and Sickles at Gettysburg." *Gettysburg Sources*. 2 Vols. Baltimore, MD: Butternut and Blue, 1987. Vol. 2, 47-66.

Feis, William B. "Secret Service, U.S.A." In David S. Heidler and Jeanne T. Heidler, *Encyclopedia of the American Civil War: A Political, Social, and Military History*. 5 Vols. Santa Barbara, CA: ABC-CLIO, Inc., 2000. Vol. 4, 1723-25.

Fishel, Edwin C. "Command Decision: Colonel Sharpe's Critical Role at Gettysburg." *North & South* (February 1998). Vol. 1, no. 3, 14-29.

Ford, Edwin. "Major General George H. Sharpe." *The Genie* (January 2000).

French, Steve. "Imboden's Advance to Gettysburg." *Gettysburg Magazine* (January 1999), Issue 20, 6-18.

——. "Hurry Was the Order of the Day: Imboden and the Wagon Train of the Wounded." *North & South* (August 1999). Vol. 2, no. 6, 35-43.

Gaddy, David Winfred. "The Confederate Signal Corps at Gettysburg." *Gettysburg Magazine* (January 1991), Issue 4, 110-112.

——. "William Norris and the Confederate Signal and Secret Service." *Maryland Historical Magazine* (Summer 1975). Vol. 70, No. 2, 167-188.

——. "Robert E. Lee: A Study in Leadership." Unpublished lecture. *Museum of American History*, November 21, 1994.

Greene, A. Wilson. "From Gettysburg to Falling Waters: Meade's Pursuit of Lee." In Gary W. Gallagher, ed. *The Third Day at Gettysburg & Beyond*. Chapel Hill, NC: University of North Carolina Press, 1994, 161-201.

Haines, Douglas Craig. "Jeb Stuart's Advance to Gettysburg." *Gettysburg Magazine*, (July 2003), Issue 29, 26-61.

——. "The Advance of Longstreet's First Corps to Gettysburg. *Gettysburg Magazine*, (July 2008), Issue 39, 7-44.

Hall, James O. "The Spy Harrison." *Civil War Times Illustrated*. Vol. 24, No. 10, 18-25.

Hyde, Bill. "Did You Get There? Capt. Samuel Johnston's Reconnaissance at Gettysburg." *Gettysburg Magazine*, (July 2003), Issue 29, 86-93.

Krolick, Marshall D. "Forgotten Field: The Cavalry Battle East of Gettysburg on July 3, 1863." *Gettysburg Magazine*, (January 1991), Issue, 4, 75-88.

Krumwiede, John F. "A July Afternoon on McPherson's Ridge." *Gettysburg Magazine*, (July 1999), Issue 21, 21-44.

Loosbrock, Richard D. "Battle of Brandy Station." In David S. Heidler and Jeanne T. Heidler, *Encyclopedia of the American Civil War: A Political, Social, and Military History*. 5 Vols. Santa Barbara, CA: ABC-CLIO, Inc., 2000. Vol. 1, 271-274.

Luvaas, Jay. "Lee at Gettysburg: A General Without Intelligence." In Michael I. Handel, *Intelligence and Military Operations*. London: Cass, 1990, 116-135.

Luvaas, Jay and Harold W. Nelson. "Intelligence in the Chancellorsville Campaign." Appendix I, *The U.S. Army War College Guide to the Battles of Chancellorsville & Fredericksburg*. Carlisle, PA: South Mountain Press, Inc., 1988, 299-314.

Moore, Wilton P. "Union Army Provost Marshals in the Eastern Theater," *Military Affairs*. (Autumn, 1962). Vol. 26, no. 3, 120-126.

Motts, Wayne E. "Pickett's Charge Revisited: 'A Brave and Resolute Force.'" *North & South* (June 1999). Vol. 2, no. 5, 27-34.

Petruzzi, J. David. "The fleeting fame of Alfred Pleasonton." *America's Civil War*. March 2005, 20-28.

Poulter, Keith. "Errors That Doomed a Campaign." *North & South* (August 1999). Vol. 2, no. 6, 82-88.

Powell, David. "Stuart's Ride: Lee, Stuart, and the Confederate Cavalry in the Gettysburg Campaign." *Gettysburg Magazine*, (January 1999), Issue 20, 27-43.

——. "A Reconnaissance Gone Awry: Capt. Samuel R. Johnston's Fateful Trip to Little Round Top." *Gettysburg Magazine*, (July 200), 88-99.

Richard Rollins. "Lee's Grand Strategy and Pickett's Charge." *North & South* (July 2002). Vol. 5, no. 5, 76-84.

——. "George Gordon Meade and the Defense of Cemetery Ridge." *Gettysburg Magazine*, (July 1998), Issue 19, 57-83.

Roland, Charles. "Lee's Invasion Strategy." *North & South*. Vol. 1, no. 6, (n.d.).

Ryan, Thomas J. "A Battle of Wits: Intelligence Operations during the Gettysburg Campaign." Part 1. *Gettysburg Magazine*, (July 2003), Issue 29, 7-25.

——. "A Battle of Wits: Intelligence Operations during the Gettysburg Campaign." Part 2. *Gettysburg Magazine*, (January 2004), Issue 30, 7-29.

——. "A Battle of Wits: Intelligence Operations during the Gettysburg Campaign." Part 3. *Gettysburg Magazine*, (July 2004), Issue 31, 6-38.

——. "A Battle of Wits: Intelligence Operations during the Gettysburg Campaign." Part 4. *Gettysburg Magazine*, (January 2005), Issue 32, 7-38.

—— "A Battle of Wits: Intelligence Operations during the Gettysburg Campaign." Part 5. *Gettysburg Magazine*, (July 2005), Issue 33, 100-127.

——. "Kilpatrick Bars Stuart's Route to Gettysburg." *Gettysburg Magazine*, (July 2002), Issue 27, 7-28.

——. "Stuart a vital force as Rebel leader." Washington *Times*, August 26, 2006

——. "Stuart's intelligence role invaluable." Washington *Times*, December 8, 2007.

Scheips, Paul J. "Union Signal Communications: Innovation and Conflict" *Civil War History*, (December 1963), Volume 9. Reprint. Arno Press. New York, 1974, 1-23.

Sears, Stephen W. "Meade Takes Command" *North & South*, (September 2002). Vol. 5, no. 6, 12-21.

Shevchuk, Paul M. "The Wounding of Albert Jenkins, July 2, 1863. *Gettysburg Magazine*, (July 1990), Issue 3, 51-64.

Smith, Karlton D. "'To Consider Every Contingency': Lt. Gen James Longstreet, Capt. Samuel R. Johnston, and the factors that affect the reconnaissance and countermarch, July 2, 1863." *The Most Shocking Battle I Have Ever Witnessed: The Second Day at Gettysburg.* Gettysburg: Gettysburg National Military Park, 2008, 98-120.

Sparks, David S. "General Patrick's Progress: Intelligence and Security in the Army of the Potomac." *Civil War History*, (December 1964). Vol. 10, 371-384.

Tidwell, William A. "Secret Service, C.S.A." In David S. Heidler and Jeanne T. Heidler, *Encyclopedia of the American Civil War: A Political, Social, and Military History*, 5 Vols. , Santa Barbara, CA: ABC-CLIO, Inc., 2000. Vol. 4, 1722-23.

Tilberg, Frederick and J. Walter Coleman. "Reconnaissance of the Confederate Right. July 2, 1863." In Douglas S. Freeman, *Lee's Lieutenants*. 3 Vols. New York: Charles Scribner's Sons. Vol. 3, 755-56.

Trimble, Tony. "Harrison: Spying for Longstreet at Gettysburg." *Gettysburg Magazine*, (July 1997), Issue 17, 17-19.

Trudeau, Noah Andre, ed. "5th Alabama Sharpshooters Taking Aim at Cemetery Hill." *America's Civil War*, (July 2001), 46-53.

Vermilyea, Peter C. "Maj. Gen. John Sedgwick and the Pursuit of Lee's Army after Gettysburg." *Gettysburg Magazine*, (January 2000), Issue 22, 112-129.

Ward, David A. "'Sedgwick's Foot Cavalry': The March of the Sixth Corps to Gettysburg." *Gettysburg Magazine*, (January 2000), Issue 22, 42-65.

Wittenberg, Eric. "Learning the Hard Lessons of Logistics: Arming and Maintaining the Federal Cavalry." *North & South*, (January 1999), 62-78.

——. "John Buford and the Gettysburg Campaign." *Gettysburg Magazine*, (July 1994), Issue 11, 19-55.

——. "The Truth About the Withdrawal of Brig. Gen. John Buford's Cavalry, July 2, 1863." *Gettysburg Magazine*, (July 2007), Issue 37, 71-82.

——. "'This was a night never to be forgotten': The Midnight Fight in the Monterey Pass, July 4-5, 1863." *North & South*, (August 1999). Vol. 2, no. 6, 44-55.

Online Sources

Abbot, Henry L. *Memoir of Dennis Hart Mahan, 1802-1871.* Read before the National Academy of Science, November 7, 1878. http://bit.ly/17RSrDm

Brown, R. J. "How the South Gathered News during the Civil War." *The History Buff*, http://www.historybuff.com/library/refgather.html

Crouch, Richard E. "The Loudoun Rangers." http://www.loudounhistory.org/history/loudoun-cw-rangers.htm

Gehris, Roy F. "Maj. Gen. David McMurtrie Gregg, Commanding Officer, 2nd Cavalry Division, Cavalry Corps, Army of the Potomac." http://www.oocities.org/mwkop/GenGregg.html

"Interrogation and the Collection of Intelligence." *International Encyclopedia of the Social Sciences* (2008). http://www.encyclopedia.com/topic/Questioning.aspx

"Lee, Robert Edward." *The Handbook of Texas Online.* http://www.tshaonline.org/handbook/online/articles/fle18

Roberts, J. A. "Blind Man's Bluff: Reconnaissance and Counter-Reconnaissance Efforts in the Gettysburg Campaign." http://www.globalsecurity.org/military/library/report/1992/RJA.htm

"Shaw, Jim." *Handbook of Texas Online*, http://www.tshaonline.org/handbook/online/articles/fsh11

Index

Thomas J. Ryan is the former president of the Central Delaware Civil War Round Table, and a longtime member of the Gettysburg Foundation and the Civil War Trust. He has published more than 125 articles and book reviews on Civil War subjects, many dealing with intelligence operations, and writes a bi-weekly column called "Civil War Profiles" for Coastal Point, a Delaware newspaper. He is the author of Essays on Delaware during the Civil War: A Political, Military and Social Perspective (2012). Ryan served three years in the United States Army and more than three decades with the U.S. Department of Defense in various intelligence operations-related capacities. Now retired, he and his wife live in Bethany Beach, Delaware.